D1158190

MODERN JAPANESE LITERATURE
IN TRANSLATION

KoKusai Bunka Kaikan, Tokyo. Toshoshitsu

MODERN JAPANESE LITERATURE IN TRANSLATION

A Bibliography

Compiled by

The International House of Japan Library

KODANSHA INTERNATIONAL LTD.

Tokyo, New York & San Francisco

R895.608016
Kokusai...

Distributed in the United States by Kodansha International/USA Ltd., through Harper & Row Publishers, Inc., 10 East 53rd Street, New York, New York 10022; in the United Kingdom by Phaidon Press Ltd., Littlegate House, St. Ebbe's Street, Oxford OXl lSQ; in Europe by Boxerbooks Inc., Limmatstrasse 111, 8031 Zurich; and in Japan by Kodansha International Ltd., 2–12–21 Otowa, Bunkyo-ku, Tokyo 112.

Published by Kodansha International Ltd., 2–12–21 Otowa, Bunkyo-ku, Tokyo 112 and Kodansha International/USA Ltd., 10 East 53rd Street, New York, New York 10022 and 44 Montgomery Street, San Francisco, California 94104. Copyright © 1979 by Kokusai Bunka Kaikan (The International House of Japan). All rights reserved. Printed in Japan.

Library of Congress Cataloging in Publication Data

Kokusai Bunka Kaikan, Tokyo. Toshoshitsu.
   Modern Japanese literature in translation.

   Includes index.
   1. Japanese literature—1868—Translations into foreign languages—Bibliography. 2. Literature, Modern—20th century—Translations from Japanese—Bibliography. I. Title.
Z3308.L5K66   1978   [PL726.55]   016.8956′08′004
ISBN   0–87011–339–9   78–66395

                                    LCC 78–66395
                                    ISBN 0–87011–339–9
                                    JBC 1591–786742–2361

First edition 1979

CREF

INTRODUCTION

The sheer volume of translation of Japanese literature into other languages is an indication of the extent of interest in Japan in some parts of the world, and a tribute to the industry and devotion of translators. However, when we consider that we have not translated or introduced the literature of many of the countries represented here, such as Finland, Turkey, Poland, Korea, and so on, it gives us pause for thought. It seems that much remains to be done to promote mutual understanding.

This is a catalogue of translations into various languages of Japanese literary works, primarily fiction, drama, poetry, and essays, published since the beginning of the Meiji period in 1868. Arrangement is alphabetical by authors' names, given in the Japanese order (family names appearing all in capitals, given names in lower case with initial capital), followed by the characters with which the names are written in Japanese, date of birth, and, in the case of authors deceased at the time of publication, of death.

Translated works are listed alphabetically in the English (Hepburn) romanization of the Japanese title, followed by the title in Japanese. Exceptions to this arrangement are poems, criticism, and essays, which follow the alphabetical listings in that order. Translations are listed by the title in the language of translation, followed by the translator's name and bibliographical information, in order of date of publication, different editions of the same work being indicated without repetition of information.

Exhaustiveness cannot be claimed. Doubtless numerous individual poems, articles, or stories in magazines have escaped notice, and in principle certain types of works, notably studies of the literature of other countries, have deliberately been excluded.

Insofar as possible orthography of the translation language has been used, but in a number of instances necessary type fonts were not available (e.g., Thai, Pakistani, Hindi, Central Asian languages) and transliteration had to be resorted to.

For authors and works listed, primary reliance has been upon *Nihon kindai bungaku daijiten* (Kodansha, 1977–8. 6v). In addition, the compiler has enjoyed the cooperation, advice, and suggestions of many institutions and libraries, whose help it is a pleasure to acknowledge in this place. The Yoshida International Education Foundation generously financed the compiler's research trips to Seoul, Taipei, and Hong Kong. The Mitsubishi Foundation also made a grant for editorial work and research in Japanese collections, and financial assistance from the Japan Foundation has made publication by Kodansha International possible. The following national central libraries have supplied invaluable information and assistance:

Biblioteca Nacional, Rio de Janeiro
Biblioteca Nacional de Lisboa, Lisbon
Biblioteca Nacional de México, Mexico City

5

Biblioteka Narodowa, Warsaw
Biblioteca Nazionale Centrale Vittorio Emanuele II, Rome
Bibliothèque Royale Albert Ier, Brussels
Cyril and Methodius National Library, Sofia
Deutsche Staatsbibliothek, Berlin
General Directorate of the National Library, Ankara
Helsingin Yliopiston Kirjasto, Helsinki
Kungliga Biblioteket, Stockholm
Narodna Biblioteka SR Srbije, Beograd
National Library of Greece, Athens
National Széchényi Library, Budapest
Österreichische Nationalbibliothek, Vienna
The Royal Library, Copenhagen
Royal University Library, Oslo
Schweizerische Landesbibliothek, Bern
State Library of the Czech Socialist Republic, Prague

The National Diet Library, Tokyo Metropolitan Central Library, Nihon Kindai Bunga-kukan, Tokyo University Library, Kyoto University Institute for Humanistic Studies, Tokyo Gakugei Daigaku Library, Waseda University Library, Toyo Bunko, Institute of Developing Economies, Japan Foundation Library, Nisso Toshokan, and the Nichi-Futsu Kaikan Library have been generous with staff time and information assistance. Yumiko Yamada, Hiroko Akutsu, Silvia Studer (Universität Zürich) and Marianne Kocks (Staatsbibliothek Preussischer Kulturbesitz) of the International House of Japan Library have labored long and hard over compilation and indexing.

Undoubtedly, despite much effort, there are numerous errors of omission and commission, for which the compiler must assume full responsibility. Nevertheless it is believed that this guide may serve as a useful reference, and if its usefulness exceeds its faults, the compiler will be amply rewarded.

October, 1978

Yukio Fujino, Librarian
International House of Japan

ま え が き

　国際文化会館図書室は創設以来25年，国外の日本研究の一助になればとの願いのもとに文献目録，便覧の編集刊行を続けてきたが，本書は10冊目の文献目録にあたる。 なお本書は1972年発行の『欧米語訳現代日本文学書目』の増補改訂版であり，今回はアジア諸国語をも収録した。

　国外における日本文学の紹介は戦後，とくに1960年代以降急速に進み，完訳を主とした質的にも水準の高い翻訳を数多く産み出している。英語訳について見るならば，漱石の代表的作品はここ10年ばかりの間にすべて完全な姿で正確に訳され，一般の手にも渡るようになったし，「暗夜行路」，鷗外の歴史小説等も読めるようになっている。これは，アメリカ，イギリスの日本研究が，日本の近代化，とくに明治以後の知識人に焦点を当てていることと無縁ではなかろう。事情はロシア語でも同様で，プロレタリア文学ばかりが訳された1950年代までとは異なり，最近では太宰治「馳込み訴へ」，三浦哲郎「忍ぶ川」なども訳されている。

　翻訳が訳者の情熱と努力の所産であることは言うまでもない。訳者はそれぞれ相当の時間と労力をそれに注ぎこんでいる。その結果，日本人の生き方，ものの考え方が少しずつでも外国に理解されてゆく。われわれとしてもこの点の認識を改めねばならないし，本書編纂の第一の目的もここにあった。文学作品を通じて日本を知りたいとするいくつかの国，たとえばフィンランド，トルコ，ポーランド，韓国などに比べ，わが国におけるこれら諸国の文学紹介がいったいどれほどあるだろうか。

　この目録は明治以降の日本文学作品外国語訳のリストである。それ以前の文学は別に考えている。収録と記述については，いくつかの点をお断りしておかねばならない。第一に，本書は翻訳され出版された作品をつきとめるための書目であって，いわゆる研究書誌ではない。訳題が同一，訳者が同じならばスペース節約のため一点づつの異同を問うていない。セミコロンの使用がこれに当る。比較研究はこれからの課題であろうが，本書目はそのための素材提供となれば幸いであると考えたからであった。

　第二に，収録はできるだけ広い範囲を心掛けたが，完全にはまだほど遠い。俳句や短歌を完璧に網羅することは不可能であったし，まだつきとめえない最近の翻訳もあろう。雑誌所載の翻訳にたいしても手をつくしたとは言えない。さらに補訂の機を得たいと考えている。本書では外国文学に関する最近の研究書・研究論文は原則として除いてある。外国語でまず発表された作品も，いくつかの例外はあるが省略した。さらに，北朝鮮その他，まったく調べのついていない地域もある。

　第三に，記載はできるだけ原綴りを使用したが，翻字を使っている場合もいくらかある。タイ語，インド・パキスタン諸語，中央アジアの言語がこれに当るが，分量が少ないためと組版のむづかしさのためであった。漢字の表記についても，訳題，書名はその国の表記によるようにしたが，若干統一せざるをえなかった場合がある。

　作家，作品については「日本近代文学大事典」（講談社 1977〜78.6冊）に依拠している。詩はそれぞれの原題をとっていない。別に索引を作るべきであろう。

　本目録の編集，出版に当ってはまことに多くの方々から協力をいただいている。吉田国際教育基金

は，中国語，韓国語訳の調査を支援して下さった。国内図書館での調査，原作との照合作業は三菱財団からの学術助成金により実現できた。さらに，国際交流基金から講談社インターナショナル株式会社への出版援助があり，この困難の多い出版が可能となった。記してお礼申し上げる次第である。

諸外国の国立中央図書館も情報提供の上で協力して下さった。オーストリア，ベルギー，ブラジル，ブルガリア，チェコスロバキア，デンマーク，フィンランド，ドイツ民主主義共和国，ギリシア，ハンガリー，イタリア，メキシコ，ノルウェー，ポーランド，ポルトガル，スウェーデン，スイス，トルコ，ユーゴスラビアの各中央図書館はこの点とくに記しておかねばならない。翻訳の多い国については，全部を記しきれないが，数多くの図書館に直接お世話になっている。とりわけ台北の国立中央図書館，香港の中文大学，ソウルの国立中央図書館ではそれぞれ数週間づつ原物を調べさせて頂いた。

国内の図書館の方々もこの計画をいろいろな面で御支援下さった。国立国会図書館，都立中央図書館，日本近代文学館，東京大学図書館，東京学芸大学図書館，京都大学人文科学研究所，早稲田大学図書館，東洋文庫近代中国研究室，大阪外国語大学英語学科，アジア経済研究所，国際交流基金図書室，日仏会館図書室，日ソ図書館にたいしてはとくに感謝の意を表しておきたい。

編集の実務は国際文化会館図書室で行なった。調査から校正，索引のすべてにわたる同職員山田由美子，阿久津弘子の両名の努力により本書はようやく仕上がったと言っても過言ではない。同図書室研修生シルヴィア・シトゥーダー（チューリヒ大学），マリアンネ・コックス（国立プロイセン文化財図書館）の協力も記しておきたい。

1978年10月

国際文化会館図書室長

藤 野 幸 雄

MODERN JAPANESE LITERATURE
IN TRANSLATION

A Bibliography

A

ABE Akira　阿部　昭　1934–

Momo　桃

'Peaches' Tr. by Jay Rubin. *Contemporary Japanese literature,* ed. by Howard Hibbett. N. Y. Knopf, 1977. p.345–353

ABE Jirō　阿部次郎　1883–1959

Santarō no nikki　三太郎の日記

「거울속의나의손」金昭影訳　서울　大裕出版社　1968. 313p.

Shintō shōkei　心頭小景

'心頭小景(抄)' 安仁吉　方坤訳　「世界随筆文学全集　4」서울　東西出版社　1969. p.296–340
'心頭小景(抄)' 鄭成煥　金泳杓訳　「世界에세이文学全集 8」서울　東西出版社　1974. p.296–340;「世界随筆文学全集 8」서울　世進出版社 1976. p.296–340

Essays　エッセイ

「마음의 그림자」金昭影訳　서울　五星出版社　1969. 175p.
「思索하는 나무가 흔들맬때」金昭影訳　서울　五星出版社 1969. 208p.

ABE Kōbō　安部公房　1924–

Akai mayu　赤い繭

'Červený kokon' Přel. V. Winkelhöferová. *Nový Orient,* v.12, no.7, 1957. p.107–110; *Červený kokon.* Praha, Odeon, 1971. p.198–203
'붉은고치' 韓光洙訳　「日本新鋭文学作家受賞作品集 2」서울　青雲社　1964. p.263–289;「戦後日本短篇文学全集 2」서울　日光出版社 1965. p.263–289;「現代日本代表文学全集 2」서울　平和出版社 1973. p.263–287
'Red coccoon' Tr. by John Nathan. *Japan Quarterly,* v.13, no.2, 1966. p.217–219; *New writing in Japan.* London, Penguin Books,

1972. p.47–50
'紅色的繭' 鐘肇政　劉慕沙訳　「砂丘之女及其他」台北 純文學出版社　1975. p.193–197
'붉은누에고치' 權逸松訳　「世界文学全集 47」서울 三省出版社　1976. p.349–350

Baberu no tō no tanuki　バベルの塔の狸

'바벨塔의너구리' 權逸松訳　「世界文学全集 47」서울 三省出版社」1976. p.374–416

Bō　棒

'Stick' Tr. by John Nathan. *Japan Quarterly,* v. 13, no.2, 1966. p.214–217; *New writing in Japan.* London, Penguin Books, 1972. p.41–46
'Hul' Přel. V. Winkelhöferová. *Červený kokon.* Praha, Odeon, 1971. p.110–115
'棍子' 鐘肇政訳　「砂丘之女及其他」台北　純文學出版社 1975. p.199–205

Bō ni natta otoko　棒になった男

'Der Mann, der zum Stock wurde' Übers. von Siegfried Schaarschmidt. *Der Mann, der zum Stock wurde.* Berlin, Literarisches Colloquium, 1969. p.45–68
'The man who turned into a stick' Tr. by Donald Keene. *The man who turned into a stick.* Tokyo, Univ. of Tokyo Press, 1975. 84p.

Chinnyūsha　闖入者

'Вторжение' Перевод Г. Ивановой. *No.36, новеллы японских писателей.* Москва, Наука, 1968. p.109–131
'Zetrelci' Přel. Vlasta Winkelhöferová. *Červený kokon.* Praha, Odeon, 1971. p.142–174

Dai yon kanpyōki　第四間氷期

Четвертый ледниковый период. Перевод С. Бережкова. Москва, Молодая Гвардия, 1965. 214p.
Neljas jääeg. Tr. from the Russian Agu Sisask. Tallin, Periodika, 1966. 175p.
Centurtais ledus laikmets. Tr. from the Russian Mirdza Gulbe. Riga, Zinatne, 1967. 283p.
A negyedik jégkorszák. Tr. from the Russian K. Sára. Budapest, Kozmosz, 1969. 232p.
Четвертый ледниковый период, на армянском языке. Перевод Г. К. Маргарян. Ереван, Ажастан, 1969. 349p.
Inter ice age 4. Tr. by E. Dale Saunders. N. Y. Knopf, 1970; London, Cape, 1971; Tokyo, Tuttle, 1971. 228p.; N. Y. Berkley Pub. 1972.
Välijääkausi 4. Suomentanut Anna Paljakka Jyväskylä. Helsinki, Gummerus, 1972. 233p.

ABE Kōbō

Het tijdperk der aquanen. Overzette door Heleen ten Holt. Antwerpen, A. W. Bruna, 1973. 219p.

Die vierte Zwischeneiszeit. Aus dem Japanischen von Siegfried Schaarschmidt. Frankfurt am Main, Insel Verlag, 1975. 231p.

Dendorokakariya　デンドロカカリヤ

'Dendrocacalia' Přel. M. Jelínková. *Nový Orient*, v.20, no.4, 1965. p.50–56

'Dendrocacalia' Ford. Sz. Holti Mária. *Modern Japán elbeszélők.* Budapest, Európa Könyvkiadó, 1967. p.403–421

'Dendrocacalia' Přel. Vlasta Winkelhöferová. *Červený kokon.* Praha, Odeon, 1971. p.175–197

Dorei gari　どれい狩り

'Охота на рабов' Перевод В. Гривнина. *Абэ Кобо, пьесы.* Москва, Искусство, 1975. p.191–272

Hako otoko　箱男

The box man. Tr. by E. Dale Saunders. N. Y. Knopf, 1974; Tokyo, Tuttle, 1975. 178p.

'Человек-ящик' Перевод В. Гривнина. *Иностранная Литература,* август 1976. p.148–192

Henkei no kiroku　変形の記録

'Zážitky zemřelého' Přel. J. Jelínek. *Nový Orient*, v.19, no.7, 1964.

Inu　犬

'The dog' Tr. by Andrew Horvat. *Japan Quarterly*, v.19, no.1, 1972. p.51–56; *Four stories by Kobo Abe.* Tokyo, Hara Shobo, 1973. p.32–56

Jigyō　事業

'事業' 權逸松訳 「世界文学全集 47」 서울 三省出版社 1976. p.368–372

Jōsai　城砦

'Крепость' Перевод Владимира Гривнина. *Абэ Кобо, пьесы.* Москва, Искусство, 1975. p.123–190

Kaban　鞄

'Der Koffer' Übers. von Siegfried Schaarschmidt. *Der Mann, der zum Stock wurde.* Berlin, Literarisches Colloquium, 1969. p.7–33

Kabe-Esu Karuma shi no hanzai　壁-S・カルマ氏の犯罪

'S・가루마씨의범죄─벽' 韓光洙訳 「日本新鋭文学作家受賞作品集 2」 서울 青雲社 1964. p.173–260; 「戦後日本短篇文学全集 2」 서울 日光出版社 1965. p.173–260; 「現代日本代表文学全集 2」 서울 平和出版社 1973. p.173–261

'S・칼마氏의犯罪' 權逸松訳 「世界文学全集 47」 서울 三省出版社 1976. p.271–347

Kake　賭

'賭博' 朴淵禧訳 「日本代表作家百人集 5」 서울 希望出版社 1966. p.154–174; 「日本短篇文学全集 6」 서울 新太陽社 1969. p.66–86

Kodomo beya　子供部屋

'Детская' Перевод В. Гривнина, *Иностранная Литература,* июнь 1972. p.66–76; *Японская новелла 1960–1970.* Москва, Прогресс, 1972. p.5–16

'Pokój dziecinny' Przeł. Jerzy Domaradzki. *Kierunki,* no.1, 1974. p.6–7

Kōzui　洪水

'洪水' 權逸松訳 「世界文学全集 47」 서울 三省出版社 1976. p.352–355

Mahō no chōku　魔法のチョーク

'Kouzelná křídla' Přel. J. Winkelhöfer a V. Winkelhöferová. *Svetová Literatura,* no.6, 1957. p.54–60

'Kouzelná křídla' Přel. V. Winkelhöferová. *Červený kokon.* Praha, Odeon, 1971. p.116–129

'魔筆' 劉慕沙訳 「破丘之女及其他」 台北 純文學出版社 1975. p.207–223

'魔法의초오크' 權逸松訳 「世界文学全集 47」 서울 三省出版社 1976. p.357–366

Moetsukita chizu　燃えつきた地図

The ruined map. Tr. by E. Dale Saunders. N. Y. Knopf, 1969; Tokyo, Tuttle, 1970; London, Cape, 1972. 299p.

'Сожденная карта' Перевод В. Гривнина. *Иностранная Литература,* 1969, номер 8, p.110–156. номер 9, p.139–173. номер 10, p.157–212

Спарена карта. Переклав И. Дзюб. Киев, Молодь, 1969. 204p.

Le plan déchiqueté. Tr. de l'anglais par Jean Gerard Chauffeteau. Paris, Stock, 1971. 265p.

Den förstörda kartan. Översätta Gunnar Barklund. Stockholm, Bonniers, 1971. 221p.

「燃燒的地圖」 鐘肇政訳 台北 遠景出版社 1977. 326p.

Mukankei na shi　無関係な死

'Smert nezheho' Přel. Vlasta Winkelhöferová. *Červený kokon.* Praha, Odeon, 1971. p.5–32

'Чужая смерть' Перевод Е. *Красная лягушка.* Москва, Наука, 1973. p.50–72

'無関係的死' 鐘肇政訳 「砂丘之女及其他」 台北 純文學出版社 1975. p.225–251

Namari no tamago　鉛の卵

'Olozene zejce' Přel. V. Winkelhöferová. *Červený kokon.* Praha, Odeon, 1971. p.33–62

Ningen sokkuri　人間そっくり

'Совсем как человек' Перевод С. Бережкова. *Продается Япония.* Москва, Мир, 1969. p.245–366

Ningyo den　人魚伝

'Legenda o morske panne' Přel. Vlasta Winkelhöferová. *Červený kokon.* Praha, Odeon, 1971. p.63–109

Omae nimo tsumi ga aru　おまえにも罪がある

'You, too, are guilty' Tr. by Ted T. Takaya. *Anthology of modern Japanese drama.* N. Y. Columbia Univ. Press, forthcoming.

Oshi musume　啞むすめ

'The deaf girl' Tr. by Andrew Horvat. *Four stories by Kobo Abe.* Tokyo, Hara Shobo, 1973. p.3–30

Purūtō no wana　プルートーのわな

'푸루토의 陷穽'　車明根訳　「日本研究」　19巻12号　1974.　p.74–77

Shijin no shōgai　詩人の生涯

'Osud básníka'　Přel. J. Winkelhöfer a V. Winkelhöferová. *Svetová Literatura*, no.6, 1958. p.61–66

'Жизнь поэта'　Перевод П. Петрова. *Японская новелла*. Москва, Изд. Иност. Лит. 1961. p.19–26

'Акун омили'　Орысшадан аударган Нурахмет Телеупов. *Хиросима касирети*. Алма-Ата, Жазушы, 1969. p.53–80

'Ocud básníka'　Přel. Vlasta Winkelhöferová. *Červený kokon*. Praha, Odeon, 1971. p.130–141

'Ein Dichterleben'　Deutsch von Jürgen Berndt und Eiitschi Yasui. *Träume aus zehn Nächten*. Berlin, Aufbau Verlag, 1975.　p.476–489

Suna no onna　砂の女

The woman in the dunes.　Tr. by E. Dale Saunders. N. Y. Knopf, 1964; London, Secker and Warburg, 1965; Tokyo, Tuttle, 1965. 241p.; N. Y. Berkley Pub. 1965. 148p.; N. Y. Random House, 1972. 1v.

Písečna zena.　Přel. Miroslav Novák. Praha, Státní Naklad. Krásné Lit. a Uměni, 1965. 182p.

Kvinden i sandet.　Oversaette Michael Tejr. København, Fremad, 1966. 180p.

'Женщина в песках'　Перевод В. Гривнина. *Иностранная Литература*, май 1966. p.8–96

La femme des sables.　Tr. par Georges Bonneau. Paris, Stock, 1967. 288p.

Die Frau in den Dünen.　Übers. von Oscar Benl und Mieko Osaki. Reinbek, Rowohlt, 1967. 219p. 1970. 135p.; Berlin, Volk und Welt, 1974. 283p.

Hiekka.　Suomentanut Antero Tiusanen. Jyväskylä, KJG, 1967. 226p.

'砂丘之女'　鐘肇政訳　「純文學」（台湾版）第1巻4期 1967.　p.1–131;　「純文學」（香港版）第1巻2期 1967.　p.1–131

「砂丘之女」　鐘肇政訳　台北 純文學月刊社 1967. 215p.; 香港　純文學月刊社　1968.　1冊;　香港 正文出版社　1968. 215p.

Kobieta z wydm.　Przeł. Mikołaj Melanowicz. Warszawa, Państowowy Instytut Wydawniczy, 1968. 172p.

Femeia nisipurilor.　În românеşte de Magdalena Levandoski-Popa. Bucureşti, Editura pentru Literatură Universală, 1968. 231p.

Moteris smėlynuose.　Tr. Verte D. Lankauskiené. Vilnius, Vaga, 1968. 263p.

Kunstiliselt kujundanud.　Tõlkinud A. Sisask. Tallinn, Raamat, 1968. 167p.

Кумдали кохтим.　Тошкент, Тослитиздат, 1968. 155p.

'모래의女人'　柳呈訳　「現代世界文学全集 12」 서울 新丘文化社 1968.　p.177–306

A homok asszonya.　Forditotta Csalló Jenő. Budapest, Magveto Könyvkiadó, 1969; 2d ed. Budapest, Európa, 1972. 161p.; Bratislava, Madách Könyvkiadó, 1972. 161p.

Женщина в песках.　Перевод В. Гривнина. Москва, Худож. Лит. 1969. 172p.

Фемеиа нисипурилор, ын молдовенеште де Б. Равий. Кишнев, Карчиа Молдовняскэ, 1969. 211p.

De vrouw in het zand.　Vertaald de Thérèse Cornips. Antwerpen, Bruna, 1969. 1v.

'모래와女人'　安壽吉訳　「오늘의世界文学 10」 서울 民

衆書館　1969.　p.1–138

'Sieviete smiltis'　Tr. from the Russian Irma Berzkalne & Laima Rumniece. *Sieviete smiltis, Svesa seja*. Riga, Liesma, 1970.

La mujer de la arena.　Tr. de Kazuya Sakai. México, Ediciones Era, 1971. 200p.

La donna di sabbia.　Tr. di Atsuko Ricca Suga. Milano, Longanesi, 1972. 206p.

A mulher da areia.　Tr. por Mário Braga. Porto, Liv. Civilização, 1974. 1v.

'砂丘之女'　鐘肇政　劉慕沙訳　「砂丘之女及其他」 台北 純文學出版社　1975.　p.1–191

Tanin no kao　他人の顔

The face of another.　Tr. by E. Dale Saunders. N. Y. Knopf, 1966. 237p.; Tokyo, Tuttle, 1967. 234p.; London, Weidenfeld and Nicolson, 1969. 239p.; Harmondsworth, Penguin Books, 1972. 224p.

'Чужое лицо'　Перевод В. Гривнина. *Иностранная Литература*, декабрь 1967. p.8–132; *Женщина в песках, Чужое лицо*. Москва, Худож. Лит. 1969. p.175–365

La face d'un autre.　Tr. par Tsunemaro Otani avec la collaboration de Louis Frédéric. Paris, Stock, 1969. 272p.

A hegyedik jégkorszak.　Oroszból ford. Karig Sára. Budapest, Kozmosz, 1969. 232p.

'Svesa seja'　Tr. from the Russian Irma Berzkalne & Laima Rumniece. *Sieviete smiltis, Svesa seja*. Riga, Liesma, 1970.

Das Gesicht des Anderen.　Deutsch von Oscar Benl. Reinbek, Rowohlt, 1971. 230p.

Svetimas veidas.　Tr. from the Russian Dalia Lankauskiené. Vilnius, Vaga, 1973. 239p.

Tanpen shōsetsu no kanōsei　短篇小説の可能性

'Время《малых жанров》?'　диалог с Кэндзабуро Оэ. Перевод И. Львовой и В. Гривнина. *Иностранная Литература*, август 1965. p.220–229

Toki no gake　時の崖

'Die Zeitklippe'　Übers. von Siegfried Schaarschmidt. *Der Mann, der zum Stock wurde*. Berlin, Literarisches Colloquium, 1969. p.34–44

'The cliff of time'　Tr. by Andrew Horvat. *Four stories by Kobo Abe*. Tokyo, Hara Shobo, 1973. p.82–111

'Urwisko czasu'　Przeł. Mikołaj Melanowicz. *Literatura na Świecie*, no.7, 1976. p.110–123

Tomodachi　友達

Friends.　Tr. by Donald Keene. N. Y. Grove Press, 1969; Tokyo, Tuttle, 1971. 94p.

'Przyjaciele'　Przeł. Henryk Lipszyc. *Dialog*, no.8, 1975. p.55–91

'Friends'　Tr. by Donald Keene. *Contemporary Japanese literature*, ed. by Howard Hibbett. N. Y. Knopf, 1977. p.54–109

Totarosukōpu　トタロスコープ

'Тоталоскоп'　Перевод С. Бережкова. *Четвертый ледниковый период*. Москва, Молодая Гвардия, 1965. p.215–236

'Totaloscopul'　În românеşte de Iacob Babin. Bucureşti, 1969.

'Totaloskop'　Przeł. Antoni Smuszkiewicz. *Problemy*, no.8, 1974. p.49–53

ABE Kōbō

Uchi naru henkyō　内なる辺境

'The frontier within' Tr. by Andrew Horvat. *Japan Quarterly*, v.22, no.2, p.135–142. v.22, no.3. 1975. p.255–265

Yume no heishi　夢の兵士

'The dream soldier' Tr. by Andrew Horvat. *Japan Quarterly*, v.19, no.1, 1972. p.56–61; *Four stories by Kobo Abe.* Tokyo, Hara Shobo, 1973. p.58–81

Yūrei wa koko ni iru　幽霊はここにいる

'Aquí esta el fantasma' Tr. por Josefina K. Ezaki. *Teatro japonés comtemporaneo.* Madrid, Aguilar, 1964. p.129–221
'Geister in Kitahama' Übers. von Jürgen Berndt. *Japanische Dramen.* Berlin, Volk und Welt, 1968. p.261–377
Geister in Kitahama. Übers. von Jürgen Berndt und Tatsuji Iwabuchi. Berlin, Bühnenvertrieb, 1971. 157p.
'To ja jestem duchem' Przeł. Stanisław Janicki & Yukio Kudo. *Dialog*, no. 1, 1972. p.31–81
'Призраки среди нас' Перевод А. Гривнина. *Абэ Кобо, пьесы.* Москва, Искусство, 1975. p.5–122

Essay　エッセイ

'小説的寫法' 鐘肇政訳 「文壇」第141期 1972. p.37–50

ABE Mitsuko　阿部光子　1912–

Ochibo hiroi　落穂拾い

'The gleaner' Tr. by Peter W. Schumacher. *Japan Christian Quarterly*, v.38, no.4, 1972. p.216–224

ABE Sueo　安倍季雄　1880–1962

Kaidan　怪談

The dying man's revenge. Tr. by Arthur Lloyd. Tokyo, Rikkyosha, 1907. 85p.
'The dying man's revenge' Tr. by Asataro Miyamori. *Representative tales of Japan.* Tokyo, Sanko Shoten, 1914. p.570–594

ABE Tomoji　阿部知二　1903–1973

Akarui tomo　明るい友

'The communist' Tr. by Grace Suzuki. *Ukiyo.* Tokyo, Phoenix Books, 1954. p.172–180; *Ukiyo.* N. Y. Vangard Press, 1963. p.225–229; London, Grosset, 1964. p.225–229

Fuyu no yado　冬の宿

Zimova kwatera. Przeł. Ewelina Tchórzewska-Adamowska. Warszawa, Książka i Wiedza, 1973. 247p.

Hoshizukiyo　星月夜

'Starry night' Tr. by Hisakazu Kaneko. *Young

forever, and five other novelettes. Tokyo, Hokuseido, 1941. p.71–97

Jinkō teien　人工庭園

'人工庭園' 崔一秀訳 「日本代表作家百人集 3」 서울 希望出版社 1966. p.200–247; 「日本短篇文学全集 3」 서울 新太陽社 1969. p.348–395

Nippon no jipushii　日本のじぷしい

'The Japanese gipsies' Tr. by Ineko Sato. *Eigo Seinen*, v.91, no.9–10, 1945. p.147–148; v.91, no.11–12, 1945. p.181–183

Shiroi bara　白いバラ

'Белая роза' Перевод С. Гутермана. *Японская новелла 1960–1970.* Москва, Прогресс, 1972. p.32–50

Shiroi tō　白い塔

Белый обелиск. Перевод В. Логуновой. Москва, Прогресс, 1966. 175p.

Criticism　評論

'亜非作家会議的成果' 李芒訳 「世界文学」 1961年5月 p.20–22

ABE Yoshishige　安倍能成　1883–1966

Essay　エッセイ

'恋愛그리고自殺' 金賢珠訳 「바이바이바다」 서울 三韓出版社 1966. p.315–323

ABURAYA Hisako　油谷緋沙子

'桂冠' 劉慕沙訳 「日本現代小説選」 台北 聯經出版 1976. p.85–119

AGAWA Hiroyuki　阿川弘之　1920–

Gunkan poruka　軍艦ポルカ

'軍艦폴카' 柳呈訳 「日本代表作家百人集 5」 서울 希望出版社 1966. p.40–50; 「日本短篇文学全集 5」 서울 新太陽社 1969. p.336–346

Hikari no mizuumi　光の湖

'光彩의湖水' 金東済訳 「日本新鋭文学作家受賞作品集 1」 서울 青雲社 1964. p.40–48; 「戦後日本短篇文学全集 1」 서울 日光出版社 1965. p.40–48;「現代日本代表文学全集 1」 서울 平和出版社 1973. p.40–47

Kōmori　蝙蝠

'박쥐' 金龍済訳 「日本新鋭文学作家受賞作品集 1」 서울 青雲社 1964. p.22–38; 「戦後日本短篇文学全集 1」 서울 日光出版社 1965. p.22–38;「現代日本代表文学全集 1」 서울 平和出版社 1973. p.22–38

Ma no isan　魔の遺産

「悪魔的遺産」 顔華訳 北京 作家出版社 1956. 216p.
Devil's heritage. Tr. by John M. Maki. Tokyo, Hokuseido, 1957. 247p.

Nennen saisai　年年歳歳

'年年歳歳' 金龍済訳 「日本新鋭文学作家受賞作品集 1」

서울 青雲社 1964. p.3–21;「戦後日本短篇文学全集 1」 서울 日光出版社 1965. p.3–21;「現代日本代表文学全集 1」 서울 平和出版社 1973. p.3–21

Tetsudō kenshūkai　鉄道研修会

'鉄道研修会' 金龍済訳「日本新鋭文学作家受賞作品集 1」 서울 青雲社 1964. p.72–86;「戦後日本短篇文学全集 1」 서울 日光出版社 1965. p.72–86;「現代日本代表文学全集 1」 서울 平和出版社 1973. p.72–85

Yamamoto Isoroku　山本五十六

「山本五十六」 曾金山 王逸石訳 嘉義 紅豆書局 1969. 233p.

Yoru no namioto　夜の波音

'밤의 波濤소리' 金龍済訳「日本新鋭文学作家受賞作品集 1」 서울 青雲社 1964. p.49–70;「戦後日本短篇文学全集 1」 서울 日光出版社 1965. p.49–70;「現代日本代表文学全集 1」 서울 平和出版社 1973. p.49–70

AIDA Tsunao　会田綱雄　1914–

Poems　詩

'休暇' 金龍済訳「日本詩集」 서울 青雲社 1960. p.44–46
'Lago salato; Scandalo' *La protesta poetica del Giappone*, a cura di Dacia Maraini e Michiko Nojiri. Roma, Officina Edizioni, 1968. p.57–59
'Wild duck; Legend' Tr. by Edith Marcombe Shiffert and Yuki Sawa. *Anthology of modern Japanese poetry*. Tokyo, Tuttle, 1972. p.109–111
'Homecoming' Remade into English by Thomas Fitzsimmons. *Japanese poetry now*. London, André Deutsch, 1972. p.32; *Japanese poetry today*. N. Y. Schocken Books, 1972. p.34

AIDA Yūji　会田雄次　1916–

Āron shūyōjo　アーロン収容所

Prisoner of the British. Tr. by Hide Ishiguro and Louis Allen. London, Cresset Press, 1966. 202p.

Essay　エッセイ

'女子大生들과의恋愛論争' 金賢珠訳 「바이바이바다」 서울 三韓出版社 1966. p.148–153

AIJIMA Kyokō　相島虚吼　1867–1935

Haiku　俳句

'3 haiku' Tr. by Asataro Miyamori. *Anthology of haiku, ancient and modern*. Tokyo, Maruzen, 1932. p.745–747
'The spring of my garden' Tr. by Asataro Miyamori. *Haiku poems, ancient and modern*. Tokyo, Maruzen, 1940. p.310
'1 haiku' Tr. by Lois J. Erickson. *Songs from the land of dawn*. N. Y. Friendship Press, 1949; Freeport, Books for Libraries Press, 1968. p.70

AIKAWA Takaaki　相川高秋　1905–

Shiina Rinzō　椎名麟三

'Rinzo Shiina: Christian novelist and thinker' *Japan Christian Quarterly*, v.24, no. 1, 1958. p.58–69

AISHINKAKURA Hiro　愛親覚羅　浩

Ruten no ōhi　流轉の王妃

「流浪王妃」 黄凡訳 台北 眞美善出版社 1973. 1冊

AIZU Yaichi　会津八一　1881–1956

Tanka　短歌

'1 tanka' Übers. von Kuniyo Takayasu und Manfred Hausmann. *Ruf der Regenpfeifer*. München, Bechtle Verlag, 1961. p.102
'3 tanka' Tr. by Edith Marcombe Shiffert and Yuki Sawa. *Anthology of modern Japanese poetry*. Tokyo, Tuttle, 1972. p.142

AKAMATSU Gessen　赤松月船　1897–

Tanka　短歌

'1 Lyrik' Übers. von Kuniyo Takayasu und Manfred Hausmann. *Ruf der Regenpfeifer*. München, Bechtle Verlag, 1961. p.84–85

AKAMATSU Mitsuo　赤松光夫　1931–

Misutēku jidai　ミステーク時代

「미스테이크時代」 呉寅泳訳 서울 隆文社 1964. 183p.

AKASHI Noriko　明石祝子

Kōfuku naru kodoku　幸福なる孤独

「幸福한孤独」 서울 新太陽社 1961. 403p.; 서울 南昌文化社 1969. 403p.

AKEDA Yasao　明田弥三夫

Poems　詩

'Grub' *An anthology of modern Japanese poetry*, ed. and tr. by Ichiro Kono and Rikutaro Fukuda. Tokyo, Kenkyusha, 1957. p.1
'Tirtil' Tercüme etmek L. Sami Akalin. *Japon şiiri*. İstanbul, Varlik Yayinevi, 1962. p.301

AKIMOTO Matsuyo　秋元松代　1911–

Hitachibō Kaison　常陸坊海尊

'Kaison, the priest of Hitachi' Tr. by David Good-

AKIMOTO Matsuyo

man. *Concerned Theatre Japan*, v.2, no.3–4, 1973. p.262–303

Reifuku 礼服

'Парадные одежды' Перевод О. Войнюш. *Современные японские пьесы.* Москва, Искусство, 1962. p.149–193

'In Gala' Übers. von Jürgen Berndt. *Japanische Dramen.* Berlin, Volk und Welt, 1968. p.6–59

AKITA Ujaku 秋田雨雀 1883–1962

Asuparagasu アスパラガス

'Asparagus（喜劇)' 楊敬慈訳 「小説月報」第14巻6号 1923. p.1–12

Bokushin to hitsuji no mure 牧神と羊の群れ

'牧神與羊羣' 張暁天訳 「小説月報」第15巻11号 1924. p.1–6

Budda no sensō 仏陀の戦争

'佛陀的戰爭' 暁天訳 「小説月報」第15巻7号 1924. p.1–4

Gaikotsu no buchō 骸骨の舞跳

'Danco de skeletoj' Tr. Kaname Suzuki. *Danco de skeletoj.* Tokyo, Japana Esperanto Instituto, 1927.

'骷髏的跳舞' 一切訳 上海 開明書店 1930. 1冊

Kan o kakomu hitobito 棺を囲む人々

Tiuj, kiuj ĉirkaŭas la ĉerkon. Tr. Junko Shibata. Tokyo, Kokusaigo Kenkyusha, 1928. 24p.

「圍着棺的人們」田漢訳 上海 金屋書店 193?. 1冊

Kitaguni no yoru 北国の夜

'北國之夜' 倪貽徳訳 「語絲」第4巻46期 1928. p.327–353

Kokkyō no yoru 国境の夜

'Nakto ce landlimo' Tr. Hajime Suzui & Kaname Suzuki. *Danco de skeletoj.* Tokyo, Japana Esperanto Instituto, 1927.

'國境之夜' 蕭崇素訳 「摩登月刊」192?.

'A night on the border' Tr. by Tadao Katayama. *The Reeds*, v.6, 1960. p.25–45

Sensei no ohaka 先生のお墓

「先生的墳」孫百剛訳 上海 開明書店 1932. 1冊

Sudara no izumi スダラの泉

'Fonto de sudroj' Tr. Hajime Suzui & Kaname Suzuki. *Danco de skeletoj.* Tokyo, Japana Esperanto Instituto, 1927.

Taiyō to hanazono 太陽と花園

「太陽與花園」林雪清訳 上海 兒童書局 1932. 1冊

Wakaki Sovēto Roshia 若きソヴェート・ロシア

「新俄遊記」文莎訶訳 上海 明月書店 1930. 1冊

Criticism 評論

'蘇聯的藝術概観' 陳直夫訳 「海風週報」第11期 1929. p.11–14

'高爾基之死' 雨田訳 「譯文」新1巻5期 1936. p.881–886

AKIYAMA Hiroshi 秋山 浩 1928–

Tokushutai 731 特殊隊七三一

Особый отряд 731. Перевод М. А. Гусева и др. Москва, Изд. Иност. Лит. 1958. 151p.

Zvláštní útvar 731. Přel. Jiří Jelínek. Praha, Naše Vojsko, 1960. 119p.

「731 細菌部人」北京編訳社訳 北京 群衆書局 1961. 116p.

AKIYAMA Kiyoshi 秋山 清 1905–

Poems 詩

'Early in spring' Tr. by Atsuhiro Sawai. *Trans-Pacific*, v.1, no.4, 1970; *Listening to Japan.* N. Y. Praeger, 1973. p.85

AKIYAMA Shun 秋山 駿 1930–

Criticism 評論

'The simple life' Tr. by Joseph and Chihoko Moran. *New writing in Japan.* London, Penguin Books, 1972. p.192–201

'A survey of literature in 1976' Tr. by Charles S. Terry. *Japanese Literature Today*, no.2, March 1977. p.1–4

AKUTAGAWA Ryūnosuke 芥川龍之介 1892–1927

Abababa あばばばば

'А-ба-ба-ба-ба' Перевод Н. Фельдман. *Акутагава, новеллы.* Москва, Гослитиздат, 1959. p.293–300; *Акутагава Рюноскэ 2.* Москва, Худож. Лит. 1971. p.111–118

Aguni no kami アグニの神

'God Agni' Tr. by Taro Ito. *Eigo Kenkyu*, v.21, no.4, 5, 6, 7, 8, 9, 11. 1928–29.

'阿格尼神' 湯鶴逸訳 「芥川龍之介小説集」上海 文化學社 192?.

'The god of Agni' Tr. by Takamasa Sasaki. *The three treasures, and other stories.* Tokyo, Hokuseido, 1944. p.74–97

'Бог Агни' Перевод И. Головнина. *Акутагава Рюноскэ 1.* Москва, Худож. Лит. 1971. p.373–381

Aki 秋

'秋' 夏丐尊訳 「東方雑誌」第23巻14期 1926. p.103–112; 「芥川龍之介集」上海 開明書店

'Autumn' Tr. by E. Omiya. *Eigo Seinen*, v.58, no.10, 11, 12, v.59, no.2, 3, 4, 5, 6, 7, 8, 9, 1928.

'The autumn' Tr. by Eric S. Bell and Eiji Ukai. *Eminent authors of contemporary Japan*, v.2. Tokyo, Kaitakusha, 1931. p.69–95

'Осень' Перевод Н. Фельдман. *Расёмон.* Ленинград, Гослитиздат, 1936. p.153–172; *Акутагава, новеллы.* Москва, Гослитиздат, 1959. p.150–162; *Акутагава Рюноскэ, 1.* Москва, Хдож. Ллт. 1971. p.306–319

'Autumn' Tr. by Hisao Kitajima and Thomas H. Carter. *Shenandoah*, Winter 1954. p.3–13

'秋' 葉笛訳 「羅生門」 台北 仙人掌出版社 1969.
p.143–158; 台北 大林書店 1973. p.143–158
'Autumn' Tr. by Norimitsu Antoku. *Eigo Eibungaku Ronshu* (Seinan Univ.), v.11, no. 3, 1970.
p.97–111
'Herbst' Übersetzt von Jürgen Berndt. *Rashomon, ausgewählte Kurzprosa.* Berlin, Volk und Welt, 1975. p.267–285

Anchū mondō 闇中問答

'Диалог во тьме' Перевод Н. Фельдман. *Акутагава, новеллы.* Москва, Гослитиздат, 1959.
p.334–342; *Акутагава Рюноскэ 2.* Москва, Худож. Лит.1971. p.265–273
'闇中問答' 葉笛訳 「地獄變」 台北 仙人掌出版社 1969. p.73–87; 台北 大林書店 1973. p.73–87
'Dialogue in darkness' Tr. by Beongcheon Yu. *East-West Review*, v.4, no.1, 1971. p.126–133

Ano koro no jibun no koto あの頃の自分の事

'Ano koro no jibun no koto' Tr. by W. J. Whitehouse. *Eigo no kenkyu to kyoju.* Tokyo, 1938.
'О себе в те годы' Перевод Б. Раскина. *Акутагава Рюноскэ 1.* Москва, Худож. Лит. 1971. p.207–227

Aru ahō no isshō 或阿呆の一生

'敗北' 沈端先訳 「日本小説集」 上海 神州書局 1930.
'某傻子的一生' 馮子韜訳 「芥川龍之介集」 上海 中華書局 1931. p.141–176; 昆明 中華書局 1934. p.141–176
'Жизнь идиота' Перевод Н. Фельдман. *Интернациональная Литература*, номер 9, 1936. p.70–83; *Расемон.* Ленинград, Гослитиздат, 1936. p.326–351; *Акутагава, новеллы.* Москва, Гослитиздат, 1959. p.372–390; *Акутагава Рюноскэ 2.* Москва, Худож. Лит. 1971. p.396–414
'Life of a certain fool' Tr. by Akio Inoue. *Posthumous works of Ryunosuke Akutagawa.* Tenri, Tenri Jihosha, 1961. p.15–37
'某傻瓜的一生' 葉笛訳 「河童」 台北 仙人掌出版社 1969. p.17–43; 台北 大林書店 1973. p.17–43
'어느바보의一生' 安仁吉 方坤訳 「世界随筆文学全集 4」 서울 東西出版社 1969. p.156–179
A fool's life. Tr. by Will Petersen. Tokyo, Mushinsha, 1970. 135p.; N. Y. Grossman, 1970. 135p.
'Життиа идиота' Переклали Иван Дзюб та Геннадии Турков. *Расьомон.* Киев, Жовтень, 1971. p.226–246
'阿呆的一生' 金溟若訳 「羅生門・河童其他六種」 台北 志文出版社 1972. p.157–186
'어느바보의一生' 鄭成換 金泳杓訳 「世界에세이 文学全集 8」 서울 東西出版社 1974. p.156–181; 「世界随筆文学全集 8」 서울 世進出版社 1976. p.156–181

Aru hi no Ōishi Kuranosuke 或日の大石内蔵助

'Оиси Кураноскэ в один из своих дней' Перевод Н. Фельдман. *Акутагава, новеллы.* Москва, Гослитиздат, 1959. p.56–66; *Акутагава Рюноскэ 1.* Москва, Худож. Лит. 1971. p.109–119

Aru katakiuchi no hanashi 或敵打の話

'Рассказ об одной мести' Перевод Н. Фельдман. *Акутагава, новеллы.* Москва, Гослитиздат, 1959. p.163–175; *Акутагава Рюноскэ 1.* Москва, Худож. Лит. 1971. p.326–339
'Die Geschichte einer Rache' Übersetzt von Jürgen Berndt. *Die Geschichte einer Rache.*

Berlin, Volk und Welt, 1973. p.129–149; *Rashomon, ausgewählte Kurzprosa.* Berlin, Volk und Welt, 1975. p.285–302

Aru kyūyū e okuru shuki 或旧友へ送る手記

'Akutagawa's last note: To my old friends' Tr. by John Matsumura. *Japan Times*, July 26, 1927.
'絶筆' 沈端先訳 「芥川龍之介集」 上海 開明書店 1927.
'致某舊友手跡' 湯鶴逸訳 「芥川龍之介小説集」 上海 文化學社 192?.
'A note forewarded to a certain old friend' Tr. by Akio Inoue. *Posthumous works of Ryunosuke Akutagawa.* Tenri, Tenri Jihosha, 1961. p.11–14
'給某舊友的手記' 葉笛訳 「河童」 台北 仙人掌出版社 1969. p.147–151; 台北 大林書店 1973. p.147–151

Aru ren'ai shōsetsu 或恋愛小説

'Любовный роман' Перевод В. Гривнина. *Акутагава Рюноскэ 2.* Москва, Худож. Лит. 1971. p.162–168

Aru shakai shugisha 或社会主義者

'Некий социалист' Перевод Н. Фельдман. *Расемон.* Ленинград, Гослитиздат, 1936. p.280–282; *Акутагава, новеллы.* Москва, Гослитиздат, 1959. p.332–333; *Акутагава Рюноскэ 2.* Москва, Худож. Лит. 1971. p.229–231

Bashō zakki 芭蕉雑記

'Notes on Basho' Tr. by Cid Corman and Susumu Kamaike. *Origin*, v.8, Jan. 1968.

Bisei no shin 尾生の信

'尾生的信' 謝六逸訳 「小説月報」 第18巻9号 1927. p.133–134; 「近代日本小品文選」 上海 開明書店 1929.
'Credo de Bisei' Tr. Yujiro Nagasaka. *Le Revuo Orienta*, Jaro, 11, 1930.
'Как верил Бисэй' Перевод Н. Фельдман. *Акутагава, новеллы.* Москва, Гослитиздат, 1959. p.147–149; *Акутагава Рюноскэ 1.* Москва, Худож. Лит. 1971. p.272–274
'The faith of Wei Sheng' Tr. by Takashi Kojima and John McVittie. *Exotic Japanese stories.* N. Y. Liveright, 1964. p.193–196
'Fidelitatea lui Wei Sheng' În românește de Ion Caraion. *Rashomon.* București, Editura pentru Literatură Universală, 1968. p.5–7
'尾生的信' 夏雲訳 「地獄變」 台北 志文出版社 1969. p.202–204
'Вирность Бисея' Переклали Иван Дзюб та Геннадий Турков. *Расьемон.* Киев, Жовтень, 1971. p.93–95
'Biseis Glaube' Übersetzt von Jürgen Berndt. *Die Geschichte einer Rache.* Berlin, Volk und Welt, 1973. p.317–320; *Rashomon, ausgewählte Kurzprosa.* Berlin, Volk und Welt, 1975. p.244–246

Bungei kōza 文芸講座

'文學一般論' 高明訳 「文藝創造講座 1」 上海 光華書局 n. d.
'文學鑑賞論' 淩堅訳 「文藝創造講座 1」 上海 光華書局 n. d.

Butōkai 舞踏会

'The ball' Tr. by Glenn W. Shaw. *Tales grotesque and curious.* Tokyo, Hokuseido, 1930. p.97–108

AKUTAGAWA Ryūnosuke

'Un bal' *Nippon*, no.6, 1936. p.25–29

'Der Chrysanthemen-Ball' Übers. von Oscar Benl und Kunihiro Kojima. *Der Chrysanthemen-Ball*. München, Nymphenburger, 1964. p.51–61

'Свиаго хризантем' Переклали Иван Дзюб та Геннадий Турков. *Расьомон*. Киев, Жовтень, 1971. p.86–72

Chōkōdo zakki 澄江堂雑記

'Из заметок «Тёкодо»' Перевод Н. Фельдман. *Акутагава Рюноскэ 2*. Москва, Худож. Лит. 1971. p.258–264

Chūtō 偸盗

'Robbers' An abridged and free translation by Tomohisa Miyahara. *Eigo Bungaku*, v.1, no. 5–6, 1918. p.9–12. v.2, no.1, 1918. p.1–6

'Die Räuber' Übers. von Hikaru Tsuji und Kohei Takahara. *Rashomon*. Tübingen, Schlichtenmayer, 1955. p.37–112; Frankfurt am Main, Fischer, 1960. p.45–142

'De rovers' Bewerkt en ingeleid door S. van Praag. *Rashomon, en andere Japanse verteilingen*. Amsterdam, Wereld, 1957. p.9–82

'The robbers' Tr. by Takashi Kojima and John McVittie. *Exotic Japanese stories*. N. Y. Liveright, 1964. p.54–127

'Hoţii' În româneşti de Ion Caraion. *Rashomon*. Bucureşti, Editura pentru Literatură Universală, 1968. p.40–113

'盗賊' 葉笛訳 「地獄變」 台北 仙人掌出版社 1969. p.89–163; 台北 大林書店 1973. p.89–163

'群盗' 権逸松訳 「世界文学全集 47」 서울 三省出版社 1976. p.43–91

Daidōji Shinsuke no hansei 大導寺信輔の半生

'大導寺信輔的半生' 葉笛訳「羅生門」台北 仙人掌出版社 1969. p.105–122; 台北 大林書店 1973. p.105–122

Dōbutsuen 動物園

'Зоологический сад' Перевод М. П. Григориева. *Событие в аду*. Дальний, Южно-Маньчж. Ж. Д. 1940. p.161–171

Dōso mondō 道祖問答

'The Ajari' Tr. by R. E. Morrell. *Young East*, v.12, no.48, 1963. p.18–22

Eiyū no utsuwa 英雄の器

'英雄の器' 謝六逸訳「小説月報」第18巻9号 1927. p.135–136;「近代日本小品文選」上海 開明書店 1929.

'英雄之器' 夏雲訳「地獄變」台北 志文出版社 1969. p.205–207

Fumi hogo 文放古

'Обрывок письма' Перевод Н. Фельдман. *Акутагава Рюноскэ 2*. Москва, Худож. Лит. 1971. p.175–179

Fushigi na shima 不思議な島

'Удивительный остров' Перевод И. Вардуля. *Акутагава Рюноскэ 2*. Москва, Худож. Лит. 1971. p.119–126

Futari Komachi 二人小町

'Futari komachi' Tr. by G. W. Shaw. *Tokyo Nichinichi*, May 15, 1923.

'Futari Komachi' Tr. by Jihei Hashiguchi. *Tokyo Nichinichi*, May 15–18, 1926.

'Futari Komachi' Tr. by T. E. Swann. *Monumenta Nipponica*, v.23, no.3–4, 1968. p.485–495

Futatsu no tegami 二つの手紙

'Du leteroj' Tr. Hirokazu Kaĵi. *La Revuo Orienta*, v.6, no.5–7, 9, 12, v.7, no.1, 3, 5–6, 1926.

Fuyu 冬

'Зима' Перевод Л. Лобачева. *Акутагава Рюноскэ 2*. Москва, Худож. Лит. 1971. p.350–357

'冬以及書信' 葉笛訳 「河童」 台北 仙人掌出版社 1969. p.53–70; 台北 大林書店 1973. p.53–70

Genkaku sanbō 玄鶴山房

'Genkaku-sanbo' Tr. by Takashi Kojima. *Japanese short stories*. N. Y. Liveright, 1961. p.145–170; N. Y. Avon Books, 1963. p.100–117

'Villa Genkaku' Tr. par Arimasa Mori. *Rashomon, et autres contes*. Paris, Gallimard, 1965. p.205–223; Paris, Livre de Poche, 1969. p.249–274

'Genkakus Bergklause' Übers. von Jürgen Berndt. *Japanische Novellen*. Berlin, Volk und Welt, 1964. p.323–345; *Rashomon, zehn Novellen*. Zürich, Diogenes, 1966. p.355–392; *Rashomon, ausgewählte Kurzprosa*. Berlin, Volk und Welt, 1975. p.464–483

'玄鶴山房' 葉笛訳 「羅生門」 台北 仙人掌出版社 1969. p.123–142; 台北 大林書店 1973. p.123–142

'Горная келья Гэнкаку' Перевод Н. Фельдман. *Акутагава Рюноскэ 2*. Москва, Худож. Лит. 1971. p.274–288

Gesaku zanmai 戯作三昧

'Absorbed in letters' Tr. by Takashi Kojima and John McVittie. *Exotic Japanese stories*. N. Y. Liveright, 1964. p.304–340

'L'illumination créatrice' Tr. par Arimasa Mori. *Rashomon, et autres contes*. Paris, Gallimard, 1965. p.163–192; Paris, Livre de Poche, 1969. p.193–231

'Cufunciat in litere' În româneşte de Ion Caraion. *Rashomon*. Bucureşti, Editura pentru Literatură Universală, 1968. p.335–369

'Das Versunkensein des Dichters' Übersetzt von Jürgen Berndt. *Die Geschichte einer Rache*. Berlin, Volk und Welt, 1973. p.321–361; *Rashomon, ausgewählte Kurzprosa*. Berlin, Volk und Welt, 1975. p.86–121

Giwaku 疑惑

'Сомнение' Перевод Н. Фельдман. *Акутагава, новеллы*. Москва, Гослитиздат, 1959. p.133–146; *Акутагава Рюноскэ 1*. Москва, Худож. Лит. 1971. p.225–268

'Der Verdacht' Übers. von Oscar Benl und Kunihiro Kojima. *Chrysanthemen-Ball*. München, Nymphenburger, 1959. p.5–27

'Zweifel' Übers. von Jürgen Berndt. *Japanische Novellen*. Berlin, Volk und Welt, 1964. p.169–189; *Rashomon, ausgewählte Kurzprosa*. Berlin, Volk und Welt, 1975. p.225–244

'疑惑' 葉笛訳 「河童」 台北 仙人掌出版社 1969. p.131–146; 台北 大林書店 1973. p.131–146

Haguruma 歯車

'歯輪' 沈端先訳 「東方雑誌」第25巻21期 1928. p.127–138, 25巻22期 1928. p.121–130

'Зубчатые колеса' Перевод Н. Фельдман. *Расемон.* Ленинград, Гослитиздат, 1936. p.283–325; *Акутагава, новеллы.* Москва, Гослитиздат, 1959. p.343–371; *Акутагава Рюноскэ 2.* Москва, Худож. Лит. 1971. p.367–395

'Los engranajes' Tr. por Kazuya Sakai. *Kappa, Los engranajes.* Buenos Aires, Mundo Nuevo, 1959.

'The cogwheel' Tr. by Beongcheon Yu. *Chicago Review,* v.18, no.2, 1965.

'歯車' 葉笛訳 「文學季刊」第5期 1967. p.172–191; 「河童」台北 仙人掌出版社 1969. p.71–110; 台北 大林書店 1973. p.71–110

'歯車' 崔泰應訳 「世界의 文學大全集 8」서울 同和出版公社 1970. p.200–236; 「羅生門外・斜陽」서울 同和出版公社 1972. p.36–85

'歯車' 金溟若訳 「羅生門・河童及其他六種」台北 志文出版社 1972. p.187–229

'톱니바퀴' 高永絢訳 「日本文学全集 10」서울 東西文化院 1975. p.20–44

'Zahnräder' Übersetzt von Jürgen Berndt. *Die Geschichte einer Rache.* Berlin, Volk und Welt, 1973. p.183–229; *Rashomon, ausgewählte Kurzprosa.* Berlin, Volk und Welt, 1975. p.549–588

Haha 母

'母親' 馮子韜訳 「芥川龍之介集」上海 中華書局 1931. p.1–22; 昆明 中華書局 1934. p.1–22

'母親' 夏雲訳 「地獄變」台北 志文出版社 1969. p.138–154

Hana 鼻

'鼻子' 魯迅訳 「現代日本小説集」上海 商務印書館 1923; 「芥川龍之介集」上海 開明書店 1927; 「日本現代小説集 3」上海 商務印書館 1930. p.309–318; 「魯迅全集 11」上海 魯迅全集出版社 1938. 作家書屋 1946. 大連 光華書店 1948. 北京 人民文學出版社 1973. 大連 光華書店 1948. 北京 人民文學出版社 1958. p.552–562; 「魯迅譯文集 1」北京 人民文學出版社 1958. p.555–562 「現代日本小説集」香港 建文書局 1959. p.145–154

'Hana' Tr. by A. Spann and A. Ennenberg. *Japan Times,* Sept. 4, 1927.

'Hana' Tr. by Haruo Endo and Eric S. Bell. *Osaka Mainichi,* Sept. 6–20, 1927.

'Le nez' Tr. par Juntaro Maruyama. *Le nez.* Tokyo, Hakusuisha, 1927. p.2–29

'Die Nase' Übers. von Alexander Spann. *Die Brücke* (Shanghai), Jahrgang 3, Nr.33–36, 1927.

'The nose' Tr. by Glenn W. Shaw. *Tales grotesque and curious.* Tokyo, Hokuseido, 1930. p.15–28; *Rashomon, and other stories.* Tokyo, Hara Shobo, 1964. p.58–83

'The nose' Tr. by Eric S. Bell and Eiji Ukai. *Eminent authors of contemporary Japan,* v.2. Tokyo, Kaitakusha, 1931. p.97–112

'Die Nase' Übers. von Heinrich Eggert. *Ostasiatische Rundschau,* Jahrgang 18, Nr.21, 1937. p.571–573

'Hana' Tr. by Shigejiro Ichikawa. *The Current of the World,* v.27, no.10, 1950. p.44–46

'The nose of Naigu Zenchi' Tr. by T. Fukuda. *Eigo Seinen,* v.98, no.7, 1952. p.313–315

'La nazo' Tr. Jasutaro Nojima. *La Revuo Orienta,* v. 83, no.4, 1952. p.122–124, no.5, 1952. p.156–159; *La kapao, kaj aliaj rakontoj.* Tokyo, Japana Esperanto Instituto, 1954.

'Le nez' Tr. par Kaze Keita. *Les Œuvres Libres,* nouv. série. no.106, 1955. p.99–107

'The nose' Tr. by Ivan Morris. *Japan Quarterly,* v.2, no.4, 1955. p.469–474

'鼻子' 新興書局編集部訳 「日本短篇小説選」台北 新興書局 1958. p.108–114; 台南 鳴宇出版社 1972. p.108–114

'Die Nase' Übers. von Oscar Benl. *Chrysanthemen-Ball.* München, Nymphenburger, 1959. p.69–80

'La nariz' Tr. por Kazuya Sakai. *El biombo del infierno, y otras cuentos.* La Mandrágora, 1959. p.9–16

'鼻子' 「日本作家十二人集」香港 新學書店 1959. p.49–57

'Nos' Přel. Vlasta Hilská. *Obraz pekla.* Praha, SNKHLU, 1960. p.81–91

'The nose' Tr. by Takashi Kojima. *Japanese short stories.* N. Y. Liveright, 1961. p.193–205; N. Y. Avon Books, 1963. p.136–143

'Le nez' Tr. par Arimasa Mori. *Rashomon, et autres contes.* Paris, Gallimard, 1965. p.68–75; Paris, Livre de Poche, 1969. p.55–66

'코' 李鐘烈訳 「日本文学選集 3」서울 知文閣 1966; 서울 韓国読書文化院 1973. p.14–25

'코' 方基煥訳 「日本代表作家百人集 1」서울 希望出版社 1966. p.205–210; 「日本短篇文学全集 1」서울 新太陽社 1969. p.205–210

'코' 崔泰應訳 「世界의 文學大全集 8」서울 同和出版公社 1970. p.191–194; 「羅生門外・斜陽」서울 同和出版公社 1972. p.18–29

'Нос' Перевод А. Стругацкого. *Акутагава Рюноскэ 1.* Москва, Худож. Лит. 1971. p.39–46

'Ніс' Переклали Іван Дзюб та Геннадій Турков. *Расьемон.* Київ, Жовтень, 1971. p.24–31

'코' 崔浩然訳 「新訳世界文学全集 48」서울 正音社 1972. p.11–17

'鼻子' 金溟若訳 「羅生門・河童其他六篇」台北 志文出版社 1972. p.22–30

'코' 高永絢訳 「日本文学大全集 10」서울 東西文化院 1975. p.11–15

'Die Nase' Übersetzt von Jürgen Berndt. *Die Geschichte einer Rache.* Berlin, Volk und Welt, 1973. p.67–78; *Rashomon, ausgewählte Kurzprosa.* Berlin, Volk und Welt, 1975. p.13–22

'鼻' 金文洙訳 「世界代表短篇文学全集 21」서울 正韓出版社 1976. p.279–285

'코' 權逸松訳 「世界文学全集 47」서울 三省出版社 1976. p.21–25

'코' 李吉鐘訳 「世界短篇文学全集 20」서울 金字堂 1976. p.21–32

'코' 陳雄基訳 「羅生門」서울 汎友社 1977. p.31–41

'Cái mũi' Bản dịch của Vũ Minh Thiều. *Lã sinh môn.* Saigon, Gió Bốn Phương, n.d. p.9–20

Hankechi 手巾

'手巾' 方光燾訳 「芥川龍之介集」上海 開明書店 1927.

'The handkerchief' Tr. by Glenn W. Shaw. *Tales grotesque and curious.* Tokyo, Hokuseido, 1930. p.29–44; *Rashomon, and other stories.* Tokyo, Hara Shobo, 1964. p.84–113

'Носовой платок' Перевод Н. Фельдман. *Расемон.* Ленинград, Гослитиздат, 1936. p.29–42; *Акутагава, новеллы.* Москва, Гослитиздат, 1959. p.34–42; *Акутагава Рюноскэ 1.* Москва, Худож. Лит. 1971. p.71–80

'Handkerchief' Tr. by Kiyoshi Morikuro. *Asia and the Americans,* v.43, 1943. p.300–303

'The handkerchief' *World of great stories.* N. Y. Crown Publishers, 1947.

'Kapesník' Přel. Vlasta Hilská. *Obraz pekla.* Praha, SNKHLU, 1960. p.203–205

'Il fazzoletto' Tr. di Mario Teti. *Kappa, e altri racconti.* Milano, Bompiani, 1961. p.111–122

'The handkerchief' Tr. by Takashi Kojima. *Eibungaku Kenkyu* (Meiji Univ), no.21, 1963. p.90–99

'The handkerchief' Tr. by Takashi Kojima and John McVittie. *Exotic Japanese stories*. N. Y. Liveright, 1964. p.140–151

'Le mouchoir' Tr. par Arimasa Mori. *Rashomon, et autres contes*. Paris, Gallimard, 1965. p.224–233; Paris, Livre de Poche, 1969. p.275–288

'The handkerchief' Tr. by Norimitsu Antoku. *Eigo Eibungaku Ronshu* (Seinan Gakuin Univ.), v.7, no.2, 1966. p.151–159

'Batista' În româneste de Ion Caraion. *Rashomon*. Bucureşti, Editura pentru Literatură Universală, 1968. p.28–39

'Хустечка' Переклали Иван Дзюб та Геннадий Турков. *Расьемон*. Киев, Жовтень, 1971. p.39–48

'手巾' 金溪若訳 「羅生門及其他六篇」 台北 志文出版社 1972. p.55–66

'Das Taschentuch' Übersetzt von Jürgen Berndt. *Die Geschichte einer Rache*. Berlin, Volk und Welt, 1973. p.151–164; *Rashomon, ausgewählte Kurzprosa*. Volk und Welt, 1975. p.54–66

'Chiếc khăn tay' Bản dịch của Vũ Minh Thiều. *Lã sinh môn*. Saigon, Gió Bốn Phương, n.d. p.77–91

Hina 雛

'Les poupées' Tr. par Serge Elisséev. *Japon et Extrême-Orient*, no.4, mars 1924. p.327–346; *Neuf nouvelles japonaises*. Paris, G. van Œst, 1924. p.55–73

'The dolls' Tr. by Takashi Kojima and John McVittie. *Exotic Japanese stories*. N. Y. Liveright, 1964. p.152–169

'Papusile' În româneşte de Ion Caraion. *Rashomon*. Bucureşti, Editura pentru Literatură Universală, 1968. p.225–242

'Die Puppen' Übersetzt von Jürgen Berndt. *Die Geschichte einer Rache*. Berlin, Volk und Welt, 1973. p.17–36; *Rashomon, ausgewählte Kurzprosa*. Berlin, Volk und Welt, 1975. p.403–420

Hōkyōnin no shi 奉教人の死

'The martyr' Tr. by Takashi Kojima. *Rashomon, and other stories*. N. Y. Liveright, 1952. p.72–89; Tokyo, Tuttle, 1952. p.53–68; Tokyo, Tuttle, 1954. p.60–75

'Morto de kredanto' Tr. Akihiko Isiguro. *Esperanto*, v.22, no.2–4, 1954. p.48–52, 80–83, 116–118

'Le martyr' Tr. de Arimasa Mori. *Rashomon, et autres contes*. Paris, Gallimard, 1965. p.147–149; Paris, Livre de Poche, 1969. p.153–170

'Смерть христианина' Перевод А. Рябкина. *Акутагава Рюноскэ 1*. Москва, Худож. Лит. 1971. p.182–192

Hōonki 報恩記

'Повесть об отплате добро' Перевод Н. Фельдман; *Расемон*. Ленинград, Гослитиздат, 1936. p.210–232; *Акутагава, новеллы*. Москва, Гослитиздат, 1959; *Акутагава Рюноскэ 2*. Москва, Худож. Лит. 1971. p.21–36

'Gratitude' Tr. by Takashi Kojima and John McVittie. *Exotic Japanese stories*. N. Y. Liveright, 1964. p.170–192

'Die Geschichte von der Vergeltung einer guten Tat' Übers. von Jürgen Berndt. *Japanische Novellen*. Berlin, Volk und Welt, 1964. p.45–68; *Rashomon, zehn Novellen*. Zürich, Diogenes, 1966. p.45–84; *Rashomon, ausgewählte Kurzprosa*. Berlin, Volk und Welt, 1975. p.358–379

'Rasplata binelui' În româneşte de Ion Caraion. *Rashomon*. Bucureşti, Editura pentru Literatură Universală, 1968. p.261–281

Hyottoko ひょっとこ

'Hyottoko' Tr. by Paul McCarthy. *Monumenta Nipponica*, v.24, no.4, 1969. p.499–505

'Маска Хёттоко' Перевод Л. Ермаковой. *Акутагава Рюноскэ 1*. Москва, Худож. Лит. 1971. p.32–38

Ikkai no tsuchi 一塊の土

'一塊土' 湯鶴逸訳 「芥川龍之介小説集」 上海 文化學社 192?.

'Клочек земли' Перевод Н. Фельдман. *Расемон*. Ленинград, Гослитиздат, 1936. p.244–259

'A clod of earth' Tr. by Richard McKinnon. *The heart is alone*. Tokyo, Hokuseido, 1957. p.118–133

'Ком земли' Перевод Н. Фельдман. *Акутагава, новеллы*. Москва, Гослитиздат, 1959. p.301–311; *Акутагава Рюноскэ 2*. Москва, Худож. Лит. 1971. p.147–157

'A clod of soil' Tr. by Takashi Kojima. *Eibungaku Kenkyu* (Meiji Univ.), no.19, 1961. p.112–124; *Japanese short stories*. N. Y. Liveright, 1961. p.78–96; N. Y. Avon Books, 1963.

'Ein Stück Erde' Übers. von Jürgen Berndt. *Rashomon, zehn Novellen*. Zürich, Diogenes, 1966. p.17–44; *Rashomon, ausgewählte Kurzprosa*. Berlin, Volk und Welt, 1975. p.441–456

'Un bulgare de pamint' În româneşte de Ion Caraion. *Rashomon*. Bucureşti, Editura pentru Literatură Universală, 1968. p.304–320

'Грудка земли' Переклали Иван Дзюб та Геннадий Турков. *Расьемон*. Киев, Жовтень, 1971. p.164–174

Imogayu 芋粥

'Yam gruel' Tr. by Takashi Kojima. *Rashomon and other stories*. N. Y. Liveright, 1952. p.45–71; Tokyo, Tuttle, 1952. p.28–52; Tokyo, Tuttle, 1954. p.35–59

'Jam kasa' Prevod Vera Ilić. *Rasomon*. Beograd, Nolit, 1958.

'Gruau d'ignames' Tr. de Arimasa Mori. *Rashomon, et autres contes*. Paris, Gallimard, 1965. p.95–114; Paris, Livre de Poche, 1969. p.95–120

'A maniókakása' Forditotta Sz. Holti Mária. *Modern Japán elbeszélők*. Budapest, Európa Könyvkiadó, 1967. p.77–90

'Crema de patate' În româneşte de Ion Caraion. *Rashomon*. Bucureşti, Editura pentru Literatură Universală, 1968. p.282–303

'Батовая каша' Перевод А. Стругацкого. *Акутагава Рюноскэ 2*. Москва, Худож. Лит. 1971. p.47–64

'죽' 崔浩然訳 「新訳世界文学全集 48」 서울 正音社 1972. p.27–43

'芋粥' 金溪若訳 「羅生門・河童及其他六篇」 台北 志文出版社 1972. p.31–54

'Der Batatenbrei' Übersetzt von Jürgen Berndt. *Die Geschichte einer Rache*. Berlin, Volk und Welt, 1973. p.237–264; *Rashomon, ausgewählte Kurzprosa*. Berlin, Volk und Welt, 1975. p.22–46

'참마즉' 權逸松訳 「世界文学全集 47」 서울 三省出版社 1976. p.27–41

Itojo oboegaki 糸女覚え書

'Показния девицы Ито о кончине благородной госпожи Сюрин...' Перевод И. Львовой. *Акутагава Рюноскэ 2*. Москва, Худож. Лит. 1971. p.137–146

Jashūmon 邪宗門

'Jashumon' Tr. by W. H. H. Norman. *Hell screen, and other stories*. Tokyo, Hokuseido, 1948. p.61–134; N. Y. Greenwood Press, 1971. p.61–134

'Dzasumon' Prevod sa engleskog Vera Ilić. *Rasomon*. Beograd, Nolit, 1958. p.48–112

'Heresy' Tr. by Takashi Kojima and John McVittie. *Exotic Japanese stories*. N.Y. Liveright, 1964. p.358–418

Jigokuhen 地獄変

'地獄變相' 江鍊百訳 「小説月報」 第18巻9号 1927. p.48–65

The horrors of hell' Tr. by Einosuke Omiya. *Eigo Seinen*, v.76, no. 4, 6, 8, 10, 12, 1937. v. 77, no.1–5, 7–10, 12, 1937.

'Муки ада' Перевод Н. Фельдман. *Расемон*. Ленинград, Гослитиздат, 1936. p.99–138; *Акутагава, новеллы*. Москва, Гослитиздат, 1959. p.84–111; *Акутагава Рюноскэ 1*. Москва, Худож. Лит. 1971. p.141–169

'Событие в аду' Перевод М. П. Григориева. *Событие в аду*. Дальний, Южно-Маньчж. Ж Д. 1940. p.19–68

'Hell screen' Tr. by W. H. H. Norman. *Hell screen, and other stories*. Tokyo, Hokuseido, 1948. p.15–60; *Modern Japanese Literature*, ed. by Donald Keene. N. Y. Grove Press, 1956. p.307–332; Tokyo, Tuttle, 1957. p.307–332; *Hell screen, and other stories*. N. Y. Greenwood Press, 1971. p.15–60

'El biombo del infierno' Tr. por Kazuya Sakai. *Rashomon*. Buenos Aires, Lopez Negri, 1959. p.39–64; *El biombo del infierno, y otras cuentos*. La Mandrágora, 1959. p.37–64

'Das Höllentor' Übers. von Hikaru Tsuji und Kohei Takahara. *Rashomon*. Tübingen, Schlichtenmayer, 1956. p.25–35; Frankfurt am Main, Fischer, 1960. p.27–43

Les portes de l'enfer. Tr. de Ivan Morris, Mlle Rosenblum et M. Beerblock. Paris, Stock, 1957.

'Dzigokuhen' Prevod sa engleskog Vera Ilić. *Rasomon*. Beograd, Nolit, 1958. p.7–47

'Helvedesskaermen' Tr. Ingeborg Stemann. *Helvedesskaermen, Rashomon*. København, Steen Hasselbalchs Forlag, 1958. p.11–45

'Die Qualen der Hölle' Übers. von Oscar Benl und Kunihiro Kojima. *Chrysanthemen-Ball*. München, Nymphenburger, 1959. p.96–148

'Obraz pekla' Přel. Vlasta Hilská. *Obraz pekla*. Praha, SNKHLU, 1960. p.21–64

El biombo infernal. Tr. por Vicente Gaos. Madrid, Arion, 1961. 75p.

'The hell screen' Tr. by Takashi Kojima. *Japanese short stories*. N. Y. Liveright, 1961. p.29–77; N. Y. Avon Books, 1963. p.24–54

'Il paravento infernale' Tr. di Mario Teti. *Kappa, e altri racconti*. Milano, Bompiani, 1961. p.153–231

'Die Qualen der Hölle' Übers. von Jürgen Berndt. *Japanische Novellen*. Berlin, Volk und Welt,

1964; *Rashomon, zehn Novellen*. Zürich, Diogenes, 1966. p.167–236; *Rashomon, ausgewählte Kurzprosa*. Berlin, Volk und Welt, 1975. p.136–175

'Figures infernales' Tr. par Arimasa Mori. *Rashomon, et autres contes*. Paris, Gallimard, 1965. p.33–67; Paris, Livre de Poche, 1969. p.11–54

'Il paravento infernale' Tr. di Atsuko Ricca Suga. *Narratori giapponesi moderni*. Milano, Bompiani, 1965. p.293–328

'Las puertas del infierno' Tr. por Alberto Luis. *Las puertas del infierno*. Barcelona, Luis de Caralt, 1965.

'地獄變' 葉笛訳 「文學季刊」 第5期 1967. p.192–211; 「地獄變」 台北 仙人掌出版社 1969. p.17–51; 台北 大林書店 1973. p.17–51

'De folteringen van de hel' Vertaald de J. J. Strating. *De folteringen van de hel; en andere griezelverhalen*. Amsterdam, Meulenhoff, 1969.

'地獄變' 夏雲訳 「地獄變」 台北 志文出版社 1969. p.7–43

'地獄變' 權逸松訳 「世界文学全集 47」 서울 三省出版社 1976. p.100–127

'地獄變' 陳雄基訳 「羅生門」 서울 汎友社 1977. p.85–132

Juriano Kichisuke じゆりあの・吉助

'Дзюриано Китискэ' Перевод Р. Кима. *Восточный сборник*, вып. 1, 1924. p.188–191

'Дзюриано Китискэ' Перевод Н. Фельдман. *Акутагава, новеллы*. Москва, Гослитиздат, 1959. p.130–132; *Акутагава Рюноскэ 1*. Москва, Худож. Лит. 1971. p.269–271

Kage 影

'影' 顧壽白訳 「小説月報」 第18巻9号 1927. p.71–79

'影子' 夏雲訳 「地獄變」台北 志文出版社 1969. p.167–187

Kaeru 蛙

'青蛙' 賴祥雲訳 「芥川龍之介的世界」 台北 志文出版社 1977. p.177–179

Kaika no ryōjin 開化の良人

'開通的丈夫' 周頌久訳 「小説月報」 第18巻9号 1927. p.91–102

'開通的丈夫' 夏雲訳 「地獄變」台北 志文出版社 1969. p.66–88

'Просвещенный супруг' Перевод Б. Раскина. *Акутагава Рюноскэ 1*. Москва, Худож. Лит. 1971. p.228–247

Kaika no satsujin 開化の殺人

'開化的殺人' 鄭心南 梁希杰訳 「小説月報」 第18巻9号 1927. p.65–70

'The old murder' *Orient-West*, v.6, no.9, 1961. p.75–79

'開化的殺人' 夏雲訳 「地獄變」 台北 志文出版社 1969. p.55–65

'Убийство в век «просвещения»' Перевод Б. Раскина. *Акутагава Рюноскэ 1*. Москва, Худож. Лит. 1971. p.170–181

'Der zivilisierte Mörder' Übersetzt von Jürgen Berndt. *Die Geschichte einer Rache*. Berlin, Volk und Welt, 1973. p.111–128; *Rashomon, ausgewählte Kurzprosa*. Berlin, Volk und Welt, 1975. p.175–189

Kamigami no bishō 神々の微笑

'Улыбка богов' Перевод М. П. Григориева.

AKUTAGAWA Ryūnosuke

Событие в аду. Дальний, Южно-Маньчж. Ж. Д. 1940. p.69–86

'Усмешка богов' Перевод Н. Фельдман. *Акутагава Рюноскэ 2.* Москва, Худож. Лит. 1971. p.5–14

Kappa 河童

'河童' 黎烈文訳「小説月報」第18巻9号 1927. p.120–132, 10号 p.63–79;「河童」上海 商務印書館 1928. p.1–109;「芥川龍之介集」上海 商務印書館 1928;「現代日本文學叢刊」上海 文化生活出版社 1936.
'河童' 馮子韜訳「芥川龍之介集」上海 中華書局 1931. p.61–139; 昆明 中華書局 1934. p.61–139
Der Kappa. Übers. von Yoshiyuki Kosaka und W. Roth. Tokyo, Shobundo Verlag, 1934. 202p.
Kappa. Tr. by Seiichi Shiojiri. Osaka, Akitaya, 1947. 154p.; Tokyo. Hokuseido, 1949. 136p.; Pasadena, Perkins, 1950. 144p.; N. Y. Greenwood Press, 1970. 136p.
'La kapao' Tr. Jasutaro Nojima. *La kapao, kaj aliaj rakontoj.* Tokyo, Japana Esperanto Instituto, 1954.
Vodnici. Přelozil Imrich Zalupsky. Bratislava, Slov. Spis, 1958. 73p.
Kapa. Prevod sa Voja Colanovic. Beograd, Rad, 1959. 116p.; 1960. 120p.
'Kappa' Traducción por Kazuya Sakai. *Kappa, Los engranajes.* Buenos Aires, Mundo Nuevo, 1959.
'Kappa, Wasserkobold' Übers. von K. Watanabe. *Japanische Meister der Erzählung.* Bremen, Dorn, 1960.
'A kappák' Fordította Lomb Kató. *A vihar kapujában.* Budapest, Európa Könyvkiadó, 1960. p.22–71
'Mezi vodniky' Přel. Vlasta Hilská. *Obraz pekla.* Praha, SNKHLU, 1960. p.137–202
'Kappa' Traduzione di Mario Teti. *Kappa, e altri racconti.* Milano, Bompiani, 1961.
В стране водяных. Перевод А. Стругацкого. Москва, Гослитиздат, 1962. 79p.; Москва, Худож. Лит. 1970. 119p
Kappy. Przełożył Mikołaj Melanowicz. Warszawa, Państowowy Instytut Wydawniczy, 1963. 99p.
'The Kappa' Tr. by Takashi Kojima and John McVittie. *Exotic Japanese stories.* N.Y. Liveright, 1964. p.209–265
'Les Kappa' Tr. par Arimasa Mori. *Rashomon, et autres contes.* Paris, Gallimard, 1965. p.234–282; Paris, Livre de Poche, 1969. p.289–349
'В стране водяных' Перевод К. Хисано. *Русский Язык,* вып. 5–6, 1965. p.20–27, 19–27
'Kappa' Übers. von Jürgen Berndt. *Rashomon, zehn Novellen.* Zürich, Diogenes, 1966. p.237–334; *Rashomon, ausgewählte Kurzprosa.* Berlin, Volk und Welt, 1975. p.493–548
'河童' 柳呈訳「世界短篇文学全集 7」서울 啓蒙社 1966. p.251–297;「世界文學全集 9」서울 三珍社 1971. p.120–166;「世界代表短篇全集 9」서울 三熙社 1976. p.120–166;「世界短篇文学全集」서울 新韓出版社 1976. p.204–280
'Kappa' În românește de Ion Caraion. *Rashomon.* București, Editura pentru Literatură Universală, 1968. p.166–224
'河童' 葉笛訳「河童」台北 仙人掌出版社 1969. p.153–211; 台北 大林書店 1973. p.153–211
Kappa. Tr. by Geoffrey Bownas. London, Peter Owen, 1970. 141p.; Tokyo, Tuttle, 1970. 141p.
'河童' 崔泰應訳「世界의文學大全集 8」서울 同和出版公社 1970. p.200–236
'В стране водяных' Перевод А. Стругацкого. *Акутагава Рюноскэ 2.* Москва, Худож. Лит.

1971. p.296–342
'河童' 金溟若訳「羅生門・河童及其他六篇」台北 志文出版社 1972. p.67–128
Kappa. Tr. por Eva Iribare Dietrich. Caracas, Editorial Tiempo Nuevo, 1971. 166p.
'У кратни водяникив' Переклали Иван Дзюб та Геннадий Турков. *Расьемон.* Киев, Жовтень, 1971. p.183–225
Víz alatti embereik. Fordította Lomb Kató. Budapest, Mágyar Helikon, 1975. 83p.
'Ngúai Điên' Bản dịch của Vũ Minh Thiều. *Lã sihn môn.* Saigon, Gió Bốn Phương, n. d. p.93–168

Kareno shō 枯野抄

'Withered fields' Tr. by Takashi Kojima and John McVittie. *Exotic Japanese stories.* N. Y. Liveright, 1964. p.291–303
'Winter field' Tr. by Hiroaki Sato. *Chanoyu Quarterly,* no.9, 1974. p.71–77

Kesa to Moritō 袈裟と盛遠

'袈裟與盛遠' 方光燾訳「芥川龍之介集」上海 開明書店 1927.
'Kessa et Morito' Tr. par Kuni Matsuo et E. Steinilber-Oberlin. *France-Japon,* année 2, no.10, 1935. p.163–166
'Kessza es Morito' Ford. Thein Alfréd. *Mai Japán dekameron.* Budapest, Nyugat, 1935. p.25–36
'Кеса и Морито' Перевод Н. Фельдман. *Расемон.* Ленинград, Гослитиздат, 1936. p.85–96; *Акутагава, новеллы.* Москва, Гослитиздат, 1959. p.76–83; *Акутагава Рюноскэ 2.* Москва, Худож. Лит. 1971. p.129–136
'Kesa and Morito' Tr. by Takashi Kojima. *Rashomon, and other stories.* N. Y. Liveright, 1952. p.90–101; Tokyo, Tuttle, 1952. p.69–79; Tokyo, Tuttle, 1954. p.76–86
'Kesa and Morito' Tr. by Howard Hibbett. *Modern Japanese literature.* N. Y. Grove Press, 1956. p.300–306; Tokyo, Tuttle, 1957. p.300–306
'Kesa en Morito' Bewerkt en ingleleid door S. van Praag. *Rashomon, en andere Japanse vertellingen.* Amsterdam, Wereld, 1957. p.97–108
'Kesa et Morito' Tr. par I. I. Morris, Mlle Rosenblum et M. Beerblock. *Les portes de l'enfer.* Paris, Stock, 1957. p.13–25
'Kesa y Moritō' Tr. por Kazuya Sakai. *Sur,* no. 249, Nov.-Dec. 1957. p.27–33; *El biombo del infierno, y otras cuentos.* Buenos Aires, La Mandrágora, 1959. p.29–35
'Kesa i Morito' Prevod sa engleskog Vera Ilić. *Rasomon.* Beograd, Nolit, 1958. p.206–216
'Kesa and Morito' Tr. by Shigeru Tadokoro. *Jinbun Kagaku* (Wakayama Univ.), no.9, 1959. p.1–12
'Kesa und Morito' Übers. von Hisashi Kojima. *Kesa und Morito, die Kindsmörderin.* Tokyo, Japanisch Deutsche Gesellschaft, 1959. p.1–23
'Kesa a Morito' Přel. Vlasta Hilská. *Obraz pekla.* Praha, SNKHLU, 1960. p.112–124
'Kesa i Morito' Przełozyła Anna Gostyńska. *Irys, opowiadania japońskie.* Warszawa, Państowowy Instytut Wydawniczy, 1960. p.88–98
'The affair between Kesa and Morito' Tr. by Shigeru Tadokoro. *France-Asie,* no.170, nov.-dec. 1961. p.2613–2619
'Lady Kesa and imperial guardsman Morito' Tr.

by Ryozo Matsumoto. *Japanese literature, new and old.* Tokyo, Hokuseido, 1961. p.75–88
'Kesa und Morito' Übersetzt von Jürgen Berndt. *Die Geschichte einer Rache.* Berlin, Volk und Welt, 1973. p.37–49; *Rashomon, ausgewählte Kurzprosa.* Berlin, Volk und Welt, 1975. p.121–132
'袈裟와盛遠' 權逸松訳 「世界文学全集 47」서울 三省出版社 1976. p.92–99

Kin shōgun　金将軍

'金将軍' 湯鶴逸訳 「芥川龍之介小説集」上海　文化學社 192?.

Kirishitohoro Shōnin den　きりしとほろ上人伝

'Der Tod des "Rôrenzo" Übers. von W. Roth. *Nippon*, Jahrgang 1, 1935. p.206–216
'Der Tod des Rorenzo' *Geschichten und Erzählungen aus Japan.* Leipzig, Fikentscher Verlag, 1950. p.156–169

Kiseru　煙管

'The pipe' Tr. by Glenn W. Shaw. *Tales grotesque and curious.* Tokyo, Hokuseido, 1930. p.109–122; *Rashomon, and other stories.* Tokyo, Hara Shobo, 1964. p.134–163
'Die Pfeife' Übers. von Oscar Benl und Kunihiro Kojima. *Chrysanthemen-Ball.* München, Nymphenburger, 1959.

Kodomo no byōki　子供の病気

'The sick infant' Tr. by Norimitsu Antoku. *Eigo Eibungaku Ronshu* (Seinan Gakuin Univ.), v.9, no.1, 1968. p.95–102
'Болезнь ребенка' Перевод Б. Раскина. *Акутагава Рюноскэ 2.* Москва, Худож. Лит. 1971. p.98–106

Kokui seibo　黒衣聖母

'黒衣聖母' 湯鶴逸訳 「芥川龍之介小説集」上海　文化學社 192?.
'Мадонна в черном' Перевод И. Львовой. *Акутагава Рюноскэ 1.* Москва, Худож. Лит. 1971. p.320–325

Konan no ōgi　湖南の扇

'湖南的扇子' 夏丏尊訳 「小説月報」第18巻9号 1927. p.106–113; 「芥川龍之介集」上海　開明書店 1927.
'Хунаньский веер' Перевод Л. Лобачева. *Акутагава Рюноскэ 2.* Москва, Худож. Лит. 1971. p.206–218
'湖南之扇' 葉笛訳 「河童」台北　仙人掌出版社 1969. p.115–130; 台北　大林書店 1973. p.115–130

Kōryōmu　黄粱夢

'黄粱夢' 謝六逸訳 「小説月報」第18巻9号 1927. p.137; 「近代日本小品文選」上海　開明書店 1929.
'黄粱夢' 夏雲訳 「地獄變」台北　志文出版社 1969. p.210–211

Kōshoku　好色

'Heichu, the amorous genius' Tr. by Takashi Kojima. *Japanese short stories.* N. Y. Liveright, 1961. p.124–144; N. Y. Avon Books, 1963. p.85–99
'好色' 權逸松訳 「世界文学全集 47」서울　三省出版社 1976. p.143–156

Kubi ga ochita hanashi　首が落ちた話

'The story of a fallen head' Tr. by Eric S. Bell and Eiji Ukai. *Japan Times*, Sept. 25, 1927; *Eminent authors of contemporary Japan, v.1.* Tokyo, Kaitakusha, 1930. p.82–108; *Eigakusei*, 1935.
'О том, как отваливалась голова' Перевод Н. Фельдман. *Расемон.* Ленинград, Гослитиздат, 1936. p.72–84
'Рассказ о том, как отвалилась голова' Перевод Н. Фельдман. *Акутагава, новеллы.* Москва, Гослитиздат, 1959. p.67–75; *Акутагава Рюноскэ 2.* Москва, Худож. Лит. 1971. p.120–128

Kumo no ito　蜘蛛の糸

'La fadeno de araneo' Tr. Kjoji Horiuchi. *La Revuo Orienta*, v.7, no. 12, 1926. p.278–280
'Le fil d'araignée' Tr. par Juntaro Maruyama. *La Smouse*, t.2, no.1–3, 1926. p.7–9, 20–23, 30–33
'The spider's web' Tr. by Eric S. Bell and Eiji Ukai. *Japan Times*, Sept. 11, 1927; *Eminent authors of contemporary Japan v.2.* Tokyo, Kaitakusha, 1931. p.61–68
'Araneajo' Tr. Machiko Kaji. *Esperanto*, Jaro 2, 1927.
'蜘蛛糸' 黎烈文訳 「文學週報」第5巻 1927. p.113–119; 「芥川龍之介集」上海　商務印書館 1928; 「河童」上海　商務印書館　1928. p.111–121
'蜘蛛糸' 湯鶴逸訳 「文學週報」第5巻3期 1928; 「芥川龍之介小説集」上海　文化學社 192?.
'The spider's thread' Tr. by Glenn W. Shaw. *Tales grotesque and curious.* Tokyo, Hokuseido, 1930. p.67–74; *Rashomon, and other stories.* Tokyo, Hara Shobo, 1964. p.164–175; *The Mentor book of modern Asian literature.* N. Y. New American Library, 1969. p.432–435
'Паутинка' Перевод М. П. Григориева. *Событие в аду.* Дальний, Южно-Маньчж. Ж. Д. 1940. p.148–153
'Il filo di ragno' Tr. di Soichi Nogami. *Yamato*, v.1, no.1, 1941. p.22–23
'The spider-thread' Tr. by F. J. Daniels. *Japanese prose.* London, Lund Humphries, 1944. p.36–49
'The spider's thread' Tr. by Takamasa Sasaki. *The three treasures, and other stories for children.* Tokyo, Hokuseido, 1944. p.45–53
'The spider's thread' Tr. by Yoshimatsu Suzuki. *Eigo Seinen*, v.96, no.2, 1950. p.66–68
'The spider's thread' Tr. by Umeyo Hirano. *Young East*, no.10, 1954; *Buddhist plays from Japanese literature.* Tokyo, CIIB Press, 1963. p.96–100
'Il filo del ragno' Tr. di Giovanni Cirillo. *Il Giappone*, anno 1, no.1–2, 1957. p.19–22
'Edderkoppertraaden' Tr. Ingeborg Stemann. *Helvedesskaermen, Rashomon, Edderkoppertraaden.* København, Steen Hasselbalchs Forlag, 1958. p.55–59
'The spider's thread' Tr. by Takashi Kojima. *Eibungaku Kenkyu* (Meiji Univ.), no.19, 1959. p.125–131; *Japanese short stories.* N. Y. Liveright, 1961. p.187–192; N. Y. Avon Books, 1963. p.130–135
'Pavouci vlakno' Přel. Vlasta Hilská. *Obraz pekla.* Praha, SNKHLU, 1960. p.92–96;
'Pokhalo' Fordította Lomb Kató. *A vihar kapujában.* Budapest, Európa Könyvkiadó, 1960. p.7–10

AKUTAGAWA Ryūnosuke

'Il filo del ragno' Tr. di Mario Teti. *Kappa, e altri raconti*. Milano, Bompiani, 1961. p.163–168

'The spider's thread' Tr. by Norimitsu Antoku. *Seinan Gakuin Joshi Tanki Daigaku Kenkyu Kiyo*, no.10, 1964. p.92–96

'Le fil d'araignée' Tr. par Arimasa Mori. *Rashomon, et autres contes*. Paris, Gallimard, 1965. p.133–136; Paris, Livre de Poche, 1969. p.145–152

'Firul de paianjen' În românește de Ion Caraion. *Rashomon*. București, Editura pentru Literatură Universală, 1968. p.256–260

'거미줄' 崔泰應訳 「世界의 文学大全集 8」 서울 同和出版公社 1970. p.197–199; 「羅生門外・斜陽」 서울 同和出版公社 1972. p.30–35

'Паутинка' Перевод В. Марковой. *Акутагава Рюноскэ 1*. Москва, Худож. Лит. 1971. p.137–147

'Паутинка' Переклалн Иван Дзюб та Геннадий Турков. *Расьемон*. Киев, Жовтень, 1971. p.49–51

'거미줄' 高永絢訳 「日本文学大全集 10」 서울 東西文化院 1975. p.17–19

'Der Faden der Spinne' Übersetzt von Jürgen Berndt. *Die Geschichte einer Rache*. Berlin, Volk und Welt, 1973. p.231–235: *Rashomon, ausgewählte Kurzprosa*. Berlin, Volk und Welt, 1975. p.132–136

'거미줄' 李吉鐘訳 「世界短篇文学全集 20」 서울 金字堂 1976. p.33–39

'蜘蛛之糸' 頼祥雲訳 「芥川龍之介的世界」 台北 志文出版社 1977. p.183–187

'Sợi tơ nhện' Bản dịch của Vũ Minh Thiều. *Lã sinh môn*. Saigón, Gió Bôn Phương, n.d. p.53–57

Majutsu 魔術

'Magic art' Tr. by Seizo Mori. *Osaka Mainichi*, Sept. 23–26, 1927.

'魔術' 侍桁訳 「現代日本小説」 上海 春潮書房 1929. p.213–229

'魔術' 湯鶴逸訳 「芥川龍之介小説集」 上海 文化學社 192?.

'魔術' 査士元訳 「日本現代名家小説集」 上海 中華書局 1930.

'Magic' Tr. by Takamasa Sasaki. *The three treasures, and other stories for children*. Tokyo, Hokuseido, 1944. p.54–73.

'Zauberkünste' Übers. von Kakuji Watanabe. *Japanische Meister der Erzählung*. Bremen, Dorn, 1960. p.47–55

'魔術' 夏雲訳 「地獄變」 台北 志文出版社 1969. p.155–166

'Чудеса магии' Перевод В. Марковой. *Акутагава Рюноскэ 1*. Москва, Худож. Лит. 1971. p.275–283

MENSURA ZOILI

'Mensura Zoili' Tr. by Tadao Katayama. *The Reeds*, v.12, 1968. p.145–152

'Mensura Zoili' Перевод Н. Фельдман. *Расемон*. Ленинград, Гослитиздат, 1936. p.64–71; *Акутагава, новеллы*. Москва, Гослитиздат, 1959. p.43–47; *Акутагава Рюноскэ 1*. Москва, Худож. Лит. 1971. p.89–94

'Mensura zoili' Tr. by W. H. H. Norman. *Hell screen, and other stories*. Tokyo, Hokuseido, 1948. p.169–176; N. Y. Greenwood Press, 1970. p.169–176

'Mensura zoili' Tr. di Mario Teti. *Kappa, e altri raconti*. Milano, Bompiani, 1961. p.153–159

'Mensura Zoili' 葉笛訳 「羅生門」 台北 仙人掌出版社 1969. p.163–170; 台北 大林書店 1973. p.163–170

Mikan 蜜柑

'Les mandarines' Tr. par Juntaro Maruyama. *La Smouse*, t.2, no.6–8, 1926. p.16–19, 11–14, 16–19

'橘子' 行澤訳 「眞美善」 第1巻10期 1928. p.1–17

'Mikan' Tr. by Tomokazu Nishira. *Corona Australis*, 1930.

'蜜柑' 高汝鴻訳 「日本短篇小説集」 上海 商務印書館 1935. p.21–26; 台北 台湾商務印書館 1969. p.21–26

'Мандарины' Перевод Н. Фельдман. *Расемон*. Ленинград, Гослитиздат. 1936. p.139–144; *Акутагава, новеллы*. Москва, Гослитиздат, 1959. p.126–129; *Акутагава Рюноскэ 1*. Москва, Худож. Лит. 1971. p.248–251

'The mandarin oranges' Tr. by T. Yuasa. *Contemporary Japan*, v.6, no. 4, 1938. p.631–634

'Мандарины' Перевод М. П. Григориева. *Событие в аду*. Дальний, Южно-Маньчж. Ж. Д. 1940. p.110–116

'Tangerines' Tr. by Ineko Sato. *Eigo Seinen*, v. 93, no.3, 1949. p.110–113

'A naranes' Fordította Lomb Kató. *A vihar kapujában*. Budapest, Európa Könyvkiadó, 1960. p.11–14

'Tangerines' *Orient-West*, v.6, no.9, 1961. p.73–75

'The tangerines' Tr. by Takashi Kojima. *Japanese short stories*. N. Y. Liveright, 1961. p.206–211; N. Y. Avon Books, 1963. p.144–148

'The oranger' Tr. by Norimitsu Antoku and Gunichi Antoku. *Seinan Gakuin Joshi Tanki Daigaku Kenkyu Kiyo*, no.10, 1964. p.96–101

'Mandarinen' Übers. von Masayuki Sugawara. *Kanazawa Daigaku Kyoyobu Ronshu, Jinbun Kagaku hen*, no.3, 1966. p.21–24

'Mandarinele' În românește de Ion Caraion. *Rashomon*. București, Editura pentru Literatură Universală, 1968. p.370–374

'The tangerines' Tr. by Norimitsu Antoku. *Eigo Eibungaku Ronshu* (Seinan Gakuin Univ.), v.9, no.2, 1969. p.115–118

'蜜柑' 葉笛訳 「地獄變」 台北 仙人掌出版社 1969. p.69–72; 台北 大林書店 1973. p.69–72

'Мандарини' Переклали Иван Дзюб та Ґеннадий Турков. *Расьемон*. Киев, Жовтень, 1971. p.82–85

'Mandarinen' Übersetzt von Jürgen Berndt. *Die Geschichte einer Rache*. Berlin, Volk und Welt, 1973. p.89–95; *Rashomon, ausgewählte Kurzprosa*. Berlin, Volk und Welt, 1975. p.221–225

'밀차' 陳雄基訳「羅生門」서울 汎友社 1977. p.61–69

'橘子' 頼祥雲訳「芥川龍之介的世界」台北 志文出版社 1977. p.135–138

'Polsom' Tr. by Nithima Apiwattanawong. *Rueng sun yeepun 1*. Bangkok, Uksornsasna, 1977. p.110–119

Mittsu no mado 三つの窓

'三個窗子' 葉笛訳 「羅生門」 台北 仙人掌出版社 1969. p.185–197; 台北 大林書店 1973. p.185–197

'Три окна' Перевод В. Гривнина. *Акутагава Рюноскэ 2*. Москва, Худож. Лит. 1971. p.358–366

Mittsu no naze 三つのなぜ

'三個為什麼' 葉笛訳 「羅生門」 台北 仙人掌出版社 1969. p.171–176; 台北 大林書店 1973. p.171–176

Mittsu no takara 三つの宝

'Les trois trésors' Tr. par Juntaro Maruyama.

Le nez. Tokyo, Hakusuisha, 1927. p.52–56
'The three treasures' Tr. by Takamasa Sasaki. *The three treasures, and other stories for children.* Tokyo, Hokuseido, 1944. p.1–23
'I tre tesori' Tr. di Leo Maquino. *Teatro Giapponese.* Milano, Nuova Accademia Editrice, 1956. p.261–279
'Три сокровища' Перевод В. Гривнина. *Акутагава Рюноскэ 2.* Москва Худож. Лит. 1971. p.76–85
'Три скарби' Переклали Иван Дзюб та Геннадий Турков. *Расьемон.* Киев, Жовтень, 1971. p.154–163

Momotarō 桃太郎

'Момотаро' *Азия и Африка Сегодня,* номер 8, 1974. p.37–39

Mōri sensei 毛利先生

'Mori sensei' Tr. by Glenn W. Shaw. *Tales grotesque and curious.* Tokyo, Hokuseido, 1930. p.123–144
'Учитель Мори' Перевод Н. Фельдман. *Акутагава, новеллы.* Москва, Гослитиздат, 1959. p.112–125; *Акутагава Рюноскэ 2.* Москва, Худож. Лит. 1971. p.193–206
'Professor Mori' Übers. von Oscar Benl und Kunihiro Kojima. *Chrysanthemen-Ball.* München, Nymphenburger, 1959. p.28–50
'Professor Mori' Übers. von Jürgen Berndt. *Japanische Novellen.* Berlin, Volk und Welt, 1964. p.291–310; *Rashomon, ausgewählte Kurzprosa.* Berlin, Volk und Welt, 1975. p.189–207

Mujina 貉

'The badger' Tr. by Glenn W. Shaw. *Tales grotesque and curious.* Tokyo, Hokuseido, 1930. p.89–96
'Jezevec' Přel. Vlasta Hilská. *Obraz pekla.* Praha, SNKHLU, 1960. p.76–80
'The badger' Tr. by Takashi Kojima and John McVittie. *Exotic Japanese stories.* N. Y. Liveright, 1964. p.353–357
'Mujina' Tr. by Yutaka Kato. *Osaka Kyoiku Daigaku Eibun Gakkaishi,* no. 9, 1964. p.53–57

Myō na hanashi 妙な話

'奇譚' 夏韞玉訳 「小説月報」 第18巻9号 1927. p.103–106
'A strange story' Tr. by Taro Ito. *Eigo to Eibungaku,* v.4, no.3, 1929. p.206–207, no.4, 1929. p.282–283, no.5, 1929. p.356–357
'Странная история' Перевод Н. Фельдман. *Акутагава, новеллы.* Москва, Гослитиздат, 1959. p.194–199; *Акутагава Рюноскэ 1.* Москва, Худож. Лит. 1971. p.391–396
'奇譚' 夏雲訳 「地獄變」台北 志文出版社 1969. p.103–109

Nankin no Kirisuto 南京の基督

'南京的基督' 鄭心南訳 「小説月報」 第18巻9号 1927. p.113–120
'南京的基督' 夏丏尊訳 「芥川龍之介集」 上海 開明書店 1927.
'南京基督' 湯鶴逸訳 「芥川龍之介小説集」 上海 文化學社 192?.
'The Christ of Nankin' Tr. by W. M. Bickerton. *Eigo Seinen,* v.65, no. 1–7, 1931.
Le Christ de Nankin. Paris, 1931. 1v.
'南京之基督' 高汝鴻訳 「日本短篇小説集」 上海 商務印書館 1935. p.1–19; 台北 台湾商務印書館 1969. p.1–19

'Нанкинский Христос' Перевод Н. Фельдман. *Акутагава, новеллы.* Москва, Гослитиздат, 1959. p.176–187; *Акутагава Рюноскэ 1.* Москва, Худож. Лит. 1971. p.355–366
'Christ in Nanking' Tr. by Saburo Haneda. *The Reeds,* v.6, 1960. p.3–22
Jesus-Christus van Nanking. Vertaald door Daniel Ellegiers. St. Andries Brugge, Verbeke-Loys, 1967. 51p.
'南京的基督' 夏雲訳 「地獄變」 台北 志文出版社 1969. p.188–201
'南京的基督' 葉笛訳 「地獄變」 台北 仙人掌出版社 1969. p.165–180; 台北 大林書店 1973. p.165–180
'Нанкинськой Христос' Переклали Иван Дзюб та Геннадий Турков. *Расьемон.* Киев, Жовтень, 1971. p.96–107

Negi 葱

'Лук' Перевод И. Головнина. *Акутагава Рюноскэ 1.* Москва, Худож. Лкт. 1971. p.284–293

Nenmatsu no ichinichi 年末の一日

'День в конце года' Перевод В. Гривнина. *Акутагава Рюноскэ 2.* Москва, Худ. Лит. 1971. p.219–222

Nezumi kozō Jirokichi 鼠小僧次郎吉

'Nezumi-kozo—the Japanese Robin Hood' Tr. by Takashi Kojima. *Japanese short stories.* N. Y. Liveright, 1961. p.97–123; N. Y. Avon Books, 1963. p.68–84
'Nezumi-kozo haiducul' În românește de Ion Caraion. *Rashomon.* București, Editura pentru Literatură Universală, 1968. p.126–148
'Jirokichi Nezumikozo' Übersetzt von Jürgen Berndt. *Die Geschichte einer Rache.* Berlin, Volk und Welt, 1973. p.265–289; *Rashomon, ausgewählte Kurzprosa.* Berlin, Volk und Welt, 1975. p.246–267

Nidai 尼提

'尼提' 葉笛訳 「羅生門」 台北 仙人掌出版社 1969. p.159–162; 台北 大林書店 1973. p.159–162

Niwa 庭

'Сад' Перевод Н. Фельдман. *Расемон.* Ленинград, Гослитиздат, 1936. p.233–243; *Акутагава, новеллы.* Москва, Гослитиздат, 1959. p.260–267; *Акутагава Рюноскэ 2.* Москва, Худож. Лит. 1971. p.42–49
'The garden' Tr. by Takashi Kojima and John McVittie. *Exotic Japanese stories.* N. Y. Liveright, 1964. p.341–352
'Der Garten' Übers. von Jürgen Berndt. *Japanische Novellen.* Berlin, Volk und Welt, 1966. p.311–322; *Rashomon, zehn Novellen.* Zürich, Diogenes, 1966. p.335–354; *Rashomon, ausgewählte Kurzprosa.* Berlin, Volk und Welt, 1975. p.379–389
'Gradina' În românește de Ion Caraion. *Rashomon.* București, Editura pentru Literatură Universală, 1968. p.114–125
'Сад' Переклали Иван Дзюб та Геннадий Турков. *Расьемон.* Киев, Жовтень, 1971. p.145–153

Numachi 沼地

'The picture of a quagmire' Tr. by Yoshimatsu

AKUTAGAWA Ryūnosuke

Suzuki. *Eigo Seinen*, v.44, no.8, no.9, 1921. p.231, 265

'沼池' 行澤訳 「眞美善」 第1巻11期 1928. p.1–6

'Marsh' Tr. by Kazuo Yamada. *Eigo Seinen*, v.81, no.9, 1939. p.277–278

'The marshland' Tr. by Beongcheon Yu. *Chicago Review*, v.18, no.2, 1965.

'Ein Moor' Übers. von Masayuki Sugawara. *Kanazawa Daigaku Kyoyo Ronshu Jinbun Kagaku hen*, no.3, 1966. p.25–27

'沼地' 葉笛訳 「文學季刊」 第5期 1967. p.220–221; 「河童」 台北 仙人掌出版社 1969. p.111–114; 台北 大林書店 1973. p.111–114

'A marsh' Tr. by Norimitsu Antoku. *Eigo Eibungaku Ronshu* (Seinan Gakuin Univ.), v.10, no.1, 1969. p.67–69

'Трясина' Перевод В. Сановича. *Акутагава Рюноскэ 1*. Москва, Худож. Лит. 1971. p.251–254

Nyotai 女体

'Тело женщины' Перевод Р. Кима. *Восточный Сборник*, вып. 1, 1924. p.188–191

'女體' 謝六逸訳 「小説月報」 第18巻9号 1927. p.134–135 「近代日本小品文選」 上海 開明書店 1929.

'A woman's body' Tr. by Takashi Kojima and John McVittie. *Exotic Japanese stories*. N. Y. Liveright, 1964. p.419–421

'女體' 夏雲訳 「地獄變」台北 志文出版社 1969. p.208–209

Ogata Ryōsai oboegaki 尾形了斎覚え書

'Le rapport d'Ogata Ryôsai' Tr. par Arimasa Mori. *Rashomon, et autres contes*. Paris, Gallimard, 1965. p.150–155; Paris, Livre de Poche, 1969. p.171–180

'Показания Огата Рёсай' Перевод И. Львовой. *Акутагава Рюноскэ 1*. Москва, Худож. Лит. 1971. p.103–108

Ogin おぎん

'O'Gin' Tr. par Juntaro Maruyama. *Le nez*. Tokyo, Hakusuisha, 1927. p.30–50

Oguim. Tr. Jose Cabral de Lacerda & Minoru Izaua. Lisboa, Imprensa Nacional, 1930. 54p.

'О-Гин' Перевод Н. Фельдман. *Расемон*. Ленинград, Гослитиздат, 1936. p.201–209; *Акутагава, новеллы*. Москва, Гослитиздат, 1959. p.287–292; *Акутагава Рюноскэ 2*. Москва, Худож. Лит. 1971. p.69–73

'Ogin' Tr. di Maria Colombina Rossi. *Il Giappone*, v.1, no.4, 1961. p.43–46; *Antologia della letteratura coreana e giapponese*. Milano, Fratelli Fabbri, 1969. p.303–308

'Ogin' Tr. par Arimasa Mori. *Rashomon, et autres contes*. Paris, Gallimard, 1965. p.156–162; Paris, Livre de Poche, 1969. p.181–192

Oitaru Susanō no Mikoto 老いたる素戔鳴尊

'Le vieux Susanoo' Tr. par Juntaro Maruyama. *Le nez*. Tokyo, Hakusuisha, 1927. p.86–134

'Les vieux jours du vénérable Susanoo' Tr. par Arimasa Mori. *Rashomon, et autres contes*. Paris, Gallimard, 1965. p.115–132; Paris, Livre de Poche, 1969. p.122–144

'Сусаноо-но-микото на склоне лет' Перевод И. Вардуля. *Акутагава Рюноскэ 1*. Москва, Худож. Лит. 1971. p.340–354

Ojigi お時儀

'The greeting' Tr. by Takashi Kojima. *Eibungaku Kenkyu* (Meiji Univ.), no.21, 1963. p.100–104

'The greeting' Tr. by Takashi Kojima and John McVittie. *Exotic Japanese stories*. N. Y. Liveright, 1964. p.284–290

'Die Verbeugung' Übers. von Klaus Altendorf. *Japan, Geistige Begegnung*. Tübingen, Erdmann, 1964. p.161–166; *Eine Glocke in Fukagawa*. Tübingen, Erdmann, 1969. p.137–166

'Die Verbeugung' Übers. von Jürgen Berndt. *Rashomon, zehn Novellen*. Zürich, Diogenes, 1966. p.137–150; *Rashomon, ausgewählte Kurzprosa*. Berlin, Volk und Welt, 1975. p.434–441

'Greeting' Tr. by Norimitsu Antoku. *Eigo Eibungaku Ronshu* (Seinan Gakuin, Univ.), v.8, no.1, 1967. p.97–102

'Поклон' Перевод А. Рябкина. *Акутагава Рюноскэ 2*. Москва, Худож. Лит. 1971. p.106–110

Ōjō emaki 往生絵巻

'Праведшая кончина' Перевод М. П. Григориева. *Событие в аду*. Дальний, Южно-Маньчж. Ж. Д. 1940. p.54–160

'Кончина праведника' Перевод И. Львовой. *Акутагава Рюноскэ 1*. Москва, Худож. Лит. 1971. p.397–401

'往生絵巻' 權逸松訳 「世界文学全集 47」서울 三省出版社 1976. p.139–141

Onna 女

'女' 湯鶴逸訳 「芥川龍之介小説集」上海 文化學社 192?.

Otomi no teisō お富の貞操

'阿富的貞操' 謝六逸訳 「小説月報」 第18巻9号 1927. p.80–86; 「接吻」 上海 大江書舗 1929.

'Otomi's virtue' Tr. by Kazuo Nishida. *Asia Scene*, Dec. 1955. p.24–26, 36–39

'Чистота О-Томи' Перевод Н. Фельдман. *Акутагава, новеллы*. Москва, Гослитиздат, 1959. p.276–286; *Акутагава Рюноскэ 2*. Москва, Худож. Лит. 1971. p.59–68

'Otomi's virginity' Tr. by Takashi Kojima. *Japanese short stories*. N. Y. Liveright, 1961. p.171–186

'Chasteté d'Otomi' Tr. par Arimasa Mori. *Rashomon, et autres contes*. Paris, Gallimard, 1965. p.193–204; Paris, Livre de Poche, 1969. p.231–248

'O-Tomi erintetlensege' Ford. Hani Kjoko. *Nagyvilág*, 1966–67. p.985–989

'O-Tomi hüsége' Ford. Sz. Holti Mária. *Modern Japán elbeszélők*. Budapest, Európa Könyvkiadó, 1967. p.91–98

'Fecioria lui Otomi' În românește de Ion Caraion. *Rashomon*. București, Editura pentru Literatură Universală, 1968. p.243–255

'阿富的貞操' 夏雲訳 「地獄變」 台北 志文出版社 1969. p.89–102

'阿富的貞操' 葉笛訳 「地獄變」 台北 仙人掌出版社 1969. p.181–196; 台北 大林書店 1973. p.181–196

'O-Tomis Keuschheit' Übersetzt von Jürgen Berndt. *Die Geschichte einer Rache*. Berlin, Volk und Welt, 1973. p.51–66; *Rashomon, ausgewählte Kurzprosa*. Berlin, Volk und Welt, 1975. p.389–403

'Tâm lòng trinh bạch của Tiêu-hũư' Bản dịch của Vũ Minh Thiều. *Lã sinh môn*. Saigon, Gió Bốn Phương, n.d. p.59–75

Rashōmon 羅生門

'Rashomon' Tr. by Glenn W. Shaw. *Eigo Seinen*, v.44, no.1–6, 1920; *Tales grotesque and curious*. Tokyo, Hokuseido, 1930. p.45–56; *Rashomon, and other stories*. Tokyo, Hara Shobo, 1964. p.8–31

'羅生門' 魯迅訳 「現代日本小説集」 上海 商務印書館 1923;「芥川龍之介集」 上海 開明書店 1927;「日本現代小説集 3」 上海 商務印書館 1930. p.319–328;「魯迅全集 11」 上海 魯迅全集出版社 1938. 作家書屋 1946. 大連 光華書店 1948. 北京 人民文学出版社 1973. p.563–572;「魯迅譯文集 1」 北京 人民文学出版社 1958. p.563–570;「現代日本小説集」 香港 建文書局 1959. p.115–164

'Rashomon' Übers. von Heinz Brasch. *Yamato*, Jahrgang 4, 1932. p.63–70

'Расёмон' Перевод Н. Фельдман. *Расемон*. Ленинград, Гослитиздат, 1936. p.19–28

'Rashomon' Tr. by Takashi Kojima. *Rashomon, and other stories*. N. Y. Liveright, 1952. p.19–27; Tokyo, Tuttle, 1952. p.19–27; *Treasury of world literature*. N. Y. Philosophical Library, 1956. p.10–15; *Masterpieces of the Orient*. N. Y. Norton, 1961. p.380–385; *The Mentor book of modern Asian literature*. N. Y. New American Library, 1969. p.380–385

'Rasho-mon' Tr. por Takeshi Ehara. *Cuentos japoneses*. Buenos Aires, Komori, 1954. p.11–22

'Rashomon' Tr. por Kazuya Sakai. *Rashomon*. Buenos Aires, Lopez Negri, 1954; *El biombo de infierno, y otras cuentos*. Buenos Aires, La Mandrágora, 1959. p.3–8

'Rashomon' Übers. von Hikaru Tsuji und Kohei Takahara. *Rashomon*. Tübingen, Schlichtenmayer, 1955. p.9–24

'羅生門'「少年の悲哀」 郁達夫等訳 台北 啓明書局 1956. p.82–87

'Rashomon' Tr. Ingeborg Stemann. *Helvedesskaermen, Rashomon*. København, Steel Hasselbalchs Forlag, 1958. p.46–54

'Rasomon' Preved sa engleskog Vera Ilić. *Rasomon*. Beograd, Nolit, 1958. p.113–121

'Ворота Расёмон' Перевод Н. Фельдман. *Акутагава, новеллы*. Москва, Гослитиздат, 1959. p.21–27; *Акутагава Рюноскэ 1*. Москва, Худож Лит. 1971. p.25–31

'Raschomon' Übers. von Kakuji Watanabe. *Japanische Meister der Erzählung*. Bremen, Dorn, 1960. p.39–46

'A Raso-kapu' Fordította Lomb Kató. *A vihar kapujában*. Budapest, Európa Könyvkiadó, 1960. p.15–21

'Rashomon' Přel. Vlasta Hilská. *Obraz pekla*. Praha, SNKHLU, 1960. p.65–75

'Rashômon' Übers. von Walter Donat. *Die fünfstöckige Pagode*. Düsseldorf, Diederichs, 1960. p.155–165; Regensburg, Pustet, n. d. p.157–165

'Rashô-mon' Tr. di Romano Vulpitta. *Il Giappone*, v.1, no.1, 1961. p.43–46

'La Rasyomon' Tr. Masao Miyamoto. *La Revuo Orienta*, v.42, no.11–12, 1961. v.43, no.1, 1962.

'Rashomon' Tr. di Mario Teti. *Kappa, e altri racconti*. Milano, Bompiani, 1961. p.21–29

'羅生門' 郭夏信訳 「世界文学全集 94」 서울 乙酉文化社 1962. p.207–213

'Rashomon' Übers. von Jürgen Berndt. *Japanische Novellen*. Berlin, Volk und Welt, 1964. p.115–124; *Rashomon, zehn Novellen*. Zürich, Diogenes, 1966. p.151–166; *Rashomon, ausgewählte Kurzprosa*. Berlin, Volk und Welt, 1975. p.5–13

'Rashômon' Tr. par Arimasa Mori. *Rashomon, et autres contes*. Paris, Gallimard, 1965. p.76–83; Paris, Livre de Poche, 1969. p.67–78

Rasiomono vartai. Tr. V. Rudokas. Vilnius, Vaga, 1965. 1v.

'羅生門' 李鐘烈訳 「日本文学選集 3」 서울 知文閣 1966; 서울 韓国読書文化院 1973. p.7–13

'羅生門' 方基煥訳 「日本代表作家百人集 1」 서울 希望出版社 1966. p.200–204;「日本短篇文学全集 1」 서울 新太陽社 1969. p.200–204

'Raşamon' Tr. Tarik Dursun K. *Raşamon*. Ankara, Bilgi Yayinevi, 1966.

'羅生門' 葉笛訳 「羅生門」 台北 仙人掌出版社 1968. p.17–25; 台北 大林書店 1973. p.17–25

'Rashomon' În românește de Ion Caraion. *Rashomon*. București, Editura pentru Literatură Universală, 1968. p.8–15

'羅生門' 崔泰應訳 「世界의文学大全集 8」 서울 同和出版公社 1970. p.183–189;「羅生門外・斜陽」 서울 同和出版公社 1972. p.7–16

'Расьемон' Переклали Иван Дзюб та Геннадий Турков. *Расьемон*. Киев, Жовтень, 1971. p.16–28

'羅生門' 金溟若訳 「羅生門・河童及其他六篇」 台北 志文出版社 1972. p.13–21

'A vihar kapujában' Ford. Gergely Ágnes. *Nagyvilág*, no.12, 1972. p.1763–1766; *A vihar kapujában*. Budapest, Európa Könyvkiadó, 1974.

'羅生門' 高永鉤訳 「日本文学大全集 10」 서울 東西文化院 1975. p.6–9

'羅生門' 趙喜娟訳 「世界名作시리즈 3」 서울 女学生出版社 1975. p.201–211

'Rašomon' Prevod od francuski Taško Strilov. *Rašomon*. Skopje, Kultura, 1976. p.286–293

'羅生門' 郭夏信訳 「日本短篇文学選」 서울 乙酉文化社 1976. p.183–195

'羅生門' 李吉鐘訳 「世界短篇文学全集 20」 서울 金字堂 1976. p.12–20

'羅生門' 金文洙訳 「世界代表短篇文学全集 21」 서울 正韓出版社 1976. p.271–276

'羅生門' 權逸松訳 「世界文学全集 47」 서울 三省出版社 1976. p.15–20

'羅生門' 陳雄基訳 「羅生門」 서울 汎友社 1977. p.21–31

'Lã-sinh-môn' Bản dịch của Vũ Minh Thiều. *Lã sinh môn*. Saigon, Gió Bốn Phương, n.d. p.23–33

Rashomon. Milano, Bocca, n.d. 1v.

Rokunomiya no himegimi 六の宮の姫君

'Барышня Рокуномия' Перевод Н. Фельдман. *Акутагава, новеллы*. Москва, Гослитиздат, 1959. p.268–275; *Акутагава Рюноскэ 2*. Москва, Худож. Лит. 1971. p.50–58

'The Lady Roku-no-miya' Tr. by Takashi Kojima and John McVittie. *Exotic Japanese stories*. N. Y. Liveright, 1964. p.197–208

'六宮姫子' 權逸松訳 「世界文学全集 47」 서울 三省出版社 1976. p.167–174

Ryū 龍

'龍' 胡可章訳 「小説月報」 第18巻9号 1927. p.86–91

'The dragon' Tr. by Takashi Kojima. *Eigo Kenkyu*, v.40, no.2, 1951. p.43–47, no.3. p.45–49. no. 4. p.44–47. no.5. p.48–50; *Rashomon, and other stories*. N. Y. Liveright, 1952. p.102–119; Tokyo, Tuttle, 1952. p.80–95; Tokyo, Tuttle, 1954. p.87–120

'Zmai' Prevod sa engleskog Vera Ilić. *Rasomon*. Beograd, Nolit, 1958. p.190–205

'Der Drache' Übers. von Jürgen Berndt. *Japanische Novellen*. Berlin, Volk und Welt, 1964. p.83–98; *Rashomon, zehn Novellen*. Zürich, Diogenes, 1966. p.109–136; *Rashomon, ausge-*

wählte Kurzprosa. Berlin, Volk und Welt, 1975. p.207–221

'Balaurul' În românește de Ion Caraion. *Rashomon*. București, Editura pentru Literatură Universală, 1968. p.321–334

'龍' 夏雲訳 「地獄變」 台北 志文出版社 1969. p.44–54

'The dragon' Tr. by Norimitsu Antoku. *Eigo Eibungaku Ronshu* (Seinan Gakuin Univ.), v.10, no.2, 1969. p.87–102

'竜' 権逸松訳 「世界文学全集 47」 서울 三省出版社 1976. p.129–136

Saigō Takamori 西郷隆盛

'Saigo Takamori' Tr. by Takashi Kojima and John McVittie. *Exotic Japanese stories*. N. Y. Liveright, 1964. p.266–283

'Saigo Takamori' În românește de Ion Caraion. *Rashomon*. București, Editura pentru Literatură Universală, 1968. p.149–165

Samusa 寒さ

'Холод' Перевод Н. Фельдман. *Акутагава, новеллы*. Москва, Гослитиздат, 1959. p.312–317; *Акутагава Рюноскэ 2*. Москва, Худож. Лит. 1971. p.169–174

'Холод' Переклали Иван Дзюб та Геннадий Турков. *Расьемон*. Киев, Жовтень, 1971. p.175–180

San'emon no tsumi 三右衛門の罪

'Преступление Санэмона' Перевод И. Львовой. *Акутагава Рюноскэ 2*. Москва, Худож. Лит. 1971. p.127–136

Saru 猿

'The monkey' *Japan Chronicle*, 1919.

'Обезьяна' Перевод Н. Фельдман. *Расемон*. Ленинград, Гослитиздат, 1936. p.42–51; *Акутагава, новеллы*. Москва, Гослитиздат, 1959. p.28–33; *Акутагава Рюноскэ 1*. Москва, Худож. Лит. 1971. p.65–71

'Der Affe' Übers. von Jürgen Berndt. *Japanische Novellen*. Berlin, Volk und Welt, 1964. p.281–290; *Rashomon, ausgewählte Kurzprosa*. Berlin, Volk und Welt, 1975. p.46–54

'Мавна' Переклали Иван Дзюб та Геннадий Турков. *Расьемон*. Киев, Жовтень, 1971. p.32–38

Saru kani gassen 猿蟹合戦

'The feud between the monkey and the crab' Tr. by Thomas E. Swann. *Monumenta Nipponica*, v.24, no.4, 1969. p.507–510

'Сражение обезьяны с крабом' Перевод Л. Ермаковой. *Акутагава Рюноскэ 2*. Москва, Худож. Лит. 1971. p.158–161

Seihō no hito 西方の人

'Western man' Tr. by Akio Inoue. *Posthumous works of Ryunosuke Akutagawa*. Tenri, Tenri Jihosha, 1961. p.38–58

'Man of the West' Tr. by Tadao Katayama. *The Reeds*, v.8, 1962. p.177–204

'西方的人' 葉笛訳 「羅生門」 台北 仙人掌出版社 1969. p.69–94; 台北 大林書店 1973. p.69–94

'西方人' 安仁吉 方坤訳 「世界随筆文学全集 4」 서울 東西出版社 1969. p.183–203

'西方的人' 金溟若訳 「羅生門・河童及其他六種」 台北 志文出版社 1972. p.129–156

'西方人' 鄭成煥 金泳杓訳 「世界에세이文学全集 8」 서

울 東西出版社 1974. p.183–203; 「世界随筆文学全集 8」 서울 世進出版社 1976. p.183–203

Seikan 清閑

'清閑' 謝六逸訳 「人間世」 第3期 1934年5月 p.36

Sennin 仙人

'Sennin' Tr. by Takamasa Sasaki. *Eigo Kenkyu*, v.39, no.5, 1950. p.35–40; *The three treasures, and other stories for children*. Tokyo, Hokuseido, 1951. p.98–109

'Il santone' Tr. di Mario Teti. *Kappa, e altri racconti*. Milano, Bompiani, 1961. p.33–39

'Sennin' Tr. by Norimitsu Antoku. *Eigo Eibungaku Ronshu* (Seinan Gakuin Univ.), v.9, no.3, 1969. p.99–104

'Святой' Перевод Л. Лобачева. *Акутагава Рюноскэ 2*. Москва, Худож. Лит. 1971. p.37–41

Shina yūki 支那游記

'中國游記' 夏丐尊訳 「芥川龍之介集」 上海 開明書店 1927.

Shinkirō 蜃気楼

'Mirage' Tr. by Beongcheon Yu. *Chicago Review*, v.18, no.2, 1965.

'I miraggi' Tr. di Guidotto Colleoni. *Il Giappone*, anno 8, 1968. p.90–96

'海市蜃樓' 葉笛訳 「羅生門」 台北 仙人掌出版社 1969. p.95–104; 台北 大林書店 1973. p.95–104

'Миражи, или у моля' Перевод Л. Лобачева. *Акутагава Рюноскэ 2*. Москва, Худож. Лит. 1971. p.289–295

'Die Fata Morgana' Übersetzt von Jürgen Berndt. *Die Geschichte einer Rache*. Berlin, Volk und Welt, 1973. p.291–300; *Rashomon, ausgewählte Kurzprosa*. Berlin, Volk und Welt, 1975. p.484–493

Shirami 虱

'Lice' Tr. by Glenn W. Shaw. *Eigo Seinen*, v.47, no.1–4, 1922. p.9, 42–43, 74, 105; *Tales grotesque and curious*. Tokyo, Hokuseido, 1930. p.57–66; *Rashomon, and other stories*. Tokyo, Hara Shobo, 1964. p.114–133

'Läuse' Übers. von Yataro Ishida. *Das junge Japan*, Band 1, Heft 6, 7–8, 1924–25. p.240–242, 257–258

'I pidocchi' Tr. di Mario Teti. *Cipangu*, 2, 1956. p.12–15; *Kappa, e altri racconti*. Milano, Bompiani, 1961. p.9–18

Shiro 白

'White the dog' Tr. by Takamasa Sasaki. *The three treasures, and other stories for children*. Tokyo, Hokuseido, 1944. p.24–26; Tokyo, Hokuseido, 1951. p.24–44

'The dog, Shiro' Tr. by Takashi Kojima and John McVittie. *Exotic Japanese stories*. N. Y. Liveright, 1964. p.128–139

Shisō 死相

'The shadow of death' Tr. by Thomas E. Swann. *Monumenta Nipponica*, v.26, no.1–2, 1971. p.191–193

Shōgun 将軍

'将軍' 湯鶴逸訳 「芥川龍之介小説集」 上海 文化學社

192?.
'将軍' 馮子韜訳 「芥川龍之介集」 上海 中華書局 1931. p.23–59; 昆明 中華書局 1934. p.23–59
'Генерал' Перевод Н. Фельдман. *Интернациональная Литература*, номер 9, 1936. p.70–83; *Расемон*. Ленинград, Гослитиздат, 1936. p.178–200; *Акутагава, новеллы*. Москва, Гослитиздат, 1959. p.219–237; *Акутагава Рюноскэ 1*. Москва, Худож. Лит. 1971. p.411–430
'The general' Tr. by W. H. H. Norman. *Hell screen, and other stories*. Tokyo, Hokuseido, 1948. p.135–168; N. Y. Greenwood Press, 1971. p.135–168
'General' Prevod sa engleskog Vera Ilić. *Rasomon*. Beograd, Nolit, 1958. p.160–189
'Der General' Übers. von Jürgen Berndt. *Japanische Novellen*. Berlin, Volk und Welt, 1964. p.191–218; *Japan erzählt*. Hamburg, Fischer, 1969. p.40–57; *Rashomon, ausgewählte Kurzprosa*. Berlin, Volk und Welt, 1975. p.314–339
'将軍' 夏雲訳 「地獄變」 台北 志文出版社 1969. p.110–137
'Генерал' Переклали Иван Дзюб та Геннадий Турков. *Расьемон*. Киев, Жовтень, 1971. p.118–138

Shōsetsu sakuhō jussoku 小説作法十則

'小説作法十則' 訒生訳 「小説月報」 第18巻9号 1927. p.138–139

Shuchū 酒虫

'The wine worm' Tr. by Glenn W. Shaw. *Tales grotesque and curious*. Tokyo, Hokuseido, 1930. p.75–88; *Rashomon, and other stories*. Tokyo, Hara Shobo, 1964. p.176–202
'Il verme del vino' Tr. di Mario Teti. *Cipangu*, 3, 1956. p.12–17; *Kappa, e altri racconti*. Milano, Bompiani, 1961.

Shuju no kotoba 侏儒の言葉

'寓語集' 宏徒訳 「小説月報」 第18巻9号 1927. p.140–143
'侏儒的話' 謝六逸訳 「近代日本小品文選」 上海 開明書店 1929.
'Aussprüche eines Pygmäen' Übers. von S. Yuasa. *Nippon*, Jahrgang 1, Heft 4, 1935. p.203–206
'Told by a pygmy' Tr. by Tadao Katayama. *The Reeds*, v.9, 1963. p.81–101
'따라지의푸념' 安仁吉 方坤訳 「世界随筆文学全集 4」 서울 東西出版社 1969. p.205–252
'Из «Слов пигмея»' Перевод Н. Фельдман. *Акутагава Рюноскэ 2*. Москва, Худож. Лит. 1971. p.232–257
'따라지의푸념' 鄭成煥 金泳杓訳 「世界에세이文学全集 8」 서울 東西出版社 1974. p.205–252; 「世界随筆文学全集 8」 서울 世進出版社 1976. p.205–252

Shūzanzu 秋山図

'Autumn mountains' *Living Age*, v.308, Feb. 5, 1921. p.337–340
'秋山圖' 湯鶴逸訳 「芥川龍之介小説集」 上海 文化學社 192?.
'The painting of an autumn mountain' Tr. by Ivan Morris. *Japan Quarterly*, v.2, no.4, 1955. p.475–481; *Modern Japanese stories*. London, Eyre and Spottiswoode, 1961. p.165–173; Tokyo, Tuttle, 1962. p.174–184
'Le tableau d'une montagne à la saison d'automne'

Tr. par I. I. Morris, Mlle Rosenblum et M. Beerblock. *Les portes de l'enfer*. Paris, Stock, 1957. p.133–147
'Jesienny pejzaż' Przełożyła Anna Gostyńska. *Irys, opowiadania japońskie*. Warszawa, Państwowy Instytut Wydawniczy, 1960. p.123–136
'Ein Berg im Herbst' Deutsch von Monique Humbert. *Nippon*, hrg. von Ivan Morris. Zürich, Diogenes, 1965. p.203–214
'秋山圖' 葉笛訳 「羅生門」 台北 仙人掌出版社 1969. p.55–67; 台北 大林書店 1973. p.55–67
'Öszi hegyoldal' Přel. Gergely Ágnes. *Nagyvilág*, no.12, 1972. p.1767–1770
'Das Bild von den Bergen im Herbst' Übersetzt von Jürgen Berndt. *Die Geschichte einer Rache*. Berlin, Volk und Welt, 1973. p.301–315; *Rashomon, ausgewählte Kurzprosa*. Berlin, Volk und Welt, 1975. p.302–314

Sōshun 早春

'Ранняя весна' Перевод Л. Ермаковой. *Акутагава Рюноскэ 2*. Москва, Худож. Лит. 1971. p.180–183

Sutego 捨児

'棄兒' 湯鶴逸訳 「芥川龍之介小説集」 上海 文化學社 192?; 「河童」 上海 文化生活出版社 192?.
'Подкидыш' Перевод Н. Фельдман. *Акутагава, новеллы*. Москва, Гослитиздат, 1959. p.188–193; *Акутагава Рюноскэ 1*. Москва, Худож. Лит. 1971. p.367–372

Tabako to akuma 煙草と悪魔

'Tobacco and the devil' Tr. by Glenn W. Shaw. *Tales grotesque and curious*. Tokyo, Hokuseido, 1930. p.1–14; *Rashomon, and other stories*. Tokyo, Hara Shobo, 1964. p.32–57
'Debel a tabok' Přel. Vlasta Hilská. *Obraz pekla*. Praha, SNKHLU, 1960. p.125–136
'Il tobacco e il diavolo' Tr. di Mario Teti. *Kappa, e altri racconti*. Milano, Bompiani, 1961. p.171–180
'Табак и дьявол' Перевод В. Сановича. *Акутагава Рюноскэ 1*. Москва, Худож. Лит. 1971. p.81–88
'Der Tabak und der Teufel' Übersetzt von Jürgen Berndt. *Die Geschichte einer Rache*. Berlin, Volk und Welt, 1973. p.5–16; *Rashomon, ausgewählte Kurzprosa*. Berlin, Volk und Welt, 1975. p.66–75
'煙草와惡魔' 金文洙訳 「世界代表短篇文学全集 21」 서울 正韓出版社 1976. p.287–296

Tegami 手紙

'冬以及書信' 葉笛訳 「河童」 台北 仙人掌出版社 1969. p.53–70; 台北 大林書店 1973. p.53–70

Tenkibo 点鬼簿

'點鬼簿' 葉笛訳 「羅生門」 台北 仙人掌出版社 1969. p.177–184; 台北 大林書店 1973. p.177–184
'Поминальник' Перевод Н. Фельдман. *Акутагава Рюноскэ 2*. Москва, Худож. Лит. 1971. p.223–228
'Das Totenregister' Übersetzt von Jürgen Berndt. *Die Geschichte einer Rache*. Berlin, Volk und Welt, 1973. p.79–88; *Rashomon, ausgewählte Kurzprosa*. Berlin, Volk und Welt, 1975. p.456–464

AKUTAGAWA Ryūnosuke

To Shishun 杜子春

'Tu Tsuchun' Tr. by Eric S. Bell and Eiji Ukai. *Eibun Tokyo Nichinichi*, Nov.27—Dec.3, 1926; *Eminent authors of contemporary Japan v.1*. Tokyo, Kaitakusha, 1930. p.109–128

'To-Sisun' Tr. Hirokazu Kaji. *La Esperanto*, Jaro 6, 1931.

'Tu Tzu-chun' Tr. by Takamasa Sasaki. *The three treasures, and other stories for children*. Tokyo, Hokuseido, 1944. p.110–142

'Tu Cucun' Tr. Yasutaro Nozima. *La kapao, kaj aliaj rakontoj*. Tokyo, Japana Esperanto Instituto, 1954. p.73–87

'Tu Tze-chun' Tr. by Takashi Kojima. *Eibungaku Kenkyu* (Meiji Univ.), no.29, 1964. p.138–149

Tu Tze-chun. Tr. by Dorothy Britton. Tokyo, Kodansha International, 1965. 55p.; London, Ward Lock, 1965. 59p.

'Tu Tzu-chun' Tr. by Norimitsu Antoku. *Eigo Eibungaku Ronshu* (Seinan Gakuin Univ.), v.8, no.2, 1968. p.131–144

'杜子春' 葉笛訳 「羅生門」 仙人掌出版社 1969. p.39–53; 台北 大林書店 1973. p.39–53

'Ду Цзы-чунь' Перевод В. Марковой. *Акутагава Рюноскэ 1*. Москва, Худож. Лит. 1971. p.294–305

'杜子春' 陳雄基訳 「羅生門」 서울 汎友社 1977. p.42–60

'Toshishun' Tr. by Wirada Tripopanun. *Rueng sun yeepun 1*. Bangkok, Urkornsasna, 1977. p.120–144

Torokko トロッコ

'Torokko' Übers. von Heinz Brasch. *Yamato*, Jahrgang 1, 1929. p.193–203

'The track' Tr. by Tomokazu Nishira. *English Society Review*, 1930.

'The wagon' Tr. by S.G. Brickley. *The writing of idiomatic English*. Tokyo, Kenkyusha, 1951. p.1–14

'La sargvagoneto' Tr. Yasutaro Nozima. *La kapao, kaj aliaj rakontoj*. Tokyo, Japana Esperanto Instituto, 1954.

'Flatcar' Tr. by Richard McKinnon. *The heart is alone*. Tokyo, Hokuseido, 1957. p.3–9

'Вагонетка' Перевод Н. Фельдман. *Акутагава, новеллы*. Москва, Гослитиздат, 1959. p.238–243; *Акутагава Рюноскэ 2*. Москва, Худож. Лит. 1971. p.15–20

'A scille' Fordította Lomb Kató. *A vihar kapujában*. Budapest, Európa Könyvkiadó, 1960. p.82–87

'The flatcar' Tr. by Takashi Kojima. *Eibungaku Kenkyu* (Meiji Univ.), no.27, 1964. p.132–137

'Die Lore' Übers. von Jürgen Berndt. *Japanische Novellen*. Berlin, Volk und Welt, 1964. p.107–114; *Rashomon, ausgewählte Kurzprosa*. Berlin, Volk und Welt, 1975. p.351–358

'Torokko, or The handcart' Tr. by Norimitsu Antoku. *Eigo Eibungaku Ronshu* (Seinan Gakuin Univ.), v.9, no.1, 1966. p.175–180

'手推車' 葉笛訳 「河童」 台北 仙人掌出版社 1969. p.45–52; 台北 大林書店 1973. p.45–52

'Вагонетка' Переклали Иван Дзюб та Геннадий Турков. *Расьемон*. Киев, Жовтень, 1971. p.139–144

'臺車' 賴祥雲訳 「芥川龍之介的世界」 台北 志文出版社 1977. p.169–175

Uma no ashi 馬の脚

'Лошадиные ноги' Перевод Н. Фельдман. *Расемон*. Ленинград, Гослитиздат, 1936. p.267–279; *Акутагава, новеллы*. Москва, Гослитиздат, 1959. p.318–331; *Акутагва Рюноскэ 2*. Москва, Худож. Лит. 1971. p.184–197

'Лошадиные ноги' Перевод М. П. Григориева. *Событие в аду*. Дальний, Южно-Маньчж. Ж. Д. 1940. p.87–109

Umi no hotori 海のほとり

'The seashore' Tr. by Susan Orpett. *Voices*, v.3, no.1, 1971. p.39–44

'У моря' Перевод В. Гривнина. *Акутагава Рюноскэ 2*. Москва, Худож. Лит. 1971. p.198–205

Un 運

'Счастье' Перевод Н. Фельдман. *Расемон*. Ленинград, Гослитиздат, 1936. p.52–56; *Акутагава, новеллы*. Москва, Гослитиздат, 1959. p.48–55; *Акутагава Рюноскэ 1*. Москва, Худож. Лит. 1971. p.95–102

'Das Schicksal' Übersetzt von Jürgen Berndt. *Die Geschichte einer Rache*. Berlin, Volk und Welt, 1973. p.97–109; *Rashomon, ausgewählte Kurzprosa*. Berlin, Volk und Welt, 1975. p.75–86

Uogashi 魚河岸

'Bordo de fisvendejoj' Tr. Keikichi Kawada. *La Revuo Orienta*, v.9, no.3, 1928. p.91–93

Yabu no naka 薮の中

'В бамбуковой чаще' Перевод Р. Кима. *Запад и Восток*, 1926, номер 1–2. p.34–44

'薮中' 章克標訳 「芥川龍之介集」 上海 開明書店 1927.

'В зарослях' Перевод М. П. Григориева. *Событие в аду*. Дальний, Южно-Маньчж. Ж. Д. 1940. p.132–147

'In a grove' Tr. by Takashi Kojima. *Rashomon, and other stories*. N. Y. Liveright, 1952. p.6–18; Tokyo, Tuttle, 1952. p.6–18; N. Y. Avon Books, 1963. p.13–25

'En el bosque' Tr. por Kazuya Sakai. *Rashomon*. Buenos Aires, Lopez Negri, 1954; *El biombo del infierno, y otras cuentos*. Buenos Aires, La Mandrágora, 1959. p.17–26

'En el bosque' Tr. por Takeshi Ehara. *Cuentos japoneses*. Buenos Aires, Komori Hermanos, 1954. p.23–37

'Yabu no naka' Übers. von Hikaru Tsuji und Kohei Takahara. *Rashômon*. Tübingen, Schlichtenmayer, 1955. p.9–24; Frankfurt am Main, Fischer, 1960. p.7–26

'Rashomon' Bewerkt en ingeleid door S. van Praag. *Rashomon, en andere Japanse vertellingen*. Amsterdam, Wereld, 1957.

'Nel bosco' Tr. di S. Merge. *Insegna del pesce d'oro*. Milano, 1958.

'U cestaru' Prevod sa engleskog Vera Ilić. *Rasomon*. Beograd, Nolit, 1958. p.122–135

'В чаще' Перевод Н. Фельдман. *Акутагава, новеллы*. Москва, Гослитиздат, 1959. p.209–218; *Акутагава Рюноскэ 1*. Москва, Худож. Лит. 1971. p.402–410

'A cserjésben' Fordította Lomb Kató. *Nagyvilág*, 1960. p.1044–1049; *A vihar kapujában*. Buda-

pest, Európa Könyvkiadó, 1960. p.72–81
'V houstine' Přel. Vlasta Hilská. *Obraz pekla.* Praha, SNKHLU, 1960. p.97–111
'In the grove' Tr. by Takashi Kojima. *Masterpieces of the Orient.* N. Y. Norton, 1961. p.385–392; *The Mentor book of modern Asian literature.* N. Y. Philosophical Library, 1969. p.385–392
'Dentro do bosque' Tr. de Katsunori Wakisaka. *Maravilhas do conto japonês.* Saõ Paulo, Editora Cultrix, 1962. p.99–109
'Mordfall im Gestrüpp' Aus dem Japanischen von Walter Scheppach. *Japan, Geistige Begegnung.* Tübingen, Erdmann, 1964. p.38–48
'Im Dickicht' Übers. von Jürgen Berndt. *Japanische Novellen.* Berlin, Volk und Welt, 1964. p.69–82; *Rashomon, zehn Novellen.* Zürich, Diogenes, 1966. p.85–108
В чаше, на армянском языке. Перевод Н. Адарьян. Ереван, Айретрат, 1964. 59p.
'En arbardensejo' Tr. Tazuo Nakamura. *El Japana literaturo.* Tokyo, Japana Esperanto Instituto, 1965. p.17–27
'Dans le fourré' Tr. par Arimasa Mori. *Rashomon, et autres contes.* Paris, Gallimard, 1965. p.85–94; Paris, Livre de Poche, 1969. p.79–94
'Intr-un bunget de padure' În româneşte de Ion Caraion. *Rashomon.* Bucureşti, Editura pentru Literatură Universală, 1968. p.16–27
'Mordfall im Gestrüpp' Übers. von Oscar Benl. *Eine Glocke in Fukagawa, und andere japanische Erzählungen.* Tübingen, Erdmann, 1969. p.38–48
'W gaszczu' Przeł. Mikołaj Melanowicz. *Przeglad Orientalistyczny*, no.1, 1969. p.33–40
'竹籔訳' 葉笛訳 「羅生門」 台北 仙人掌出版社 1969. p.27–38; 台北 大林書店 1973. p.27–38
В чаше, на грузинском языке. Тбилиси, Детиуниздат Груз. ССР, 1969. 18p.
'У чагарнику' Переклали Иван Дзюб та Геннадий Турков. *Расьетон.* Киев, Жовтень, 1971. p.108–117
'Im Dickicht' Deutsch von Jürgen Berndt. *Träume aus zehn Nächten.* Berlin, Aufbau-Verlag, 1975. p.193–203; *Rashomon, ausgewählte Kurzprosa.* Berlin, Volk und Welt, 1975. p. 339–351
'대금이야기' 權逸松訳 「世界文学全集 47」 서울 三省出版社 1976. p.157–166
'竹籔中' 賴祥雲訳 「芥川龍之介的世界」 台北 志文出版社 1977. p.155–167
'덤불속' 陳雄基訳 「羅生門」 서울 汎友社 1977. p.70–84
'竹籔中' 「文鳥・夢十夜」 英紹唐編 n.d. p.107–136
'Trong rừng rậm' Ban dịch của Vū Minh Thiều. *Lã sinh môn.* Saigon, Gió Bốn Phương, n.d. p.35–51

Yamashigi 山鴫

'La bécassine' Tr. par Daigaku Horiguchi. *Japon et Extrême-Orient*, no.7–8, 1924. p.1–12
'山鴫' 湯鶴逸訳 「小説月報」 第18巻2号 1927. p.1–6; 「芥川龍之介小説集」 上海 文化學社 192?.
'Вальдшнеп' Перевод М. П. Григориева. *Событие в аду.* Дальний, Южно-Маньчж. Ж. Д. 1940. p.117–131
'Вальдшнеп' Перевод Н. Фельдман. *Акутагава, новеллы.* Москва, Гослитиздат, 1959. p.200–208; *Акутагава Рюноскэ 1.* Москва, Худож. 1971. p.382–390
'山鴫' 葉笛訳 「文學季刊」 第5期 1967年11月 p.212–218; 「地獄變」 台北 仙人掌出版社 1969. p.53–67; 台北 大林書店 1973. p.53–67
'山鴫' 賴祥雲訳 「芥川龍之介的世界」 台北 志文出版社 1977. p.139–153

Yasukichi no techō kara 保吉の手帳から

'La honte' Tr. par Juntaro Maruyama. *La Smouse*, t.2, no. 4–5, 1926. p. 2–4, 13–15
'Из записок Ясукити' Перевод В. Гривнина. *Акутагава Рюноскэ 2.* Москва, Худож. Лит. 1971. p.86–97
'Nach Aufzeichnungen Yasukichis' Übersetzt von Jürgen Berndt. *Die Geschichte einer Rache.* Berlin, Volk und Welt, 1973. p.165–182; *Rashomon, ausgewählte Kurzprosa.* Berlin, Volk und Welt, 1975. p.420–434

Yonosuke no hanashi 世之介の話

'The story of Yonosuke' Tr. by Takashi Kojima. *Eibungaku Kenkyu* (Meiji Univ.), v.1, no.2, 1954. p.1–9; *Eigo Seinen*, v.101, no.9–11, 1955. p.413–415, 462–464, 513–514; *Japanese short stories.* N. Y. Liveright, 1961. p.212–224; *Pacific Spectator*, v.9, no.2, 1965. p.192–198

Yuki 雪

'雪' 葉笛訳 「文學季刊」 5期 1967年11月 p.219
'雪' 賴祥雲訳 「芥川龍之介的世界」 台北 志文出版社 1977. p.181–182

Yume 夢

'Сон' Перевод В. Гривнина. *Акутагава Рюноскэ 2.* Москва, Худож. Лит. 1971. p.343–349

Yuri 百合

'Lilies' Tr. by Marvin J. Suomi. *Solidarity*, v.8, no.2, 1973. p.83–86

Yūwaku 誘惑

'San Sebastian' Tr. by Arthur Waley. *Horizon*, no.20, Sept. 1949. p.190–200; *The real tripitaka, and other pieces.* London, Allen and Unwin, 1952. p.224–232

Zoku seihō no hito 続西方の人

'Western man continued' Tr. by Akio Inoue. *Posthumous works of Ryunosuke Akutagawa.* Tenri, Tenri Jihosha, 1961. p.59–70

Haiku 俳句

'20 haiku' Tr. by Makoto Ueda. *Modern Japanese haiku, an anthology.* Tokyo, Univ. of Tokyo Press, 1976. p.99–108

AMANO Tadashi 天野 忠 1909–

Poems 詩

'Rice; Beware; The philosopher; The cry' *Postwar Japanese poetry*, ed. and tr. by Harry and Lynn Guest and Shozo Kajima. London, Penguin Books, 1972. p.38–40
'Философ' Перевод Анатолия Мамонова. *Вкус хризантемы.* Москва, Восточная Литература, 1976. p.19

AMATA Guan 天田愚庵 1854–1904

Tanka 短歌

'2 tanka' Tr. by V. H. Viglielmo. *Japanese literature in the Meiji era*. Tokyo, Obunsha, 1955. p.369

AMAZAWA Taijirō 天沢退二郎 1936–

Poems 詩

'Nato dal sógno' *La protesta poetica del Giappone*, a cura di Dacia Maraini e Michiko Nojiri. Roma, Officina Edizioni, 1968. p.151–152

'Seat; Revolution; Blood Sunday' *Postwar Japanese poetry*, ed. and tr. by Harry and Lynn Guest and Shozo Kajima. London, Penguin Books, 1972. p.149–152

ANDŌ Ichirō 安藤一郎 1907–1972

Pojishion ポジシオン

'Position' *An anthology of modern Japanese poetry*, ed. and tr. by Ichiro Kono and Rikutaro Fukuda. Tokyo, Kenkyusha, 1957. p.3–6

'Position' Tr. par Karl Petit. *La poésie japonaise*. Paris, Seghers, 1959. p.238

'Five poems from "The position" *United Asia*, v.12, no. 2, 1960. p.174–175

'Posítion 30, 35' Tr. por Kikuya Ionesawa. *Poesia japonesa contemporanea*. Bogotá, Colombia Editoriales de Librería, 1965.

Poems 詩

'A flash of lightning; The still life of an arm; To the pupil; The melting distance; Butterfly' *An anthology of modern Japanese poetry*, ed. and tr. by Ichiro Kono and Rikutaro Fukuda. Tokyo, Kenkyusha, 1957. p.1–7

'Mariposa' *Sur*, no.249, Nov.-Dec. 1957. p.90

'Two poems from "Experiences"; Two poems from "On love"; The still life of an arm; A butterfly' *United Asia*, v.12, no.2, 1960. p.173, 176–177

'Şimşek çakiyor; Pozisyon 21' Tercüme etmek L. Sami Akalin. *Japon şiiri*. İstanbul, Varlik Yayinevi, 1962. p.292

'나비의사랑; 눈동자의映像; 나의품안으로' 崔一秀訳 「기다리고있네」 서울 韓国政経社 1966. p.90–92, 187–188, 204–206

'Es una rosa' Tr. por Kikuya Ionesawa. *Poesia japonesa contemporanea*. Bogotá, Colombia Editoriales de Librería, 1965.

'Lynglimt' Til norsk ved Paal Brekke. *Moderne japansk lyrikk*. Oslo, Norske Bokklubben, n.d. p.65

Criticism 評論

'Modern Japanese poems—introduction' *Japan Quarterly*, v.3, no.1, 1956. p.79–81

'A new tendency in modern Japanese poetry' *KBS Bulletin*, no.24, 1957. p.1–4

'Modern Japanese poetry' *Today's Japan*, v.3, June, 1958. p.15–16

ANDŌ Mikio 安藤美紀夫 1930–

Ondori to nimai no kinka おんどりと二まいのきんか

The cock and the two gold coins. N. Y. Holt, Rinehart and Winston, n.d. 1v.

'Kouzelná kamenná sekera' Přel. Ivan Krouský a Z. K. Slabý. *Modré vánoce*. Praha, Albatros, 1975.

ANDŌ Tsuguo 安東次男 1919–

Poems 詩

'Alternation; 樹木開花' 辛東門訳 「世界戦後文学全集 9」 서울 新丘文化社 1962. p.239

'Tubers' *Modern Japanese poetry*, by Donald Keene. Ann Arbor, Center for Japanese Studies, Univ. of Michigan, 1964. p.33; *Landscapes and portraits*, by Donald Keene. Tokyo, Kodansha International, 1971. p.151

'La notte verde di giugno del cinquantaque' *La protesta poetica del Giappone*, a cura di Dacia Maraini e Michiko Nojiri. Roma, Officina Edizioni, 1968. p.63–64

'Three blooming; Note from the dead' Remade into English by Thomas Fitzsimmons. *Japanese poetry now*. London, André Deutsch, 1972. p.76–78; *Japanese poetry today*. N. Y. Schocken Books, 1972. p.78–80

ANDŌ Tsuruo 安藤鶴夫 1908–1969

Bunraku 文楽

Bunraku, the puppet theater. Tr. by Charles J. Dunn. Tokyo, Weatherhill, 1970. 222p.

Essay エッセイ

'Ye olde Kabuki advertising' *This is Japan*, v.13, 1966. p.132–133

ANDŌ Wafū 安藤和風 1866–1936

Haiku 俳句

'6 haiku' Tr. by Asataro Miyamori. *Anthology of haiku, ancient and modern*. Tokyo, Maruzen, 1932. p.804–808

'A symphony of love; Different ears; The glove' Tr. by Asataro Miyamori. *Haiku poems, ancient and modern*. Tokyo, Maruzen, 1940. p.310–312

'1 haiku' Tr. by Lois J. Erickson. *Songs from the land of dawn*. N. Y. Friendship Press, 1949; Freeport, Books for Libraries Press, 1968. p.71

'1 haiku' Tr. by Peter Beilenson. *Japanese haiku*. Mount Verson, Peter Pauper Press, 1955. p.41

'Haiku' Tercüme etmek L. Sami Akalin. *Japon şiiri*. İstanbul, Varlik Yayinevi, 1962. p.234

'2 haiku' Übers. von Gerolf Coudenhove. *Japanische Jahreszeiten*. Zürich, Manesse Verlag, 1963. p.93, 295

ANNO Mitsumasa　安野光雅　1926–

ABC no hon　ABC の本

Anno's alphabet. London, Bodley Head, 1974. 1v.; N. Y. Crowell, 1974. 1v.

Fushigi na e　ふしぎなえ

Topsy-turvies. N. Y. Walker, 1970. 30p.; Tokyo, Weatherhill, 1970. 30p.
Jeux de construction. Paris, L'École des Loisirs, 1970. 1v.
Zwerggespuk. Zürich, Atlantis Verlag, 1971. 1v.
Den tossede bog. København, Høst, 1974. 1v.

Fushigi na sākasu　ふしぎなサーカス

Dr. Anno's magical midnight circus. Tokyo, Weatherhill, 1972. 27p.

Sakasama　さかさま

Upside-downers. Adapted into English by Meredith Weatherby and Suzanne Turnbull. Tokyo, Weatherhill, 1971. 27p.
Château de cartes. Paris, L'École des Loisirs, 1974. 1v.

Tabi no ehon　旅の絵本

Anno's journey. Cleveland, Collins and World, 1978. 1v.; London, Bodley Head, 1978. 1v.
Ce jour là . . . Paris, L'École des Loisirs, 1978. 1v.
De Reis van Anno. Rotterdam, Ploegsma, 1978. 1v.
En rejse. København, Høst, 1978. 1v.
Wo ist der Reiter? Zürich, Artemis Verlag, 1978. 1v.

ANZAI Fuyue　安西冬衛　1898–1965

Poems　詩

'The warship "Mari"' Tr. by D. J. Enright. *Bulletin of the Japan Society of London*, no.20, Oct. 1955. p.9
'Spain III' Tr.by S. Sato and C. Urdang. *Poetry*, May 1956. p.97
'A birthday; Spring; A peaceful essay on women; The battleship Marie; Furniture a hundred years old' *An anthology of modern Japanese poetry*, ed. and tr. by Ichiro Kono and Rikutaro Fukuda. Tokyo, Kenkyusha, 1957. p.7–9
'Birthday again; The warship Mari; The gulf of Tartary and a butterfly' *The poetry of living Japan, an anthology*, by Takamichi Ninomiya and D. J. Enright. London, John Murray, 1957. p.67–69
'여크브의점정사닥다리' 金龍済訳 「日本詩集」 서울 青雲社 1960. p.137–139
'Frühling' Übers. von Kuniyo Takayasu und Manfred Hausmann. *Ruf der Regenpfeifer.* München, Bechtle Verlag, 1961. p.92
'百年의家具；콤과；흰박쥐雨傘；수레；下市어子애서' 柳呈訳 「世界戦後文学全集 9」 서울 新丘文化社 1962. p.213–215
'Kadinlar hakkinda mülâyim bir deneme; Doğum günü' Tercüme etmek L. Sami Akalin. *Japon şiiri.* İstanbul, Varlik Yayinevi, 1962. p.263

'物；樫樹裏的火；電漫髪' 徐和隣訳 「現代詩解説」 台北 葡萄園詩刊社 1970. p.53–55
'生日' 金光林訳 「現代詩学」 第4巻3号 1972.

ANRYŪ Suharu　安立スハル　1923–

Tanka　短歌

'1 tanka' *The burning heart*, tr. and ed. by Kenneth Rexroth and Ikuko Atsumi. N.Y. Seabury Press, 1977. p.73

ANZAI Hitoshi　安西　均　1919–

Poems　詩

'Signal' *An anthology of modern Japanese poetry*, ed. and tr. by Ichiro Kono and Rikutaro Fukuda. Tokyo, Kenkyusha, 1957. p.10
'아침；전화가울린다' 金龍済訳 「日本詩集」 서울 青雲社 1960. p.13–14
'꽃과마음' 崔一秀訳 「기다리고있네」 서울 韓国政経社 1966. p.144–146
'아침市場；아침；電話가울린다' 辛東門訳 「世界戦後文学全集 9」 서울 新丘文化社 1962. p.236–237
'The poetry of Anzai Hitoshi; Snow; Rain; Sanetomo; Nightingale; Hitomaro; Saigyo; Blinded city; Sunflower; Summer 1945; Woman of Sagami; Trap; Signal; Overcoat; Night shower; Haiku; Homework' Tr. by Atsumi Ikuko and Graeme Wilson. *Japan Quarterly*, v.17, no.1, 1970. p.65–71
'Disused railway station' Tr. by Ikuko Atsumi and Graeme Wilson. *Quadrant*, Nov.-Dec. 1970. p.58–59
'The discarded horse; The flower shop' *Anthology of modern Japanese poetry*, tr. and comp. by Edith Marcombe Shiffert and Yuki Sawa. Tokyo, Tuttle, 1972. p.118–119
'Bed that smells of sunshine; Morning phone rings' Remade into English by Thomas Fitzsimmons. *Japanese poetry now.* London, André Deutsch, 1972. p.103–104; *Japanese poetry today.* N. Y. Schocken Books, 1972. p.105–106
'Snow; Rain; Sanetomo; Nightingale; Hitomaro; Saigyo; Blinded city; Sunflower; Summer 1945; Trap; Signal; Night shower; Overcoat; Haiku; Homework; My eyes; Disused railway station; Young water; Golden arm; Woman of Sagami' Tr. by Graeme Wilson and Atsumi Ikuko. *Three contemporary Japanese poets.* London, Magazine Editions, 1972. p.16–35
'Rain; Nightingale; Hitomaro' Tr. by Atsumi Ikuko and Graeme Wilson. *New writing in Japan.* London, Penguin Books, 1972. p.205–207
'Blinded city; Sunflower; Summer, 1945; Trap; Like a signal; Night shower; Overcoat; Homework; Jealousy; In the morning; The telephone rings; A new razor' Tr. by Ikuko Ayusawa. *The poetry of postwar Japan.* Iowa City, Univ. of Iowa Press, 1975. p.33–40

ANZAI Ōkaishi　安斎桜磈子　1886–1953

Haiku　俳句

'3 haiku' Tr. by V. H. Viglielmo. *Japanese*

ANZAI Ōkaishi

literature in the Meiji era. Tokyo, Obunsha, 1955. p.442, 448

AOKI Getto　青木月斗　1879–1949

Haiku　俳句

'5 haiku' Tr. by Asataro Miyamori. *Anthology of haiku, ancient and modern.* Tokyo, Maruzen, 1932. p.745–750

'New Year's day; Insects' Tr. by Asataro Miyamori. *Haiku poems, ancient and modern.* Tokyo, Maruzen, 1940. p.344–345

'Dancers of old Kyoto' Tr. by Harold Stewart. *A net of fireflies.* Tokyo, Tuttle, 1960. p.45

'3 haiku' Übers. von Gerolf Coudenhove. *Japanische Jahreszeiten.* Zürich, Manesse Verlag, 1963. p.13, 37, 221

'Autumn insects; Winter tempest' Tr. by Kenneth Yasuda. *A pepper-pod.* Tokyo, Tuttle, 1976. p.88–89

AOKI Shigeru　青木　茂　1897–

Santa monogatari　三太物語

'Santa and Miss Hanaogi play baseball' Tr. by Kojima Takashi. *Eigo Kenkyu,* v.43, no.5, 1954. p.48–51; v.43, no.8, 1954. p.46–49; v.43, no.9, 1954. p.57–59

AONO Suekichi　青野季吉　1890–1961

Criticism　評論

'関于智識階級' 魯迅訳 「語絲」 第4巻4期 1928. p.171–174;「壁下譯叢」上海 北新書局 1929;「魯迅全集 16」上海 魯迅全集出版社 1938. 作家書屋 1946. 大連 光華書店 1948. 北京 人民文学出版社 1973. p.253–256;「魯迅譯文集 5」北京 人民文学出版社 1958. p.327–329

'藝術的革命與革命的藝術' 魯迅訳 「壁下譯叢」上海 北新書局 1929;「魯迅全集 16」上海 魯迅全集出版社 1938. 作家書屋 1946. 大連 光華書店 1948. 北京 人民文学出版社 1973. p.241–252;「魯迅譯文集 5」北京 人民文学出版社 1958. p.318–327

'現代文學的十大缺陥' 魯迅訳 「壁下譯叢」上海 北新書局 1929;「魯迅全集 16」上海 魯迅全集出版社 1938. 作家書屋 1946. 大連 光華書店 1948. 北京 人民文学出版社 1973. p.257–270;「魯迅譯文集 5」北京 人民文学出版社 1958. p.330–340;

「藝術簡論」汪馥泉訳 上海 大江書局 1930. 1冊

「新興藝術概論」王集叢訳 上海 辛墾書局 1930. 1冊

「観念形態論」若俊訳 上海 南強書店 193?. 1冊

'An outline of postwar Japanese literature' *United Asia,* v. 8, no. 4, Sept. 1956. p.255–259

'关于 "源氏物語" 錢稲孫訳 「譯文」 1957年8月 p.81–88

'德永直君的死' 梅韜訳 「譯文」 1958年4月 p.5–6

AOYAGI Nobuo　青柳信雄　1903–

Dai issei　第一声

'第一聲' 陳勺水訳 「日本寫實派代表傑作集」 上海 樂羣雑誌社 1929.

AOYAMA Nobutoshi　青山延敏　1888–

Poems　詩

'Das Meer der Träume; Die Sehnsucht' Übers. von Ludwig Harold Schutz. *The living garland,* ed. by Makoto Sangu. Tokyo, Hokuseido, 1957. p.9–10

ARA Masahito　荒　正人　1913–

Criticism　評論

'Translated Japanese literature' *Oriental Economist,* no.25, 1957. p.588–589

'Писатели вышли из своих кабинетов' *Иностранная Литература,* сентябрь 1961. p.193–195

'On "Michikusa" *Essays on Natsume Soseki's works.* Tokyo, Japan Society for the Promotion of Science, 1972. p.67–76

ARAI Kiichi　新井紀一　1890–1966

Akubī　悪日

'La journée malheureuse' Tr. par Serge Elisséev. *Le jardin des pivoines.* Paris, Au Sans Pareil, 1927. p.17–45

Kuma no i　熊の瞻

'Bear's gall' *Osaka Mainichi,* August 14–18, 1925.

ARAI Masao　新井正夫　1905–

Poems　詩

'Сезон дождей' Перевод Анатолия Мамонова. *Вкус хризантемы.* Москва, Восточная Литература, 1976. p.20

ARIMA Takashi　有馬　敲　1931–

Poems　詩

'Сонет об усах' Перевод Анатолия Мамонова. *Вкус хризантемы.* Москва, Восточная Литература, 1976. p.21

ARIMA Yorichika　有馬頼義　1918–

Misshitsu　密室

「密室」 文瑛訳 서울 金字閣 1968. 2冊

Shōsoku　消息

'痲瘋病患者' 廖清秀訳 「投水自殺營救業」 台北 蘭開書局 1968. p.33–45

ARISHIMA Ikuma　有島生馬　1882–1974

Hato kau musume　鳩飼ふ娘

'飼鴿姑娘'「日本作家十二人集」 香港　新學書店　1959. p.135–146

Jizō bosatsu　地蔵菩薩

'Il volto a santo Jizo' Tr. di Salvatore Merge. *Il Giappone*, anno 3, no.1–2, 1959. p.30–40

Criticism　評論

Tōson Shimazaki, su personalidad y sus obras. Tr. de Yoshio Shinya. Buenos Aires, 1937. 17p.

ARISHIMA Takeo　有島武郎　1878–1923

Aru onna　或る女

Cette femme-là. Tr. par M. Yoshitomi et Albert Maybon. Paris, Flammarion, 1926. 246p.
Эта женщина. Перевод. Е. З. Брок и Г. П. Брок. Москва, Время, 1927. 139p.; Токио, Наука, 1973. 139p.
'A certain woman' Tr. by S. G. Brickley. *The writing of idiomatic English*. Tokyo, Kenkyusha, 1951. p.15–18
Женщина. Перевод А. Рябкина. Москва, Гослитиздат, 1962. 382p.; 1967. 342p.
Moteris. Tr. from the Russian P. Griskevicius. Vilnius, Goslitizdat, 1964. 371p.
Жинка. Переклав Иван Чирко. Киев, Днерпо, 1970. 309p.
「어느女人」 郭昌信訳 서울　乙酉文化社　1974. 464p.
A certain woman. Tr. by Kenneth Strong. Tokyo, Univ. of Tokyo Press, 1978. 388p.

Chiisaki mono e　小さき者へ

'與幼少者' 魯迅訳「現代日本小説集」上海　商務印書館　1923;「日本現代小説集 2」上海　商務印書館　1930. p.129–146;「魯迅全集 11」上海　魯迅全集出版社 1938. 作家書屋 1948. 大連　光華書店 1948. 北京　人民文学出版社 1973. p.446–463;「魯迅譯文集 1」北京　人民文学出版社 1958. p.472–485
'Meinem Kleinen' Übers. von Oscar Benl. *Flüchtiges Leben*. Berlin, Landsmann, 1942.
'與幼少者'「少年的悲哀」郁達夫等訳　台北　啓明書局 1656. p.55–64
'Al miaj etuloj' Tr. Yukio Isobe. *El Japana literaturo*. Tokyo, Japana Esperanto Instituto, 1962. p.28–39
'어린것들에게' 郭昌信訳「世界文学全集 94」서울 乙酉文化社 1962. p.193–205;「日本短篇文学選」서울 乙酉文化社 1976. p.101–181
'어린것들에게' 趙演鉉訳「世界短篇文学全集 7」서울 啓蒙社 1966. p.180–190;「世界短篇文学全集 9」서울 三珍社 1971. p.28–38;「世界代表短篇文学全集 9」서울 三熙社 1976. p.28–38;「世界短篇文学全集 9」서울 新羅出版社 1976. p.52–71
'To my little sons' Tr. by Yoshikazu Ueno. *The Reeds*, v.13, 1972. p.53–69
'與幼少者'「散文欣賞」台北　大孚書局 1977. p.49–61

Domomata no shi　ドモ又の死

「吃嘴阿又之死」 侍桁訳　上海　193?. 1冊

Gaisen　凱旋

'Triumph' Übers. von Heinz Brasch. *Nippon*, Jahrgang 1, 1935. p.32–42

'Triumph' *Geschichten und Erzählungen aus Japan*, hrg. von B. Matsumoto. Leipzig, Fikentscher Verlag, 1950. p.143–155
'Triumph' Übers. von Margarete Donath. *Japan erzählt*. Hamburg, Fischer, 1969. p.58–66

Geijutsu o umu tai　芸術を生む胎

'生藝術的胎' 魯迅訳「莽原」第9期　1926. p.365–377;「壁下譯叢」上海　北新書局 1929;「魯迅全集 16」上海　魯迅全集出版社 1938. 作家書屋 1946. 大連 光華書店 1948. 北京 人民文学出版社 1973. p.110–120;「魯迅譯文集 5」北京 人民文学出版社 1958. p.211–219

Hitofusa no budō　一房の葡萄

'A bunch of grapes' Tr. by Hideichi Ono and John McVittie. *The Japanese image v.2*, ed. by M. Schneps and A. D. Coox. Tokyo, Orient West, 1966. p.155–159

Jikkenshitsu　実験室

'實驗室' 金溟若訳「小説月報」第19巻11期　1928. p.1301–1312

Kain no matsuei　カインの末裔

'該隠的末裔' 沈端先訳「有島武郎集」上海　中華書局 1935. p.1–68
'Descendants of Cain' Tr. by John W. Morrison. *Modern Japanese fiction*. Salt Lake City, Univ of Utah Press, 1955. p.117–171
'카인의後裔' 方基煥訳「日本代表作家百人集 1」서울 希望出版社 1966. p.262–292;「日本短篇文学全集 1」서울 新太陽社 1969. p.262–292
'Потомок Каина' Перевод А. Рябкина. *Женщина, Потомок Каина*. Москва, Гослитиздат, 1967. p.345–383
'카인의後裔' 洪淳基訳「日本文学大全集 10」서울 東西文化院 1975. p.133–164
'Ein Nachkomme Kains' Deutsch von Jürgen Berndt. *Träume aus zehn Nächten*. Berlin, Aufbau-Verlag, 1975. p.110–158

Kodomo no negao　小児の寝顔

'小兒的睡相' 魯迅訳「莽原」第12期 1926. p.485;「魯迅全集 16」上海　魯迅全集出版社 1938. 作家書屋 1946. 大連 光華書店 1948. 北京 人民文学出版社 1973. p.804–805;「魯迅譯文集 10」北京 人民文学出版社 1958. p.487

Oshimi naku ai wa ubau　惜しみなく愛は奪ふ

Senbedaŭre amo rabas. Tr. T. Tooguu. Tokyo, Japana Esperanto Instituto, 1931. 103p.
「아낌없이사랑을뺏는다」 趙演鉉訳 서울　正音社 1975. 197p.

Osue no shi　お末の死

'阿末的死' 魯迅訳「現代日本小説集」上海　商務印書館　1923;「日本現代小説集 2」上海　商務印書館 1930. p.147–181;「魯迅全集 11」上海　魯迅全集出版社 1938. 作家書屋 1946. 大連 光華書店 1948. 北京 人民文学出版社 1973. p.464–498;「魯迅譯文集 1」北京 人民文学出版社 1958. p.486–512;

Rubekku to Irine no sonogo　ルベックとイリーネのその後

'盧勃克和伊里納的後來' 魯迅訳「小説月報」第19巻 1号 1928. p.75–77;「壁下譯叢」上海　北新書局 1929;「魯迅全集 16」上海　魯迅全集出版社 1938. 作家書屋 1946. 大連 光華書店 1948. 北京 人民文学出版社 1973. p.121–128;「魯迅譯文集 5」北京 人民文学出版社 1958. p.220–225

ARISHIMA Takeo

Sengen 宣言

Deklaracio. Tr. T. Tooguu. Leipzig, 1924. 125p.
「宣言」緑蕉訳 上海 啓智書局 1929. 1冊

Sengen hitotsu 宣言一つ

'宣言一篇' 魯迅訳 「壁下譯叢」 上海 北新書局 1929;
「魯迅全集 16」 上海 魯迅全集出版社 1938. 作家
書屋 1946. 大連 光華書店 1948. 北京 人民文
学出版社 1973. p.153–160;「魯迅譯文集 5」北京
人民文学出版社 1958. p.245–251

Shi 死

'Death' *New plays from Japan*, ed. and tr. by
Yozan T. Iwasaki and Glenn Hughes. London,
Ernest Benn, 1930. p.15–71

Shiogiri 潮霧

'潮霧' 周作人訳 「東方雑誌」 第19巻1期 1922.
p.134–139;「兩條血痕」上海 開明書店 192?;「近
代日本小説集」 上海 商務印書館 192?.

Shi to sono zengo 死と其前後

'死及其前後' 張定璜訳 「東方雑誌」第20巻19期 1923.
p.101–120; 第20巻24期 1923. p.91–100

Ugokanu tokei 動かぬ時計

'不走的鐘' 夏蘊五訳 「東方雑誌」 第20巻16期 1923.
p.109–116

Umare izuru nayami 生れ出る悩み

'出生的煩悩' 沈端先訳 「有島武郎集」上海 中華書局
1935. p.69–170
'The agony of coming into the world' Tr. by Seiji
Fujita. *Eigo Seinen*, v.97, no.5, 1951. p.210–212
The agony of coming into the world. Tr. by Seiji
Fujita. Tokyo, Hokuseido, 1955. 97p.

Criticism 評論

「生活與文學」 張我軍訳 上海 北新書局 1929. 1冊
'以生命寫成的文章' 魯迅訳 「壁下譯叢」 上海 北新書
局 1929;「魯迅全集 16」 上海 魯迅全集出版社
1938. 作家書屋 1946. 大連 光華書店 1948. 北京
人民文学出版社 1973. p.161;「魯迅譯文集 5」北
京 人民文学出版社 1958. p.252
'關于藝術的感想' 魯迅訳 「壁下譯叢」 上海 北新書局
1929;「魯迅全集16」 上海 魯迅全集出版社 1938.
作家書屋 1946. 大連 光華書店 1948. 北京 人
民文学出版社 1973. p.143–152;「魯迅譯文集 5」
北京 人民文学出版社 1959. p.244
'伊孛生的工作態度' 魯迅訳 「壁下譯叢」 上海 北新書
局 1929;「魯迅全集 16」 上海 魯迅全集出版社
1938. 作家書屋 1946. 大連 光華書店 1948. 北京 人
民文学出版社 1973. p.129–142;「魯迅譯文集 5」
北京 人民文学出版社 1958. p.226–236
「有島武郎論文集」 任伯濤訳 上海 神州書局 1933. 1冊
「生活與文學」 汪馥泉訳 上海 大江書舖 193?. 1冊

ARIYOSHI Sawako 有吉佐和子 1931–

Eguchi no sato 江口の里

'The village of Eguchi' Tr. by Yukio Sawa and
Herbert Glazer. *Japan Quarterly*, v.18, no.4,
1971. p.427–442

Hanaoka Seishū no tsuma 華岡青洲の妻

The doctor's wife. Tr. by Wakako Hironaka and
Ann Siller Kostant. Tokyo, Kodansha International, 1978. 174p.

Jiuta 地唄

'지우다' 李蓉姫訳 「日本新鋭文学作家受賞作品選集 5」
서울 青雲社 1964. p.119–148;「戦後日本短篇
文学全集 5」 서울 日光出版社 1965. p.119–149
'地唄' 李蓉姫訳 「現代日本代表文学全集 5」 서울 平
和出版社 1973. p.119–148
'Jiuta' Tr. by Yukio Sawa and Herbert Glazer.
Japan Quarterly, v.22, no.1, 1975. p.40–58
'地歌' 文洁若訳 「有吉佐和子小説选」北京 人民文学出
版社 1977. p.1–44

Kitō 祈禱

'祈禱' 刘德有訳「世界文学」1961年7月 p.18–52
'기도' 李蓉姫訳 「日本新鋭文学作家受賞選集 5」 서
울 青雲社 1964. p.178–217;「戦後日本短篇文
学全集 5」 서울 日光出版社 1965. p.178–216;
「現代日本代表文学全集 5」 서울 平和出版社 1973.
p.178–215

Kōkotsu no hito 恍惚の人

'Love the old as yourself' Tr. by F. Uyttendaele.
Japan Missionary Bulletin, v.26, no.10, 1972.
p.602–604
'恍惚的人' 余阿勲訳 台北 皇冠雑誌社 1973. 267p.
'恍惚的人' 柳麗華訳 台北 天人出版社 1973. 1冊
'황홀의인생' 金永哲訳 서울 韓進文化社 1973. 343p.
'恍惚의人生' 權一鶴訳 서울 文潮社 1975. 379p.

Kuroko 黒衣

'黒衣' 文洁若訳 「有吉佐和子小説选」 北京 人民文
学出版社 1977. p.134–174

Mizu to hōseki 水と宝石

'물과보석' 李蓉姫訳 「日本新鋭文学作家受賞作品選集 5」
서울 青雲社 1964. p.150–176;「戦後日本短篇文
学全集 5」 서울 日光出版社 1965. p.150–177;
「現代日本代表文学全集 5」 서울 平和出版社 1973.
p.150–177

Nidai no ikeri 二代の生けり

'Дважды рожденный' Перевод В. Логуновой.
Иностранная Литература, декабрь 1971.
p.3–28

Ningyō jōruri 人形浄瑠璃

「木偶浄瑠璃」 錢稲孫 文潔若訳 北京 作家出版社 1965.
74p.
'木偶浄瑠璃' 叶渭渠訳 「有吉佐和子小説选」 北京 人
民文学出版社 1977. p.45–133

Sumi 墨

'The ink stick' Tr. by Mildred Tahara. *Japan Quarterly*, v.22, no.4, 1975. p.348–369
'墨' 叶渭渠訳 「有吉佐和子小説选」北京 人民文学出
版社 1977. p.175–220

Tomoshibi ともしび

'호롱불' 申智植訳 「日本代表作家百人集 5」 서울 希望
出版社 1966. p.344–356;「日本短篇文学選集 6」
서울 新太陽社 1969. p.256–268
'Laternchen' Übers. von Margarete Donath. *Japan
erzählt.* Hamburg, Fischer, 1969. p.77–93

Umikura 海暗

'海暗' 梅韜訳 「七十年代月刊」 第45期 1973年10月
p.74–80; 第46期 1973年11月 p.71–76; 第47期
1973年12月 p.73–79
'海暗' 明洛訳 「七十年代月刊」(香港版) 第43期 1973
年8月 p.72–30; 第44期 1973年9月 p.72–78
「暗流」 梅韜訳 香港 七十年代雑誌社 1974. 301p.

Essays エッセイ

'年輕的母亲, 劳动模范罗淑珍' 李直訳 「世界文学」1966
年1月 p.95–105
"보이프렌드" 와술을마실때' 金賢珠訳 「바이바이바더」
서울 三韓出版社 1966. p.91–94
'我所看見的中國文字改革' 澄明訳 「明報」 第6巻3期
1971. p.70–73
'Danchi life as seen by Ariyoshi Sawako: letters'
Japan Missionary Bulletin, v.26, no.5, 1972.
p.321–327

ASADA Teruhiko 浅田晃彦 1915–

Hiroku Kaura no bōdō 秘録カウラの暴動

The night of a thousand suicides. Tr. and ed. by Ray
Cowan. London, Angus and Robertson, 1970;
N. Y. St. Martin's Press, 1972. 125p.

ASAHARA Rokurō 浅原六朗 1895–1977

Aru jisatsu kaikyūsha 或る自殺階級者

'某自殺階級者' 査士驤訳 「東方雜誌」第27巻19期 1970.
p.110–126

Kurofuku no otoko to watashi 黒服の男と私

'黒衣男子和我' 査士驤訳 「東方雜誌」 第27巻5期 1930.
p.97–104

Rigō 離合

'離合' 王賓蓀訳 「中國公論」 第1巻5期 1939. p.127–
133; 第1巻6期 1939. p.155–164

Essay エッセイ

'蚤' 謝宏徒訳 「當代文藝」 第1巻3期 1931. p.539–540

ASAKURA Isamu 朝倉 勇 1931–

Poems 詩

'파울·크레에 ; 그림의부처서' 金龍済訳 「日本詩集」 서
울 青雲社 1960. p.103–108

ASHIDA Takako 芦田高子 1907–

Kitaguni 北辺

'Из сборника «Северный край»' *Асида Такако,
избранное.* Москва, Изд. Иност. Лит. 1963.
p.11–22

Uchinada 内灘

'Из сборника «Утинада»' *Асида Такако,
избранное.* Москва, Изд. Иност. Лит. 1963.
p.25–39

Tanka 短歌

'Пятистишия' Перевод Анатолия Мамонова.
Вкус хризантемы. Москва, Восточная Литература, 1976. p.22

ATSUMI Ikuko 渥美育子 1940–

Poems 詩

'Interchange; Platform' Tr. by the author. *Prism
International*, Winter 1965. p.11–12
'False creek; Willing a murder' Tr. by Ikuko
Atsumi and Graeme Wilson. *Quadrant*, Nov.
Dec. 1970. p.61
'At Manila airport in summer' *Solidarity*, August
1971. p.20
'The ring; Different dimensions' *The burning heart*,
tr. and ed. by Kenneth Rexroth and Ikuko
Atsumi. N.Y. Seabury Press, 1977. p.127–
128

AWANO Seiho 阿波野青畝 1899–

Haiku 俳句

'16 haiku' *A history of haiku v.2*, by R. H. Blyth.
Tokyo, Hokuseido, 1964. p.215–223

AYUKAWA Nobuo 鮎川信夫 1920–

Poems 詩

'어느記念写真에서' 金龍済訳 「日本詩集」 서울 青雲社
1960. p.18–22
'Off the harbor; Distant life-buoy' Tr. by Makoto
Ueda. *Literary Review*, v.6, no.1, 1962.
p.106–107
'天国의 이야기 ; 秋思 ; 다리위의사람' 辛東門訳 「世界戦
後文学全集 9」 서울 新丘文化社 1962. p.235–236
'깊은밤에' 崔一秀訳 「기다리고있네」 서울 韓国政経社
1966. p.211–213
'Uomo morto' *La protesta poetica del Giappone*,
a cura di Dacia Maraini e Michiko Nojiri.
Roma, Officina Edizioni, 1968. p.75–76
'The evening sun; Leaving harbor; A wanderer'
Anthology of modern Japanese poetry, tr. and
comp. by Edith Marcombe Shiffert and Yuki
Sawa. Tokyo, Tuttle, 1972. p.121–124
'Barcelona; Ishmael' Tr. by Thomas Fitzsimmons.
Japanese poetry now. London, André Deutsch,
1972. p.82–83; *Japanese poetry today.* N. Y.
Schocken Books, 1972. p.84–85
'Saigon 1942; Maritime graves; The dead man;
Morning song at the Marine Hotel' Tr. by
Harry and Lynn Guest and Shozo Kajima.
Post-war Japanese poetry. Harmondsworth,
Penguin Books, 1972. p.63–68
'Wartime buddy; Morning song on a floating hotel
tied to its moorings; In Saigon; The end of
the night; Beyond your death; Why did my
hand; Ode on waves, clouds, and a girl' Tr.
by J. Thomas Rimer and others. *The poetry of
postwar Japan.* Iowa City, Univ. of Iowa
Press, 1975. p.60–73

Criticism 評論

'詩란무엇인가' 金光林訳 「現代詩学」 第4巻2号 1972.

AZUMI Ryōsai 安積りょうさい

Poems 詩

'The old examiner' Tr. by Kinussa and Charlotte
M. A. Peake. *Lotus and chrysanthemum.* N.
Y. Liveright, 1928. p.155–156

B

BABA Akiko　馬場あき子　1928-

Tanka　短歌

'3 tanka' *The burning heart*, tr. and ed. by
Kenneth Rexroth and Ikuko Atsumi. N.Y.
Seabury Press, 1977. p.74–75

BABA Bun'ei　馬場文英

Kaikoku shidan　開国史談

Japan 1853–1864, or, Genji yume monogatari. Tr.
by Sir Ernest Mason Satow. Tokyo, Naigai
Shuppan Kyokai, 1905. 242p.

BABA Noboru　馬場のぼる　1925–

Jūippiki no neko　じゅういっぴきのねこ

Eleven hungry cats. Tr. by Albin Tresselt. N. Y.
Parents, Magazine Press, 1970. 39p.

BEN-DASAN, Isaiah　イザヤ・ベンダサン

Nihonjin to Yudayajin　日本人とユダヤ人

「日本人과유태人」 全吉秀訳 서울 世宗出版公社 1971.
308p.
The Japanese and the Jews. Tr. by Richard L.
Gage. Tokyo, Weatherhill, 1972. 193p.

BETTCHAKU Minoru　別役 実　1937–

Idō　移動

'The move' Tr. by Ted T. Takaya. *Anthology of
modern Japanese drama*. N. Y. Columbia
Univ. Press, forthcoming.

Zō　象

'The elephant' Tr. by David Goodman. *Concerned
Theatre Japan*, v.1, no.3, 1970. p.72–143

C

CHIBA Kameo　千葉亀雄　1878–1935

Criticism　評論

'波蘭文學的特性' 海鏡訳 「小説月報」 第13巻7号 1922.
p.1–7
'1928年世界文藝界概觀' 魯迅訳 「朝花週刊」 第2巻8期
1928;「魯迅全集 16」上海 魯迅全集出版社 1938.
作家書屋 1946. 大連 光華書店 1948. 北京 人民
文学出版社 1973. p.405–422;「魯迅譯文集 10」北京
人民文学出版社 1958. p.184–197
「現代世界文學大綱 上」張我軍訳 上海 神州書局 1930.
1冊
'現代希蠟文學概觀' 武陵訳 「文藝月刊」 第4巻6期 1933.
p.125–132
「大戰後之世界文學」 徐翔訳 上海 光華書局 1933. 1冊

CHIBA Taneaki　千葉胤明　1864–1953

Tanka　短歌

'The rising sun' Tr. by Asataro Miyamori. *Masterpieces of Japanese poetry, ancient and modern*. Tokyo, Maruzen, 1936; Tokyo,
Taiseido, 1956; N. Y. Greenwood Press,
1971. p.620–621

CHICHIBU no miya　秩父宮　1902–1953

Tanka　短歌

'1 tanka' Tr. par Roger Bersihand. *La littérature
japonaise*. Paris, Presses Universitaires de
France, 1956. p.106
'1 tanka' Tr. from the French by Unity Evans.
Japanese literature. N. Y. Walker, 1965.
p.90

CHICHIBU no miya hi　秩父宮妃　1909–

Tanka　短歌

'3 tanka' Tr. by Shigeshi Nishimura. *Eigo Seinen*,
v.62, no.11, 1930. p.402; v.66, no.11, 1932.
p.380
'1 tanka' Tr. par Roger Bersihand. *La littérature
japonaise*. Paris, Presses Universitaires de
France, 1956. p.107
'1 tanka' Tr. from the French by Unity Evans.
Japanese literature. N. Y. Walker, 1965.
p.91
'Slope' Tr. by Kyoko Yamasaki. *Poetry Nippon*,
no.39 & 40, 1977. p.18

CHIGIRI Kōsai　知切光歳　1902–

Kōbō Daishi　弘法大師

'Kobo Daishi' Tr. by Umeyo Hirano. *Buddhist plays from Japanese literature*. Tokyo, CIIB Press, 1962. p.53–59

Myōe Shōnin　明恵上人

'Myoe Shonin' Tr. by Umeyo Hirano. *Buddhist plays from Japanese literature*. Tokyo, CIIB Press, 1962. p.75–95

Oda Tokunō　織田得能

'Tokuno Oda' Tr. by Umeyo Hirano. *Buddhist plays from Japanese literature*. Tokyo, CIIB Press, 1962. p.60–74

Yamato no Seikurō　大和の清九郎

'Seikuro of Yamato' Tr. by Umeyo Hirano. *Buddhist plays from Japanese literature*. Tokyo, CIIB Press, 1962. p.38–52

CHIKAMATSU Shūkō　近松秋江　1876–1944

Kurokami　黒髪

'Das schwarze Haar' Übers. von Oscar Benl. *Der Kirschblütenzweig*. München, Nymphenburger, 1965. p.346–381

'黒髪' 郭夏信訳 「世界文学全集 94」 서울 乙酉文化社 1962. p.457–483

CHIKANO Toshio　ちかの・としお

Poems　詩

'С войной я близко не знаком' Перевод А. Долина. *Иностранная Литература*, сентябрь 1976. p.115

CHIN Shunshin　陳舜臣 (Chen Shun-chen)　1924–

Hisha shōnen　飛車少年

'飛車少年' 朱佩蘭訳 「撒旦的玩笑」 台南 豊生出版社 1975. p.213–239

Kuroi Himaraya　黒いヒマラヤ

「黒色喜馬拉雅山」 劉慕沙訳 台北 皇冠雜誌社 197?. 328p.

Seigyoku shishi kōro　青玉獅子香炉

'青玉獅子香爐' 朱佩蘭訳 「夏流」 台北 純文學出版社 1969. p.171–254

CHINO Masako　茅野雅子　1880–1946

Mekura fukurō　めくら梟

'Mekura fukuroo' Tr. by Yasutaro Jinbo. *Eisakubun Zasshi*, March, April 1922.

Tanka　短歌

'The spring moon; I feel joyful' Tr. by Asataro Miyamori. *Masterpieces of Japanese poetry, ancient and modern*. Tokyo. Maruzen, 1936; Tokyo, Taiseido, 1956; N. Y. Greenwood Press, 1971. p.772–773

'2 tanka' Tr. by V. H. Viglielmo. *Japanese literature in the Meiji era*. Tokyo, Obunsha, 1955. p. 386

'1 tanka' *The burning heart*, tr. and ed. by Kenneth Rexroth and Ikuko Atsumi. N.Y. Seabury Press, 1977. p.68

CHINO Shōshō　茅野蕭々　1883–1946

Tanka　短歌

'2 tanka' Tr. by V. H. Viglielmo. *Japanese literature in the Meiji era*. Tokyo, Obunsha, 1955. p.387

D

DAIGOBŌ Toshio　大悟法利雄　1898–

Tanka　短歌

'A bright smile; A young girl; The light: Her image; A light breeze; Autumn stars; Middle school boys' Tr. by Asataro Miyamori. *Masterpieces of Japanese poetry, ancient and modern*. Tokyo, Maruzen, 1936; Tokyo, Taiseido, 1956; N. Y. Greenwood Press, 1971. p.792–796

'2 tanka' Übers. von Gerolf Coudenhove. *Japanische Jahreszeiten*. Zürich, Manesse Verlag, 1963. p.101, 174

DAN Ikuma　団　伊玖麿　1924–

Essay　エッセイ

'紙的圓舞' 洛海璇訳 「海洋文藝」 第4期 1973年12月 p.115–126

DAN Kazuo　檀　一雄　1912–1976

Moyuru kusabune　燃ゆる草舟

'불타는草舟' 表文台訳 「日本代表作家百人集 4」 서울 希望出版社 1966. p.246–258; 「日本短篇文学全集 5」 서울 新太陽社 1969. p.86–98

Poems　詩

'惜別' 崔一秀訳 「기다리고있네」 서울 韓国政経社 1966. p.41–46

DATE Gen'ichirō**

DATE Gen'ichirō 伊達源一郎 1874–

Kanshō no haru 感傷の春

'感傷之春' 謝位鼎訳 「小説月報」 第15巻5号 1924.

Criticism 評論

'近代文學' 張聞天訳 「小説月報」 第15巻1号 1924.
'近代文學' 趙光栄訳 「文學週報」 第7巻30期 1929.
「近代文學」 張聞天 汪馥泉訳 上海 商務印書館 1935.
1冊

DATE Yutaka 伊達ゆたか

Poems 詩

'Фейерверк' Перевод Анатолия Мамонова. *Вкус хризантемы.* Москва, Восточная Литература, 1976. p.29

DAZAI Osamu 太宰 治 1909–1948

Asa 朝

'Morning' Tr. by David J. Brudnoy and Yumi Oka. *Monumenta Nipponica*, v.24, no.4, 1969. p.519–522

Chichi 父

'The father' Tr. by David J. Brudnoy and Kazuko Shimizu. *Monumenta Nipponica*, v.24, no.4, 1969. p.511–518

Chōchō 蝶蝶

'胡蝶' 具滋雲訳 「現代日本代表文学全集 6」 서울 平和出版社 1973. p.186–187

Dasu gemaine ダス・ゲマイネ

'Das Gemaine' Перевод Т. Делюшной. *И была любовь, и была ненависть.* Москва, Наука, 1975. p.126–151

Gyofukuki 魚服記

'Metamorphosis' Tr. by Thomas J. Harper. *Japan Quarterly*, v.17, no.3, 1970. p.285–288
'魚服記' 具滋雲訳 「現代日本代表文学全集 6」 서울 平和出版社 1973. p.177–181
'Одежда из рыбьей чешуи' Перевод Т. Делюшной. *И была любовь, и была ненависть.* Москва, Наука, 1975. p.167–174

Ha 葉

'Leaves' Tr. by Eric Gangloff. *Chicago Review*, no.20, 1968. p.31–41

Haha 母

'Mother' Tr. by David J. Brudnoy and Yumiko Oka. *Monumenta Nipponica*, v.24, no.3, 1969. p.327–335

Hakumei 薄明

'Šero na úsvitu' Přel. Vlasta Winkelhöferová. *Světová Literatura*, v.20, no.2, 1975. p.142–152

Hannin 犯人

'The criminal' Tr. by Takashi Kojima. *Ei-Bei Bungaku* (Meiji Univ.), no.2, 1956. p.1–11

Hashire Merosu 走れメロス

'Wing Maeloswing' Tr. by Ummaratna Chongkanchana. *Rueng sun yeepun 1.* Bangkok, Urkornsasna, 1977. p.233–259

Hazakura to mateki 葉桜と魔笛

'Листья вишни и флейта' Перевод Т. Делюшной. *И была любовь, и была ненависть.* Москва, Наука, 1975. p.183–189

I can speak

'I can speak' Tr. by David J. Brudnoy and Kazuko Shimizu. *Monumenta Nipponica*, v.24, no.3, 1969. p.337–339

Kassai 喝采

'Applausi' Tr. di Mario Scalise. *Il Giappone*, anno 15, 1975. p.63–76

Kakekomi uttae 駆込み訴へ

'I accuse' Tr. by Tadao Katayama. *The Reeds*, v.4, 1958. p.69–88
'A denúncia' Tr. de Antônio Nojiri. *Maravilhas do conto japonês.* São Paulo, Editôra Cultrix, 1962. p.170–183
'Придаю к вашим стопам' Перевод Т. Делюшной. *И была любовь, и была ненависть.* Москва, Наука, 1975. p.152–166

Katei no kōfuku 家庭の幸福

'Rodinne stesti' Přel. Karel Fiala. *Nový Orient*, no.2, 1970. p.50–54

Kyōō fujin 饗応夫人

'Hostitelka' Přel. Vlasta Winkelhöferová. *Zapadající slunce.* Praha, Odeon, 1972. p.149–159

Mangan 満願

'La plenumigo de voto' Tr. Tacuo Hugimoto. *El japana literaturo.* Tokyo, Japana Esperanto Instituto, 1965. p.40–42
'Fulfilment of a vow' Tr. by David J. Brudnoy and Kazuko Shimizu. *Monumenta Nipponica*, v.24, no.1–2, 1969. p.181–182
'顧' 具滋雲訳 「現代日本代表文学全集 6」 서울 平和出版社 1973. p.183–184

Matsu 待つ

'Waiting' Tr. by David J. Brudnoy and Kazuko Shimizu. *Monumenta Nipponica*, v.24, no.1–2, 1969. p.183–185

Mesu ni tsuite 雌について

'Of women' Tr. by Edward Seidensticker. *Encounter*, v.1, no.1, 1953. p.23–28; *Atlantic Monthly*, Jan. 1955. p.145–147

Ningen shikkaku 人間失格

No longer human. Tr. by Donald Keene. N. Y. New Directions, 1958. 177p.; London, Peter Owen, 1957. 154p.; London, Four Square Press, 1961. 1v.

「人間失格」方基煥訳 서울 新太陽社 1961. 340p.
La déchéance d'un homme. Tr. par Gaston Re-
nondeau. Paris, Gallimard, 1962. 181p.
Ya no humano. Tr. de José María Aroca. Barcelona,
Seix y Barral, 1962. 152p.
Lo squalificato. Tr. dell'inglese di Luciano Bian-
ciardi. Milano, Feltrinelli, 1962. 193p.
'Lo squalificato' Tr. di Luciano Bianciardi.
Il sole di spegne, Lo squalificato. Milano, Fel-
trinelli, 1966. p.164–310

Omoide 思い出

'생각나는일들' 具滋雲訳 「現代日本代表文学全集 6」 서
울 平和出版社 1973. p.143–175

Osan おさん

'Osan' Tr. by E. G. Seidensticker. *Japan Quarterly*, v.5, no.4, 1958. p.478–487; *Modern
Japanese short stories.* Tokyo, Japan Publications Trading Co. 1960. p.38–51; Rev. ed.
1970. p.31–41
'Osan' Přel. Vlasta Hilská. *Nový Orient*, no.7,
1965.
'Osan' Přel. Vlasta Winkelhöferová. *Zapadají́cí
slunce.* Praha, Odeon, 1972. p.180–196

Ōtō 桜桃

'Cherries' Tr. by Edward Seidensticker. *Encounter*,
v.1, no.1, 1953. p.23–28
'앵두' 趙演鉉訳 「世界短篇文学全集 7」 서울 啓蒙社
1966. p.394–400; 「世界短篇文学全集 9」 서울 三
珍社 1971. p.268–273; 「世界代表短篇文学全集 9」
서울 三熙社 1976. p.268–273; 「世界短篇文学全
集 10」 서울 新韓出版社 1976. p.82–91
'Вишни' Перевод А. Бабинцева. *Красная лягушка.* Москва, Наука, 1973. p.96–101

Romanesuku ロマネスク

'Romanesque' Tr. by John Nathan. *Japan Quarterly*, v.12, no. 3, 1965. p.331–346

Sange 散華

'Fallen flowers' Tr. by T. E. Swann. *Monumenta
Nipponica*, v.24, no.1–2, 1969. p.168–179

Sarugashima 猿ケ島

'Monkey island' Tr. by Aileen Gatten. *Voices*,
v.3, no.1, 1971. p.33–38
'Обезьяний остров' Перевод Т. Делюшной. *И
была любовь, и была ненависть.* Москва,
Наука, 1975. p.175–182

Shayō 斜陽

The declining sun. Tr. by Takehide Kikuchi.
Tokyo, Nire Shobo, 1950. 138p.
The setting sun. Tr. by Donald Keene. Norfork,
Conn. J. Laughlin, 1956. 189p.; N. Y. New
Directions, 1956. 189p.; London, Peter Owen,
1958. 189p.; London, Four Square Press,
1961. 128p.: Calcutta, Rupa, 1961. 151p.;
Tokyo, Hara Shobo, 1965. 235p.
Die sinkende Sonne. Übers. von Oscar Benl.
München, Hanser, 1958. 167p.
Il sole di spegne. Tr. di Luciano Bianciardi. Milano,
Feltrinelli, 1959. 190p.
El sol que declina. Tr. por Kazuya Sakai. Buenos
Aires, Sur, 1960. lv.
Soleil couchant. Tr. par Hélène de Sarbois et G.
Renondeau. Paris, Gallimard, 1961. 201p.

'斜陽' 辛東門訳 「世界戦後文学全集 7」 서울 新丘文化
社 1962. p.217–291
Astagāmī sūrya. Tr. into Bengali by Kalpana
Ray. Calcutta, Rupa, 1962. 150p.
Namato sūraj. Tr. into Gujarati by Jayant Parekh
and Anirudh Brahmabhatt. Baroda, Chetan,
1962. 244p.
'The declining sun' Tr. by · Takehide Kikuchi.
Info, v.9, no.6, 1963—v.10, no.1, 1964.
Večerno sonce. Tr. Katarina Pucova. Ljubljana,
Mladinska Knjiga, 1964. 139p.
Laskeva aurinko. Suomentanut luota engl. Kyllikki
Härkäpää. Helsinki, Weilin ja Göös, 1965.
168p.
'Il sole di spegne' Tr. dall'inglese di Luciano
Bianciardi. *Il sole di spegne, Lo squalificato.*
Milano, Feltrinelli, 1966. p.1–162
El sol poniente. Havana, 1966. lv.
'Il testamento di Naoji' Tr. di Luciano Bianciardi.
Antologia della letteratura coreana e giapponese.
Milano, Fratelli Fabbri, 1969. p.319–326
'斜陽' 閔丙山訳 「世界의文学全集 8」 서울 同和出版公
社 1970. p.265–351; 「羅生門外・斜陽」 서울 同
和出版公社 1972. p.87–260
'Zapadají́cí slunce' Přel. Vlasta Winkelhöferová.
Zapadají́cí slunce. Praha, Odeon, 1972. p.5–147
'斜陽' 權逸松訳 「世界文学全集 47」 서울 三省出版社
1976. p.175–268

Shin'yū kōkan 親友交歓

'Wizyta' Przeł. Anna Gostyńska. *Irys, opowi-
adania japońskie.* Warszawa, Pánstwowy In-
stytut Wydawniczy, 1960. p.99–122
'The courtesy call' Tr. by Ivan Morris. *Modern
Japanese stories.* London, Eyre and Spottis-
woode, 1961; Tokyo, Tuttle, 1962. p.465–480;
The world of Japanese fiction. N. Y. Dutton,
1973. p.265–279
'Ein Besucher' Deutsch von Monique Humbert.
Nippon. Zürich, Diogenes, 1965. p.487–508
'The visitor' Tr. by Ivan Morris. *The Japanese
image*, ed. by M. Schneps and A. D. Coox.
Tokyo, Orient West, 1965. p.177–189
'Zdvořilostní návštěva starého přítele' Přel. Vlasta
Winkelhöferová. *Zapadají́cí slunce.* Praha,
Odeon, 1972. p.197–220

Tokatonton トカトントン

'A sound of hammering' Tr. by Frank T. Motofuji. *Japan Quarterly*, v.16, no.2, 1969.
p.194–202
'Bušení' Přel. Vlasta Winkelhöferová. *Zapadají́c
slunce.* Praha, Odeon, 1972. p.160–179

Tōkyō hakkei 東京八景

'Le otto vedute di Tokyo' Tr. di Maria Teresa
Orsi. *Annali dell' Instituto Universitario
Orientale di Napoli*, 1972. p.133–154
'東京八景' 具滋雲訳 「現代日本代表文学全集 6」 서울
平和出版社 1973. p.188–209

Tsugaru 津軽

'Tsugaru' Tr. par Paul Anouilh. *Bulletin de L'
Association des Français du Japon*, no.10,
automne, 1978. p.3–10 (à suivre)

Uso 嘘

'A lie' Tr. by Toshihiko Sato. *Today's Japan*,
v.5, May-June 1960. p.25–30; *The Japanese
image*, ed. by M. Schneps and A. D. Coox.
Tokyo, Orient West, 1966. p.138–144

DAZAI Osamu

Viyon no tsuma　ヴィヨンの妻

'Villon's wife'　Tr. by Donald Keene. *New Directions*, 15, 1955. p.176–195; *Modern Japanese literature*. N. Y. Grove Press, 1956; Tokyo, Tuttle, 1957. p.398–414

'La mujer de Villon'　Tr. por Miguel Alfredo Olivera. *Sur*, no. 249, Nov.-Dec. 1957. p.65–78

'Жена Вийона'　Перевод Кима Минэ. *Японская новелла*. Москва, Изд. Иност. Лит. 1961. p.40–59

'Villonova žena'　Přel. M. Novák. *Světová Literatura*, no.4, 1962. p.144–155

'La moglie di Villon'　Tr. di Atsuko Ricca Suga. *Narratori giapponesi moderni*. Milano, Bompiani, 1965. p.393–416

'비용의아내'　金龍済訳　「日本代表作家百人集 4」　서울 希望出版社　1966. p.10–27; 「日本短篇文学全集 4」　서울　新太陽社　1969. p.236–253

'Villon felesege'　Fordította Sz. Holti Mária. *Modern Japan elbészelők*. Budapest, Európa Könyvkiadó, 1967. p.272–289

'비용의妻'　具滋雲訳　「現代日本代表文学全集 6」　서울 平和出版社　1973. p.119–140

'Die Frau Villon'　Deutsch von Jürgen Berndt. *Träume aus zehn Nächten*. Berlin, Aufbau Verlag, 1975. p.363–390

'비용의아내'　金文洙訳「世界代表短篇文学全集 21」서울 正韓出版社　1976. p.299–325

'Mój mąż Villon'　Przeł. Krystyna Okazaki. *Literatura na Świecie*, no.10, 1976. p.200–228

Yuki no yo no hanashi　雪の夜の話

'A snowy night's tale'　Tr. by T. E. Swann. *Monumenta Nipponica*, v.22, no.1–2, 1967. p.211–215

Zakkan　雑感

'Citaty'　Přel. Karel Fiala. *Nový Orient*, no.2, 1970.

Poems and Haiku　詩, 俳句

'Hlas z dali'　Přel. Karel Fiala. *Nový Orient*, no.2, 1970.

'2 haiku'　Tr. by Rieko Okamura. *Poetry Nippon*, no.35 & 36, 1976. p.14

Essay　エッセイ

'Z miłości'　Przeł. Zdzisław Rzeszelewski. *Fakty*, no.25–26, 1977. p.6

DOI Bansui　土井晩翠　1871–1952

Poems　詩

'Sur le orme dell'ippogrifo'　Tr. di H. Shimoi. *Sakura*, 2, 1920. p.31–36

'Femme japonaise; Chant d'une nuit de clair de lune, au bord du lac du bourget; Etoiles et fleurs; Cloches au crépuscule; L'amour éternel'　Tr. par Kuni Matsuo et Steinilber-Oberlin. *Anthologie des poètes japonais contemporains*. Paris, Mercure de France, 1939. p.21–27

'The mighty foe comes nigh!'　Tr. by Shigeshi Nishimura. *The Current of the World*, v.21, no.10, 1944. p.46–49

'Moonlight over a ruined castle'　Tr. by Henry H. Armstrong. *Jijo Eigo Kenkyu*, v.2, no.9, 1947. p.19

'The moon over the ruined castle'　Tr. by Shigeshi Nishimura. *The Current of the World*, v.28, no.11, 1951. p.29

'Sorrow and pleasure'　Tr. by Shigeshi Nishimura. *The Current of the World*, v.30, no.6, 1953. p.43

'The moon on the ruined castle; Fair Japan'　*The poetry of living Japan*, by Takamichi Ninomiya and D. J. Enright. London, John Murray, 1957. p.19–21

'Moon over the ruined castle'　Tr. by Geoffrey Bownas and Anthony Thwaite. *The Penguin book of Japanese verse*. Harmondsworth, Penguin Books, 1964. p.177

'별과꽃'「永遠한世界名詩全集 2」黄錦燦編　서울 翰林出版社　1969. p.101; 「永遠한世界名詩全集 5」黄錦燦編　서울　翰林出版社　1973. p.101

'Green breeze'　Tr. by Kenneth Yasuda. *A pepperpod*. Tokyo, Tuttle, 1976. p.95

'The moon over the castle ruins'　Tr. by Gaku Kojima. *Eigo Seinen*, v. 123, no. 1, 1977. p. 24

'Star and flower'　Tr. by Hideo Naito. *Poetry Nippon*, no.37 & 38, 1977. p.23

DOI Kōchi　土居光知　1886–

Criticism　評論

「現代文壇的怪傑」　馮次行訳　上海　現代書局　1929. 1冊

DOI Daisuke　土井大助　1927–

Poems　詩

'Война и мир'　Перевод Анатолия Мамонова. *Вкус хризантемы*. Москва, Восточная Литература, 1975. p.30

E

EDOGAWA Ranpo　江戸川乱歩　1894–1965

Akai heya　赤い部屋

'The red chamber'　Tr. by James B. Harris. *Japanese tales of mystery and imagination*. Tokyo, Tuttle, 1956. p.143–170

Akuma no monshō　悪魔の紋章

「魔鬼的標誌」方圓客訳　三重市　明志出版社　1962. 229p.

Dangai　断崖

'The cliff'　Tr. by James B. Harris. *Japanese tales of mystery and imagination*. Tokyo, Tuttle, 1956. p.88–106

Dēzaka no satsujin jiken　D坂の殺人事件

'D언덕의 殺人'　李英朝訳　「心理試験」　서울　豊林出版社 1974. p.57–91

Hakuhatsuki　白髪鬼

「白髪鬼」　永思訳　台北　現代文藝社　1956. 96p.

Horikoshi sōsa daiichi kachō dono 堀越捜査第一課長殿

'捜査第一課長貴下' 權純萬訳 「日本代表作家百人集 2」 서울 希望出版社 1966. p.260–291; 「日本短篇文学全集 2」 서울 新太陽社 1969. p.324–355

Ichimai no kippu 一枚の切符

Unu bileto. Tr. J. Simomura. Tokyo, Esperanto Kenkyusha, 1930. 41p.

Ichimai 芋虫

'The caterpillar' Tr. by James B. Harris. *Japanese tales of mystery and imagination.* Tokyo, Tuttle, 1956. p.65–88

Injū 陰獣

'陰獣' 姜龍俊訳 「世界推理文学全集 5」 서울 河西出版社 1974. p.211–301

Jigoku no dōkeshi 地獄の道化師

「地獄的傀儡」 永思訳 台北 現代文藝社 1956. 84p.

Kagami jigoku 鏡地獄

'The hell of mirrors' Tr. by James B. Harris. *Japanese tales of mystery and imagination.* Tokyo, Tuttle, 1956. p.107–122
'거울地獄' 李英朝訳 「心理試験」 서울 豊林出版社 1974. p.253–278

Kotō no oni 孤島の鬼

「岩屋島」 餘蔭訳 台北 皇冠出版社 1962. 176p.

Kumo otoko 蜘蛛男

「蜘蛛男」 黃宏籌訳 上海 南京書店 192?. 1冊
Démon. Praha, 1942. 138p.
「蜘蛛人」 耕實訳 三重市 明志出版社 1963. 3冊

Ni haijin 二廃人

'Two crippled men' Tr. by James B. Harris. *Japanese tales of mystery and imagination.* Tokyo, Tuttle, 1956. p.171–194
'Два инварида' *Азия и Африка Сегодня,* 1974, номер 4. p.29–31

Ningen hyō 人間豹

「人豹」 耕實訳 台北 明志出版社 1963. 125p.

Ningen isu 人間椅子

'Human chair' Tr. by James B. Harris. *Japanese tales of mystery and imagination.* Tokyo, Tuttle, 1956. p.1–24
'Чедовек-кресдо' Перевод Т. Виноградовой. *Японская новелла.* Москва, Изд. Иност. Лит. 1961. p.432–443
'Inimtooi' *Elada.* Tallinn, Eest Ruklik Kirjastas, 1962. p.186–198
'Кресло-адам' Аударган К. Ормандаева. *Жапон енгимелери.* Алма-Ата, Жазушы, 1965. p. 142–153
'W objęciach fotela' Przeł. Blanka Yonekawa. *Przekrój,* no.1536, 1974. p.15–16
'人間椅子' 李英朝訳 「心理試験」 서울 豊林出版社 1974. p.195–219

Nisen dōka 二銭銅貨

'二錢銅貨' 姜龍俊訳 「世界推理文学全集 5」 서울 河西

出版社 1974. p.337–402
'二錢銅貨' 李英朝訳 「心理試験」 서울 豊林出版社 1974. p.93–121

Ogon kamen 黄金仮面

Ora masko. Tr. J. Simomura, Tokyo, Japana Esperantista Associo, 1931. 110p.

Oshie to tabi suru otoko 押絵と旅する男

'The traveller with the pasted rag picture' Tr. by James B. Harris. *Japanese tales of mystery and imagination.* Tokyo, Tuttle, 1956. p.195–222

Osoroshiki sakugo 恐ろしき錯誤

'무서운錯誤' 李英朝訳 「心理試験」 서울 豊林出版社 1974. p.173–193

Shinri shiken 心理試験

'The psychological test' Tr. by James B. Harris. *Japanese tales of mystery and imagination.* Tokyo, Tuttle, 1956. p.25–64
'心理試験' 姜龍俊訳 「世界推理文学全集 5」 서울 河西出版社 1974. p.303–335
'心理試験' 李英朝訳 「心理試験」 서울 豊林出版社 1974. p.13–55

Sōseiji 双生児

'The twins' Tr. by James B. Harris. *Japanese tales of mystery and imagination.* Tokyo, Tuttle, 1956. p.123–142

Tsuki to tebukuro 月と手袋

'月亮和手套' 徐白訳 「日本短篇譯集 1」 台北 晩蟬書店 1969. p.103–164

Yaneura no sanposha 屋根裏の散歩者

'天障위의散歩' 姜龍俊訳 「世界推理文学全集 5」 서울 河西出版社 1974. p.337–374
'다락방의散歩者' 李英朝訳 「心理試験」 서울 豊林出版社 1974. p.123–171

Yōchū 妖虫

「美女與野獣」 台北 集文書局 1963. 1冊

'完全犯罪의名手' 李英朝訳 「心理試験」 서울 豊林出版社 1974. p.221–251

EGUCHI Kan 江口 漢 1887–1975

Aru onna no hanzai ある女の犯罪

'某女人的犯罪' 張資平訳 「資平譯品集」 上海 193?.
「某女人的犯罪」 張資平訳 上海 楽羣雜誌社 193?. 1冊

Hanayome to uma ippiki 花嫁と馬一匹

'The surplus bride' Tr. by E. Seidensticker. *Atlantic Monthly,* v.195, 1955. p.160–164
「新娘子和一匹馬」 張夢麟訳 北京 作家出版社 1964. 115p.

Koi to rōgoku 恋と牢獄

Любовь и тюрьма. Перевод Е. Терновской. Москва, Московский Рабочий, 1927. 120p.
「戀愛與牢獄」 錢歌川訳 上海 北新書局 1930. 1冊

Kyōkoku no yoru 峡谷の夜

'峽谷的夜' 魯迅訳 「現代日本小説集」 上海 商務印書館

EGUCHI Kan

1923. 「日本現代小説集 3」 上海 商務印書館
1930. p.255–279;「魯迅全集 11」上海 魯迅全集出
版社 1938. 作家書屋 1946. 大連 光華書店 1948.
北京 人民文学出版社 1973. p.499–523; 「魯迅
譯文集 1」北京 人民文学出版社 1958. p.513–532

Essay エッセイ

'憶愛羅先珂華希理君' 魯迅訳 「晨報副刊」 1922年5月;
「魯迅譯文集 10」 北京 人民文学出版社 1958.
p.462–469

EI Rokusuke 永 六輔 1933–

Poems 詩

'Love's creed' (from *Nihon no oto*) Tr. by Jose
Civasaqui. *Poetry Nippon*, no.11, 1970. p.7

EMA Nakashi 江馬 修 1889–1975

Aru jisatsu 或る自殺

'自殺' 張資平訳 「洪水」 復刊第1巻4期 1925. p.1–
10; '別宴」 武昌 時中合作社 1926; 「襯衣」 上
海 光華書局 1928.

Chiisai hitori 小さい一人

'小小的一個人' 周作人訳 「新青年」 第5巻6期 1918.
p.623–630; '點滴」 北京 北京大學 1920; 「日本現
代小説集 2」 上海 商務印書館 1930. p.245–254

Kōri no kawa 氷の河

「冰河 第一部」 力生訳 北京 新文艺 1958. 239p.

EMA Shōko 江間章子 1913–

Poems 詩

'서글픈約束 ; 순수한사람' 崔一秀訳 「기다리고있네」 서
울 韓国政経社 1966. p.51–52, 179–181

EMI Suiin 江見水蔭 1869–1934

Himitsu sekai 秘密世界

「地中秘」 鳳仙女史訳 上海 廣智書局 1906. 1冊

ENCHI Fumiko 円地文子 1905–

Aijō no keifu 愛情の系譜

「愛情都市」 서울 平和文化社 1965. 310p.
「愛情의系譜」 裵弼相訳 서울 白潮出版社 1965. 1冊;
서울 裕林社 1965. 325p.
「愛情戦線」 서울 平和出版社 1965. 316p.

Gendai kōshoku ichidai onna 現代好色一代女

「現代好色一代女」 崔林訳 서울 受験社 1964. 343p.
「푸른果實」 崔林訳 서울 受験社 1966. 343p.
「어머니의秘密」 李光熙訳 서울 尚志文化社 1974. 343p.

Himojii tsukihi ひもじい月日

'배고픈歳月' 金潤成訳 「日本代表作家百人集 3」 서울
希望出版社 1966. p.410–426; 「日本短篇文学全
集 4」 서울 新太陽社 1969. p.170–186

Onnazaka 女坂

The waiting years. Tr. by John Bester. Tokyo,
Kodansha International, 1971. 203p.

Yō 妖

'Enchantress' Tr. by John Bester. *Japan Quarterly*,
v.5, no.3, 1958. p.339–357; *Modern Japanese
short stories*. Tokyo, Japan Publications Trading Co. 1960. p.90–117; Rev. ed. 1970. p.72–
93

Essay エッセイ

'一分의길이' 金賢珠訳 「바이바이바디」 서울 三韓出版
社 1966. p.122–125

ENCHI Terutake 遠地輝武

Poems 詩

'돌' 金龍済訳 「日本詩集」 서울 青雲社 1960. p.27–
29

ENDA Keiichirō えんだ・けいいちろう

Poems 詩

'Любовь' Перевод Анатолия Мамонова. *Свобод-
ный стих в японской поэзии.* Москва,
Книга, 1971. p.123; *Вкус хризантемы.*
Москва, Восточная Литература, 1976. p.172

ENDŌ Shūsaku 遠藤周作 1923–

Chinmoku 沈黙

Silence. Tr. by William Johnston. Tokyo, Sophia
Univ. 1969; Tokyo, Tuttle, 1969; London,
Prentice-Hall, 1970. 306p.
'Milczenie' Przeł. Izabella Denysenko. *Przeglad
Orientalistyczny*, no.2, 1969. p.151–158
Silence. Tr. par Henriette Guex-Rolle. Paris,
Calmann-Lévy, 1971. 275p.
Taus himmel. Oversette Erik Gunnes. Oslo, Gyl-
dendal, 1971. 216p.
Tystnad. Översätta Magnus K. Lindberg. Stock-
holm, Forum, 1971. 187p.
Milczenie. Przeł. Izabella Denysenko. Warszawa,
Pax, 1971. 236p.
Silenzio. Tr. di Bonaventura G. Tonutti. Tokyo,
privately pub. 1972. 262p.
Stilte. Tr. Frans Uyttendaele. Brugge, Emmaüs,
1972. 303p.
Tavshed. Tr. Ingeborg Stemann. Hellerup, DMS
Forlag, 1972. 240p.
Silencio. Tr. por Jaime Fernández y José Miguel
Vara. Madrid, Atenas, 1973. 230p.
Silensió. Roma, Cánes, 1973. 1v.
「沈默」 朱佩蘭訳 台北 道聲出版社 1973. 225p.
「침묵」 金潤成訳 서울 聖바오로出版社 1973. 253p.
Schweigen. Übers. von Ruth Linhart. Wien,
Styria, 1977. 248p.

Fuda no Tsuji 札の辻

'Fuda no Tsuji' Tr. by Frank Hoff and James
Kirkup. *Japan P.E.N. News*, no.14, Jan. 1965.
p.1–9

Haha naru mono 母なるもの

'Mothers' Tr. by Francis Mathy. *Japan Christian Quarterly*, v.40, no.4, 1974. p.186–204

Iesu no shōgai イエスの生涯

「耶穌的生涯」余阿勲訳 台北 新理想出版社 1973. 166p.
Vita di Gesù. Tr. di L. Muratori e F. Moriguci. Brescia, Queriniana, 1977. 182p.

Ihōjin no kunō 異邦人の苦悩

'The anguish of an alien' Tr. by the Japan Christian Quarterly editor. *Japan Christian Quarterly*, v.40, no.4, 1974. p.179–185

Jinari 地なり

'地震」表文台訳 「日本代表作家百人集 5」서울 希望出版社 1966. p.82–95; 「日本短篇文学全集 5」서울 新太陽社 1969. p.378–391

Kagebōshi 影法師

「오따마쥬리아」成玉泉訳 서울 弘信文化社 1973. 212p.

Kazan 火山

Volcano. Tr. by Richard A. Schuchert. London, Peter Owen, 1978. 175p.

Kekkon 結婚

Супружеская жизнь. Перевод З. Рахима. Москва, Прогресс, 1965. 126p.
Мкки дил. Перевод на узвекском языке. Тошкент, Гослитиздат, 1968. 160p.
'Seimyninis gyvenimas' Tr. from the Russian Viktoras Bufas. *Seimyninis gyvenimas, Moteria, kuria as pameciau.* Vilnius, Vaga, 1970.
Ажел зулеги. Перевод Субыкан Сосанов. Алма-Ата, Жазушы, 1970. 136p.

Menamu gawa no nipponjin メナム河の日本人

'I Giapponesi del Menam' Tr. di Adriana Boscaro. *Il Giappone*, anno 16, 1976. p.123–184

Nikushin saikai 肉親再会

'Младшая сестра' Перевод С. Гутермана. *Японская новелла 1960–1970.* Москва, Прогресс, 1972. p.418–434

Obaka san おバカさん

Wonderful fool. Tr. by Francis Mathy. London, Peter Owen, 1974. 237p.; Tokyo, Tuttle, 1975. 237p.
Szaleniec? Przeł. Izabella Denysenko. Warszawa, Pax, 1976. 179p.

Ōgon no kuni 黄金の国

The golden country. Tr. by Francis Mathy. Tokyo, Tuttle, 1970. 128p.

Otoko to kyūkanchō 男と九官鳥

'L'uomo e il kyukancho' Tr. di Adriana Boscaro. *Il Giappone*, anno 14, 1974. p.119–138
'Die Männer und ein Vogel' Deutsch von Jürgen Berndt und Eiko Saito-Berndt. *Träume aus zehn Nächten.* Berlin, Aufbau Verlag, 1975. p.591–616

Shiroi hito 白い人

'白色人' 鄭漢淑訳 「世界戦後文学全集 7」서울 新丘文化社 1962. p.13–48
'흰사람' 李鐘烈訳 「日本新鋭文学作家受賞作品選集 4」서울 青雲社 1964. p.125–177; 「戦後日本短篇文学全集 4」서울 日光出版社 1965. p.125–178; 「現代日本代表文学全集 4」서울 平和出版社 1973. p.125–176

Shurudan byōin シュルダン病院

'В больнице Журден' Перевод З. Рахима. *Японская новелла.* Москва, Изд. Иност. Лит. 1961. p.444–471
'Журден ауруханасында' Орыссадан аударган Нырахмет Телеупов. *Хиросима касирети.* Алта-Ата, Жазушы, 1969. p.36–52

Uchi no nyōbō uchi no musuko うちの女房うちの息子

「吾妻吾子」劉慕沙訳 台中 慧龍出版社 1977. 206p.

Umi to dokuyaku 海と毒薬

'Море и яд' Перевод П. Петрова. *Иностранная Литература*, август 1964. p.114–175
'바다와毒薬' 李鐘烈訳 「日本新鋭文学作家受賞作品選集 4」서울 青雲社 1964. p.179–294; 「戦後日本短篇文学全集 4」서울 日光出版社 1965. p.179–294; 「現代日本代表文学全集 4」서울 平和出版社 1973. p.179–293
Море и яд. Перевод П. Петрова. Москва, Молодая Гвардия, 1964. 125p.
Meri ja mürk. Jaapani keelest tõlkinud Agu Sisask. Tallinn, Perioodika, 1965. 103p.
Море и яд, на армянском языке. Ереван, Аиастан, 1967. 136p.
'바다와毒薬' 金潤成訳 「現代世界文学全集 18」서울 新丘文化社 1968.
Море и яд, на грузинском языке С. Кетелаури. Тбилиси, Сабчота Сакартвело, 1970. 130p.
The sea and the poison. Tr. by Michael Gallagher. London, Peter Owen, 1972. 167p.; Tokyo, Tuttle, 1973. 167p.
Morze i trucizna. Przeł. Izabella Denysenko. Warszawa, Pax, 1974. 164p.
Meer und Gift. Übers. von Jürgen Berndt. Berlin, Volk und Welt, 1976. 197p.

Watashi ga suteta onna 私が・棄てた・女

「내가버린女人」李時哲訳 서울 知性社 1964. 282p.
Женщина, которую я бросил. Перевод К. Рехо. Москва, Прогресс, 1968. 142p.
'Moteris, kuria as pameciau' Tr. from the Russian Viktoras Bufas. *Seimyninis gyvenimas, Moteris, kuria as pameciau.* Vilnius, Vaga, 1970.
Sieviete, kuru es pametu. Tr. from the Russian Edgars Katajs. Riga, Liesma, 1971. 231p.

Watashi no mono 私のもの

'Mine' Tr. by Peter W. Schumacher. *Japan Christian Quarterly*, v. 40, no. 4, 1974. p.205–213

Yonjussai no otoko 四十歳の男

'四十歳的男人' 江上訳 「日本名家小説選」高雄 大舞台書苑 1976. p.59–88

「사랑이오고갈때」文德守訳 서울 新潮文化社 1963. 243p.; 1964. 250p.
「첫사랑」文熙訳 서울 上智社 1967. 279p.
「바림받은女人」李時哲訳 서울 無等出版社 1969. 282p.

ENDŌ Yoshimoto

ENDŌ Yoshimoto 遠藤嘉基 1905–

Nihon bungakushi shinkō 日本文学史新講

「日本文学史」 楊春霖訳 台北 榮文出版社 1973. 130p.

ENOMOTO Torahiko 榎本虎彦 1866–1916

Raizan 来山

'Raizan' Tr. by A. L. Sadler. *Japanese plays.* Sydney, Angus and Robertson, 1934. p.261–283

Tōkō Kakiemon 陶工柿右衛門

'The potter Kakiemon' Tr. by A. L. Sadler. *Japanese plays.* Sydney, Angus and Robertson, 1934. p.193–238

Tsuzumi no sato 鼓の里

'The village of drummakers' Tr. by A. L. Sadler. *Japanese plays.* Sydney, Angus and Robertson, 1934. p.239–260

ENYA Uhei 塩谷鵜平 1877–1940

Haiku 俳句

'2 haiku' Tr. by V. H. Viglielmo. *Japanese literature in the Meiji era.* Tokyo, Obunsha, 1955. p.450, 451

ETŌ Jun 江藤 淳 1933–

Criticism 評論

'An undercurrent in modern Japanese literature' *Journal of Asian Studies*, v.23, no.3, May 1964. p.433–445
'Modern Japanese literary criticism' *Japan Quarterly*, v.12, no. 2, 1965. p.177–186
'Natsume Soseki: a Japanese Meiji intellectual' *American Scholar*, v. 34, 1965. p.603–619
'The International Symposium on the Short Story, Japan' *Kenyon Review*, v.31, no.1, 1969. p.63–68
'A Japanese Meiji intellectual: an essay on Kokoro' *Essays on Natsume Soseki's works.* Tokyo, Japan Society for the Promotion of Science, 1972. p.49–65

F

FUCHIGAMI Mōsen 淵上毛銭 1915–1950

Poems 詩

'Rogers' bronze-leaf; Insanity' *An anthology of*

modern Japanese poetry, ed. and tr. by Ichiro Kono and Rikutaro Fukuda. Tokyo, Kenkyusha, 1957. p.10–11

FUJI Masaharu 富士正晴 1913–

Chūgoku no inja 中国の隠者

「中國的隠者」 張良澤訳 高雄 大皇出版社 1975. 140p.

FUJII Chikugai 藤井竹外 1807–1866

Poems 詩

'Going down the Yodo river on a flowery morn' Tr. by Tetsuzo Okada. *Chinese and Sino-Japanese poems.* Tokyo, Seikanso, 1937. p.96

FUJII Kenjirō 藤井健治郎 1872–1931

Jinsei no shukuzu 人生の縮図

'Human life pictured in miniature' Tr. by F. J. Daniels. *Japanese prose.* London, Lund Humphries, 1944. p.64–79

FUJII Masumi 藤井真澄 1889–1962

Shin maō 新魔王

Nova Satano. Tr. Ichiro Sakurada. Kyoto, Kaniya, 1924. 27p.

Criticism 評論

'戯曲的種類' 甄乃力訳 「北平晨報劇刊」 123期 1933.

'春宵' 野如訳 「語絲」 第5巻40期 1929. p.26–44

FUJII Shiei 藤井紫影 1868–1945

Haiku 俳句

'3 haiku' Tr. by Asataro Miyamori. *Anthology of haiku, ancient and modern.* Tokyo, Maruzen, 1932. p.712–713
'Young bamboos' Tr. by Asataro Miyamori. *Haiku poems, ancient and modern.* Tokyo, Maruzen, 1940. p.329
'1 haiku' Tr. by Lois J. Erickson. *Songs from the land of dawn.* N. Y. Friendship Press, 1949; Freeport, Books for Libraries Press, 1968. p.76

FUJIKAWA Gyō 藤川ぎょう

Dyreborn. København, Illustrations Forlaget, 1964. 22p.

FUJIKO Fujio　藤子不二雄

Obake no Q-tarō　おばけのQ太郎

Q the spook.　Tokyo, Labo-Teaching Information Center, 1971.　56p.

FUJIMORI Seikichi　藤森成吉　1892–1977

Aru taisō kyōshi no shi　ある体操教師の死

'一位體操教員之死'「日本短篇小説選」香港　藝美圖書公司　1959. p.1–11
'一位體操教員之死'　高汝鴻訳「日本短篇小説集」台北　台湾商務印書館　1969. p.111–126

Dassōsha　脱走者

'Беглец' Перевод Елены Терновской. Ад. Москва, Московский Рабочий, 1929.　p.159–189

Gisei　犠牲

「犠牲」沈端先訳　上海　北新書局　1929. 1冊

Hako basha　箱馬車

'馬車' 張資平訳「資平譯品集」上海　現代書局　192?.

Hakushu shinai otoko　拍手しない男

'The man who did not applause'　The cannery boat, and other Japanese short stories. N. Y. International Publications, 1933; London, Martin Lawrence, 1933; N. Y. Greenwood Press, 1968. p.61–66
'Человек, который не аплодировал' Перевод Н. Фельдман. Японская революционная литература. Москва, Худож. Лит. 1934. p.185–196
'Der Mann, der nicht klatschte'　Deutsch von Jürgen Berndt. Träume aus zehn Nächten. Berlin, Aufbau Verlag, 1975. p.241–243

Higasa　日傘

'遮陽傘與老師' 新興書局編集部訳「日本短篇小説選」台北　新興書局　1958. p.36–41; 台南　鳴宇出版社　1972. p.36–41
'陽傘' 高汝鴻訳「日本短篇小説集」台北　台湾商務印書館　1969. p.127–137

Jinushi　地主

'地主' 張資平訳「資平譯品集」上海　現代書局　192?.

Kusama Chūi　草間中尉

'Lieutenant Kusama'　The cannery boat, and other Japanese short stories. N. Y. International Publications, 1933; London, Martin Lawrence, 1933: N. Y. Greenwood Press, 1968. p.245–252

Sōrenki　相恋記

'相戀記' 江珠訳「人魚的悲戀」台中　中央書局　1955. p.63–102

Watanabe Kazan　渡辺崋山

On Watanabe Kazan.　Tr. by F. Hawley. Tokyo, Nippon Bunka Chuo Renmei, 1939. 27p.

Criticism　評論

「文藝新論」張資平訳　上海　聯合書局　1928. 1冊

Essay　エッセイ

'О себе' Перевод Елены Терновской. Ад. Москва, Московский Рабочий, 1929. p.159–189

「藤森成吉集」魯森堡訳　上海　現代書局　1933. 1冊

FUJIMORI Yasukazu　藤森安和　1940–

Jūgosai no ijōsha　15歳の異常者

「十五歳의異常者」姜敏訳 서울 徽文出版社　1962. 125p.

Poems　詩

'그로테스크한空想家；멋대가리없는입맞춤의가을' 辛東門訳「戦後世界文学全集 9」서울 新丘文化社 1962. p.263–264
'Words death gone'　Tr. by Thomas Fitzsimmons. Japanese poetry now. London, André Deutsch, 1972. p.32; Japanese poetry today. N. Y. Schocken Books, 1972. p.34

FUJIMURA Misao　藤村 操　1886–1903

Gantō no kan　巖頭の感

「삶과죽음의對話」崔崑崗訳 서울　大学社　1964. 85p.

FUJINO Kohaku　藤野古白　1871–1895

Haiku　俳句

'2 haiku'　Tr. by V. H. Viglielmo. Japanese literature in the Meiji era. Tokyo, Obunsha, 1955. p.427

FUJINO Tokuko　藤野登久子　1908–

Hana no dorei　花の奴隷

'꽃의奴隷' 金鐘仁訳「戦後日本新人受賞作品選」서울 隆文社　1960. p.155–193

FUJISAWA Eiko　藤沢えい子　1885–

Yamahime no mai　山姫の舞

'The dance of the mountain princess' Tr. by F. J. Daniels. Japanese prose. London, Lund Humphries, 1944.　p.26–35

FUJISAWA Kosetsu　藤沢古雪

Garashia　がらしあ

Gracia, historia dramo. Tr. Tomoyuki Murakami. Kyushu Esperanto Renmei, 1930. 22p.

FUJISAWA Takeo 藤沢桓夫 1904–

Fukanzen na hanzai 不完全な犯罪

‘不完全的犯罪’ 徐白訳 「日本短篇譯集 2」 台北 晩蟬書
店 1969. p.27–59

Kindan no kajitsu 禁断の果実

‘禁断의열매’ 金龍済訳 「日本代表作家百人集 3」 서울
希望出版社 1966. p.262–279; 「日本短篇文学全
集 4」 서울 新太陽社 1969. p.22–39

Ki no nagai tomodachi 気の永い友達

‘A slow-witted fellow’ Tr. by Tomokazu Nishira.
English Society Review, 1931.

Shūkaku nikki 収穫日記

‘Das Erntetagebuch’ Übers. von Kurt Meissner.
Der Tanzfächer, hrg. von K. Meissner. Tokyo,
1943. p.221–232

Utsukushii kisetsu 美しい季節

「아름다운季節」 金奎東訳 서울 韓一出版社 1961. 183p

Yōsei wa hana no nioi ga suru 妖精は花の匂いがする

「天鵝夢」 謝新發訳 三重市 明志出版社 1963. 2冊

FUJISHIMA Udai 藤島宇内 1924–

Poems 詩

‘夕陽의少女’ 崔一秀訳 「기다리고있네」 서울 韓国政経
社 1966. p.153–162

FUJITA Sōnosuke 藤田草之助

Awajimachi shinjū 淡路町心中

‘Awaji machi shinju, oder, der Liebesselbstmord
in der Awajistraße’ Übers. von Maria Piper.
Die Schaukunst der Japaner. Berlin, Gruyter,
1927. p.177–191

FUJITA Tamao 藤田圭雄 1905–

The boy and the bird. Tr. by Kiyoko Tucker. N. Y.
John Day, 1972. 24p.

FUJITOMI Yasuo 藤富保男 1928–

Poems 詩

‘Really; Explanation’ Tr. by Harry and Lynn
Guest and Shozo Kajima. *Post-war Japanese
poetry*. Harmondsworth, Penguin Books,
1972. p.116–118

FUJIWARA Hitoshi 藤原 等

Poems 詩

‘Ты не должен молчать’ Перевод А. Долина.
Иностранная Литература, сентябрь 1976.
p.114

FUJIWARA Sadamu 藤原 定 1905–

Poems 詩

‘A transparent autumn’ *An anthology of modern
Japanese poetry*, ed. and tr. by Ichiro Kono
and Rikutaro Fukuda. Tokyo, Kenkyusha,
1957. p.11

‘그한마디가；보이지않는다는；사랑의骸骨’ 辛東門訳 「世
界戰後文学全集 9」 서울 新丘文化社 1962. p.234–
235

FUJIWARA Saitarō 藤原宰太郎 1932–

Gofunkan misuterī 五分間ミステリー

「추억！五分間」 李千載訳 서울 知焰林 1977. 289p.

FUJIWARA Tei 藤原てい 1918–

Nagareru hoshi wa ikite iru 流れる星は生きている

‘흐르는별은살아있다 第一部’ 陳明仁訳 「民聲」 第5巻
8号 1949.
「내가넘은三八線」 鄭広鉉訳 서울 首都文化社 1952.
215p.；1964. 220p.
‘Le stelle cadenti vivono. . .’ Tr. di Giuseppe
Morichini. *Il Giappone*, anno 2, no.3–4, 1958.
p.41–54

FUKADA Kyūya 深田久弥 1903–1971

G.S.L. kurabu G.S.L. クラブ

‘G.S.L. club’ Tr. by Kiyoshi Maekawa. *Young
forever, and five other novelettes*, ed. by Japan
Writers’ Society. Tokyo, Hokuseido, 1941.
p.20–44

FUKAGAWA Munetoshi 深川宗俊 1921–

Poems 詩

‘Сопротивление; Хиросима’ Перевод В. Марковой. *Японская поэзия*. Москва, Гослитиздат,
1954. p.370–371; Изд. 2. 1956. p.470–471;
Поэты Азии. Москва, Гослитиздат 1957.
p.876–877

‘Руки трянутся ввысь’ Перевод А. Мамонова.
Песня Хиросимы, Москва, Худож. Лит.
1964. p.13

‘Хиросимские пятистишия’ Перевод А. Мамонова.
Иностранная Литература, август 1966.
p.3–4

‘Из цикла «6 август 1945 года» и другие позмы’

Перевод Анатолия Мамонова. *Три поэта из Хиросимы.* Москва, Наука, 1970. p.80–135
'Yuki-chan and a dove; This bone of pretty shape; A keloid face' Tr. by Miyao Ohara. *The songs of Hiroshima.* Tokyo, Taihei Shuppan-sha, 1971. p.63–77
'Хиросимские пятистишия' Перевод Анатолия Мамонова. *Вкус хризантемы.* Москва, Восточная Литература, 1976. p.147

FUKAGAWA Shōichirō 深川正一郎 1905–

Haiku 俳句

'1 haiku' Tr. by Mayumi Hara. *Poetry Nippon,* no.29 & 30, 1975. p.18

FUKAO Sumako 深尾須磨子 1893–1974

Eien no kyōshū 永遠の郷愁

'Из «Вечная тоска»' Перевод Евгения Винокурова. *Фукао Сумако.* Москва, Прогресс, 1966. p.45–54

Hanmyō 斑猫

'Из сборник «Пятнистая кошка»' Перевод Евгения Винокурова. *Фукао Сумако.* Москва, Прогресс, 1966. p.11–15

Juso 呪詛

'Из сборника «Проклятие»' Перевод Евгения Винокурова. *Фукао Сумако.* Москва, Прогресс, 1966. p.19–26

Mendori no shiya 牝鶏の視野

'Из сборника «Крутозор курицы»' Перевод Евгения Винокурова. *Фукао Сумако.* Москва, Прогресс, 1966. p.37–42

Ranqu to hana 洋燈と花

'Из «Лампа и цветы»' Перевол Евгения Винокурова. *Фукао Сумако.* Москва, Прогресс, 1966. p.77–89
Lampa i cvetja. Perevede Jordan Jankov. Sofiia, Narod. Kultura, 1972. 160p.

Shi wa majutsu de aru 詩は魔術である

'Из «Стихи—это жизнь»' Перевод Евгения Винокурова. *Фукао Сумако,* Москва, Прогресс, 1966. p.99–109

Shinwa no musume 神話の娘

'Из «Девушка из мифологии»' Перевод Евгения Винокурова. *Фукао Сумако.* Москва, Прогресс, 1966. p.57–73

Shōsō 焦躁

'Из «Нетерпение»' Перевод Евгения Винокурова. *Фукао Сумако,* Москва, Прогресс, 1966. p.29–34

Poems 詩

'Jour nuageux; Jour de brouillard; Premiers jours d'automne; Mourasaki; Soliloque; Septembre; Midi; Tentation; La nuit; Le visage; Champs de vision d'une poule' Tr. par Kuni Matsuo et Steinilber-Oberlin. *Anthologie des poètes japonais contemporains.* Paris, Mercure de France, 1939. p.222–232
'My fondly Nippon' *United Asia,* v.8, no.4, 1956. p.367
'Presentiment; Human talks' *An anthology of modern Japanese poetry,* ed. and tr. by Ichiro Kono and Rikutaro Fukuda. Tokyo, Kenkyu-sha, 1957. p.12
'Will-o'-the wisp; Dante's scourge' *The poetry of living Japan.* Tr. by Takamichi Ninomiya and D. J. Enright. London, John Murray, 1957. p.84–85
'La tentation; Le fouet de Dante' *La poésie japonaise,* par Karl Petit. Paris, Seghers, 1959. p.214–215
'Die Geißel Dantes' Übertragen von Shin Aizu. *Der schwermütige Ladekran.* St. Gallen, Tschudy Verlag, 1960. p.43
'İnsanlarm konuşmalari' Tercüme etmek L. Sami Akalin. *Japon şiiri.* İstanbul, Varlik Yayinevi, 1962. p. 260
'長歌 《日，月，星》 三部曲' 李芒訳「世界文学」1963年 12月 p.13–15
'Presentimiento' Tr. por Kikuya Ionesawa. *Poesia japonesa contemporanea.* Bogotá, Colombia Editoriales de Librería, 1965.
'愛戀；呂' 崔一秀訳「기다리고있네」서울 韓国政経社 1966. p.23–24, 132–134
'Суцкумдуу Япониям; Имне, Бала; Жашыл инир; Тунку маек; Гогорек стои; Айнуру; Тан уру; Естее; Коздун жашу; Эске тушуруу; Терт мезгил; Жаз келетат' Которгон С. Жусуев. *Хиросима кектери.* Фрунзе, Кыргызстан, 1969. p.64–71
'Bright house' *The burning heart,* tr. and ed. by Kenneth Rexroth and Ikuko Atsumi. N. Y. Seabury Press, 1977. p.88
'Ispita; Himera; Biciul lui Dante' Tr. Violeta Zamfirescu. *Din lirica japoneză.* Bucureşti, Editura Univers, n.d. p.178–179

FUKAZAWA Shichirō 深沢七郎 1914–

Aki no yagumo uta 安芸の八雲唄

'Az aki-ridék felhöénekei' Ford. Holti Mária. *Zarándokének.* Budapest, Európa, 1965. p.243–248
'Восьмицветные облака' Перевод А. Стерлинг. *Японская новелла 1960–1970.* Москва, Прогресс, 1972. p.412–417

Chōsenfū serenāde 靹鮮風小夜曲

'Koreai szerenád' Ford. Sz. Holti Mária. *Kósui bölcsödal.* Budapest, Európa, 1968. p.131–154

Fuefuki gawa 笛吹川

'Der Fluss Fuefukigawa' Analyse und übers. von Eduard Klopfenstein. *Asiatische Studien,* Band 23, no.3–4, 1969. p.118–138
'A hömpölygö Fuefuki' Fofd. Holti Mária. *Zarándokének.* Budapest, Európa, 1965. p.74–178

Fūryū mutan 風流夢譚

'Nyári almon története' Ford. Holti Mária.

FUKAZAWA Shichirō

Zarándokének. Budapest, Európa, 1965. p.212–227

Kagerō bayashi かげろう囃子

'Árnyjáték' Ford. Sz. Holti Mária. *Modern Japán elbeszélők*. Budapest, Európa, 1967. p.525–537

Kōshū komoriuta 甲州子守唄

'Kósui bölcsödal' Ford. Sz. Holti Mária. *Kósui bölcsödal*. Budapest, Európa, 1968. p.3–130

Nankin kozō 南京小僧

'Zsák fickók' Ford. Holti Mária. *Zarándokének*. Budapest, Európa, 1965. p.41–44
'Nankin kozo' Tr. di Francesco Marrano. *Annali della Facoltà di Lingue e Letterature Straniere di Ca' Foscari*, 16, Serie Orientale 8, 1977.

Narayamabushi kō 楢山節考

'The oak mountain song' Tr. by John Bester. *Japan Quarterly*, v.4, no.2, 1957. p.200–233
'Zarándokének' Ford. Szenczei László. *Nagyvilág*, 1958. p.791–813
Etude à propos des chansons de Narayama. Tr. par Bernard Frank. Paris, Gallimard, 1959. 121p.
'나라야마부시考' 金鐘仁訳 「戦後日本新人受賞作品選」 서울 隆文社 1960. p.45–79
'The songs of oak mountain' Tr. by Donald Keene. *Three modern Japanese short novels*. N. Y. Viking Press, 1961. p.3–50
Le canzoni di Narayama. Tr. di Bianca Garufi. Roma, Einaudi, 1961. 84p.
'나라야마부시考' 桂鎔黙訳 「世界戦後文学全集 7」 서울 新丘文化社 1962. p.155–181
Schwierigkeiten beim Verständnis der Narayama Lieder. Übers. aus dem Französischen von Klaudia Rheinhold. Reinbek, Rowohlt, 1964. 104p.; Berlin, Volk und Welt, 1970. 99p.
'Zarándokének' Ford. Holti Mária. *Zarándokének*. Budapest, Európa, 1965. p.5–40
'楢山節考' 鐘肇政訳 「戦後日本短篇小説選」 台北 台湾商務印書館 1968. p.1–54
Jabal al-Sindian. Tr. from the French by Anwar Cozac. Damascus, Ministère de la Culture, 1973. 87p.
'Zarándokének' Ford. Szenczi László. *A világirodalom legszebb elbeszélései III*. Budapest, Európa, 1973. p.419–446
Valfarten til. Overs. av Halldis Moren Vesaas. Oslo, Norsk Rikskringkasting, 1975. 83p.

Otōmyō no shimai お燈明の姉妹

'Az isteni lampion-beli testvérek' Ford. Holti Mária. *Zarándokének*. Budapest, Európa, 1965. p.228–242

Senshūraku 千秋楽

'Ezerösz játéka' Ford. Sz. Holti Mária. *Kósui bölcsödal*. Budapest, Európa, 1968. p.177–272

Tōhoku no zummu tachi 東北の神武たち

'Gli Zummu del Tohoku' Tr. di Atsuko Ricca Suga. *Narratori giapponesi moderni*. Milano, Bompiani, 1965. p.603–646
'Zummuk észak japánban' Ford. Holti Mária. *Zarándokének*. Budapest, Európa, 1965. p.45–73

Tōkyo no purinsu tachi 東京のプリンスたち

'Tokjó hercegei' Ford. Holti Mária. *Zarándokének*. Budapest, Európa, 1965. p.179–211

Tsuki no Apenin san 月のアペニン山

'Měsiční Apeniny' Přel. M. Jelinková. *Nový Orient*, no.4, 1966. p.82–87

Yakiniku monogatari 焼肉物語

'Avagy a hússütés hétköznapjai' Ford. Shinobu Itomi. *Nagyvilág*, no.3, 1972. p.384–386

Yureru ie 搖れる家

'The house which rocked' Tr. by G. W. Sargent. *Eigo Seinen*, v.104, no.1–7, 1958.
'Ringó ház' Ford. Holti Mária. *Kósui bölcsödal* Budapest, Európa, 1968. p.155–176

'A sominok hős cselekedetei' Ford. Sz. Holti Mária. *Modern Japán elbeszélők*. Budapest, Európa, 1967. p.538–556

FUKIYA Kōji 蔀谷虹児 1898–

Poems 詩

'坦波林之歌' 魯迅訳 「奔流月刊」 第1巻6期 1928; 「魯迅全集 16」 上海 魯迅全集出版社 1938. 作家書屋 1946. 大連 光華書店 1948. 北京 人民文学出版社 1973. p.855–857; 「魯迅譯文集 10」 北京 人民文学出版社 1958. p.741–742
'萌芽; 旅人; 月光波; 金合歓樹之別; 傀儡子的外套; 幻影船; 宵星; 春天; 病在野間的小島' 魯迅訳 「藝苑朝華」 第1巻2期 1929; 「魯迅譯文集 10」 北京 人民文学出版社 1958. p.743–750

FUKUCHI Ōchi 福地桜痴 1841–1906

Tagai no giwaku 互ひの疑惑

'The green eyed monster' Tr. by Kenzo Wadagaki. *Stray leaves*. Tokyo, 1908; *Gleanings from Japanese literature*. Tokyo, Nampokusha, 1919. p.246–294

FUKUDA Eiichi 福田栄一 1909–1975

Tanka 短歌

'1 tanka' Tr. by H.H. Honda. *The Reeds*, v.5, 1959. p.87

FUKUDA Kiyoto 福田清人 1904–

Nichirin heisha 日輪兵舎

'Sun-shaped barracks' Tr. by T. Iwado. *Contemporary Japan*, v.10, no.9, Sept. 1941. p.1188–1199

FUKUDA Masao 福田正夫 1893–1952

Poems 詩

'Песнь о курсе' Перевод Е. Спалвина. *Восточный Студия* (Владивосток), 1925, номер
13. p.274–275
'Stars winging over the earth' Tr. by Hisakazu
Kaneko. *Orient-West*, v.9, no.3, 1964. p.61

FUKUDA Rikutarō 福田陸太郎 1916–

Poems 詩

'European summer' *An anthology of modern
Japanese poetry*, ed. and tr. by Ichiro Kono
and Rikutaro Fukuda. Tokyo, Kenkyusha,
1957. p.13
'Avrupa yazi' Tercüme etmek L. Sami Akalin.
Japon şiiri. İstanbul, Varlik Yayinevi, 1962.
p.297

Criticism 評論

'The aesthetic experience underlying Japanese
literature' *Eigo Seinen*, v.118, no. 10, 1973.
p.558–563
'Ezra Pound and the Orient' Tr. by Burton
Watson. *Eigo Seinen*, v.119, no.1, 1973. p.13–
16

FUKUDA Shōji 福田章二（庄司　薫）1937–

Sōshitsu 喪失

'喪失' 金鐘仁訳 「戦後日本新人受賞作品選」 서울　隆文
社 1960. p.5–41

FUKUDA Sumako 福田須磨子 1922–1974

Poems 詩

'Снег' Перевод Анатолия Мамонова. *Вкус хризантемы.* Москва, Восточная Литература,
1976. p.150

FUKUDA Tsuneari 福田恆存 1912–

Chūgoku no subete 中国のすべて

「日本人看中國」 福田恆存撰　劉水秀訳　台北　中日関係
研究会　1974. 234p.

Kitei taifū キテイ颱風

'El tifon Kitty' Traduccion por Josefina Keiko
Ezaki. *Teatro japonés contemporaneo*. Madrid,
Aguilar, n. d. p.287–373

Nihon no chishiki kaikyū 日本の知識階級

'The intellectual class of Japan' *Journal of Social
and Political Ideas in Japan*, v.2, no.1, 1964.
p.21–23

FUKUDA Tsutomu 福田勗 1905–

Poems 詩

The hanging bridge. Tokyo, Hokuseido, 1971. 1v.
'The big shadow; My watch; Sunlight' Tr. by
James Kirkup. *Listening to Japan.* N. Y.
Praeger, 1973. p.83, 86

FUKUDA Yoshiyuki 福田善之 1931–
FUJITA Asaya ふじた・あさや 1934–

Fuji sanroku 富士山麓

'У горы Фудзи' Перевод Г. Ивановой. *Современные японские пьесы.* Москва, Искусство,
1962. p.77–147

FUKUDA Yūsaku 福田夕咲 1886–1948

Poems 詩

The painter-priest of the "White-cloud hermitage'" Tr. by Shigeshi Nishimura. *The Current
of the World*, v.30, no.10, 1953. p.46

FUKUHARA Kiyoshi 福原清 1901–

Poems 詩

'Sea-gull; You are far away' *An anthology of
modern Japanese poetry*, ed. and tr. by Ichiro
Kono and Rikutaro Fukuda. Tokyo, Kenkyusha, 1957. p.13
'Uzaklardasiniz' Tercüme etmek L. Sami Akalin.
Japon şiiri. İstanbul, Varlik Yayinevi, 1962.
p. 271

FUKUHARA Rintarō 福原麟太郎 1894–

Essay エッセイ

'人生의幸福' 金賢珠訳 「바이바이바다」 서울　三韓出版
社　1966. p.65–70

FUKUI Hisako 福井久子 1929–

Poems 詩

'If the time to die comes to me; Fruit and knife;
A boat; Your words; Two tableaus' Tr. by
Hisako Fukui. *The poetry of postwar Japan.*
Iowa City, Univ. of Iowa Press, 1975. p.154–
158
'Now is the time' *The burning heart*, tr. and ed.
by Kenneth Rexroth and Ikuko Atsumi. N.Y.
Seabury Press, 1977. p.104

FUKUMOTO Kazuya

FUKUMOTO Kazuya 福本和也 1928–

'海棺' 劉慕沙訳 「日本現代小説選」 台北 聯經出版社
1976. p.203–280

FUKUNAGA Takehiko 福永武彦 1918–

Kaishi 海市

「海市蜃楼」 余阿勲訳 台北 中国時報社 1968. 322p.

Kusa no hana 草の花

「花草」 余阿勲訳 台北 晨鐘出版社 1973. 191p.

FUKUNAKA Tomoko 福中都生子 1928–

Poems 詩

'It's not the same' *The burning heart*, tr. and
ed. by Kenneth Rexroth and Ikuko Atsumi.
N. Y. Seabury Press, 1977. p.102–103

FUKUSHI Kōjirō 福士幸次郎 1889–1946

Poems 詩

'A hunter; Who knows?' *An anthology of modern
Japanese poetry*, ed. and tr. by Ichiro Kono
and Rikutaro Fukuda. Tokyo, Kenkyusha,
1957. p.14–15
'Kim kestirebilir' Tercüme etmek L. Sami Akalin.
Japon şiiri. İstanbul, Varlik Yayinevi, 1962.
p.246

FUKUSHIMA Keiko 福島慶子 1900–

Uchi no yadoroku うちの宿六

'我家宿六, 続我家宿六' 徐白訳 「日本短篇譯集 3」 台北
晩蟬書店 1969. p.161–186

FUKUZAWA Yukichi 福沢諭吉 1834–1901

Bunmeiron no gairyaku 文明論之概略

An outline of theory of civilization. Tr. by David
A. Dilworth and G. Cameron Hurst. Tokyo,
Sophia Univ. 1973. 205p.

Fukuō hyakuwa 福翁百話

'L'homme dans la nature' *Anthologie de la littérature japonaise des origines au XXᵉ siècle*, ed. et
tr. par Michel Revon. Paris, Delagrave, 1910.
p.431–434

Fukuō jiden 福翁自伝

The autobiography of Fukuzawa Yukichi. Tr. by
Eiichi Kiyooka. Tokyo, Hokuseido, 1934.
380p.; Rev. ed. 1940; Re-rev. ed. 1948; New
translation, 1960. 401p.

Eine autobiographische Lebensschilderung. Übers.
von Gerhard Linzbichler. Tokyo, Japanisch-
Deutsche Gesellschaft, 1971. 387p.

Gakumon no susume 学問のすすめ

An encouragement of learning. Tr. by David A.
Dilworth and Umeyo Hirano. Tokyo, Sophia
Univ. 1969. 128p.

Kyūhanjō 旧藩情

'The kyuhanjo of Fukuzawa Yukichi' Tr. by Car-
men Blacker. *Monumenta Nipponica*, v.9,
1953. p.304–329

Shin onna daigaku 新女大学

'Ein Wegweiser für moderne Frauen und Mädchen' Übers. von Takahira Tsuji. *Mitteilungen des Seminars für orientalische Sprachen
an der König. Wilhelms-Universität*, Bd.11,
Heft.1, 1908. p.265–270

Speeches 演説

The speeches of Fukuzawa. Tr. by Wayne H.
Oxford. Tokyo, Hokuseido, 1973. 281p.

FUNABASHI Seiichi 舟橋聖一 1904–1976

Aru onna no enkei ある女の遠景

Das Mädchen Tsunako. Übers. von Oscar Benl.
Tübingen, Erdmann, 1964. 367p.; Basel,
Erdmann, 1967. 267p.

Gamō 鵞毛

'Thistle down' Tr. by Edward Seidensticker.
Japan Quarterly, v.8, no.4, 1961. p.431–459
'Distelwolle' Aus dem Japanischen von Maria
von Gemmingen. *Japan, Geistige Begegnung*.
Tübingen, Erdmann, 1964. p.313–353

Kaoshi 顔師

'舞台化粧師' 金龍済訳 「日本代表作家百人集 3」 서울
希望出版社 1966. p.300–316; 「日本短篇文学全集
4」 서울 新太陽社 1969. p.60–76

Kuroi kafun 黒い花粉

「黒色的花粉」 擁白訳 三重市 明志出版社 1963. 208p.

FUNAKATA Hajime 舟方 一 1912–1957

Poems 詩

'이른봄바람' 金龍済訳 「日本詩集」 서울 青雲社 1960.
p.157–158

FUNAKI Hitoshi 船木 仁

Poems 詩

'Fuhkei: a landscape' Tr. by Onsey Nakagawa.
Poetry Nippon, no.33 & 34, 1967. p.5

FUNAKI Shigenobu　舟木重信　1893-1975

Kyūji no tako　給仕のたこ

「僕歐章魚」「標準日本名著選讀」孫文斗編　台北　大新
書局　1969.　p.144-162

FUNAYAMA Kaoru　船山馨　1914-

Hanjūshin　半獣神

'Assassin: a story from Hanjushin' *Contemporary
Japan*, Jan.-Mar. 1948. p.43-60

Ishikari heiya　石狩平野

「激流人生」安東民訳「大経略 1」서울　文海出版社
1975. 356p.

――――――――――

「大経略」安東民訳　서울　文海出版社　1975. 10冊

FURUGAKI Tetsurō　古垣鉄郎　1900-

Poems　詩

'This rain; In peace and happiness; Feuille morte'
The lyric garland, ed. by Makoto Sangu. Tokyo,
Hokuseido, 1957. p.18-20

FURUI Yoshikichi　古井由吉　1937-

Tsumagomi　妻隠

'Wedlock' Tr. by Howard Hibbett. *Japan Quarterly*, v.24, no.3, 1977. p.317-346; *Contemporary Japanese literature*, ed. by Howard Hibbett.
N. Y. Knopf, 1977. p.4-40

Yōko　杳子

「杳子」路人訳「純文學」(香港版)　第10巻2期　1972.
p.173-192

FURUTA Miyuki　古田　幸　1955-

Okaasan no baka　おかあさんのばか

Why, mother, why? Tr. by Harold P. Wright.
Tokyo, Kodansha International, 1965. 63p.;
London, Ward Lock, 1965. 63p.

FURUYA Tsunatake　古谷綱武　1908-

Essay　エッセイ

「人生的春天」竹南　七燈出版社　1976. 204p.

FUTABATEI Shimei　二葉亭四迷　1864-1909

Heibon　平凡

'Studienreise nach Tokyo' Übers. von K. Koike.
Maske, und Studienreise nach Tokyo. Tokyo,
Nankodo, 1918. p.1-141
'Storia di un cagnolino' Tr. di Harukichi Shimoi.
Sakura, no.1, 1920. p.49-51
Mediocrity. Tr. by Glenn Shaw. Tokyo, Hoku-
seido, 1927. 195p.
Mediocrità. Torino, Giulio Einaudi, 1941. 171p.
'Dva z Tókja' Přelozila Vlasta Hilská. *Dva z
Tókja, Jeho podoba*. Praha, Čin, 1943.
Všednost. Přelozila Vlasta Hilská. Praha, SNK-
HLU, 1957. 193p.
「平凡」石堅白　秦柯訳「二叶亭四迷小説集」北京　人民
文学出版社　1962. p.343-462
'Mittelmass' Übers. von Oscar Benl. *Der Kirsch-
blütenzweig*. München, Nymphenburger,
1965. p.218-255

Sono omokage　其面影

An adopted husband. Tr. by Buhachiro Mitsui and
Gregg M. Sinclair. N. Y. Knopf, 1919; Tokyo,
Eigo Kenkyusha, 1926. 275p.; N. Y. Green-
wood Press, 1969. 275p.
'Jeho podoba' Přelozila Vlasta Hilská. *Dva z
Tókja, Jeho podoba*. Praha, Čin, 1943.
「面影」石堅白　秦柯訳「二叶亭四迷小説集」北京　人民
文学出版社　1962. p.163-342

Ukigumo　浮雲

'The drifting clouds' Tr. by Donald Keene.
Modern Japanese literature, ed. by D. Keene.
N. Y. Grove Press, 1956; Tokyo, Tuttle,
1957. p.59-69
「浮云」石堅白　秦柯訳「二叶亭四迷小説集」北京　人民
文学出版社　1962. p.1-162
'Ukigumo' Tr. by Marleigh G. Ryan. *Japan's
first modern novel*. N. Y. Columbia Univ.
Press, 1967. p.197-356
'Il turbine' Tr. di R. Vulpitta. *Antologia della
letteratura coreana e giapponese*. Milano, Fratelli Fabbri, 1969. p.225-230

Yo ga honyaku no hyōjun　余が翻訳の標準

'Мои принципы художественного перевода'
Перевод Р. Карлиной. *Восточный альманах 1*. Москва, Худож. Лит. 1957. p.384-388

FUTAMATA Eigorō　二俣英五郎

Nezumi wa tsukamaru ka　ねずみはつかまるか

How not to catch a mouse. Tokyo, Weatherhill,
1972. 43p.

G

GENJI Keita　源氏鶏太　1912-

Asu wa nichiyōbi　明日は日曜日

「公司裡的羅曼斯」蔡茂豊訳　高雄　則中出版社　1960.
216p.

51

GENJI Keita

「花前月下」蔡茂豊訳　高雄　則中出版社　1961. 216p.
「明天星期日」李朝熙訳　台北　大新書局　1967. 783p.

Botan to hankachi　ボタンとハンカチ

「모란이피기까지」尹淑姫訳　서울　上智社 1967. 339p.

Eigoya san　英語屋さん

'The English interpreter'　Tr. by Hugh Cortazzi. *The guardian god of golf.*　Tokyo, Japan Times, 1972. p.57–94

Gokurō san　御苦労さん

'Taken for a ride'　Tr. by Hugh Cortazzi. *The ogre, and other stories of Japanese salaryman.* Tokyo, Japan Times, 1972.　p.9–28

Hana　鼻

'The nose'　Tr. by Hugh Cortazzi. *The ogre, and other stories of Japanese salaryman.* Tokyo, Japan Times, 1972. p.113–131

Hōpu san　ホープさん

'The hope of the company'　Tr. by Hugh Cortazzi. *The guardian god of golf.* Tokyo, Japan Times. 1972. p.95–124

Jūnen　十年

'Десять лет' Перевод В. Логуновой. *Японская новелла.* Москва, Изд. Иност. Лит. 1961. p.121–132
'Он жыл' Орышадан аударган Нырахмет Телеупов. *Хиросима касирети.* Алма-Ата, Жазушы, 1969. p.125–136

Kekkon no jōken　結婚の条件

「肉体의告白」鄭泰鎮訳　서울　漢陽出版社 1964. 338p.

Kōfuku san　幸福さん

「행복을가르쳐준여인」李鐘烈訳　서울　美林出版社 1969. 255p.

Kohan no hito　湖畔の人

「湖畔人」孫鐵齋訳　高雄　大衆書局　1963. 207p.
'湖畔人' 孫鐵齋訳 「世界文學名著」台北　大衆書局 1966. p.1–207

Mikka mitsuki sannen　三日三月三年

「三日三月三年」李明求訳　서울　徽文出版社 1963. 323p.

Mukyū shokutakushitsu kaisan　無給嘱託室解散

'無給嘱託室解散' 朴松訳 「日本代表作家百人集 4」서울 希望出版社　1966. p.286–296; 「日本短篇文学全集 5」서울　新太陽社　1969. p.126–136

Nijūyonsai no yūutsu　二十四歳の憂鬱

「二十四歳의憂鬱」張宥晟訳　서울　受験社　1963. 343p.
「女子의十字架」張宥晟訳　서울　受験社　1966. 343p.
「二十四歳의우울」李光熙訳　서울　尚志文化社　1974. 344p.

Okashina yume　おかしな夢

'The guardian god of golf'　Tr. by Hugh Cortazzi.

The guardian god of golf. Tokyo, Japan Times, 1972. p.177–204

Oni kachō　鬼課長

'The ogre'　Tr. by Hugh Cortazzi. *The ogre, and other stories of Japanese salaryman.* Tokyo, Japan Times, 1972. p.132–194

Onjōha no oihagi　温情派の追はぎ

'The kind hearted robber'　Tr. by Hugh Cortazzi. *The guardian god of golf.* Tokyo, Japan Times, 1972. p.125–130

Rakkī san　ラッキーさん

'The lucky one'　Tr. by Hugh Cortazzi. *The ogre, and other stories of Japanese salaryman.* Tokyo, Japan Times, 1972. p.29–67

Santō jūyaku　三等重役

「三等重役」李剛祿訳　서울　人文閣　1966. 1冊
'三等重役' 李剛祿訳 「日本文学選集 6」서울　知文閣 1967. p.7–280 ; 서울　韓国読書文化院　1973. p.7–283
「三等重役」金家平訳　서울　有文出版社　1969. 5冊

Shachō banzai　社長万歳

'Three cheers for the company president'　Tr. by Hugh Cortazzi. *The ogre, and other stories of Japanese salaryman.* Tokyo, Japan Times, 1972. p.92–112

Shachō fujin no kagami　社長夫人の鏡

'A model company president's wife'　Tr. by Hugh Cortazzi. *The guardian god of golf.* Tokyo, Japan Times, 1972. p.205–230

Shachō no yūshōki　社長の優勝旗

'The championship banner of the company president'　Tr. by Hugh Cortazzi. *The ogre, and other stories of Japanese salaryman.* Tokyo, Japan Times, 1972. p.68–91

Shichinin no teki ari　七人の敵あり

「행복을가르쳐준여인」李鐘烈訳　서울　美林出版社 1969. 255p.

Shikarare yaku　叱られ役

'The scapegoat'　Tr. by Hugh Cortazzi. *The guardian god of golf.* Tokyo, Japan Times, 1972. p.131–150

Teinen taishoku　停年退職

「停年退職」羅炳廈訳　서울　徽文出版社　1963. 362p.

Tōkyō monogatari　東京物語

「東京夜話」許昭榮訳　台北　水牛出版社　1967. 240p.

Uwaki no tabi　浮気の旅

'A business trip with a girl friend'　Tr. by Hugh Cortazzi. *The guardian god of golf.* Tokyo, Japan Times, 1972. p.9–30

Yūrei ni natta otoko 幽霊になった男

'The man who became a ghost' Tr. by Hugh Cortazzi. *The guardian god of golf.* Tokyo, Japan Times, 1972. p.151–171

Zento ryōen 前途遼遠

'前途遼遠' 徐白訳 「日本短篇譯集 2」 台北 晚蟬書店 1969. p.1–25

Zuikō san 随行さん

'The president's temporary A.D.O.' Tr. by Hugh Cortazzi. *The guardian god of golf.* Tokyo, Japan Times, 1972. p.31–56

「진짜와가짜」 李鐘烈訳 서울 世光出版社 1966. 273p.

GŌHARA Hiroshi 郷原 宏 1942–

Poems 詩

'As far as Cannan' Tr. by Onsey Nakagawa. *Poetry Nippon,* no.28, 1974. p.4

GOMI Yasusuke 五味康祐 1921–

Sōshin 喪神

'喪神' 金京鈺訳 「芥川賞小説集」 서울 新丘文化社 1960. p.123–138 ; 「깊은江」 서울 三耕社 1971. p.123–138

Yagyu bugeichō 柳生武芸帳

「虎俠誌」 臥龍人訳 서울 五倫出版社 1968. 335p.

GOMIKAWA Junpei 五味川純平 1916–

Jiyū tono keiyaku 自由との契約

「自由와의契約」 金栗峰訳 서울 白文社 1956. 1冊 1960. 6冊 ; 서울 文暎閣 1968. 6冊 「自由와의契約」金光州訳 서울 啓明文化社 1960. 3冊 ; 서울 아카데미出版社 1973. 3冊

Kodoku no kake 孤独の賭け

「孤独의賭博」 鄭成煥訳 서울 白文社 1963–64. 2冊

Ningen no jōken 人間の条件

「日本人」 劉遠崎 溫亜蘭訳 基隆 衡光出版社 1959. 204p. 「人間의條件」 蔡謀栗等訳 高雄 公益出版社 1959. 2冊 「人間의条件」 李昌潤 李時哲訳 서울 正向社 1960– 64. 6冊 'Казнь' отрывок из романа. Перевод Б. Поспе- рова. *Японская новелла.* Москва, Изд. Иност. Лит. 1961. p.27–39 「人間의条件」 金鐘和訳 서울 青山文化社 1962. 485p. 「人間의条件」 金相浩訳 서울 합동出版社 1962. 323p. ; 서울 不二出版社 1967. 2冊 *Условия человеческого существования.* Перевод З. Рахима и И. Львовой. Москва. Прогресс, 1964. 799p. 「人間의条件」 李昌潤訳 서울 世宗出版公社 1972. 3冊 「人間的條件」 古梅書摘訳 「世界文學名著鑑賞」 台北 黎明文化事業 1973. p.151–212 「人間의条件」 李日葉訳 서울 開拓社 1974. 2冊 「人間의条件」 韓義史訳 서울 主婦生活社 1974. 3冊

Rekishi no jikken 歴史の実験

「大地에서꿈을지고」 鄭成煥訳 서울 日善閣 1964. 381p. 「大野望」 鄭雲舜訳 서울 文昌社 1971. 2冊

Sensō to ningen 戦争と人間

「戦争과人間」 李賢一訳 서울 아리랑社 1965–67. 8冊 ; 서울 大洋書籍 1970. 5冊 「戦争과人間」 李時哲訳 서울 唯文閣 1965. 「戦争과人間 第一部」 千不乱訳 서울 上智社 1965. 257p. 「戦争과人間」 鄭成煥訳 서울 集賢閣 1976. 2冊

Essay エッセイ

'Rethinking Showa's half-century' Tr. by Wayne Root and Takechi Manabu. *Japan Interpreter,* v.9, no.3, 1975. p.351–353

GOTŌ Chūgai 後藤宙外 1866–1938

Nokoru hikari のこる光

'The remaining light' *Representative tales of Japan,* comp. and tr. by Asataro Miyamori. Tokyo, Sanko Shoten, 1917. p.192–238

GOTŌ Kiichi 後藤紀一 1915–

Shōnen no hashi 少年の橋

'少年之橋' 劉慕沙訳 「芥川賞作品選集 1」 台北 大地出版社 1972. p.3–66

GOTŌ Miyoko 五島美代子 1898–1978

Tanka 短歌

'1 tanka' Tr. by Shigeshi Nishimura. *The Current of the World,* v.36, no.3, 1959. p.28

'2 tanka' *The burning heart,* tr. and ed. by Kenneth Rexroth and Ikuko Atsumi. N. Y. Seabury Press, 1977. p.71

H

HACHIYA Michihiko 蜂谷道彦 1903–

Hiroshima nikki ヒロシマ日記

Hiroshima diary. Tr. and ed. by Warner Wells. Chapel Hill, Univ. of North Carolina Press, 1955. 238p.

Diario de Hirosima. Tr. de inglés por J. C. Torres. Buenos Aires, Emece, 1957. 266p.

「廣島日記」 曉萌 王無為訳 北京 世界知識 1958. 224p.

Hirosimsky dennik. Tr. from the English. Bosanski Petrovac, Kultura, 1960. 280p.

'完全한沈黙과어둠' 「世界에세이文学全集 8」 서울 東西出版社 1974. p.394–404; 「世界随筆文学全集 8」 서울 世進出版社 1976. p.394–404

HAGIWARA Kyōhei　萩原恭平　1898-1969

Poems　詩

'Meditations; Reflections'　Tr. by Shigeshi Nishimura. *The Current of the World*, v.24, no.8, 11, 12, 1947.

HAGIWARA Kyōjirō　萩原恭次郎　1899-1938

Poems　詩

'The family; I will suffer from what my father suffered from'　Tr. by S. Sato and C. Urdang. *Poetry*, May 1956. p.87-88

HAGIWARA Sakutarō　萩原朔太郎　1886-1942

Aoneko　青猫

'Blue cat' Tr. by Hiroaki Sato. *Howling at the moon*. Tokyo, Univ. of Tokyo Press, 1978. p.73-142

Neko machi　猫町

Cat town.　Tr. by George Saito. Tokyo, Jujiya, 1948. 25p.

Shi no genri　詩の原理

「詩底原理」	孫俍工訳	上海　中華書局	1933.	1冊
「詩的原理」	程鼎聲訳	上海　知行書店	1933.	1冊
「詩的原理」	徐佛観訳	台北　正中書局	1956.	132p.
'詩的原理'	王世高訳	「人生」	1965年4-5月	p.82, 84

Tsuki ni hoeru　月に吠える

'Howling at the moon' Tr. by Hiroaki Sato. *Howling at the moon*. Tokyo, Univ. of Tokyo Press, 1978. p.1-71

Poems　詩

'Cimetière hallucinant; Flûte verte; Triste nuit de clair de lune; Grenouilles; Le cadavre d'un chat; Bouddha ou l'énigme du monde; Le chat' Tr. par Kuni Matsuo et Steinilber-Oberlin. *Anthologie des poètes japonais contemporains.* Paris, Mercure de France, 1939. p.125-131

'The deathless octopus; The clock in the country; The sea' Tr. by Junsaku Ozawa. *Eigo Kenkyu*, v.39, no.9, 1950. p.12-15

'Tortoise; Song without a name; Littoral zone; Death of a frog; The white moon; A dish of skylarks' Tr. by S. Sato and C. Urdang. *Poetry*, May 1956. p.102-104

'Night train; Cats; Harmful animals; The corpse of a cat; The new road of Koide' Tr. by Donald Keene. *Modern Japanese literature.* N. Y. Grove Press, 1956; Tokyo, Tuttle, 1957. p.377

'An octopus which did not die; Is thought just a pattern?; At a post-office window; A journey; The sick face in the bowels of the earth' *An anthology of modern Japanese poetry*, ed. and tr. by Ichiro Kono and Rikutaro Fukuda. Tokyo, Kenkyusha, 1957. p.18-20

'Late autumn; Night train; A leisurely indulgence; Woman's tortoise; A sick face below the surface of the earth' *The poetry of living Japan, an anthology*, by Takamichi Ninomiya and D. J. Enright. London, John Murray, 1957. p.47-51

'Tren nocturno; El cadáver de un gato; El nuevo camino de Koide' *Sur*, no.249, Nov.-Dec. 1957. p.91-92

'Cimetière hallucinant; Femme; Automne tardif; La lune blanche; Le cadavre du chat' *La poésie japonaise*, tr. par Karl Petit. Paris, Seghers, 1959. p.203-205

'Der Bambus; Die traurige Mondnacht; Nachtzug' Übertragen von Shin Aizu. *Der schwermütige Ladekran.* St. Gallen, Tschudy Verlag, 1960. p.9-31

'Stilleben; Haustier; Rambus' Übers. von Kuniyo Takayasu und Manfred Hausmann. *Ruf der Regenpfeifer.* München, Bechtle Verlag, 1961. p.82-83

'Geceleyin bir bar; Postahanenin penceresinde' Tercüme etmek L. Sami Akalin. *Japon şiiri.* İstanbul, Varlik Yayinevi, 1962. p.244-245

'Sick face at the base of the earth' Tr. by Geoffrey Bownas and Anthony Thwaite. *The Penguin book of Japanese verse.* Harmondsworth, Penguin Books, 1964. p.186

'The corpse of a cat' *Modern Japanese poetry*, by Donald Keene. Ann Arbor, Center for Japanese Studies, Univ. of Michigan, 1964. p.28

'El pulpo que no murio' Tr. por Kikuya Ionesawa. *Poesia japonesa contemporanea.* Bogotá, Colombia Editoriales de Librería, 1965.

'Still life; The duel' Tr. by Graeme Wilson. *Japan Quarterly*, v.12, no.2, 1965. p.186

'Death of a frog' Tr. by William L. Clark. *Jiji Eigo Kenkyu*, v.21, no.1, 1966. p.69

'Night in spring; Suicide by hanging in heaven' Tr. by Makoto Ueda. *East-West Review*, v.2, no.3, 1966. p.232-233

'Sea shell; Swimmer; Toad' Tr. by Graeme Wilson. *Japan Quarterly*, v.13, no.1, 1966. p.16, 70, 75

'Ai ren; Winter; Eggs; In the bar at night; Person who loves love; These animals are dangerous; Death of a frog; Sad moonlit night; Rotten clam; To dream of a butterfly; The cafe of the drunken moon; Fieldmouse; With a gift; An elegant appetite; Turtle' Tr. by Graeme Wilson. *Japan Quarterly*, v.13, no.4, 1966. p.496-506

'愛憐'　崔一秀訳　「기다리고있네」　서울　韓国政経社 1966. p.214-216

'Face at the bottom of the world; Skyscrape; Night train' Tr. by Graeme Wilson. *Japan P.E.N. News*, no. 20, Sept. 1967. p.7

'Goldfish; Domestic animals; Seedling; Dwarf landscape' Tr. by Graeme Wilson. *Japan Quarterly*, v.14, no.3, 1967. p.296, 310, 317, 332

'Bamboos; White moon; Woman; Person who digs the ground; Divine wisdom; Chair' Tr. by Graeme Wilson. *Japan Quarterly*, v.14, no.4, 1967. p.421, 428, 468, 489, 497, 509

'Polished metal hands; Portrait; New road at Koide' Tr. by Graeme Wilson. *East-West Review*, v.3, no.3, Winter 1967-68. p.281-283

'La vongola malata; Il pensiero e solo una forma; Una faccia malata negli intestini della terra; Un viaggio' *La protesta poetica del Giappone*, a cura di Dacia Maraini e Michiko Nojiri. Roma, Officina Edizioni, 1968. p.27-30

'Three poems' Tr. by Harold P. Wright. *Malahat Review*, no.6, April 1968. p.39-40

'Spring night; Seaside hotel; Blue flame' Tr. by Graeme Wilson. *Japan Quarterly*, v.15, no.1, 1968. p.21, 41, 61

'Being afraid of the country; Seed in the palm; Birds' Tr. by Graeme Wilson. *Japan Quarterly*, v.15, no.2, 1968. p.179, 186, 232
'Dead man in May' Tr. by Graeme Wilson. *Japan Quarterly*, v.15, no.3, 1968. p.329
'Heavenly suicide by hanging; Portrait of a hand; In the mountains; Hunting fireflies' Tr. by Graeme Wilson. *Japan Quarterly*, v. 15, no.4, 1968. p.455, 461, 480, 497
'Ai ren; White night' Tr. by Graeme Wilson. *Encounter*, Nov. 1968. p.27
'Barking at the moon' Tr. by Graeme Wilson. *Encounter*, Dec. 1968. p.32
Tworczosc Hagiwara Sakutaro. Przeł. Mikołaj Melanowicz. Warszawa, Univ. Warszawa, 1968. 382p.
Face at the bottom of the world. Tr. by Graeme Wilson. Tokyo, Tuttle, 1969; London, Prentice-Hall, 1969. 83p.
'Night train; Harmful animals; The new road of Koide' Tr. by Donald Keene. *The mentor book of modern Asian literature*, ed. by D. B. Shimer. N. Y. New American Library, 1969. p.127–128
'The ninth small poem; Field landscape; Will with teeth; Nature study; Crime that I committed' Tr. by Graeme Wilson. *Japan Quarterly*, v.16, no.1, 1969. p.24, 52, 60, 63, 92
'Murder case; Green flute; To dream of a butterfly; Dawn; Seaside hotel; In the mountains' Tr. by Graeme Wilson. *Hudson Review*, v.22, Summer 1969. p.253–259
'Poems' Tr. by Graeme Wilson. *Delos*, no.3, 1969. p.57–59
'Poems' *Literature East and West*, v.13, Dec. 1969. p.423–428
'Minimal spring; White night; Grass stem; Flute' Tr. by Graeme Wilson. *Japan Quarterly*, v.16, no.2, 1969. p.147, 169, 179, 221
'Diseased fish and shellfish; Penitentiary; Terrible mountain; Dinner at the empty house' Tr. by Graeme Wilson. *Japan Quarterly*, v.16, no.3, 1969. p.285, 296, 313, 343
'Insects' Tr. by James H. Sanford. *Japan Quarterly*, v.16, no.3, 1969. p.330–331
'Heart; The soured chrysanthemum: The voluptuous soul; A dream; A farewell' Tr. by Reiko Tsukimura. *Literature East and West*, v.13, no.3 & 4, 1969. p.425–428
'Arm-chair; Pine; Double feature; At a corner of the barley field' Tr. by Graeme Wilson. *Japan Quarterly*, v.16, no.4, 1969. p.396, 405, 422, 453
'Death; Dangerous walk' Tr. by Harold P. Wright. *Poetry Nippon*, no.5 & 6, 1969. p.8,12
'여상; 여정' 「永遠한世界名詩全集 2」 黃錦燦編 서울 翰林出版社 1969. p.193, 260–264 ; 「永遠한世界名詩全集 5」 黃錦燦編 서울 翰林出版社 1973. p.193, 260–264
'Five poems' Tr. by Graeme Wilson. *Malahat Review*, no.14, April 1970. p.81–83
'Four poems by Hagiwara Sakutaro' Tr. by Graeme Wilson. *Poetry*, Aug.-Sept. 1970. p.370–373
'Loneliness; Toy box—evening; Near Mount Futago; Angler' Tr. by Graeme Wilson. *Japan Quarterly*, v. 17, no. 1, 1970. p.17, 26, 36, 91
'Home; Barleys; At market' Tr. by Graeme Wilson. *Japan Quarterly*, v.17, no.2, 1970. p.138, 159, 182
'Toy box—morning; The third patient; Corpse

and bamboo; Moonlit night; Ultramarine; Toothache' Tr. by Graeme Wilson. *Japan Quarterly*, v.17, no.3, 1970. p.260, 271, 275, 284, 307, 327
'Water rite; Autumn cricket; Amakusa; Ghosts; Hirose River; Mountain top' Tr. by Graeme Wilson. *Japan Quarterly*, v.17, no.4, 1970. p.382, 420, 442, 450, 466, 473
'Hand turning ghost' Tr. by Graeme Wilson. *Quadrant*, Nov.-Dec. 1970. p.57–58
'Death of an alcholic' Tr. by Harold P. Wright. *Poetry Nippon*, no.9 & 10, 1970. p.11
'The corpse of a cat' Tr. by Donald Keene. *Landscapes and portraits*. Tokyo, Kodansha International, 1971. p.147
'Miracle; Ancestors; Viewpoint; Death wish; Blue snow' Tr. by Graeme Wilson. *Japan Quarterly*, v.18, no.1, 1971. p.17, 31, 38, 92, 111
'Bottles; To drown in the mountains' Tr. by Graeme Wilson. *Japan Quarterly*, v.18, no.2, 1971. p.167, 213
'Blue sky; Suddenly; Grass nerve; The most primitive feeling; Shining in the sky; Disturbed person; Sea spa in late autumn; Face; A dish of skylarks; Senescence; Shining road of disease' Tr. by Graeme Wilson. *Japan Quarterly*, v.18, no.4, 1971. p.391, 401, 407, 413, 426, 448, 454, 471, 478, 487
'青猫；乃木坂倶楽部；珈琲店酔月；旅上낮선개' 金巢雲訳 「世界의文学大全集 34」 서울 同和出版公社 1971. p.508–510
'The swimmer; Death of a frog; You frogs; Wanting to be walking among crowds; Buddha' *Anthology of modern Japanese poetry*, tr. and comp. by Edith Marcombe Shiffert and Yuki Sawa. Tokyo, Tuttle, 1972. p.48–51
'Under the peach blossoms—from Laotse's illusions' Tr. by Hideo Yamaguchi. *Kobe Jogakuin Daigaku Ronshu*, v.18, no.3, 1972. p.47–49
'Autumn; Cherry blossoms; Sunset; Howling at the moon; Sparrows; Idealism; Small town Geisha; Shining hand' Tr. by Graeme Wilson. *Japan Quarterly*, v.19, no.1, 1972. p.27, 35, 40, 62, 72, 87, 91, 98
'Group of three persons; Village where the flute is playing; Pinefield by the river Tone; Garden of the dreamt empty house; Balloonist's dream; Club Nogisaka; Night; Tiger; Useless book; Homecoming; New Maebashi railway station; Hand turning ghost' Tr. by Graeme Wilson. *Japan Quarterly*, v.19, no.2, 1972. p.170–181
'White cock; Water weed; House; On the bridge at Maebashi; Human body' Tr. by Graeme Wilson. *Japan Quarterly*, v.19, no.3, 1972. p.280, 300, 306, 315, 372
'In the dreadfully gloomy woods; Climbing a mountain' Tr. by Graeme Wilson. *Japan Quarterly*, v.20, no.1, 1973. p.29, 38
'Under green shadow; Mountain pilgrims; When I awoke' Tr. by Graeme Wilson. *Japan Quarterly*, v.20, no.2, 1973. p.142, 175, 182
'Double feature' Tr. by Graeme Wilson. *Solidarity*, v.8, no.2, 1973. p.67
'Cracksman' Tr. by Graeme Wilson. *Japan Quarterly*, v.20, no.3, 1973. p.323
'Small boat; Whose house' Tr. by Graeme Wilson. *Japan Quarterly*, v.20, no.4, 1973. p.381, 396
'Turtle' Tr. by Jim Cogswell. *Poetry Nippon*, no.22, 1973. p.18
'Chrysanthemum gone sour; Frog's death; The reason the person inside looks; The chair;

HAGIWARA Sakutarō

Spring night; The world of bacteria; The swimmer; Daybreak; Sunny spring; Afraid of the countryside' Tr. by Hiroaki Sato. *Ten Japanese poets.* Hanover, N.H. Granite Publications, 1973. p.68–79

'Sickroom; Garden; Descent of man; By the river Tone' Tr. by Graeme Wilson. *Japan Quarterly*, v.21, no.1, 1974. p.18, 27, 35, 57

'Landscape with disgusting objects; That nape's a fish' Tr. by Graeme Wilson. *Japan Quarterly*, v.21, no.2, 1974. p.134, 151

'Blue cat and stone bamboo; Decomposing body; Dog' Tr. by Graeme Wilson. *Japan Quarterly*, v.21, no.3, 1974. p.234, 257, 293

'Withering crime' Tr. by Graeme Wilson. *Japan Quarterly*, v.22, no.1, 1975. p.21

'In dreams' Tr. by Graeme Wilson. *Japan Quarterly*, v.22, no.2, 1975. p.134

'Zołw; Zwiedła chryzantema' Przeł. Mikołaj Melanowicz. *Rocznik Orientalistyczny*, t.33, z.2, 1975. p.18–19

'7 tanka' Tr. by Reiko Tsukimura. *Journal of the Association of Teachers of Japanese*, v.11, no.1, 1976. p.47–63

'Лягушки; Смерть лягушки; Золотая рыбка' Перевод Анатолия Мамонова. *Вкус хризантемы*. Москва, Восточная Литература, 1976. p.151–152

'The stem; Bamboo' Tr. by Stephen Wolfe. *Poetry Nippon*, no.41 & 42, 1978. p.12–13

'Drunken death; Dried up crime' Tr. by Stephen Wolfe. *Poetry Nippon*, no.43 & 44, 1978. p.41–42

'Sykt ansikt i jordens innvoller; Den ättearmede blekksprut; Kystbelte; Nattog' Til norsk ved Paal Brekke. *Moderne japansk lyrikk.* Oslo, Norske Bokklubben, n.d. p.26–29

'Toamnă tîrzie; Broaşte; Stîrvul pisicii; O faţă bolnavă sub fata pămîntului' Traducerea Virgil Teodorescu. *Din lirica japoneză.* Bucureşti, Editura Univers, n.d. p.158–160

Criticism 評論

'主觀與客觀' 孫俍工訳 「現代文學」 第1卷4期 1930.
'詩人與藝術家' 孫俍工訳 「青年界」 第1卷1期 1931.
'描寫與情象' 程鼎聲訳 「青年界」 第1卷5期 1931.
'詩與小説' 孫俍工訳 「現代文學評論」 創刊号 1931.
'近代詩的派別' 孫俍工訳 「青年界」 第2卷1期 1932.
'藝術的若干問題' 王世高訳 「人生」 第5卷11–12期 1953. 第6卷1–2期 1953. 1964年8–10月

HAMADA Hirosuke 浜田広介 1893–1973

Konezumi choro choro こねずみちょろちょろ

The little mouse who didn't come home. London, Hamlyn, 1968. 1v.
The little mouse who tarried. Tr. by Alvin Tresselt. N. Y. Parents' Magazine Press, 1971. 32p.

Ryū no me no namida 竜の目のなみだ

Dragon's tears. Tokyo, Tuttle, 1964. 1v.
The tears of the dragon. Tr. by Alvin Tresselt. N. Y. Parents' Magazine Press, 1967. 32p.

Sarawareta oningyō さらわれたおにんぎょう

Minote, the beautiful doll. London, Hamlyn, 1968. 1v.

'I disoccupati' Tr. di Takuya Okuno. *Cipangu*, 7, 1957. p.22–23

HAMAGUCHI Kunio 浜口国雄 1920–

Poems 詩

'Пейзаж' Перевод В. Н. Марковой. *Японская поэзия.* Москва, Гослитиздат, 1954. p.352–354

HANADA Hiroshi 花田比露思 1882–1967

Tanka 短歌

'Insects; Poems of ancient masters; Cloudy days' Tr. by Asataro Miyamori. *Masterpieces of Japanese poetry, ancient and modern.* Tokyo, Maruzen, 1936; Tokyo, Taiseido, 1956; N. Y. Greenwood Press, 1971. p.698–699

HANATO Kobako 花登 筐 1928–

Doterai yatsu どてらい男

「大成 1, 2」 尹淑寧訳 서울 大河出版社 1974. 2冊

Zeni no hana 銭の花

「여자의길」 文仁子訳 서울 大河出版社 1971. 289p.
「女子의運命」 李文壽訳 서울 無等出版社 1977. 6冊

HANAWA Sakuraku 塙 作楽 1913–

Ihin 遺品

'Все, что осталось' Перевод Г. Ивановой. *Красная лягушка.* Москва, Наука, 1973. p.88–95

HANDA Yoshiyuki 半田義之 1911–1970

Haru no hanazono 春の花園

「春天的花園」 瞿麥訳 台北 兒童讀物 1956. 32p.

'深秋' 刘振瀛訳 「世界文学」 1964年6月 p.22–39, 7月 p.113–136

HANI Setsuko 羽仁説子 1903–

Oshō to kozō 和尚と小僧

Бонза и маленький послушник. Перевод П. Равленчева. Москва, Детгиз, 1956. 32p.
「大和尚和小和尚」 王山訳 北京 少年児童 1957. 24p.
Бонза и маленький послушник, на грузинском

языке. Перевод Г. Чрелошвили. Тбилиси, Детиунизд, 1959. 31р.

Бонза и маленький послушник, на молдавском языке. Кишнев, Изд. Култур Моллав. 1961. 32р.

Бонза и маленький послушник, на тазикском языке. Сталинабад, Тадзик. Госиздат, 1961. 32р.

HANIYA Yutaka 埴谷雄高 1910–

Uchū no kagami 宇宙の鏡

'Cosmic mirror' Tr. by Geoffrey Bownas. *New writing in Japan*. Harmondsworth, Penguin Books, 1972. p.32–40

HARA Asao 原 阿佐緒 1888–1969

Tanka 短歌

'My complaint; My child in sleep' Tr. by Asataro Miyamori. *Masterpieces of Japanese poetry, ancient and modern*. Tokyo, Maruzen, 1936; Tokyo, Taiseido, 1956; N. Y. Greenwood Press, 1971. p.760–761

HARA Gesshū 原 月舟 1889–1920

Haiku 俳句

'A goldfish vendor' Tr. by Asataro Miyamori. *Anthology of haiku, ancient and modern*. Tokyo, Maruzen, 1932; Tokyo, Taiseido, 1957. p.695

'1 haiku' Tr. by Peter Beilenson and Harry Behn. *Haiku harvest*. Mount Verson, Peter Pauper Press, 1962. p.49

HARA Sekitei 原 石鼎 1886–1951

Haiku 俳句

'5 haiku' Tr. by Asataro Miyamori. *Anthology of haiku, ancient and modern*. Tokyo, Maruzen, 1932; Tokyo, Taiseido, 1957. p.796–799

'Kites; Men's voices' Tr. by Asataro Miyamori. *Haiku poems, ancient and modern*. Tokyo, Maruzen, 1940. p.346–347

'Updraught' Tr. by Harold Stewart. *A net of fireflies*. Tokyo, Tuttle, 1960. p.96

'1 haiku' Übers. von Gerolf Coudenhove. *Japanische Jahreszeiten*. Zürich, Manesse Verlag, 1963. p.324

'8 haiku' *A history of haiku v.2*, by R. H. Blyth. Tokyo, Hokuseido, 1964. p.168–171

'5 haiku' Tr. by Geoffrey Bownas and Anthony Thwaite. *Penguin book of Japanese verse*. Harmondsworth, Penguin Books, 1964. p.169

'2 haiku' Til norsk ved Paal-Helge Haugen.

Blad frå ein austleg hage. Oslo, Det Norske Samlaget, 1965. p.86

'3 haiku' Traducere Virgil Teodorescu. *Din lirica japoneză*. Bucureşti, Editura Univers, n. d. p.155–156

HARA Tamiki 原 民喜 1905–1951

Genbaku shōkei 原爆小景

'Из цикла «Атомные пейзажи»' Перевод Анатолия Мамонова. *Три поэта из Хиросимы*. Москва, Наука, 1970. p.22–27

'Из цикла «Атомные пейзажи»' Перевод Анатолия Мамонова, *Вкус хризантемы. Москва*, Восточная Литература, 1976. p.155–157

Ma no hitotoki 魔のひととき

'Из цикла «Дьявольский миг»' Перевод Анатолия Мамонова. *Три поэта из Хиросимы*. Москва, Наука, 1970. p.28–47

Natsu no hana 夏の花

'The summer flower' Tr. by George Saito. *Pacific Spectator*, v.7, no.2, Spring 1953. p.202–210

'Летние цветы' Перевод Л. Часовичиной. *Японская новелла*. Москва, Изд. Иност. Лит. 1961. p.366–379

'Summer flower' Tr. by George Saito. *Literary Review*, v.6, no.1, 1962. p.25–34; *The shadow of sunrise*, selected by Shoichi Saeki. Tokyo, Kodansha International, 1966; London, Ward Lock, 1966. p.119–131

'A nyár virága' Ford. Sz. Holti Mária. *Modern Japán elbeszélők*. Budapest, Európa, 1967. p.290–303; *Pokolraszállás*. Budapest, Európa, 1975. p.205–217

'Хиросима касирети' Орусшадан аударган Ныбрахмет Телеупов. *Хиросима касирети*. Алма-Ата, Жазушы, 1969. p.3–16

'Kwiaty lato' Przeł. Mikołaj Melanowicz. *Cień wschodzącego słońca*. Warszawa, Książka i Wiedza, 1972.

'Sommerblumen' Deutsch von Edith Shimomura. *Träume aus zehn Nächten*. Berlin, Aufbau Verlag, 1975. p.391–410

Shingan no kuni 心願の国

'Testamentum' Ford. Sz. Holti Mária. *Modern Japán elbeszélők*. Budapest, Európa, 1967. p.304–308

Poems 詩

'This is a human being' *An anthology of modern Japanese poetry*, ed. and tr. by Ichiro Kono and Rikutaro Fukuda. Tokyo, Kenkyusha, 1957. p.21

'Telegraphenstange in Hiroshima; Inschrift' Übers. von Kuniyo Takayasu und Manfred Hausmann. *Ruf der Regenpfeifer*. München, Bechtle Verlag, 1961. p.92–93

'Bu insanoğlu bu' Tercüme etmek L. Sami Akalin. *Japon şiiri*. İstanbul, Varlik Yayinevi, 1962. p.283

'이것이 人間인것입니다 ; 碑銘' 辛東門訳 「世界戦後文学全集 9」 서울 新丘文化社 1962. p.233

'In the fire, a telegraph pole; Glittering fragments' Tr. by Geoffrey Bownas and Anthony Thwaite.

HARA Tamiki

The Penguin book of Japanese verse. Harmondsworth, Penguin Books, 1964. p.221

'Дайте воды!' Перевод Анатолия Мамонова. *Песни Хиросимы.* Москва, Худож. Лит. 1964. p.9–10

'Esto es un ser humano' Tr. por Kikuya Ionesawa. *Poesia japonesa contemporanea.* Bogotá, Colombia Editoriales de Librería, 1965.

'Из цикла «В тот час»; Из цикла «Маленький сад»' Перевод Анатолия Мамонова. *Три поэта из Хиросимы.* Москва, Наука, 1970. p.16–22

'Eternal green; A moment bewitched' Tr. by Miyao Ohara. *The songs of Hiroshima.* Tokyo, Taihei Shuppansha, 1971. p.32–35

'Вечер; Тропинка; Засохшее поле; Заря; Молодой месяц; В тот час' Перевод Анатолия Мамонова. *Вкус хризантемы.* Москва, Восточная Литература, 1976. p.153–154

'Из цикла «Маленький сад»' Перевод Анатолия Мамонова. *Вкус хризантемы.* Москва, Восточная Литература, 1976. p.154–155

'Brokker lystes opp; En telegrafstolpe; Dette er et menneske' Til norsk ved Paal Brekke. *Moderne japansk lyrikk.* Oslo, Norske Bokklubben, n. d. p.62–64

'Bucăţi scînteietoare, et al' Traducerea Virgil Teodorescu. *Din lirica japoneză.* Bucureşti, Editura Univers, n.d. p.206

HARADA Setsuko 原田節子

Poems 詩

'The square rain is tapping' Tr. by Miyao Ohara. *The songs of Hiroshima.* Tokyo, Hokuseido, 1957. p.21

HARADA Yasuko 原田康子 1928–

Banka 挽歌

Elegy. Boston, Beacon Press, 1957. 1v.
「挽歌」 李顯子訳 서울 科学社 1960. 1冊
「挽歌」 林玉仁訳 서울 新太陽社 1960. 276p.
Chant d'automne. Tr. par Fumiko Issomura et Henriette Valot. Paris, Albin Michel, 1964. 292p.
'挽歌' 金芝郷訳 「日本文学大全集 7」 서울 東西文化社 1975. p.184–386

Bōkyō 望郷

「望郷」 朱佩蘭訳 台北 小説創作社 1967. 334p.

Haien 廃園

'廢園' 李蓉姫訳 「日本文学選集 5」 서울 知文閣 1966. p.109–189
'戀園' 金芝郷訳 「日本文学大全集 7」 서울 東西文化院 1975. p.388–448

Hi no tori 火の鳥

「火鳥」 李範洌訳 서울 創文社 1967. 336p.

Rinshō 輪唱

「輪唱」 林玉仁訳 서울 新太陽社 1960. 357p.
'輪唱' 鄭清茂訳 台北 学生書局 1961. 225p.

HARAJŌ Akiko 原条あきこ 1923–

Poems 詩

'그이를기다리며 ; 追憶의그날 ; 사랑하는그이 ; 서글픈戀人' 崔一秀訳 「기다리고있네」 서울 韓国政経社 1966. p.17–19, 55–57, 119–121, 126–128

HARUKAWA Tetsuo 春川鉄男

Rōdōsha 労働者

「日本労働者」 梅韜訳 北京 作家出版社 1955. 136p.

HARUYAMA Yukio 春山行夫 1902–

Poems 詩

'Cauliflowers' *An anthology of modern Japanese poetry,* ed. and tr. by Ichiro Kono and Rikutaro Fukuda. Tokyo, Kenkyusha, 1957. p.21
'廣場 ; 花等' 徐和隣訳 「現代詩解説」 台北 葡萄園詩刊社 1970. p.40–43

Criticism 評論

'近代象徴詩的源流' 陳勻水訳 「樂羣月刊」 第1巻4期 1929.

HASEGAWA Izumi 長谷川 泉 1918–

Criticism 評論

'Mori Ogai' *Japan Quarterly,* v.12, no.2, 1965. p.237–244

HASEGAWA Kanajo 長谷川かな女 1887–1969

Haiku 俳句

'One haiku' Tr. by Asataro Miyamori. *Anthology of haiku, ancient and modern.* Tokyo, Maruzen, 1932; Tokyo, Taiseido, 1957. p.816

HASEGAWA Nyozekan 長谷川如是閑 1875–1969

Jokyū 女給

'La fille du café' Tr. par Serge Elisséev. *Le jardin des pivoines.* Paris, Au Sans Pareil, 1927. p.65–99
'A kaveház leanya' Ford. Thein Alfréd. *Mai Japán dekameron.* Budapest, Nyugat, 1935. p.41–63

Nihonteki seikaku 日本的性格

The Japanese character. Tr. by John Bester. Tokyo, Kodansha International, 1965. 157p.

Ushinawareta Nihon 失はれた日本

'The lost Japan the new Japan' *Sources of the Japanese tradition,* comp. by Ryusaku Tsunoda and others. N. Y. Columbia Univ. Press, 1958. p.891–900

Utsukushii baka 美しい馬鹿

'Beautiful stupidity' Tr. by Takeshi Tezuka. *Eigo Kenkyu*, v.24, no.11, 1932. p.1027–1029

Zōya no Kume san 象やの粂さん

'Le cornac' Tr. par Serge Elisséev. *Japon et Extrême-Orient*, no.7–8, 1924. p.13–55; *Neuf nouvelles japonaises*. Paris, G. van Œst, 1924. p.103–145

Criticism 評論

'埜野猪' 魯迅訳 「旭光旬刊」 第4期 1925；「魯迅譯文集 10」 北京 人民文学出版社 1958. p.481–483
'歳首' 魯迅訳 「國民新報副刊」 1926年1月；「魯迅譯文集 10」 北京 人民文学出版社 1958. p.484–486
'羅素的社會思想與中國' 劉叔琴訳 「東方雜誌」 第23巻13期 1926. p.61–72
'Japan's "Cultural democracy"' Tr. by William Candlewood. *Atlantic*, v.195, Jan. 1955. p.170–173

HASEGAWA Reiyoshi 長谷川零余子 1886–1928

Haiku 俳句

'1 haiku' *A history of haiku v.2*, by R. H. Blytk. Tokyo, Hokuseido, 1964. p.168

HASEGAWA Ryūsei 長谷川龍生 1928–

Poems 詩

'Revolution' Tr. by Makoto Ueda. *Literary Review*, v.6, no.1, 1962. p.111
'La gelosia' *La protesta poetica del Giappone*, a cura di Dacia Maraini e Michiko Nojiri. Roma, Officina Edizioni, 1968. p.115–117
'At the barber' Tr. by Thomas Fitzsimmons. *Japanese poetry now*. London, André Deutsch, 1972. p.84; *Japanese poetry today*. N. Y. Schocken Books, 1972. p.86
'New-style terrorist; An owl looks down; At the barber's' Tr. by Harry and Lynn Guest, and Shozo Kajima. *Post-war Japanese poetry*. Harmondsworth, Penguin Books, 1972. p.119–123
'A tale of the squid falling night' *Chicago Review*, v.25, no.2, 1973. p.97–98
'The pursuer; Pavlov's cranes; Summer mushroom; My burial song; Hand of death' Tr. by Hajime Kijima, Hiroaki Sato and Takako Ayusawa. *The poetry of postwar Japan*. Iowa City, Univ. of Iowa Press, 1975. p.145–153

HASEGAWA Shirō 長谷川四郎 1909–

Aku Tadashi no hanashi 阿久正の話

'Vyprávění o Dobroději Spatném' Přel. V. Winkelhöferová. *Světová Literatura*, no.4, 1962. p.115–128

Chō Tokugi 張徳義

'Чжан Дэ-и' Перевод Т. Виноградовой. *Японская новелла*. Москва, Изд. Иност. Лит. 1961. p.380–394
'Чжан Дэ-И' Аударган Х. Сыздуков. *Жапон енгимелери*. Алма-Ата, Жазушы, 1965. p.112–127

Takarabune 宝船

'Такарабунэ' Перевод Д Бугаевой. *Красная лягушка*. Москва, Наука, 1973. p.21–35

Tsuru 鶴

'A crane' Tr. by Tsuneo Masaki. *The Reeds*, v.11, 1967. p. 93–126
'A daru' Ford. Sz. Holti Mária. *Modern Japán elbeszélők*. Budapest, Európa, 1967. p.436–458
'Jeřáb' Přel. Vlasta Winkelhöferóva. *Světová literatura*, v.19, no.2, 1974. p.134–145

Poems 詩

'Traveller's song; Watchman's song' Tr. by Thomas Fitzsimmons. *Japanese poetry now*. London, André Deutsch, 1972. p.101–102; *Japanese poetry today*. N. Y. Schocken Books, 1972. p.103–104
'Ballad of soldiers; Traveller's song; Watchman's song; Song of a cat; Song of a ribbon; Song of a patient' Tr. by Hajime Kijima, Thomas Fitzsimmons and David Goodman. *The poetry of postwar Japan*. Iowa City, Univ. of Iowa Press, 1975. p.12–18
'Песня странника' Перевод Анатолия Мамонова. *Вкус хризантемы*. Москва, Восточная Литература, 1976. p.158

HASEGAWA Sosei 長谷川素逝 1907–1946

Haiku 俳句

'3 haiku' *A history of haiku v.2*, by R. H. Blyth. Tokyo, Hokuseido, 1964. p.251

HASHIDA Tōsei 橋田東声 1886–1930

Tanka 短歌

'Spring' Tr. by Asataro Miyamori. *Masterpieces of Japanese poetry, ancient and modern*. Tokyo, Maruzen, 1936; Tokyo, Taiseido, 1956; N. Y. Greenwood Press, 1971. p.744
'1 tanka' Übers. von Gerolf Coudenhove. *Japanische Jahreszeiten*. Zürich, Manesse Verlag, 1963. p.121

HASHIMOTO Eikichi 橋本英吉 1898–

Hottan 発端

'發端' 陳勹水訳 「日本新寫實派代表傑作集」 上海 樂羣雜誌社 1929.

Criticism 評論

'高爾基評傳' 森堡訳 「徴音月刊」 第2巻5期 1932.

HASHIMOTO Shinobu

HASHIMOTO Shinobu 橋本 忍 1918–

Mahiru no ankoku 真昼の暗黒

「暗無天日」 李正倫訳 北京 中國戏剧 1957. 106p.

HASHIMOTO Takako 橋本多佳子 1899–1963

Haiku 俳句

'2 haiku' *A history of haiku v.2*, by R. H. Blyth. Tokyo, Hokuseido, 1964. p.237–238
'2 haiku' *Anthology of modern Japanese poetry*, tr. and comp. by Edith Marcombe Shiffert and Yuki Sawa. Tokyo, Tuttle, 1972. p.169
'1 haiku' *The burning heart*, tr. and ed. by Kenneth Rexroth and Ikuko Atsumi. N. Y. Seabury Press, 1977. p.81

HASHIZUME Ken 橋爪 健 1900–1964

Kōbe hyōhakusha 神戸飄泊者

'神戸飄泊者' 徐雲濤訳 「當代日本小説選」 台南 經緯書局 1954. p.183–204;「當代日本創作小説」 台南 經緯書局 1961. p.183–204;「當代日本短篇小説選」 台南 大行出版社 1973. p.183–204

HATANO Isoko 波多野勤子 1905–1978

Shōnenki 少年期

L'enfant d'Hiroshima. Tr. par S. Motono. Paris, Editions du Temps, 1959. 194p.
Mother and son. Tr. from the French by Margaret Shenfield. Boston, Houghton Mifflin, 1962. 195p.
Dziecko Hiroszimy. Přzel. franc. Elzbieta Wassongowa. Warszawa, Min. Obrony Narod, 1962. 225p.
El hijo de Hirosima. Tr. por Alfredo Crespo. Barcelona, Plaza y Janés, 1964. 287p.
「어머니나를이해해주세요」 鄭基淑訳 서울 三一閣 1973. 217p.; 서울 三英社 1975. 217p.

HATSUI Shizue 初井しづ枝 1900–

Tanka 短歌

'2 tanka' *The burning heart*, tr. by Kenneth Rexroth and Ikuko Atsumi. N. Y. Seabury Press, 1977. p.72

HATTA Tomonori 八田知紀 1799–1873

Tanka 短歌

'The cherry-blossoms on Mount Yoshino; The swallow; The cherry-flowers on Mount Arashi; Cherry-flowers' Tr. by Asataro Miyamori. *Masterpieces of Japanese poetry, ancient and modern.* Tokyo, Maruzen, 1936; Tokyo, Taiseido, 1956; N. Y. Greenwood Press, 1971. p.590–594
'1 tanka' Übers. von Gerolf Coudenhove. *Japa-*

nische Jahreszeiten. Zürich, Manesse Verlag, 1963. p.113

HATTORI Bushō 服部撫松 1841–1908

Tōkyō shin hanjōki 東京新繁昌記

'The western peep show' Tr. by Donald Keene. *Modern Japanese literature.* N. Y. Grove Press, 1956; Tokyo, Tuttle, 1957. p.34–36

HATTORI Kakō 服部嘉香 1886–1975

Poems 詩

'Mr. Edmund Blunden; The Tenryu gorge; Disappointed and lost' Tr. by Makoto Sangu. *The lyric garland.* Tokyo, Hokuseido, 1957. p.21

HATTORI Motoharu 服部躬治 1875–1925

Tanka 短歌

'2 tanka' Tr. by V. H. Viglielmo. *Japanese literature in the Meiji era.* Tokyo, Obunsha, 1955. p.378

HATTORI Sōgai 服部蒼外

Ōgonbutsu 黄金仏

'The golden Buddha' Tr. by Iwao Matsubara. *Tokyo Nichinichi,* March 17–21, 1925; *Eigo Kenkyu,* v.24, no.7–9, 1931, v.24, no.10–11, 1932.

HAYAKAWA Sesshū 早川雪州 1889–1973

Musha shugyō sekai o yuku 武者修行世界をゆく

Der Sohn des Samurai. Übers. von Alastair. Stuttgart, Goverts, 1963. 208p.; Berlin, Deutsche Buchgemeinschaft, 1965. 168p.

HAYAMA Yoshiki 葉山嘉樹 1894–1945

Fune no inu Kain 船の犬「カイン」

'船狗迦菌' 陳勺水訳 「日本新寫實派代表傑作集」 上海 樂羣雜誌社 1929.

Inbaifu 淫売婦

'Проститутка' Перевод Елены Терновской. *Ад.* Москва, Московский Рабочий, 1929. p.116–135
'賣淫婦' 張我軍訳 「日本小説集」 上海 北新書局 1930.
'Az utcalány' Ford. Sz. Holti Mária. *Modern Japán elbeszélők.* Budapest, Európa, 1967. p.107–118

Indo no kutsu 印度の靴

'印度的鞋子' 沈端先訳 「初春的風」 上海 大江書店 193?.

Kosakunin no inu to jinushi no inu 小作人の犬と地主の犬

'佃戸的狗和地主的狗' 陳勺水訳 「日本新寫實派代表傑作集」上海 樂羣雜誌社 1929.

Rōdōsha no inai fune 労働者のいない船

'Карабль без матросов' Перевод Елены Е. Терновской. *Ад.* Москва, Московский Рабочий, 1929. p.136–151

'没有勞働者的船' 馮憲章訳 「拓荒者」 第1巻1期 1930. p.211–230

'Судно без матросов' *Японская пролетарская литература.* Москва, 1936. p.11–13

Sakura no saku koro 桜の咲く頃

'櫻花時節' 張我軍訳 「北新半月刊」 第3巻16号 1929. p.79–108

Semento daru no naka no tegami セメント樽の中の手紙

'Письмо из цементной бочки' Перевод Е. Терновской. *Японо-Советское искусство*, 2, 1927; *Красная Нива*, номер 20, 1927. p.6; *Ад.* Москва, Московский Рабочий, 1929. p.111–115

'Кровавый цемент' Перевод Л. Руставелли. *На досуге*, номер 3, 1928. p.3

'洋灰桶裏的一封信' 張我軍訳 「語絲」 第5巻28期 1929. p.72–83

'土敏土罐裏的一封信' 張資平訳 「資平譯品集」 上海 現代書局 192?.

'A letter in a cement bag' Tr. by Takashi Kojima. *Ei-Bei Bungaku* (Meiji Univ.), no.1, 1955. p.8–11

'Dopis ze sudu na cement' Přel. J. V. Neustupný. *Nový Orient*, v.16, no.7, 1961. p.166–171

'Surat di-dalam tong sěmen' Děngan kata pěngantar oleh James Kirkup. *Shoji.* Kuala Lumpur, Oxford Univ. Press, 1961. p.17–22

'Letter found in a cement-barrel' Tr. by Ivan Morris. *Modern Japanese stories.* London, Spottiswoode, 1961; Tokyo, Tuttle, 1962. p.205–210

'Der Brief im Zementfass' Deutsch von Monique Humbert. *Nippon.* Zürich, Diogenes, 1965. p.239–244

'Letero el cementbarelo' Tr. Kei Kurisu. *El japana literaturo.* Tokyo, Japana Esperanto Instituto, 1965. p.43–46

'Der Brief im Zementfass' Deutsch von Jürgen Berndt. *Träume aus zehn Nächten.* Berlin, Aufbau Verlag, 1975. p.206–209

Sumubeki tokoro o motomete 住むべき所を求めて

'В пойсках пристанища' *Красная Панорама*, 32, 1928. p.4–5

Essay エッセイ

'Автобиография' Перевод Елены Терновской. *Ад.* Москва, Московский Рабочий, 1928. p.109–110

「葉山嘉樹選集」 馮憲章訳 上海 現代書局 1930. 1冊

HAYASHI Fumiko 林 芙美子 1903–1951

Aru onna no hansei 或る女の半生

「어느女人의半生」 玄一民訳 서울 百忍社 1962. 268p.

Bangiku 晩菊

'Late chrysanthemum' Tr. by John Bester. *Japan Quarterly*, v.3, no.4, 1956. p.468–486; *Modern Japanese short stories.* Tokyo, Japan Publications Trading Co. 1960. p.236–262; Rev. ed. 1970. p.188–208

'Поздние хризантемы' Перевод И. Львовой. *Восточный альманах*, выпуск 2. Москва, Худож. Лит. 1958. p.371–387

'Поздная хризантема' Перевод Д. Андреева. *Хаяси Фумико.* Москва, Изд. Иност. Лит. 1960. p.73–92

'晩菊' 表文台訳 「日本代表作家百人集 2」 서울 希望出版社 1966. p.404–417; 「日本短篇文学全集 3」 서울 新太陽社 1969. p.90–103

'Späte Chrysanthemen' Deutsch von Jürgen Berndt. *Träume aus zehn Nächten.* Berlin, Aufbau Verlag, 1975. p.411–435

'晩菊' 劉賢鐘訳 「日本文学大全集 10」 서울 東西文化院 1975. p.45–60

Boruneo daiya ボルネオ・ダイヤ

'Алмазы Борнео' Перевод З. Рахима и А. Хмельницкого. *Хаяси Фумико.* Москва, Изд. Иност. Лит. 1960. p.40–57

Bungakuteki jijoden 文学的自叙伝

'林芙美子自傳' 斐琴訳 「人間生」 第2期 1936年4月 p.23–28

Daun taun 下町

'Tokyo' Tr. by Ivan Morris. *Modern Japanese literature*, ed. by D. Keene. N. Y. Grove Press, 1956; Tokyo, Tuttle, 1957. p.415–428

'En los bajos de Tokio' Tr. por Miguel Alfredo Olivera. *Sur*, no.249, Nov.-Dec. 1957. p.79–90

'Tokio' Przeł. Anna Gostyńska. *Irys, opowiadania japońskie.* Warszawa, Pánstwowy Instytut Wydawniczy, 1960. p.179–199

'Čtvrt chudiny' Přel. Z. Vasiljevová. *Deset novel z Asie a Afriky.* Praha, Spisovatel, 1961.

'Tokyo' Děngan kata pěngantar oleh James Kirkup. *Shoji.* Kuala Lumpur, Oxford Univ. Press, 1961. p.93–113

'Downtown' Tr. by Ivan Morris. *Modern Japanese stories*, ed. by I. Morris. London, Spottiswoode, 1961; Tokyo, Tuttle, 1962. p.350–364

'На окраине' Перевод П. Петрова. *Японская новелла.* Москва, Изд. Иност. Лит. 1961. p.395–408

'La periferia' Tr. di Atsuko Ricca Suga. *Narratori giapponesi moderni.* Milano, Bompiani, 1965. p.417–434

'Tokio' Deutsch von Monique Humbert. *Nippon.* Zürich, Diogenes, 1965. p.387–404

'Кара шетинде' Аударган К. Орманбаева. *Жапон енгимелери.* Алма-Ата, Жазушы, 1965. p.128–141

Gunka 軍歌

'Марш' Перевод Д. Андреева и З. Рахима. *Халси Фумико.* Москва, Изд. Иност. Лит. 1960. p.58–72

Gyūniku 牛肉

'Макиэ' Перевод Я. Берлина и З. Рахима. *Хаяси Фумико.* Москва, Изд. Иност. Лит. 1960. p.107–134

HAYASHI Fumiko

Hone 骨

'Bones' Tr. by Ted T. Takaya. *The shadow of sunrise*, comp. by Shoichi Saeki. Tokyo, Kodansha International, 1966; London, Ward Lock, 1966. p.133–154

'Kości' Przeł. Mikołaj Melanowicz. *Cień wschodzącego słońca*. Warszawa, Książka i Wiedza, 1972.

Hōrōki 放浪記

「放浪記」 崔萬秋訳 上海 啓明書局 1937. 72p; 上海 大江書店 1937. 1冊

'Journal of a vagabond' Tr. by S. G. Brickley. *The writing of idiomatic English*. Tokyo, Kenkyusha, 1951. p.19–23

「放浪記」 啓明書局編集部訳 台北 啓明書局 1956. 70p.

'Putino kaj mangajo' Tr. Masao Hukuta. *El japana literaturo*. Tokyo, Japana Esperanto Instituto, 1965. p.47–55

「放浪記」 李蓉姫訳 「日本文学選集 3」 서울 知文閣 1966. p.383–477; 서울 韓国読書文化院 1973. p.383–477

Kareha 枯葉

「枯葉」 張建華訳 上海 文化生活出版社 1973. 1冊

Kawa 川

'Im Strom' Übers. von Kurt Meissner. *Der Tanzfächer*, von K. Meissner. Tokyo, 1943. p.145–161

Nomugi no uta 野麦の唄

'У протины' Перевод В. Смирнова. *Хаяси Фумико*. Москва, Изд. Иност. Лит. 1960. p.93–106

Nureta ashi 濡れた葦

'젖은갈대' 朴在森訳 「世界短篇文学全集 7」 서울 啓蒙社 1966. p.353–366; 「世界短篇文学全集 9」 서울 三珍社 1971. p.227–240; 「世界代表短篇文学全集 9」 서울 三熙社 1976. p.227–240; 「世界短篇文学全集 10」 서울 新韓出版社 1976. p.14–36

Seihin no sho 清貧の書

'清貧의書' 方基煥訳 「20世紀女流文学選集 3」 서울 新太陽社 1967. p.133–157

Ukigumo 浮雲

'Floating cloud' Tr. by Yasushi Wuriu. *Info*, v.2, no. 4–12, 1956.

Floating cloud. Tr. by Yoshiyuki Koitabashi. Tokyo, Information Pub. 1957. 110p.

「浮雲」 石桂香訳 서울 圓覚光 1960. 348p.

The floating clouds. Tr. by Yoshiyuki Koitabashi and Martin C. Collcott. Tokyo, Hara Shobo, 1965. 217p.

Uruwashiki sekizui 麗わしき脊髄

'Splendid carrion' Tr. by Sakae Shioya. *Western Humanities Review*, Summer 1952; *Eigo Seinen*, v.99, no.9, 1953. p.420–422, v.99, no.12, 1953. p.575–578

Yaen 夜猿

'Ночные обезьяны' Перевод Д. Андреева и З. Рахима. *Хаяси Фумико*. Москва, Изд. Иност. Лит. 1960. p.11–39

Yoru 夜

'Noc' Przeł. Mikołaj Melanowicz. *Widnokręgi*, no.2, 1972. p.95–99

Poems 詩

'Song in despair' *An anthology of modern Japanese poetry*, ed. and tr. by Ichiro Kono and Rikutaro Fukuda. Tokyo, Kenkyusha, 1957. p.23

'Homecoming' Tr. by Hisakazu Kaneko. *Orient West*, v.8, no.1, May-June 1963. p.48; *The Japanese image*, ed. by M. Schneps and A. D. Coox. Tokyo, Orient West, 1965. p.349; *London Magazine*, v.7, no.7, Oct. 1967. p.34

'The Lord Budda' *The burning heart*, tr. and ed. by Kenneth Rexroth and Ikuko Atsumi. N. Y. Seabury Press, 1977. p.89

'達凱愛爾路' 黄源訳 「文學季刊」 第2巻1期 1935. p.253–257

'雨天挿話' 紀生訳 「中國公論」 第1巻1期 1939. p.154–160

'達凱愛爾路' 「日本作家十二人集」 香港 新學書店 1959. p.159–168

HAYASHI Fusao 林 房雄 1903–1975

E no nai ehon 絵のない絵本

'Книга картин без каритнок' Перевод А. Лейферт. *Книга картин без картинок*. Москва, Госиздат, 1928. p.3–35

'Книжка с картинками, в которой нет картинок' Перевод Елены Терновской. *Ад*. Москва, Московский Рабочий, 1929. p.58–87; *Японская пролетарская литература*. Москва, 1936. p.8–13

Bildlibro sen bildoj. Tr. Hirokazu Kaĵi. Tokyo, Esperanto Kenkyusha, 1933. 35p.

'没有畫的畫本' 「日本短篇小説選」 香港 藝美圖書公司 1959. p.53–73

Enu kangoku chōbatsu nisshi N監獄懲罰日誌

'Дневник надзирателя Нагасакской тюрьмы' Перевод А. Лейферт. *Книга картин без картинок*. Москва, Госиздат, 1928. p.146–162

Kōen no aibiki 公園の媾曳

'Такой свидание в парке' Перевод А. Лейферт. *Книга картин без картинок*. Москва, Госиздат, 1928. p.132–145

'Парк свидании' Перевод Елены Терновской. *Ад*. Москва, Московский Рабочий, 1929. p.97–108

Kotenteki na tegami 古典的な手紙

'一束古典的情書' 林伯脩訳 「一束古典的情書」 上海 現代書局 1933

Kuroda Kurō shi no aikokushin 黒田九郎氏の愛国心

'黒田九郎氏的愛國心' 吶吶鷗訳 「色情文化」 上海 水沫書店 1928

Mayone Yonekichi shi no dōzō　間米米吉氏の銅像

'間米米吉氏底銅像'　趙冷訳　「小説月報」　第21巻7号　1930. p.1067–1074

Mayu　繭

'Кокон'　Перевод А. Лейферт. *Книга картин без картинок.* Москва, Госиздат, 1928. p.115–131

'繭'　郁達夫訳　「奇零集」　上海　開明書局　1928.

'Коконы'　*Интернациональные Молодежи,* 1932, номер 5. p.15–17; *Литература Мировой Революции,* 1932, номер 3. p.42–45; *Сборник японской революционной литературы.* Москва, Гослитиздат, 1933. p.139–145

'Cocoons'　*The cannery boat, and other Japanese short stories.* N. Y. International Publishers, 1933; London, Martin Lawrence, 1933; N. Y. Greenwood Press, 1968. p.253–266

'繭'　林伯脩訳　「一束古典的情書」　上海　現代書局 1933.

'Кокон'　Перевод Н. Фельдман. *Японская революционная литератра.* Москва, Худож. Лит. 1934. p.197–205; *Японская пролетарская литература.* Москва, 1966. p.197–204

Ringo　林檎

'Яблоко'　Перевод А. Лейферт. *Книга картин без картинок.* Москва, Госиздат, 1928. p.102–114

'Яблоко'　Перевод Елены Терновской. *Ад.* Москва, Московский Рабочий, 1929. p.88–96

Rōgoku no gogatsusai　牢獄の五月祭

'牢獄的五月祭'　林伯脩訳　「一束古典的情書」　上海　現代書局　1933.

Shin Isoppu monogatari　新いそっぷ物語

'Новые рассказы Эзопа'　Перевод А. Лейферт. *Книга картин без картинок.* Москва, Госиздат, 1928. p.64–101

Seinen　青年

「青年」　張庸吾訳　上海　太平書局　1943. 1冊

Shuhai　酒盃

'Бокар'　Перевод А. Лейферт. *Книга картин без картинок.* Москва, Госиздат, 1928. p.178–198

Tessō no hana　鉄窓の花

'鐵窗之花'　高汝鴻訳　「日本短篇小説集」　台北　台湾商務印書館　1969. p.183–206

Tokai sōkyokusen　都会双曲線

「都會雙曲線」　石兄訳　上海　神州書局　1932. 1冊

'Na křižovatkách velkoměšta'　Přel. A. Pultr. *Nový Orient,* v.5, 1950. v.6, 1951.

Umi no arubamu　海のアルバム

'바다의앨범'　表文台訳　「日本代表作家百人集 3」　서울　希望出版社　1966. p.250–259; 「日本短篇文学全集 4」　서울　新太陽社　1969. p.10–19

Yuriko no kōun　百合子の幸運

'百合子的幸運'　適夷訳　「小説月報」　第21巻4号　1930. p.727–731

'愛的開脱'　林伯脩訳　「一束古典的情書」　上海　現代書局　1933.

'密會'　林伯脩訳　「一束古典的情書」　上海　現代書局　1933.

「林房雄集」　林伯脩訳　上海　現代書局　1933. 1冊

「林房雄集」　適夷訳　上海　開明書店　1933. 1冊

'愛的觧脱'　「日本短篇小説選」　台北　新書書局　1958. p.31–35; 台南　鳴宇出版社　1972. p.31–35

'丈夫的獨白'　傅寶齢訳　「勲章」　台北　文壇社　1960. p.12–24

'꽃피는金'　鄭乙炳訳　「日本文学選集 6」　서울　知文閣 1966. p.285–494; 「日本文学選集 6」　서울　韓国読書文化院　1973. p.285–494

HAYASHI Kyōko　林　京子　1930–

Futari no bohyō　二人の墓標

'両人的墓標'　游禮毅訳　「祭場」　台南　豊生出版社　1975. p.85–128

Kumoribi no kōshin　曇り日の行進

'陰天的行進'　游禮毅訳　「祭場」　台南　豊生出版社　1975. p.131–164

Matsuri no ba　祭りの場

'祭場'　游禮毅訳　「祭場」　台南　豊生出版社　1975. p.9–81

'祭場'　劉蔡沙訳　「祭場」　台北　皇冠出版社　1975. p.13–84

'祭壇'　金后蘭訳　「70年代芥川賞小説集」　서울　玄岩社 1976. p.239–297; 「新鋭世界文学選集20世紀 9」 서울　玄岩社　1977. p.239–297

'Ritual of death'　Tr. by Kyoko Selden. *The Japan Interpreter,* v.12, no.1, 1978. p.54–93

HAYASHI Seigo　林　青梧　1929–

Kiga kakumei　飢餓革命

「人間火山」　林仁洙　金佑圭訳　서울　正信社　1960. 204p.

HAYASHI Torao　林　虎雄　1902–

Chinurareta kiroku　血ぬられた記録

Кровавый документ. Москва, Московский Рабочий, 1930. 248p.; Токио, Наука, 1973. 248p.

HAYASHI Yukiko　林　ゆき子

Poems　詩

'Небо над Хиросимой'　Перевод Анатолия Мамонова. *Свободный стих в японской поэзии.* Москва, Наука, 1971. p.175–178; *Вкус хризантемы.* Москва, Восточная Литература, 1976. p.160

HIDAKA Teru　日高てる　1920–

Poems　詩

'밤'　崔一秀訳　「기다리고있네」　서울　韓国政経社　1960. p.163–165

HIGUCHI Ichiyō 樋口一葉 1872–1896

Jūsanya 十三夜

'The thirteenth night' Tr. by Hisako Tanaka. *Monumenta Nipponica*, v.14, no.3–4, 1960–61. p.157–174

'La tredicesima notte' Tr. di Atsuko Ricca Suga. *Narratori giapponesi moderni*. Milano, Bompiani, 1965. p.53–72; *Antologia della letteratura coreana e giapponese*. Milano, Fratelli Fabbri, 1969. p.240–245

Nigorie にごりえ

'Palude mortifera' Tr. di Harukichi Shimoi. *Sakura*, no.5 & 6, 1920. p.123–126

'Borongo felhok' Ford. Thein Alfréd. *Mai Japán dekameron*. Budapest, Nyugat, 1935. p.69–116

'Muddy bay' Tr. by Hisako Tanaka. *Monumenta Nipponica*, v.14, no.1–2, 1958. p.173–204

'In the gutter' Tr. by Seizo Nobunaga. *Takekurabe*. Tokyo, Information Pub. 1960. 25p.

'흐린江어귀' 表文台訳 「日本代表作家百人集 1」 서울 希望出版社 1966. p.120–138; 「日本短篇文学全集 1」 서울 新太陽社 1969. p.120–138

'V kalném proudu' Přel. Miriam Jelínková. *5 japonských novel*. Praha, Odeon, 1969. p.9–35

'Trübe Wasser' Deutsch von Jürgen Berndt. *Träume aus zehn Nächten*. Berlin, Aufbau Verlag, 1975. p.5–39

Ōtsugomori 大つごもり

'The last day of the year' Tr. by Tei Fujiu. *Hanakatsura*. Tokyo, Ikuseikai, 1903. p.37–68

'Под новый год' Перевод И. Львовой. *Восточный альманах 1*. Москва, Худож. Лит. 1957. p.366–380

'大年夜' 「日本作家十二人集」 香港 新學書店 1959. p.1–18

Takekurabe たけくらべ

'They compare heights' Tr. by W. M. Bickerton. *Transactions of the Asiatic Society of Japan*. 2d series, v.7, 1930. p.131–137

'Takekurabe' Tr. by Miss Sato. *Sekai to Josei*, 1935.

'Growing up' Tr. by Edward Seidensticker. *Modern Japanese literature*, ed. by D. Keene. N. Y. Grove Press, 1956; Tokyo, Tuttle, 1957. p.70–110

'Teenagers vying for tops' Tr. by Seizo Nobunaga. *Takekurabe*. Tokyo, Information Pub. 1960. 41p.

'Die Liebe der kleinen Midori' Übers. von Oscar Benl. *Der Kirschblütenzweig*. München, Nymphenburger, 1965. p.171–217

Wakare michi わかれ道

'The parting of the ways' Tr. by W. M. Bickerton. *Transactions of the Asiatic Society of Japan*. 2d series, v.7, 1930. p.120–130

Yami zakura 闇桜

'Kirschblüte in der Dämmerung' Übers. von Shigeko Matsuno. *Das Junge Japan*, Band 2, 1925. p.73–75, 99–103

「樋口一葉選集」 蕭蕭訳 北京 人民文学出版社 1962. 1冊

HIKAGE Jōkichi 日影丈吉 1908–

Kitsune no tori 狐の鶏

'狐鶏' 劉慕沙訳 「狐鶏」 台北 林白出版社 1969. p.170–234

HINATSU Kōnosuke 日夏耿之介 1890–1971

Poems 詩

'Colline grise; Voyageur au crépuscule; La couleur noire; Ce fut une nuit où je n'entendis pas la flûte; Mon minuit' Tr. par Kuni Matsuo et Steinilber-Oberlin. *Anthologie des poètes japonais contemporains*. Paris, Mercure de France, 1939. p.184–191

'5 poèmes' *Histoire de la littérature japonaise contemporaine*, par Georges Bonneau. Paris, Payot, 1944. p.245–246

'Viaggio di un eremita sulla luna; Tosse' Tr. di R. Beviglia. *Antologia della letteratura coreana e giapponese*. Milano, Fratelli Fabbri, 1969. p.279–280

'Tosse' *Il simbolismo nella poesia giapponese dell'era Meiji*, di Rosaria Beviglia. Roma, Istituto Italiano per il Medio ed Estremo Oriente, 1971. p.169

'Ochi negri; Ab intra; Miez de noapte' Traducerea Virgil Teodorescu. *Din lirica japoneză*. Bucureşti, Editura Univers, n.d. p.166–167

HINO Ashihei 火野葦平 1907–1960

Fukushū 復讐

'復讐' 崔泰應訳 「日本代表作家百人集 2」 서울 希望出版社 1966. p.432–447; 「日本短篇文学全集 3」 서울 新太陽社 1969. p.118–134

Hana to heitai 花と兵隊

Flowers and soldiers. Tr. by Lewis Bush. Tokyo, Kenkyusha, 1939. 213p.

Kỹetiny a vojác. Přel. Vlasta Praskova-Novotna. Praha, Sfinx, 1940. 360p.

'Blumen und Soldaten' Übers. von A. von Choinatzky und Teisuke Kojima. *Weizen und Soldaten*. Leipzig, T. G. Gotts'sche Buchhandlung, 1942. p.125–331; *Japan, Tradition und Gegenwart*. Stuttgart, Deutsche Volksbücher, 1942. p.158–176

Kamishibai 紙芝居

'Bildertheater' Übers. von Kurt Meissner. *Der Tanzfächer*, von. K. Meissner. Tokyo, 1943. p.109–126

Mugi to heitai 麦と兵隊

「麥田裡的兵隊」 雪笠訳 新京 満州國通信社 1939. 1冊

Barley and soldiers. Tr. by K. Bush and L. W. Bush. Tokyo, Kenkyusha, 1939. 207p.

Orze e soldati. Tr. di Luciano Fabbri. Milano, Bompiani, 1940. 305p.

Пшеница и солдаты. Перевод Г. К. Юшкова. Дальний, Южно-Маньчж. Ж. Д. 1941. 214p.

'Weizen und Soldaten' Übers. von A. von Choinatzky und Teisuke Kojima. *Weizen und Solda-*

ten. Leipzig, T. G. Gotta'sche Buchhandlung, 1942. p.335–495
Corn and soldiers. Tr. by Shigeo Inouye. Tokyo, Kenkyusha, 1943. 265p.
Orzo e soldati. Tr. di Shigeo Inouye. Tokyo, Kenkyusha, 1943. 265p.
Wheat and soldiers. Tr. by Shidzue Ishimoto. N. Y. Rinehart, n.d. 1v.

Ryūkyū monogatari 琉球物語

'Отрезанная Окинава' Перевод И. Львовой и В. Марковой. *Дружба Народов*, номер 9, 1958. p.98–137

Tabako to heitai 煙草と兵隊

'Cigarettes and soldiers' *Contemporary Japan*, v.8, 1939. p.229–239

Tsuchi to heitai 土と兵隊

Mud and soldiers. Tr. by Lewis Bush. Tokyo, Kenkyusha, 1939. 160p.
「土與兵隊」 金石訳 北京 東方書店 1939. 1冊
'La requisizione di Kichizo' (da Terra e soldati) Tr. di R. Claratti. *Asiatica*, 6, 1940.
Fanti nel fango. Dal giapponese di Soiti Nogami. Milano, Garzanti, 1942. 1v.
'Erde und Soldaten' Übers. von A. von Choinatzky und Teisuke Kojima. *Weizen und Soldaten.* Leipzig, T. G. Gotta'sche Buchhandlung, 1942. p.11–122
'Tuti to heitai (part)' Tr. by F. J. Daniels. *Japanese prose.* London, Lund Humphries, 1944. p.6–25
'Earth and soldiers' Tr. by Shidzue Ishimoto. *Modern Japanese literature*, ed. by D. Keene. N. Y. Grove Press, 1956; Tokyo, Tuttle, 1957. p.357–365; *The Mentor book of modern Asian literature*, ed. by D. B. Shimer. N. Y. New American Library, 1969. p.239–246

Poems 詩

'1 poem' Tr. by Donald Keene. *Landscapes and portraits.* Tokyo, Kodansha International, 1971. p.311

'Венок' Перевод В. Логуновой. *Огонек*, номер 39, 1958. p.20–23

HINO Keizō 日野啓三 1929–

Ano yūhi あの夕陽

'그저녁놀' 印泰星訳 「그저녁놀」 서울 中央日報社 1968. p.80–131
'那夕陽' 劉慕沙訳 「祭場」 台北 皇冠出版社 1975. p.89–131.
'그저녁놀' 洪完基訳 「世界文学속의 韓国 12」 서울 正韓出版社 1975. p.79–123
'거 夕陽' 崔一秀訳 「70年代芥川賞小説集」 서울 玄岩社 1976. p.197–237; 「新鋭世界文学選集20世紀 9」 서울 玄岩社 1977. p.197–236

Kaze no chihei 風の地平

'바람의地平' 洪完基訳 「世界文学속의 韓国 12」 서울 正韓出版社 1975. p.221–290

Kono kishi no ie 此岸の家

'此岸의집' 印泰星訳 「그저녁놀」 서울 中央日報社 1968. p.13–78

'此岸의집' 洪完基訳 「世界文学속의 韓国 12」 서울 正韓出版社 1975. p.292–344

Kumo no hashi 雲の橋

'구름다리' 印泰星訳 「그저녁놀」 서울 中央日報社 1968. p.168–230
'구름다리' 洪完基訳 「世界文学속의 韓国 12」 서울 正韓出版社 1975. p.171–220

Nokoshienu kotoba 遺しえぬ言

'남길수없는말' 印泰星訳 「그저녁놀」 서울 中央日報社 1968. p.134–165
'남길수없는말' 洪完基訳 「世界文学속의 韓国 12」 서울 正韓出版社 1975. p.345–352

Ukabu heya 浮ぶ部屋

'떠오르는房' 崔貞順訳 「文学思想」 26巻11号 1974. p.288–316
'떠 있는房' 洪完基訳 「世界文学속의 韓国 12」 서울 正韓出版社 1975. p.123–170
'떠오르는房' 金巣雲訳 「故郷을어이잊으리까」 서울 文学思想出版部 1977. p.238–288

HINO Sōjō 日野草城 1901–1956

Haiku 俳句

'7 haiku' *A history of haiku v.2*, by R. H. Blyth. Tokyo, Hokuseido, 1964. p.240–242
'20 haiku' *Modern Japanese haiku: an anthology*, comp. and tr. by Makoto Ueda. Tokyo, Univ. of Tokyo Press, 1976. p.135–144
'In the grove of plum-flowers' Tr. by Kenneth Yasuda. *A pepper-pod.* Tokyo, Tuttle, 1976. p.100

HIRABAYASHI Hatsunosuke 平林初之輔 1892–1931

Criticism 評論

'民衆藝術底理論和實際' 海晶訳 「小説月報」 第12巻11号 1921. p.8–16
'現代文化論' 希聖訳 「北新半月刊」 第2巻11号 1927. p.1183–1211
'文學及藝術之技術的革命' 陳望道訳 「小説月報」 第19巻2号 1928. p.224–232
「文學之社會學的研究」方光燾訳 上海 大江書局 1929. 1冊
'政治底價値與藝術底價値' 胡秋原訳 「小説月報」 第21巻1号 1930. p.65–70
'法國浪漫派の評論' 張資平訳 「學藝」 第10巻7期 1930.
'藝術家的離婚問題批評' 丁鴻勛訳 「南開週刊」 99期 1924.
'自然主義文學底理論的體系' 陳望道訳 「文藝研究」 創刊号 1930.
'法國自然派的文學評論' 張我軍訳 「讀書雜誌」 第2巻9期 1932. p.1–14
「近代社會思想史要」 施復亮 鍾復光訳 上海 大江書局 193?.
'文學之社會學的研究方法及其適用' 林駟訳 「太平洋」 193?.

HIRABAYASHI Taiko 平林たい子 1905–1972

Hito no inochi 人の命

'A man's life' Tr. by George Saito. *Modern Japanese stories*, ed. by Ivan Morris. London, Spottiswoode, 1961; Tokyo, Tuttle, 1962. p.366–382
'Das Leben eines Menschen' Deutsch von Moni-

que Humbert. *Nippon*. Zürich, Diogenes, 1965. p.403–426

Kishimojin 鬼子母神

'The goddess of children' Tr. by Ken Murayama. *Pacific Spectator*, v.6, no.4, 1952. p.451–457
'鬼子母神' 朴在森訳 「20世紀女流文学選集 3」 서울 新太陽社 1967. p.159–166

Kuroi nenrei 黒い年令

'The black age' Tr. by Edward Seidensticker. *Japan Quarterly*, v.10, no.4, 1963. p.479–493; *Comment*, no.20, 1963. p.39–51; *Solidarity,* March 1958. p.11–19

Nage suteyo 投げすてよ

'抛棄' 沈端先訳 「初春の風」 上海 大江書局 193?.

Nagurareru aitsu 殴られるあいつ

'殴打' 陳勺水訳 「日本寫實派代表傑作集」 上海 楽羣雑誌社 1929.

Sairen サイレン

'汽笛' 秦覺訳 「小説月報」 第22巻1号 1931. p.177–184

Seryōshitsu nite 施療室にて

「在施療室」 沈端先訳 上海 水沫書店 1929. 1冊

Ujina chikaku 宇品ちかく

'우지나근방' 柳呈訳 「日本代表作家百人集 3」 서울 希望出版社 1966. p.378–386; 「日本短篇文学全集 4」 서울 新太陽社 1969. p.138–146

Waga tomo 我が友

'我的朋友' 劉吶鷗訳 「人間月刊」 第1巻1期 1929.

Watashi wa ikiru 私は生きる

'I mean to live' Tr. by Edward Seidensticker. *Japan Quarterly*, v.10, no.4, 1963. p.469–479; *Asian P.E.N. anthology*, ed. by F. S. Jose. N. Y. Taplinger, 1966. p.144–154; *Solidarity*, v.8, no.2, 1973. p.2–10

Essay エッセイ

'Modern Japanese literature' *Oriental Economist*, July 1962. p.418–419
'큰사고의보도' 金賢珠訳 「바이바이바다」 서울 三韓出版社 1966. p.110–111

────────

「平林泰子集」 沈端先訳 上海 現代書局 1933. 1冊

HIRAFUKU Hyakusui 平福百穂 1877–1933

Tanka 短歌

'Icicles' Tr. by Asataro Miyamori. *Masterpieces of Japanese poetry, ancient and modern*. Tokyo, Maruzen, 1936; Tokyo, Taiseido, 1956; N. Y. Greenwood Press, 1971. p.668

HIRAIWA Yumie 平岩弓枝 1932–

Aki no hi 秋の日

'秋日' 朱佩蘭訳 「撒旦的玩笑」 台南 豊生出版社 1975.

p.75–99

────────

'人慈花美' 朱佩蘭訳 「伊豆的舞娘」 嘉義 明山書局 1969. p.91–108
'溺愛' 朱佩蘭訳 「伊豆的舞娘」 嘉義 明山書局 1969. p.109–129
'萬博之縁' 朱佩蘭訳 「撒旦的玩笑」 台南 豊生出版社 1975. p.101–124

HIRAKI Jirō 平木二六 1903–

Poems 詩

'Death and I' *An anthology of modern Japanese poetry*, ed. and tr. by Ichiro Kono and Rikutaro Fukuda. Tokyo, Kenkyusha, 1957. p.24
'Ölüm ve ben' Tercüme etmek L. Sami Akalin. *Japon şiiri*. İstanbul, Varlik Yayinevi, 1962. p.276

HIRANO Banri 平野万里 1885–1947

Tanka 短歌

'The ocean; The breeze in Musashi Plain; At Akakura' Tr. by Asataro Miyamori. *Masterpieces of Japanese poetry, ancient and modern*. Tokyo, Maruzen, 1936; Tokyo, Taiseido, 1956; N. Y. Greenwood Press, 1971. p.725–727
'2 tanka' Tr. by V. H. Viglielmo. *Japanese literature in the Meiji era*. Tokyo, Obunsha, 1955. p.387–388

HIRANO Ken 平野 謙 1907–1978

Criticism 評論

'On acting, revised' Tr. by George Saito. *Japan P.E.N. News*, no. 17, Feb. 1966. p.1–7
'Kenzaburo Oye' *New Japan*, v.24, 1972. p.84–85

HIRATO Renkichi 平戸廉吉 1893–1922

Poems 詩

'Impressions à l'hôpital K.; Oiseau volant' Tr. par Kuni Matsuo et Steinilber-Oberlin. *Anthologie des poètes japonais contemporains*. Paris, Mercure de France, 1939. p.218–221

HIRATSUKA Un'ichi 平塚運一 1895–

Tabi no kaisō 旅の回想

Recollections of travel. Tr. by George Saito. Tokyo, Meiji Shobo, 1951. 68p.

HIROE Yaezakura 広江八重桜 1879–1945

Haiku 俳句

'The hearth of my house' Tr. by Asataro Miya-

mori. *Anthology of haiku, ancient and modern.* Tokyo, Maruzen, 1932. p.821
'3 haiku' Tr. by V. H. Viglielmo. *Japanese literature in the Meiji era.* Tokyo, Obunsha, 1955. p.442, 448
'1 haiku' Tercüme etmek L. Sami Akalin. *Japon şiiri.* İstanbul, Varlik Yayinevi, 1962. p.235

HIROIKE Akiko　広池秋子　1919–

Ai to yūki no meigenshū　愛と勇気の名言集

「愛的表現」劉慕沙訳　台北　純文學出版社　1973. 1冊
「愛與勇氣」劉慕沙訳　台北　純文學出版社　1973. 1冊

Onna ga kangaete irukoto　女が考えていること

「女人心」劉慕沙訳　台北　革欣文化事業中心　1973. 226p.

HIROTSU Kazuo　広津和郎　1891–1968

Aru yo　ある夜

'One night' Tr. by William E. Naff. *The heart is alone*, ed. by Richard N. McKinnon. Tokyo, Hokuseido, 1957. p.115–117

Izumi e no michi　泉への道

「到泉水去的道路」生生訳　上海　上海文艺出版社　1961. 323p.

Kunren saretaru ninjō　訓練されたる人情

「訓練成的感情」秦水訳「世界文学」1962年5月　p.58–74

Mandorin shōjo　マンドリン少女

「만돌린少女」張壽哲訳　「日本代表作家百人集 2」서울 希望出版社　1966. p.304–321;「日本短篇文学全集 2」서울　新太陽社　1969. p.368–385

HISAMATSU Sen'ichi　久松潜一　1894–1976

Criticism　評論

'Fujiwara Shunzei and literary theories of the Middle Ages' *Acta Asiatica*, no.1, 1960. p.29–42
The vocabulary of Japanese literary aesthetics. Tokyo, Centre for East Asian Cultural Studies, 1963. 112p.
'The characteristics of beauty in the Japanese Middle Ages' *Acta Asiatica*, no.8, 1965. p.40–53
Concepts of Kami in Japanese ancient songs and poems, by Senichi Hisamatsu and Nobuyoshi Shida. Tokyo, Daiichi Shobo, 1967. 410p.
Biographical dictionary of Japanese literature. Tokyo, Kodansha International, 1976. 437p.

HISAO Jūran　久生十蘭　1902–1957

Boshi zō　母子像

「母子像」傳寶齢訳「勲章」台北　文壇社　1960. p.146–147

'Madre e figlio' Tr. di Olga Ceretti Borsini. *Novelle giapponesi.* Milano, Martello, 1969. p.35–48

HISHIYAMA Shūzō　菱山修三　1909–1967

Poems　詩

'Home' *An anthology of modern Japanese poetry*, ed. and tr. by Ichiro Kono and Rikutaro Fukuda. Tokyo, Kenkyusha, 1957. p.24
'High summer' *The poetry of living Japan*, comp. and tr. by Takamichi Ninomiya and D. J. Enright. London, John Murray, 1957. p.83
'Ev' Tercüme etmek L. Sami Akalin. *Japon şiiri.* İstanbul, Varlik Yayinevi, 1962. p.294
'쏜아지는落葉에게 ; 아카시아나무는 ; 딸리아가피는마을 ; 敗北' 鄭漢模　辛東門訳「世界戦後文学全集 9」서울　新丘文化社　1962. p.230–231

HITOMI Katsu　人見　克

Hahaoya　母親

'母親' 蘇儀貞訳「小説月報」第17巻11号　1926. p.16–18

HITOMI Tōmei　人見東明　1883–1974

Poems　詩

'Dans la clairière' Tr. par Nico D. Horiguchi. *The lyric garland*, ed. by Makoto Sangu. Tokyo, Hokuseido, 1957. p.22

HŌJŌ Tamio　北条民雄　1914–1937

Inochi no shoya　いのちの初夜

'Die erste Nacht eines neuen Lebens' Übers. von Oscar Benl. *Flüchtiges Leben, moderne japanische Erzählungen.* Berlin, Landsmann, 1942.
'生命의初夜' 崔白山訳　「日本代表作家百人集 1」서울 希望出版社　1966. p.428–451;「日本短篇小説全集 2」서울　新太陽社　1969. p.48–71

Rai kazoku　癩家族

'癩患者家族' 郭夏信訳「世界文学全集 94」서울 乙酉文化社　1969. p.359–381;「日本短篇文学選」서울 乙酉文化社　1976. p.225–257

HONDA Akira　本多顕彰　1898–

Criticism　評論

'德國人與莎士比亞' 王執鐘訳「譯文」新1巻4期　1936. p.746–751
'文學的形態' 陳淑女訳「人生」1970年5月　p.205

HONDA Katsuichi　本多勝一　1931–

Betonamu kiko　ベトナム紀行

'北越紀行' 英慧訳「七十年代月刊」第36期　1973. p.4–6

HONDA Katsuichi

Senjō no mura 戦場の村

'Villages in the battlefield, the Vietnam war and the people' *Japan Quarterly,* v.15, no.2, 1968. p.159–179
Vilaĝoj en batalkampo. Tr. Gaku Konishi. Tokyo, Japana Esperanta Librokooperativo, 1970. 63p.
Vilaĝoj en lai batalkampo. Tr. Chiba Univ. Esperanto-kai. Chiba, 1970. 88p.

HONJŌ Kasō 本荘可宗 1891–

Criticism 評論

'藝術與哲學・倫理' 魯迅訳 「世界文化月刊」 1930年 9月; 「魯迅全集 16」 上海 魯迅全集出版社 1939. 作家書屋 1946. 大連 光華書店 1948. 北京 人民文学出版社 p.495–523; 「魯迅譯文集 10」 北京 人民文学出版社 1958. p.333–345

HONMA Hisao 本間久雄 1886–

Ōshū kindai bungei shichō gairon 欧州近代文芸思潮概論

「歐州近代文藝思潮」 沈端先訳 上海 開明書店 1928. 1冊

Shin bungaku gairon 新文学概論

「新文學概論」 章錫琛訳 上海 商務印書館 1925. 1冊
「新文學概論」 汪馥泉訳 上海 東亞図書館 1925. 1冊
「文學概論」 台湾開明書店訳 台北 開明書店 1957. 250p.
「新文學概論」 章錫光訳 台北 台湾商務印書館 1968. 134p.

Criticism 評論

「文藝概論」 章錫琛訳 上海 開明書店 1930. 1冊
「文學研究法」 李自珍訳 北平 星雲堂 1932. 1冊
'生活美化論' 從予訳 「東方雜誌」 第21巻11期 1924. p.80–93
'文學研究法' 朱雲影訳 「讀書雜誌」 第1巻9期 1931. p.1–38

HONPŌ Shūrin 本方秀鱗 1881–1932

Haiku 俳句

'3 haiku' Tr. by Asataro Miyamori. *Anthology of haiku, ancient and modern.* Tokyo, Maruzen, 1932. p.702–704
'The spring in Iki; Men's voices' Tr. by Asataro Miyamori. *Haiku poems, ancient and modern.* Tokyo, Maruzen, 1940. p.325–326
'Still and clear' Tr. by Harold Stewart. *A net of fireflies.* Tokyo, Tuttle, 1960. p.62
'3 haiku' Tr. by Peter Beilenson and Harry Behn. *Haiku harvest.* Mount Vernon, Peter Pauper Press, 1962. p.48

HORI Hidehiko 堀 秀彦 1902–

Essays エッセイ

'넌센스 (人生의意味)' 金賢珠訳 「바이바이바다」 서울 三韓出版社 1966. p.22–27
'浮気講座' 徐白訳 「日本短篇譯集 3」 台北 晩蟬書店 1969. p.133–145

HORI Tatsuo 堀 辰雄 1904–1953

Kaze tachinu 風立ちぬ

'The wind has risen' Tr. by Ineko Sato. *Eigo Seinen,* v.93, no.1, 4, 8, 12, 1947.
'The wind rises' Tr. by Eiichi Hayashi. *The Reeds,* v.4, 1958. p.91–126
'The wind awakes' Tr. by Gerard S. Barry. *Selected works of Tatsuo Hori.* Tokyo, Privately print. 1967. p.37–77
'The wind rises' Tr. by Seiji Takenaka. *The Reeds,* v.14, 1976. p.57–71

Kōya 曠野

'曠野' 李相魯訳 「日本代表作家百人集 2」 서울 希望出版社 1966. p.420–429; 「日本短篇文学全集 3」 서울 新太陽社 1969. p.106–115
'The waste land' Tr. by Hiroo Tagawa. *The Reeds,* v.13, 1972. p.71–87

Moyuru hoho 燃ゆる頬

'Moyuru hoho' Tr. by Hisatoshi Takada. *Eigo to Eibungaku,* 1938.

Naoko 菜穂子

'Naoko' Tr. by Gerard S. Barry. *Selected works of Tatsuo Hori.* Tokyo, Privately print. 1967. p.88–135

Utsukushii mura 美しい村

'Beaútiful village' Tr. by Gerard S. Barry. *Selected works of Tatsuo Hori.* Tokyo, Privately print. 1967. p.1–33

Poems 詩

'Die Krankheit' Übertragen von Shin Aizu. *Der schwermütige Ladekran.* St. Gallen, Tschudy Verlag, 1960. p.44

HORIE Ken'ichi 堀江謙一 1938–

Taiheiyō hitoribotchi 太平洋ひとりぼっち

Kodoku: sailing alone across the Pacific. Tr. by Alfredo Takuichi Ito and Kaoru Ogimi. Tokyo, Tuttle, 1964. 223p.
Kodoku. Milano, Bompiani, 1964. 250p.

HORIGUCHI Daigaku 堀口大学 1892–

Poems 詩

Tankas, petits poèmes japonais. Tr. de l'auteur. Paris, Fauconnier, 1921. 119p.
'重荷; 故郷; 歎息' 周作人訳 「新青年」 第9巻4期 1921. p.36; 「陀螺」 上海 北新書局 192?.
Tankas. Tr. from the French by Louise Kidder Sparrow. London, MacDonald, 1925. 72p.
Tanka, poesias japonesas de Nico D. Horiguchi. Tr. por Munio Nisay. Tokyo, Yuraku Insatsusha, 1925. 69p.
'Femme dansant; Le rat bouceux; Femme du souvenir; Le suffisant . . . ; Jours sans amour; Mon moi; Hamac; Flûte de deux sous' Tr. par Georges Bonneau. *Rythmes japonais,* par G. Bonneau. Paris, Paul Geuthner, 1935. p.

74–83; *Lyrisme du temps présent*, par G. Bonneau. Paris, Paul Geuthner, 1935. p.64–75; *Anthologie de la poésie japonaise*. Paris, Paul Geuthner, 1935. p.196–207

'Soul hunger: The coconut tree' Tr. by Tatsue Fujita. *Aoba no fue*. Honolulu, Univ. of Hawaii, 1937. n. p.

'Моего аз; Има дни без любовь; Блатнииат плех; Люлка; Жената от спомела' Превод от франз. Никола Джеров. *Песните на Ямато*. София, Корали, 1937. p.69–74

'Etoile filante; Une femme danse; Pêche aux étoiles; Eventail; Moi; Une femme dans mes souvenirs; L'arc-en-ciel' Tr. par Kuni Matsuo et Steinilber-Oberlin. *Anthologie des poètes japonais contemporains*. Paris, Mercure de France, 1939. p.202–206

'5 poèmes' *Histoire de la littérature japonaise contemporaine*, par George Bonneau. Paris, Payot, 1944. p.242–243

'Two poems' Tr. by Joseph K. Yamagiwa. *Atlantic Monthly*, v.195, Jan. 1955. p.107

'A morning spectrum; A pillow of sand; Palm trees; Fox; The necklace; Sung in a cold garden; Grief; Ash Wednesday' *An anthology of modern Japanese poetry*, ed. and tr. by Ichiro Kono and Rikutaro Fukuda. Tokyo, Kenkyusha, 1957. p.26–31

'Le lion; Actualisme; Corbeau; Le palmier' *The lyric garland*, ed. by Makoto Sangu. Tokyo, Hokuseido, 1957. p.23–25

'Parasz; Elet; Jajoso' *Kinai es Japán koitok*. Budapest, Szepirodalmi, 1957. p.213–214

'La femme de mes souvenirs; La danseuse; Le miroir; Association d'idées; Regrets; Vision ensoleillée' *La poésie japonaise*, par Karl Petit. Paris, Seghers, 1959. p.212–213

'Im Schwingnety' Übers. von Günther Debon. *Im Schnee die Fähre*. München, R. Piper, 1960. p.54

'Basne' Přel. J. V. Neustupný. *Nový Orient*, v.17, no.10, 1962. p.229

'Gerdanlik; Kum yastiği; Soğuk bahçenin türküsü; Palmiyeler; Bir sabah tayfi; Ash Wednesday' Tercüme etmek L. Sami Akalin. *Japon şiiri*. İstanbul, Varlik Yayinevi, 1962. p.252–257

'Landscape; Hammock; Memories' Tr. by Geoffrey Bownas and Anthony Thwaite. *The Penguin book of Japanese verse*. Harmondsworth, Penguin Books, 1964. p.192–193

'First snow' Tr. by Graeme Wilson. *Japan Quarterly*, v.12, no.3, 1965. p.323

'Girl dancing; Loneliness; Fan' Tr. by Graeme Wilson. *Japan Quarterly*, v.12, no.4, 1965. p.437, 462, 490

'The national flag of the sky' Tr. by Graeme Wilson. *Japan Quarterly*, v.13, no.4, 1966. p.512

'Palm-trees' Tr. by Hisakazu Kaneko. *London Magazine*, v.6, no.9, 1966. p.22–23

'乳房；銀河の戀情' 崔一秀訳 「가다리고있네」 서울 韓國政経社 1966. p.84–85, 169

'戀愛；等待及約會；手風琴；橄欖樹；母親的聲音' 徐和隣訳 「現代詩解説」 台北 葡萄園詩刊社 1970. p.23–28

'水浴女人；까마귀；人生이란' 金巣雲訳 「世界의文学大全集 34」 서울 同和出版公社 1971. p.515–516

'Sea scene; Poetry' Tr. by James Kirkup. *Poetry Nippon*, no.39 & 40, 1977. p.16–17

'Dansatoarea; Regrete; Pescuit de stele; Evantaiul, et al' Traducerea Dan Constantinescu. *Din lirica japoneză*. Bucureşti, Editura Univers, n. d. p.170–173

HORIKAWA Masami 堀川正美 1931–

Poems 詩

'Ammonizione del libro' *La protesta poetica del Giappone*, a cura di Dacia Maraini e Michiko Nojiri. Roma, Officina Edizioni, 1968. p.129–130

'Voice; Touching a box of dreams' Tr. by Thomas Fitzsimmons. *Japanese poetry now*. London, André Deutsch, 1972. p.107–108; *Japanese poetry today*. N. Y. Schocken Books, 1972. p.109–110

'Waves; Letter from an old friend' Tr. by Harry and Lynn Guest and Shozo Kajima. *Post-war Japanese poetry*. Harmondsworth, Penguin Books, 1972. p.126–129

HORIUCHI Seiichi 堀内誠一

Chi no hanashi ちのはなし

Darihal darah. Kuala Lumpur, Dewan Bahasa, 1975. 1v.

HOSHI Shin'ichi 星 新一 1926–

Ashiato no nazo 足あとのなぞ

'The mysterious footprints' Tr. by Bernard Susser and Tomoyoshi Genkawa. *The spiteful planet, and other stories*. Tokyo, Japan Times, 1978. p.33–39

Bokko chan ボッコちゃん

'Bokko' Tr. by Bernard Susser and Tomoyoshi Genkawa. *The spiteful planet, and other stories*. Tokyo, Japan Times, 1978. p.203–207

Chigai ちがい

'The difference' Tr. by Bernard Susser and Tomoyoshi Genkawa. *The spiteful planet, and other stories*. Tokyo, Japan Times, 1978. p.82–89

Chōsei 調整

'Fine tuning' Tr. by Bernard Susser and Tomoyoshi Genkawa. *The spiteful planet, and other stories*. Tokyo, Japan Times, 1978. p.20–25

Fuyu kitarinaba 冬きたりなば

'Когда придет весна' Перевод З. Рахима. *Времена Хокусая*. Москва, Мир, 1967. p.227–235

'Cind va veni primăvara' In româneşte de Iacob Babin. *Cind va veni primăvara*. Bucureşti, Revista Stiinta şi Tehnica, 1967.

'Kaiateis pavasaris' *Hokusajaus laikai*. Vilnius, Vaizde, 1969. p.173–179

'If winter comes...' Tr. by Bernard Susser and Tomoyoshi Genkawa. *The spiteful planet, and other stories*. Tokyo, Japan Times, 1978. p.73–81

Ganbō 願望

'The wish' Tr. by Bernard Susser and Tomoyoshi

HOSHI Shin'ichi

Genkawa. *The spiteful planet, and other stories*. Tokyo, Japan Times, 1978. p.159–166

Gendai 現代

'The present age' Tr. by Bernard Susser and Tomoyoshi Genkawa. *The spiteful planet, and other stories*. Tokyo, Japan Times, 1978. p.26–28

Ijiwaruna hoshi いじわるな星

'The spiteful planet' Tr. by Bernard Susser and Tomoyoshi Genkawa. *The spiteful planet, and other stories*. Tokyo, Japan Times, 1978. p.13–19

Jakku to mame no ki ジャックと豆の木

'Jack and the beanstalk' Tr. by Bernard Susser and Tomoyoshi Genkawa. *The spiteful planet, and other stories*. Tokyo, Japan Times, 1978. p.102–109

Jōnetsu 情熱

'Enthusiasm' Tr. by Bernard Susser and Tomoyoshi Genkawa. *The spiteful planet, and other stories*. Tokyo, Japan Times, 1978. p.132–141

Kachi kensaki 価値検査機

'The universal evaluator' Tr. by Bernard Susser and Tomoyoshi Genkawa. *The spiteful planet, and other stories*. Tokyo, Japan Times, 1978. p.128–131

Keihin 景品

'Премия' Перевод З. Рахима. *Времена Хокусая*. Москва, Мир, 1967. p.89–96
'Premiul' In româneşte de Iacob Babin. *Cind va veni primăvara*. Bucureşti, Revista Stiinta şi Tehnica, 1967.
'Premija' *Hokusajaus laikai*. Vilnius, Vaizde, 1969. p.65–70
'The premium' Tr. by Bernard Susser and Tomoyoshi Genkawa. *The spiteful planet, and other stories*. Tokyo, Japan Times, 1978. p.51–56

Keiyaku jidai 契約時代

'The age of contracts' Tr. by Bernard Susser and Tomoyoshi Genkawa. *The spiteful planet, and other stories*. Tokyo, Japan Times, 1978. p.142–150

Kibō 希望

'Надежда' Перевод З. Рахима. *Времена Хокусая*. Москва, Мир, 1967. p.147–154
'Viltis' *Hokusajaus laikai*. Vilnius, Vaizde, 1969. p.110–116

Kiki 危機

'Кризис' Перевод З. Рахима. *Времена Хокусая*. Москва, Мир, 1967. p.147–154
'Krize' *Hokusajaus laikai*. Vilnius, Vaizde, 1969. p.164–172

Kimagure robotto 気まぐれロボット

'The wild robot' Tr. by Bernard Susser and Tomo-

yoshi Genkawa. *The spiteful planet, and other stories*. Tokyo, Japan Times, 1978. p.70–72

Kowai ojisan こわいおじさん

'The boogeyman' Tr. by Bernard Susser and Tomoyoshi Genkawa. *The spiteful planet, and other stories*. Tokyo, Japan Times, 1978. p.167–171

Kyōhansha 共犯者

「共犯者」廖清秀訳 台北 鴻儒堂出版社 1976. 1冊

Muryō no denwaki 無料の電話機

'The toll-free telephone' Tr. by Bernard Susser and Tomoyoshi Genkawa. *The spiteful planet, and other stories*. Tokyo, Japan Times, 1978. p.90–95

Naruhodo なるほど

'I see!' Tr. by Bernard Susser and Tomoyoshi Genkawa. *The spiteful planet, and other stories*. Tokyo, Japan Times, 1978. p.186–191

Nemuri usagi ねむりウサギ

'The tortoise and the hare' Tr. by Bernard Susser and Tomoyoshi Genkawa. *The spiteful planet, and other stories*. Tokyo, Japan Times, 1978. p.57–69

Ningenteki 人間的

'All too human' Tr. by Bernard Susser and Tomoyoshi Genkawa. *The spiteful planet, and other stories*. Tokyo, Japan Times, 1978. p.180–185

Ōi, detekōi おーい，でてこーい

'Hey, come out!' Tr. by Bernard Susser and Tomoyoshi Genkawa. *The spiteful planet, and other stories*. Tokyo, Japan Times, 1978. p.197–202

Purezento プレゼント

'The gift' Tr. by Bernard Susser and Tomoyoshi Genkawa. *The spiteful planet, and other stories*. Tokyo, Japan Times, 1978. p.29–32

Raihōsha 来訪者

'The visitor' Tr. by Bernard Susser and Tomoyoshi Genkawa. *The spiteful planet, and other stories*. Tokyo, Japan Times, 1978. p.151–158

Rappa no oto ラツパの音

'The bugle's call' Tr. by Bernard Susser and Tomoyoshi Genkawa. *The spiteful planet, and other stories*. Tokyo, Japan Times, 1978. p.48–50

Shiawase na yatsu しあわせなやつ

'Lucky guy' Tr. by Bernard Susser and Tomoyoshi Genkawa. *The spiteful planet, and other stories*. Tokyo, Japan Times, 1978. p.125–127

Shinpo 進歩

'Progress' Tr. by Bernard Susser and Tomoyoshi Genkawa. *The spiteful planet, and other stories*. Tokyo, Japan Times, 1978. p.119–124

Sōnan 遭難

'Emergency landing' Tr. by Bernard Susser and Tomoyoshi Genkawa. *The spiteful planet, and other stories.* Tokyo, Japan Times, 1978. p.40–47

Sora eno mon 空への門

'The portals of space' Tr. by Bernard Susser and Tomoyoshi Genkawa. *The spiteful planet, and other stories.* Tokyo, Japan Times, 1978. p.192–196

Subarashii tentai すばらしい天体

'The heavenly body' Tr. by Bernard Susser and Tomoyoshi Genkawa. *The spiteful planet, and other stories.* Tokyo, Japan Times, 1978. p.172–179

Tabako タバコ

'Табак' Перевод З. Рахима. *Времена Хокусая.* Москва, Мир, 1967. p.137–146
'Tabakas' *Hokusajaus laikai.* Vilnius, Vaizde, 1969. p.102–109
'Cigarettes' Tr. by Bernard Susser and Tomoyoshi Genkawa. *The spiteful planet, and other stories.* Tokyo, Japan Times, 1978. p.110–118

Takarabune 宝船

'Корабль сокровищ' Перевод З. Рахима. *Продается Япония.* Москва, Мир, 1969. p.95–99

Uchū no otoko tachi 宇宙の男たち

'Мужчина в космосе' Перевод З. Рахима. *Времена Хокусая.* Москва, Мир, 1967. p.97–109
'Vyriskis kosmose' *Hokusajaus laikai.* Vilnius, Vaizde, 1969. p.71–80

Yakkaina sōchi やっかいな装置

'An infernal machine' Tr. by Bernard Susser and Tomoyoshi Genkawa. *The spiteful planet, and other stories.* Tokyo, Japan Times, 1978. p.96–101

'Pasiunea unui proprietar de bar' In românește de Sintimbreanu. *A se feri de umezeala.* București, 1965. p.25–28
'Jaśnie wielmożny pan hipoputam' Przeł. Blanka Yonekawa. *Przekrój*, no.1665, 1977. p.15
'Рационалист' Перевод З. Рахима. *Продается Япония.* Москва, Мир, 1969. p.206–210

HOSHINO Tatsuko 星野立子 1903–

Haiku 俳句

'Falling leaves' Tr. by Kenneth Yasuda. *A pepper-pod.* Tokyo, Tuttle, 1976. p.104
'1 haiku' *The burning heart,* tr. and ed. by Kenneth Rexroth and Ikuko Atsumi. N. Y. Seabury Press, 1977. p.83

HOSODA Genkichi 細田源吉 1891–1974

Honshin 本心

'Le vrai coeur' Tr. par M. Yoshitomi. *Anthologie de la littérature japonaise contemporaine.* Grenoble, Xavier Drevet, 1924. p.141–170

Kūgai 空骸

「空虚」 張資平 鄭佐蒼訳 上海 新宇宙書局 193?. 1冊

HOSOI Wakizō 細井和喜蔵 1897–1925

Bōsekikō Kōji 紡績工江治

Кодзи. Перевод Н. И. Фельдман. Ленинград, Прибой, 1927. 287p.; Токио, Наука, 1973. 287p.
Текстильщик Кодзи. Перевод. Н. Фельдман. Москва, Московский Рабочий, 1930. 40p.
Текстильщик Кодзи, на еврейском языке. Москва, Эмес, 1931. 190p.
Текстильщик Кодзи, на татарском языке. Казань, Татарск. Изд. 1931. 159p.
Текстильщик Кодзи, на таджикском языке. Сталинабад, 1931. 159p.
Текстильщик Кодзи, на украинском языке. Одесса, Молодой Большевик, 1932. 184p.

Nagai namae ながい名前

Длинное имя, на украинском языке. Перевод И. Нехода. Киев, Детгиз, 1957. 15p.

HOSOKAWA Kaga 細川加賀 1924–

Haiku 俳句

'1 haiku' Tr. by Tsutomu Fukuda. *Eigo Kenkyu,* v.63, no.4, 1974. p.19

HOTTA Kiyomi 堀田清美 1922–

Shima 島

「島」 陳北鷗訳 北京 中国戯劇 1959. 67p.
'Остров' Перевод Е. Пинус. *Современные японские пьесы.* Москва, Искусство, 1962. p.3–75

HOTTA Yoshie 堀田善衛 1918–

Dansō 断層

'Пропасть' Перевод С. Гутермана. *Японская новелла.* Москва, Изд. Иност. Лит. 1961. p.409–431
「断層」 權純萬訳 「日本代表作家百人集 4」 서울 希望出版社 1966. p.452–464; 「日本短篇文学全集 5」 서울 新太陽社 1969. p.292–304

Hiroba no kodoku 広場の孤独

'Solitude in the plaza' Tr. by Yoshiro Shirakawa.

HOTTA Yoshie

Review (Otaru Univ. of Commerce), no.10, 1955. p.1–62, no.12, 1956. p.199–226
「廣場의孤獨」 辛東門訳 「芥川賞小説集」 서울 新丘文化社 1960. p.253–329; 「깊은江」 서울 三耕社 1971. p.253–330

Jikan 時間

'Время' Перевод Т. Григорьевой и др. *Шестерны, Время*. Ташкент, Гослитиздат, 1958. n. p.

Kage no bubun 影の部分

'Shadow pieces' Tr. by P. G. O'Neill. *Japan Quarterly*, v.13, no.3, 1966. p.348–365
'Teile eines Schatten' Deutsch von Jürgen Berndt. *Träume aus zehn Nächten*. Berlin, Aufbau Verlag, 1975. p.506–540

Kibukijima 鬼無鬼島

「鬼无鬼島」 李芒 文潔若訳 北京 作家出版社 1963. 92p.

Kinenhi 記念碑

Памятник. Перевод Я. Берлина и З. Рахима. Москва, Изд. Иност. Лит. 1962. 246p.
Malestussammas. Tr. from the Russian K. Kivi. Tallin, Estgosizdat, 1963. 256p.

Sharin 車輪

'Шестерни' Перевод А. Стругацкого. *Шестерни, Время*. Ташкент, Гослитиздат, 1958. n. p.

Shinpan 審判

Суд. Перевод З. Рахима. Москва, Прогресс, 1969. 575p.
Сад. Превела от руски Ана Беливанова. София, Изд. на Отечествения Фронт, 1973. 575p.

Uminari no soko kara 海鳴りの底から

Из грубины бушующего моря. Перевод И. Львовой. Москва, Худож. Лит. 1968. 383p.

I

IBARAGI Noriko 茨木のり子 1926–

Poems 詩

'보이지않는配達夫' 金龍済訳 「日本詩集」 서울 青雲社 1960. p.127–130
'六月；은밀하게' 辛東門訳 「世界戦後文学全集 9」 서울 新丘文化社 1962. p.239–240
'Soul; Invisible mailmen' Tr. by Makoto Ueda. *Literary Review*, v.6, no.1, 1962. p.115–117
'Dialogo; L'anima' *La protesta poetica del Giappone*, a cura di Dacia Maraini e Michiko Nojiri. Roma, Officina Edizioni, 1968. p.103–104
'Мен сулуу, жанжаш кезимде' Которгон Ж. Алыбаев. *Хиросима кектери*. Фрунзе, Кыргызстан, 1969. p.50–51
'Когда я была красивой' Перевод А. И. Мамонова. *Свободный стих в японской поэзии.*

Москва, Наука, 1971. p.174–175; *Вкус хризантемы*. Москва, Восточная Литература, 1976. p.39
'Children; Invisible messengers' Tr. by Harry and Lynn Guest and Shozo Kajima. *Postwar Japanese poetry*. Harmondsworth, Penguin Books, 1972. p.103–105
'Soul; The invisible mailmen; My camera; Outran; Suicide by hanging' Tr. by Fukuko Kobayashi and Hajime Kijima. *The poetry of postwar Japan*. Iowa City, Univ. of Iowa Press, 1975. p.107–112
'Dialogue; What a little girl had on her mind' *The burning heart*, tr. and ed. by Kenneth Rexroth and Ikuko Atsumi. N. Y. Seabury Press, 1977. p.100–101

IBUSE Masuji 井伏鱒二 1898–

Hakuchō no uta 白鳥の歌

'Swan song' Tr. by G. W. Sargent. *Eigo Seinen*, v.102, no.9, 10, 11, 12, 1956.

Henrō yado へんろう宿

'Pilgrims' inn' Tr. by John Bester. *Lieutenant Lookeast, and other stories*. Tokyo, Kodansha International, 1971; London, Secker and Warburg, 1971. p.53–58

Honjitsu kyūshin 本日休診

'No consultation today' Tr. by Edward Seidensticker. *Japan Quarterly*, v.8, no.1, 1961. p.50–79; *No consultation today*. Tokyo, Hara Shobo, 1964. p.8–123

Iwata kun no kuro 岩田君のクロ

'Kuro, the fighting-cock' Tr. by Yokichi Miyamoto with Frederick Will. *Chicago Review*, v.19, no.1, 1966. p.83–89

Jon Manjirō hyōryūki ジョン万次郎漂流記

John Manjiro, the cast-away; his life and adventure. Tr. by Hisakazu Kaneko. Tokyo, Hokuseido, 1940. 136p.

Jū no bangō 銃の番号

'Номер винтовки' Перевод А. Бабинцева. *Рассказ писателей Востока*. Ленинград, Лениздат, 1958. p.333–346

Kaikon mura no Yosaku 開墾村の与作

'Yosaku, the settler' Tr. by John Bester. *Lieutenant Lookeast, and other stories*. Tokyo, Kodansha International, 1971; London, Secker and Warburg, 1971. p.113–129

Kakitsubata カキツバタ

'The crazy iris' Tr. by Ivan Morris. *Encounter*, v.6, no.5, 1956. p.92–93
'Irys' Przeł. Anna Gostyńska. *Irys, opowiadania japońskie*. Warszawa, Państwowy Instytut Wydawniczy, 1960. p.152–178

Kan'ya 寒夜

'A cold night' Tr. by George Saito. *Japan P.E.N.*

News, no.18, March 1966. p.1–6

Kappa sōdō 河童騒動

'Catching a Kappa, or water imp' Tr. by Kiyoaki Nakao. *Two stories by Masuji Ibuse*. Tokyo, Hokuseido, 1970. p.4–28

Koi 鯉

'Carp' Tr. by John Bester. *Lieutenant Lookeast, and other stories*. Tokyo, Kodansha International, 1971; London, Secker and Warburg, 1971. p.91–95
'잉어' 韓榮珣訳 「世界短篇文学全集 9」 서울 三珍社 1971. p.204–206; 「世界代表短篇文学全集 9」 서울 三熙社 1976. p.204–207; 「世界短篇文学全集 9」 서울 新韓出版社 1976. p.340–349
'鯉' 「文鳥・夢十夜」 英紹唐編 n.p. p.70–80

Kuroi ame 黒い雨

'Black rain' Tr. by John Bester. *Japan Quarterly*, v.14, no.2–4, 1967; v.15, no.1–3, 1968.
Black rain. Tr. by John Bester. Tokyo, Kodansha International, 1969; London, Secker and Warburg, 1971. 300p.
Czarny deszcz. Przeł. Mikołaj Melanowicz. Warszawa, Książka i Wiedza, 1971. 330p.
Schwarzer Regen. Übers. aus dem Engl. von Brandstädter. Berlin, Aufbau Verlag, 1974. 378p.

Noheji no Mutsugorō ryakuden 野辺地の睦五郎略伝

'The life of Mutsugoro of Noheji' Tr. by Kiyoaki Nakao. *Two stories by Masuji Ibuse*. Tokyo, Hokuseido, 1970. p.32–72

Noriai jidōsha 乗合自動車

'Autobus' Przeł. Anna Gostyńska. *Irys, opowiadania japońskie*. Warszawa, Państwowy Instytut Wydawniczy, 1960. p.137–151
'The charcoal bus' Tr. by Ivan Morris. *Modern Japanese stories*, ed. by I. Morris. London, Spottiswoode, 1961; Tokyo, Tuttle, 1962. p.212–222
'Bas arang' Děngan kata pěngantar oleh James Kirkup. *Shoji*. Kuala Lumpur, Oxford Univ. Press, 1961. p.23–36
'Автобус' Перевод О. Войнюш. *No.36, новеллы японских писателей*. Москва, Наука, 1968. p.21–30

Nyonin raihō 女人来訪

'Besuch einer Frau' Übers. von Oscar Benl. *Der Kirschblütenzweig*. München, Nymphenburger, 1965. p.401–421

Sanshōuo 山椒魚

'The salamander' Tr. by Tadao Katayama. *The Reeds*, v.2, 1956. p.51–64
'The salamander' Tr. by Leon Zolbrod. *The East*, v.1, no.2, 1964. p.21–23
'La salamandra' Tr. di Atsuko Ricca Suga. *Narratori giapponesi moderni*. Milano, Bompiani, 1965. p.329–338
'Salamandra' Tr. de Antônio Nojiri. *Maravilhas do conto japonês*. São Paulo, Editóra Cultrix, 1962. p.110–116
'Salamandro' Tr. Hideo Jamanaka. *El japana literaturo*. Tokyo, Japana Esperanto Instituto, 1965. p.56–62
'Salamander' Tr. by Sadamichi Yokoo and San-

ford Goldstein. *Japan Quarterly*, v.13, no.1, 1966. p.71–75
'Salamander' Tr. by John Bester. *Lieutenant Lookeast, and other stories*. Tokyo, Kodansha International, 1971; London, Secker and Warburg, 1971. p.59–65
'A szalamandra' Ford. Jamaji Masanori & Apor Éva. *Égtájak*. Budapest, Európa, 1977. p.136–141
'Plasunsho' Tr. Marasri Saengnikorn. *Rueng sun yeepun 1*. Bangkok, Uksornsasna, 1977. p.194–206

Shiraga 白毛

'Bílé vlasy' Přel. A. Líman. *Nový Orient*, v.19, no.5, 1964.

Tajinko mura 多甚古村

'Tagebuch eines Dorfpolizisten' Übers. von Oscar Benl. *Eine Glocke in Fukagawa, und andere japanische Erzählungen*. Tübingen, Erdmann, 1964. p.49–113
'Tajinko village' Tr. by John Bester. *Lieutenant Lookeast, and other stories*. Tokyo, Kodansha International, 1971; London, Secker and Warburg, 1971. p.135–247

Tange shi tei 丹下氏邸

'At Mr. Tange's' Tr. by Sadamichi Yokoo and Sanford Goldstein. *Literature East and West*, v.13, no.1–2, 1969. p.167–181
'Life at Mr. Tange's' Tr. by John Bester. *Lieutenant Lookeast, and other stories*. Tokyo, Kodansha International, 1971; London, Secker and Warburg, 1971. p.97–111

Urashima Tarō 浦島太郎

'Urashima Taro' *Nippon*, Band 3, 1933. p.45–48

Ushitora jiisan 丑寅爺さん

'Old Ushitora' Tr. by John Bester. *Lieutenant Lookeast, and other stories*. Tokyo, Kodansha International, 1971; London, Secker and Warburg, 1971. p.67–89

Warui nakama 悪い仲間

'頑童' 「日本作家十二人集」 香港 新學書店 1959. p.185–195
'頑童' 高汝鴻訳 「日本短篇小説集」 台北 台湾商務印書館 1969. p.233–246

Yane no ue no sawan 屋根の上のサワン

'Schwan auf dem Dache' Übers. von Oscar Benl. *Flüchtiges Leben, moderne japanische Erzählungen*. Berlin, Landsmann, 1942.
'Sawan on the roof' Tr. by Yokichi Miyamoto with Frederic Will. *Chicago Review*, v.19, no.1, 1966. p.51–54
'Sawan on the rooftop' Tr. by Tadao Katayama. *The Reeds*, v.11, 1967. p.127–134
'Savan on the roof' Tr. by John Bester. *Lieutenant Lookeast, and other stories*. Tokyo, Kodansha International, 1971; London, Secker and Warburg, 1971. p.129–134

Yofuke to ume no hana 夜ふけと梅の花

'Plum blossom by night' Tr. by John Bester.

IBUSE Masuji

Lieutenant Lookeast, and other stories. Tokyo, Kodansha International, 1971; London, Secker and Warburg, 1971. p.11–22

Yōhai taichō 遙拝隊長

'A far-worshipping commander' Tr. by Glenn Shaw. *Japan Quarterly*, v.1, no.1, 1954. p.53–73; *No consultation today.* Tokyo, Hara Shobo, 1964. p.126–213
'遙拝队長' 刘仲平訳 「譯文」 1957年6月 p.112–133
'Верноподданный командир' Перевод Г. Иммерман. *Японская новелла.* Москва, Изд. Иност. Лит. 1961. p.60–76
'Кулдыкшыл командир' Аударган Е. Сатыбалдиев. *Жапон енгимелери.* Алма-Ата, Жазушы, 1965. p.3–21
'The far-worshiping commander' Tr. by Glenn Shaw. *The shadow of sunrise*, ed. by Shoichi Saeki. Tokyo, Kodansha International, 1966; London, Ward Lock, 1966. p.157–186
'遙拝隊長' 李相魯訳 「日本代表作家百人集 3」 서울 希望出版社 1966. p.82–101; 「日本短篇文学全集 3」 서울 新太陽社 1969. p.230–249
'Lieutenant Lookeast' Tr. by John Bester. *Lieutenant Lookeast, and other stories.* Tokyo, Kodansha International, 1971; London, Secker and Warburg, 1971. p.23–51
'Dowódca' Przeł. Mikołaj Melanowicz. *Cień wschodzącego słońca.* Warszawa, Książka i Wiedza, 1972.
'Ehrerbietung aus der Ferne' Deutsch von Jürgen Berndt. *Träume aus zehn Nächten.* Berlin, Aufbau Verlag, 1975. p.444–475

Poems 詩

'Die Lawine' Übers. von Kuniyo Takayasu und Manfred Hausmann. *Ruf der Regenpfeifer.* München, Bechtle Verlag, 1961. p.91

Essay エッセイ

'아가씨' 金賢珠訳 「바이바이바다」 서울 三韓出版社 1966. p.209–212

'Landschaftsschildern in den Bergen' Übers. von Kurt Meissner. *Der Tanzfächer*, von K. Meissner. Tokyo, 1943. p.1–16

ICHIKO Teiji 市古貞次 1911–

Criticism 評論

'A study of medieval stories' *Japan Science Review, literature, philosophy and history*, no.8, 1957. p.12–15
'History of literary studies' *Le Japon au XIᵉ Congrès International des Sciences Historiques à Stockholm.* Tokyo, Nippon Gakujutsu Shinkokai, 1960. p.91–99
'Otogi and literature' *Acta Asiatica*, no.4, 1963. p.32–42

ICHINOSE Ichiya 市之瀬いちや

Haiku 俳句

'1 haiku' Übers. von Gerolf Coudenhove. *Japa-*

nische Jahreszeiten. Zürich, Manesse Verlag, 1963. p.135

IENAGA Saburō 家永三郎 1913–

Nihon bunka shi 日本文化史

История японской культуры. Перевод Б. В. Поспелова. Москва, Прогресс, 1972. 228p.

IGARASHI Chikara 五十嵐 力 1874–1947

Tanka 短歌

'The Myogi mountains; Rain on a spring night; The death of a beautiful goldfish' Tr. by Asataro Miyamori. *Masterpieces of Japanese poetry, ancient and modern.* Tokyo, Maruzen, 1936; Tokyo, Taiseido, 1956; N. Y. Greenwood Press, 1971. p.647–649
'Rain on a spring night' *Japanese love poems*, ed. by Jean Bennett. Garden City, Doubleday, 1976. p.12

IIDA Dakotsu 飯田蛇笏 1885–1962

Haiku 俳句

'3 haiku' Tr. by Asataro Miyamori. *Anthology of haiku, ancient and modern.* Tokyo, Maruzen, 1932. p.810–811
'Peach-blossoms' Tr. by Asataro Miyamori. *Haiku poems, ancient and modern.* Tokyo, Maruzen, 1940. p.351
'1 haiku' Tr. by Lois J. Erickson. *Songs from the land of dawn.* N. Y. Friendship Press, 1949; Freeport, Books for Libraries Press, 1968. p.69
'5 haiku' Tr. by Geoffrey Bownas and Anthony Thwaite. *Penguin book of Japanese verse.* Harmondsworth, Penguin Books, 1964. p.168–169
'9 haiku' *A history of haiku v.2*, by R. H. Blyth. Tokyo, Hokuseido, 1964. p.162–165
'2 haiku' *Anthology of modern Japanese poetry*, tr. and comp. by Edith Marcombe Shiffert and Yuki Sawa. Tokyo, Tuttle, 1972. p.166
'20 haiku' *Modern Japanese haiku, an anthology*, comp. and tr. by Makoto Ueda. Tokyo, Univ. of Tokyo Press, 1976. p.111–119
'1 haiku' Traducerea Virgil Teodorescu. *Din lirica japoneză.* Bucureşti, Editura Univers, n. d. p.155

IIDA Ryūta 飯田龍太 1920–

Haiku 俳句

'1 haiku' Tr. by Tsutomu Fukuda. *Eigo Kenkyu*, v.63, no.4, 1974. p.19

IIJIMA Kōichi 飯島耕一 1930–

Poems 詩

'모든싸움의끝' 辛東門訳 「世界戦後文学全集 9」 서울 新丘文化社 1962. p.237–238
'Il cielo altrui; Nella sabbia; Cereare' *La protesta poetica del Giappone*, a cura di Dacia Maraini e Michiko Nojiri. Roma, Officina Edizioni, 1968. p.119–121
'The end of the war to end all wars; The sky; Just once' Tr. by Harry and Lynn Guest and Shozo Kajima. *Post-war Japanese poetry*. Harmondsworth, Penguin Books, 1972. p. 124–125
'Remembering a poet named Blake; Seeing the invisible; Stranger's sky' Tr. by Thomas Fitzsimmons. *Japanese poetry now*. London, André Deutsch, 1972. p.113–119; *Japanese poetry today*. N. Y. Schocken Books, 1972. p.115–121

IKEDA Daisaku 池田大作 1928–

Kinō kyō きのうきょう

Yesterday, today and tomorrow. Tr. by Robert Epp. Santa Monica, World Tribune Press, 1973. 228p.

Ningen kakumei 人間革命

The human revolution. Tokyo, Seikyo Press, 1965–66. 2v.; Tokyo, Weatherhill, 1972–76. 3v.
La révolution humaine. Tokyo, Seikyo Presse, 1966–67. 3v.; Sceaux, Nichiren Shoshu Française, 1972–74. 5v.
Revolucão humana. Traducão de Fumio Tiba. São Paulo, Editora Brasil Seikyo, 1973. lv.
「人間革命」 陳鮑瑞訳 香港 香港佛教日蓮正宗 1974. 1冊
「人間革命 上」 韓国日蓮正宗佛教会訳 서울 鶴人社 1974. 280p.

Waga kokoro no uta わが心の詩

Songs from my heart. Tr. by Burton Watson. Tokyo, Weatherhill, 1978. 111p.

IKEDA Katsumi 池田克己 1912–1953

Poems 詩

'天津的一日' 徐和隣訳 「現代詩解説」 台北 葡萄園詩刊 社 1970. p.13–18

IKEDA Masuo 池田満寿夫 1934–

Ēgekai ni sasagu エーゲ海に捧ぐ

'에게海에바친다' 洪東菩訳 「에게海에바친다 外」 서울 世代文庫社 1977. p.5–51

IKEDA Some 池田そめ

Poems 詩

'Umeboshi' Tr. by James Kirkup and Michio Nakano. *Poetry Nippon*, no.11, 1970. p.1

IKENAGA Takeshi 池長 孟 1891–

Oran おらん

'O-Ran: a foreigner's concubine' Tr. by Yasushi Wuriu. *Info*, Sept.-Oct. 1960–May 1961 in 7 parts.

IKENOUCHI Takeshi 池内たけし 1889–1974

Haiku 俳句

'1 haiku' *A history of haiku v. 2*, by R. H. Blyth. Tokyo, Hokuseido, 1964. p.172
'Irises' Tr. by Kenneth Yasuda. *A pepper-pod.* Tokyo, Tuttle, 1976. p.101

IKENOUCHI Tomojirō 池内友次郎 1906–

Haiku 俳句

'1 haiku' Tr. by Harold Gould Henderson. *The bamboo broom.* Tokyo, Thompson, 1933; London, Kegan Paul, 1933. p.120

IKETANI Shinzaburō 池谷信三郎 1900–1933

Hashi 橋

'橋' 吶吶鷗訳 「色情文化」 上海 水沫書店 1928.

Shibai 芝居

'Make belief' Tr. by Kazuo Yamada. *Eigo Kenkyu*, v.25, no.9, 1932. p.825–827

IKOMA Shisen 生駒紫泉 1894–

Haiku 俳句

'A cucumber' Tr. by Asataro Miyamori. *Anthology of haiku, ancient and modern.* Tokyo, Maruzen, 1932. p.833; *Haiku poems, ancient and modern.* Tokyo, Maruzen, 1940. p.354

IKUSHIMA Jirō 生島治郎 1933–

Oitsumeru 追いつめる

「追」 朱佩蘭訳 台北 皇冠出版社 1968. 233p.

IKUTA Naochika 生田直親 1929–

Tsundora 凍原

「凍原」 朱佩蘭訳 嘉義 新高出版社 1968. 264p.

IKUTA Shungetsu 生田春月 1892–1930

Kanshō no haru 感傷の春

'感傷之春 選譯' 謝位鼎訳 「小説月報」 第15巻5号 1924. p.1–8

75

IKUTA Shungetsu

Poems 詩

'小悲劇；燕子' 周作人訳 「新青年」 第9巻4期 1921.
p.38–39；「陀螺」 上海 北新書局 192?.
'L'amour moderne; Les loups; Roses des champs;
Admiration du printemps; Les nuages' Tr.
par Kuni Matsuo et Steinilber-Oberlin.
Anthologie des poètes japonais contemporains.
Paris, Mercure de France, 1939. p.197–201

Criticism 評論

'現代的斯干底那維亜文學' 李達訳 「小説月報」 第12巻6
号 1921. p.1–11
'現代德奥兩國的文學' 無明訳 「小説月報」 第14巻12号
1923. p.1–10

IMAE Yoshitomo 今江祥智 1932–

Aoi Kurisumasu 青いクリスマス

'Modré vánoce' Přel. Ivan Krouský a Z. K.
Slabý. *Modré vánoce.* Praha, Albatros, 1975.

Chōcho musubi ちょうちょむすび

'Vousy na mašličku' Přel. Ivan Krouský. *Třicet
ctříbrných klíčů.* Praha, Prace, 1971. p.17–19
'Vousy na mašličku' Přel. Ivan Krouský a Z. K.
Slabý. *Vousy na mašličku.* Praha, Lidové
nakladatelství, 1973.

No no uma 野の馬

'Houpací kůň' *Modré vánoce.* Přel. Ivan Krouský
a Z. K. Slabý. Praha, Albatros, 1975.

Poketto ni ippai ポケットにいっぱい

'O moři, které se vešlo do kapsy' Přel. Ivan
Krouský. *Třicet ctříbrných klíčů.* Praha, Prace,
1971. p.13–16

IMAI Kuniko 今井邦子 1890–1948

Tanka 短歌

'Images of Kwannon; My children in sleep; Water-
birds; My younger sister's tomb' Tr. by
Asataro Miyamori. *Masterpieces of Japanese
poetry, ancient and modern.* Tokyo, Maruzen,
1936; Tokyo, Taiseido, 1956; N. Y. Greenwood Press, 1971. p.768–771

IMANAKA Fūkei 今中楓渓 1883–1963

Tanka 短歌

'On the birth of the crown prince; An elegy on
Admiral Togo; Lespedeza flowers; Lines sent
to my eldest son Goitsu' Tr. by Asataro
Miyamori. *Masterpieces of Japanese poetry,
ancient and modern.* Tokyo, Maruzen, 1936;
Tokyo, Taiseido, 1956; N. Y. Greenwood
Press, 1971. p.801–803

IMANISHI Sukeyuki 今西祐行 1923–

Mizuumi wa naze kōru みずうみはなぜこおる

The moon and the fishes. Tr. by Ann Herring. Tokyo,
Gakken, 1973. 27p.

IMOTO Nōji 伊本納技

'良夜幽情曲' 杜衡訳 「小説月報」 第19巻5号 1928.
p.607–616

INADA Kōzō 稲田耕三 1949–

Kōkō hōrōki 高校放浪記

「高校放浪記」 李素民訳 서울 立文閣 1975. 2冊：서울
端音出版社 1976. 2冊

INADA Sadao 稲田定雄 1909–

Tanka 短歌

'Пятистишия' Перевод Анатолия Мамонова. *Вкус
хризантемы.* Москва, Восточная Литература, 1976. p.41

INAGAKI Taruho 稲垣足穂 1900–1977

Ikarusu イカルス

'Icarus' Tr. by Geoffrey Bownas. *New writing in
Japan.* Harmondsworth, Penguin Books,
1972. p.27–31

INOUE Fumio 井上文雄 1800–1871

Tanka 短歌

'The devil in the mind; The summer shower; Plovers' Tr. by Asataro Miyamori. *Masterpieces
of Japanese poetry, ancient and modern.* Tokyo,
Maruzen, 1936; Tokyo, Taiseido, 1956; N. Y.
Greenwood Press, 1971. p.594–595

INOUE Hisashi 井上ひさし 1934–

Bun to fun ブンとフン

'Boon and Phoon' Tr. by Roger Pulvers. *Japan
Quarterly,* v.25, no.1, 1978. p.73–104; v.25,
no.2, 1978. p.181–211

INOUE Mitsuharu 井上光晴 1926–

Akai temari 赤い手毬

'Rote Bälle' Deutsch von Jürgen Berndt. *Träume
aus zehn Nächten.* Berlin, Aufbau Verlag,
1975. p.617–643

Ninpu tachi no ashita 妊婦たちの明日

'Tomorrow for those women' Tr. by Tsuneo Masaki. *The Reeds,* v.12, 1968. p.111–143

Yuki to parasoru 雪とパラソル

'Снег и летний зонтик' Перевод Г. Максимовой.

No.36, новеллы японских писателей. Москва, Наука, 1968. p.67–78

Criticism 評論

'Die innere Entwicklung zur "Modernisierung" bei den Schriftstellern im Alter zwischen dreissig und vierzig' *Kagami*, Band 2, Heft 3, 1963–64. p.95–107

INOUE Mitsuko 井上充子

Poems 詩

'Minerva's whispering' Tr. by K. Kitasono. *New World Writing*, no.6, 1956. p.62–63
'당신은오지않고' 崔一秀訳 「기다리고있네」 서울 韓国政経社 1966. p.49–50
'Get angry, compass' *The burning heart,* tr. and ed. by Kenneth Rexroth and Ikuko Atsumi. N. Y. Seabury Press, 1977. p.106

INOUE Tetsujirō 井上哲次郎 1855–1944

Poems 詩

'At the age of twenty-six' Tr. by Tetsuzo Okada. *Chinese and Sino-Japanese poems.* Tokyo, Seikanso, 1937. p.98–99

Criticism 評論

'日本左翼文壇之進展' 「大公報文藝副刊」 1931.

Essay エッセイ

'General Nogi and ghost stories' Tr. by Kazutomo Takahashi. *Eigo Kenkyu*, v.23, no.12, 1931. p.1142–1147

INOUE Tomoichirō 井上友一郎 1909–

Katō dōbutsu 下等動物

'下等動物' 權純萬訳 「日本代表作家百人集 4」 서울 希望出版社 1966. p.106–127; 「日本短篇文学全集 4」 서울 新太陽社 1969. p.332–353

INOUE Toshio 井上俊夫 1922–

Poems 詩

'Мы больше не солдаты-рабы' Перевод В. Н. Марковой. *Японская поэзия.* Москва, Гослитиздат, 1954. p.332–333
'Majusi emlek' Ford. Sövény Aladár. *Nagyvilág,* no.5, 1958. p.761
'Шелуха от семян репы' Перевод Е. Винокурова. *Иностранная Литература*, июнь 1964. p.156
'Солдат емее, курлбуз биз' Которгон Ж. Абдукалыков. *Хиросима кектери.* Фрунзе, Кыргызстан, 1969. p.18–19

INOUE Yasushi 井上 靖 1907–

Aru gisakka no shōgai ある偽作家の生涯

'The counterfeiter' Tr. by Leon Picon. *The counterfeiter, and other stories.* Tokyo, Tuttle, 1965; London, Prentice-Hall, 1965. p.15–69
'一个冒名画家的生涯' 唐月梅訳 「井上靖小説选」 北京 人民文学出版社 1977. p.46–97

Aru rakujitsu ある落日

'Splendid sunset' Tr. by Fuki Uramatsu. *The Yomiuri*, April 16–August 9, 1960.

Eitai kōshu no kubikazari 永泰公主の頸飾り

'泰公主的項錬' 鐘肇政訳 「戦後日本短篇小説選」 台北 台湾商務印書館 1968. p.223–244

Fūtō 風濤

'風濤' 李元燮訳 「現代世界文学全集 6」 서울 新丘文化社 1968. p.9–175; 「世界文学속의韓国 3」 서울 正韓出版社 1975. p.17–278
'風濤' 崔浩然訳 「新訳世界文学全集 48」 서울 正音社 1972. p.333–500
'風濤' 朴尚均訳 「日本文学大全集 4」 서울 東西文化院 1975. p.310–463

Hatō 波濤

「사랑」 趙一峰訳 서울 百忍社 1962. 308p.

Hira no shakunage 比良のシャクナゲ

'The azaleas of Hira' Tr. by Edward Seidensticker. *Japan Quarterly*, v.2, no.3, 1955. p.322–347; *Modern Japanese short stories.* Tokyo, Japan Publications Trading Co. 1960. p.141–177. Rev. ed. 1970. p.112–140
'La azalèe dello Hira' Tr. di Sergio Rustichelli. *Almanacco Letterario.* Milano, Bompiani, 1961. p.50–62
'La montagna Hira' Tr. di Atsuko Ricca Suga. *La montagna Hira.* Milano, Bompiani, 1964. p.183–234
'Die Azaleen von Hira' Deutsch von Monique Humbert. *Nippon.* Zürich, Diogenes, 1965. p. 427–472
'히라山의石南花' 林鐘國訳 「日本研究」 第19巻12号 1974. p.34–58
'比良山的石楠花' 唐月梅訳 「井上靖小説选」 北京 人民文学出版社 1977. p.1–45

Hyōheki 氷壁

'Icy crag' Tr. by Jukichi Suzuki. *Jiji Eigo Kenkyu*, v.22, no.4, 1967. p.22–25; v.22, no.5, 1967. p.22–27; v.22, no.6, 1967. p.22–25; v.22, no.7, 1967. p.22–26
Die Eiswand. Übers. von Oscar Benl. Frankfurt am Main, Suhrkamp, 1968. 416p.; Berlin, Volk und Welt, 1973. 421p.
「冰壁」 鐘肇政訳 高雄 三信出版社 1974. 380p.

Kakō 河口

'河口' 方春海訳 「日本文学選集 3」 서울 知文閣 1966. p.267–441; 서울 韓国読書文化院 1973. p.267–441
'河口' 申庚林訳 「日本文学大全集 4」 서울 東西文化院 1975. p.168–306

Kaze 風

'The wind' Tr. by Tsutomu Fukuda. *Eigo Kenkyu*, v.55, no.4, p.28–32; no.5, p.38–42; no.6, p.34–35, 1966.

INOUE Yasushi

Kōreru ki 凍れる樹

'凍結的樹' 江上訳 「日本名家小説選」 高雄 大舞台書苑 1976. p.203–247

Kōzui 洪水

'Flood' Tr. by John Bester. *Japan P.E.N. News*, no.4, Dec. 1959. p.1–10; *Flood*. Tokyo, Hara Shobo, 1964. p.8–75

Kurumi bayashi 胡桃林

'核桃林' 梅韜訳 「世界文学」 1962年1–2月号 p.71–97
'核桃林' 唐月梅訳 「井上靖小説选」 北京 人民文学出版社 1977. p.98–138

Mangetsu 満月

'The full moon' Tr. by Leon Picon. *The counterfeiter, and other stories*. Tokyo, Tuttle, 1965; London, Prentice-Hall, 1965. p.99–124

Michite kuru shio 満ちて来る潮

「涙渦」 施翠峯訳 台中 中央書局 1967. 517p.

Mukashi no onjin 昔の恩人

'Un vècchio debito' Tr. di Olga Ceretti Borsini. *Novelle giapponesi*. Milano, Martello, 1969. p.49–64

Obasute 姥捨

'Obasute' Tr. by Leon Picon. *The counterfeiter, and other stories*. Tokyo, Tuttle, 1965; London, Prentice-Hall, 1965. p.73–96
'弃老' 唐月梅訳 「井上靖小説选」 北京 人民文学出版社 1977. p.139–162

Oroshiya koku suimutan おろしや国酔夢譚

'Сны о России' Перевод Б. Раскина. *Иностранная Литература*, фев. 1974. p.121–163
Сны о России. Перевод Б. Раскина. Москва, Прогресс, 1977. 231p.

Rōran 樓蘭

'Lou-lan' Tr. by E. G. Seidensticker. *Japan Quarterly*, v.6, no.4, 1959. p.460–489; *Lou-lan*. Tokyo, Hara Shobo, 1964. p.8–123
'樓蘭' 劉興堯訳 「現代日本小説選」 台北 雲天出版社 1970. p 55–98
'樓蘭' 文太久訳 「世界代表文学全集 9」 서울 高麗出版社 1976. p.536–568

Ryōjū 猟銃

Das Jagdgewehr. Übers. von Oscar Benl. Frankfurt am Main, Suhrkamp, 1958. 97p.
The hunting gun. Tr. by Sadamichi Yokoo and Sanford Goldstein. Tokyo, Tuttle, 1961; London, Prentice-Hall, 1961. 74p.
'Shotgun' Tr. by George Saito. *Modern Japanese stories*, ed. by I. Morris. London, Spottiswoode, 1961; Tokyo, Tuttle, 1962. p.416–451
Le fusil de chasse. Tr. par Sadamichi Yokoo, Sanford Goldstein et Gisèle Bernier. Paris, Stock, 1961. 106p.
'A espingarda' Tr. de José Yamashiro. *Maravilhas do conto japonês*. São Paulo, Editôra Cultrix, 1962. p.200–240
'Il fucile da caccia' Tr. di Atsuko Ricca Suga. *La montagna Hira*. Milano, Bompiani, 1964. p.107–179; *Antologia della letteratura coreana e giapponese*. Milano, Fratelli Fabbri, 1969. p.327–332

Haori. Przeł. Anna Gostyńska. Warszawa, Czytelnik, 1966. 64p.
Metsästyskivääri. Kääntää Hikki Mäki. Helsinki, Weilin ja Göös, 1966. 76p.
'獵銃' 方基換訳 「日本代表作家百人集 4」 서울 希望出版社 1966. p.30–66; 「日本短篇文学全集 4」 서울 新太陽社 1969. p.256–292
Puşcă de vînătoare. În româneşte de Lia şi Platon Pardau. Bucureşti, Editura pentru Literatura Universală, 1969. 83p.
'엽총' 李圭植訳 「世界短篇文学全集 9」 서울 三珍社 1971. p.309–352; 「世界代表短篇文学全集 9」 서울 三熙社 1976. p.309–351; 「世界短篇文学全集 9」 서울 新韓出版社 1976. p.152–218
'獵銃' 朴敬勛訳 「日本文学大全集 4」 서울 東西文化院 1975. p.132–166

Saiiki monogatari 西域物語

Journey beyond Samarkand. Tr. by Gyo Furuta and Gordon Sager. Tokyo, Kodansha International, 1971. 130p.

Sōkara kuni engi 僧伽羅国縁起

'How came Ceylon to be founded?' Tr. by Yutaka Kato. *Konan Joshi Daigaku Eibungaku Kenkyu*, no.5, 1969. p.52–63

Tenpyō no iraka 天平の甍

'天平之甍 (选譯)' 楼適夷譯 「世界文学」 1963年4月 p.40–67
「天平之甍」 楼適夷訳 北京 作家出版社 1963. 85p.
The roof tile of Tempyo. Tr. by James T. Araki. Tokyo, Univ. of Tokyo Press, 1975. 140p.

Tōgyū 闘牛

'La lotta dei tori' Tr. di Atsuko Ricca Suga. *La montagna Hira*. Milano, Bompiani, 1964. p.7–104; *Narratori giapponesi moderni*. Milano, Bompiani, 1965. p.467–534
'闘牛' 劉慕沙訳 「芥川賞作品選集 1」 台北 大地出版社 1972. p.219–295
Der Stierkampf. Übers. von Oscar Benl. Frankfurt am Main, Suhrkamp, 1971. 127p.; Berlin, Volk und Welt, 1975. 128p.

Tonkō 敦煌

'悲願' 李俊凡訳 서울 新興出版社 1962. 263p.
'敦煌' 金光植訳 「오늘의世界文学 10」 서울 民衆書館 1969. p.371–520
'敦煌' 李鍾烈訳 「日本文学選集 5」 서울 知文閣 1967; 서울 韓国読書文化院 1973. p.195–366
'敦煌' 崔浩然訳 「新譯世界文学全集 48」 서울 正音社 1972. p.193–231
'敦煌' 申庚林訳 「日本文学大全集 4」 서울 東西文化社 1975. p.2–130
Tun-huang. Tr. by Jean Oda Moy. Tokyo, Kodansha International, 1978. 201p.

Wadatsumi わだつみ

'Wadatsumi' Tr. by John Bester. *The East*, v.2, no.5–6, 1966; v.3, no.2–6, 1967; v.4, no.1–6, 1968.

Yama no mizuumi 山の湖

「노을진湖水」 朴淑英訳 서울 文音社 1969. 308p.

Yōkihi den 楊貴妃伝

「楊貴妃」 朴智帥訳 서울 青山文庫 1968. 2冊; 서울 明文堂 1975. 2冊

Poems 詩

'Runoja phojoisesta maasta' Suomentanut Kai
Nieminen. *Parnasso*, 1975. p.545–546

'Пора цветения слив; Транспортный корабль'
Перевод Анатолия Мамонова. *Вкус хризантемы*. Москва, Восточная Литература, 1976.
p.42

'A friend' Tr. by Kyoko Yukawa. *Poetry Nippon*,
no.35 & 36, 1976. p.10

'On New Year's day' Tr. by Kyoko Yukawa.
Poetry Nippon, no. 37 & 38, 1977. p.22–23

'The first day of spring' Tr. by Kyoko Yukawa.
Poetry Nippon, no. 41 & 42, 1978. p.14–15

'The sea' Tr. by Kyoko Yukawa. *Poetry Nippon*,
no.43- 44, 1978. p.40

Essay エッセイ

'My thoughts on Chanoyu' *Chanoyu Quarterly*,
v.1, no.1, 1970. p.14–15

INUI Naoe 乾 直恵 1901–1958

Poems 詩

'終焉' 金龍済訳 「日本詩集」 서울 青雲社 1960.
p.154–156

INUI Tomiko いぬい・とみこ 1924–

Hokkyoku no Mushika to Mishika ほっきょくのムシ
カとミシカ

Eskymacek tajaut a medvedi. Přel. Ivan Krouský.
Praha, Albatros, 1971. 105p.

Kawa to Norio 川とノリオ

'Река и Норио' Перевод Г. Ронской. *Лети
журавлик!* Москва, Дет. Лит. 1966. p.7–18

'Reka a Norio' Přel. Ivan Krouský. *Zlaty Maj*,
no.11, 1964. p.1–8

Kokage no ie no kobito tachi 木かげの家の小人たち

Le secret du verre bleu. Tr. par Noriyasu Nakamura. Paris, F. Nathan, 1971. 192p.

Τό γαλάζιο κυπελλο. Είκουογράφηόη Patrice Har-
ispe. Athens, Kedros, 1974. 170p.

Umineko no sora うみねこの空

Песнь о чайках. Перевод А. Коломиец и И.
Кожевникова. Москва, Дет. Лит. 1968. 206p.

「小企鵝历険記」 周維権訳 北京 少年兒童 1957. 64p.

'Mésto plné hub' *Modré vánoce.* Přel. Ivan
Krouský a Z. K. Slabý. Praha, Albatros, 1975.

INUKAI Michiko 犬養道子 1921–

Ojōsan hōrōki お嬢さん放浪記

「아가씨世界放浪記」 尹相根訳 서울 法通社 1964. 274p.

Essay エッセイ

'麵包與義大利的勞働者' 東方人訳 「大學生活」 1963年
1月16日 p.39–41

INUZUKA Gyō 犬塚 堯 1924–

Poems 詩

'What was eaten at the South Pole' Tr. by Thomas
Fitzsimmons. *Japanese poetry now.* London,
André Deutsch, 1972. p.22; *Japanese poetry
today.* N. Y. Schocken Books, 1972. p.24

IOKI Hyōtei 五百木飄亭 1870–1937

Haiku 俳句

'3 haiku' Tr. by Asataro Miyamori. *Anthology
of haiku, ancient and modern.* Tokyo, Maruzen, 1932. p.743–745

'Insects; The summer shower' Tr. by Asataro
Miyamori. *Haiku poems, ancient and modern.*
Tokyo, Maruzen, 1940. p.316–317

'3 haiku' Tr. by V. H. Viglielmo. *Japanese literature in the Meiji era.* Tokyo, Obunsha, 1955.
p.427

IRIE Tamemori 入江為守 1868–1936

Tanka 短歌

'Billows' Tr. by Asataro Miyamori. *Masterpieces
of Japanese poetry, ancient and modern.* Tokyo,
Maruzen, 1936; Tokyo, Taiseido, 1956; N. Y.
Greenwood Press, 1971. p.624–625

IRIZAWA Yasuo 入沢康夫 1931–

Poems 詩

'Prima notte' *La protesta poetica del Giappone*,
a cura di Dacia Maraini e Michiko Nojiri.
Roma, Officina Edizioni, 1968. p.133

'Night' Tr. by Thomas Fitzsimmons. *Japanese
poetry now.* London, André Deutsch, 1972.
p.48; *Japanese poetry today.* N. Y. Schocken
Books, 1972. p.50

'Shining; Song two; Song five' Tr. by Harry and
Lynn Guest and Shozo Kajima. *Postwar
Japanese poetry.* Harmondsworth, Penguin
Books, 1972. p.130–132

ISHIDA Hakyō 石田波郷 1913–1969

Haiku 俳句

'2 haiku' *A history of haiku v.2,* by R. H. Blyth.
Tokyo, Hokuseido, 1964. p.244–245, 248

'3 haiku' Tr. by Geoffrey Bownas and Anthony
Thwaite. *The Penguin book of Japanese verse.*
Harmondsworth, Penguin Books, 1964. p.173

'2 haiku' *Anthology of modern Japanese poetry,*
tr. and comp. by Edith Marcombe Shiffert
and Yuki Sawa. Tokyo, Tuttle, 1972. p.173

'20 haiku' *Modern Japanese haiku, an anthology,*
comp. and tr. by Makoto Ueda. Tokyo, Univ.
of Tokyo Press, 1976. p.207–216

'1 haiku' Traducerea Virgil Teodorescu. *Din
lirica japoneză.* București, Editura Univers,
n. d. p.210

ISHIDA Shizue

ISHIDA Shizue 石田志つ枝

Tanka 短歌

'1 tanka' Tr. by Shigeshi Nishimura. *Eigo Seinen*, v.91, no.3, 1946. p.81

ISHIGAKI Rin 石垣りん 1920–

Poems 詩

'Tragedy; Nursery rhyme; Cocoon; Nameplate' Tr. by Gregory Campbell, Hajime Kijima and Takako Ayusawa. *The poetry of postwar Japan.* Iowa City, Univ. of Iowa Press, 1975. p.56–59

'Shellfish; Walking-with-a-cane-pass' *The burning heart,* tr. and ed. by Kenneth Rexroth and Ikuko Atsumi. N. Y. Seabury Press, 1977. p.96–98

ISHIGURO Mitsuko 石黒みつ子

Tanka 短歌

'1 tanka' Tr. by Shigeshi Nishimura. *Eigo Seinen*, v.92, no.3, 1946. p.81

ISHIHAMA Tomoyuki 石浜知行 1895–1950

Criticism 評論

'日本無産階級作家論' 胡行之訳 「北新半月刊」 第4巻6期 1928.

'機械與藝術' 汪馥泉訳 「現代文學」 第1巻3期 1930.

'機械和藝術' 森堡訳 「當代文藝」 第2巻3期 1931. p.457–467

'女性社會史考' 方天白訳 「讀書雜誌」 第1巻3期 1931. p.1–25

'經済與文藝' 高明訳 「微音」 第2巻3・4期 1932.

ISHIHARA Shintarō 石原慎太郎 1932–

Daimei no nai barādo 題名のないバラード

'Ballata senza nome' Tr. di Ester Maimeri. *Novelle giapponesi.* Milano, Martello, 1969. p.77–108

'Ambush' Tr. by Noah S. Brannen and William I. Elliott. *New writing in Japan.* Harmondsworth, Penguin Books, 1972. p.133–151

'Lying in wait' Tr. by Noah S. Brannen and William I. Elliott. *Listening to Japan,* ed. by Jackson H. Bailey. N. Y. Praeger, 1973. p.68–82

Gesshoku 月蝕

「月蝕」 崔壯圭訳 서울 太白社 1961. 230p.

Ikari no zō 怒りの像

「怒吼的畫像」 朱佩蘭訳 嘉義 明山書局 1969. 338p.

Kamo 鴨

'Kacsák' Ford. Hani Kjoko és Holti Mária.

Nagyvilág, no.6, 1964. p.822–840

'Vadkacsák' Ford. Sz. Holti Mária. *Modern Japán elbeszélők.* Budapest, Európa Könyvkiadó, 1967. p.489–524

Kanzen na yūgi 完全な遊戯

'完全한遊戯' 申東漢訳 「日本代表作家百人集 5」 서울 希望出版社 1966. p.358–377; 「日本短篇文学全集 6」 서울 新太陽社 1969. p.270–289

'完全한遊戯' 李元秀訳 「日本新鋭文学作家受賞作品選集 4」 서울 靑雲社 1964. p.87–108; 「戦後日本短篇文学全集 4」 서울 日光出版社 1965. p.87–108; 「現代日本代表文学全集 4」 서울 平和出版社 1973. p.87–107

'完全한遊戯' 宋赫訳 「日本文学大全集 10」 서울 東西文化院 1975. p.341–360

Kuroi mizu 黒い水

'검은潮流' 閔丙山訳 「日本研究」 第19巻12号 1974. p.98–113

Otoko dake 男だけ

'Men without women' Tr. by Kohji Ōi. *The Reeds,* v.6, 1960. p.85–96

'清一色的男人' 傅寶齡訳 「勲章」 台北 文壇社 1960. p.189–197

Seishun no kate 青春のかて

「歓喜」 李承雨訳 서울 惠明出版社 1967. 2冊

「歓喜」 姜慧妍訳 서울 韓一出版社 1967. 336p.

Seishun no ki 青春の樹

「젊음은불꽃처럼」 李承雨訳 서울 合同出版社 1962. 293p.

Seishun towa nanda 青春とはなんだ

「青春頌」 施翠峯訳 台北 青文出版社 1968. 557p.

「푸른教室」 安東民訳 서울 東民文化社 1971. 437p.

Shokei no heya 処刑の部屋

'La chambre de tortures' Tr. par Kuni Matsuo. *La saison du soleil.* Paris, Juillard, 1958. p.99–154

'處刑室' 李元秀訳 「日本新鋭文学作家受賞作品集 4」 서울 靑雲社 1964. p.44–85; 「戦後日本短篇文学全集 4」 서울 日光出版社 1965. p.44–86; 「現代日本代表文学全集 4」 서울 平和出版社 1973. p.87–107

'The punishment room' Tr. by John G. Mills, Toshie Takahama, and Ken Tremayne. *Season of violence.* Tokyo, Tuttle, 1966; London, Prentice-Hall, 1966. p.61–107

Suparuta kyōiku スパルタ教育

「斯巴達教育」 蘇錫淇訳 台北 水牛出版社 1972. 243p.

Taiyō no kisetsu 太陽の季節

'La saison du soleil' Tr. par Kuni Matsuo. *La saison du soleil.* Paris, Juillard, 1958. p.35–98

'太陽의季節' 哲理文化社編輯部訳 「芥川賞受賞作品集」 서울 哲理文化社 1960. p.7–75

「太陽의季節」 榮文社編集部訳 서울 榮文社 1960. 72p.

'太陽의季節' 千世旭訳 「太陽의季節」 서울 科学社 1960.

'太陽의季節' 辛東門訳 「世界戦後文学全集 7」 新丘文化社 1962. p.49–79; 「世界代表短篇文学全集 21」 서울 正韓出版社 1976. p.299–325

'太陽의季節' 李元秀訳 「日本新鋭文学作家受賞作品集 4」 서울 靑雲社 1964. p.3–42; 「戦後日本短篇文学全集 4」 서울 日光出版社 1965. p.3–43; 「現代日本代表文学全集 4」 서울 平和出版社 1973. p.3–41

'Season of violence' Tr. by John G. Mills, Toshie Takahama and Ken Tremayne. *Season of violence*. Tokyo, Tuttle, 1966; London, Prentice-Hall, 1966. p.13–57
「太陽의季節」李圭楨訳 「世界短篇文学全集 9」 서울 三珍社 1971. p.369–421; 「世界代表短篇文学全集 9」 서울 三珍社 1976. p.396–412; 「世界短篇文学全集 9」 서울 新韓出版社 1976. p.248–316
「太陽的季節」 葉笛訳 高雄 大業書店 1967. 1冊
「太陽의季節」 李圭楨訳 서울 経林出版社 1975. 193p.

Tamashii o ueru kyōiku 魂を植える教育

「培養靈性的教育」 蘇錫淇訳 台北 開山書店 1973. 212p.

Yogoreta yoru 汚れた夜

「阱陷的夜」 方圓客訳 台北 交通出版社 1963. 2冊

Yokubō no kaikyō 欲望の海峡

「어느사랑의이야기」 尹素姫訳 서울 漢陽出版社 1971. 336p.

Yotto to shōnen ヨットと少年

'Le yacht et jeune homme' Tr. par Kuni Matsuo. *La saison du soleil*. Paris, Juillard, 1958. p.155–209
'The yacht and the boy' Tr. by John G. Mills, Toshie Takahama and Ken Tremayne. *Season of violence*. Tokyo, Tuttle, 1966; London, Prentice-Hall, 1966. p.111–153

Essays エッセイ

'Lament for the samisen' *This is Japan*, v.11, 1964. p.77–79
'갓고싶은청춘기념비' 金賢珠訳 「바이바이바디」 서울 三韓出版社 1966. p.29–30
'潜意識的自我醒讓' 余阿勳訳 「純文學」(台灣版) 第2巻 3号 1967. p.56–57
「人生的陶冶」 鄭端容 林秀地訳 台北 新太出版部 1974. 290p.

「이것이戀愛다」 李俊凡訳 서울 白文社 1962. 220p.

ISHIHARA Yoshirō 石原吉郎 1915–1977

Poems 詩

'Funeral train; That morning in Samarkand' Tr. by Harry and Lynn Guest and Shozo Kajima. *Post-war Japanese poetry*. Harmondsworth, Penguin Books, 1972. p.45–48
'Horse and riot; Commerce in the Caucasus: a retribution; The last enemy; Sancho Panza's homecoming; Song of the ringing in the ear; Mist and town; The sniper; You heard him say lonely, now; Nights' invitation' Tr. by Hiroaki Sato. *Ten Japanese poets*. Hanover, N.H. Granite Publications, 1973. p.80–91
'Beasts in Siberia; The wind and the marriage; Funeral train; The greeting of the tree; Though Demetriarde died at the prison of Baikal in 1950' Tr. by Shigenori Nagatomo. *The poetry of postwar Japan*. Iowa City, Univ. of Iowa Press, 1975. p.26–32
'Funeral train; Facts' Tr. by Akiko Matsumura. *Japan Christian Quarterly*, v.41, no.4, 1975. p.231–233

ISHII Kenkichi 石井憲吉

Poems 詩

'Младшие братья' Перевод Анатолия Мамонова. *Вкус хризантемы*. Москва, Восточная Литература, 1976. p.43

ISHII Momoko 石井桃子 1907–

Issun bōshi いっすんぼうし

Issun boshi, the inchling. Retold by Momoko Ishii. Tr. by Yone Mizuta. N. Y. Walker, 1967. 1v.

Kaeru no ie sagashi かえるのいえさがし

'Jak žáby přezimovaly' *Modré vánoce*. Přel. Ivan Krouský a Z. K. Slabý. Praha, Albatros, 1975.

Nonchan kumo ni noru ノンちゃんくもにのる

Nobbi, Erlebnisse einer kleinen Japanerin. Übers. von Aenne Sano Gerber. Reutlingen, Ensslin und Laiblin, 1956. 207p.
「阿信坐在云彩上」 梅韜訳 北京 少年兒童 1958. 101p.

Sangatsu hina no tsuki 三月ひなのつき

The dolls' day for Yoshiko. Tr. by Yone Mizuta. London, Oxford Univ. Press, 1965. 64p.
The doll's day. Tr. by Yone Mizuta. Chicago, Follett, 1966. 94p.

'Jak mraveneček nesl jahodu' *Modré vánoce*. Přel. Ivan Krouský a Z. K. Slabý. Praha, Albatros, 1975.

ISHII Rogetsu 石井露月 1873–1928

Haiku 俳句

'The bandit's wife; The cricket' Tr. by Asataro Miyamori. *Anthology of haiku, ancient and modern*. Tokyo, Maruzen, 1932. p.700–701
'The outlaw's wife; The cricket' Tr. by Asataro Miyamori. *Haiku poems, ancient and modern*. Tokyo, Maruzen, 1940. p.321–322
'3 haiku' Tr. by V. H. Viglielmo. *Japanese literature in the Meiji era*. Tokyo, Obunsha, 1955. p.431
'1 haiku' Tr. by Peter Beilenson and Harry Behn. *Haiku harvest*. Mount Vernon, Peter Pauper Press, 1962. p.58
'1 haiku' *A history of haiku v.2*, by R. H. Blyth. Tokyo, Hokuseido, 1964. p.150–151
'1 haiku' Übers. von Erwin Jahn. *Fallende Blüten*. Zürich, Arche, 1968. p.60

ISHII Yutaka 石井ゆたか 1940–

Poems 詩

'Forest' Tr. by Harry and Lynn Guest and Shozo Kajima. *Post-war Japanese poetry*. Harmondsworth, Penguin Books, 1972. p.162

ISHIJIMA Kijirō　石島雉子郎　1887–1941

Haiku　俳句

'3 haiku' Tr. by Asataro Miyamori. *Anthology of haiku, ancient and modern.* Tokyo, Maruzen, 1932. p.817–819
'Chain-mail' Tr. by Harold Stewart. *A net of fireflies.* Tokyo, Tuttle, 1960. p.76
'1 haiku' Übers. von Günther Debon. *Im Schnee die Fähre.* München, Piper, 1960. p.48
'Cercuri în apă; Ciinele uriaş; Zmeul' Traducerea Dan Constantinescu. *Din lirica japoneză.* Bucureşti, Editura Univers, n.d. p.156

ISHIKAWA Itsuko　石川逸子　1933–

Poems　詩

'Перед императорским дворцом' Перевод Е. Винокурова. *Иностранная Литература,* июнь 1964. p.155–156
'Bird' *Asian P.E.N. anthology,* ed. by F. Sionil Jose. N. Y. Taplinger, 1966. p.324

ISHIKAWA Jun　石川　淳　1899–

Shion monogatari　紫苑物語

'Asters' Tr. by Donald Keene. *Three modern Japanese short novels.* N. Y. Viking Press, 1961. p.119–172
'La storia delle settembrine' Tr. di Atsuko Ricca Suga. *Narratori giapponesi moderni.* Milano, Bompiani, 1965. p.647–698

ISHIKAWA Kin'ichi　石川欣一　1895–1959

Essays　エッセイ

'The home town of Bobbin Burns' Tr. by Kazuo Yamada. *Eigo Seinen,*v.110, no.4, 1964. p.218–220; v.110, no.6, 1964. p.436–438
'Carlyle's house' Tr. by Kazuo Yamada. *Eigo Seinen,* v.112, no.5, 1966. p.284–287

ISHIKAWA Sanshirō　石川三四郎　1876–1956

Criticism　評論

'土民藝術論' 毛一波訳 「新時代」 第1巻3期 192?.

ISHIKAWA Takuboku　石川啄木　1886–1912

Futasuji no chi　二筋の血

'兩條的血痕' 周作人訳 「東方雜誌」 第19巻15期 1922. p.103–118
'兩條血痕' 周作人訳 「近代日本小説集」 上海　商務印書館 192?.; 「兩条血痕」 上海　開明書店 192?.

Ichiaku no suna　一握の砂

A handful of sand. Tr. by Shio Sakanishi. Boston, Marshall Jones, 1934. 93p.; Tokyo, Dokusho Tenbosha, 1947. 113p.
'Из книги «Горсть песка»' Перевод Веры Марковой. *Исикава Такубоку, стихи.* Москва, Гослитиздат, 1957. p.7–181; *Исикава Такубоку, избранная лирика.* Москва, Молодая Гвардия, 1971. p.9–56
'歌集「한줌의모래」에서' 金龍済訳 「石川啄木歌集」 서울　新太陽社 1960. p.83–155
'Handful of sand' Tr. by Carl Sesar. *Takuboku, poems to eat.* Tokyo, Kodansha International, 1966; London, Ward Lock, 1966. p.25–87
'Гросгь песка' Перевод Веры Марковой. *Исикава Такубоку, лирика.* Москва, Худож. Лит. 1966. p.25–148
'한줌의모래' 呉英珍訳 「石川啄木歌集」 서울　壯文社 1976. p.5–152

Kanashiki gangu　悲しき玩具

'Из книги «Грустная игрушка»' Перевод Веры Марковой. *Исикава Такубоку, стихи.* Москва, Гослитиздат, 1957. p.185–222; *Исикава Такубоку, избранная лирика.* Москва, Молодая Гвардия, 1971. p.57–76
'歌集「슬픈장난감」에서' 金龍済訳 「石川啄木歌集」 서울　新太陽社 1960. p.217–256
A sad toy. Tr. by Hiroshi Takamine. Tokyo, Tokyo News Service, 1962. 154p.
'Sad toy' Tr. by Carl Sesar. *Takuboku, poems to eat.* Tokyo, Kodansha International, 1966; London, Ward Lock, 1966. p.89–131
'Грустная игрушка' Перевод Веры Марковой. *Исикава Такубоку, лирика.* Москва, Худож. Лит. 1966. p.151–172
'슬픈장난감' 呉英珍訳 「石川啄木歌集」 서울　壯文社 1976. p.157–212

Michi　みち

'길' 張壽哲訳 「日本代表作家百人集 1」 서울　希望出版社 1966. p.148–170; 「日本短篇文学全集 1」 서울　新太陽社 1969. p.148–170

Okeya no Shinta　桶屋の新太

'The cooper's son' Tr. by S. G. Brickley. *The writing of idiomatic English.* Tokyo, Kenkyusha, 1951. p.24–32

Rōmaji nikki　ローマ字日記

'The romaji diary' Tr. by Donald Keene. *Modern Japanese literature,* ed. by D. Keene. N. Y. Grove Press, 1956; Tokyo, Tuttle, 1957. p.211–231
'El diario romaji' Tr. por Carla Viola Soto. *Sur,* no. 249, Nov.-Dec. 1957. p.12–18
Diario in alfabeto latino. Tr. di Mario Teti. Milano, Il Saggiatore, 1957. 1v.
'Diario in alfabeto latino' Tr. di M. Teti. *Antologia della letteratura coreana e giapponese.* Milano, Fratelli Fabbri, 1969. p.265–270

Warera no ichidan to kare　我等の一団と彼

'我們的一團與他' 畫室訳 上海　光華書局 193?.
「我們的一伙和他」 叔昌訳 北京　人民文学出版社 1962. 36p.

Tanka and poems　短歌・詩

'無結果的議論之後；科科的一瓢；激論；舊的提包；飛機' 周作人訳 「新青年」 第9巻4期 1921. p.29–31; 「陀螺」 上海　北新書局 193?.
'四篇短歌' 周作人訳 「小説月報」 第14巻1号 1923. p.6

'2 tanka' Tr. by A. Naito. *La Semeuse* (Tokyo), Année 1, no.4, 1925. p.5–6

「石川啄木底歌」汪馥泉訳「小説月報」第16巻1号 1925. p.11–12

'墓碑名' S.F. 訳「奔原」第2巻2期 1927. p.806–809

'1 tanka' Tr. by Yu Tezuka. *Eigo Seinen*, v.59, no.5, 1928. p.169

'2 waka' Tr. by I. U. Verda. *Parnaso*. Tokyo, Japana Esperanto Instituto, 1932. p.84

'끝없는討論한귀' 金相回訳「新東亜」第2巻2号 1932. p.100

'2 tanka' Tr. par Georges Bonneau. *Rythmes japonais*. Paris, Geuthner, 1933. p.46–47; *La sensibilité japonaise*. Tokyo, Maison Franco-Japonaise, 1934. p.351–353

'Mais moi, sous chaque jour. . .; Dune; Symbole; Le fil coupé; Traces; Falaise; L'enfant prodigue; Paroles; Homme libre toujours. . .; Jeu; Le crabe; Flûte; Pauvreté; Pleureuse; Le chemin vers la mer' Tr. par Georges Bonneau. *Lyrisme du temps présent*, par G. Bonneau. Paris, Geuthner, 1935. p.22–33; *Anthologie de la poésie japonaise*. Paris, Geuthner, 1935, p.118–129

'13 tanka' Tr. by Asataro Miyamori. *Masterpieces of Japanese poetry, ancient and modern*. Tokyo, Maruzen, 1936; Tokyo, Taiseido, 1956; N. Y. Greenwood Press, 1971. p.730–737

'Всеки гень; Дюна; Симбол; Звесдите гаснат; Далече от херага; Свободен и винаги сам; Флейта; В срдцето ми' Преведе от франц. Никола Джеров. *Песните на Ямато*. София, Корали, 1937. p.58–60

Takuboku no uta. Übers. von Hiroshi Sakurai. Morioka, 1937. 1v.

'On the hill-top' Tr. by Shigeshi Nishimura. *The Current of the World*, v.15, no.5, 1938. p.100–101

'The white bird and the sea of blood' Tr. by Saburo Katayama. *English Aoyama*, 1938.

'4 shintaishi et 8 tanka' Tr. par Kuni Matsuo et Steinilber-Oberlin. *Anthologie des poetes japonais contemporains*. Paris, Mercure de France, 1939. p.98–107

'啄木短歌二十一首' 周作人訳「陀螺」上海 北新書局 193?.

'Traces; Homme libre toujours; Jeu; Le crabe' *Histoire de la littérature japonaise contemporaine*, par Georges Bonneau. Paris, Payot, 1940. p.238

'3 tanka' Tr. by Kenneth Yasuda. *Lacquer box*. Tokyo, 1952. p.105–106

'1 waka' Suomentanut G. J. Ramstedt. *Japanilaisia runoja*. Helsinki, Werner Söderström, 1953. p.24

'Памяти адмирала Макарова; 49 танка; После бесконечных споров; Надгробная надпись' Перевод А. Е. Глускиной и В. Н. Марковой. *Японская поэзия*. Москва, Гослитиздат, 1954. p.234–290

'The poetry of Takuboku' Tr. by H. H. Honda. *The Reeds*, v.1, 1955. p.36–43

'Das Herz meiner Jugend; Leben; Das arme Kind; Liebe; Sand; Soldaten; Glück' Übers. von Günther Debon. *Im Schnee die Fähre*. München, Piper, 1955. p.39–50

'7 tanka' Tr. by V. H. Viglielmo. *Japanese literature in the Meiji era*. Tokyo, Obunsha, 1955. p.405–407

'1 tanka et 2 poèms' Tr. par Roger Bersihand. *La littérature japonaise*. Paris, Presses Universitaires de France, 1956. p.115

'6 tanka' Tr. by H. H. Honda. *The Reeds*, v.3, 1957. p.15, 21, 22

'Wake not; A fist; Eleven waka poems' Tr. by Shio Sakanishi. *Modern Japanese literature*, ed. by D. Keene. N. Y. Grove Press, 1956; Tokyo, Tuttle, 1957. p.203–204, 207–209

'3 tanka' Tr. by Kenneth Rexroth. *In defense of the earth*. N. Y. New Directions, 1956. p.86

'Édesanyám; Sárkany; Tékozló fiu' *Kinai és Japan költök*. Budapest, 1957. p.210–211

'An old man; A clenched fist; Better than crying' *An anthology of modern Japanese poetry*, ed. and tr. by Ichiro Kono and Rikutaro Fukuda. Tokyo, Kenkyusha, 1957. p.31–33

'Un puño' *Sur*, no.249, Nov.-Dec. 1957. p.31–33

'Стихи из разных книг' Перевод Веры Марковой. *Исикава Такубоку, стихи*. Москва, Гослитиздат, 1957. p.225–245

'A paraszt' Ford. Sövény Aladár. *Nagyvilág*, no.5, 1958. p.701

'4 tanka' Kääntää Marta Keravuori. *Kirnikankukkia*. Helsinki, Werner Söderström, 1958. p.65–66

The poetry of Ishikawa Takuboku. Tr. by H. H. Honda. Tokyo, Hokuseido, 1959. 100p.

'Le poing; Découragement; Précieux fardeau' *La poésie japonaise*, par Karl Petit. Paris, Seghers, 1959. p.189–190

'Ein heller Nachmittag' Übertragen von Shin Aizu. *Der schwermütige Ladekran*. St. Gallen, Tschudy Verlag, 1960. p.24

「石川啄木歌集」金龍済訳編 서울 新太陽社 1960. 1冊

'3 tanka' Übers. von Kuniyo Takayasu und Manfred Hausmann. *Ruf der Regenpfeifer*. München, Bechtle Verlag, 1961. p.99

'İhtiyar adamin biri' Tercüme etmek L. Sami Akalin. *Japon şiiri* İstanbul, Varlik Yayinevi, 1962. p.241–242

「石川啄木詩歌集」周啓明 卞立強訳 北京 人民文学出版社 1962. 138p.

'2 tanka' Übers. von Gerolf Coudenhove. *Japanische Jahreszeiten*. Zürich, Manesse Verlag, 1963. p.181, 182

'13 tanka; After a fruitless argument; Rather than cry' Tr. by Geoffrey Bownas and Anthony Thwaite. *The Penguin book of Japanese verse*. Harmondsworth, Penguin Books, 1964. p.161–163, 182–183

'1 tanka' *Modern Japanese poetry*, by Donald Keene. Ann Arbor, Center for Japanese Studies, Univ. of Michigan, 1964. p.35

'2 poems and 2 tanka' Tr. from the French by Unity Evans. *Japanese literature*. N. Y. Walker, 1965. p.98

'Soldaten' *Lyrik des Ostens*, hrg. von Wilhelm Gundert. München, Hanser, 1965. p.473

'Other poems' Tr. by Carl Sesar. *Takuboku, poems to eat*. Tokyo, Kodansha International, 1966; London, Ward Lock, 1966. p.133–159

'Мураедегу жазуу; Адмирал Макаровдун встелигине' Которгон С. Фмурбаев. *Хиросима кектери*. Фрунзе, Кыргызстан, 1969. p.11–17

Танка, на грузинском языке. Тбилиси, Накадули, 1970. 124p.

'한줌의모래; 사향' 「永遠한世界名詩全集 2」黄錦燦編 서울 翰林出版社 1969. p.25; 「永遠한世界名詩全集 5」黄錦燦編 서울 翰林出版社 p.25

'Стихи из разных книг и стихи, не вошедшие в сборники' Перевод В. Марковой. *Исикава Такубоку, избранная лирика*. Москва, Молодая Гвардия, 1971. p.77–78

'2 tanka' Tr. by Donald Keene. *Landscapes and portraits*. Tokyo, Kodansha International, 1971. p.153, 165

ISHIKAWA Takuboku

'24 tanka' Przeł. Andrzej Novák. *Przegląd Orientalistyczny*, no.2, 1972. p.142, 164–167
'1 tanka' Tr. by Tsutomu Fukuda. *Eigo Kenkyu*, v.63, no.4, 1974. p.19
'3 haiku' Tr. by Carl Sesar. *Japanese love poems*, ed. by Jean Bennett. Garden City, Doubleday, 1976. p.51, 62
'1 tanka' *Japanese love poems*, ed. by Jean Bennett. Garden City, Doubleday, 1976. p.92

「石川啄木小説集」 豊子愷等訳 北京 人民文学出版社 1958. 252p.

ISHIKAWA Tatsuzō 石川達三 1905–

Akujo no shuki 悪女の手記

「悪女의手記」 崔林訳 서울 受験社 1963. 209p.
「悪女의手記」 安炳燮訳 서울 尚志文化社 1974. 209p.

Aku no tanoshisa 悪の愉しさ

Evil for pleasure. Tr. by Paul T. Konya. Tokyo, Yohan Publications, 1972. 356p.

Aoiro kakumei 青色革命

「青色革命」 李環薫訳 서울 普成社 1963. 272p.

Bokutachi no shippai 僕たちの失敗

「나와나의失敗」 呉東燁訳 서울 極東出版社 1965. 375p.

Doro ni mamirete 泥にまみれて

「女子가幸福할때」 洪英姫訳 서울 三育出版社 1971. 186p.
'婦道' 張文平訳 「日本文学大全集 3」 서울 東西文化院 1975. p.236–324

Ikiteiru heitai 生きてゐる兵隊

Vivantaj soldatoj. Tr. Teru Hasegaua. Chungching, Heroldo de Ĉinio, 1941. 144p.; Tokyo, Esperanto Tsushinsha, 1954. 95p.

Jibun no kao 自分の顔

'Свое лицо' Перевод В. Логуновой. *Японская новелла 1960–1970.* Москва, Прогресс, 1972. p.64–93

Jiyū shijin 自由詩人

'自由詩人' 表文台訳 「日本代表作家百人集 3」 서울 希望出版社 1966. p.336–357; 「日本短篇文学全集 4」 서울 新太陽社 1969. p.94–117

Kaze ni soyogu ashi 風にそよぐ葦

Тросик под ветром. Перевод И. Львовой. Москва, Гослитиздат, 1960. 639p.

Kekkon no jōken 結婚の条件

「結婚의条件」 鄭白煥訳 서울 百忍社 1962. 259p.

Kekkon no seitai 結婚の生態

「카민의사랑」 薛益洙訳 서울 新友文化社 1969. 375p.

Kinkanshoku 金環蝕

「金環蝕」 張幸勲訳 서울 精研社 1967. 341p.

Kiseki 奇蹟

'神迹' 石堅白訳 「世界文学」 1961年3月 p.22–35; 「知識分子」 第63期 1970年10月 p.28–33
'神迹' 「當代亜菲拉小説選」 香港 中流出版社 1977. p.399–413

Kōtaiki 交替期

'교체기' 趙演鉉訳 「世界短篇文学全集 7」 서울 啓蒙社 1966. p.368–377; 「世界短篇文学全集 9」 서울 三珍社 1971. p.242–251; 「世界代表短篇文学全集 9」 서울 三熙社 1976. p.242–251; 「世界短篇文学全集10」 서울 新韓出版社 1976. p.38–56
'Fuszako öröksége' Ford. Klaudy Kinga. *Égtájak.* Budapest, Európa, 1974. p.141–151

Mitasareta seikatsu 充たされた生活

「充足된生活」 崔林訳 서울 受験社 1963. 312p.
「独身女」 全湖訳 서울 西欧社 1963. 306p.
「어느女人의告白」 安炳訳 서울 尚志文化社 1974. 312p.
'충족되지않는欲望' 張文平訳 「日本文学大全集 3」 서울 東西文化院 1975. p.326–467

Ningen no kabe 人間の壁

「人間의壁」 睦順福訳 서울 普成社 1961–63. 3冊
Стена человеческая. Перевод Т. П. Григорьева, В. М. Константинова, Л. З. Левина и В. В. Логунова. Москва, Гослитиздат, 1960. 639p.; Москва, Изд. Иност. Лит. 1963. 639p.

Shijū hassai no teikō 四十八歳の抵抗

Resistance at forty-eight. Tr. by Kazuma Nakayama. Tokyo, Hokuseido, 1960. 343p.
「四十八歳의抵抗」 李鐘烈他訳 서울 人文閣 1966. 1冊
'四十八歳의抵抗' 李鐘烈訳 「日本文学選集 7」 서울 知文閣 1967; 서울 韓国読書文化院 1973. p.7–231
'四十八歳의抵抗' 李浩訳 「現代日本代表文学全集 7」 서울 平和出版社 1973. p.3–176

Shin Nihon minwashū 新日本民話集

'New folk tales of Japan' Tr. by Kohji Ōi. *The Reeds*, v.5, 1959. p.89–110

Yōgan 熔岩

'Похититель велосипедов' Перевод Г. Ивановой. *Рассказ писателей Востока.* Ленинград, Лениздат, 1958. p.319–332

Essays エッセイ

'Thoughts in the dark' Tr. by Brewster Horwitz. *New world writing 3*, 1953. p.23–26
'마침내나도희생자가' 金賢珠訳 「바이바이바다」 서울 三韓出版社 1966. p.259–263
'見故人原稿而痛心' 余阿勲訳 「純文學」 第3巻1期 1968. p.32–34
'我對共産主義的疑惑' 樊菊聲訳 「東西風」 第9期 1973年7月 p.8–10

'Тайфун' Перевод В. Логуновой. *Японская новелла.* Москва, Изд. Иност. Лит. 1961. p.77–91
'The affair of the arabesque inlay' Tr. by Makoto Momoi and Jay Gluck. *Ukiyo*, ed. by Jay Gluck. N. Y. Vangard Press, 1963. p.120–132
「사랑이끝날때면」 尹相根訳 서울 徽文出版社 1963. 291p.
「언제까지나섧음을」 陸順福訳 서울 普成社 1963. 320p.
「아까시아피는언덕」 南小珍訳 서울 文音社 1968. 255p.
'Тайфун' Аударган Г. Оспанов. *Жапон енгимелери.* Алма-Ата, Жазушы, 1965. p.22–36.

'Una strega' Tr. di Orsola Fenghi. *Novelle giapponesi.* Milano, Martelo, 1969. p.65–75
'Дузахда узгариш; 'Хужумни кандаи даф килиш мукин' Собир Юнусов таржимаси. *Ижро етилмаган хукм.* Тошкент, Госиздат, 1971. p.125–139, 140–161

ISHIKAWA Yū 石川 湧 1906–1976

Criticism 評論

'説述自己的記徳' 魯迅訳 「譯文」 第1巻第2期 1934;「魯迅全集 16」 上海 魯迅全集出版社 1938. 作家書屋 1946. 大連 光華書店 1948. 北京 人民文学出版社 1973. p.851–852;「魯迅譯文集10」 北京 人民文学出版社 1958. p.551–552

ISHIKAWA Zensuke 石川善助 1901–1932

Poems 詩

'Scene from a subarctic zone; A maidservant; A prostitute of the sea' *An anthology of modern Japanese poetry*, ed. and tr. by Ichiro Kono and Rikutaro Fukuda. Tokyo, Kenkyusha, 1957. p.34
'Dneiz orospusu' Tercüme etmek L. Sami Akalin. *Japon şiiri.* İstanbul, Varlik Yayinevi, 1962. p.293
'En hushjelp; En havets hore' Til norsk ved Paal Brekke. *Moderne japansk lyrikk.* Oslo, Norske Bokklubben, n. d. p.66–67

ISHIKURE Chimata 石榑千亦 1869–1942

Tanka 短歌

'The coronation of the Emperor; During a voyage; The northern sea; Longing for my departed wife' Tr. by Asataro Miyamori. *Masterpieces of Japanese poetry, ancient and modern.* Tokyo, Maruzen, 1936; Tokyo, Taiseido, 1956; N. Y. Greenwood Press, 1971. p.625–627

ISHIMORI Nobuo 石森延男 1897–

Iesusama no ohanashi いえすさまのおはなし

As Jesus grew. Tr. by Valerie Bannert. Valley Forge, Judson Press, 1975. 1v.

ISHIMURE Michiko 石牟礼道子 1927–

Kugai jōdo 苦海浄土

'Pure land, poisoned sea' Tr. by James Kirkup and Nakano Michio. *Japan Quarterly*, v.18, no.3, 1971. p.299–306

ISHIZAKA Yōjirō 石坂洋次郎 1900–

Aitsu to watashi あいつと私

「那個傢伙與我」 江柏峰訳 鹿港鎮 鴻文出版社 1969. 295p.

Ame no naka ni kiete 雨の中に消えて

「비속으로사라지다」 崔錦淑訳 서울 徵文出版社 1963. 307p.
「비속에지다」 李愚榮訳 서울 漢陽出版社 1964. 206p.
「비속으로사라지다」 許文寧訳 서울 善瓊図書 1964. 206p.

Aoi sanmyaku 青い山脈

'푸른山脈' 李剛録訳 「日本文学選集 2」 서울 知文閣 1966; 서울 韓国読書文化院 1973. p.279–477
'푸른山脈' 洪潤基訳 「日本文学大全集 5」 서울 東西文化院 1975. p.292–444
'푸른산맥' 金永壽訳 「金閣寺外」 서울 主婦生活社 1976. p.161–309

Hana to kajitsu 花と果実

「꽃과과일」 孫玟訳 서울 進明出版社 1967. 243p.; 서울 漢陽出版社 1972. 243p.

Hi no ataru sakamichi 陽のあたる坂道

'That guy' Tr. by Fuki Uramatsu. *The Yomiuri*, Sept. 21–Dec. 22, 1959.
「家庭教師」 李時哲訳 서울 文光社 1962. 378p.; 서울 權徳出版社 1974. 379p.
'陽地바른언덕길' 洪潤基訳 「日本文学大全集 5」 서울 東西文化院 1975. p.2–289

Hoshikusa guruma 干草ぐるま

'乾草馬車' 閔丙山訳 「日本代表作家百人集 3」 서울 希望出版社 1966. p.172–187; 「日本短篇文学全集 3」 서울 新太陽社 1969. p.320–335

Ishinaka sensei gyōjōki 石中先生行状記

Mr. Ishinaka tells tales of rural drollery. Tr. by Paul T. Konya. Tokyo, Yohan Publications, 1971. 213p.

Kiken na nenrei 危険な年齢

'危險的年齢' 黄錦堂訳 「荒絹」 台北 大明王氏出版公司 1972. p.161–177

Mizuiro no seishun 水色の青春

'Pale youth' Tr. by Shuzo Nakanishi. *Eigo Kenkyu*, v.42, no.1–6, 1953.

Taifū to zakuro 颱風とざくろ

「颱風과石榴」 尹龍成訳 서울 東西文化社 1968. 324p.
「個人教授」 尹龍成訳 서울 高麗出版社 1973. 324p.

Wakai hito 若い人

「젊은사람」 李鳳九訳 서울 新太陽社 1961. 2冊

Wakai kawa no nagare 若い川の流れ

「下一代的女性」 純浩訳 三重市 明志出版社 1962. 153p.

Essay エッセイ

"프랑스어" 를국어로' 金賢珠訳 「바이바이바다」 서울 三韓出版社 1966. p.247–250

「젊음이흐르는江・주운아침」 崔錦淑訳 서울 徵文出版社 1963. 324p.
「青春教室」 李時哲訳 서울 文光社 1963. 347p.

ISHIZAKA Yōjirō

「영름한사람들」千世旭訳 서울 王子出版社 1963. 237p.
「原罪」 河小苑訳 서울 不二出版社 1966. 358p.
「初愛」 曹信鏑訳 서울 現代思潮社 1967. 1冊
「호느끼는太陽」 林龍澤訳 서울 高麗文化社 1973. 306p.
「별들의사랑」 尹龍済訳 서울 五倫出版社 1974. 324p.
「再婚」 李禹榮訳 서울 大興出版社 1974. 205p.

ISHIZAWA Eitarō　石沢英太郎　1916–

Uwasa o atsume sugita otoko　噂を集め過ぎた男

'Too much about too many' *Japanese golden dozen*,
ed. by Ellery Queen. Tokyo, Tuttle, 1978.
p.15–37

ISHIZUKA Tomoji　石塚友二　1906–

Haiku　俳句

'1 haiku' *A history of haiku v.2*, by R. H. Blyth.
Tokyo, Hokuseido, 1964. p.250

ITAGAKI Takaho　板垣鷹穂　1894–1966

Criticism　評論

'機械美' 陳望道訳 「當代文藝」 第1巻3期 1931. p.419–
423
'美術的表現與背景' 蕭石君訳 193?.

ITŌ Einosuke　伊藤永之介　1903–1959

Uguisu　鶯

'Nightingale' Tr. by Geoffrey Sargent. *Modern
Japanese stories*, ed. by Ivan Morris. London,
Spottiswoode, 1961; Tokyo, Tuttle, 1962.
p.258–301
'Auf der Polizeiwache' Deutsch von Monique
Humbert. *Nippon*. Zürich, Diogenes, 1965.
p.289–348
'The song bird' Tr. by Geoffrey Sargent. *The
Japanese image,* ed. by M. Schneps and A. D.
Coox. Tokyo, Orient West, 1965. p.109–143

ITŌ Hisashi　伊藤尚志　1923–

Poems　詩

'Coffee/no sugar; Veronica' Remade into English
by Thomas Fitzsimmons. *Japanese poetry now*.
London, André Deutsch, 1972. p.97–99;
Japanese poetry today. N. Y. Schocken Books,
1972. p.99–101

ITŌ Keiichi　伊藤桂一　1917–

Hotaru no kawa　螢の河

'반디의江' 金洙暎訳 「日本代表作家百人集 4」 서울 希
望出版社 1966. p.402–416; 「日本短篇文学全集
5」 서울 新太陽社 1969. p.242–256

'山谷鐘鳴時' 劉慕沙訳 「日本現代小説選」 台北 聯經
出版 1976. p.1–36

ITŌ Kōtarō　伊藤光太郎

Saisho ni harareta fuda　最初に貼られた札

'Das anfangs angeklebte Schild' Übers. von Kurt
Meissner. *Der Tanzfächer,* von K. Meissner.
Tokyo, 1943. p.233–239

ITŌ Masao　伊藤まさお

Poems　詩

'Мешок песен' Перевод Веры Марковой. *Восточный альманах 6*. Москва, Худож. Лит.
1963. p.331

ITŌ Masanori　伊藤正徳　1889–

Rengō kantai no saigo　連合艦隊の最後

The end of the Imperial Japanese Navy. Tr. by
Andrew Y. Kuroda and Roger Pineau. N. Y.
W. W. Norton, 1956. 240p.
La Marina Imperiale Giapponese. Tr. di Lucia
Bilancini. Milano, Club degli Editori, 1969.
361p.

ITŌ Masashi　伊藤　正　1921–

Guamu tō　グアム島

Les derniers soldats. Tr. par Jean Bourdier. Paris,
La Table Ronde, 1967. 219p.

ITŌ Sachio　伊藤左千夫　1864–1913

Hamagiku　濱菊

'Hamagiku' Tr. by Saburo Yamamura. *Eigo
Kenkyu*, v.63, no.11, 1975. p.36–38; v.63, no.12,
1975. p.27–29

Ushikai no uta　牛飼の歌

Songs of a cowherd. Tr. by Shio Sakanishi. Boston,
Marshall Jones, 1936. 88p.

Tanka　短歌

'Cowherds' poetry; My children' Tr. by Asataro
Miyamori. *Masterpieces of Japanese poetry,
ancient and modern*. Tokyo, Maruzen, 1936;
Tokyo, Taiseido, 1956; N. Y. Greenwood
Press, 1971. p.620–621
'5 tanka' Tr. by V. H. Viglielmo. *Japanese literature in the Meiji era*. Tokyo, Obunsha, 1955.
p.398–399
'4 tanka' Übers. von Kuniyo Takayasu und Man-

fred Hausmann. *Ruf der Regenpfeifer*. München, Bechtle Verlag, 1961. p.95
'5 tanka' Tr. by Geoffrey Bownas and Anthony Thwaite. *The Penguin book of Japanese verse*. Harmondsworth, Penguin Books, 1964. p.158

ITŌ Sei 伊藤 整 1905–1969

Bishōjo 美少女

'Красивая' Перевод Д. Бугаевой. *No.36, новеллы японских писателей*. Москва, Наука, 1968. p.79–87

Hi no tori 火の鳥

'Firebird' Tr. by John G. Mills and Mifune Okumura. *Eigo Seinen*, v. 109, no.7–12, 1963.
'火鳥' 崔象德訳 「日本文学選集 3」 서울 知文閣 1966. p.195–378; 서울 韓国読書文化院 1973. p.195–381

Niji 虹

'虹' 傅寶齡訳 「勲章」 台北 文壇社 1960. p.158–175

Shukke tonsei no kokorozashi 出家遁世の志

'出家遁世' 金龍済訳 「日本代表作家百人集 3」 서울 希望出版社 1966. p.360–376; 「日本短篇文学全集 4」 서울 新太陽社 1969. p.120–136

Poems 詩

'Native village; Again; For a later day' *An anthology of modern Japanese poetry*, ed. and tr. by Ichiro Kono and Rikutaro Fukuda. Tokyo, Kenkyusha, 1957. p.35–36
'Yenibaştan' Tercüme etmek L. Sami Akalin. *Japon şiiri*. İstanbul, Varlik Yayinevi, 1962. p.285
'달밤 ; 사과밭의六月' 崔一秀訳 「기다리고있네」 서울 韓国政経社 1966. p.28–29, 129–131
'Melancholy summer; A night frozen hard; A night of the moon again' *Anthology of modern Japanese poetry*, tr. and comp. by Edith Marcombe Shiffert and Yuki Sawa. Tokyo, Tuttle, 1972. p.102–104

Criticism 評論

'Modern Japanese literature, pre-Meiji and early Meiji era' *Japan Quarterly*, v.1, no.1, 1954. p.74–86
'Modern Japanese literature, development in journalism in Meiji era' Tr. by V. H. Vigliemo. *Japan Quarterly*, v.2, no.1, 1955. p.94–107
'Pioneers of the new literature' Tr. by V. H. Viglielmo. *Japan Quarterly*, v.2, no.2, 1955. p.224–234
'Ozaki Koyo and his circle' Tr. by V. H. Viglielmo. *Japan Quarterly*, v.2, no.3, 1955. p.355–364
'Rise of naturalism' Tr. by Charles S. Terry. *Japan Quarterly*, v.2, no.4, 1955. p.509–515
'Lovable topknot' *Japan Quarterly*, v.8, no.4, 1961. p.473–476
'Modes of thought in contemporary Japan' *Japan Quarterly*, v.12, no.4, 1965. p.501–514
'Natsume Soseki, his personality and works' *Essays on Natsume Soseki's works*. Tokyo, Japan Society for the Promotion of Science, 1972. p.1–18

ITŌ Shizuo 伊東静雄 1906–1953

Poems 詩

'Naturally, naturally enough' *An anthology of modern Japanese poetry*, ed. and tr. by Ichiro Kono and Rikutaro Fukuda. Tokyo, Kenkyusha, 1957. p.37
'Evening sea; Picture drawn by a boy' *The poetry of living Japan*, by Takamichi Ninomiya and D. J. Enright. London, John Murray, 1957. p.89–90
'저녁노을 ; 詩作뒤 ; 늦여름 ; 帰路 ; 들의갈나무 ; 긴療養生活' 鄭漢模 辛東門訳 「世界戦後文学全集 9」 서울 新丘文化社 1962. p.228–230
'The cicada in the garden' Tr. by Greg Campbell. *TransPacific*, no.5, 1970. p.19
'帰省者 ; 작은手帖에서' 金巢雲訳 「世界의文学大全集 34」 서울 同和出版社 1971. p.534–535
'Watching the beam of a lighthouse; Locusts in the garden' *Anthology of modern Japanese poetry*, tr. and comp. by Edith Marcombe Shiffert and Yuki Sawa. Tokyo, Tuttle, 1972. p.105–106

ITŌ Shōu 伊藤松宇 1859–1943

Haiku 俳句

'9 haiku' Tr. by Asataro Miyamori. *Anthology of haiku, ancient and modern*. Tokyo, Maruzen, 1932. p.706–712
'2 haiku' Tr. by Gladys Seabury. *Aoba no fue*. Honolulu, Univ. of Hawaii, 1937. n.p.
'A summer shower; Birds; Snow and pine-trees; On the battlefield of Seki-ga-hara' Tr. by Asataro Miyamori. *Haiku poems, ancient and modern*. Tokyo, Maruzen, 1940. p.326–328
'2 haiku' Tr. by R. H. Blyth. *Haiku v.2*. Tokyo, Hokuseido, 1950. p.27, 40
'1 haiku' Tr. by Peter Beilenson and Harry Behn. *Haiku harvest*. Mount Vernon, Peter Pauper Press, 1962. p.46
'4 haiku' Übers. von Gerolf Coudenhove. *Japanische Jahreszeiten*. Zürich, Manesse Verlag, 1963. p.26, 54, 101, 260
'1 haiku' Übers. von Erwin Jahn. *Fallende Blüten*. Zürich, Arche, 1968. p.31, 92
'Shower; New Year's morn' Tr. by Kenneth Yasuda. *A pepper-pod*. Tokyo, Tuttle, 1976. p.81

ITŌ Sukenobu 伊藤祐命 1834–1889

Tanka 短歌

'The road under pine trees' Tr. by Asataro Miyamori. *Masterpieces of Japanese poetry, ancient and modern*. Tokyo, Maruzen, 1936; Tokyo, Taiseido, 1956; N. Y. Greenwood Press, 1971. p.605

ITŌ Takashi 伊東 敬 1906–

Poems 詩

'Лежень' Перевод Анатолия Мамонова. *Вкус*

ITŌ Takashi

хризантемы. Москва, Восточная Литература, 1976. p.45

ITSUKI Hiroyuki 五木寛之 1932–

Seishun no mon 青春の門

「青春의門」 李爓訳 서울 自由文学社 1977. 2冊

IWAI Sannosuke 祝 算之介 1915–

Poems 詩

'Fruit' Tr. by S. Sato and C. Urdang. *Poetry*, May 1956. p.71

IWAMOTO Shūzo 岩本修蔵 1968–

Poems 詩

'Любовь; Будущее' Перевод Е. Винокурова. *Иностранная Литература*, июнь 1964. p.157

IWANO Hōmei 岩野泡鳴 1873–1920

Dokuyaku o nomu onna 毒薬を飲む女

'Žena, která si vzala jed' Přel. Miroslav Novák. *5 japonských novel*. Praha, Odeon, 1969. p.37–147

Geisha Kotake 芸者小竹

'사랑이나쿰이나' 郭夏信訳 「世界文学全集 94」 서울 乙酉文化社 1962. p.147–169; 「日本短篇文学選」 서울 乙酉文化社 1976. p.71–117

Poems 詩

'3 poems' *The spirit of Japanese poetry*, by Yone Noguchi. London, John Murray, 1914. p.106, 109
'Yearning for spring; "Tankyoku"' Tr. by Yone Noguchi. *Lotus and chrysanthemum*. N. Y. Liveright, 1928. p.170
'La pierre silencieuse; Lune et chat; Les bruits stridents de mon coeur; Le soleil rouge, tout rouge; Le criquet' Tr. par Kuni Matsuo et Steinilber-Oberlin. *Anthologie des poètes japonais contemporains*. Paris, Mercure de France, 1939. p.39–44
'Kara sevda, kara turku' Tercüme etmek L. Sami Akalin. *Japon şiiri*. İstanbul, Varlik Yayinevi, 1962. p.236

IWASA Tōichirō 岩佐東一郎 1905–1974

Poems 詩

'Change of seasons; The snow; The grapes; My poems; Autumn wind; Song of a child; Woven cloth' *An anthology of modern Japanese poetry*, ed. and tr. by Ichiro Kono and Rikutaro Fukuda. Tokyo, Kenkyusha, 1957. p.37–39

'Sürlerim; Sonbahar rüzgâri; Mevsimlerin değişimi' Tercüme etmek L. Sami Akalin. *Japon şiiri*. İstanbul, Varlik Yayinevi, 1962. p.284

IWASA Wakako 岩佐和歌子

Tanka 短歌

'1 tanka' Tr. by Shigeshi Nishimura. *Eigo Seinen*, v.93, no.3, 1947. p.120

IWASAKI Akira 岩崎 昶 1903–

Criticism 評論

'現代電影與有産階級' 魯迅訳 「萌芽」 第1巻3期 1930; 「魯迅譯文集 10」 北京 人民文学出版社 1958. p.307–332

IWASAKI Chihiro 岩崎ちひろ 1918–1974

Akachan no kuru hi あかちゃんのくる日

A brother for Momoko. London, Bodley Head, 1970. 24p.
A new baby is coming to my house. N. Y. McGraw-Hill, 1972. 1v.

Ame no hi no orusuban あめの日のおるすばん

Momoko's lovely day. London, Bodley Head, 1969. 1v.
Staying home alone on a rainy day. N. Y. McGraw-Hill, 1969. 1v.

Kotori no kuru hi ことりのくるひ

Momoko and the pretty bird. London, Bodley Head, 1972. 1v.; Chicago, Follett, 1972. 25p.

IWASHITA Shunsaku 岩下俊作 1906–

Muhōmatsu no isshō 無法松の一生

L'uomo del rikscio. Tr. di Mario Teti. Milano, Mondadori, 1959. 120p.

IWATA Hiroshi 岩田 宏 1932–

Poems 詩

'房' 金龍済訳 「日本詩集」 서울 青雲社 1960. p.113–114
'未婚；大砲；処女' 辛東門訳 「世界戦後文学全集 9」 서울 新丘文化社 1962. p.241–242
'Il mare' *La protesta poetica del Giappone*, a cura di Dacia Maraini e Michiko Nojiri. Roma, Officina Edizioni, 1968. p.139–140
'Seaside experiment; Tyranny; Damn song; Saturday night date' Tr. by Thomas Fitzsimmons. *Japanese poetry now*. London, André Deutsch, 1972. p.61–68; *Japanese poetry today*. N. Y. Schocken Books, 1972. p.63–70

'Auf der Spitze des Felsens; Stierkopf; Ah, Trompete; An der Stirm des Menschen' Übers. von Helmut Gross. *Internationales Jahrbuch fur Literatur*, Ensemble 8, 1977. p.102

IWAYA Kuchinashi　岩谷山梔子　1883–1944

Haiku　俳句

'2 haiku' Tr. by V. H. Viglielmo. *Japanese literature in the Meiji era*. Tokyo, Obunsha, 1955. p.448

IWAYA Sazanami　厳谷小波　1870–1933

Berurin hyakutan　ベルリン百談

Briefe eines Japaners aus Deutschland. Übers. von August Gramatzky. Tokyo, 1904. 1v.

Nihon mukashi banashi　日本昔噺
Nihon otogi banashi　日本お伽噺

'Tsukushimbo; Saimyoji; Hibariyama' Übers. von Hilda von Fallot. *Die Wahrheit*, v.5, 1904. p.114–117, 128–137, 154–159
Der Spiegel aus Matsuyama. Berlin, Tägliche Rundschau, 1906. 1v.
「花笑翁」梅秀峰訳　北京　東亜公司 1907. 1冊
Iwaya's fairy tales of old Japan. Tokyo, Bunyodo, 1914. 1v.
'Deyama monogatari' Tr. by Sakujiro Yamakawa. *Chuto Eigo*, Jan. 1924.
'Himejima no todai' Tr. by Taro Ito. *Jokyu Eigo*, July and Aug. 1928.
The crab's revenge, and others. Tokyo, Hokuseido, 1938. 11 issues.
Nippon satusetäkertoo: valikomia japanlaisia satuja. Toimittanut ja suomentanut Marta Keravuori. Helsinki, Otava, 1952. 93p.
Japanese fairy tales. Tokyo, Hokuseido, 1954. 180p.
'Девятихвостая лиса' Перевод В. Горегляда. *Восточная новелла*. Москва, Изд. Иност. Лит. 1963. p.84–93
Сказания древней Японии. Перевод В. М. Мендрина. Петербург, n.d. 254p.

Haiku　俳句

'5 haiku' Tr. by Asataro Miyamori. *Anthology of haiku, ancient and modern.* Tokyo, Maruzen, 1932. p.781–784
'Born a man; The bugle; Chrysanthemums and maple leaves' Tr. by Asataro Miyamori. *Haiku poems, ancient and modern.* Tokyo, Maruzen, 1940. p.314–316
'1 haiku' Tr. by R. H. Blyth. *Haiku v.4.* Tokyo, Hokuseido, 1952. p.52
'2 haiku' Tr. by V. H. Viglielmo. *Japanese literature in the Meiji era.* Tokyo, Obunsha, 1955. p.437
'1 haiku' Tercüme etmek L. Sami Akalin. *Japon şiiri.* İstanbul, Varlik Yayinevi, 1962. p.235
'2 haiku' Übers. von Gerolf Coudenhove. *Japanische Jahreszeiten.* Zürich, Manesse Verlag, 1963. p.117, 245
'1 haiku' Tr. by William Howard Cohen. *To walk in seasons.* Tokyo, Tuttle, 1972. p.89
'Heavy snow' Tr. by Kenneth Yasuda. *A pepperpod.* Tokyo, Tuttle, 1976. p.91

IZU Toshihiko　伊豆利彦　1926–

Gendai Nihon bungakushi　現代日本文学史

История современной японской литературы. Перевод Р. Г. Карлиной и В. Н. Марковой. Москва, Иностранная Литература, 1961. 429p.

IZUMI Daihachi　泉　大八　1928–

Kūsō tōin　空想党員

'假想党員'　文洁若訳　「世界文学」　1959年12月　p.18–26

Yokubō no rasshu　欲望のラッシュ

「欲望의라쉬」威大植訳　서울　世昌出版社 1968. 251p.

IZUMI Katsuo　和泉克雄　1916–

Poems　詩

'恋歌'　崔一秀訳　「기다리고있네」　서울　韓国政経社 1966. p.76–81

IZUMI Kyōka　泉　鏡花　1873–1939

Kōya hijiri　高野聖

'The Koya priest' Tr. by Eiichi Hayashi. *The Reeds,* v.5, 1959. p.17–60; v.6, 1960. p.97–131
'Der Wanderpriester' Übers. von Walter Donat. *Die fünfstöckige Pagode.* Düsseldorf, Eugen Diederichs, 1960. p.75–112; Regensburg, Friedrich Pustet, n.d. p.75–112
'Il monaco di Koya' Tr. di Atsuko Ricca Suga. *Narratori giapponesi moderni.* Milano, Bompiani, 1965. p.73–130

Mayukakushi no rei　眉かくしの霊

'눈섭가린귀신'　金龍済訳　「日本代表作家百人集 1」　서울　希望出版社 1966.　p.172–197;「日本短篇文学全集 1」　서울　新太陽社 1969. p.172–197

Sannin no mekura no hanashi　三人のめくらの話

'A tale of three who were blind' Tr. by Edward Seidensticker. *Modern Japanese literature,* ed. by D. Keene. N. Y. Grove Press, 1956; Tokyo, Tuttle, 1957. p.242–253

Yakō junsa　夜行巡査

'夜行巡査'　郭夏信訳　「世界文学全集 94」　서울　乙酉文化社　1962.　p.269–283;「日本短篇文学選」　서울　乙酉文化社　1976. p.197–223

'Roman Geishi'　*Novellist,* no.5, 1901. p.5–6

J

JINBŌ Kōtarō 神保光太郎 1905–

Poems 詩

> '花河；독수리' 金巢雲訳 「世界의文学大全集 34」 서울 同和出版公社 1971. p.528–530

JŌ Samon 城 左門 1904–1976

Poems 詩

> 'Seeking after truth' Tr. by Hisakazu Kaneko. *London Magazine,* v.7, no.7, Oct. 1967. p.32–33

JŌ Susumu 城 侑 1932–

Poems 詩

> '벼랑과딸기' 金龍済訳 「日本詩集」 서울 青雲社 1960. p.41–43

JUGAKU Bunshō 寿岳文章 1900–

Criticism and essay 評論・エッセイ

> 'The sound of rain' *Chanoyu Quarterly,* v.1, no.3, 1970. p.60–69
> 'Japanese literature in English translation' *J.O.L.* v.6, no.2, 1955. p.36–40
> 'William Blake and Japan' *Eigo Seinen,* v.103, no.10, 1957. p.38–39

JŪICHIYA Gisaburō 十一谷義三郎 1897–1937

Criticism 評論

> '英雄主義' 秋濤訳 「文藝月刊」 第3巻12期 1933. p.1793–1799

K

KADOKURA Satoshi 門倉 訣 1935–

Poems 詩

> '桑田的憤怒和誓言' 石麟訳 「世界文学」 1962年12月 p.52–53
> '祖国–1962年10月21日' 李芒訳 「世界文学」 1963年7月 p.57–60

'Память' Перевод Анатолия Мамонова. *Новый Мир,* август 1973.
'Долой водородную бомбу!' Перевод А. Мамонова. *Вкус хризантемы.* Москва, Восточная Литература, 1976. p.46

KADOMATSU Shōichi 門松正一

Kōshukei 絞首刑

> 「絞首刑」 尤光先訳 台北 春齋書屋 1953. 70p.

KAGA Kōji 加賀耿二 1899–1974

Wata 綿

> '棉花' 胡風訳 「譯文」 新2巻3期 1936.

KAGA Otohiko 加賀乙彦 1929–

Kaerazaru natsu 帰らざる夏

> *Die Hand des Riesen.* Übertragen von Helmut Erlinghagen. Stuttgart, Deutsche Verlags Anstalt, 1976. 328p.

KAGAWA Fubō 香川不抱 1889–1917

Tanka 短歌

> '5 tanka' Tr. by Shigeshi Nishimura. *The Current of the World,* v.15, no.6, 1938. p.103
> 'The door of glass' Tr. by Asataro Miyamori. *Masterpieces of Japanese poetry, ancient and modern.* Tokyo, Maruzen, 1936; Tokyo, Taiseido, 1956; N. Y. Greenwood Press, 1971. p.759–760

KAGAWA Shigeru 香川 茂 1920–

Setoro no umi セトロの海

> 「冰海小鯨」 余阿勲訳 台北 國語日報 1972. 162p.

KAGAWA Toyohiko 賀川豊彦 1888–1960

Chichi to mitsu no nagaruru sato 乳と蜜の流るる里

> *Landet som flyter av mjölk.* Översätta Hugo Hultenberg. Stockholm, Svensk. Kristl. Stud. 1937. 240p.

Chikurin no bi 竹林の美

> 'The beauty of bamboo groves' Tr. by Isoh Yamagata. *The Current of the World,* v.32, no.11, 1955. p.64–65

Hinminkutsu nite utau 貧民窟にて歌う

> *Songs from the slums.* Interpretation by Lois J. Erickson. Nashville, Cokesbury Press, 1935. 97p.

Songs from the land of dawn. Tr. by Lois J. Erickson. Nashville, Cokesbury Press, 1935. 96p.; N. Y. Friendship Press, 1949. 91p.; N. Y. Books for Libraries Press, 1968. 78p.
Sånger från slummen. Tr. from the English Jenny Holmåsen. Uppsala, Lindblad, 1936. 64p.
Cantos de los barrios bajos. Tr. por Lois J. Erickson. México, Casa Unida de Publicaciones, 1953. 94p.

Hirō 疲労

'Fatigue' Tr. by Isoh Yamagata. *The Current of the World,* v.33, no.8, 1956. p.74

Hitotsubu no mugi 一粒の麦

A grain of wheat. Tr. by Marion R. Draper. London, Hodder and Stoughton, 1933. 313p.; N. Y. Abingdon Press, 1936. 155p.
Ett sädeskorn. Översättä Astrid Hallstrom. Stockholm, Fahlcrantz, 1934. 296p.
Et hvedekorn. København, Frederik E. Pedersen, 1934. 304p.
Et hvetekorn. Treeken (from the English) Frithjov Iversen. Oslo, De Unges Forlag, 1939. 176p.; 1961. 262p.; 1970. 240p.
Ein Weizenkorn. Übers. von R. A. Egon Hessel. Basel, Basler Missions-Buchhandlung, 1954: Stuttgart, Evang. Missionsverlag. 1954, 175p. 2. Aufl. 1956. 175p.

Kabe no koe kiku toki 壁の声聞く時

'The rice riots' *Japan Chronicle,* March 20, 21, 1925.

Kami to shokuzai ai eno kangeki 神と贖罪愛への感激

The challenge of redemptive love. Tr. by M. Draper. N. Y. Abingdon Press, 1940.

Seirei ni tsuite no meisō 聖霊に就ての瞑想

Meditations on the Holy Spirit. Tr. by C. A. Logan. Nashville, Cokesbury Press, 1939.

Shisen o koete 死線を越えて

'Across the death-line' Tr. by I. Fukumoto and T. Satchell. *Japan Chronicle,* Jan. 29–Sept. 17, 1922.
Across the death-line. Tr. by I. Fukumoto and T. Satchell. Kobe, Japan Chronicle, 1922. 188p.; London, 1935. 1v.
Before the dawn. Tr. by I. Fukumoto and T. Satchell. London, Chatto and Windus, 1925; N. Y. Doran, 1925. 398p.
Auflehnung und Opfer. Übers. von Wilhelm Gundert. Stuttgart, Gundert Verlag, 1929. 366p.
Avant l'aube. Paris, Je Sers, 1931. 2v.
Innan dagen grydde. Översättä Teresia Eurén. Stockholm, Svensk. Kristl. Stud. 1933. 334p.
Vzpoura a cbĕt. Přel. Jan Vanek. Praha, Sfinx, 1935. 314p.
「死線을넘어서」金素影訳 서울 新教出版社 1956. 368p.; 서울 螢雪文化社 1963. 280p.
「死線을넘어서」 韓仁煥 張倍徳訳 서울 韓宗出版社 1975. (上・中) 2冊

Taiyō o iru mono 太陽を射るもの

'A shooter at the sun' *Japan Chronicle,* Dec. 2, 1923.
A shooter at the sun. Tr. by T. Satchell. Kobe,

Japan Chronicle, 1925. 116p.
Solskytten. Översätta Teresia Euren. Stockholm, Diakonistyr, 1934. 325p.
L'archer tirant contre le soleil. Tr. par Ch. Guillon. Paris, Société Commerciale d'Edition et de Librairie, 1936. 237p.

Tenjō ura no nezumi 天井裏の鼠

'Rat behind the ceiling' Tr. by Isoh Yamagata. *The Current of the World,* v.35, no.6, 1958. p.44–45

Zakuro no kataware ざくろのかたわれ

Ein Stück Granatapfel. Übers. von Karl Weidinger. Berlin, Ostasien Mission, 1933. 88p.

Criticism 評論

Love and the law of life. Tr. by J. F. Gressitt. Philadelphia, Winston, 1929.
The religion of Jesus. Tr. by Helen F. Topping. Philadelphia, Winston, 1931.
New life through God. Tr. by Elizabeth Kilburn. N. Y. Revell, 1931. 210p.
Christ and Japan. Tr. by William Axling. N. Y. Friendship Press, 1934.
The two kingdoms. London, Lutterworth Press, 1941. 350p.
Se det menneske. Oversette Aage Hallsberg. Oslo, Norsk Litteraturselskap, 1949. 342p; Oslo, De Unge, 1971. 2v.
Meditations. Tr. by Jiro Takenaka. N. Y. Harper, 1950.
Se människan. Översätta Elisabet Akasson. Uppsala, J. A. Lindblad, 1950. 348p.
「나는왜크리스챵이되었는가」大韓基督教書会訳 서울 大韓基督教書会 1952. 160p.
Kristendom i praksis. Overs. av E. Agnes. Oslo, Norsk Litteraturselskap, 1973. 63p.
「한알의길」 安英埈訳 서울 三良社 1977. 342p.

KAIKŌ Takeshi 開高 健 1930–

Aoi getsuyōbi 青い月曜日

Горькое похмелье. Перевод А. Раскина. Москва, Прогресс, 1975. 317p.
Горькое похмелье. Перевод с русс. А. Поращкас. Вильнюс, 1977. 279p.

Funkorogashi フンコロガシ

'쇠똥구리' 金龍済訳 「日本代表作家百人集 5」 서울 希望出版社 1966. p.306–326; 「日本短篇文学全集 6」 서울 新太陽社 1969. p.218–238

Hadaka no ōsama 裸の王様

'裸體國王' 傅寶齡訳 「勲章」 台北 文壇社 1960. p.217–289
'벌거숭이임금님' 金東立訳 「世界戰後文学全集 7」 서울 新丘文化社 1962. p.81–121
'벌거벗은王' 金龍済訳 「日本新鋭文学作家受賞作品選集 5」 서울 青雲社 1964. p.3–56; 「戰後日本短篇文学全集 5」 서울 日光出版社 1965. p.3–57; 「現代日本代表文学全集 5」 서울 平和出版社 1973. p.3–56
'Голый король' Перевод З. Рахима. *Голый король.* Москва, Худож. Лит. 1966. p.131–208
'The naked king' Tr. by Howard Curtis. *Japan Quarterly,* v.24, no.2, 1977. p.185–224

KAIKŌ Takeshi

Heishi no hōshū　兵士の報酬

'Награда солдата' Перевод З. Рахима. *Японская новелла 1960–1970.* Москва, Прогресс, 1972. p.100–121

Kyojin to gangu　巨人と玩具

'Гиганты и игрушки' Перевод З. Рахима. *Голый король.* Москва, Худож. Лит. 1966. p.7–68
'Гигантлар ви ыиинчоклар' Собир Юнусов таржи. *Мхрсо атилызган хукм.* Тошкент, 1971. p.73–126

Natsu no yami　夏の闇

Darkness in summer. Tr. by Cecilia Segawa Seigle. N. Y. Knopf, 1973. 210p.

Nihon sanmon opera　日本三文オペラ

Japanische Dreigroschen Oper. Deutsch von Jürgen Berndt. Berlin, Volk und Welt, 1967. 360p.
Японская трехгрошовая опера. Перевод З. Рахима. Москва, Худож. Лит. 1971. 220p.
Japońska opera za trzy grosze. Przeł. Zuzanna Melicka. Warszawa, Państwowy Instytut Wydawniczy, 1973. 231p.

Panikku　パニック

'Паника' Перевод З. Рахима. *Голый король.* Москва, Худож. Лит. 1966. p.71–128
'Panic' Tr. by Charles Dunn. *Panic, and The runaway.* Tokyo, Univ. of Tokyo Press, 1977. p.1–56

Rubōki　流亡記

'流亡記' 金龍済訳 「日本新鋭文学作家受賞作品選集 5」 서울 青雲社 1964. p.58–105; 「戦後日本短篇文学全集 5」 서울 日光出版社 1965. p.58–105; 「現代日本代表文学全集 5」 서울 平和出版社 1973. p.58–104
'The runaway' Tr. by Charles Dunn. *Panic, and The runaway.* Tokyo, Univ. of Tokyo Press, 1977. p.59–122

Essay　エッセイ

'과겨를말하지않는사나이' 金賢珠訳 「바이바이바디」 서울 三韓出版社 1966. p.74–81

KAIONJI Chōgorō　海音寺潮五郎　1901–1977

Ten to chi to　天と地と

「実録大河小説 大志 7–10」 安東民訳 서울 大河出版社 1973. 4冊

KAJI Wataru　鹿地 亘　1903–

Poems　詩

'Из «Дневника секретного узника»' Перевод В. Н. Марковой. *Японская поэзия.* Москва, Гослитиздат, 1954. p.364–365; Изд.2. 1956. p.466–467
'富士山' 南冠訳 「譯文」 1956年6月 p.64–65
'Дети' Перевод В. Марковой. *Поэты Азии.* Москва, Гослитиздат, 1957. p.842
'要更高更高的速度' 適夷訳 「世界文学」 1959年9月 p.14–15

'憤怒的詩' 適夷訳 「人民文学」 1960年7月 p.39–41

KAJII Motojirō　梶井基次郎　1901–1932

Ame　雨

'Rain' Tr. by Saburo Shimada. *Kenmei Joshi Gakuin Tandai Kenkyu Kiyo,* no.2, 1960. p.62–69

Remon　檸檬

'Citrón' Přel. M. Novák. *Nový Orient,* v.17, no.8, 1962. p.174–176
'La limono' Tr. Yasujiro Nozima. *El japana literaturo.* Tokyo, Japana Esperanto Instituto, 1965. p.88–94

Rojō　路上

'Pěšina' Přel. M. Jelínková. *Nový Orient,* no.4, 1965.

Sakura no ki no shita niwa　桜の木の下には

'Beneath the cherry trees' Tr. by John Bester. *Japan P.E.N. News,* no.12, Feb. 1964. p.7–8

KAJIMA Shōzō　加島祥造　1923–

Poems　詩

'Autumn in Claremont, California' Tr. by Thomas Fitzsimmons. *Japanese poetry now.* London, André Deutsch, 1972. p.90; *Japanese Poetry today.* N. Y. Schocken Books, 1972. p.92

KAJINO Hideo　かじの・ひでお　1937–

Poems　詩

'Stone' Tr. by Harry and Lynn Guest and Shozo Kajima. *Post-war Japanese poetry.* Harmondsworth, Penguin Books, 1972. p.154

KAJITA Hakuhyō　梶田薄氷

Oni senbiki　鬼千匹

'One thousand devils' Tr. by Tei Fujiu. *Hanakatsura.* Tokyo, Ikuseikai, 1903. p.69–98

KAJIWARA Hashin　梶原芭臣　1864–

Haiku　俳句

'Snowfall' Tr. by Asataro Miyamori. *Anthology of haiku, ancient and modern.* Tokyo, Maruzen, 1932. p.833; *Haiku poems, ancient and modern.* Tokyo, Maruzen, 1940. p.329
'1 haiku' Tr. by Peter Beilenson. *Japanese haiku.* Mount Vernon, Peter Pauper Press, 1955. p.55

'1 haiku' Tercüme etmek L. Sami Akalin. *Japon şiiri*. İstanbul, Varlik Yayinevi, 1962. p.222
'1 haiku' Übers. von Gerolf Coudenhove. *Japanische Jahreszeiten*. Zürich, Manesse Verlag, 1963. p.342
'Eine haiku' Übers von Erwin Jahn. *Fallende Blüten*. Zürich, Arche, 1968. p.86
'1 haiku' Tr. by William Howard Cohen. *To walk in seasons*. Tokyo, Tuttle, 1972. p.89

KAJIYAMA Toshiyuki　梶山季之　1929–1975

Akai daiya　赤いダイヤ

「人間経営 1–2」李京南訳 서울 平和文化社 1974. 2冊

Aku no yūsha　悪の勇者

「経営大望 13.巨物大欲」康曙海訳 서울 鮮京図書 1975. 448p.

Akujo no jōken　悪女の条件

「人間経営 23.運命條件」李京南訳 서울 平和文化社 1975. 462p.

Akunin shigan　悪人志願

「経営大望 5.無資巨富」康曙海訳 서울 鮮京図書 1975. 452p.
「人間経営 18.悪人志願」李京南訳 서울 平和文化社 1975. 481p.

Aoi safaiya　青いサファイヤ

「人間経営 21.商才修業」李京南訳 서울 平和文化社 1975. 446p.

Aru fukushū　ある復讐

'어떤 復讐' 李貞變訳 「李朝残影」 서울 内外出版社 1966. p.217–269

Hanzai nisshi　犯罪日誌

「人間経営 29.一大賭博」李京南訳 서울 平和文化社 1975. 463p.

Hijō kaidan　非常階段

「人間経営 4.経営速戦」 李京南訳 서울 平和文化社 1974. 468p.

Hitozuma dakara　人妻だから

「人間経営 26.活火山性」李京南訳 서울 平和文化社 1975. 448p.

Jimenshi　地面師

'地官' 李貞變訳 「李朝残影」 서울 内外出版社 1966. p.271–316

Kage no kyōki　影の凶器

「人間経営 22.猪突猛進」 李京南訳 서울 平和文化社 1975. 439p.

Kurai hanamichi　暗い花道

「経営大望 9.経世大望」康曙海訳 서울 鮮京図書 1975. 466p.
「大物人間 8.攻略의 名人」李京南訳 서울 韓音社 1976. 435p.
「人間経営 38.人間大学」李京南訳 서울 平和文化社 1976. 435p.

Kuroi dokku　黒い船渠

「人間経営 39.商敵大胆」李京南訳 서울 平和文化社 1976. 433p.

Kuro no shisōsha　黒の試走車

「人間経営 9.大器晩成」李京南訳 서울 平和文化社 1974. 458p.

Nigi nigi jinsei　にぎにぎ人生

「大物人間 1.無頼의 名人 2.背徳의 名人」李京南訳 서울 韓音社 1976. 2冊
「人間経営 31.弱肉強食 32.背徳時代 33.欲望読本」李京南訳 서울 平和文化社 1976. 3冊

Nihonjin koko ni ari　日本人ここにあり

「人間経営 44.金脈人脈」李京南訳 서울 平和文化社 1976. 426p.

Niji o tsukamu　虹を摑む

「人間経営 27.黄金探索」李京南訳 서울 平和文化社 1975. 436p.

Noruka soruka　のるかそるか

「人間経営 24.野望点火」李京南訳 서울 平和文化社 1975. 442p.

Omachinasee　お待ちなせえ

「人間経営 11.快速走破 12.猛烈人生」서울 平和文化社 1975. 2冊

Onna no keisatsu　女の警察

「人間経営 19.起死悦楽」李京南訳 서울 平和文化社 1975. 460p.

Onna no shatō　女の斜塔

「석양이비웃을때」成香基訳 서울 文映閣 1968. 295p.
「大物人間 6.破壊의 名人 7.投銭의 名人」李京南訳 서울 韓音社 1976. 2冊
「人間経営 36.破戒攻略 37.投銭一手」李京南訳 서울 平和文化社 1976. 2冊

Otori　囮

「経営大望 18.社長天下」康曙海訳 서울 鮮京図書 1975. 498p.

Richō zan'ei　李朝残影

'李朝残影' 李貞變訳 「李朝残影」 서울 内外出版社 1966. p.15–91
'李朝残影' 閔丙山訳 「世界文学속의韓国 6」 서울 正韓出版社 1975. p.25–100

Shikima　色魔

「人間経営 5.千面能手 6.商魂怪物」李京南訳 서울 平和文化社 1974. 2冊

Teki wa doitsu da　敵はどいつだ

「人間経営 8.商売心得」 李京南訳 서울 平和文化社 1974. 565p.

Teyandee　てやんでえ

「人間経営 3.財覚破型」李京南訳 서울 平和文化社 1974. 486p.

Tokin shinshi　と金紳士

「大物人間 4.術数의 名人 5.集金의 名人」李京南訳 서울 韓音社 1976. 2冊
「人間経営 34. 鍍金紳士 35. 集金戦法」李京南訳 서울 平和文化社 1976. 2冊

Yamibune　闇船

'密船' 閔丙山訳 「世界文学속의韓國 6」 서울 正韓出版社 1975. p.175–236

KAJIYAMA Toshiyuki

Yarazu buttakuri　やらずぶったくり

「人間経営　15.一攫千金　16.疾風怒濤」李京南訳　平和
文化社　1975. 2冊

Yoru no haitō　夜の配当

「大物人間　9.商才의名人」李京南訳　서울　韓音社　1976.
433p.
「밤의配当」趙弼鎬訳　서울　広智院　1977. 328p.

Yuganda eikō　歪んだ栄光

'일그러진栄光'李貞變訳　「李朝残影」서울　内外出版社
1966. p.161-215

Yume no chōtokkyū　夢の超特急

「人間経営　17.黒字力学」李京南訳　서울　平和文化社
1975. 403p.

Zokufu　族譜

'族譜'「世代」第3巻7号 1965.
'族譜'李貞變訳　「李朝残影」서울　内外出版社 1966.
p.93-159
'族譜'表文台訳　「日本代表作家百人集 5」서울　希望出
版社 1966. p.236-276；「日本短篇文学全集 6」
서울　新太陽社 1969. p.148-188
'族譜'閔丙山訳　「世界文学속의韓国 6」서울　正韓出版
社 1975. p.101-174

Essay　エッセイ

'白人"컴플랙스"金賢珠訳　「바이바이바디」서울　三
韓出版社 1966. p.161-164

'무지개같은개념'成香基訳　서울　文映閣 1967. 295p.
'遅来의幸運'廖清秀訳　「投水自殺営救業」台北　蘭開書
局 1968. p.66-79
'金嬉老'金浄煕訳　「世代」第7巻11号 1969.
「人間経営　7.社長小学」李京南訳　서울　平和文化社 1974.
453p.
「人間経営　10.人間勝負」李京南訳　서울　平和文化社
1974. 572p.
「人間経営　13.出世戦略　14.大願成就」李京南訳　서울
平和文化社 1975. 2冊
「人間経営　20.人間征服」李京南訳　서울　平和文化社
1975. 499p.
「人間経営　25.心機一転」李京南訳　서울　平和文化社
1975. 452p.
「人間経営　28.乱世挑戦」李京南訳　서울　平和文化社
1975. 449p.
「人間経営　30.人間機熟」李京南訳　서울　平和文化社
1975. 456p.
'나는半島人'閔丙山訳　「世界文学속의韓國 6」서울　正
韓出版社 1975. p.237-264
「大物人間　11.挑戦의名人　12.黒字의名人」李京南訳　서
울　韓音社 1976. 2冊
「人間経営　40.死角脱出」李京南訳　서울　平和文化社
1976. 444p.
「大物人間 10.勝負의名人」李京南訳　서울　韓音社 1976.
444p.
「人間経営　41.獅子奮闘」李京南訳　서울　平和文化社
1976. 431p.
「人間経営　42.業界探険」李京南訳　서울　平和文化社
1976. 434p.
「大物人間 13.権謀의名人　14.強食의名人」李京南訳　서
울　韓音社 1976. 2冊
「人間経営　43.異常繁栄」李京南訳　서울　平和文化社
1976. 416p.

KAKO Satoshi　加古里子　1926-

Daruma chan to kaminari chan　だるまちゃんとかみな りちゃん

It's a funny funny day.　English version by Anita

M. Teeter. Tokyo, Labo-Teaching Information Center, 1969. 27p.

KAKURAI Akio　加倉井秋を　1909-

Haiku　俳句

'1 haiku'　*A history of haiku v.2*, by R. H. Blyth.
Tokyo, Hokuseido, 1964. p.252

KAMEI Katsuichiro　亀井勝一郎　1907-1966

Ai no mujō ni tsuite　愛の無常について

'愛之無情'司馬長風訳　「明報」第4巻2期 1969. p.88-93
'사랑의無常에대하여'鄭成煥　金冰杓訳　「世界에세이文
学全集 8」서울　東西出版社 1974. p.102-154；
「世界随筆文学全集 8」서울　世進出版社 1976.
p.102-154
「美的思索」王家成訳　台北　新理想出版社 1975. 204p.
'사랑의無常에対하여'姜敏訳「世界随想録全集 12」서울
百萬社 1976. p.1-238
「사랑의無常에대하여」張炅龍訳　서울　文芸出版社 1976.
237p.

Pekin no hoshi　北京の星

「北京的星星」李芒　祖秉和訳　北京　作家出版社 1958.
39p.
'北京的星星'文洁若訳　「世界文学」1962年5月　p.49-
56

Poems　詩

'詠萬里長城（長歌）'「明報」第4巻4期 1969. p.45-48

Essay　エッセイ

'Return to the East'　*Sources of the Japanese tradition*, comp. by Ryusaku Tsunoda and others.
N. Y. Columbia Univ. Press, 1958. p.900-906
'櫻花树下忆友誼忧虑日本文化的危机'李芒訳「世界文学」
1964年6月　p.102-112
「'我'之迷惑」司馬長風訳　「明報」第4巻6期 1969.
p.81-86.
'愛情易變人易老'顧竹君訳　「東西風」第9期 1973年7
月 p.31-34

KAMICHIKA Ichiko　神近市子　1888-

Fuan　不安

'Éloignement'　Tr. par M. Yoshitomi. *Femmes
japonaises et leur littérature*. Paris, Chariot,
1924. p.57-93

KAMIMURA Hajime　上村　肇　1910-

Poems　詩

'The way my poetry should go; Song of the light-
bulb; The foot of the mountain; Firefly;
Poor quarter psalm'　Tr. by Harry and Lynn
Guest and Shozo Kajima. *Post-war Japanese
poetry*. Harmondsworth, Penguin Books,
1972. p.41-44

KAMIMURA Hiro　上村ひろ　1932–

Poems　詩

'Water and ice'　Tr. by Harry and Lynn Guest and Shozo Kajima. *Post-war Japanese poetry*. Harmondsworth, Penguin Books, 1972. p.144

KAMITSUKASA Shōken　上司小剣　1874–1947

Rokubei no sainan　六兵衛の災難

'Rokubei no sainan'　Tr. by Yasutaro Kanzaki. *Eisakubun Zasshi*, Oct. 1921.

KAMURA Isota　嘉村礒多　1897–1933

Tojō　途上

'途上' 郭夏信訳 「世界文学全集 94」 서울　乙酉文化社 1962. p.329–357

KANAGAKI Robun　仮名垣魯文　1829–1894

Agura nabe　安愚楽鍋

'The beef eater'　Tr. by Donald Keene. *Modern Japanese literature*, ed. by D. Keene. N. Y. Grove Press, 1956; Tokyo, Tuttle, 1957. p.31–33

KANAI Choku　金井　直　1926–

Poems　詩

'도라지꽃' 金龍済訳 「日本詩集」 서울　青雲社　1960. p.47–49
'Small tune on snow, impromptu'　Tr. by Thomas Fitzsimmons. *Japanese poetry now*. London, André Deutsch, 1972. p.81; *Japanese poetry today*. N. Y. Schocken Books, 1972. p.83

KANAI Mieko　金井美恵子　1947–

Poems　詩

'The house of Madam Juju'　Tr. by Christopher Drake. *Contemporary Japanese literature*, ed. by Howard Hibbett. N. Y. Knopf, 1977. p.342–343
'In the town with catshaped maze' *The burning heart*, tr. and ed. by Kenneth Rexroth and Ikuko Atsumi. N. Y. Seabury Press, 1977. p.129–131

KANBARA Ariake　蒲原有明　1876–1952

Poems　詩

'5 poems' *The spirit of Japanese poetry*, by Yone Noguchi. London, John Murray, 1914. p.102–104
'Un oiseau sur l'eau; Chanson d'automne; La vie de la jeunesse; Trois visages de l'hiver; Le matin est là'　Tr. par Kuni Matsuo et Steinilber-Oberlin. *Anthologie des poètes japonais contemporains*. Paris, Mercure de France, 1939. p.53–60
'The jar; Adoration'　Tr. by Shigeshi Nishimura. *The Current of the World*, v.29, no.8, 1952. p.31; v.29, no.11, 1952. p.36
'When the wise physiognomist looked at me; The oyster shell' *The poetry of living Japan*, by Takamichi Ninomiya and D. J. Enright. London, John Murray, 1957. p.27–28
'Un oiseau sur l'eau; La matin est là . . .' *La poésie japonaise,* par Karl Petit. Paris, Seghers, 1959. p.187–189
'Gedanken; Wasser im Krug; An einem solchen Tag wird der Winter scheiden; Epitaph' Übers. von Kuniyo Takayasu und Manfred Hausmann. *Ruf der Regenpfeifer*. München, Bechtle Verlag, 1961. p.77–79
'Koyu kirmizi gölgeler'　Tercüme etmek L. Sami Akalin. *Japon şiiri*. İstanbul, Varlik Yayinevi, 1962. p.238
'Oyster shell'　Tr. by Geoffrey Bownas and Anthony Thwaite. *The Penguin book of Japanese verse*. Harmondsworth, Penguin Books, 1964. p.180
'Guardandomi il saggio indovino' Tr. di R. Beviglia. *Antologia della letteratura coreana e giapponese*. Milano, Fratelli Fabbri, 1969. p.272; *Il simbolismo nella poesia giapponese dell'era Meiji*. Roma, Istituto Italiano per il Medio ed Estremo Oriente, 1971. p 141–142
'겨울풍경; 봄노래 「永遠한世界名詩全集 2」 黄錦燦編 서울　翰林出版社　1964. p.114, 248–252; 「永遠한世界名詩全集 5」 黄錦燦編 서울　翰林出版社 1973. p.114, 248–252

KANBAYASHI Akatsuki　上林　暁　1902–

Banshun nikki　晩春日記

'Diary for late spring'　Tr. by G. W. Sargent. *Eigo Seinen*, v.103, no.1–5, Jan.–May, 1957.

Bara tōnin　薔薇盗人

'Похититель розы' Перевод В. Сановича. *Японская новелла*. Москва, Изд. Иност. Лит. 1961. p.99–107
'Роза гулин урлаушы' Орыссадан аударган Нурахмет Телеупов. *Хиросима касирети*. Алма-Ата, Жазушы, 1969. p.101–124

Haru no saka　春の坂

'Vision in spring'　Tr. by John Bester. *Japan P.E.N. News*, no.3, July 1959. p.1–7

Maigo fuda　迷ひ子札

'迷兒標' 金龍済訳 「日本代表作家百人集 3」 서울　希望出版社　1966. p.190–197; 「日本短篇文学全集 3」 서울　新太陽社　1969. p.338–346

Shiroi yakatabune　白い屋形船

'A stately white barge'　Tr. by Warren Carlisle. *Japan P.E.N. News*, no.17, Feb. 1966. p.8–13

Shōsetsu seinensha sonogo　小説青年社その後

'小説青年社・ユ後' 張壽哲訳 「新世界」 第2巻11号 p.306–320

KANDA Yuki 神田 雪

Poems 詩

'新緑之月' 文沽若訳 「詩刊」 第4期 1961. p.61-62

KANEI Fuhō 兼井芙峰 1886-

Haiku 俳句

'A moonlight night' Tr. by Asataro Miyamori. *Anthology of haiku, ancient and modern.* Tokyo, Maruzen, 1932. p.834; *Haiku poems, ancient and modern.* Tokyo, Maruzen, 1940. p.351

KANEKO Chikusui 金子筑水 1870-1937

Criticism 評論

'最年青的徳意志的藝術運動' 歴昌訳 「小説月報」 第12巻 8号 1921. p.14-20
'新時代與文藝' 魯迅訳 「莽原」 1925; 「壁下譯叢」 上海 北新書局 1929; 「魯迅全集 16」 上海 魯迅全集出版社 1938. 作家書屋 1946. 大連 光華書店 1948. 北京 人民文学出版社 1973. p.183-193; 「魯迅譯文集 5」 北京 人民文学出版社 1958. p.271-279
'教育與文藝' 李自珍訳 「北平晨報」 1930.
'理想主義與藝術' 胡雪訳 「新壘月刊」 第1巻2-3期 1933.

KANEKO Kun'en 金子薫園 1876-1951

Tanka 短歌

'Когда у двери, где цветут' *Огонек,* 1925, номер 30. p.7
'Peach-blossoms; A watershed; Fuji; The wind; My heart; The summer willow; Saint Nichiren' Tr. by Asataro Miyamori. *Masterpieces of Japanese poetry, ancient and modern.* Tokyo, Maruzen, 1936; Tokyo, Taiseido, 1956; N. Y. Greenwood Press, 1971. p.655-659
'Tanka' Tr. par Kuni Matsuo et Steinilber-Oberlin. *Anthologie des poètes japonais contemporains.* Paris, Mercure de France, 1939. p.264-265
'1 tanka' Tr. by Shigeshi Nishimura. *The Current of the World,* v.17, no.2, 1940. p.131
'4 tanka' Tr. by V. H. Viglielmo. *Japanese literature in the Meiji era.* Tokyo, Obunsha, 1955. p.389, 391
'1 tanka' Tr. by H. H. Honda. *The Reeds,* v.5, 1959. p.87
'Pfirsichblüten' Übers. von Günther Debon. *Im Schnee die Fähre.* München, Piper, 1960. p.30
'1 tanka' Übers. von Gerolf Coudenhove. *Japanische Jahreszeiten.* Zürich, Manesse Verlag, 1963. p.217
'Peach-blossoms' *Japanese love poems,* ed. by Jean Bennett. Garden City, Doubleday, 1976. p.9

KANEKO Mitsuharu 金子光晴 1895-1975

Poems 詩

'Demons and a poet' Tr. by S. Sato and C. Urdang. *Poetry,* May 1956. p.72
'The soap bubbles' Tr. by Rikutaro Fukuda.

Japan Quarterly, v.3, no.1, 1956. p.84-86
'The song of placenta; The soap bubbles' *An anthology of modern Japanese poetry,* ed. and tr. by Ichiro Kono and Rikutaro Fukuda. Tokyo, Kenkyusha, 1957. p.40-41
'Les bulles de savon' *La poésie japonaise,* par Karl Petit. Paris, Seghers, 1959. p.222-223
'Fuji' Übertragen von Shin Aizu. *Der schwermütige Ladekran.* St. Gallen, Tschudy Verlag, 1960. 0.46-47
'День призыва в японскую армию' Перевод Веры Марковой. *Иностранная Литература,* сентябрь 1960. p.150-151
'假面具之歌；另一个假面具之歌' 楼適夷 郁挈訳 「世界文学」 1962年5月 p.47-48
'真空を그리ㅇㄴ래；海底를헤매ㅇㄴㅡㄴ基督；鬼児誕生；곰팡이；鬼（抄）' 具滋雲訳 「世界戦後文学全集 9」 서울 新丘文化社 1962. p.209-213
'Song of the tart; Ascension; Opposition' Tr. by Geoffrey Bownas and Anthony Thwaite. *The Penguin book of Japanese verse.* Harmondsworth, Penguin Books, 1964. p.197-199
'La protesta' *La protesta poetica del Giappone,* a cura di Dacia Maraini e Michiko Nojiri. Roma, Officina Edizioni, 1968. p.39
'Война; Ночь; Песня, сложенная на берегу озера; Маяк' Перевод А. Долина. *Иностранная Литература,* ноябрь 1970. p.113-117
'海狗；臉盆；一個願望' 徐和隣訳 「現代詩解説」 台北 葡萄園詩刊社 1970. p.61-70
'손；飄泊의노래' 金巣雲訳 「世界의文学大全集 34」 서울 同和出版公社 1971. p.517-519
'A song of loneliness; My parachute; Bay' Tr. by James R. Morita. *Literature East and West,* v.15, no.4, v.16, no.1 & 2. 1971-72. p.806-815
'Song of a jellyfish; Cuckoos; To a certain unmarried woman; Recitative—a lakeshore poem; Mount Fuji' *Anthology of modern Japanese poetry,* tr. and comp. by Edith Marcombe Shiffert and Yuki Sawa. Tokyo, Tuttle, 1972. p. 60-67
'세수대야' 金光林訳 「現代詩学」 第4巻3号 1972.
'Moth I; Moth II; Moth III; Moth IV; The parachute; Night; Songs of loneliness; Standing amid the ruins of Tokyo' Tr. by Keiko Takagi. *Japan Quarterly,* v. 23, no.3, 1976. p.275-282
'Song of loneliness; The sun; The receiver' Tr. by Howard Hibbett and James R. Morita. *Contemporary Japanese literature,* ed. by Howard Hibbett. N. Y. Knopf, 1977. p.311-317
'Tøser; Såpeboblene' Til norsk ved Paal Brekke. *Moderne japansk lyrikk.* Oslo, Norske Bokklubben, n. d. p.35-38
'Urcuş' Traducerea Virgil Teodorescu. *Din lirica japoneză.* Bucureşti, Editura Univers, n.d. p.183

KANEKO Motoomi 金子元臣 1868-1944

Tanka 短歌

'Whistles of barley stalks; Violets' Tr. by Asataro Miyamori. *Masterpieces of Japanese poetry, ancient and modern.* Tokyo, Maruzen, 1936; Tokyo, Taiseido, 1956; N. Y. Greenwood Press, 1971. p.623-624
'Die Flöte von Stroh' Übers. von Günther Debon. *Im Schnee die Fähre.* München, Piper, 1960. p.20

KANEKO Tōta 金子兜太 1919–

Haiku 俳句

'20 haiku' *Modern Japanese haiku, an anthology*, comp. and tr. by Makoto Ueda. Tokyo, Univ. of Tokyo Press, 1976. p.254–263

KANEKO Yōbun 金子洋文 1894–

Jigoku 地獄

'Ад' Перевод Елены Терновской. *Ад*. Москва, Московский Рабочий, 1929. p.18–63
「地獄」 沈端先訳 上海 春野書局 192?. 1冊

Jūka 銃火

'銃火' 沈端先訳 「初春的風」 上海 大江書局 192?.

Kono jinsei wa この人生は

'Автобиография' Перевод Елены Терновской. *Ад*. Москва, Московский Рабочий, 1929. p.15–17

Me 眼

'Augen' Deutsch von Jürgen Berndt. *Träume aus zehn Nächten*. Berlin, Aufbau Verlag, 1975. p.204–205

Onna 女

'女人' 張資平訳 「資平譯品集」 上海 現代書局 192?.

Sentakuya to shijin 洗濯屋と詩人

Lavisto kaj poeto. Tr. T. Tooguu. Tokyo, Esperanto Kenkyusha, 1927. 40p.
'洗衣老板與詩人' 楊騷訳 「語絲」 第4巻45期 1928. p.273–307; 「日本戯曲集」 上海 南強書店 1929.
「洗衣老板與詩人」 楊騷訳 上海 南強書店 1929. 1冊

Shuppan 出帆

'Weighing anchor' Tr. by Kazuo Yamada. *Japan Times*, September 14, 1930; *Eigo Kenkyu*, v.23, no.7, 1930. p.607–609, v.23, no.8, 1930. p.746–748; *The roofgarden, and other one-act plays*. Tokyo, Shijo Shobo, 1934. p.31–70

'勞働家的金銀' 兪寄凡訳 「東方雑誌」 第18巻22期 1921. p.103–106

KANEOYA Kiyoshi 金親 清 1907–

'星光下的札記' 何华訳 「世界文学」 1966年1月 p.41–60

KANŌ Sakujirō 加能作次郎 1885–1941

Amazake 甘酒

'甘酒' 黎烈文訳 「東方雑誌」 第25巻13期 1928. p.123–130

Shatsu 襯衣

'襯衣' 張資平訳 「別宴」 武昌 時中合作社 1926; 「襯衣」 上海 光華書局 1928.

KANZAWA Toshiko 神沢利子 1924–

Dareka ga pai o tabe ni kita だれかがパイをたべにきた

The selfish old woman. Indianapolis, Bobbs-Merrill, 1971. 32p.

Itazura rakko no Rokko いたずらラッコのロッコ

'Uličník Rokko' *Modré vánoce*. Přel. Ivan Krouský a Z. K. Slabý. Praha, Albatros, 1975.

KARA Jūrō 唐 十郎 1940–

Jon Shirubā ジョン・シルバー

'John Silver: the beggar of love' Tr. by David Goodman. *Concerned Theatre Japan*, v.1, no.2, 1970. p.146–211

KARAKI Junzō 唐木順三 1904–

Criticism and essays 評論・エッセイ

'芥川龍之介在思想史上的位置' 侍桁訳 「文藝研究」 創刊号 1930.
'The feeling of awe' *Nippon*, August 1964. p.48–52; *Journal of Social and Political Ideas in Japan*, v.3, no.2, August 1965. p.80–82
'The spirit of wabi' *Chanoyu Quarterly*, v.2, no.3, 1971. p.1–6
'On "Meian"' *Essays on Natsume Soseki's works*. Tokyo, Japan Society for the Promotion of Science, 1972. p.77–118

KASAI Zenzō 葛西善蔵 1887–1928

Bafun seki 馬糞石

'馬糞石' 高汝鴻訳 「日本短篇小説集」 台北 台湾商務印書館 1969. p.67–85

Chi o haku 血を吐く

'Chrleni krve' Přel. M. Jelínková. *Nový Orient*, no.4, 1965.

Norowareta te 呪われた手

'The cursed hand' Tr. by Max Bickerton. *Eigo Seinen*, v.69, no.1–3, 1933.

Yūdō enboku 遊動円木

'遊動圓木' 劉石克訳 「新壘月刊」 創刊号 1933.

KASHIMA Ōkō 鹿島桜巷

「美人島」 張論訳 上海 羣學社 1910. 1冊

KASUGAI Ken 春日井 建 1938–

Tanka 短歌

'1 tanka' *Modern Japanese poetry*, by Donald Keene. Ann Arbor, Center for Japanese Studies, Univ. of Michigan, 1964. p.37

KASUGAI Ken

'1 tanka' Tr. by Donald Keene. *Landscapes and portraits*. Tokyo, Kodansha International, 1971. p.154

KASUYA Masahiro　かすや昌宏　1937–

Kurisumasu　くりすます

Long ago in Bethlehem. Tr. by Peggy Blakeley. London, Black, 1973. 1v.
The way Christmas came. Tr. by Chieko Funakoshi. N. Y. Judson Press, 1973. 1v.
Barnet i krubban. Översätta Britt G. Hallqvist. Örebro, I.P.C. 1973. 24p.

KATAGIRI Yuzuru　片桐ユズル　1931–

Poems　詩

'Ненависть' Перевод А.Мамонова. *Иностранная Литература*, июнь 1966. p.104

KATAKAMI Noboru　片上　伸　1884–1928

Criticism　評論

'新時代的豫感' 魯迅訳 「春潮月刊」 第1巻6期 1929; 「魯迅全集 16」上海 魯迅全集出版社 1938. 作家書屋 1946. 大連 光華書店 1948. 北京 人民文学出版社 1973. p.423–438; 「魯迅譯文集 10」北京 人民文学出版社 1958. p.198–209
'北歐文學的原理；階級藝術的問題；「否定」的文學' 魯迅訳 「壁下譯叢」上海 北新書局 1929; 「魯迅全集 16」上海 魯迅全集出版社 1938. 作家書屋 1946. 大連 光華書店 1948. 北京 人民文学出版社 1973. p.194–240;「魯迅譯文集 5」北京 人民文学出版社 1958. p.280–317
'現代新興文學的諸問題' 魯迅訳 上海 大江書舖 1929. 1冊
「文學的作者與讀者」汪馥泉訳 上海 大江書舖 193?. 1冊
「文學與社會」雪峰訳 上海 光華書局 193?. 1冊

KATAOKA Teppei　片岡鉄兵　1894–1944

Aru ketsumatsu　ある結末

'一個結局' 章克標訳「小説月報」第21巻2号 1930. p.435–438

Ayasato mura kaikyoroku　綾里村快挙録

'Повесть о мирном житье-бытье деревни Киори' Перевод Н. Фельдман. *Японская революционная литература*. Москва, Худож. Лит. 1934. p.137–161

Onna no sesugata　女の背姿

'女人的背影' 劉大杰訳 「新月刊」 第3巻2期 1931.
'女人的背景'「日本短篇小説選」香港 藝美圖書公司 1959. p.75–81

Shikijō bunka　色情文化

'色情文化' 吶吶鷗訳 「色情文化」上海 水沫書店 1928.

Shōnibyō　小児病

'小児病' 高汝鴻訳「日本短篇小説集」 台北 台湾商務印書館 1969. p.207–232

KATAOKA Yoshikazu　片岡良一　1897–1957

Criticism　評論

'日本之個人主義文學及其淵源' 張資平訳 「絜茜」 創刊号 19??.
'個人主義文學的輪廓' 張資平訳 「橄欖月刊」 第2巻8期 19??.
'The study of naturalism' *Japan Science Review, Humanistic Studies*, no.10, 1959. p.29–32

KATAYAMA Koson　片山孤村　1879–1933

Criticism　評論

'大戦與德國國民性及其文化文藝' 李達訳 「小説月報」 第12巻8号 1921. p.20–24
'思索的惰性；自然主義的理論及技巧；表現主義' 魯迅訳 「壁下譯叢」上海 北新書局 1929;「魯迅全集 16」上海 魯迅全集出版社 1938. 作家書屋 1946. 大連 光華書店 1948. 北京 人民文学出版社 1973. p.13–60;「魯迅譯文集 5」北京 人民文学出版社 1958. p.135–172

KATAYAMA Sen　片山　潜　1859–1933

Jiden　自伝

Катаяма Сэн, воспоминания. Москва, Наука, 1964. 770p.

Waga kaisō　わが回想

Катаяма Сэн, моя жизнь. Перевод С. Мятежного. Москва, 1921. 80p.
'Пройденный путь' Перевод П. П. Топеха. *Катаяма Сэн, статьи и мемуалы*. Москва, Восточная Литература, 1959. p.176–294

KATAYAMA Shōzō　片山昌造　1911–

Akatsuki no ko ra　あかつきの子ら

Дети зари. Перевод И. Львовой. Москва, Детгиз, 1960. 159p.

KATAOKA Yoshikazu (右欄)

Shusse banashi　出世ばなし

'立志' 章克標訳 「東方雑誌」 第26巻22期 1929. p.113–120

Tsūshin kōshu　通信工手

'Монтеры' Перевод Н. Фельдман. *Литература Мировой Революции*, номер 6, 1932. p.53–58; *Японская революционная литература*. Москва, Худож. Лит. 1934. p.206–217
'Linesmen' *The cannery boat, and other Japanese short stories*. N. Y. International Publishers, 1933; London, Martin Lawrence, 1933; N. Y. Greenwood Press, 1968. p.171–192

Criticism　評論

'普羅列塔利亜小説作法' 筱江訳 「新亜洲月刊」 第1巻2号 1930.
'新興小説的創作理論' 謝六逸訳 「現代文學」第1巻2–5号 1935.
「普羅小説創作論」 謝六逸訳 上海 前夜書局 193?.

Paikesetsosumaa lapsed. Tr. from the Russian L. Seo. Tallin, Estgosizdat, 1961. 159p.
Дети зари, на литовском языке. Перевод Л. Гребликене. Вильнюс, Гослитиздат, 1962. 202p.
Дети зари, на украинском языке. Перевод Н. Сизоренко. Киев, Детгиз, 1962. 182p.
Kinder der Morgenröte. Übers. von Horst Scherenschmidt. Berlin, Kinderbuchverlag, 1963. 165p.
Басагони субкыш фируз. Перевод О. Ходжаева. Душанбе, Тоджикгосиздат, 1963. 184p.

KATAYAMA Toshihiko　片山敏彦　1898–1961

Poems　詩

'Evening sea' *An anthology of modern Japanese poetry,* ed. and tr. by Ichiro Kono and Rikutaro Fukuda. Tokyo, Kenkyusha, 1957. p.44

KATŌ Kazuo　加藤一夫　1887–1951

Mura ni osou nami　村に襲う波

'Под натиском волн' Перевод Н. Фельдман. *Вестник японской литературы,* номер 3, 1930. p.52–129
Под натиском волн. Перевод Н. Фельдман. Москва, Молодая Гвардия, 1931. 152p.

KATŌ Masao　加藤まさを　1897–

Poems　詩

'A woman and a grass; On resigning a post; Dream or reality?; Monica's hill' *The lyric garland,* ed. by Makoto Sangu. Tokyo, Hokuseido, 1957. p.30–31

KATŌ Shūichi　加藤周一　1919–

Shisendō shi　詩仙堂志

'The pavilion of great poets' Tr. by Hilda Kato. *Japan Quarterly,* v.13, no.4, 1966. p.476–489

Criticism　評論

'Zur Situation der modernen japanischen Literatur' *Nachrichten* (Gesellschaft für Natur- und Völkerkunde Ostasiens, Nr.75, 1953. p.35–46
'Homo viator' *Japan Quarterly,* v.8, no.2, 1961. p.219–221
'Problèmes des écrivains japonais d'aujourd'hui' *Les Temps Modernes,* 24, no.272, Feb. 1969. p.1480–1490
'Modern Japanese civilization in history' *The Japan Interpreter,* v.6, no.1, 1970. p.29–44
Form, style, tradition. Tr. by John Bester. Berkeley, Univ. of California Press, 1971. 216p.
The Japan-China phenomenon. Tr. by David Chibbett. Tokyo, Kodansha International, 1975. 103p.

KATŌ Shūson　加藤楸邨　1905–

Haiku　俳句

'5 haiku' Tr. by Haxon Ishii. *Eigo Seinen,* v.88, no.6, 1942. p.179
'3 haiku poems' Tr. by Donald Keene. *Modern Japanese literature,* ed. by D. Keene. N. Y. Grove Press, 1956; Tokyo, Tuttle, 1957. p.382
'3 haiku' Tr. by Geoffrey Bownas and Anthony Thwaite. *The Penguin book of Japanese verse.* Harmondsworth, Penguin Books, 1964. p.172
'3 haiku' Tr. by Donald Keene. *The Mentor book of modern Asian literature,* ed. by D. B. Shimer. N. Y. New American Library, 1969. p.125
'3 haiku' Tr. by Takamasa Sasaki. *Eigo Seinen,* v.122, no.5, 1976. p.231
'20 haiku' *Modern Japanese haiku: an anthology,* comp. and tr. by Makoto Ueda. Tokyo, Univ. of Tokyo Press, 1976. p.219–228

KATŌ Takeo　加藤武雄　1888–1956

Aiken monogatari　愛犬物語

'愛犬故事' 謝六逸訳 「小説月報」 第9巻1号 1928. p.46–55

Kyōshū　郷愁

'郷愁' 周作人訳 「小説月報」 第12巻1号 1921. p.16–19; 「日本現代小説集 3」 上海 商務印書館 1930. p.356–363; 「日本小説集」 上海 商務印書館 193?.
'一篇稿子' 「少年的悲哀」 郁達夫等訳 台北 啓明書局 1956. p.88–93
'郷愁' 新興書局編集部訳 「日本短篇小説選」 台南 鳴宇出版社 1972. p.1–5
'郷愁' 「日本作家十二人集」 香港 新學書店 1959. p.79–85

Matsuri no yo no dekigoto　祭の夜の出来事

'祭夜的意外' 黎烈文訳 「東方雑誌」 第24巻24期 1927. p.91–102
'В праздничную ночь' Перевод Н. Фельдман. *Вестник японской литературы,* номер 2, 1930. p.145–154

Shūressha　終列車

'最後列車' 張資平訳 「別宴」 武昌 時中合作社 1926.
'最後的列車' 張資平訳 「襯衣」 上海 光華書局 1928.

Criticism　評論

'関於新興藝術派' 李自珍訳 「北平晨報學園」 1931.

「接吻」 謝六逸訳 上海 大江書舗 1929. 1冊
「她的肖像」 葉作舟訳 上海 開華書房 192?.

KATSU Genzō　勝 諺蔵　1844–1902

Nikaigasa Yagyū jikki　二蓋笠柳生実記

'The fencing master' Tr. by Thomas R. H. McClatchie. *Japanese plays.* Yokohama, H. M.'s Consular Service, 1879. p.115–136; London, Allen and Unwin, 1890. p.117–141

KATSU Kaishū

KATSU Kaishū 勝 海舟 1823–1899

Tanka 短歌

'Recollections of the battle of Ueno; The anchor-rope' Tr. by Asataro Miyamori. *Masterpieces of Japanese poetry, ancient and modern.* Tokyo, Maruzen, 1936; Tokyo, Taiseido, 1956; N. Y. Greenwood Press, 1971. p.596–598

KATSUMINE Shinpū 勝峰晋風 1887–1954

Haiku 俳句

'2 haiku' Tr. by Asataro Miyamori. *Anthology of haiku, ancient and modern.* Tokyo, Maruzen, 1932. p.791–792
'1 haiku' Tr. by R. H. Blyth. *Haiku v.4.* Tokyo, Hokuseido, 1952. p.294

KATSUMOTO Masaakira 勝本正晃 1895–

Poems 詩

'Am Kriegsende' *The lyric garland,* ed. by Makoto Sangu. Tokyo, Hokuseido, 1957. p.32

KATSUO Kin'ya 勝尾金弥 1927–

Tenpō no hitobito 天保の人々

People of the Tenpo era: a story. Tr. by A. T. Yoshimura. Kanazawa, Santo no Kai, 1970. 194p.

KATSURA Yoshihisa 桂 芳久 1929–

Poems 詩

'Черный пепел Хиросимы' *Иностранная Литература,* октябрь 1960. p.181–182

KATSUTA Kōgetsu 勝田香月 1899–1966

Poems 詩

'Song of departure' Tr. by Henry H. Armstrong. *Jiji Eigo Kenkyu,* v.2, no.7, 1947. p.21

KAWABATA Bōsha 川端茅舎 1897–1941

Haiku 俳句

'6 haiku' Tr. by Geoffrey Bownas and Anthony Thwaite. *The Penguin book of Japanese verse.* Harmondsworth, Penguin Books, 1964. p.170–171
'26 haiku' *A history of haiku v.2,* by R. H. Blyth. Tokyo, Hokuseido, 1964. p.272–280
'20 haiku' *Modern Japanese haiku, an anthology,* comp. and tr. by Makoto Ueda. Tokyo, Univ. of Tokyo Press, 1976. p.183–192

'1 haiku' Tr. by Takamasa Sasaki. *Eigo Seinen,* v.122, no. 5, 1976. p.231
'1 haiku' Traducerea Virgil Teodorescu. *Din lirica japoneză.* Bucureşti, Editura Univers, n. d. p.189

KAWABATA Yasunari 川端康成 1899–1972

Aki no ame 秋の雨

'Jesienny deszcz' Przeł. Krystyna Okazaki. *Literatura na Świecie,* no.7, 1972. p.119

Amagasa 雨傘

'The umbrella' Tr. by Minoru Kohda. *The Reeds,* v.14, 1976. p.22–23

Arigatō 有難う

'Köszönöm' Ford. István Benko. *Vigilia,* Jún. 1970. p.390–391
'Подяка' Переклав Иван Дзюб. *Всесвет,* номер 8, 1971. p.97–98

Asa no tsume 朝の爪

'Nagels in de ochtend' Vertaald von C. Ouwehand. *Nagels in de ochtend.* Amsterdam, Meulenhoff, 1971. p.12–13
'Paznokcie' Przeł. Krystyna Okazaki. *Literatura na Świecie,* no.7, 1972.

Batta to suzumushi バッタと鈴虫

'Grasshopper and bell-ring' Tr. by Minoru Kohda. *The Reeds,* v.14, 1976. p.23–27

Bi no sonzai to hakken 美の存在と発見

'美之存在與發現' 伍木盛訳 「文藝月刊」 第44期 1962. p.122–132, 第45期 1962. p.124–138
The existence and discovery of beauty. Tr. by V. H. Viglielmo. Tokyo, Mainichi Shimbunsha, 1969. 109p.
'Существование и открытие красоты' Перевод Т. Григорьевой. *И была любовь, и была ненависть.* Москва, Наука, 1975. p.249–275
'Über das Vorhandensein und die Entdeckung von Schönheit' *Asiatische Studien,* Band 29, Teil 1, 1975. p.2–38

Bōshi jiken 帽子事件

'A hat incident' Tr. by Shohei Shimada. *The Reeds,* v.6, 1960. p.60–64
'Die Geschichte mit dem Strohhut' Übers. von Oscar Benl. *Tagebuch eines Sechzehnjährigen.* München, Nymphenburger, 1969. p.289–292
'帽子事件' 余翼等訳 「川端康成短篇選」 台北 水晶出版社 1969. p.145–150

Bungaku teki jijoden 文学的自叙伝

'文学的自叙傳' 金世煥訳 「世界베스트셀라북스 1」 서울 三耕社 1968. p.327–340; 「노오벨賞文学全集10」 서울 新丘文化社 1971. p.491–505; 「川端康成全集 4」 서울 新丘文化社 1969. p.355–369

Fuji no hatsuyuki 富士の初雪

'Der erste Schnee auf dem Fuji-Berg' Übers. von Oscar Benl. *Der Kirschblütenzweig.* München, Nymphenburger, 1965. p.422–444
'Первий снег на Фудзи' Переклав М. Федоришин.

Жовтень, номер 2, 1973. p.72–81

Futari 二人

'Twee' Vertaald door C. Ouwehand. *Nagels in de ochtend.* Amsterdam, Meulenhoff, 1971. p.116–125

Fuyu chikashi 冬近し

'Tél van' Ford. Thein Alfréd. *Mai Japán dekameron.* Budapest, Nyugat, 1935. p.121–129
'Vorwinter' Übers. von Oscar Benl. *Tagebuch eines Sechzehnjährigen.* München, Nymphenburger, 1969. p.293–297

Gekka bijin 月下美人

'The cereus' Tr. by Edward Seidensticker. *Contemporary Japanese literature.* N. Y. Knopf, 1977. p.308–309

Haha no hatsukoi 母の初恋

'母親的初戀' 章安蘋訳 「知識分子」 第25期 1969年3月 p.33–35, 第26期 1969年4月 p.33–35, 第27期 1969年5月 p.33–35
'母親的初戀' 余翼等訳 「川端康成短篇小説選」 台北 水晶出版社 1969. p.153–186
'母親的初戀' 劉慕沙訳 「水月」 高雄 文皇出版社 1971. p.111–142

Hana no warutsu 花のワルツ

'꽃의왈츠' 具滋雲訳 「川端康成全集 1」 서울 新丘文化社 1969. p.89–141
'꽃의왈츠' 崔浩然訳 「新訳世界文学全集 48」 서울 正音社 1972. p.67–191
'꽃의왈츠' 朴仁植訳 「世界短篇文学大系 29」 서울 尚書閣 1975. p.281–380

Hi mo tsuki mo 日も月も

'날마다달마다' 金光福訳 「川端康成全集 3」 서울 新丘文化社 1969. p.323–439

Hi ni yuku kanojo 火に行く彼女

'A girl who goes towards the fire' Tr. by Minoru Kohda. *The Reeds,* v.13, 1972. p.48–49

Hinata 日向

'The sunny place' Tr. by Shohei Shimada. *The Reeds,* v.6, 1960. p.65–67

Hinja no koibito 貧者の恋人

'Возлюбленная бедника' на латышском языке. *Тарибине Мотерис,* номер 6, 1969. p.14–15

Hitori no kōfuku 一人の幸福

'The happiness of one person' Tr. by Kiyoaki Nakao. *Eigo Kenkyu,* v.55, no.8, 1966. p.34–38, no.9, p.34–36

Hokuro no tegami ほくろの手紙

'The mole' Tr. by Edward Seidensticker. *Japan Quarterly,* v.2, no.1, 1955. p.86–93; *Modern Japanese literature.* N. Y. Grove Press, 1956. Tokyo, Tuttle, 1957. p.366–374; *Modern Japanese short stories.* Tokyo, Japan Publications Trading Co. 1960. p.190–200. Rev. ed. Tokyo, Japan Publications Trading Co. 1970. p.151–159; *The Izu dancer.* Tokyo, Hara Shobo, 1963. p.133–162

'Il neo' Tr. di Atsuko Ricca Suga. *Narratori giapponesi moderni.* Milano, Bompiani, 1965. p.355–366
'黒痣的信' 余翼等訳 「川端康成短篇小説選」 台北 水晶出版社 1969. p.113–125
'A szemolcs' Ford. Dudas Kalman. *Nagyvilág* no.12, 1970. p.1808–1812
'Das Mal auf der Schulter' Übers. von Siegfried Schaarschmidt. *Träume im Kristall.* Frankfurt am Main, Suhrkamp, 1974. p.111–125

Itaria no uta イタリアの歌

'Песнь об Италии' Перевод С. Гутерман. *Ясунари Кавабата.* Москва, Прогресс, 1971. p.332–344
'Песния об Италии' Перевод с русс. Т. Токмагамбетова. *Жалын,* номер 1, 1972. p.121–130

Izu no odoriko 伊豆の踊子

'Die kleine Tänzerin von Izu' Übers. von Oscar Benl. *Flüchtiges Leben.* Berlin, Landsmann, 1942.
'The Izu dancer' Tr. by Edward Seidensticker. *Atlantic Monthly,* v.195, 1955. p.108–114; *The Izu dancer.* Tokyo, Hara Shobo, 1963. p.7–68; *The Izu dancer, and other stories.* Tokyo, Tuttle, 1974. p.9–38
'The dancing girl of Izu' Tr. by Eiichi Hayashi. *The Reeds,* v.3, 1957. p.71–106
Danceur de Izu. Paris, Albin Michel, 1957.
'伊豆的舞女' 傅寶齡訳 「勲章」 台北 文壇社 1960. p.75–106
'A pequena dançarina de Izu' Tr. de Antônio Nojiri. *Maravilhas do conto japonês.* São Paulo, Editôra Cultrix, 1962. p.117–144
'Dancistino de Izu' Tr. Gaku Konisi. *El japana literaturo.* Tokyo, Japana Esperanto Instituto, 1965. p.63–87
'La danzatrice di Izu' *Le piu belle novelle di tutti i paesi.* Milano, 1965.
'Die Tänzerin von Izu' Übers. von Oscar Benl. *Die Tänzerin von Izu, Tausend Kraniche, Schneeland, Kyoto.* München, Carl Hanser, 1968. p.5–34
Die Tänzerin von Izu. Übers. von Oscar Benl. Stuttgart Reclam, 1968. 45p.
İzu dansözü. Almanca'dan çeviren Azra Erhat. İstanbul, Cem Yayinevi, 1968. 166p.
'伊豆의舞妓' 柳呈訳 「世界베스트셀라북스 1」 서울 三耕社 1968. p.173–193; 「川端康成全集 3」 서울 新丘文化社 1969. p.3–23; 「노오벨賞文学全集 10」 서울 新丘文化社 1971. p.173–193
'As Izui tancosno' Ford. Vihar Judit. *Nagyvilág,* no.2, 1969. p.168–171
'La danzarina di Izu' Tr. del aleman de Ana M. de la Fuente. *Kioto, La danzatrina de Izu.* Barcelona, Plaza y Janés, 1969.
'La danzatrice di Izu' Tr. di K. Toguchi e E. Maimeri. *Novelle giapponesi.* Milano, Martello, 1969. p.7–34
De danseres uit Izu. Vertaald van engl. von H. C. ten Berge. Amsterdam, Van Gennep, 1969. 31p.
'伊豆의舞娘' 朱佩蘭訳 「伊豆的舞娘」 嘉義 明山書局 1969. p.221–253
'伊豆舞孃' 余翼等訳 「川端康成短篇小説選」 台北 水晶出版社 1969. p.7–39
'La danzarina de Izu' Tr. por Jaime Fernández. *Los premios Novel de Literatura, v.12.* Barcelona, Plaza y Janés, 1970.
'伊豆的舞娘' 劉與亮訳 「現代日本小説選」 台北 雲天出版社 1970. p.202–234
'Танцовщица из Иззу' Перевод З. Рахима. *Ясу-*

нари Кавабата. Москва, Прогресс, 1971. p.287–310

'Танцивниця з Идзу' Переклав Иван Дзюб. *Всесвет*, номер 8, 1971. p.88–97

'伊豆的舞嬢' 瑞宏訳 「水月」 高雄 文皇出版社 1971. p.42–72

'伊豆의舞妓' 金容浩訳 「노벨賞文学大全集 10」 서울 高麗出版社 1971. p.23–43; 「世界代表文学全集 9」 서울 高麗出版社 1976. p.23–43

'이즈의춤아가씨' 崔浩然訳 「新訳世界文学全集 48」 서울 正音社 1972. p.45–65

'La danseuse d'Izu' Tr. par Sylvie Regnault-Gatier et al. *La danseuse d'Izu*. Paris, Albin Michel, 1973. p.9–60

'이즈의舞妓' 李圭植訳 서울 鮮文出版社 1973. 188p.

'Die Tänzerin von Izu' Deutsch von Oscar Benl. *Träume aus zehn Nächten*. Berlin, Aufbau-Verlag, 1975. p.210–240

'伊豆의舞娘' 朴仁植訳 「世界短篇文学大系 29」 서울 尚書閣 1975. p.13–49

'이즈의춤추는少女' 閔丙山訳 「世界文学全集 20」 서울 三省出版社 1975. p.426–446

'伊豆의춤추는少女' 李吉鐘訳 「世界短篇文学全集 20」 서울 金字堂 1976. p.69–102

'이즈의춤추는少女' 姜敏訳 「世界代表短篇文学全集 22」 서울 正韓出版社 1976. p.179–205

'Nangrabamisu' Tr. Orasa Sripruksamas. *Rueng sun yeepun 1*. Bangkok, Uksornsasna, 1977. p.145–193

Jojōka 抒情歌

'抒情歌' 千祥炳訳 「世界베스트셀러북스 1」 서울 三耕社 1968. p.257–275; 「川端康成全集 3」 서울 新丘文化社 1969. p.153–171

'Lyric poem' Tr. by Francis Mathy. *Monumenta Nipponica*, v.26, no.3–4, 1971. p.287–305

'Элегия' Перевод З. Рахима. *Ясунари Кавабата*. Москва, Прогресс, 1971. p.311–331

'Élégie' Tr. par Sylvie Regnault-Gatier et al. *La danseuse d'Izu*. Paris, Albin Michel, 1973. p.61–96

'Lirika' Tr. di Nicoletta Spadavecchia. *Il Giappone*, anno 15, 1975. p.39–62

'抒情歌' 姜敏訳 「世界代表短篇文学全集 22」 서울 正韓出版社 1976. p.241–264

Jūroku sai no nikki 十六歳の日記

'16歳의日記' 鄭漢模訳 「世界베스트셀러북스 1」 서울 三耕社 1968. p.295–315; 「川端康成全集 3」 서울 新丘文化社 1969. p.173–193; 「世界代表短篇文学全集 22」 서울 正韓出版社 1976. p.295–323

'Tagebuch eines Sechzehnjährigen' Übers. von Oscar Benl. *Tagebuch eines Sechzehnjährigen*. München, Nymphenburger, 1969. p.259–288

'Diario de un muchacho' Tr. por Angel Sabrido. *Diario de un muchacho*. Barcelona, Plaza y Janés, 1971.

Kaikō kinenbi 開校記念日

'開校記念日' 「묏 불」 第1巻6号 1969年6月

Kakesu かけす

'The jay' Tr. by Edward Seidensticker. *Contemporary Japanese literature,* ed. by Howard Hibbett. N. Y. Knopf, 1977. p.300–303

Kami 髪

'The hair' Tr. by Minoru Kohda. *The Reeds*, v.14, 1976. p.21

Kami wa nagaku 髪は長く

'一把長髪' 劉慕沙訳 「水月」 高雄 文皇出版社 1971. p.73–82

Kataude 片腕

'One arm' Tr. by Edward Seidensticker. *Japan Quarterly*, v.14, no.1, 1967. p.60–71; *House of the sleeping beauties, and other stories*. Tokyo, Kodansha International, 1969; London, Quadriga Press, 1969; N. Y. Ballantine Books, 1970; London, Sphere, 1971. p.103–124

'De arm' Vertaald von C. Ouwehand. *Nagels in de ochtend*. Amsterdam, Meulenhoff, 1971. p.137–158

'한쪽팔' 金容浩訳 「노벨賞文学大全集 10」 서울 高麗出版社 1971. p.493–511

'Kataude' Tr. di Mario Teti. *La casa delle belle addormentate*. Milano, Mondadori, 1972.

'Ein Arm' Übers. von Siegfried Schaarschmidt. *Träume im Kristall*. Frankfurt am Main, Suhrkamp, 1974. p.76–110

'한쪽팔' 朴仁植訳 「世界短篇文学大系 29」 서울 尚書閣 1975. p.245–279

Kinjū 禽獣

'금수' 李炯基訳 「世界短篇文学全集 7」 서울 啓蒙社 1966. p.334–351; 「世界短篇文学全集 9」 서울 三珍社 1971. p.208–225; 「世界代表短篇文学全集 9」 서울 三熙社 1976. p.208–225; 「世界短篇文学全集 9」 서울 新韓出版社 1976. p.350–377

'禽獣' 李炯基訳 「世界베스트셀러북스 1」 서울 三耕社 1968. p.277–293; 「川端康成全集 3」 서울 新丘文化社 1969. p.195–211

'Of birds and beasts' Tr. by Edward G. Seidensticker. *House of the sleeping beauties, and other stories*. Tokyo, Kodansha International, 1969. p.127–148. London, Quadriga Press, 1969. N. Y. Ballantine Books, 1970. London, Sphere, 1971. p.135–158

'禽獣' 余翼等訳 「川端康成短篇小説選」 台北 水晶出版社 1969. p.41–73

'禽獣' 劉慕沙訳 「水月」 高雄 文皇出版社 1971. p.83–110

'Kinju' Tr. di Mario Teti. *La casa delle belle addormentate*. Milano, Mondadori, 1972.

'Bestiaire' Tr. par Sylvie Regnault-Gatier et al. *La danseuse d'Izu*. Paris, Albin Michel, 1973. p.97–132

'Von Vögeln und Tieren' Übers. von Siegfried Schaarschmidt. *Träume im Kristall*. Frankfurt am Main, Suhrkamp, 1974. p.126–159

'禽獣' 李吉鐘訳 「世界短篇文学全集 20」 서울 金字堂 1976. p.40–68

'禽獣' 姜敏訳 「世界代表短篇文学全集 22」 서울 正韓出版社 1976. p.219–239

Ki no ue 木の上

'In de boom' Vertaald door C. Ouwehand. *Nagels in de ochtend*. Amsterdam. Meulenhoff, 1971. p.134–136

Kinsen no michi 金銭の道

'生財有道' 施翠峯訳 「知識分子」 第56期 1970年7月 p.31–32

Kita no umi kara 北の海から

'С северного моря' Перевод на литовском В. Скогалите. *Литература ир мианас*, 1965, янв. 25

'북녁바다' 姜敏訳 「世界베스트셀러북스 1」 서울 三耕社 1968. p.317–325; 「世界代表短篇文学全集 22」 서울 正韓出版社 1976. p.207–217; 「川端康成全集 3」 서울 新丘文化社 1969. p.213–220

Kōbai 紅梅

'The plum' Tr. by Edward Seidensticker. *Con-*

temporary Japanese literature, ed. by Howard Hibbett. N. Y. Knopf, 1977. p.299–300

Koji no kanjō 孤児の感情

'孤兒的感情' 江上訳 「日本名家小説選」 高雄 大舞台書苑 1976. p.1–21

Kokyō 故郷

'故郷' 余翼訳 「川端康成短篇小説選」 台北 水晶出版社 1969. p.101–110

Koto 古都

Kyoto, oder, Die jungen Liebenden in der alten Kaiserstadt. Übers. von Walter Donat. München, Carl Hanser, 1965; Reinbek, Rowohlt, 1969. 138p.; Frankfurt am Main, Büchergilde Gutenberg, 1967. 245p.

Kyoto eller de unge elskande i den gamle kejserstad. Oversaette Karina Windfeld-Hansen. København, Hasselbalch, 1965. 190p.

Kioto. Kääntää Eeva-Liisa Manner. Helsinki, Tammi, 1968. 192p.; Helsinki, Suuri Suomalainen Kirjakerho, 1972. 196p.

Koto. Tr. di Mario Teti. Milano, Rizzoli, 1968. 155p.

Kyoto, eller, De unga älskande i den gamla kejsarstaden. Översätta Vanja Lantz. Stockholm, Bonniers, 1968. 214p.

'Kyoto' Übers. von Walter Donat. Die Tänzerin von Izu, Tausend Kraniche, Schneeland, Kyoto. München, Carl Hanser, 1968. p.257–431

Kiyoto. Çeviren Esat Nermi. İstanbul, Cem Yayinevi, 1968. 176p.

「古都」 台北 立志出版社 1968. 1冊

'Kioto' Tr. por Ana de la Fuente. Kioto, La danzarina de Izu. Barcelona, Plaza y Janés, 1969. p.5–268

'Koto' Tr. di Mario Teti. Antologia della letteratura coreana e giapponese. Milano, Fratelli Fabbri, 1969. p.346–361

Kyoto, eller, de unge elskende i den gamle Keiser. Oversette Inger Inadomi. Oslo, Oyldendal Norsk Forlag, 1969. 188p.

Kyoto. Tr. de Virgilio Martinho. Lisboa, Don Quixote, 1969. 226p.

Kiraz çiçekleri. Dilimize çeviren Ahmet Hisarli. İstanbul, Altin Kitaplar Yayinevi, 1969. 352p.

「古都」 趙長年訳 台北 正文出版社 1969. 208p.

「古都」 張秀英訳 台北 立志出版社 1969. 254p.

「古都」 施翠峯訳 台北 東方出版社 1969. 221p.

'古都' 李元燮 金潤成訳 「川端康成全集 1」 서울 新丘文化社 1969. p.291–422

'古都' 趙長年訳 「川端康成諾貝爾文学奨全集」 三重市 大立書店 1969. p.1–208

'L'ancienne capitale' Tr. par Philippe Pons. Nouvelle Revue Française, no.210, juin 1970. p.838–874

'Kioto' Tr. por Jaime Fernández. Los premios novel de literatura, v.12. Barcelona, Plaza y Janés, 1970.

Kyoto. În românești de Vasile Spoială. București, Univers, 1970. 240p.

Kyoto. Tr. par Philippe Pons. Paris, Albin Michel, 1971. 253p.; Genève, Editions Sari, 1973. 256p.

Kioto. Tr. por Ana M. de la Fuente. Barcelona, Plaza y Janés, 1971. 229p.

Kyoto. Übers. von Walter Donat, mit Kawai Yuzuru. Leipzig, Reclam, 1974. 187p.

Kiotói szerelmesek. Fordította Jászay Gabriella. Budapest, Kozmosz, 1975. 211p.

Kotsu hiroi 骨拾い

'Botten rapen' Vertaald von C. Ouwehand. Nagels in de ochtend. Amsterdam, Meulenhoff, 1971. p.7–11

Kyūchō no tantei 級長の探偵

'級長의探偵' 「횃불」 第1巻6号 1969年6月

Maihime 舞姫

'Az ererdaru minta' Fordította Sz. Holti Mária. Modern Japán elbeszélők. Budapest, Európa Könyvkiadó, 1967. p.348–402

'Die Tänzerinnen' Übers. von Oscar Benl. Tagebuch eines Sechzehnjährigen. München, Nymphenburger, 1969. p.75–258

'舞姫' 李元壽訳 「川端康成全集 2」 서울 新丘文化社 1969. p.87–223

Matsugo no me 末期の眼

'마지막눈길' 漢戊淑訳 「川端康成全集 2」 서울 新丘文化社 1969. p.405–416

Meigetsu 明月

'Volle maan' Vertaald door C. Ouwehand. Nagels in de ochtend. Amsterdam, Meulenhoff, 1971. p.93–98

Meijin 名人

'名人' 閔丙山訳 「川端康成全集 3」 서울 新丘文化社 1969. p.61–151

The master of Go. Tr. by Edward G. Seidensticker. N. Y. Knopf, 1972; London, Secker and Warburg, 1973. 188p.; Tokyo, Tuttle, 1973. 187p.; N. Y. Berkley Pub. 1974. 186p.

Le maître, ou le tournoi de Go. Tr. par Sylvie Regnault-Gatier. Paris, Albin Michel, 1975. 214p.

Mizuumi みずうみ

'湖水' 金世煥訳 「川端康成全集 3」 서울 新丘文化社 1969. p.243–321; 「노오벨賞文学全集 10」 서울 新丘文化社 1971. p.231–309

The lake. Tr. by Reiko Tsukimura. Tokyo, Kodansha International, 1974. 160p.

Le lac. Tr. par Michel Bourgeot et Jacques Serguine. Paris, Albin Michel, 1978. 208p.

Natsu no kutsu 夏の靴

'Summer shoes' Tr. by Yamada Kazuo. Eigo Seinen, v.97, no.2, 1951. p.62–64

Natsu to fuyu 夏と冬

'Zomer en winter' Vertaald door C. Ouwehand. Nagels in de ochtend. Amsterdam, Meulenhoff, 1971. p.87–92

'Summer and winter' Tr. by Edward Seidensticker. Contemporary Japanese literature, ed. by Howard Hibbett. N. Y. Knopf, 1977 p.303–306

Nemureru bijo 眠れる美女

'The sleeping beauty' Tr. by J. I. Ackroyd and Hiro Mukai. Eastern Horizon, v.4, March 1965. p.53–64

'잠자는美女' 金龍済訳 「日本代表作家百人集 3」 서울 希望出版社 1966. p.104–160; 「日本短篇文学全集 3」 서울 新太陽社 1969. p.252–308

De schone slaapsters. Vertaald door C. Ouwehand. Amsterdam, Van Gennep, 1968. 120p.

'잠든美女' 柳呈訳 「世界베스트셀라북스 1」 서울 三耕社 1968. p.195–255; 「川端康成全集 4」 서울 新丘文化社 1969. p.293–353

'잠자는 美女' 朴仁根訳 「雪国外」 서울 話題社 1968. p.135–211

'House of the sleeping beauties' Tr. by Edward Seidensticker. *House of the sleeping beauties, and other stories.* Tokyo, Kodansha International, 1969. p.13–99; London, Quadriga Press, 1969; London, Sphere, 1971; N. Y. Ballantine Books, 1970. p 13–99

Huset med de sovande skönheterna. Övers. av Erik Sundström. Stockholm, Bonniers, 1969. 157p.

'睡美人' 邱素臻訳 「睡美人」 台北 林白出版社 1969. p.1–99

Les belles endormies. Tr. par René Sieffert. Paris, Albin Michel, 1970. 186p.

'Śpiące krásavice' Přeložil Viktor Krupa. *Kawabata Yasunari, śpiące krásavice.* Blatislava, Slovensky Spisovatel, 1971.

Uykuda sevilen kizlar. Çeviren Samih Tiryakioğlu. İstanbul, Varlik Yayinevi, 1971. 160p.

'잠든美女' 金容浩訳 「노벨賞文学大全集 10」 서울 高麗出版社 1971. p.257–315

'La casa delle belle addormentate' Tr. di Mario Teti. *La casa delle belle addormentate.* Milano, Mondadori, 1972.

「잠든美女」 柳呈訳 서울 三耕社 1972. 351p.

「잠자는美女」 李仁光訳 서울 世昌書館 1974. 290p.; 서울 裕林堂 1976. 277p.

'잠든美女' 朴仁根訳 「世界短篇文学大系 29」 서울 尚書閣 1975. p.51–166

Rumah perawan. Jakarta, Pustaka Jaya, 1976. 93p.

'Śpiące piękności' Przeł. Mikołaj Melanowicz. *Literatura na świecie.* Warszawa, Październik, no.10, 1976. p.18–117

Niji 虹

'무지개' 楊明文訳 「川端康成全集 3」 서울 新丘文化社 1969. p.25–59; 「노오벨賞文学全集 10」 서울 新丘文化社 1971. p.195–229

'무지개' 崔浩然訳 「新訳世界文学全集 48」 서울 正音社 1972. p.159–191

Niji ikutabi 虹いくたび

「多色的虹」 廖清秀訳 台北 一文出版社 1969. 153p.

Niou musume 匂う娘

'Het geurende meisje' Vertaald door C. Ouwehand. *Nagels in de ochtend.* Amsterdam, Meulenhoff, 1971. p.126–133

Nokogiri to shussan 鋸と出産

'A saw and childbirth' Tr. by Minoru Kohda. *The Reeds,* v.13, 1972. p.49–52

Okujō no kingyo 屋上の金魚

'De goudvissen op het dak' Vertaald door C. Ouwehand. *Nagels in de ochtend.* Amsterdam, Meulenhoff, 1971. p.14–16

Onna de aru koto 女であること

「女人과女人과」 韓文聲訳 서울 大衆実話社 1969. 353p.

'女子라느것' 崔昌熙他訳 「川端康成全集 4」 서울 新丘文化社 1969. p.3–291

「最難懂女人心」 黃季媛訳 台北 道聲出版社 1973. 561p.

「아름다운女人과애처러운女人」 韓文聲訳 서울 泰運文化社 1977. 353p.

Onsen yado 温泉宿

'Het badhotel' Vertaald door C. Ouwehand. *Nagels in de ochtend.* Amsterdam, Meulenhoff, 1971. p.17–57

Rigō 離合

'離合' 章安蘋 「知識分子」 第23期 1969年2月 p.34–35, 第24期 1969年3月 p.33–35

'離合' 余翼等訳 「川端康成短篇小説選」 台北 水晶出版社 1969. p.77–97

'離合' 江上訳 「日本名家小説選」高雄 大舞台書苑 1976. p.23–45

Saikai 再会

'Rediscovery' Tr. by Leon Picon. *Orient-West,* v.8, no.4, 1963. p.37–47; *The Japanese image.* Tokyo, Orient West, 1965. p.197–211

'Reencounter' Tr. by Leon Picon. *The Izu dancer.* Tokyo, Hara Shobo, 1963. p.69–132

'Het weerzien' Vertaald door C. Ouwehand. *Nagels in de ochtend.* Amsterdam, Meulenhoff, 1971. p.66–86

'Retrouvailles' Tr. par Sylvie Regnault-Gatier, S. Suzuki et H. Suematsu. *La danseuse d'Izu.* Paris, Albin Michel, 1973. p.133–164

Saikonsha 再婚者

'Ihre zweite Ehe' Übers. von Oscar Benl. *Tagebuch eines Sechzehnjährigen.* München, Nymphenburger, 1969. p.7–74

'再婚者' 金容浩訳 「노벨賞文学大全集 10」 서울 高麗出版社 1971. p.209–255

Sasabune 笹舟

'The bamboo leaves' Tr. by Edward Seidensticker. *Contemporary Japanese literature,* ed. by Howard Hibbett. N. Y. Knopf, 1977. p.306–307

Sazanka さざん花

'The camellia' Tr. by Edward Seidensticker. *Contemporary Japanese literature,* ed. by Howard Hibbett. N. Y. Knopf, 1977. p.295–299

Senbazuru 千羽鶴

Tausend Kraniche. Übers. von Sachiko Yatsushiro. München, Hanser, 1956. 146p.; Frankfurt am Main, Fischer, 1959. 149p.; Reinbek, Rowohlt, 1970. 183p.

Thousand cranes. Tr. by Edward G. Seidensticker. N. Y. Knopf, 1958. 147p.; London, Secker and Warburg, 1959. 144p.; Tokyo, Tuttle, 1960. 147p.; N. Y. Berkley Pub. 1964. 144p.

Nuée d'oiseaux blancs. Tr. par Bunkichi Fujimori. Paris, Librairie Plon, 1960. 206p.; Lausanne, La Guilde du Livre, 1969. 267p.

De duizend kraanvogels. Vertaald door C. Ouwehand. Lochem, Tijdstroom, 1961. 139p.; Leuven, Davidsfonds, 1970. 141p.

'Tisuću ždralova' Prevesti Zlatko Gorjan. *Tisuću ždralova, Zemlja snijega.* Zagreb, Matica Hrvatska, 1961. p.7–124

Una grulla en la taza de te. Version por Luis de Salvador. Barcelona, Vergara, 1962. 228p.; Barcelona, Circulo de Lectures, 1968. 223p.

Mille gru. Tr. di Mario Teti. Milano, Mondadori, 1965. 168p.

Tisoč žerjavov. Prevesti Jože Kranjc. Ljubljana, Prešernova Družba, 1965. 116p.

De tusind traner. Oversatta Karina Windfeld-Hansen. København, Hasselbalch, 1966. 150p.

Tusen tranor. Övers. av Olov Jonason. Stockholm, Bonniers, 1966. 165p.

'Tausend Kraniche' Übers. von Sachiko Yatsushiro. *Die Tänzerin von Izu, Tausend Krani-*

che, Schneeland, Kyoto. München, Carl Hanser, 1968. p.35–135

Bin beyaz turna. Almanca'dan çeviren Zeyyat Selimoğlu. İstanbul, Čem Yayinevi, 1968. 129p.

'千羽鶴' 「中央」（台北） 第1巻9期 1968年12月
「千羽鶴」 張秀英訳 台北 立志出版社 1968. 171p.
「千羽鶴」 何瑞雄訳 台北 開山書店 1968. 181p.
'千羽鶴' 李浩哲訳 「世界베스트셀러북스 1」 서울 三耕社 1968. p.89–171; 「川端康成全集 2」 서울 新丘文化社 1969. p.3–86; 「노오벨賞文学全集 10」 서울 新丘文化社 1971. p.89–171

'Thousand cranes' Tr. by E. G. Seidensticker. Snow country, and Thousand cranes. N. Y. Knopf, 1969. p.1–147; Harmondsworth, Penguin Books, 1971.

'Tausend Kraniche' Übers. von Oscar Benl, und Sachiko Yatsushiro. Tausend Kraniche. Schneeland. Zürich, Ex Libris, 1969. p.7–105; Berlin, Volk und Welt, 1971.

Tuhat kurkea. Suomentanut Eeva-Liisa Manner. Helsinki, Tammi, 1969. 149p.

Ena synnefo aspra poulia. Tr. from the English by Kosmas Polites. Athenai, Korali, 1969. 242p.

Xú tuyết. Tr. from the French by Chu-Viêt. Saigon, Trinh-Bāy, 1969. 236p.

Hnin pwint taingpye. Tr. from the English by Nandathu. Rangoon, Daw Daw & Sons, 1969. 242p.

「千隻鶴」 趙長年訳 台北 正文出版社 1969. 154p.
「千羽鶴」 施絜峰訳 台北 東方出版社 1969. 153p.
'千羽鶴' 趙長年訳 「川端康成諾貝爾文学奨全集」 三重市 大立書店 1969. p.1–154
'千羽鶴' 金巣雲訳 「世界의文学大全集 8」 서울 同和出版公社 1970. p.105–182; 「雪国・千羽鶴」 서울 同和出版公社 1972. p.169–329
'千羽鶴' 金容浩訳 「노벨賞文学大全集 10」 서울 高麗出版社 1971. p.127–206; 「世界代表文学全集 9」 서울 高麗出版社 1976. p.127–207

'Tisíčžeiavov' Přeložil Viktor Krupa. Kawabata Yasunari, spiace krásovice. Blatislava, Slovenský Spisovatel, 1971.

'Тысячекрылый журавль' Перевод З. Рахима. Ясунари Кавабата. Москва, Прогресс, 1971. p.16–179

Uykuda sevilen kizlar. Dilimize çeviren Samih Tiryakioğlu. İstanbul, Varlik Yayinevi, 1971. 160p.

'Stol de păsări albe' În româneşti de Pericle Martinescu. Stol de păsări albe, Vuietul muntelui Bucureşti, Minerva, 1973.

「千羽鶴」 金鎮郁訳 서울 三中堂 1975. 298p.
'千羽鶴' 李吉鐘訳 「世界短篇文学全集 20」 서울 金字堂 1976. p.103–251
'千羽鶴' 金鎮郁訳 「新選世界文学全集 19」 서울 三珍社 1976. p.93–173

'Hiljada žeravi' Tr. Bojka Elitova & Georgi Stoev. Snežnata strana i Hiljada žeravi. Plovdiv, H. G. Danov, 1977.

'Мин канаттуу турна' Которгон Ш. Келгенбаев. Мин канаттуу турна. Фрунзе, Кыргызстан, 1977. p.3–197

Shimen 死面

'The death-mask' Tr. by George Saito. Japan P.E.N. News, no.23, Oct. 1970. p.2–3; Asian and Pacific short stories. Seoul, Cultural and Social Centre for the Asian and Pacific Region, 1974; Tokyo, Tuttle, 1974. p.81–83

Shinjū 心中

'Serce' Przeł. Zdzisław Rzeszelewski. Przekrój, no.1538, 1974. p.15

Shirayuki 白雪

'白雪' 金光鏞訳 「川端康成全集 3」 서울 新丘文化社 1969. p.223–241; 「世界代表短篇文学全集 22」 서울 正韓出版社 1976. p.269–293

Shitai shōkainin 死体紹介人

'屍体紹介人' 金容浩訳 「노벨賞文学大全集 10」 서울 高麗出版社 1971. p.513–551
'屍体紹介人' 崔浩然訳 「新訳世界文学全集 48」 서울 正音社 1972. p.121–157
'屍体紹介人' 朴仁植訳 「世界短篇文学大系 29」 서울 尚書閣 1975. p.169–243

Shizen 自然

'Природа' Перевод С. Гутерман. Ясунари Кавабата. Москва, Прогресс, 1971. p.345–358

Shojo no inori 処女の祈り

'Ууздай кыздарын дубасы' Которгон Ш. Келгенбаев. Мин канаттуу турна. Фрунзе, Кыргызстан, 1977. p.321–323

Suigetsu 水月

'The moon in the water' Tr. by George Saito. United Asia, v.8, no.4, 1956. p.260–264; Diliman Review, v.6, no.2–4, 1958. p.460–472

'El lunar' Tr. por Miguel Alfredo Olivera. Sur, no.249, Nov.-Dec. 1957. p.57–64

'水月' 傅實齢訳 「勲章」 台北 文壇社 1960. p.40–53

'The moon on the water' Tr. by George Saito. Modern Japanese stories. London, Spottiswoode, 1961; Tokyo, Tuttle, 1962. p.246–257; The Izu dancer. Tokyo, Hara Shobo, 1963. p.163–199; The world of Japanese fiction. N. Y. Dutton, 1973. p.280–290

'Bulan di-pěrmjkaan ayer' Děngan kata pěngantar oleh James Kirkup. Shoji. Kuala Lumpur, Oxford Univ. Press, 1961. p.37–51

'Mond auf dem Wasser' Übers. von Annelotte Piper. Japan, Geistige Begegnung. Tübingen, Erdmann, 1964. p.282–294; Eine Glocke in Fukagawa. Tübingen, Erdmann, 1969. p.282–294

'Der Mond auf dem Wasser' Deutsch von Monique Humbert. Nippon. Zürich, Diogenes, 1965. p. 275–288

'Holdtükör' Forditotta Sz. Holti Mária. Modern Japán elbeszélők. Budapest, Európa Könyvkiadó, 1967. p.339–347; Szerelmesek. Budapest, Kozmosz, 1975. p.220–229

'Otblesk luny' Perevod E. Katai na latyshskom iazyke. Literatura yn maksla, Okt. 4, 1969. p.10–11

'水月' 「諾貝爾奨小説選」 台北 水晶出版社 1969. p.3–14

'水月' 鐘肇政訳 「水月」 高雄 文皇出版社 1971. p.28–41

'La lune dans l'eau' Tr. par Sylvie Regnault-Gatier, S. Suzuki et H. Suematsu. La danseuse d'Izu. Paris, Albin Michel, 1973. p.165–184

'La luna en el agua' Tr. por Oscar Montes. Estudios Orientales, v.9, no.3, 1974. p.353–368

Suishō gensō 水晶幻想

'Träume im Kristall' Übers. von Siegfried Schaarschmidt. Träume im Kristall, Erzählungen. Frankfurt am Main, Suhrkamp, 1974. p.7–52

Take no koe momo no hana 竹の声桃の花

'Голос бамбука, цветок персика' Перевод Б

Раскина. *Иностранная Литература*, номер 6, 1972. p.62–66; *Японская новелла 1960–1970*. Москва, Прогресс, 1972. p.94–99

Taki 滝

'Waterfall' Tr. by Leon Zolbrod. *The East*, v.2, no.1, 1965. p.62–64

Tenohira no shōsetsu 掌の小説

'妻的遺容, 化粧' 鄭清文訳 「純文學」（台灣版）第4巻5期 1968. p.166–168;「水月」 高雄 文皇出版社 1971. p.189–193
'掌篇小説' 柳呈 洪性裕訳 「川端康成全集 4」 서울 新丘文化社 1969. p.371–412
'Рассказы величикой с ладонь:Случай с мертвым лицом, Аригато, Сердце, Молитва, Мужи-чина, который не смеется, Камелия, Кораб-лики' Перевод С. Гутерман. *Ясунари Каваба-та*. Москва, Прогресс, 1971. p.359–382
「小小小説一百篇」 施翠峯訳 台北 東方出版社 1973. 1冊
'帽子事件, 祈禱, 海, 懺悔, 屋上的金魚, 紅梅' 藍影訳 「沉船余生記」 台北 益羣書店 1973. p.155–183
「川端康成袖珍小説選」 喬遷 張好訳 台北 幼獅文化事業公司 1977. 152p.

Tōkyo no hito 東京の人

「東京사람」 金京鈺 崔仁勲訳 서울 新丘文化社 1969. 2冊（川端康成全集 5, 6）

Tsubakuro no dōjo 燕の童女

'飛燕號的女孩' 鄭清文訳 「水月」 高雄 文皇出版社 1971. p.164–178

Umi 海

'바다' 金文洙訳 「世界文学속의韓国 6」 서울 正韓出版社 1975. p.17–22;「世界代表短篇文学全集 22」 서울 正韓出版社 1976. p.266–268

Utsukushii Nihon no watakushi 美しい日本の私

「日本的美與我」 喬炳南訳 台北 台湾商務印書館 1968. 128p.
'Japan, the beautiful, and myself' Tr. by Edward G. Seidensticker. *Jiji Eigo Kenkyu*, v.24, no.3, 1969. p.19–27; *Social Education*, v.33, no.7, 1969. p.827–829
Japan the beautiful and myself. Tr. by E. G. Seiden-sticker. Tokyo, Kodansha, 1969. 74p.
'日本之美與我' 安萍訳 「明報」 第5巻7期 1970. p.90–96
'Красотой Японии рожденный' Перевод С. Григорьева. *Ясунари Кавабата*. Москва, Прогресс, 1971. p.385–398

Utsukushisa to kanashimi to 美しさと哀しみと

「美麗與哀愁」 朱佩蘭訳 台北 皇冠出版社 1969. 249p.
「美麗的悲哀」 金溟若訳 台北 志文出版社 1969. 242p.
'아름다움과애처로움과' 柳呈 安東林訳 「川端康成全集 1」 서울 新丘文化社 1969. p.143–288
Beauty and sadness. Tr. by Howard Hibbett. N. Y. Knopf, 1976. 206p.; Tokyo, Tuttle, 1976. 206p.

Yama no oto 山の音

'The sound of the mountain' Tr. by Edward Sei-densticker. *Japan Quarterly*, v.11, no.3, 1964. p.309–330, v.11, no.4, 1964. p.446–457
El clamor de la montaña. Tr. por Jaimé Fernández y Satur Ochoa. Barcelona, Plaza y Janés, 1969. 364p.; Barcelona, Ediciones G. P. 1973. 312p.

Le grondement de la montagne. Tr. par Sylvie Regnault-Gatier et Hisashi Suematsu. Paris, Albin Michel, 1969. 269p.; Lausanne, La Guilde du Livre, 1969. 264p.
Ein Kirschbaum im Winter. Übers. von Siegfried Schaarschmidt. München, Carl Hanser, 1969. 366p.
Il suono della montagna. Tr. di Atsuko Ricca Suga. Milano, Bompiani, 1969. 286p.
'山의소리'「횃불」 第1巻1号 1969年1月
'山소리' 柳呈訳 「川端康成全集 2」 서울 新丘文化社 1969. p.225–413;「노오벨賞文学全集 10」 서울 新丘文化社 1971. p.311–489
The sound of the mountain. Tr. by Edward Seiden-sticker. N. Y. Knopf, 1970; London, Peter Owen, 1970; Tokyo, Tuttle, 1970; London, Secker and Warburg, 1971. 276p.; London, Penguin Books, 1974. 218p.
'El clamor de la montaña' Tr. por Jaimé Fernán-dez. *Los premios novel de literatura*, v.12. Barce-lona, Plaza y Janés, 1970.
'Hlas hory' Preložil Viktor Krupa. *Kawabata Yasunari, Spiace krasovice*. Blatislava, Slo-vensky Spisovatel, 1971.
'山소리' 金容浩訳 「노벨賞文学大全集 10」 서울 高麗出版社 1971. p.317–491;「世界代表文学全集 9」 서울 高麗出版社 1976. p.209–383
'Vuietul muntelui' În româneşti di Pericle Marti-nescu. *Stol de păsări albe, Vuietul muntelui*. Bucureşti, Minerva, 1973.
'Стон горы' Перевод В. Гривнина. *Иностранная Литература*, сентябрь 1973. p.25–95, ок-тябрь 1973. p.119–188
Vuoren jyly. Suomentanut Eeva-Liisa Manner. Helsinki, Tammi, 1973. 220p.
Стон горы. Перевод В. Гривнина. Москва, Ху-дож. Лит. 1975. 238p.
'山의소리' 河在麟訳 「日本文学大全集 3」 서울 東西文化院 1971. p.76–234

Yokochō 横町

'小巷' 傅賓齡訳 「勲章」 台北 文壇社 1960. p.54–74
'De zijstraat' Vertaald door C. Ouwehand. *Nagels in de ochtend*. Amsterdam, Meulenhoff, 1971. p.99–115
'小巷' 瑞宏訳 「水月」 高雄 文皇出版社 1971. p.143–163

Yowaki utsuwa 弱き器

'A weak vessel' Tr. by Minoru Kohda. *The Reeds*, v.13, 1972. p.47–48

Yukiguni 雪国

Snow country. Tr. by Edward G. Seidensticker. N. Y. Knopf, 1956. 175p.; London, Secker and Warburg, 1957. 188p.; Tokyo, Tuttle, 1957. 175p.; N. Y. Berkley Pub. 1960. 142p.
Schneeland. Übers. von Oscar Benl. München, Carl Hanser, 1957. 178p.; Reinbek, Rowohlt, 1961. lv.
Snöns rike. Övers. från engelskan av per Erik Wahlund. Stockholm, Bonniers, 1957. 185p.; 1967. 142p.
Lumen maa. Suomentanut Yrjö Kivimies. Hel-sinki, Tammi, 1958. 171p.; 2d ed. 1963. 145p.; 1970. 158p.
Il paese delle nevi. Dall'inglese di Luca Lambert. Torino, Einaudi, 1959. 197p.; 1969. 145p.; Milano, Mondadori, 1971. 154p.; 2d ed. 1968. 149p.
「雪鄉」 趙長年訳 台北 正文出版社 1959. 150p.
「雪鄉」 施翠峰訳 台北 東方出版社 1959. 161p.

Pays de neige. Tr. par Bunkichi Fujimori et Armel Guerne. Paris, Albin Michel, 1960. 253p.

'Zemlja snijega' Preveo Zlatko Gorjan. *Tisuĉu zdralova, Zemlja snijega.* Zagreb, Matica Hrvatska, 1961. p.127–252

Sneeuwland. Vertaald door C. Ouwehand. Lochem, Tijdstroom, 1963. 136p.

Kráina sniegu. Preł. Wiesław Kotański. Warszawa, Państwowy Instytut Wydawniczy, 1964. 192p.; 1969. 155p.

「雪国」金龍済訳 「日本文学選集 5」 서울 知文閣 1966. p.7–106; 서울 韓國読書文化院 1967. p.7–108

'Schneeland' Übers. von Oscar Benl. *Die Tänzerin von Izu, Tausend Kraniche, Schneeland.* München, Carl Hanser, 1968. p.137–255

Karlar ülkesi. Dilimize çeviren Nihal Yeğinobali. İstanbul, Altin Kitaplar Yayinevi, 1968. 284p.

「雪郷」 李鐘求訳 「新東亜」 52期 1968年12月

「雪国」 林昌雄訳 「月刊文学」 第1巻2期 1968年12月

「雪郷」 金淇若訳 台北 立志出版院 1968. 175p.; 台北 水芙蓉出版社 1969. 175p.

「雪国」 金龍済訳 서울 東西文化社 1968. 264p.

「雪国」 朴仁根訳 「雪国外」 서울 話題社 1968. p. 23–133

「雪国」 金世煥訳 「世界베스트셀라북스 1」 서울 三耕社 1968. p.7–87; 「川端康成全集 1」 서울 新丘文化社 1969. p.7–87; 「노오벨賞文学全集 10」 서울 新丘文化社 1971. p.7–87

「雪国」 서울 善瓊図書出版社 1968. 336p.

「雪国」 朴永姫訳 서울 文音社 1968. 359p.

「雪国」 李剛緑訳 서울 新明文化社 1968. 178p.

「雪国」 서울 康友出版社 1968. 236p.

「雪国」 金宇烈訳 서울 博英社 1968. 211p.; 1976. 184p.

「雪国」 朴敬勛訳 서울 東西文化院 1968. 357p.

「설국」 金世煥訳 서울 話題社 1968. 352p.

「雪国」 朴仁根訳 서울 話題社 1968. 317p.

「雪国」 李福澤訳 서울 선경도出版社 1968. 336p.

Hóország. Ford. Jólesz László. Budapest, Magvetö, 1969. 171p.

Terre de neve. Tr. por Armando da Silva Garralho. Lisboa, Don Quixote, 1969. 177p.

'Schneeland' Übers. von Oscar Benl und Sachiko Yatsushiro. *Tausend Kraniche, Schneeland.* München, Ex Libris, 1969. p.109–225

'Sněhová země' Přeložila Vlasta Hilská. *5 japonských novel.* Praha, Odeon, 1969. p.229–332

'Snow country' Tr. by E. G. Seidensticker. *Snow country and Thousand cranes.* N. Y. Knopf, 1969. p.1–175; London, Penguin Books, 1971.

「雪国」 喬遷訳 台北 三民書局 1969. 173p.

「雪郷」 台南 王家出版社 1969. 110p.

「雪郷」 趙長年訳 「川端康成諾貝爾文学奬全集」 三重市 大立書店 1969. p.1–150

Zemjata na snegot. Tr. from the French Tasko Sirilor. Skopje, Nova Makedonija, 1970. 216p.

País de nieve. La Habana, Instituto del Libro, 1970. 196p.

「雪国」 金巣雲訳 「世界의 文学大全集 8」 서울 同和出版公社 1970. p.23–103; 「雪国・千羽鶴」 서울 同和出版公社 1972. p.5–166

Neĝa lando. Tr. Gaku Konisi. Tokyo, Japan Esperanto Instituto, 1971. 118p.

País de la nieve. Tr. de César Durán. Barcelona, Imp. Moderna, 1971. 247p.

Sniegynu šalis. Tr. Virginija Niparaite. Vilnius, Vaga, 1971. 141p.

Karlar ülkesi. Tercüme etmek Nihal Yeğinobali. İstanbul, Altin Kitaplar Yayinevi, 1971. 284p.

'Снежная страна' Перевод З. Рахима. *Ясунари Кавабата.* Москва, Прогресс, 1971. p.180–284

「雪国」 金容浩訳 「노벨賞文学大全集 10」 서울 高麗出版社 1971. p.45–125; 「世界代表文学全集 9」 서울 高麗出版社 1976. p.45–125

Natyra me borë. Tr. Abdullah Karjagdiu. Prishtinë, Rilindja, 1972. 127p.

Hemuntakam. Tr. Chun Prabhavivadhand. Bangkok, Praepitaya, 1972. 305p.

Tusār grām. Tr. into Bengali by Sandipkumar Thakur. Calcutta, Rupa, 1972. 142p.

Negeri salju. Diterjemarhkan dan diberi pengantar oléh Anas Ma'ruf. Jakarta, Pustaka Jaya, 1972. 147p.

'雪国' 金字烈訳 「現代日本代表文学全集 6」 서울 平和出版社 1973. p.3–103

Tara zăpezilor. În românești de Stanca Cionca. București, Editura Univers, 1974. 157p.

「雪国」 柳呈訳 서울 主婦生活社 1974. 277p.

「雪国」 姜敏訳 「日本文学大全集 3」 서울 東西文化院 1975. p.2–74

「雪国」 閔丙山訳 「世界文学全集 20」 서울 三省出版社 1975. p.337–425

「雪国」 金鎮郁訳 서울 三中社 1975. 298p.

「雪国」 趙喜娟訳 「世界名作시리즈 3」 서울 女学生 1975. p.7–197

「雪国」 李吉鐘訳 「世界短篇文学全集 20」 서울 金字堂 1976. p.254–405

「雪国」 金鎮郁訳 「新選世界文学全集 19」 서울 三珍社 1976. p.11–91

'Snežnata strana' Tr. Bojka Elitova & Georgi Stoev. *Snežnata strana i Hiljada žeravi.* Plovdiv, H. G. Danov, 1977. p.198–320

'Кар чумкэгэн элкэ' Которгон Шералы Келгенбаев. *Мин канаттуу турна.* Фрунзе, Кыргызстан, 1977. p.198–320

Yuku hito ゆくひと

'送行' 余翼等訳 「川端康成短篇小説選」 台北 水晶出版社 1969. p.129–141

'Zij die wegging' Vertaald door C. Ouwehand. *Nagels in de ochtend.* Amsterdam, Meulenhoff, 1971. p.58–65

'送行' 林浦訳 「世界短篇小説精華」 三重市 大立書店 1971. p.192–201

Yume no ane 夢の姉

'Der Schatten der älteren Schwester' Übers. von Siegfried Schaarschmidt. *Träume im Kristall, Erzählungen.* Frankfurt am Main, Suhrkamp, 1974. p.53–75

Yumiura shi 弓浦市

'Бухта Лука' Перевод Я. Берлина и З. Рахима. *Японская новелла.* Москва, Изд. Иност. Лит. 1961. p.92–98

'Město Jumiura' Přel. M. Novák. *Světova Literatura,* no.4, 1962. p.157–160

'Садак койнвуы' Аударган Г. Оспанов. *Жапон енгимелери.* Алма-Ата, Жазущы, 1965. p.38–45

Zakuro ざくろ

'Owoc granatu' Przeł. Krystyna Okazaki. *Literatura na Świecie,* no.7, 1972.

'Granátové jablko' Přel. S.M. Vačkář. *Lidová Demokracie,* 3. 3. 1973. p.3

'The pomegranate' Tr. by Edward Seidensticker. *Contemporary Japanese literature,* ed. by Howard Hibbett. N. Y. Knopf, 1977. p.293–295

Poems 詩

'Yukiguni' Tr. by Marvin J. Suomi. *Solidarity,* v.8, no.2, 1973. p.82

KAWABATA Yasunari

Criticism 評論

'文章論' 「世代」 第6巻12号 1968.
'小説の本質' 葉泥訳 「文藝」 第1期 1969. p.157–166
'小説之構成' 葉泥訳 「文藝月刊」 第7期 1970. p.26–32
'論性格' 葉泥訳 「文藝月刊」 第8期 1970. p.37–44,
　第9期 1970. p.74–82, 第11期 1970. p.57–66, 第13
　期 1970. p.41–47
'文學之美' 章萍訳 「知識分子」 第66期 1970. p.31–34
'論環境' 葉泥訳 「文藝月刊」 第21期 1971. p.17–27

KAWACHI Sensuke　河内仙介　1898–1954

Sazanka 山茶花

'Sazanka' Tr. by Grace Suzuki. *Ukiyo.* Tokyo, Phoenix Books, 1954. p.112–125; *Ukiyo,* ed. by J. Gluck. N. Y. Vanguard Press, 1963. p.195–202; London, Universal Library, 1964. p.195–202

KAWAGUCHI Hiroshi　川口　浩　1905–

Criticism 評論

'德國的新興文學' 憑憲章訳 「拓荒者」 第1巻2期 1930. p.713–735
'到科學的美學的路' 鳴心訳 「微音月刊」 第2巻5号 1932.
'報告文學論' 沈端先訳 「北斗月刊」 第2巻1期 1932.
'文學的黨派性' 張英白訳 「文藝月刊」 創刊号 1933.
「藝術方法論」 森堡訳 上海 大江書舗 193?.

KAWAGUCHI Matsutarō　川口松太郎　1899–

Fukagawa no suzu 深川の鈴

'A bell in Fukagawa' Tr. by Edward G. Seidensticker. *Japan Quarterly,* v.6, no.2, 1959. p.211–227; *Modern Japanese short stories.* Tokyo, Japan Publications Trading Co. 1960. p.15–37; Rev. ed. Tokyo, Japan Publications Trading Co. 1970. p.12–30
'Eine Glocke in Fukagawa' Übers. von Tatsuji Iwabuchi und Noburo Koshibe. *Japan, Geistige Begegnung.* Tübingen, Erdmann, 1964. p.137–160; *Eine Glocke in Fukagawa.* Tübingen, Erdmann, 1969. p.137–160

Essay エッセイ

'돈을구어다와' 金賢珠訳 「바이바이바다」 서울 三韓出版社 1966. p.256–258

KAWAHIGASHI Hekigotō　河東碧梧桐　1873–1937

Haiku 俳句

'3 haiku' Tr. by Asataro Miyamori. *Anthology of haiku, ancient and modern.* Tokyo, Maruzen, 1932. p.733–735
'Haiku' Tr. par Kuni Matsuo et Steinilber-Oberlin. *Anthologie des poètes japonais contemporains.* Paris, Mercure de France, 1939. p.285–287
'19 haiku' Tr. by V. H. Viglielmo. *Japanese literature in the Meiji era.* Tokyo, Obunsha, 1955. p.429–430, 441, 447, 449, 450, 451
'The crimson carpet' Tr. by Harold Stewart. *A net of fireflies.* Tokyo, Tuttle, 1960. p.83
'1 haiku' Übers. von Gerolf Coudenhove. *Japanische Jahreszeiten.* Zürich, Manesse Verlag, 1963. p.313
'2 haiku' Tr. by Geoffrey Bownas and Anthony Thwaite. *The Penguin book of Japanese verse.* Harmondsworth, Penguin Books, 1964. p.166
'12 haiku' *A history of haiku v.2,* by R. H. Blyth. Tokyo, Hokuseido, 1964. p.189–193
'2 haiku' *Anthology of modern Japanese poetry,* tr. and comp. by Edith Marcombe Shiffert and Yuki Sawa. Tokyo, Tuttle, 1972. p.161
'20 haiku' *Modern Japanese haiku, an anthology,* comp. and tr. by Makoto Ueda. Tokyo, Univ. of Tokyo Press, 1976. p.62–71
'Tea-plants; Violent gale; Migrating birds; Moonlit shower; In autumn; Maple leaves' Tr. by Kenneth Yasuda. *A pepper-pod.* Tokyo, Tuttle, 1976. p.86–87

KAWAI Suimei　河井酔茗　1874–1965

Poems 詩

'Moi' Tr. par Nico D. Horiguchi. *The lyric garland.* Tokyo, Hokuseido, 1957. p.33
'Things left behind' *An anthology of modern Japanese poetry,* ed. and tr. by Ichiro Kono and Rikutaro Fukuda. Tokyo, Kenkyusha, 1957. p.44
'Geride kalanlar' Tercüme etmek L. Sami Akalin. *Japon şiiri.* İstanbul, Varlik Yayinevi, 1962. p.237
'山的歡喜' 「標準日本名著選讀」 孫文斗編　台北　大新書局　1969. p.61–63

KAWAJI Ryūkō　川路柳虹　1888–1959

Poems 詩

'Забравени неща' Преведе Никола Джеров. *Песните на Ямато.* София, Корали, 1937. p.79
'Premier amour; La mort; Chardons; Jour de pluie; Rêves; Chanteur ambulant; Choses oubliées; Coeur d'amour; Sentiment; Monologue; Soir de printemps; Le ciel bleu; Le temps passe; Saule' Tr. par Kuni Matsuo et Steinilber-Oberlin. *Anthologie des poètes japonais contemporains.* Paris, Mercure de France, 1939. p.114–124
'Entrée a la caserne' *Histoire de là littérature japonaise contemporaine,* par Georges Bonneau. Paris, Payot, 1944. p.248
'Burning books' *United Asia,* v.8, no.3, 1956. p.268
'Burning books; Camel' *An anthology of modern Japanese poetry,* ed. and tr. by Ichiro Kono and Rikutaro Fukuda. Tokyo, Kenkyusha, 1957. p.45–46
'La pierre; La mort' Tr. par Kuni Matsuo et Steinilber-Oberlin. *The lyric garland,* ed. by Makoto Sangu. Tokyo, Hokuseido, 1957. p.34
'Monologue' *La poésie japonaise,* par Karl Petit. Paris, Seghers, 1959. p.206
'春頌' 崔一秀訳 「기다리고있네」 서울 韓国政経社 1966. p.239–240
'Ноги дождя' Перевод Веры Марковой. *Восточный альманах 6.* Москва, Худож. Лит.

1963. p.328; *Птица, птица красная.*
Москва, Дет. Лит. 1967.
'Brennende bøker' Til norsk ved Paal Brekke.
Moderne japansk lyrikk. Oslo, Norske Bok-
klubben, n.d. p.26–29
'Inima dragostei' Traducerea Virgil Teodorescu.
Din lirica japoneză. Bucureşti, Editura Uni-
vers, n.d. p.157

Criticism 評論

'不規則的詩派' 馥泉訳 「小説月報」 第13巻9号 1922.
p.10–15
'Dry 한詩趣' 金龍済訳 「日本詩集」 서울 青雲社 1960.
p.172–198

KAWAMATA Kōji 川俣晃自 1917–

Hannya shinkyō 般若心経

'般若心経' 金鐘仁訳「戦後日本新人受賞作品選」 서울 隆
文社 1961. p.81–109

KAWAMURA Akira 川村 晃 1927–

Bidan no shuppatsu 美談の出発

'聖家族' 劉慕沙訳 「芥川奨作品選集 1」 台北 晩蟬書店
1969. p.149–175
'小家族' 劉慕沙訳 「芥川賞作品選集 2」 台北 大地出版
社 1974. p.151–178

KAWAMURA Jirō 川村二郎 1928–

Criticism 評論

'A survey of literature in 1977' *Japanese Literature
Today*, no.3, March, 1978. p.1–4

KAWAMURA Karyō 川村花菱 1884–1954

Tōjin Okichi 唐人お吉

'Die "Ausländer" Okichi' Übers. von Maria
Piper. *Das japanische Theater.* Frankfurt am
Main, Societäts Verlag, 1937. p.23–34

KAWANO Jun 川野 順

Ibara no michi いばらの道

「荊棘의半生記」 辛定夏訳 서울 三一閣 1975. 175p.

KAWASAKI Chōtarō 川崎長太郎 1901–

Wakareta onna 別れた女

'以後的女人' 吶吶鷗訳 「色情文化」 上海 水沫書店
1928.

KAWASAKI Daiji 川崎大治 1902–

「変成花呀，変成路！」 瞿麥訳 北京 少年兒童 1957.
50p.

KAWASAKI Hiroshi 川崎 洋 1930–

Poems 詩

'Look/come/closer' Tr. by Thomas Fitzsimmons.
Japanese poetry now. London, André Deutsch,
1972. p.81–82; *Japanese poetry today.* N. Y.
Schocken Books, 1972. p.83–84

KAWATA Jun 川田 順 1882–1966

Tanka 短歌

'The future life; The crane; A crane in zoological
gardens; My joy' Tr. by Asataro Miyamori.
*Masterpieces of Japanese poetry, ancient and
modern.* Tokyo, Maruzen, 1936; Tokyo,
Taiseido, 1956; N. Y. Greenwood Press,
1971. p. 695–697
'The image of Ippen the Saint' Tr. by Shigeshi
Nishimura. *The Current of the World*, v.26,
no.1, 1949. p.59
'9 tanka' Tr. by H. H. Honda. *The Reeds*, v.3,
1957. p.9, 10, 16, 17, 19, 24
'Vor dem gemeinsamen Liebestod' Übers. von
Günther Debon. *Im Schnee die Fähre.* München, Piper, 1960. p.31
'1 tanka' Übers. von Gerolf Coudenhove. *Japanische Jahreszeiten.* Zürich, Manesse Verlag,
1963. p.78
'1 tanka' Tr. by Donald Keene. *Landscapes and
portraits.* Tokyo, Kodansha International,
1971. p.305

KAWAUCHI Kōhan 川内康範 1920–

Ai wa oshiminaku 愛は惜しみなく

「사랑은아낌없이」 沈在文訳 서울 三美出版社 1970.
365p.
「사랑한다는것 믿는다는것」 沈在文訳 서울 三友春秋社
1970. 279p.

KAYAMA Shigeru 香山 滋 1909–1975

「死亡谷」 曙光訳 台北 龍門出版社 1956. 46p.

KAZAKI Untarō 風木雲太郎 1913–

Poems 詩

'Суудагы ай; Кыш ыры' Которгон Ж. Алыши.
Хиросима кектери. Фрунзе, Кыргызстан,
1969. p.26–27

KIDA Minoru

KIDA Minoru　きだ・みのる　1895-1975

Kichigai buraku shūyū kikō　気違い部落周游紀行

'Il maestro del tempio, acquistata la fama di spia, trovasi negli impicci'　Tr. di Morichini. *Il Giappone*, v.2, no.1-2, 1958. p.41-47
Viaggio intorno a un borgo di fango. Milano, Bocca, n. d. lv.

Essays　エッセイ

'The laws of the buraku'　*Japan Quarterly,* v.4, no.1, 1957. p.77-88
'Buraku in Japan'　Tr. by James Kirkup and Fumiko Miura. *Japan Quarterly,* v.15, no.3, 1968. v.15, no.4, 1968. v.16, no.1, 1969. v.16, no. 2, 1969.

KIDO Rei　城戸　礼　1910-

Kaze yo kono hi o kesanaide　風よこの灯を消さないで

「바람아등불을끄지말아다오」方基煥訳 서울　新太陽社 1963. 293p.
「無情한바람아이등불을끄지말아다오」金思達訳 서울　徽文出版社　1963. 375p.
「바람아이등불을끄지말아다오」方基煥訳 서울　真文出版社　1966. 273p.; 서울　五倫出版社 1972. 273p.

KIGI Takataro　木々高太郎　1879-1969

Kare no motomeru kage　彼の求める影

「追跡者」李文賢訳 서울　弘益出版社　1974. 289p.

Waga jogakusei jidai no tsumi　わが女学生時代の罪

「肉體의彷徨」尹岐浩訳 서울　真文出版社 1964. 210p.

KIHARA Kōichi　木原孝一　1922-

Poems　詩

'The birthplace; Thither'　*An anthology of modern Japanese poetry,* ed. and tr. by Ichiro Kono and Rikutaro Fukuda. Tokyo, Kenkyusha, 1957. p.47-48
'O noktaya'　Tercüme etmek L. Sami Akalin. *Japon şiiri.* İstanbul, Varlik Yayinevi, 1962. p.299
'予感；그대'辛東門訳 「世界戦後文学全集 9」서울　新丘文化社　1962. p.243
'Hacia alla; El sitio de nacimiento'　Tr. por Kikuya Ionesawa. *Poesia japonesa contemporanea.* Bogotá, Colombia Editoriales de Librería, 1965.
'Revelation'　Remade into English by Thomas Fitzsimmons. *Japanese poetry now.* London, André Deutsch, 1972. p.33: *Japanese poetry today.* N. Y. Schocken Books, 1972. p.35

KIJIMA Hajime　木島　始　1928-

Kawaii mendori　かわいいめんどり

Little white hen, a folk tale, adapted by Hajime

Kijima. N. Y. Harcourt, 1969. 27p.; London, Macdonald, 1969. 30p.
Den kloke hønen. Oversette Grete Grieg Wiersholm. Oslo, Gyldendal, 1968. 27p.
Den kloge høne. Oversaette Ib Permin. København, Høst, 1968. 28p.

Yaseta buta　やせたぶた

'O hubeném prasátku'　*Modré vánoce.* Přel. Ivan Krouský a Z. K. Slabý. Praha, Albatros, 1975.

Poems　詩

'Голубь；Хозяйка'　Перевод Е. Винокурова. *Иностранная Литература,* июнь 1964. p.158
'Айалдар；Ак кептер；Жаз' Которгон Ж. Алыбаев. *Хиросима кектери.* Фрунзе, Кыргызстан, 1969. p.32-33
'Отражение' Перевод А. И. Мамонова. *Свободный стих в японской поэзии.* Москва, Наука, 1971. p.130
'Dream; Raison d'être of red; Cattle; Omen; Falling star; Ask again; Honesty covered with flame; The hand of velocity for Kajiyama Toshio; Message to the flying; Human air; So free; From now on; Vie; Outside the circle; Encounter for Ruiko and her pictures'　Tr. by Hajime Kijima and Hiroaki Sato. *The poetry of postwar Japan.* Iowa City, Univ. of Iowa Press, 1975. p.130-144
'Ранняя весна; Отражение; Послевоенное (1946 год)' Перевод Анатолия Мамонова. *Вкус хризантемы.* Москва, Восточная Литература, 1976. p.50-51

'Upovídaný zloděj'　*Modré vánoce.* Přel. Ivan Krouský a Z. K. Slabý. Praha, Albatros, 1975.

KIKUCHI Chiyū　菊池知勇　1889-1972

Tanka　短歌

'A fish'　Tr. by Asataro Miyamori. *Masterpieces of Japanese poetry, ancient and modern.* Tokyo, Maruzen, 1936; Tokyo, Taiseido, 1956; N. Y. Greenwood Press, 1971. p.766

KIKUCHI Kan　菊池　寛　1888-1948

Aru katakiuchi no hanashi　ある敵討の話

'A katakiuchi'　Tr. by S. Okabe. *Tsurisuto,* 1919.
'復讐的話'魯迅訳 「現代日本小説集」上海　商務印書館 1923；「日本現代小説集 3」上海 商務印書館 1930. p.293-308；「魯迅全集 11」上海　魯迅全集出版社　1938. 作家書屋　1938. 大連　光華書店 1948. 北京　人民文学出版社　1973. p.537-552；「魯迅譯文集 1」北京　人民文学出版社　1958. p.543-554
'殺父之仇'新興書局編集部訳 「日本短篇小説選」台北　新興書局　1958. p.21-30；台南　鳴宇出版社 1972. p.21-30
'復仇的故事' 「日本作家十二人集」香港 新學書店 1959. p.60-71

Aru kōgisho　ある抗議書

'어떤抗議書'韓榮珣訳 「世界短篇文学全集 9」서울　三珍社　1971. p.78-97；「世界代表短篇文学全集 9」

110

서울 三熙社 1976. p.78–97; 「世界短篇文学全集 9」서울 新韓出版社 1976. p.138–168

Chichi kaeru 父帰る

'The father returns' Tr. by Glenn W. Shaw. *Tojuro's love, and four other plays.* Tokyo, Hokuseido, 1925. p.99–117

La patro revenas. Tr. Hirokazu Kaĵi. Tokyo, Esperanto Kenkyusha, 1927. 30p.

「父帰」田漢訳 「日本現代劇選」 上海 中華書局 192?.

Der Vater kehrt zurück. Übers. von E. Ackermann. Tokyo, Schobundo, 1935. 51p.

'Возвращение отца' Перевод М. П. Григориева. *По ту сторону мести.* Дальний, Южно-Маньчж. Ж. Д. 1941. p.134–153

'La patro revenas' Tr. Hirokazu Kaĵi. *El japana literaturo.* Tokyo, Japana Esperanto Instituto, 1965. p.95–106

'Return of the father' Tr. by Ichiro Nishizaki. *Eigo Kenkyu,* v.54, no.4–no.9, 1965 in 6 parts.

Chichi no mokei 父の模型

「父親的模型」「標準日本名著選讀」 孫文斗編 台北 大新書局 1969. p.34–60

Daini no seppun 第二の接吻

「再和我接個吻」葛祖蘭訳 上海 商務印書館 1928. 1冊

「再和我接個吻罷」鶯鸞子訳 上海 澄衷校 193?. 1冊

「二度吻」楊召愚訳 台北 野風出版社 1951. 122p

「再和我接個吻」潤壁訳 三重市 明志出版社 1962. 356p.

「第二의接吻」方春海訳 「日本文学選集 3」서울 知文閣 1966. p.27–189; 서울 韓國読書文化院 1973. p.27–193

「花文子小姐」謝蘭萍訳 台北 正文出版社 1968. 198p.

Engeki ron 演劇論

「戯劇之研究」沈辛白訳 上海 良友図書 193?. 1冊

Gimin Jinbei 義民甚兵衛

'Подвиг Дзимбея' *Прожектор,* номер 24, 1929. p.19–21

Gokuraku 極楽

'Рай' Перевод М. П. Григориева. *По ту сторону мести.* Дальний, Южно-Маньчж. Ж. Д. 1941. p.90–104

Hagoromo 羽衣

「羽衣」章克標訳 「菊池寛集」 上海 開明書店 1929. p.59–66

'Hagoromo' Übers. von Wilhelm Lietzke. *Nippon,* Jahrgang 2, 1936. p.165–169

「羽衣」 「少年的悲哀」郁達夫等訳 台北 啓明書局 1956. p.49–54

Irefuda 入れ札

「投票」仲持訳 「東方雑誌」 第18巻6期 1921. p.97–104; 「近代日本小説集」上海 商務印書館 192?.

「投票」 「標準日本名著選讀」 孫文斗編 台北 大新書局 1969. p.1–33

'Saikanan' Tr. Pakorn Limpanusorn. *Rueng sun yeepun 1.* Bangkok, Uksornsasna, 1977. p.85–109

Jigoku no Don Fuan 地獄のドン・ファン

「地獄的侫玄」羅江訳 「小説月報」 第20巻10号 1929. p.1631–1639

Junange 受難華

'Junange' Tr. by G. S. Rawlings and K. Takeu-chi. *Osaka Mainichi,* April 18–August 5, 1928.

Katakiuchi ijō 仇討以上

'Better than revenge' Tr. by Glenn W. Shaw. *Tojuro's love, and four other plays.* Tokyo, Hokuseido, 1925. p.29–78

Keikichi no yūwaku 啓吉の誘惑

'Keikichi's temptation' Tr. by Ryozo Matsumo-to. *Japanese literature, new and old.* Tokyo, Hokuseido, 1961. p.1–30

'Kiusaus' Suomentanut Kari Jalonen. *Kiusaus ja Nautinto.* Hämeenlinna, 1973.

Kekkon nijūsō 結婚二重奏

「結婚二重奏」浩然訳 上海 長城書局 1933. 1冊

Kiseki 奇蹟

'The miracle' Tr. by Glenn W. Shaw. *Tokyo Nichinichi,* Jan. 13–17, 1925; *Tojuro's love, and four other plays.* Tokyo, Hokuseido, 1925. p.119–138

Magotsuku sensei まごつく先生

'Magotsuku sensei' Tr. by Glenn W. Shaw. *English,* Dec. 1925–Feb. 1926.

Minage kyūjogyō 身投げ救助業

'The trade of rescuing drowning men' Tr. by Kanichi Ando. *Eigo Seinen,* v.53, no.1–no.7, 1925 in 7 parts.

「投水救助業」章克標訳 「菊池寛集」 上海 開明書店 1929. p.47–57

'A profissão de salva-vidas' Tr. de Antônio Nojiri. *Maravilhas do conto japonês.* São Paulo, Editôra Cultrix, 1962. p.91–98

'Aki menti az öngyilkost' Ford. Sz. Holti Mária. *Modern Japán elbeszélők.* Budapest, Európa Könyvkiadó, 1967. p.99–106

「投水自殺營救業」廖清秀訳 「投水自殺營救業」 台北 蘭開書局 1968. p.1–9

Miura Uemon no saigo 三浦右衛門の最期

「三浦右衛門的最後」魯迅訳 「新青年」 第9巻3期 1921. p.1–9; 「現代日本小説集」上海 商務印書館 1923; 「日本現代小説集 3」 上海 商務印書館 1930. p.280–292; 「魯迅全集 11」 上海 魯迅全集出版社 1938. 作家書屋 1946. 大連 光華書店 1948. 北京 人民文学出版社 1973. p.524–536; 「魯迅譯文集 1」 北京 人民文学出版社 1958. p.533–542

Mumei sakka no nikki 無名作家の日記

「無名作家的日記」「現代世界小説選」台北 1971. p.300–326

「無名作家的日記」 「現代世界短篇小説傑作選」 台北 徳華出版社 1975. p.287–310

Okujō no kyōjin 屋上の狂人

'The housetop madman' Tr. by Glenn W. Shaw. *Eibun Mainichi,* May 1, 1923; *Tojuro's love, and four other plays.* Tokyo, Hokuseido, 1925. p.79–97

'The madman on the roof' Tr. by Yozan Iwasaki and Glenn Hughes. *Three modern Japanese plays.* Cincinnati, Stewart Kidd, 1923. p.57–75; *Modern Japanese literature,* ed. by D. Keene. N. Y. Grove Press, 1956; Tokyo, Tuttle, 1957. p.278–287; *Treasury of world literature,* ed. by D. D. Runes. N. Y. Philosophical

Library, 1956. p.700–705; *The Mentor book of modern Asian literature*, ed. by D. B. Shimer. N. Y. New American Library, 1969. p.163–171.

'屋上的狂人' 田漢訳 「日本現代劇選」 上海 中華書局 192?.

'The madman on the roof' Tr. by Ichiro Nishizaki. *Helicon* (Ochanomizu Univ.) no. 9, 1958.

Il matto sul tetto. Tr. di Mario Teti. Milano, Il Saggiatore, 1962. 1v.

Ono no Komachi 小野小町

'Ono no Komachi' Tr. by Jihei Hashiguchi. *Tokyo Nichinichi*, April 12, 1923.

'Ono no Komachi' Übers. von Alexander Spann. *Die Brücke*, Band 3, 1927. p. 202–203

Onsenba shōkei 温泉場小景

'温泉場小景' 田漢訳 「日本現代劇選」 上海 中華書局 192?.

'Une scène d'une station thermale' Tr. par M. Yoshitomi. *Anthologie de la littérature japonaise contemporaine*. Grenoble, Xavier Drevet, 1924. p.203–221

Onshū no kanata ni 恩讐の彼方に

'The serene realm beyond passions' Tr. by Kanichi Ando. *Eigo Seinen*, v.43, no.1–no.12, 1920, v.44, no.1–no.12, 1920–21 in 24 parts.

'Piu che la vendetta' Tr. di H. Shimoi. *Sakura*, 1920.

The serene realm beyond passions. Tr. by Kanichi Ando. Tokyo, Kenkyusha, 1922. 1v.

'Jenseits von Hass und Liebe' Übers. von Alexander Spann. *Das Junge Japan*, Band 2, 1925. p.18–21, 48–50, 62–72, 88–99

'恩怨之外' 鄭心南訳 「小説月報」 第21巻1号 1930. p.297–311

'По ту сторону мести' Перевод М. П. Григориева. *По ту сторону мести*. Дальний, Южно-Маньчж. Ж. Д. 1941. p.9–66

'The realm beyond' Tr. by John Bester. *Japan Quarterly*, v.7, no.3, 1960. p.317–342; *The realm beyond*. Tokyo, Hara Shobo, 1964. p.7–108

'Jenseits von Liebe und Hass' Übers. von Walter Donat. *Die fünfstöckige Pagode*. Düsseldorf, Diederichs, 1960. p.167–205

Beyond the pale of vengeance. Tr. by Teru Kikuchi. Ube, Karin Bunko, 1961. 73p.

'恩怨을넘어서' 金龍済訳 「日本代表作家百人集 1」 서울 希望出版社 1966. p.384–405; 「日本短篇文学全集 1」 서울 新太陽社 1969. p.366–387

'恩讎' 徐白訳 「日本短篇譯集 1」 台北 晩蟬書店 1969. p.1–38

'И была любовь, и была ненависть' Перевод В. Скальника. *И была любовь, и была ненависть*. Москва, Наука, 1975. p.2–54

'恩怨을넘어서' 宋赫訳 「日本文学大全集 10」 서울 東西文化院 1975. p.110–132

'Au delà des représailles' Tr. par Chiyo Machii. *Le pays des cerisiers*. Paris, n.d. p.61–109

Rangaku koto hajime 蘭学事始

'Il Rangaku koto hajime de Kikuchi Kan' Tr. di Maria Teresa Orsi. *Il Giappone*, anno 14, 1974. p.73–102

Ren'aibyō kanja 恋愛病患者

'L'amour est une maladie' Tr. par Juntaro Maruyama. *L'amour est une maladie*. Tokyo, Haku-

suisha, 1927. p.2–54

'戀愛病患者' 劉大杰訳 「戀愛病患者」 上海 北新書局 192?.

Ren'ai kekkon 恋愛結婚

'The love match' *Contemporary Japan*, v.1, no.4, 1933. p.687–695

Sehyō 世評

'公論' 章克標訳 「菊池寛集」上海 開明書店 1929. p.99–186

'輿論' 劉大杰訳 「戀愛病患者」 上海 北新書局 192?.

Shimabara shinjū 島原心中

'Le double suicide de Shimabara' Tr. par Serge Elisséev. *Japon et Extrême-Orient*, no.9, 1924. p.123–147; *Neuf nouvelles japonaises*, par S. Elisséev. Paris, G. van Œst, 1924. p.146–170

'島原心中' 章克標訳 「菊地寛集」 上海 開明書店 1929. p.69–96

Shindō 新道

'Gomu to kaze' Tr. by Kenkichi Sudo. *The Youth's Companion*, v.2, no.1–3, 1947.

Shinju 新珠

「新珠」 周白棣訳 上海 大陸書店 193?. 1冊

Shinju fujin 真珠夫人

Портрет дамы с жемчугами. Перевод М. Огуси. Москва, Худож. Лит. 1977. 274p.

Shisha o warau 死者をわらふ

'Laughing at the dead' Tr. by Michael Y. Matsudaira. *The heart is alone*, ed. by Richard N. McKinnon. Tokyo, Hokuseido, 1957. p.10–16

Shōbu goto 勝負事

'Sieg und Niederlage' Übers. von Maria Piper. *Das japanische Theater*. Frankfurt am Main, Societäts Verlag, 1937. p.84–92

'Games of chance' Tr. by John Bester. *Japan P.E.N. News*, no.6, Dec. 1960. p.1–3

Shōhai 勝敗

Victory or defeat. Tr. by Kiichi Nishi. Tokyo, Kairyudo, 1934. 289p.

Shunkan 俊寛

'Shunkan' Tr. di R. Vulpitta. *Antologia della letteratura coreana e giapponese*. Milano, Fratelli Fabbri, 1969. p.282–292

Sōji 相似

'模仿' 劉大杰訳 「戀愛病患者」 上海 北新書局 192?.

Tadanao kyō gyōjōki 忠直卿行状記

'On the conduct of Lord Tadanao' Tr. by Geoffrey Sargent. *Today's Japan*, v.6, no.3, 1961. p.15–34; *Modern Japanese stories*, ed. by I. Morris. London, Spottiswoode, 1961; Tokyo, Tuttle, 1962. p.102–137; *The realm beyond*. Tokyo, Hara Shobo, 1964. p.109–231

'Sul comportamento del Sire Tadanao' Tr. di Atsuko Ricca Suga. *Narratori giapponese moderni*. Milano, Bompiani, 1965. p.185–226

'Über das Benehmen von Lord Tadanao' Deutsch

von Monique Humbert. *Nippon*. Zürich, Diogenes, 1965. p.117–166

Ten no haizai 天の配剤

'Ten no haizai' Tr. by Glenn W. Shaw. *English*, July, 1925.

Tōjūrō no koi 藤十郎の恋

'Tojuro's love' Tr. by Glenn Shaw. *Eigo Seinen*, v.48, no.2–no.12, 1922–23, v.49, no.1–no.3, 1923 in 12 parts; *Tojuro's love, and four other plays*. Tokyo, Hokuseido, 1925. p.1–27
'Tojuros Liebe' Übers. von Naoto Yonezawa und A. Spann. *Das Junge Japan,* Band 2, 1925. p.1–17
「藤十郎之戀」 章克標訳 「菊池寛集」 上海 開明書局 1929. p.1–27
「藤十郎的戀」 胡仲侍訳 上海 現代書局 1929. 1冊
'Amo de Toojuuroo' Tr. J. Simomura. *Amo de Toojuuroo, kaj du aliaj teatrajoy*. Budapest, Literatura Monde, 1934.

Toki no ujigami 時の氏神

'時間之神' 葛綏成訳 「東方雑誌」 第23巻8期 1926. p.117–130
'La providence du moment' Tr. par Juntaro Maruyama. *L'amour est une maladie*. Tokyo, Hakusuisha, 1927. p.55–114
'The savior of the moment' Tr. by Noboru Hidaka. *The passion*. Honolulu, Oriental Literature Society, 1933; N. Y. Greenwood Press, 1971. p.55–86

Toki to ren'ai 時と恋愛

'時間與戀愛' 文運訳 「戀愛病患者」 上海 北新書局 192?.

Tsuma 妻

'妻' 劉大杰訳 「戀愛病患者」 上海 北新書局 192?.

Umi no yūsha 海の勇者

'海之勇者' 田漢訳 「日本現代劇選」 上海 中華書局 193?.

Uwasa no hassei 噂の発生

'謠言的發生' 侍桁訳 「小説月報」 第20巻4号 1929. p.681–693

Wagaya no inu tachi 我家の犬達

'Our dogs' Tr. by Kyohei Hagiwara. *Eigo Seinen*, v.76, no.12, 1937. p.407–408

Wakasugi saibanchō 若杉裁判長

'若杉裁判長' 章克標訳 「菊池寛集」 上海 開明書店 1929. p.29–45
'Der Richter Wakasugi' Übers. von K. Sano und A. Sano. *Nippon*, Band 2, 1935. p.36–37, 40–41

Warai 笑

'Laughter' *Selections from modern Japanese writers*, by A. L. Sadler. Sydney, Australian Medical Pub. 1943. p.48–58
'Смех' Перевод М. П. Григориева. *По ту сторону мести*. Дальний, Южно-Маньчж. Ж. Д. 1941. p.67–89

Yuranosuke yakusha 由良之助役者

'The actor who was Yuranosuke' Tr. by S. G. Brickley. *The writing of idiomatic English*. Tokyo, Kenkyusha, 1951. p.33–50

Criticism 評論

'文藝與人生' 周柏棣訳 「貢献」 第1巻5期 1927.
'文學上的諸主義' 朱雲影訳 「讀書雑誌」 第1巻1号 1931. p.1–12
'志賀直哉氏的作品' 謝六逸訳 「志賀直哉集」 上海 中華書局 1935. p.1–12
'歴史小説論' 洪秋雨訳 「文藝創作講座 1」 上海 193?.
「世界文學大綱」 朱應會訳 上海 崑崙書局 193?. 1冊
History and trends of modern Japanese literature. Tokyo, Kokusai Bunka Shinkokai, 1936. 18p.
Tendencias de la literatura contemporanea del Japón. Tr. de G. Yoshio Shinya. Tokyo, Kokusai Bunka Shinkokai, 1935. 5p.

Essay エッセイ

'母之夢' 王潜訳 「中國公論」 第1巻2期 1939. p.121–129

「菊池寛戯曲集」 黄九如訳 上海 中華書局 1934. 1冊

KIKUCHI Keikin 菊池溪琴 1798–1881

Poems 詩

'At Yanagase' Tr. by Tetsuzo Okada. *Chinese and Sino-Japanese poems*. Tokyo, Seikanso, 1937. p.96

KIKUCHI Yūhō 菊池幽芳 1870–1947

Chikyōdai 乳姉妹

「乳姉妹」 韻琴訳 上海 商務印書館 1926. 2冊

KIKUMURA Itaru 菊村 到 1925–

Fuhō shoji 不法所持

'不法所持' 玄相杰訳 「日本新鋭文学作家受賞作品選集 3」 서울 青雲社 1964. p.153–205; 「戦後日本短篇文学全集 3」 서울 日光出版社 1965. p.153–206; 「現代日本代表文学全集 3」 서울 平和出版社 1973. p.153–205

Iwōjima 硫黄島

'Iwojima' Tr. by John Bester. *Japan Quarterly*, v.7, no.1, 1960. p.66–88
'硫黄島' 崔玄植訳 「芥川賞小説集」 서울 新丘文化社 1960. p.11–37; 「깊은江」 서울 三耕社 1971. p.11–37
'硫黄島' 玄相杰訳 「日本新鋭文学作家受賞作品選集 3」 서울 青雲社 1964. p.207–246; 「戦後日本短篇文学全集 3」 서울 日光出版社 1965. p.207–246; 「現代日本代表文学全集 3」 서울 平和出版社 1973. p.207–246
'硫磺島' 劉蔡沙訳 「芥川賞作品選集 1」 台北 大地出版社 1972. p.185–218
'硫黄島' 李喜春訳 「日本文学大全集 10」 서울 東西文化院 1975. p.397–420

Korosanai de 殺さないで

'Non uccidere' Tr. di Ester Maimeri. *Novelle giapponesi*. Milano, Martello, 1969. p.109–138

Kurenai no tsubasa 紅の翼

'붉은날개' 玄相杰訳 「日本新鋭文学作家受賞作品選集 3」 서울 青雲社 1964. p.247–302; 「戦後日本短篇文学全集 3」 서울 日光出版社 1965. p.247–302;

KIKUMURA Itaru

「現代日本代表文学全集 3」 서울 平和出版社 1973.
p.247–301

'甜姑娘' 徐白訳 「日本短篇譯集 2」 台北 晩蟬書店 1969.
p.169–190

KIKUOKA Kuri 菊岡久利 1909–1970

Poems 詩

'Pass through' 崔一秀訳 「기다리고있네」 서울 韓
国政経社 1966. p.233–235
'蝦夷覧古；什麼島；事件' 徐和隣訳 「現代詩解説」 台北
葡萄園詩刊社 1970. p.80–90

KIKUTA Kazuo 菊田一夫 1908–1973

Kimi no na wa 君の名は

「그대의름은」 李圭植訳 서울 啓明文化社 1960. 2冊；
1963. 708p.；서울 韓国読書文化院 1974. 2冊
「그대의름은」 韓民教訳 서울 哲理文化社 1961. 351p.；
서울 합동出版社 1962. 2冊；서울 泰文堂 1963.
2冊；서울 不二出版社 1967. 2冊
「기다리에서」 文德守訳 서울 青雲出版社 1963. 2冊

KIMATA Osamu 木俣 修 1906–

Masaoka Shiki 正岡子規

'Shiki Masaoka, his haiku and tanka' Tr. by
Shin Ohara. *Philosophical Studies of Japan,*
no.8, 1967. p.41–66

Tanka 短歌

'1 tanka' *Modern Japanese poetry,* by Donald
Keene. Ann Arbor, Center for Japanese
Studies, Univ. of Michigan, 1964. p.37
'1 tanka' Tr. by Donald Keene. *Landscapes and
portraits.* Tokyo, Kodansha International,
1971. p.154

KIMISHIMA Hisako 君島久子

Ine ni natta tennyo いねになったてんにょ

The princess of the rice fields. N. Y. Walker, 1970.
1v.; Tokyo, Weatherhill, 1970. 1v.

Māryan to mahō no fude マーリャンとまほうのふで

Ma Lien and the magic brush. English version by
Alvin Tresselt. N. Y. Parents' Magazine
Press, 1968. 32p.
The magic brush. Retold by Jane Carruth. Lon-
don, Hamlyn, 1969. 1v.

Yama ippai no kinka やまいっぱいのきんか

Lum Fu and the golden mountain Tr. by Alvin
Tresselt. N. Y. Parents' Magazine Press,
1971. 32p.

KIMURA Ayako 木村あや子

Tanka 短歌

'1 tanka' Tr. by Shigeshi Nishimura. *Eigo Seinen,*
v.93, no.3, 1947. p.120

KIMURA Ki 木村 毅 1894–

Nichi-Bei bunka kōshōshi 日米文化交渉史

*Japanese literature: manners and customs in Meiji-
Taisho era,* comp. and ed. by Kimura Ki. Tr.
and adapted by Philip Yampolsky. Tokyo,
Obunsha, 1957. 277p.

Shōsetsu kenkyū jūrokkō 小説研究十六講

「小説研究十六講」 高明訳 上海 北新書局 193?. 1冊

Shōsetsu no sōsaku to kanshō 小説の創作と鑑賞

「小説底創作及鑑賞」 高明訳 上海 神州書局 1931. 1冊

Criticism 評論

「世界文學大綱」 朱應會訳 上海 崑崙書局 1929. 1冊
「東西小説發達史」 美子訳 上海 世界文藝社 1930. 1冊
'眞個提綱絜領的世界文學大綱' 朱應會訳 「新書月報」第
1巻2期

Essays エッセイ

'The Japanese "Mayflower"' *Japan Quarterly,*
v.7, no.3, 1960. p.302–309
'The legacy of Rizal' *Japan Quarterly,* v.9, no.3,
1962. p.301–309
'Diplomacy by revelry' *This is Japan,* v.10,
1963. p.124–127

KIMURA Masakoto 木村正辞 1827–1913

Tanka 短歌

'Mount Yoshino' Tr. by Asataro Miyamori.
*Masterpieces of Japanese poetry, ancient and
modern.* Tokyo, Maruzen, 1936; Tokyo,
Taiseido, 1956; N. Y. Greenwood Press,
1971. p.602

KIMURA Shōshū 木村小舟 1881–1955

Essay エッセイ

'冤兒的衣服' 秋藝訳 「小説月報」 第16巻11号 1925.
p.1–2

KIN Tatsuju 金 達寿 (Kim Darsu) 1919–

Boku Tatsu no saiban 朴達の裁判

Суд над Пак Талем. Перевод В. Логунова.
Москва, Прогресс, 1967. 63p.
'Ижеро етилмаган хукм' Азиз Абдуллаев таржимаси. *Ижеро етилмаган хукм.* Тошкент,
1971. p.7–72

KIN Soun 金 素雲 **(Kim Soun)** 1907–

Negi o ueta hito ネギをうえた人

The story bag. Tr. by Setsu Higashi. Tokyo, Tuttle, 1955. 229p.

KINOSHITA Junji 木下順二 1914–

Kawazu shōten 蛙昇天

Успение лягушки. Перевод И. Львовой. Москва, Искусство, 1958. 169p.

Yūzuru 夕鶴

Twilight of a crane. Tr. by Takeshi Kurahashi. Tokyo, Miraisha, 1952. 51p.
'Журавлиные перья' Перевод И. Львовой и В. Марковой. *Театр,* номер 12, 1955. p.3–16; *Современные японские пьесы.* Москва, Искусство, 1962. p.195–217
'Twilight crane' Tr. by A. C. Scott. *Playbook,* N. Y. New Directions, 1956. p.137–159
'夕鶴' 周浩如訳 「譯文」1957年6月 p.3–18
「夕鶴」 陳北鷗訳 北京 中國戏剧 1961. 17p.
'夕鶴' 辛東門訳 「世界戦後文学全集 10」 서울 新丘文化社 1962. p.101–113
'Twilight crane' Tr. by Ryoichi Nakagawa. *Eigo Kenkyu,* v.56, no.1–no.6, 1967 in 6 parts.
'Der Abendkranich' Übers. von Jürgen Berndt. *Japanische Dramen.* Berlin, Volk und Welt, 1968. p.145–167
'La grulla crepuscular' Tr. por Josefina Keiko Ezaki. *Teatro japonés contemporaneo.* Madrid, Aguilar, n.d. p.101–121
'Yuzuru' Tr. di Mario Teti. Milano, Einaudi, n.d. 1v.

Essay エッセイ

'战斗的友誼' 聞逖訳 「世界文学」 1963年7月 p.16–20

「民間故事劇」 錢稲孫訳 北京 作家出版社 1963. 57p.
'螃蟹的故事' 錢稲孫訳 「世界文学」 1964年6月 p.120 –124

KINOSHITA Mokutarō 木下杢太郎 1885–1945

Poems 詩

'路上；睡醒；剳青，石竹花' 周作人訳 「新青年」 第9巻 4期 1921. p.37–38; 「陀螺」 上海 北新書局 193?.
'Sherry; Ryogoku; This side and that side' *The poetry of living Japan,* by Takamichi Ninomiya and D. J. Enright. London, John Murray, 1957. p.37–38
'Discussione centrale' Tr. di R. Beviglia. *Antologia della letteratura coreana e giapponese.* Milano, Fratelli Fabbri, 1969. p.274

KINOSHITA Naoe 木下尚江 1869–1937

Hi no hashira 火の柱

Pillar of fire. Tr. by Kenneth Strong. London, George Allen and Unwin, 1972. 199p.

Rinka no bijin 隣家の美人

'Красивая соседка' *Вестник Знания,* номер 10, 1910. p.1090–1094

Ryōjin no jihaku 良人の自白

The confessions of a husband. Tr. by Arthur Lloyd. Tokyo, Yurakusha, 1905–6. 2v.

KINOSHITA Rigen 木下利玄 1886–1925

Tanka 短歌

'Autumn stirs; The crematory' Tr. by Asataro Miyamori. *Masterpieces of Japanese poetry, ancient and modern.* Tokyo, Maruzen, 1936; Tokyo, Taiseido, 1956; N. Y. Greenwood Press, 1971. p.745–746
'1 tanka' Tr. by H. H. Honda. *The Reeds,* v.3, 1957. p.24

KINOSHITA Soshi 木下蘇子 1868–1953

Haiku 俳句

'2 haiku' Tr. by Asataro Miyamori. *Anthology of haiku, ancient and modern.* Tokyo, Maruzen, 1932. p.824–825

KINOSHITA Yūji 木下夕爾 1914–1965

Poems 詩

'An evening; At a table in the country; A boy; A winter fountain; Youth' *An anthology of modern Japanese poetry,* ed. and tr. by Ichiro Kono and Rikutaro Fukuda. Tokyo, Kenkyusha, 1957. p.48–50
'Kirda bir masada' Tercüme etmek L. Sami Akalin. *Japon şiiri.* İstanbul, Varlik Yayinevi, 1962. p.296
'Late summer' Tr. by Geoffrey Bownas and Anthony Thwaite. *The Penguin book of Japanese verse.* Harmondsworth, Penguin Books, 1964. p.226
'Country table; A lad; At an inn; The field; Village in Izumo; In younger days; Meadow-lark's nest; Memories' Tr. by Robert Epp. *Literature East and West,* v.15, no.4, v.16, no.1 & 2, 1971–72. p.816–820
'Late summer' Tr. by Tsutomu Fukuda. *Eigo Kenkyu,* v.63, no.4, 1974. p.18
'Miez de vară' Traducerea Virgil Teodorescu. *Din lirica japoneză.* Bucureşti, Editura Univers, n.d. p.211
'Sensommer; Ved et bord på landet' Til norsk ved Paal Brekke. *Moderne japansk lyrikk.* Oslo, Norsk Bokklubben, n.d. p.68–69

KIRISHIMA Yōko 桐島洋子 1937–

Botomuresu USA ボトムレス USA

'性海探奇録' 「東西風」 第1期11号 1972—第6期4号 1973.

KISABA Jun 喜舎場　順　1934–

Kurai hana 暗い花

'Цветы горя' Перевод Г. Ивановой. *Красная лягушка.* Москва, Наука, 1973. p.73–79

KISARAGI Shin 衣更着　信　1920–

Poems 詩

'賭博師' 金龍済訳 「日本詩集」 서울 青雲社 1960. p.109–112
'The form of summer; Cold wind; A short train' Tr. by Harry and Lynn Guest and Shozo Kajima. *Post-war Japanese poetry.* London, Penguin Books, 1972. p.49–51

KISHI Nami 岸　なみ　1912–

Oni no yomesan おにのよめさん

The ogre and his bride. English version by Alvin Tresselt. N. Y. Parents' Magazine Press, 1971. 32p.

KISHI Yamaji 貴司山治　1899–1973

Awa no kojima 阿波の小島

'Die Insel Kojima in Awa' Übers. von Kurt Meissner. *Der Tanzfächer,* von K. Meissner. Tokyo, 1943. p.89–109

Darakan yōkō su ダラ幹洋行す

'The misleader goes abroad' *The cannery boat, and other Japanese short stories.* N. Y. International Publishers, 1933; London, Martin Lawrence, 1933; N. Y. Greenwood Press, 1968. p.193–210

Kinenhi 記念碑

'Памятник' Перевод Г. Горбштейн. *Литература Мировой Революции,* 1931, номер 4. p.70–84
'The monument' *The cannery boat, and other Japanese short stories.* N. Y. International Publishers, 1933; London, Martin Lawrence, 1933; N. Y. Greenwood Press, 1968. p.141–170

Kōfuku na rōjin 幸福な老人

'Egy boldog aggastyán' Ford. Thein Alfréd. *Mai Japán dekameron.* Budapest, Nyugat, 1935. p.163–181

Teishuku na saikun 貞淑な妻君

'貞淑的妻' 高汝鴻訳 「日本短篇小説集」 台北 台湾商務印書館 1969. p.159–167

KISHIDA Eriko 岸田衿子　1929–

Jojo no kanmuri ジョジォのかんむり

The lion and the bird's nest. London, Bodley Head,

1972. 1v.; N. Y. Thomas Y. Crowell, 1973. 22p.
Der Löwe und das Vogelnest. Zürich, Atlantis, 1972. 1v.
Løven med fuglereden. Oversaette Ib Permin, København, Høst, 1972. 23p.

Kabakun かばくん

Hippopotamus. Tr. by Masako Matsuno. Englewood Cliffs, N. J. Prentice-Hall, 1963. 27p.
Hippo. Zürich, Atlantis, 1964. 1v.
Debout! mon brave hippopotame. Tr. par le père Castor. Paris, Flammarion, 1965. 28p.
Wake up Hippopotamus. London, Bodley Head, 1967. 28p.
God morgen flodhest. Oversaette Viggio Nørgaar-Jepsen. København, Høst, 1967. 28p.

Kabakun no fune かばくんのふね

Hippos Boot. Augsburg, Verlag Lebendiges Wort, 1966. 27p.
Hippo boat. London, Bodley Head, 1967. 1v.; Harmondsworth, Penguin Books, 1971. 31p.
The hippo boat. N. Y. World Publishing Co. 1968. 1v.
Hjaelp os, flodhest. Oversaette Viggo Norgaard-Jepsen. København, Høst, 1968. 28p.

KISHIDA Kunio 岸田国士　1890–1954

Asu wa tenki 明日は天気

'It will be fine tomorrow' Tr. by Eric S. Bell and Eiji Ukai. *Osaka Mainichi,* August 8–12, 1928; *Eminent authors of contemporary Japan v.2.* Tokyo, Kaitakusha, 1931. p.31–59

Chiroru no aki チロルの秋

'Autumn in the Tyrol' Tr. by Koji Oi. *The Reeds,* v.11, 1967. p.75–92

Hi tomoshi koro 灯ともし頃

'Towards nightfall' Tr. by Koji Oi. *The Reeds,* v.12, 1968. p.67–71

Kami fūsen 紙風船

'Le ballon de papier' Tr. par Marguerite Guillemot. *Nippon,* 13, 1937. p.33–37
'A paper balloon' Tr. by Koji Oi. *The Reeds,* v.10, 1965. p.81–97

Nyonin katsugō 女人渇仰

'Adoration' Tr. by Richard McKinnon. *Literary Review,* v.6, no.1, 1962. p.122–143

Ochiba nikki 落葉日記

'Fallen leaves, a diary' Tr. by Tadao Katayama. *The Reeds,* v.7, 1961. p.145–180

Okujō teien 屋上庭園

'The roof garden' Tr. by Noboru Hidaka. *The passion, and three other Japanese plays.* Honolulu, Oriental Literature Society, 1933. p.1–22
'The roof-garden' Tr. by Kazuo Yamada. *The roof-garden, and other one-act plays.* Tokyo, Shijo Shobo, 1934. p.1–29

Shinnen kyōsō kyoku 新年狂想曲

'A New Year rhapsody' Tr. by Koji Oi. *The Reeds*, v.12, 1968. p.71–76

Criticism 評論

'包多麗許研究' 予倩訳 「戯劇」 第2巻2期 1930. p.79–84

「戯劇概論」 陳瑜訳 上海 中華書局 1933. 1冊

KITA Morio 北 杜夫 1927–

Haari no iru oka 羽蟻のいる丘

'Mraveniste krialatych mravencu' Přel. M. Jelínková. *Nový Orient,* no.2, 1965. p.103–106

Iwaone nite 岩尾根にて

'嶺背上' 鐘肇政訳 「戦後日本短篇小説選」 台北 台湾商務印書館 1968. p.83-99

'On the rock ridge' Tr. by Clifton Royston. *Japan Quarterly*, v.16, no.4, 1969. p.423–430

'На скалистом гребне' Перевод М. Певзнера. *Красная лягушка.* Москва, Наука, 1973. p.36–49

'바위稜線' 權英鉉訳 「日本研究」 第19巻12号 1974. p.88–97

Kiiroi fune 黄色い船

'Желтый корабль' Перевод Б. Раскина. *Японская новелла 1960–1970.* Москва, Прогресс, 1972. p.122–141

Otamajakushi おたまじゃくし

'Голобастики' Перевод В. Гривнина. *Иностранная Литература,* июнь 1971. p.125–128

Taimu mashin タイム・マシン

'Машина времени' Перевод З. Рахима. *Иностранная Литература,* январь 1967. p.158–169; *Времена Хокусая.* Москва, Мир, 1967. p.110–136

'Laiko masina' *Hokusajaus laikai.* Vilnius, Vaizdo, 1969. p.81–101

Tanjō 誕生

'Birth' Tr. by Clifton Royston. *Japan Quarterly*, v.16, no.4, 1969. p.414–422

Tenjō ura no kodomo tachi 天井裏の子供たち

'天障속의少年들' 李柱訓訳 「日本代表作家百人集 5」 서울 希望出版社 1966. p.210–233; 「日本短篇文学全集 6」 서울 新太陽社 1969. p.122–145

Yoru to kiri no sumi de 夜と霧の隅で

'밤과안개의구석에서' 哲理文化社編輯部訳 「芥川賞受賞作品選」 서울 哲理文化社 1961. p.79–214

KITAGAWA Fuyuhiko 北川冬彦 1900–

Kyodai na ibukuro no naka 巨大な胃袋の中

Im Bauch des Riesen, Übers. von Siegfried Schaarschmidt. Neuwied, Luchterhand, 1965. 27p.

Shi no hanashi 詩の話

「現代詩解説 什麼是現代詩」 徐和隣訳 台北 葡萄園詩刊社 1970. 170p.

Poems 詩

'Vers le plateau; Rivière; Le printemps; La neige du printemps; Sur le même sujet; En rêve, dessins de diables; Une branche; Sur le même sujet; Poésie lyrique; Sur le même sujet; Le printemps prématuré; Admiration du bambou; Le serpent; Campanules à grandes fleurs; La vie; L'enter; La fête; Mont Mihara' Tr. par Kuni Matsuo et Steinilber-Oberlin. *Anthologie des poètes japonais contemporains.* Paris, Mercure de France, 1939. p.155–168

'A downpour' Tr. by Thomas T. Ichinose. *New world writing,* no.6, 1954.

'Spring snow; Early spring' Tr. by Donald Keene. *Modern Japanese literature,* ed. by D. Keene. N. Y. Grove Press, 1956; Tokyo, Tuttle, 1957. p.378–379

'A morning; On the blue sea; A war; A machine; A whale; A scene; Diamond-shaped legs; A railway toward destruction; A song of despair; Horse and landscape; The spring snow; A razor; The sore moon; The whisper of a bird' *An anthology of modern Japanese poetry,* ed. and tr. by Ichiro Kono and Rikutaro Fukuda. Tokyo, Kenkyusha, 1957. p.50–55

'The rush hour; Festivals; Faces in the procession' *The poetry of living Japan,* by Takamichi Ninomiya and D. J. Enright. London, John Murray, 1957. p.70–71

'Festival; A horse and the landscape' Tr. by S. Sato and Constance Urdang. *Poetry,* May 1956. p.85–86

'Nieve de primavera' *Sur,* no.249. Nov.-Dec. 1957. p.93

'Le cheval et le paysage; Neige de printemps; La fête' *La poésie japonaise,* par Karl Petit. Paris, Seghers, 1959. p.225–226

'Hiei-san; Vogelschau; Eis; Der Krieg' Übertragen von Shin Aizu. *Der schwermütige Ladekran.* St. Gallen, Tschudy Verlag, 1960. p.20, 36, 45, 48

'진눈깨비의季節' 金龍済訳 「日本詩集」 서울 青雲社 1960. p.131–132

'Das Pferd' Übers. von Kuniyo Takayasu und Manfred Hausmann. *Ruf der Regenpfeifer.* München, Bechtle Verlag, 1961. p.29

'Mavi denizde; Çengel gibi bacaklar' Tercüme etmek L. Sami Akalin. *Japon şiiri.* İstanbul, Varlik Yayinevi, 1962. p.270–271

'먼山脈; 접데기; 돌아온사람; 얼굴; 豪雨; 새의一瞥; 새의속삭임' 柳呈訳 「世界戦後文学全集 9」 서울 新丘文化社 1962. p.215–217

'Pulnocni probuzeni a poloha stolu' Přel. M. Novák. *Nový Orient,* v.19, no.1, 1964. p.10

'El murmullo de un pajaro; Una maquina' Tr. por Kikuya Ionesawa. *Poesia japonesa contemporanea.* Bogotá, Colombia Editoriales de Libreria, 1965.

'A stone' Tr. by Hisakazu Kaneko. *London Magazine,* v.7, no.7, 1967. p.32

'Early spring' Tr. by Donald Keene. *The Mentor book of modern Asian literature,* ed. by D. B. Shimer. N. Y. New American Library, 1969. p.129

'Gama sennin (a hermit toad)' Tr. by Tsutomu Fukuda. *Poetry Nippon,* no.8, 1969. p.21

'잡초; 얼굴' 「永遠한世界名詩全集 2」 黄錦燦編 서울 翰林出版社 1969. p.181, 228; 「永遠한世界名詩

KITAGAWA Fuyuhiko

全集 5」서울 翰林出版社 1973. p.181, 228

'Vitr' Přel. M. Novák. *Nový Orient*, no.1, 1970.

'A view' Tr. by Greg Campbell. *TransPacific*, no.5, 1970. p.21

'愛情；橡樹的果實' 徐和隣訳 「現代詩解説」台北 葡萄園詩刊社 1970. p.18–22

'Face; Bubbles; Weeds' *Anthology of modern Japanese poetry*, tr. and comp. by Edith Marcombe Shiffert and Yuki Sawa. Tokyo, Tuttle, 1972. p.84–86

'戦争' 金光林訳 「現代詩学」 4巻3号 1972.

'Война; Час пик' Перевод Анатолия Мамонова. *Вкус хризантемы.* Москва, Восточная Литература, 1976. p.53

'Ninsoare de primăvară; Feţe în procesiune; Copacii; Calul şi peisajul' Traducerea Dan Constantinescu & Virgil Teodorescu. *Din lirica japoneză.* Bucureşti, Editura Univers, n.d. p.187–188

'Togskinner mot ødeleggelsen; Prosesjonen; Fortvilesse' Til norsk ved Paal Brekke. *Moderne japansk lyrikk.* Oslo, Norske Bokklubben, n.d. p.47–49

Criticism 評論

'抒情은詩의本質인가' 金光林訳 「現代詩学」 第4巻2号 1972.

KITAHARA Hakushū 北原白秋 1885–1942

Poems 詩

'望火臺，鳳仙花' 周作人訳 「新青年」 第9巻4期 1921. p.36–37；'陀螺' 上海 北新書局 192?.

'The sparrow' Tr. by Yonejiro Noguchi. *Tokyo Nichinichi*, July 1, 1924.

'Crépuscule; Près d'un jet d'eau; Route de sable; Ruine; La montagne; Nuit' Tr. par Georges Bonneau. *Rythmes japonais,* par G. Bonneau. Paris, Geuthner, 1933. p.86–93; *Lyrisme du temps présent,* par G. Bonneau. Paris, Geuthner, 1935. p.76–83; *Anthologie de la poésie japonaise.*Paris, Geuthner, 1935. p.208–217

'The river of heaven; A clay dove; Summer has come; A firefly; Bread and roses; Spring birds; A water wheel' Tr. by Asataro Miyamori. *Masterpieces of Japanese poetry, ancient and modern.* Tokyo, Maruzen, 1936; Tokyo, Taiseido, 1956; N. Y. Greenwood Press, 1971. p.737–741

'The aegle flowers; This road' Tr. by Haxon Ishii. *Eigo Seinen,* v.72, no.12, 1935. p.409; v.73, no.1, 1935. p.9

'That moment; Tomorrow' Tr. by Jane Nakano. *Aoba no fue.* Honolulu, Univ. of Hawaii, 1937. n.p.

'Запустелата градина; Говата' Преведе от франц. Никола Джеров. *Песните на Ямато.* София, Корали, 1937. p.77–78

'Le visage d'octobre; Parce que j'avais envie de pleurer; Un tel jour si tendre; Camélias affolés; Le soleil se couche dans sa splendeur; Ombre et lumière; Jardin désert; Le faucon; Chrysanthèmes blancs; Mélèze; Petite image; L'ondée; Solitude; Glycines blanches; Admirant toute la longue journée; L'été; Sen-no-Rikyu; Rishikoun: Clair de lune; Pèlerinage; La nuit tardive; Lao-Tseu; Sous la vague clarté lunaire; et tanka' Tr. par Kuni Matsuo et Steinilber-Oberlin. *Anthologie des poètes japonais contemporains.* Paris, Mercure de France, 1939. p.81–97, 272–273

'Kaido-tosei' *Cultural Nippon*, v.1, 1941. p.77–116

'間；新月；雨中小景' 張我軍訳 「藝文雜誌」 第1巻1号 1943. p.16–17

'Ruine; Près d'un jet d'eau' *Histoire de la littérature japonaise contemporaine,* par G. Bonneau. Paris, Payot, 1944. p.241–242

'The larches' Tr. by Shigeshi Nishimura. *The Current of the World,* v.29, no. 9, 1952. p.41

'Okaru and Kampei' Tr. by D. J. Enright. *Bulletin of the Japan Society of London,* no.20, Oct. 1955. p.8

'7 tanka' Tr. by V. H. Viglielmo. *Japanese literature in the Meiji era.* Tokyo, Obunsha, 1955. p.408–410

'Secret song of the heretics; One-sided love' Tr. by Donald Keene. *Modern Japanese literature,* ed. by D. Keene. N. Y. Grove Press, 1956; Tokyo, Tuttle, 1957. p.204–205

'The water surface; Okaru and Kampei' Tr. by S. Sato and C. Urdang. *Poetry,* May 1956. p.99–101

'1 poème' Tr. by Roger Bersihand. *La littérature japonaise.* Paris, Presses Universitaires de France, 1956. p.116

'Земля и море; Торопливый брадобрей; Почтальон; Конкон' Перевод В. Марковой. *Японская поэзия.* Москва, Худож. Лит. 1956. p.406–411

'Caoción secreta de los heréticos' *Sur,* no.249, Nov.-Dec. 1957. p.94

'Voros' *Kinai es Japán koltok.* Budapest, Szepirodalmi, 1957. p.211

'Younger days; A red apple; Roses' *An anthology of modern Japanese poetry,* ed. and tr. by Ichiro Kono and Rikutaro Fukuda. Tokyo. Kenkyusha, 1957. p.56

'The precious music of heresy; Okaru and Kampei; Spinning wheel' *The poetry of living Japan,* by Takamichi Ninomiya and D. J. Enright. London, John Murray, 1957. p.29–32

'Camélias affolés; Mélèzes; Été' *La poésie japonaise,* par Karl Petit. Paris, Seghers, 1959. p.200–202

'Okaru und Kampei' Übertragen von Shin Aizu. *Der schwermütige Ladekran.* St. Gallen, Tschudy Verlag, 1960. p.40–41

'Tiefrot am Himmel' Übers. von Günther Debon. *Im Schnee die Fähre.* München, Piper, 1960. p.50

'1 lyrik und 1 tanka' Übers. von Kuniyo Takayasu und Manfred Hausmann. *Ruf der Regenpfeifer.* München, Bechtle Verlag, 1961. p.82, 101

'Güller; Kirmizi elma; İlk gençlik günleri' Tercüme etmek L. Sami Akalin. *Japon şiiri.* İstanbul, Varlik Yayinevi, 1962. p.243

'Лунной ночью' Перевод Веры Марковой. *Восточный альманах 6.* Москва, Худож. Лит. 1963. p.327

'Rain on Castle Island; Larches' Tr. by Geoffrey Bownas and Anthony Thwaite. *The Penguin book of Japanese verse.* Harmondsworth, Penguin Books, 1964. p.184–185

'2 poems' *Modern Japanese poetry,* by Donald Keene. Ann Arbor, Center for Japanese Studies, Univ. of Michigan, 1964. p.24–25

'Fever; Red fruit; Fireworks' Tr. by Harold P. Wright. *The Japanese image,* ed. by M. Schneps and A. D. Coox. Tokyo, Orient West, 1965. p.358–361

'Tiefrot am Himmel; Höhere Lust' *Lyrik des Ostens,* hrg. von Wilhelm Gundert usw. München, Carl Hanser, 1965. p.473–474

'1 poem' Tr. from the French by Unity Evans. *Japanese literature.* N. Y. Walker, 1965. p.99

'Лунной ночью; Птица, птица красная' Перевод Веры Марковой. *Птица, птица красная.* Москва, Дет. Лит. 1967.

'L'arcolaio: un giorno d'autunno' Tr. di R. Beviglia. *Antologia della letteratura coreana e giapponese.* Milano, Fratelli Fabbri, 1969. p.273

'Secret song of the heretics' Tr. by Donald Keene. *The Mentor book of modern Asian literature,* ed. by D. B. Shimer. N. Y. New American Library, 1969. p.126

'귀뚜라미 ; 단장 ; 모란꽃 ; 모라향기 ; 분꽃' 「永遠한世界名詩全集 2」黃錦燦編 서울 翰林出版社 1969; 「永遠한世界名詩全集 5」 서울 翰林出版社 1973. p.49, 89, 113, 169, 189, 209

'落葉松 ; 疊日 ; 보리내음' 金巣雲訳 「世界의文学大全集 34」서울 同和出版公社 1970. p.499–501

'3 poems' Tr. by Donald Keene. *Landscapes and portraits.* Tokyo, Kodansha International, 1971. p.143–145

'L'arcolaio; Un giorno d'autunno' *Il simbolismo nella poesia giapponese dell'era Meiji,* di Rosaria Beviglia. Roma, Istituto Italiano per il Medio ed Estremo Oriente, 1971. p.147

'Disillusion; Whisky' Tr. by Kazuko Takei and Marie Philomène. *Poetry Nippon,* no.20, 1972. p.9

'Větvičky' Přel. J. Brukner. *Mateřídouška,* v.28, no.4, 1972. p.7

'Vörös' Ford. Kosztolányi Dezsö. *Noé vessze je, a világirodalom gyöngyszemei.* Budapest, Kozmosz Könyvek, 1972. p.69

'Soot' Tr. by Kazuko Takei and Marie Philomene. *Poetry Nippon,* no.22, 1973. p.7–8

'The earth seen from the moon' Tr. by Mariko Hashimoto. *Poetry Nippon,* no.27, 1974. p.21–22

'The foundling' Tr. by Mariko Hashimoto. *Poetry Nippon,* no.29 & 30, 1975. p.27–28

'Whisky; The foundling; Night; Fall; Snow in the night; The palm of the hand; Disillusion; The sky in the early fall; A shower in late autumn; Migratory birds; Sky o'er the landscape garden; Nostalgia in the snow; Bamboo rising above the snow; Soot; Spring; Arranging flowers; The earth seen from the moon' Tr. by Kazuko Takei and Mariko Hashimoto. *Japanese songs of innocence and experience.* Tokyo, Hokuseido, 1975. p.59–73

'Camelii speriate; Vara; Ploaie pe insula castelului; Amurg; Tipătul pescăruşului; După ce mi-au dat lacrimile; Grădina pustie; Clar de lună; Noaptea' Traducerea Virgil Teodorescu. *Din lirica japoneză.* Bucureşti, Editura Univers, n.d. p.149–154

KITAHARA Takeo 北原武夫 1907–1973

Kiken na nikki 危険な日記

「危険한日記」 金惠林訳 서울 韓一出版社 1968. 1冊
「에겐行」 金惠林訳 서울 韓一出版社 1969. 424p.

Sei kazoku 聖家族

'The holy family' Tr. by William L. Clark. *Jiji Eigo Kenkyu,* v.12, no.2–9, 1957.

Taiatari josei ron 体当たり女性論

「男과女」 金文影 林石淵訳 서울 真文出版社 1972. p.199–340

「男性과女性의条件」 孔仲仁訳 서울 徽文出版社 1962. 280p.
「알쏭달쏭」 孔仲仁訳 서울 徽文出版社 1962. 341p.
「조용한離別」 서울 東民文化社 1971. 302p.

KITAKŌJI Isamitsu 北小路功光 1901–

Dōji Terumaro 童子照麿

'The child Terumaro' *Selections from modern Japanese writers,* by A. L. Sadler. Sydney, Australian Medical Publications, 1943. p.71–81

KITAMURA Kihachi 北村喜八 1898–1960

Criticism 評論

'英美의左傾文學' 土驤訳 「語絲」 第5卷39期 1929. p.649–658
'現代美國의文學' 方天白訳 「北新月刊」 第3卷18期 1929. p.47–63
'表現主義的藝術' 張資平訳 「當代文藝」 創刊号 1931. p.23–28; 第1卷2期 1931. p.381–385; 第1卷3期 1931. p.439–445
'The Japanese theatre—old and new' *United Asia,* v.8, no.4, 1956. p.281–284

KITAMURA Komatsu 北村小松 1901–1964

Mayonaka no sakaba 真夜中の酒場

'Die Mitternachtsbar' Übers. von Maria Piper. *Das japanische Theater.* Frankfurt am Main, Societäts Verlag, 1937. p.35–42

KITAMURA Tarō 北村太郎 1922–

Poems 詩

'A man in the grave; The rain' *An anthology of modern Japanese poetry,* ed. and tr. by Ichiro Kono and Rikutaro Fukuda. Tokyo, Kenkyusha, 1957. p.57–58

'Дождь' Перевод Веры Марковой. *Иностранная Литература,* сентябрь 1960. p.152–153

'조그만눈동자 ; 1952년의이미쥐' 辛東門訳 「世界戰後文学全集 9」 서울 新丘文化社 1962. p.242

'Birds' Tr. by Thomas Fitzsimmons and Rikutaro Fukuda. *Orient West,* v.9, no.5, 1964. p.59

'Rain; Garden, short poems; An autumn holiday; Evening to night' Tr. by Harry and Lynn Guest and Shozo Kajima. *Post-war Japanese poetry.* London, Penguin Books, 1972. p.81–86

'Birds; One in a graveyard' Tr. by Thomas Fitzsimmons. *Japanese poetry now.* London, André Deutsch, 1972. p.85–86; *Japanese poetry today.* N. Y. Schocken Books, 1972. p.87–88

'Май-сережки из полированной зелени; Некто, играющий на фортепьяно' Перевод Анатолия Мамонова. *Вкус хризантемы.* Москва, Восточная Литература, 1976. p.54

KITAMURA Tōkoku　北村透谷　1868–1894

Shukkonkyō　宿魂鏡

'Shukkonkyo, or, the magic mirror'　Tr. by Kenneth Strong.　*Monumenta Nipponica,* v.21, no.3–4, 1966.　p.392–409

Poems　詩

'The single butterfly'　Tr. by Shigeshi Nishimura. *Eigo Seinen,* v.92, no.11, 1946.　p.337
'Three butterfly poems'　Tr. by Shigeshi Nishimura.　*Language and Literature,* no.1, 1955. p.97–109
'반닷불' 「永遠한世界名詩全集 2」 黄錦燦編 서울 翰林出版社 1969. p.70; 「永遠한世界名詩全集 5」 서울 翰林出版社 1973. p.70

Criticism　評論

'萬物之聲與詩人' 侍桁訳 「語絲」 第4巻8期 1928. p.369–374

KITANI Rikka　喜谷六花　1877–1968

Haiku　俳句

'3 haiku'　Tr. by V. H. Viglielmo. *Japanese literature in the Meiji era.* Tokyo, Obunsha, 1955. p.443, 448

KITANI Shigeteru　喜谷繁暉　1929–

Poems　詩

'A castle for sale'　Tr. by Sanehide Kodama. *TransPacific,* no.5, 1970.　p.24

KITASATO Ran　北里　蘭

Kokoro　こころ

'A modern Japanese problem play: Kokoro'　Tr. by Arthur Lloyd.　*Transactions of the Asiatic Society of Japan,* v.33, part 1, 1905.　p.1–85

KITASONO Katsue　北園克衛　1902–1978

Poems　詩

'Poetry going out'　Tr. by the poet. *Atlantic Monthly,* Jan. 1955.　p.151
'Moonlight night in a bay'　*New World Writing,* 6th, 1956.　p.63
'The elements of a night; Night à la zorzicoz'　*An anthology of modern Japanese poetry,* ed. and tr. by Ichiro Kono and Rikutaro Fukuda. Tokyo, Kenkyusha, 1957. p.59–62
'Blau weiß schwarz gelb' Übertragen von Shin Aizu. *Der schwermütige Ladekran.* St. Gallen,

Tschudy Verlag, 1960. p.50
'白色装置' 金龍済訳 「日本詩集」 서울 青雲社 1960. p.64–69
'죽음과우산의詩；가을의立体；華麗한여름의단추；稀薄한바이올린' 鄭漢模訳 「世界戦後文学全集 9」 서울 新丘文化社 1962. p.218–219
'Two poems'　Tr. by Sam Grolmes. *Literature East and West,* v.12, no.2–4, 1968. p.249–254
'仙人掌島；開始腐敗的誹謗；街' 徐和隣訳 「現代詩解説」 台北 葡萄園詩刊社 1970. p.34–39

KIYAMA Shōhei　木山捷平　1904–1968

Hatsukoi　初恋

'첫사랑' 李圭楨訳 「世界短篇文学全集 9」 서울 三珍社 1971. p.275–289; 「世界代表短篇文学全集 9」 서울 三熙社 1976. p.275–290; 「世界短篇文学全集 9」 서울 新韓出版社 1976. p.94–120

KIYOOKA Takayuki　清岡卓行　1922–

Poems　詩

'Midnight; At a bar'　Tr. by Makoto Ueda. *Literary Review,* v.6, no.1, 1962. p.112–114
'자장가를위한북；얼은불꽃' 辛東門訳 「戦界戦後文学全集 9」 서울 新丘文化社 1962. p.243–244
'Cinepresa bizzarra'　*La protesta poetica del Giappone,* a cura di Dacia Maraini e Michiko Nojiri. Roma, Officina Edizioni, 1968. p.83–84
'Drum for a lullaby'　Tr. by Thomas Fitzsimmons. *Japanese poetry now.* London, André Deutsch, 1972. p.105; *Japanese poetry today.* N. Y. Schocken Books, 1972. p.107

Criticism　評論

'論吉野弘的詩' 陳千武訳 「笠」 第53期 1962. p.114–119

KIYOSAWA Manshi　清沢満之　1863–1903

Waga shinnen　わが信念

'My faith'　Tr. by Shojun Bando. *The Eastern Buddhist,* New series, v.5, no.2, 1972. p.148–152

KIZU Toyotarō　木津豊太郎

Poems　詩

'1 poem'　*New World Writing,* 6th, 1956. p.62

KŌ Haruto　耕　治人　1906–

Gunji hōtei　軍事法廷

'Black market blues'　Tr. by Grace Suzuki. *Ukiyo.* Tokyo, Phoenix Books, 1954. p.74–99; *Ukiyo.* ed. by J. Gluck. N. Y. Vanguard Press, 1963. p.133–148; London, Universal Library, 1964. p.133–148

KOBAYASHI Hajime　小林はじめ

Poems　詩

'Токио–Москва' Перевод Анатолия Мамонова. *Вкус хризантемы.* Москва, Восточная Литература, 1976. p.55

KOBAYASHI Hideo　小林秀雄　1902–

Criticism and essays　評論・エッセイ

'Naoya Shiga' *Nippon,* Band 9, 1936. p.48–49
'Aus Essay "Meine Lebensauffassung" Übers. von Oscar Benl und Horst Hammitzsch. *Japanische Geisteswelt.* Baden Baden, Holle Verlag, 1956. p.328–329
"뉴욕"에간 "사르트르" 金賢珠訳 「바이바이바디」 서울 三韓出版社 1966. p.165–166

KOBAYASHI Masaru　小林　勝　1927–1971

Chōji　弔辞

'弔辭' 梅翰譯 「譯文」 1955年4月 p.224–244
'弔辭' 「當代亜非拉小説選」 香港 中流出版社 1977. p.354–372

Hizume no wareta mono　蹄の割れたもの

'쪽발이' 閔丙山訳 「世界文学속의韓國 6」 서울 正韓出版社 1975. p.17–75

KOBAYASHI Takiji　小林多喜二　1903–1933

Bōsetsurin　防雪林

'Снегозащитная роща' Перевод Т. Чегодарь. *Такидзи Кобаяси, избранное.* Москва, Гослитиздат, 1957. p.5–84

Fuzai jinushi　不在地主

'在外地主' 震先訳 「小林多喜二选集」 北京 作家出版社 1956.
'The absentee landlord' Tr. by Frank Motofuji. *The factory ship, and The absentee landlord.* Tokyo, Univ. of Tokyo Press, 1973; Seattle, Univ. of Washington Press, 1973. p.85–185
「在外地主」 李芒訳 北京 人民文学出版社 1973. 152p.

Kani kōsen　蟹工船

「蟹工船」 潘念之訳 上海 大江書舗 1930. 1冊
Крабоконсервная фактория. Москва, МОПР, 1932. 80p.
'The cannery boat' *The cannery boat, and other Japanese short stories.* N. Y. International Publishers, 1933; London, Martin Lawrence, 1933. p.1–60; *Modern Japanese literature,* ed. by D. Keene. N. Y. Grove Press, 1956; Tokyo, Tuttle, 1957. p.333–338; *The cannery boat, and other Japanese short stories.* Reprint ed. N. Y. Greenwood Press, 1968. p.1–60
Крабоконсервная фактория, на украинском языке. Харьков, Рабочее Изд. 1934. 92p.
'Краболов' Перевод Н. Фельдман. *Японская революционная литература.* Москва, Худож. Лит. 1934. p.13–82; *Японская пролетарская литература.* Москва, 1936. p.33–42; *Рассказы.* Ленинград, Гослитиздат,
1938; *Кобаяси Такидзи, избранное.* Москва, Гослитиздат, 1957. p.85–154
Lod na kraby. Přel. Vlasta Hilská. Praha, Svoboda, 1947. 125p.
Polawiacze krabow. Tłumaczyc Andrzej Kamien. Warszawa, Czytelnik, 1953. 95p.
「蟹工船」 適夷訳 北京 作家出版社 1955. 216p.
Krabbenfischer. Übers. von Alfons Mainka. Berlin, Volk und Welt, 1958. 138p.
Краболов. Перевод А. Стругацкого. Владивосток, Приморское Книжное Изд. 1960. 75p.
'Lod na kraby' Přel. Vlasta Hilská. *Citanka svetove literatury.* Praha, Státní Pedagogiske Nakládatelství, 1970.
'The factory ship' Tr. by Frank Motofuji. *The factory ship, and The absentee landlord.* Tokyo, Univ. of Tokyo Press, 1973; Seattle, Univ. of Washington Press, 1973. p.1–83
「蟹工船」 叶渭渠訳 北京 人民文学出版社 1973. 118p.

Kōjō saibō　工場細胞

'Фабличная ячейка' Перевод Н. Фельдман. *Рассказы.* Ленинград, Гослитиздат, 1938.
'Фабличная ячейка' Перевод Е. Пинус. *Такидзи Кобаяси, избранное.* Москва, Гослитиздат, 1957. p.155–239

Numajiri mura　沼尻村

'Деревня Нумадзири' Перевод Н. Фельдман. *Рассказы.* Ленинград, Гослитиздат, 1938.
'Деревня Нумадзири' Перевод Р. Карлиной. *Такидзи Кобаяси, избранное.* Москва, Гослитиздат, 1957. p.300–361
「沼尻村」 李徳純訳 北京 人民文学出版社 1973. 104p.

Orugu　オルグ

'Организатор' Перевод Н. Фельдман. *Рассказы.* Ленинград, Гослитиздат, 1938.
'Организатор' Перевод И. Львовой. *Такидзи Кобаяси, избранное.* Москва, Гослитиздат, 1957. p.240–299

1928 nen sangatsu jūgo nichi　1928年3月15日

Der 15 März 1928. Berlin, Mopr Verlag, 1932. 46p.
'The fifteenth of March, 1928' *The cannery boat, and other Japanese short stories.* N. Y. International Publishers, 1933; London, Martin Lawrence, 1933; N. Y. Greenwood Press, 1968. p.67–90
15 марта в Отару. Москва, МОПР, 1934. 31p.
'Пятнадцатое марта 1928 года' Перевод Н. Фельдман. *Японская революционная литература.* Москва, Худож. Лит. 1934. p.83–136
「一九二八年三月十五日」 適夷訳 北京 人民文学出版社 1958. 50p.

Shimin no tame ni　市民のために

'For the sake of the citizens' *The cannery boat, and other Japanese short stories.* N. Y. International Publishers, 1933; London, Martin Lawrence, 1933; N. Y. Greenwood Press, 1968. p.131–140
'替市民' 「日本短篇小説選」 香港 藝美圖書公司 1959. p.12–17
'替市民' 高汝鴻訳 「日本短篇小説集」 台北 台湾商務印書館 1969. p.139–147

KOBAYASHI Takiji

Tō seikatsusha　党生活者

'Жизнь для партия' Перевод И. Львовой. *Таки-дзи Кобаяси, избранное*. Москва, Гослитиздат, 1957. p.362–454; *Японские повести* Москва, Молодая Гвардия, 1957. p.15–122

'Партияга жон фидо' Торжимаси У. Шамсиму-хамедов. *Япон повестлари*. Тошкент, Бадии Адабиет, 1960. p.15–116

Život pro ty druhé. Přel. Vlasta Hilská. Praha, Noso Vojsko, 1963. 106p.

'Живот за партията' Преведе от русс. Монел Наков. *Трябва да живея*. София, Народ Култура, 1964.

Criticism　評論

'新寫實主義與形式' 式鈞訳 「開拓」 第1巻3–4期 1931.

'新寫實主義的根本態度' 式鈞訳 「開拓」 第1巻6期 1931.

'战爭與文学' 卞立強訳 「世界文学」 1963年2月 p.12–16

Letters　書翰

'書簡六封' 申非 刘仲平訳 「譯文」 1958年2月 p.106–112

「小林多喜二选集」 金中等訳 北京 人民文学出版社 1958. 266p.

「小林多喜二选集」 適夷等訳 北京 人民文学出版社 1958–59. 3冊

「小林多喜二小説选」 適夷 李克異訳 北京 人民文学出版社 1965. 1冊

KOBORI Jinji　小堀甚二　1901–1959

Criticism　評論

'大衆文藝小品' 陶晶孫訳 「大衆文藝」 第1巻6期 1928.

KŌDA Aya　幸田 文　1904–

Kuroi suso　黒い裾

'The black skirt' Tr. by E.G. Seidensticker. *Japan Quarterly*, v.3, no.2, 1956. p.196–212

'The black kimono' Tr. by Edward Seidensticker. *Modern Japanese short stories*. Tokyo, Japan Publications Trading Co. 1960. p.118–140; Rev. ed. Tokyo, Japan Publications Trading Co. 1970. p.94–111

'검은옷자락' 金洙暎訳 「日本代表作家百人集 4」 서울 希望出版社 1966. p.312–328; 「日本短篇文学全集 5」 서울 新太陽社 1969. p.152–168

KŌDA Rohan　幸田露伴　1867–1947

Gojū no tō　五重塔

The pagoda. Tr. by Sakae Shioya. Tokyo, Okura Shoten, 1909. 167p.

'The gojiu no to, the pagoda' Tr. by Sakae Shioya. *The treasury of Japanese literature*, ed. by Tokichi Watanabe. Tokyo, Jippoh-kaku, 1933. p.310–323

'Gozyuu-no-too (chapter 31 and 32)' Tr. by F. J. Daniels. *Selections from Japanese literature*. London, Lund Humphries, 1959. p.176–183

'Die fünfstöckige Pagode' Übers. von Walter Donat. *Die fünfstöckige Pagode*. Düsseldorf, Diederichs, 1960. p.25–73; Regensburg, Pustet, n.d. p.25–73

Shutsuro　出盧

Leaving the hermitage. Tr. by Jiro Nagura. London, Allen and Unwin, 1925. 205p.

Yuki tataki　雪たたき

'Vigyázz a lábbelidre!' Ford. Sz. Holti Mária. *Modern Japán elbeszélők*. Budapest, Európa Könyvkiadó, 1967. p.214–233

Essay　エッセイ

'Matsushima' Tr. by Yaichiro Isobe. *Chugai Eigo*, November 1922.

'Before and after snow' Tr. by Kazutomo Takahashi. *Eigo Seinen*, v.62, no.3, 1929. p.86; v.62, no.4, 1929. p.132

'Lodging for a night' Tr. by Miyamori Asataro. *Representative tales of Japan*. Tokyo, Sanseido, 1914; Tokyo, Sanko Shoten, 1917. p.392–422

KODAMA Kagai　児玉花外　1874–1943

Poems　詩

'Кровь, слезы, сердце; Больная чайка; Прекрасное дитя' Перевод В. Н. Марковой. *Японская поэзия*. Москва, Гослитиздат, 1954. p.231–233; Изд. 2. 1956. p.340–342

KOGA Saburō　甲賀三郎　1893–1945

Kōya　荒野

La dezerto. Tr. Ŝ. Minami. Tokyo, Privata eldono, 1932. 42p.

KŌGŌ Nagako　皇后良子　1903–

Tanka　短歌

'12 tanka' Tr. by Shigeshi Nishimura. *Eigo Seinen*, v.54, no.11, 1926. p.347; v.62, no.11, 1930. p.402; v.64, no.11, 1931. p.366; v.66, no.11, 1932. p.381; v.72, no.12, 1935. p.409; v.74, no.12, 1936. p.413; v.76, no.11, 1937. p.389; v.84, no.11, 1941. p.337; v.88, no.11, 1943; v.95, no.4, 1949. p.107; v.99, no.8, 1953. p.368; v.101, no.3, 1955. p.113

'2 tanka' Tr. par Roger Bersihand. *La littérature japonaise*. Paris, Presses Universitaires de France, 1956. p.106, 107

'2 tanka' Tr. by Shigeshi Nishimura. *The Current of the world*, v.36, no.3, 1959. p.28; v.38, no.3, 1961. p.48

'2 tanka' Tr. from the French by Unity Evans. *Japanese literature*. N. Y. Walker, 1965. p.90, 91

KOGURE Katsuhiko 小暮勝彦 1930–

Poems 詩

'The face' *An anthology of modern Japanese poetry*, ed. and tr. by Ichiro Kono and Rikutaro Fukuda. Tokyo, Kenkyusha, 1957. p.63

KOIDE Shōgo 小出正吾 1897–

Noroma na rōrā のろまなローラー

Den langsomme vejtromle. København, Høst, 1967. 27p.

KOIDE Tsubara 小出 粲 1833–1908

Tanka 短歌

'Cherry flowers' Tr. by Asataro Miyamori. *Masterpieces of Japanese poetry, ancient and modern*. Tokyo, Maruzen, 1936; Tokyo, Taiseido, 1956; N. Y. Greenwood Press, 1971. p.605

'1 tanka' Übers. von Gerolf Coudenhove. *Japanische Jahreszeiten*. Zürich, Manesse Verlag, 1963. p.121

KOIKE Fumiko 小池富美子 1921–

Kosumosu no saku ie コスモスの咲く家

「大波斯菊盛开的人家」王廷齢訳 北京 新文艺 1958. 66p.

KOIZUMI Chikashi 古泉千樫 1886–1927

Tanka 短歌

'Quiet rain; A flock of herons' Tr. by Asataro Miyamori. *Masterpieces of Japanese poetry, ancient and modern*. Tokyo, Maruzen, 1936; Tokyo, Taiseido, 1956; N. Y. Greenwood Press, 1971. p.746–747

'1 tanka' Tr. by V. H. Viglielmo. *Japanese literature in the Meiji era*. Tokyo, Obunsha, 1955. p.412

'Verselets' Tr. by H. H. Honda. *The Reeds*, v.5, 1959. p.86

KOJIMA Masajirō 小島政二郎 1894–

Hata 旗

'旗' 徐白訳 「日本短篇譯集 1」 台北 晩蟬書店 1969. p.39–76

Meiji Tennō 明治天皇

「明治天皇」 李學熙訳 台北 水牛出版社 1970. 290p.

San bijin 三美人

'風月堂二世' 朴容淑訳 「日本代表作家百人集 2」 서울 希望出版社 1966. p.358–374；「日本短篇文学全集 3」 서울 新太陽社 1969. p.44–60

Essay エッセイ

'Once there was a moon' *This is Japan*, v.11, 1964. p.218–220

KOJIMA Nobuo 小島信夫 1915–

Amerikan sukūru アメリカン・スクール

'아메리칸 스쿨' 車凡錫訳 「芥川賞小説集」 서울 新丘文化社 1960. p.59–89；「깊은 江」 서울 三耕社 1971. p.59–89

'아메리칸·수쿨' 玄相杰訳 「日本新鋭作家受賞作品集 3」 서울 青雲社 1964. p.93–137；「戦後日本短篇文学全集 3」 서울 日光出版社 1965. p.93–137；「現代日本代表文学全集 3」 서울 平和出版社 1973. p.93–135

'美國學校' 劉慕沙訳 「芥川賞作品選集 1」 台北 晩蟬書店 1969. p.77–120；「芥川賞作品選集 2」 台北 大地出版社 1974. p.77–121

'The American school' Tr. by Bernard Susser. *Japan Interpreter*, v.11, no.4, 1977. p.467–492

'The American school' Tr. by William F. Sibley. *Contemporary Japanese literature*, ed. by Howard Hibbett. N. Y. Knopf, 1977. p.120–144

Kami no ayamachi 神のあやまち

'神의 過誤' 玄相杰訳 「日本新鋭作家受賞作品集 3」 서울 青雲社 1964. p.36–91；「戦後日本短篇文学全集 3」 서울 1965. p.36–91；「現代日本代表文学全集 3」 서울 平和出版社 1973. p.36–91

Kisha no naka 汽車の中

'汽車속' 玄相杰訳 「日本新鋭作家受賞作品集 3」 서울 青雲社 1964. p.3–34；「戦後日本短篇文学全集 3」 서울 日光出版社 1965. p.3–34；「現代日本代表文学全集 3」 서울 平和出版社 1973. p.3–35

Shōjū 小銃

'Винтовка' Перевод С. Гутермана. *Японская новелла*. Москва, Изд. Иност. Лит. 1961. p.103–120

'Винтовка' Аударган Ж. Мухамеджанов. *Жапон енгимелери*. Алма-Ата, Жазушы, 1965. p.46–58

'小銃' 具洋淑訳 「日本研究」 第19巻12号 1974. p.65–73

Sorin eno michi 疎林への道

'疎林으로가는길' 金龍済訳 「日本代表作家百人集 4」 서울 希望出版社 1966. p.390–400；「日本短篇文學全集 5」 서울 新太陽社 1969. p.230–240

KOJIMA Tsutomu 小島 勗 1900–1933

Chihei ni arawareru mono 地平に現れるもの

「平地風波」 張資平 鄭佐蒼訳 上海 楽羣書局 193?. 1冊

KOMAI Gonnosuke 駒井権之助

Poems and haiku 詩・俳句

'Love's librarian; A spring morning; Butterfly; The temple bell; Cherry-blossoms; To the lotus-bloom; Azalea; Fuji-yama' Tr. by

KOMAI Gonnosuke

William N. Porter. *Lotus and chrysanthemum.*
N. Y. Liveright, 1928. p.156–158
'4 poems and 1 haiku' *Japanese love poems,* ed. by
Jean Bennett. Garden City, Doubleday, 1976.
p.20, 50, 76, 92
Fuji-yama, and other poems. London, Eastern Press,
n.d. 215p.

KOMATSU Kiyoshi　小松　清　1900–1962

Criticism　評論

'論歌劇' 楚橋訳 「北平晨報劇刊」 1931年3月
'歌劇的歴史' 楚橋訳 「北平晨報劇刊」 1931年4月
'十九世紀的歌劇' 楚橋訳 「北平晨報劇刊」 1931年5月
'歌劇的發展' 楚橋訳 「北平晨報劇刊」 1931年6月
'East and West in Japanese literature' *Oriental
Economist,* March 1956. p.134–135

KOMATSU Sakyō　小松左京　1931–

Ana　穴

'Dziura' Przeł. Blanka Yonekawa. *Przekrój,* no.
1515, 1974. p.15–17

Asu dorobō　明日泥棒

Похитители завтрашнего дня. Перевод З.
Рахима. Москва, Мир, 1970. 317p.
A holnap elrablói. Oroszbol ford. Török Piroska.
Budapest, Kossuth, 1971. 284p.
Rytdienos grobikai. Tr. from the Russian Arvydas
Ališauskas. Vilnius, Vaga, 1973. 199p.

Chi niwa heiwa o　地には平和を

'Мир-земле' Перевод З. Рахима. *Времена Хокусая.* Москва, Мир, 1967. p.236–286
'Zemei-taika' *Hokusajaus laikai.* Vilnius, Vaizdo,
1969. p.180–220

Gosenzosama banzai　御先祖様万歳

'Да здравствуют предки' Перевод З. Рахима.
Продается Япония. Москва, Мир, 1969.
p.131–183

Hokusai no sekai　ホクサイの世界

'Времена Хокусая' Перевод З. Рахима. *Времена
Хокусая.* Москва, Мир, 1967. p.13–18
'Hokusajaus laikai' *Hokusajaus laikai.* Vilnius,
Vaizdo, 1969. p.5–9

Ikamono gui　いかもの食い

'Sami swói . . .' Przeł. Zdzisław Rzeszelewski.
Szpilki, no.1, 1975. p.11–12

Kamagasaki 2013 nen　釜が崎 2013年

'Камагасаки 2013 года' Перевод З. Рахима.
Продается Япония. Москва, Мир, 1969.
p.219–244

Kami ka kami ka　紙か髪か

'Бумага или волосы?' Перевод З. Рахима. *Времена Хокусая.* Москва, Мир, 1967. p.19–47

'Popierius ar plankai?' *Hokusajaus laikai.* Vilnius,
Vaizdo, 1969. p.10–31

Mechakucha na kigeki　めちゃくちゃな喜劇

'Хаотическая комедия' Перевод З. Рахима. *Времена Хокусая.* Москва, Мир, 1967. p.184–
215
'Chaotiska komedija' *Hokusajaus laikai.* Vilnius,
Vaizdo, 1969. p.139–163

Nihon urimasu　日本売ります

'Продается Япония' Перевод З. Рахима. *Продается Япония.* Москва, Мир, 1969. p.18–38
'Japan till salu' Övers. av Saburo Oishi och Karin
Johansson. *Japan till salu.* Tumba, Hedenlans,
1972.

Nihon chinbotsu　日本沈没

「日本沈没」 余阿勲 左秀霊訳 台北 林白出版社 1973.
350p.
「日本沈没」 林正翼訳 서울 旺文社 1973. 399p.
「日本沈没」 高平國訳 서울 汎友社 1973. 425p.
Japan sinks. Tr. by Michael Gallagher. N. Y.
Harper and Row, 1976. 184p.
La submersion du Japon. Paris, Albin Michel,
1977. 256p.

Orochi　おろち

'Orochi (Il drago)' Tr. di Maria Teresa Orsi.
Il Giappone, anno 15, 1975. p.77–100

Soshite daremo shinaku natta　そして誰もしなくなった

'Теперь, как сказать, свой…' Перевод З. Рахима. *Продается Япония.* Москва, Мир,
1969. p.211–218

Yōshi daisakusen　養子大作戦

'Провестка о мобилизация' Перевод З. Рахима.
Продается Япония. Москва, Мир, 1969.
p.39–71

Essay　エッセイ

'It's there but we can't use it' Tr. by Robert
Wargo. *Japan Interpreter,* v.8, no.4, 1974.
p.484–487

'Разбоплощенная' Перевод З. Рахима. *Продае-
тся Япония.* Москва, Мир, 1969. p.80–99
'Новый товарь' Перевод З. Рахима. *Продается
Япония.* Москва, Мир, 1969. p.184–205
'Zagłada jaszczurów' Przeł. Andrzej Stoff. *Pro-
blemy,* no.5, 1972. p.53–56

KOMINE Taiu　小峰大羽　1873–

Haiku　俳句

'Telephone' Tr. by Asataro Miyamori. *Anthology
of haiku, ancient and modern.* Tokyo, Maruzen,
1932. p.835
'The New Year's compliments' Tr. by Asataro
Miyamori. *Haiku poems, ancient and modern.*
Tokyo, Maruzen, 1940. p.333

KOMIYAMA Akitoshi 小宮山明敏 1902–1931

Criticism 評論

'新興文學的發生過程' 海若訳 「現代文學」創刊号 1933.
'普羅列塔利亜藝術發達史概論' 楊沖牒訳 「新地月刊」創刊号

KOMURO Kutsuzan 小室屈山 1858–1908

Jiyū no uta 自由の歌

'Из «Песни свободы»' Перевод В. Н. Марковой. *Японская поэзия*. Москва, Гослитиздат, 1954. p.191–193
'Ode to liberty (part)' Tr. by G. Sansom. *Modern Japanese poetry*, by Donald Keene. Ann Arbor, Center for Japanese Studies, Univ. of Michigan, 1964. p.15

KON Hidemi 今 日出海 1903–

Chi no rozario 血のロザリオ

'피묻은黙珠' 申東漢訳 「日本代表作家百人集 3」 서울 希望出版社 1966. p.450–473; 「日本短篇文学全集 4」 서울 新太陽社 1969. p.210–233

Kono jūnen この十年

'These ten years' Tr. by Makoto Momoi and Jay Gluck. *Orient Digest*, Sept.-Oct. 1955. p.101–102, 117–127; *Ukiyo*, ed. by J. Gluck. N. Y. Vanguard Press, 1963. p.19–42; London, Universal Library, 1964. p.19–42

Tennō no bōshi 天皇の帽子

'A császár kalapja' Ford. Sz. Holti Mária. *Modern Japán elbeszékők*. Budapest, Európa Könyvkiadó, 1967. p.422–435

KON Tōkō 今 東光 1898–1977

Essay エッセイ

'신판 "바걸"의노래' 金賢珠訳 「바이바이바디」 서울 三韓出版社 1966. p.130–140

KONAGAYA Kiyomi 小長谷清実 1936–

Poems 詩

'A search for a shirt; Until the ache goes' Tr. by Fukuda Rikutaro. *Japanese Literature Today*, no.3, March, 1978. p.11–12

KONDŌ Azuma 近藤 東 1904–

Poems 詩

'Poem; The country afternoon' Tr. by S. Sato and C. Urdang. *Poetry*, May, 1956. p.82–84
'A woman of the Mediterranean' *United Asia*, v.8, no.4, 1956. p.267

'A girl of the port; The country; The fire; A cab; A Mediterranean girl; A low hurdle; A girl; An escape; Girl and grapes; At a sea-port town; A white dog; The civilized nation' *An anthology of modern Japanese poetry*, ed. and tr. by Ichiro Kono and Rikutaro Fukuda. Tokyo, Kenkyusha, 1957. p.64–71
'Cette nation civilisée' *La poésie japonaise*, par Karl Petit. Paris, Seghers, 1959. p.237
'Az a bizonyos müvelt nemzet' Ford. Illyés Gyula. *Nagyvilág*, no.10, 1960.
'Liman kizi; O medenî millet' Tercüme etmek L. Sami Akalin. *Japon şiiri*. İstanbul, Varlik Yayinevi, 1962. p.281–282
'Mediterranean woman; Fire' Tr. by Geoffrey Bownas and Anthony Thwaite. *The Penguin book of Japanese verse*. Harmondsworth, Penguin Books, 1964. p.217
'拂暁；晝；悪夢' 徐和隣訳 「現代詩解説」 台北 葡萄園詩刊社 1970. p.50–53
'Această naţie civilizată; Femeia mării Mediterane' Traducerea Virgil Teodorescu. *Din lirica japoneză*. Bucureşti, Editura Univers, n.d. p.202–203
'Den siviliserte nasjonen' Til norsk ved Paal Brekke' *Moderne japansk lyrikk*. Oslo, Norske Bokklubben, n.d. p.61

KONDŌ Keitarō 近藤啓太郎 1920–

Amabune 海人舟

'海人舟' 桂鎔黙訳 「芥川賞小説集」 서울 新丘文化社 1960. p.187–215; 「깊은江」 서울 三耕社 1971. p.187–215
'海人舟' 劉慕沙訳 「芥川奨作品選集 1」 台北 晩蟬書店 1969. p.177–213; 「芥川賞作品選集 2」 台北 大地出版社 1974. p.179–215

KONDŌ Kōjin 近藤耕人 1933–

Criticism 評論

'사뮤엘·베케트의말' 「現代詩学」 第2巻3号 1970

KONDŌ Yoshimi 近藤芳美 1913–

Tanka 短歌

'Ёсими Кондо, избранное' Перевод Вадима Сикорского. *Из современной японской поэзии*. Москва, Прогресс, 1971. p.171–220

KONISHI Gaku 小西 学

Essay エッセイ

'Sennorama' Przeł. Tyburcjusz Tyblewski. *Problemy*, no.8, 1974. p.53–56

KONISHI Jin'ichi 小西甚一 1915–

Essay エッセイ

'Furyu: an ideal of Japanese esthetic life' *The*

KONISHI Jin'ichi

Japanese image, ed. by M. Schneps and A. D. Coox. Tokyo, Orient West, 1965. p.271–278

KŌNO Ichirō 河野一郎 1930–

Poems 詩

'Andante; Portrait of a lady; Love song' *An anthology of modern Japanese poetry*, ed. and tr. by Ichiro Kono and Rikutaro Fukuda. Tokyo, Kenkyusha, 1957. p.71–73
'Andante; Bir kadinin portresi' Tercüme etmek L. Sami Akalin. *Japon şiiri*. İstanbul, Varlik Yayinevi, 1962. p.300
'Retrato de una mujer' Tr. por Kikuya Ionesawa. *Poesia japonesa contemporanea*. Bogotá, Colombia Editoriales de Librería, 1965.

KŌNO Makoto 河野 実 1941–

Ai to shi o mitsumete 愛と死を見つめて

「愛與死」 江柏峰訳 彰化 鴻文出版社 1966. 349p.; 1974. 347p.
Michiko, cronica de amor y muerte, por Makoto Kono y Michiko Oshima. Tr. por José Miguel Vara. Madrid, Sociedad de Educación Atenas, 1971. 246p.
「愛與死的日記」 文珪訳 彰化 鴻文出版社 1976. 1冊

KŌNO Taeko 河野多恵子 1926–

Hone no niku 骨の肉

'Bone meat' Tr. by Lucy Lower. *Contemporary Japanese literature*, ed. by Howard Hibbett. N. Y. Knopf, 1977. p.42–52

Kani 蟹

'蟹' 劉慕沙訳 「芥川賞作品選集 1」 台北 大地出版社 1972. p.67–107
'게' 徐槿培訳 「新思想」 第2巻8号 p.406–427

KŌRA Rumiko 高良留美子 1932–

Poems 詩

'In this country' Tr. by Thomas Fitzsimmons and Rikutaro Fukuda. *Orient West*, v.9, no.5, 1964. p.61
'Первый снег; Луна; В нашей стране; Неведомый' Перевод А. Долина. *Иностранная Литература*, Февраль, 1973. p.89–92
'The tree; Awakening; Autumn; She; The moon; The friend' Tr. by Rumiko Kora. *The poetry of postwar Japan*. Iowa City, Univ. of Iowa Press, 1975. p.199–203
'Woman' *The burning heart*, tr. and ed. by Kenneth Rexroth and Ikuko Atsumi. N.Y. Seabury Press, 1977. p.123

KŌRI Torahiko 郡 虎彦 1890–1924

Kanawa 鉄輪

The incantation. London, Gowans and Gray, 1918. 22p.

Yoshitomo ki 義朝記

The toils of Yoshitomo. London, Selwyn and Blount, 1922. 87p.
Yoshitomo. Paris, Stock, 1923. 77p.
Yoshitomo. Tr. di Mario Maria Martini. Milano, Alpes, 1929. 1v.
'Yoshitomo' Tr. di Leo Magnino. *Teatro giapponese*. Milano, Nuòva Accademia, 1956. p.211–259

KOSUGI Tengai 小杉天外 1865–1952

Kaisōki 回想記

'My sister' Tr. by Asataro Miyamori. *Representative tales of Japan*. Tokyo, Sanko Shoten, 1917. p.163–191

KŌTAISHI Akihito 皇太子明仁 1933–

Tanka 短歌

'2 tanka' Tr. by Shigeshi Nishimuta. *Eigo Seinen*, v.99, no.8, 1953. p.368; v.101, no.3, 1955. p.113
'1 tanka' Tr. par Roger Bersihand. *La littérature japonaise*. Paris, Presses Universitaires de France, 1956. p.107
'2 tanka' Tr. by Shigeshi Nishimura. *The Current of the World*, v.36, no.3, 1959. p.28; v.38, no.3, 1961. p.48
'1 tanka' Tr. from the French by Unity Evans. *Japanese literature*. N. Y. Walker, 1965. p.91

KOTANI Tsuyoshi 小谷 剛 1924–

Fudan bonō 不断煩悩

'放心不下' 徐白訳 「日本短篇譯集 1」 台北 晩蟬書店 1969. p.191–216

KŌTOKU Shūsui 幸徳秋水 1871–1911

Tanka 短歌

'Накануне казни' Перевод В. Марковой. *Японская поэзия*. Изд. 2. Москва, Худож. Лит. 1956. p.405

KOYAMA Itoko 小山いと子 1901–

Kōgō sama 皇后さま

Nagako, empress of Japan. Tr. by Atsuo Tsuruoka. N. Y. John Day, 1958. 189p.

Teiden 停電

'Black out' Tr. by Grace Suzuki. *Ukiyo*. Tokyo, Phoenix Books, 1954. p.58–73; *Ukiyo*, ed. by J. Gluck. N. Y. Vanguard Press, 1963. p.110–119; London, Universal Library, 1964. p.110–119

KOYAMA Katsukiyo 小山勝清 1896–1965

Sorekara no Musashi それからの武蔵

'嚴流島後的宮本武蔵' 金溟若訳 「中華日報」 1976; 「香港時報」 1976.
「嚴流島後的宮本武蔵」 金溟若訳 台北 四季出版公司 1977. 2冊

KŌYAMA Yoshiko 香山美子 1928–

Ariko no ki あり子の記

Příběh dívky Ariko. Přel. Ivan Krouský. Brno, Blok, 1974. 140p.

KOZAKAI Fuboku 小酒井不木 1890–1929

'鬍子的謎' 黄宏壽訳 「橄欖月刊」 第17期 192?.
'懐中的瀕死者' 黄宏壽訳 「橄欖月刊」 第17期 192?.

KUBO Inokichi 久保猪之吉 1874–1939

Tanka 短歌

'Grapes; Ayu' Tr. by Asataro Miyamori. *Masterpieces of Japanese poetry, ancient and modern*. Tokyo, Maruzen, 1936; Tokyo, Taiseido, 1956; N. Y. Greenwood Press, 1971. p.649–650

KUBOKAWA Tsurujirō 窪川鶴次郎 1903–1974

Essay エッセイ

'悼念徳永直' 梅韜訳 「譯文」 1958年4月 p.6–7

KUBOTA Kuhonta 久保田九品太 1881–1926

Haiku 俳句

'2 haiku' Tr. by Asataro Miyamori. *Anthology of haiku, ancient and modern*. Tokyo, Maruzen, 1932. p.697–698
'A toy-kite' Tr. by Asataro Miyamori. *Haiku poems, ancient and modern*. Tokyo, Maruzen, 1940. p.324
'1 haiku' Tr. by R. H. Blyth. *Haiku v.2*. Tokyo,

Hokuseido, 1952. p.153
'1 haiku' Tr. by Peter Beilenson and Harry Behn. *Haiku harvest*. Mount Vernon, Peter Pauper Press, 1962. p.49
'1 haiku' Übers. von Gerolf Coudenhove. *Japanische Jahreszeiten*. Zürich, Manesse Verlag, 1963. p.56

KUBOTA Mantarō 久保田万太郎 1899–1963

Mijikayo 短夜

'短夜' 章克標訳 「日本戲曲集」 台北 中華書局 1934. p.207–245

Shoka 初夏

'L'été qui commence' Tr. par Serge Elisséev. *Japon et Extrême-Orient*, no.6, 1924. p.471–484; *Neuf nouvelles japonaises*. Paris, G. van Œst, 1934. p.89–102

KUBOTA Sei 窪田 精 1921–

Tōi Reite no umi 遠いレイテの海

'Далекое море Лейте' Перевод В. Логуновой. *Японская новелла 1960–1970*. Москва, Прогресс, 1972. p.142–161

Essay エッセイ

'我从河内来' 思一訳 「人民文学」 1965年3月 p.2–6

KUBOTA Shōji 窪田正次

Essay エッセイ

'The greengrocer' Tr. by Takeji Wakameda. *Tourist*, 1943.

KUBOTA Utsuho 窪田空穂 1877–1967

Tanka 短歌

'Tanka' Tr. by Shigeshi Nishimura. *The Current of the World*, v.13, 1936.
'The fountain; The waterfall; When my mother passed away; An entrance examination; A white heron; My little son; The dead child; Noonday sleep' Tr. by Asataro Miyamori. *Masterpieces of Japanese poetry, ancient and modern*. Tokyo, Maruzen, 1936; Tokyo, Taiseido, 1956; N. Y. Greenwood Press, 1971. p.669–674
'1 tanka' Tr. by Chizu Kurokawa. *Aoba no fue*. Honolulu, Univ. of Hawaii, 1937. n.p.
'3 tanka' Tr. by V. H. Viglielmo. *Japanese literature in the Meiji era*. Tokyo, Obunsha, 1955. p.403–404
'Die Quelle' Übers. von Günther Debon. *Im Schnee die Fähre*. München, Piper, 1960. p.26
'1 tanka' Übers. von Gerolf Coudenhove. *Japanishce Jahreszeiten*. Zürich, Manesse Verlag, 1963. p.175

KUJŌ Takeko 九条武子 1887–1928

Tanka 短歌

'Songs of the Baroness Kujo' Tr. by Glenn Hughes and Yozan T. Iwasaki. *New Orient*, v.3, no.1, 1925. p.18–24

'4 tanka' Tr. by Takeshi Tezuka. *Eigo Seinen*, v.64, no.11, 1931. p.366; v.65, no.1, 1931. p.25

'Takeko Kujo' Tr. by Glenn Hughes and Yozan Iwasaki. *Three women poets of modern Japan*. Seattle, Univ. of Washington Book Store, 1932. p.35–43

'Parting; A visitor; My mind; Heaven and earth; My footsteps; The great earthquake and fire of 1923; Spring has come again; Joking' Tr. by Asataro Miyamori. *Masterpieces of Japanese poetry, ancient and modern*. Tokyo, Maruzen, 1936; Tokyo, Taiseido, 1956; N. Y. Greenwood Press, 1971. p.750–754

'Abschied' Übers. von Günther Debon. *Im Schnee die Fähre*. München, Piper, 1960. p.46

'2 tanka' Übers. von Gerolf Coudenhove. *Japanische Jahreszeiten*. Zürich, Manesse Verlag, 1963. p.42, 282

'1 tanka' *The burning heart*, tr. and ed. by Kenneth Rexroth and Ikuko Atsumi. N.Y. Seabury Press, 1977. p.69

KUMAGAI Takeo 熊谷武雄 1883–1936

Tanka 短歌

'An atmospheric depression; Whalers' Tr. by Asataro Miyamori. *Masterpieces of Japanese poetry, ancient and modern*. Tokyo, Maruzen, 1936; Tokyo, Taiseido, 1956; N. Y. Greenwood Press, 1971. p.646–647

KUME Masao 久米正雄 1891–1952

Abukuma shinjū 阿武隈心中

'阿武隈心中' 章克標訳 「日本戲曲集」 台北 中華書局 1934. p.153–205

Gakusei jidai 学生時代

'学生時代' 李元秀訳 「日本文学選集 5」 서울 知文閣 1966. p.370–473; 「日本文学選集 5」 서울 韓国 読書文化院 1973. p.369–475

'学生時代' 朴仁根訳 「雪国外」 서울 話題社 1968. p.213–316

Tejinashi 手品師

'魔術師' 大立書店編集部訳 「世界短篇小説精華」 台北 大立書店 1971. p.102–111

Tora 虎

'The tiger' Tr. by Robert H. Brower. *Modern Japanese literature*, ed. by D. Keene. N. Y. Grove Press, 1956; Tokyo, Tuttle, 1957. p.288–299

'La tigre' Tr. di Franco Corsi. *Il Giappone*, anno 5, 1965. p.107–113

KUNIKIDA Doppo 国木田独歩 1871–1908

Bajō no tomo 馬上の友

'A friend on horseback' Tr. by Taro Ito. *Osaka Mainichi*, Feb. 7–12, 1928.

Dai sansha 第三者

'Love as cruel as the grave' Tr. by Asataro Miyamori. *Representative tales of Japan*. Tokyo, Sanko Shoten, 1917. p.249–302

'第三者' 夏丏尊訳 「國木田獨歩集」 上海 開明書店 1927.

Fūfu 夫婦

'夫婦' 夏丏尊訳 「東方雜誌」 第19巻18期 1922. p.112–126; 第19巻19期 1922. p.100–108; 「近代日本小説集」 上海 商務印書館 1923; 「國木田獨歩集」 上海 開明書店 1927.

Gen oji 源叔父

'Uncle Gen' Tr. by Akira Ota. *New World*, August 1946.

'Old Gen' Tr. by Sam Houston Brock. *Modern Japanese literature*, ed. by D. Keene. N. Y. Grove Press, 1956; Tokyo, Tuttle, 1957. p.111–121

'Il vecchio Gen' Tr. di Atsuko Ricca Suga. *Narratori giapponesi moderni*. Milano, Bompiani, 1965. p.131–150; *Antologia della letteratura coreana e giapponese*. Milano, Fratelli Fabbri, 1969. p.231–234

'Old Gen' Tr. by Jay Rubin. *Monumenta Nipponica*, v.27, no.3, 1972. p.280–293

Дядя Генн. Перевод Л. Мчедлисвили. Тбилиси, Накадули, 1973. 27р.

Gōgai 号外

'Экстренный выпуск' Перевод Т. Топеха. *Куникида Доппо, избранные рассказы*. Москва, Гослитиздат, 1958. p.144–150

Gyūniku to jagaimo 牛肉と馬鈴薯

'Beef and potatoes' Tr. by Arthur Lloyd. *Model translations and dialogues*. Tokyo, Eigo Kenkyusha, 1913. p.62–118

'牛肉與馬鈴薯' 夏丏尊訳 「東方雜誌」 第22巻7期 1925. p.116–130; 「國木田獨歩集」 上海 開明書店 1927.

'Meat and potatoes' Tr. by Leon Zolbrod. *The heart is alone*, ed. by Richard McKinnon. Tokyo, Hokuseido, 1957. p.49–73; *Orient West*, v.9, no.3, 1964. p.28–38; *The Japanese image v.2*, ed. by M. Schneps and A. D. Coox. Tokyo, Orient West, 1966. p.175–189

Haru no tori 春の鳥

'Haru no tori' Tr. by Takamasa Sasaki. *Eigo no kenkyu to kyoju*. Tokyo, 1940.

'春鳥' 魏都麗訳 「中日文化月刊」 第2巻1期 1942. p.111–116

'Spring birds' Tr. by Tsutomu Fukuda. *Pacific Spectator*, v.8, no.3, 1954. p.249–255; *Sansho dayu, and other stories*. Tokyo, Hokuseido, 1970. p.67–82

'Pássaros na primavera' Tr. de Fuyou Koyama. *Maravilhas do conto japonês*. São Paulo, Editôra Cultrix, 1962. p.61–70

'Birdoj de la printempo' Tr. Yosio Oosima.

El Japan literaturo. Tokyo, Japana Esperanto Instituto, 1965. p.107–116

'The spring bird' Tr. by Atsumu Kanayama. *The Reeds*, no.10, 1965. p.65–80

'Birds of spring' Tr. by David G. Chibbett. *Monumenta Nipponica*, v.26, no.1–2, 1971. p.195–203

'Vihoknaivasun' Tr. Piyachit Tadang. *Rueng sun yeepun 1*. Bangkok, Uksornsasna, 1977. p.1–20

Hibon naru bonjin 非凡なる凡人

'Необыкновенный обыкновенный человек' Перевод Т. Топеха. *Куникида Доппо, избранные рассказы*. Москва, Гослитиздат, 1958. p.133–143

Hirō 疲労

'疲労' 夏丏尊訳 「國木田獨歩集」 上海 開明書店 1927.

Jonan 女難

'Petticoat dangers' Tr. by Arthur Lloyd. *Model translations and dialogues*. Tokyo, Eigo Kenkyusha, 1913. p.119–194

'女難' 夏丏尊訳 「小説月報」 第12巻12号 1921. p.7–25; 「日本小説集」 上海 商務印書館 1923; 「國木田獨歩集」 上海 開明書店 1927.

'女難' 新興書局編集部訳 「日本短篇小説選」 台北 新興書局 1958. p.49–73; 台南 鳴宇出版社 1972. p.49–73

'女難' 「日本作家十二人集」 香港 新學書店 1959. p.19–47

Junsa 巡査

'巡査' 仲密訳 「北京晨報」 1921年10月

'巡査' 周作人訳 「日本現代小説集 1」 上海 商務印書館 1930.

'Der Schutzmann' Übers. von Hiroshi Terano. *Nippon*, Jahrgang 3, 1937. p.216–222

'巡査' 「少年的悲哀」 郁達夫等訳 台北 啓明書局 1956. p.8–13

Kikyorai 帰去来

'Heimwärts' Übers. von Alexander Spann. *Das Junge Japan*, Band 1, 1925. p.279–288, 329–338, 381–388

'Скиталец' Перевод Т. Топеха. *Куникида Доппо, избранные рассказы*. Москва, Гослитиздат, 1958. p.39–71

Kōgai 郊外

'The suburbs' Tr. by Jay Rubin. *Monumenta Nipponica*, v.27, no.3, 1972. p.305–317

Kyūshi 窮死

'Driven to death' Tr. by Iwao Matsubara. *Tokyo Nichinichi*, Oct. 24, 1924.

'Der Tod eines armen Mannes' Übers. von S. Yuasa. *Nippon*, Jahrgang 3, 1937. p.91–100

'窮死' 錢端義訳 「藝文雑誌」 第1巻3期 1943. p.48–51

'Жалкая смерть' Перевод Т. Топеха. *Куникида Доппо, избранные рассказы*. Москва, Гослитиздат, 1958. p.151–158

'Tod aus Verzweiflung' Deutsch von Jürgen Berndt. *Träume aus zehn Nächten*. Berlin, Aufbau Verlag, 1975. p.40–50

'窮死' 「文鳥・夢十夜」 英紹唐編 n.d. p.81–106

Musashino 武蔵野

'La panura di Musashi' Tr. di Harukichi Shimoi. *Sakura*, no.4, 1920. p.57–61

'Musashino' Tr. by Kyohei Yamamoto. *Living English*, 1932.

'Равнина Мусаси' Перевод Т. Топеха. *Куникида Доппо, избранные рассказы*. Москва, Гослитиздат, 1958. p.19–38

Musashino nikki 武蔵野日記

'A diary of Musashino' Tr. by Kazutomo Takahashi. *Eigo Seinen*, v.62, no.9, 1930. p.319; v.62, no.10, 1930. p.357

Naki warai 泣き笑い

'Le rire dans les larmes' Tr. par M. Yoshitomi. *Anthologie de la littérature japonaise contemporaine*. Grenoble, Xavier Drevet, 1924. p.117–125

'Sunbeams through the mist' Tr. by Iwao Matsubara. *Eigo Seinen*, v.58, no.7, 1928. p.242; v.58, no.8, 1928. p.274–275; v.58, no.9, 1928. p.312–313

Nami no oto 波の音

'La voce delle onde' Tr. di Harukichi Shimoi. *Sakura*, no.4, 1920.

Ni rōjin 二老人

'Два старика' Перевод Т. Топеха. *Куникида Доппо, избранные рассказы*. Москва, Гослитиздат, 1958. p.180–187

Okamoto no shuki 岡本の手記

'Taccuino di Okamoto' Tr. di Harukichi Shimoi. *Sakura*, no.4, 1920.

Oyako 親子

'Vater und Tochter' Übers. von Hiroshi Terano. *Das Junge Japan*, Band 2, no.5, 1915. p.1–9

'Vater und Tochter' Übers. von Alexander Spann. *Japan: Tradition und Gegenwart*. Stuttgart, Deutsche Volksbücher, 1942. p.123–134

Sabaku no ame 沙漠の雨

'沙漠之雨' 黎烈文訳 「文學週報」 第5巻10期 1928. p.365–367

Shi 死

'Death' Tr. by Thomas E. Swann. *Monumenta Nipponica*, v.24, no.3, 1969. p.315–325

Shōjiki mono 正直者

'Der Biedermann' Übers. von Heinz Brasch. *Yamato*, Jahrgang 3, 1931. p.6–18

'Der Biedermann' *Geschichten und Erzählungen aus Japan*, hrg. von B. Matsuoka. Leipzig, Fikentscher Verlag, 1950. p.179–196

'Верность' Перевод Т. Топеха. *Куникида Доппо, избранные рассказы*. Москва, Гослитиздат, 1958. p.159–164

'An honest man' Tr. by Jay Rubin. *Monumenta Nipponica*, v.27, no.3, 1972. p.318–327

Shōnen no hiai 少年の悲哀

'少年的悲哀' 周作人訳 「新青年」 第8巻5期 1921.

p.705–712; 「現代日本小説集」 上海 商務印書館 1923;「日本現代小説集 1」上海 商務印書館 1930.
'La tristesse d'un enfant' Tr. par M. Yoshitomi. *Anthologie de la littérature japonaise contemporaine*. Grenoble, Xavier Drevet, 1924. p.186–202
'Das Leid eines Knaben' Übers. von Masatora Sakurai. *Nippon*, Jahrgang 3, 1937. p.41–47
'少年の悲哀' 「少年的悲哀」 郁達夫等訳 台北 啓明書局 1956. p.1–7
'Печали детства' Перевод Т. Топеха. *Куникида Доппо, избранные рассказы*. Москва, Гослитиздат, 1958. p.72–79
'少年의슬픔' 金洙暎訳 「日本代表作家百人集 1」 서울 希望出版社 1966. p.140–146; 「日本短篇文学全集 1」 서울 新太陽社 1969. p.140–146
'少年的悲哀' 林浦生訳 「世界短篇小説精華」 三重市 大立書店 1971. p.184–191
'少年的悲哀' 「世界著名作家小説選」 香港 上海書局 1977. p.383–391

Shuchū nikki 酒中日記

'Дневник пьяницы' Перевод Т. Топеха. *Куникида Доппо, избранные рассказы*. Москва, Гослитиздат, 1958. p.80–111

Sorachigawa no kishibe 空知川の岸辺

'Sul fiume Sorachi' Tr. di Harukichi Shimoi. *Sakura*, no.4, 1920.

Take no kido 竹の木戸

'Бамбуковая калитка' Перевод Т. Топеха. *Восточный альманах 1*. Москва, Худож. Лит. 1957. p.351–364; *Куникида Доппо, избранные рассказы*. Москва, Гослитиздат, 1958. p.165–179
'The bamboo gate' Tr. by John Bester. *Japan P.E.N. News*, no.13, Oct. 1964. p.1–9
'The bamboo gate' Tr. by Jay Rubin. *Monumenta Nipponica*, v.27, 1972. p.325–341

Takibi たき火

'The bonfire' Tr. by Thomas E. Swann. *Asian Studies*, v.6, April 1968. p.102–107
'The bonfire' Tr. by Jay Rubin. *Monumenta Nipponica*, v.25, no.1–2, 1970. p.197–202

Teisō 貞操

'La chasteté' Tr. par M. Yoshitomi. *Anthologie de la littérature japonaise contemporaine*. Grenoble, Xavier Drevet, 1924. p.138–140

Tomioka sensei 富岡先生

'Tomioka Sensei' Tr. by Arthur Lloyd. *Model translations and dialogues*. Tokyo, Eigo Kenkyusha, 1913. p.1–61

Unmei ronja 運命論者

'The fatalist' Tr. by Tsutomu Fukuda. *Eigo Kenkyu*, v.42, no.10, no.12, 1953; v.43, no.2, no.3, 1954.
'Фаталист' Перевод Т. Топеха. *Куникида Доппо, избранные рассказы*. Москва, Гослитиздат, 1958. p.112–132
'運命論者' 郭夏信訳 「世界文学全集 94」 서울 乙酉文化社 1962. p.109–131; 「日本短篇文学選」 서울 乙酉文化社 1976. p.27–68

Wasure enu hitobito 忘れえぬ人々

'Men I shall never forget' Tr. by Arthur Lloyd. *Japan Magazine*, v.1, 1910. p.50–53, 108–111, 217–220
'Unforgettable people' Tr. by Jay Rubin. *Monumenta Nipponica*, v.27, no.3, 1972. p.294–304

Yugawara yori 湯ケ原より

'Letter from Yugawara' Tr. by Arthur Lloyd. *Model translations and dialogues*. Tokyo, Eigo Kenkyusha, 1913. p.195–215
'湯原通信' 美子訳 「小説月報」 第13巻2号 1922. p.37–42;「日本小説集」 上海 商務印書館 193?.

Poems 詩

'In the woodland freedom exists' Tr. by Shigeshi Nishimura. *The Current of the World*, v.30, no.1, 1953. p.37
'Freedom in the mountains; Entering into the woods' Tr. by James R. Morita. *Journal of the Association of Teachers of Japanese*, v.10, no.2 & 3, 1975. p.198–199

'Opere' Napoli, 1920. 1v.

KUNO Keiji 久能啓二 1929–

'殺人信箱' 文良出版社訳 「推理小説 日本偵探小説」 台南 文良出版社 1969. p.97–135

KURAHARA Korehito 蔵原惟人 1902–

Criticism 評論

'訪革命後的托爾斯泰故郷記' 魯迅訳 「奔流月刊」 第1巻7期 1928;「魯迅譯文集 10」 北京 人民文学出版社 1958. p.517–531
'普羅列塔利亜藝術的内容與形式' 林伯脩訳 「海風週報」 第10期 1929. p.1–8, 第11期 1929. p.6–8
'新興藝術論的論文' 不文訳 「語絲」 第5巻15期 1929. p.95–104
'俄羅斯文學最高頂點的要素' 方炎武訳 「北新半月刊」 第3巻17期 1929. p.47–53
'新藝術形式之探求' 江伯玉訳 「新亜州月刊」 創刊号 1930.
'新興藝術論的文獻' 不文訳 「語絲」 第5巻15期 1930.
「文藝政策」 魯迅訳 上海 水沫書店 1930. 1冊
「新寫實主義論文集」 之本訳 上海 現代書局 1930. 1冊
'浪漫主義以後的俄國文學' 毛一波訳 「新時代月刊」 創刊号 1931.
'関于《毀滅》' 魯迅訳 「毀滅」 上海 三閑書屋 1931;「魯迅全集 18」 上海 魯迅全集出版社 1938. 作家書屋 1940. 大連 光華書店 1948. 北京 人民文学出版社 1973. p.265–274;「魯迅譯文集 7」北京 人民文学出版社 1958. p.192–199
'帝国主義與藝術' 曉風訳 「微音月刊」 第1巻9–10期 1931.
'法兒耶夫底小説潰滅' 洛陽訳 「萌芽」 第2巻 1931.
'関于藝術作品底評價問題' 王集叢訳 「北國月刊」 第1巻2期 1932.
'到新寫實主義的路' 林伯脩訳 「太陽月刊」 第7巻
「新興藝術概論」 馮憲章訳 上海 現代書局 193?. 1冊
「新興藝術論」 上海 辛墾書局 193?. 1冊
'Японская демократическая литература после второй мировой войны' *Советская Востоковедения*, номер 2, 1958. p.88–93
'小林多喜二的現代意义' 申非訳 「譯文」 1958年2月 p.116–121
'論日本戰後文学' 「譯文」 1958年10月

Статьи о современной японской литературе. Перевод Л. А. Часовичной и др. Москва, Изд. Восточной Литературы, 1959. 194p.
'小林多喜二的文学' 陳九仁訳 「世界文学」 1963年2月 p.9–12

KURAHARA Shinjirō 蔵原伸二郎 1899–1965

Poems 詩

'The afternoon of a solar eclipse' *Asian P.E.N. anthology*, ed. by F. Sionil Jose. N. Y. Taplinger, 1966. p.322
'辺土；詩人；四月우박' 金巣雲訳 「世界의 文学大全集 34」 서울 同和出版社 1971. p.521–523
'The fox; Footprints; A secret code' *Anthology of modern Japanese poetry*, tr. and comp. by Edith Marcombe Shiffert and Yuki Sawa. Tokyo, Tuttle, 1972. p.77–78

KURAHASHI Yumiko 倉橋由美子 1935–

Kakō ni shisu 河口に死す

'To die at the estuary' Tr. by Dennis Keene. *Contemporary Japanese literature*, ed. by Howard Hibbett. N. Y. Knopf, 1977. p.248–281

Parutai パルタイ

'Partei' Tr. by Saburo Haneda. *The Reeds*, v.7, 1961. p.85–108
'脱党' 金鍾仁訳 「戦後日本新人受賞作品選」 서울 隆文社 1961. p.197–213

Sei shōjo 聖少女

「聖少女」 崔林訳 서울 王子出版社 1965. 268p.
「聖少女」 李顯子訳 서울 兄弟出版社 1965. 244p.

KURATA Hyakuzō 倉田百三 1891–1943

Ai to ninshiki tono shuppatsu 愛と認識との出発

'愛與認識的出發' 徐祖正訳 「葬原」 第2巻10期 1927. p.361–381
「사랑과認識의出発」 金壽影訳 서울 文藝出版社 1970. 255p.
「사랑과認識의出発」 張炅龍訳 서울 文藝出版社 1975. 310p.

Shinran 親鸞

Shinran. Tr. by Umeyo Hirano. Tokyo, CIIB Press, 1964. 250p.

Shukke to sono deshi 出家とその弟子

The priest and his disciples. Tr. by Glenn W. Shaw. Tokyo, Hokuseido, 1922; London, Ernest Benn, 1927; Tokyo, Hokuseido, 1955. 246p.
「出家及其弟子」 孫百剛訳 上海 創造社 1930. 1冊
Le prêtre et ses disciples. Tr. par Kuninosuke Matsuo et Emile Steinilber-Oberlin. Paris, Rieder, 1932. 291p.
A zarándok és tanitvanyai. Budapest, Stádium, 1943. 219p.

Shunkan 俊寛

'Shunkan' Tr. by Kanichi Ando. *Eigo Seinen.* v.47, no.3–no.12, 1922; v.48, no.1–no.12,

1922–23; v.49, no.1–no.12, 1923; v.50, no.1–no.12, 1923–24; v.51, no.1–no.11, 1924.
Shunkan, a play. Tr. by Kanichi Ando. Tokyo, Kenkyusha, 1925. 141p.

Tanabata matsuri 七夕祭

'Das Tanabata-Fest' Übers. von Kiyoshi Sasaki. *Das Junge Japan*, Band 1, 1924. p.26–32, 60–63, 103–114, 149–153

Essay エッセイ

'사랑을잃은者가걸을길；이웃으로서의사랑；땅위의男女' 鄭成煥 金泳杓訳 「世界에세이文学全集 8」 서울 東西出版社 1974. p.342–392；「世界随筆文学全集 8」 서울 世進出版社 1976. p.342–392

KURATOMI Chizuko 蔵富千鶴子

Donkuma san どんくまさん

Remember Mr. Bear. London, Macdonald, 1967. 25p.
Helpful Mr. Bear. N. Y. Parents' Magazine Press, 1968. 1v.
Meneer Beer helpt. 's-Gravenhage, Junk, 1973. 25p.

Donkuma san no otetsudai どんくまさんのおてつだい

Mr. Bear and the robbers. London, Macdonald, 1971. 24p.
Meneer Beer en de rovers. 's-Gravenhage, Junk, 1973. 24p.

Donkuma san no rappa どんくまさんのらっぱ

Mr. Bear's trumpet. London, Macdonald, 1969. 25p.; N. Y. Judson Press, 1969. 1v.

Donkuma san sora e iku どんくまさんそらへいく

Mr. Bear in the air. London, Macdonald, 1969. 25p.; N. Y. Judson Press, 1969. 1v.

Donkuma san umi e iku どんくまさんうみへいく

Mr. Bear goes to sea. London, Macdonald, 1968. 25p.; N. Y. Judson Press, 1968. 1v.

Donkuma san wa ekichō san どんくまさんはえきちょうさん

Mr. Bear, station-master. London, Macdonald, 1972. 25p.

Jamu jamu Donkuma san じゃむじゃむどんくまさん

Mr. Bear and apple jam. London, Macdonald, 1973. 25p.

Okaasan wa doko おかあさんはどこ

Have you seen my mother? English version by Anne Maley. N. Y. Lerner, 1969. 1v.

KURIBAYASHI Issekiro 栗林一石路 1894–1961

Haiku 俳句

'2 haiku' *A history of haiku v.2*, by R. H. Blyth. Tokyo, Hokuseido, 1964. p.204–206

KURIHARA Sadako　栗原貞子

Poems　詩

'Let's help them bear; I would be a witness for Hiroshima'　Tr. by Miyao Ohara. *The songs of Hiroshima*. Tokyo, Taihei Shuppansha, 1971. p.94

'Дерево; Инвалиды войны' Перевод Анатолия Мамонова. *Вкус хризантемы*. Москва, Восточная Литература, 1976. p.57–58

KURIYAGAWA Hakuson　厨川白村　1880–1923

Bungei shichōron　文芸思潮論

'文藝思潮論' 汪馥泉訳 「覚悟」 1922年2月
「文藝思潮論」 樊從予訳　上海　商務印書館　1924. 1冊
「文藝思想論」 汪馥泉訳　上海　民智書局 193?. 1冊
'文藝思潮論' 樊仲雲訳 「文學週報」 102期–120期 193?.

Jūji gaitō o yuku　十字街頭を往く

「走向十字街頭」 緑焦 劉大杰訳　上海 啓智書局 1928. 1冊

Kindai bungaku jukkō　近代文学十講

「近代文學十講」 羅迪先訳　上海　學術研究會　1921. 2冊；上海 啓智書局 193?. 2冊
「近代文學十講」 楊開渠訳　上海 現代書局　1931. 1冊
「西洋近代文藝思想」 陳暁南訳　台北 志文出版社 1975. 385p.

Kindai no ren'ai kan　近代の恋愛観

'戀愛論' 任伯濤訳 「小説月報」 第15巻10号 1924.
「近代的戀愛觀」 夏丏尊訳　上海 開明書店 1928. 1冊
「戀愛論」 任伯濤訳　上海 學術研究會 193?. 1冊

Kumon no shōchō　苦悶の象徴

'苦悶的象徴' 魯迅訳 「晨報副刊」 1924；「苦悶的象徴 出了象牙之塔」 北京 新潮社 1924；「魯迅全集 13」 上海 魯迅全集出版社 1938. 作家書屋 1946. 大連 光華書店 1948. 北京 人民文学出版社 1973. p.17–91；「魯迅譯文集 3」 北京 人民文学出版社 1958. p.3–91
「苦悶的象徴」 魯迅訳　北京 未名社 1924. 1冊
「苦悶的象徴」 豊子愷訳　上海 商務印書館 1926. 1冊
「苦悶的象徴」 徐雲濤訳　台北 經緯出版社 1957. 84p.
'苦悶的象徴' 慕容蕳訳 「苦悶的象徴」 台北 常春樹書坊 1973. p.1–90
「苦悶的象徴」 德華出版社訳　台北 德華出版社 1975. 101p.

Zōge no tō o dete　象牙の塔を出て

'出了象牙之塔' 魯迅訳 「苦悶的象徴・出了象牙之塔」 北京 新潮社 1924；「魯迅全集 13」 上海 魯迅全集出版社 1938. 作家書屋 1946. 大連 光華書店 1948. 北京 人民文学出版社 1973. p.155–381；「魯迅譯文集 3」 北京 人民文学出版社 1958. p.107–286
「出了象牙之塔」 魯迅訳　北京 未名社 1924. 1冊
「出了象牙之塔」 金溟若訳　台北 志文出版社 1968. 228p.
'象牙塔을나서면서' 安仁吉 方坤訳 「世界随筆文学全集 4」 서울 東西出版社 1969. p.254–292
'象牙塔을나서면서' 鄭成煥 全泳杓訳 「世界에세이文学全集 8」 서울 東西出版社 1974. p.254–294；「世界随筆文学全集 8」 서울 世進出版社 1976. p.254–294

Criticism　評論

'文藝的進化' 朱希祖訳 「新青年」 第6巻6期 1919. p.581–584
'宣傳與創作' 任伯濤訳 「小説月報」 第15巻10号 1924. p.1–4

'文藝上幾箇根本問題的考察' 仲雲訳 「東方雜誌」 第21巻 20期 1924. p.72–84
'文藝創作論' 樊仲雲訳 「學燈」 1924年7号–9号；「文學週報」 第128–129期
'東西之自然詩觀' 魯迅訳 「莽原」 第1巻2期 1926. p.45–55；「壁下譯叢」 上海 北新書局 1929；「魯迅全集 16」 上海 魯迅全集出版社 1938. 作家書屋 1946. 大連 光華書店 1948. 北京 人民文学出版社 1973. p.72–81；「魯迅譯文集 5」北京 人民文学出版社 1958. p.181–188
'西班牙劇壇的将星' 魯迅訳 「小説月報」 第16巻1期 1925. p.1–8；「壁下譯叢」 上海 北新書局 1929；「魯迅全集 16」 上海 魯迅全集出版社 1938. 作家書屋 1946. 大連 光華書店 1948. 北京 人民文学出版社 1973. p.82–93；「魯迅譯文集 5」 北京 人民文学出版社 1958. p.189–198
'病的性慾與文學' 仲雲訳 「小説月報」 第16巻5号 1925. p.1–9
'文藝與性慾' 仲雲訳 「小説月報」 第16巻7号 1925. p.1–4
「歐州文藝思想史」 黄新民訳 厦門 國際學術書社 1928. 1冊
「北美印象記」 沈端先訳　上海 金屋書店 1929. 1冊
「歐美文學評論」 夏綠焦訳　上海 大東書局 1931. 1冊
'英國的戰世詩派' 東聲訳 「文藝月刊」 第4巻6期 1933. p.112–125
'小泉八雲及其他' 綠焦訳　上海 啓智書局 193?. 1冊
'女性的表情美' 李慧訳 「摩爾寧」 創刊号 193?.
'小泉八雲' 金溟若訳 「純文學」 （台湾版） 第4巻2期 1968. p.40–59
'Essay' 周豫才訳 「世界名作家散文選」 香港 上海 書局 1977. p.1–8

KURODA Kio　黒田喜夫　1926–

Poems　詩

'Imaginary guerrilla'　Tr. by Thomas Fitzsimmons and Rikutaro Fukuda. *Orient West*, v. 9, no. 5, 1964. p.59–60

'Il licenziamento'　*La protesta poetica del Giappone*, a cura di Dacia Maraini e Michiko Nojiri. Roma, Officina Edizioni, 1968. p.111–112

'Daydream guerrilla'　Tr. by Harry and Lynn Guest and Shozo Kajima. *Post-war Japanese poetry*. Harmondsworth, Penguin Books, 1972. p.111–112

'The breeding of poisonous worms; Imaginary guerrilla; Hungarian laughter'　Tr. by Thomas Fitzsimmons. *Japanese poetry now*. London, André Deutsch, 1972. p.50–57; *Japanese poetry today*. N. Y. Schocken Books, 1972. p.52–59

'Imaginary guerrilla; Hungarian laughter; The breeding of poisonous worms'　Tr. by Thomas Fitzsimmons. *The poetry of postwar Japan*, ed. by Kajima Hajime. Iowa City, Univ. of Iowa Press, 1975. p.120–129

'Burning giraffe'　Tr. by James Kirkup. *Poetry Nippon*, no.39 & 40, 1977. p.14–15

'Vor dem Schrei; Ich wollte; Schrei und Tad' Übers. von Helmut Gross. *Internationales Jahrbuch für Literatur*, Ensemble 8, 1977. p.97–98

KURODA Kiyotsuna　黒田清綱　1830–1917

Tanka　短歌

'Globeflowers'　Tr. by Asataro Miyamori. *Masterpieces of Japanese poetry, ancient and modern*. Tokyo, Maruzen, 1936; Tokyo, Taiseido, 1956; N. Y. Greenwood Press, 1971. p.603–604

KURODA Reiji 黒田礼二 1890–1937

Criticism 評論

'霧鼮運動' 海鏡訳 「小説月報」 第12巻6号 1921. p.1–11

KURODA Saburō 黒田三郎 1919–

Poems 詩

'I have been changed so much' *An anthology
  of modern Japanese poetry*, ed. and tr. by
  Ichiro Kono and Rikutaro Fukuda. Tokyo,
  Kenkyusha, 1957. p.74
'There's a seat there' Tr. by J. G. Mills and
  Rikutaro Fukuda. *Japan Quarterly*, v.6,
  no.3, 1959. p.340–341
'저녁 나절 三十分' 金龍済訳 「日本詩集」 서울 青雲社
  1960. p.140–143
'Çok değiştim' Tercüme etmek L. Sami Akalin.
  Japon şiiri. İstanbul, Varlik Yayinevi, 1962.
  p.298
'당신도 單純한；나를 責望하는것' 辛東門訳 「世界戦後文
  学全集 9」 서울 新丘文化社 1962. p.244–245
'Я стал совсем другим' Перевод Е. Винокурова.
  Иностранная Литература, июнь 1964.
  p.157
'Nothing more to be lost' Tr. by Thomas Fitzsim-
  mons and Rikutaro Fukuda. *Orient West*,
  v.9, no.5, 1964. p.58
'한女人에게' 崔一秀訳 「기다리고있네」 서울 韓国政
  経社 1966. p.37–38
'Non importa; La penitenza' *La protesta poetica
  del Giappone*, a cura di Dacia Maraini e
  Michiko Nojiri. Roma, Officina Edizioni,
  1968. p.67–68
'The sea; Nature; Hide and seek' *Anthology of
  modern Japanese poetry*, tr. and comp. by
  Edith Marcombe Shiffert and Yuki Sawa.
  Tokyo, Tuttle, 1972. p.116–117
'Half an hour in the evening; Nothing but a poet;
  Nothing more to be lost' Remade into English
  by Thomas Fitzsimmons. *Japanese poetry
  now*. London, André Deutsch, 1972. p.87–89;
  Japanese poetry today. N. Y. Schocken Books,
  1972. p.89–91
'The stake; Only a poet; Suddenly; In a light
  breeze' Tr. by Harry and Lynn Guest and
  Shozo Kajima. *Post-war Japanese poetry*.
  London, Penguin Books, 1972. p.52–58

Criticism 評論

'詩人과言語' 金龍済訳 「日本詩集」 서울 青雲社
  1960. p.159–171

KUROIWA Jūgo 黒岩重吾 1924–

Ori o deta yajū 檻を出た野獣

'우리를나온野獣' 張壽哲訳 「日本代表作家百人選 5」 서
  울 希望出版社 1966. p.134–152; 「日本短篇文学
  全集 6」 서울 新太陽社 1969. p.46–64

'紅色的夜花' 振江訳 「黒色幻惑」 台南 文良出版社
  1966. p.40–76
'鬼船' 劉慕沙訳 「狐鶏」 台北 林白出版社 1969. p.2–
  37

KUROIWA Ruikō 黒岩涙香 1862–1920

「天際落花」 褚靈辰訳 上海 商務印書館 1891. 1冊
「寒桃記」 呉檮訳 上海 商務印書館 1906. 2冊
「鴛鴦離合記」 上海 商務印書館 1926. 2冊
「懺悔記」 上海 商務印書館 192?. 2冊

KURONUMA Ken 黒沼 健 1902–

Shinpi to gensō monogatari 神秘と幻想物語

「奇幻世界」 李朝熙訳 台北 大立書店 1970. 166p.

KUROSAWA Akira 黒沢 明 1910–

Dodesukaden どですかでん
(with Hideo Oguni and Shinobu Hashimoto)

Dodesukaden. Tr. by Don Kenny. Tokyo, Kinema
  Junposha, 1970. 138p.
Под стук трамвайных колес. Перевод М.
  Доли и Л. Завяровко. Москва, Искусство,
  1974. 143p.

Hakuchi 白痴
(with Eijiro Hisaita)

'The idiot' Tr. by Don Kenny. *Complete works of
  Akira Kurosawa 6*. Tokyo, Kinema Junposha,
  1971. p.5–104

Ikiru 生きる
(with Shinobu Hashimoto and Hideo Oguni)

Ikiru. Ed. by Donald Richie. London, Lorrimer,
  1968. 84p.
'Ikiru' Tr. by Don Kenny. *Complete works of
  Akira Kurosawa 6*. Tokyo, Kinema Junpo-
  sha, 1971. p.105–176
'Ikiru' Tr. by Donald Richie. *Contemporary
  Japanese literature*, ed. by Howard Hibbett.
  N. Y. Knopf, 1977. p.146–188
'Жить' Перевод М. Доли. *Акира Куросава*.
  Москва, Искусство, 1977. p.117–180

Kakushi toride no san akunin 隠し砦の三悪人
(with S. Hashimoto, H. Oguni and R. Kikushima)

'Three badmen in a hidden fortress' Tr. by Don
  Kenny. *Complete works of Akira Kurosawa 9*.
  Tokyo, Kinema Junposha, 1971. p.5–108

Norainu 野良犬
(with Ryuzo Kikushima)

'Stray dog' Tr. by Don Kenny. *Complete works
  of Akira Kurosawa 4*. Tokyo, Kinema Junposha, 1971. p.67–152

Rashōmon 羅生門
(with Shinobu Hashimoto)

Rashomon. N. Y. Grove Press, 1952. 255p.
Rasomon. Beograd, Sportska Knjiga, 1953. 32p.

Shichinin no samurai 七人の侍

Seven samurai. Tr. by Donald Richie. London,
  Lorrimer, 1970. 224p.; N. Y. Simon and
  Schuster, 1970. 224p.

KUROSAWA Akira

Shizuka naru kettō 静かなる決闘
(with Senkichi Taniguchi)

'Quiet duel' Tr. by Don Kenny. *Complete works of Akira Kurosawa 4*. Tokyo, Kinema Junposha, 1971. p.5–66

Subarashiki nichiyōbi 素晴らしき日曜日
(with Keinosuke Uekusa)

'One wonderful Sunday' Tr. by Don Kenny. *Complete works of Akira Kurosawa 3*. Tokyo, Kinema Junposha, 1971. p.6–60

Sugata Sanshirō 姿三四郎

'Sanshiro Sugata' Tr. by Kimi Aida. *Complete works of Akira Kurosawa 2*. Tokyo, Kinema Junposha, 1971. p.6–64

Waga seishun ni kui nashi わが青春に悔いなし
(with Eijiro Hisaita)

'No regrets for our youth' Tr. by Miyahiko Miki. *Complete works of Akira Kurosawa 2*. Tokyo, Kinema Junposha, 1971. p.65–120

Warui yatsu hodo yoku nemuru 悪い奴ほどよく眠る
(with H. Oguni, E. Hisaita, R. Kikushima, S. Hashimoto)

'The bad sleep well' Tr. by Don Kenny. *Complete works of Akira Kurosawa 9*. Tokyo, Kinema Junposha, 1971. p.109–232

Yoidore tenshi 酔いどれ天使
(with Keinosuke Uekusa)

'Drunken angel' Tr. by Don Kenny. *Complete works of Akira Kurosawa 3*. Tokyo, Kinema Junposha, 1971. p.61–120

KUROSHIMA Denji 黒島伝治 1898–1943

Fudō suru chika 浮動する地価

'波動の地價' 「泛濫」 香港 上海書局 1970. p.96–125

Hanran 氾濫

'氾濫' 陳勺水訳 「日本新寫實派代表傑作集」 上海 楽羣雑誌社 1929.
'泛濫' 「泛濫」 香港 上海書局 1970. p.42–95

kokkyō 国境

'На границе' Перевод. Н. Фельдман. *Вокруг Света*, номер 6, 1934. p.23–27

Nisen dōka 二銭銅貨

'A copper' Tr. by Atsumu Kanayama. *The Reeds*, v.9, 1963. p.71–79
'両分銭' 「泛濫」 香港 上海書局 1970. p.1–8

Tongun 豚群

'猪羣' 「泛濫」 香港 上海書局 1970. p.25–41

Umi no dai jūichi kōjō 海の第十一工場

'The factory in the sea' *The cannery boat, and other Japanese short stories*. N. Y. International Publishers, 1933; London, Martin Lawrence, 1933; N. Y. Greenwood Press, 1968. p.91–130
'Фабрика в море' *Сборник японской революц-ионной литературы*. Москва, Гос. Изд. Худож. Лит. 1933. p.119–136
'Завод в море' Перевод Н. Фельдман. *Японская революционная литература*. Москва, Худож. Лит. 1934. p.169–194

Urabon zengo 盂蘭盆前後

'過節前後' 「泛濫」 香港 上海書局 1970. p.9–24
'過節前後' 「當代亜非拉小説選」 香港 中流出版社 1977. p.335–344

Yuki no Shiberia 雪のシベリア

'風雪西伯利亜' 「泛濫」 香港 上海書局 1970. p.126–144

Zenshō 前哨

'Головной дозор' Перевод Р. Кима. *Знамя*, номер 6, 1934. p.100–105

「黒島傳治短篇小説集」 李芒等訳 北京 作家出版社 1964. 1冊

KUSANO Shinpei 草野心平 1903–

Fujisan 富士山

Fujisan. Tokyo, Iwasaki Bijutsu, 1966. 64p.
'Fujisan' Tr. by S. Kamaike and Cid Corman. *Japan P.E.N. News*, no.19, June 1967. p.2–5
'Muntele Fuji' Traducereă Virgil Teodorescu. *Din lirica japoneză*. Bucureşti, Editura Univers, n.d. p.199

Kaeru 蛙

Selected frogs. Tr. by Susumu Kamaike and Cid Corman. Kyoto, Origin Press, 1963. 38p.
'Selected frogs' Tr. by S. Kamaike and Cid Corman. *Japan P.E.N. News*, no.19, 1966. p.1–2
Frogs and others. Tr. by Cid Corman and Susumu Kamaike. Tokyo, Tuttle, 1968. 124p.; Tokyo, Mushinsha, 1969; N. Y. Grossman, 1969. 124p.
Rane e altre cose. Versione di Cid Corman, Susumu Kamaike e M. Datini. Parma, Guanda, 1969. 82p.

Poems 詩

'Stone' Tr. by Thomas T. Ichinose. *Japan Quarterly*, v.3, no.1, 1956. p.91
'Remorse' *An anthology of modern Japanese poetry*, ed. and tr. by Ichiro Kono and Rikutaro Fukuda. Tokyo, Kenkyusha, 1957. p.75
'Queroqué la rana' *Sur*, no.249, Nov.-Dec. 1957. p.95
'Queroqué the frog; An autobiography; Conversation on an autumn night; The frog' *The poetry of living Japan*, by Takamichi Ninomiya and D. J. Enright. London, John Murray, 1957. p.81–82
'Window' Tr. by J. G. Mills and Rikutaro Fukuda. *Japan Quarterly*, v.4, no.4, 1957. p.465
'Pierre; Queroqué la grenouille' *La poésie japonaise*, par Karl Petit. Paris, Seghers, 1959. p.235–236
'Der Marienkäfer; Durchs Fenster; Das Atom' Übertragen von Shin Aizu. *Der schwermütige Ladekran*. St. Gallen, Tschudy Verlag, 1960.

p.8, 18–19, 49

'Keroke, a béka' Ford. Illyés Gyula. *Nagyvilág*, no.10, 1960.

'검정개구리' 金龍済訳 「日本詩集」 서울 青雲社 1960. p.54–56

'時空; 原子; 上小川村; 머물지않는時間속을; 中華民国 의藍에판하여' 柳呈訳 「世界戦後文学全集 9」 서울 新丘文化社 1962. p.220–222

'Mount Fuji, opus 5; Stone' Tr. by Geoffrey Bownas and Anthony Thwaite. *The Penguin book of Japanese verse*. Harmondsworth, Penguin Books, 1964. p.216

'The sea at night' *Modern Japanese poetry*, by Donald Keene. Ann Arbor, Center for Japanese Studies, Univ. of Michigan, 1964. p.31

'Pietra; Fammi dormine' *La protesta poetica del Giappone*, a cura di Dacia Maraini e Michiko Nojiri. Roma, Officina Edizioni, 1968. p.49–50

'祭蛇進行曲; 生殖; 蟻; 牡丹園' 徐和隣訳 「現代詩解説」 台北 葡萄園詩刊社 1970. p.55–60.

'The stone' Tr. by Toshiaki Fukuhara. *Poetry Nippon*, no.15, 1971. p.11

'The sea at night' Tr. by Donald Keene. *Landscapes and portraits*. Tokyo, Kodansha International, 1971. p.149

'가을밤의대화; 窓; 五月; 言語' 金巢雲訳 「世界의文学 大全集 34」 서울 同和出版公社 1971. p.532–534

'窓' 金光林訳 「現代詩学」 第4巻3号 1972.

'Steinen; Anger' Til norsk ved Paal Brekke. *Moderne japansk lyrikk*. Oslo, Norske Bokklubben, n.d. p.56–57

KUSHIDA Magoichi 串田孫一 1915–

Poems 詩

'午前의햇살' 辛東門訳 「世界戦後文学全集 9」 서울 新丘文化社 1962. p.231–232

Essay エッセイ

'Stillness' *Chanoyu Quarterly*, v.1, no.4, 1970. p.1–3

KUSUDA Toshirō 楠田敏郎 1890–1951

Tanka 短歌

'Labourers; The spirit of rivalry' Tr. by Asataro Miyamori. *Masterpieces of Japanese poetry, ancient and modern*. Tokyo, Maruzen, 1936; Tokyo, Taiseido, 1956; N. Y. Greenwood Press, 1971. p.771–772

KUSUYAMA Masao 楠山正雄 1884–1950

Kitsune to shishi 狐と獅子

'Kitsune to shishi' Tr. by Yasutaro Kanzaki. *Eisakubun Zasshi*, Nov. 1921.

Shin Kaguyahime 新かぐや姫

Princezna Zářící paprsek. Přel. Z. Mareckova. Praha, SNDK, 1959. 84p.

Criticism 評論

'近代戯劇의開展與分化' 乃力訳 「文藝戦線」 第42期—44期

KUWATA Masakazu 桑田雅一 1926–

Momotarō 桃太郎

Momotaro. English version by Eric Sackheim. Tokyo, Kodansha International, 1963. 45p.

Tsuru no ongaeshi 鶴の恩がえし

The grateful crane. English version by Eric Sackheim. Tokyo, Kodansha International, 1963. 43p.

KYO Nanki 許 南麒 (Ho Nam-gi) 1918–

Poems 詩

'The river Rizan' *An anthology of modern Japanese poetry*, ed. and tr. by Ichiro Kono and Rikutaro Fukuda. Tokyo, Kenkyusha, 1957. p.25

'Песня в яблоневом саду' Перевод Анатолия Мамонова. *Вкус хризантемы*. Москва, Восточная Литература, 1976. p.48

KYŪ Eikan 邱 永漢 1924–

Essay エッセイ

'왜사는가' 金賢珠訳 「바이바이바디」 서울 三韓出版 社 1966. p.33–41

M

MAEDA Fura 前田普羅 1884–1954

Haiku 俳句

'1 haiku' Tr. by Asataro Miyamori. *Anthology of haiku, ancient and modern*. Tokyo, Maruzen, 1932. p.820

'3 haiku' *A history of haiku v.2*. Tokyo, Hokuseido, 1964. p.171–172

MAEDA Hiromasa 前田宏昌

Aru wakare 或る別れ

'訣別' 劉慕沙訳 「日本現代小説選 1」 台北 聯經出版事業公司 1976. p.255–316

MAEDA Mieko 前田三恵子 1930–

Itazura usagi no bōken いたずらうさぎのぼうけん

How rabbit tricked his friends. N. Y. Parents' Magazine Press, 1969. 32p.

MAEDA Yūgure　前田夕暮　1883–1951

Tanka　短歌

'A green tree; The sunflower; April; My sorrow; A prison-house' Tr. by Asataro Miyamori. *Masterpieces of Japanese poetry, ancient and modern.* Tokyo, Maruzen, 1936; Tokyo, Taiseido, 1956; N. Y. Greenwood Press, 1971. p.704–706

'Tanka' Tr. par Kuni Matsuo et Steinilber-Oberlin. *Anthologie des poètes japonais contemporains.* Paris, Mercure de France, 1939. p.270–271

'4 tanka' Tr. by V. H. Viglielmo. *Japanese literature in the Meiji era.* Tokyo, Obunsha, 1955. p.402–403

'2 tanka' Übers. von Kuniyo Takayasu und Manfred Hausmann. *Ruf der Regenpfeifer.* München, Bechtle Verlag, 1961. p.101

'2 tanka' Übers. von Gerolf Coudenhove. *Japanische Jahreszeiten.* Zürich, Manesse Verlag, 1963. p.121, 222

Essay　エッセイ

'The Chinese parasol tree and the boy' Tr. by Iwao Matsubara. *Eigo Seinen* v.76, no.7, 1937. p.225–226

MAEDAKŌ Hiroichirō　前田河広一郎　1888–1957

Kureopatora　クレオパトラ

'克羅帕特拉' 陳勺水訳 「新的歴史戯曲集」 上海 楽羣書局 n.d.

Rasupūchin no shi　ラスプーチンの死

'拉思蒲琴的死' 陳勺水訳 「新的歴史戯曲集」 上海 楽羣書局 n.d.

Santō senkyaku　三等船客

'Пассажиры третьего класса' Перевод Н. Фельдман. *Альманах,* номер 2, 1930. p.72–97

Taiyō no kokuten　太陽の黒点

'Пятна на солнце' Перевод Н. Фельдман. *Вестник Иностранной Литературы,* номер 3, 1929. p.3–38

'土耳其最後的王國' 陳勺水訳 「新的歴史戯曲集」 上海 楽羣書局 n.d.

MAEKAWA Yasuo　前川康男　1921–

Nigedashita raion　にげだしたライオン

The lion who ran away. Retold by Laurence Collinson. London, Hamlyn, 1969. 1v.

MAENO Shigeru　前野　茂　1897–

Ikeru shikabane　生ける屍

「살아있는人間무덤」 李嶺一訳 서울 清潮文化社 1966. 396p.

「살아있는송장」 蔡榮哲訳 서울 泰西出版社 1966. 3冊；서울 藝術文化社 1970. 3冊

MAJIMA Setsuko　真島節子　1937–

Umeboshi no uta　うめぼしのうた

Song of the sour plum. N. Y. Walker, 1968. 1v.

MAKABE Jin　真壁　仁　1907–

Poems　詩

'赤手空拳的戦闘；富士山' 南冠訳 「譯文」 1956年6月 p.63–65

'彈道下的村子' 思ған訳 「詩刊」 第4期 1961. p.59–60

MAKIMURA Hiroshi　槇村　浩　1912–1938

Poems　詩

'間島游击队之歌；寄異邦的中國詩人' 林犀訳 「世界文学」 1963年11月 p.21–27

MAKINO Shin'ichi　牧野信一　1896–1936

Kinada mura　鬼涙村

'鬼涙村' 郭夏信訳 「世界文学全集 94」 서울 乙酉文化社 1962. p.311–327

'Ördögkönnyfalva' Ford. Sz. Holti Mária. *Modern Japán elbeszélők.* Budapest, Európa Könyvkiadó, 1967. p.119–131

MAKINO Yoshiharu　牧野吉晴　1904–1957

'新生之路' 徐雲濤訳 「當代日本小説選」 台南 經緯書局 1954. p.72–94；「當代日本創作小説」 台南 經緯書局 1961. p.72–94；「當代日本短篇小説選」 台南 大行出版社 1973. p.72–94

'新月' 徐雲濤訳 「當代日本小説選」 台南 經緯書局 1954. p.205–222；「當代日本創作小説」 台南 經緯書局 1961. p.205–222；「當代日本短篇小説選」 台南 大行出版社 1973. p.205–222

MAMIYA Mosuke　間宮茂輔　1899–1975

Fun'en no moto ni　噴煙の下に

「在噴烟之下」 張夢麟訳 北京 中國青年 1958. 205p.

MANZŌJI Hitoshi　万造寺　斉　1886–1957

Tanka　短歌

'Peonies; Wandering' Tr. by Asataro Miyamori. *Masterpieces of Japanese poetry, ancient and modern.* Tokyo, Maruzen, 1936; Tokyo, Taiseido, 1956; N. Y. Greenwood Press, 1971. p.749–750

'1 tanka' Übers. von Gerolf Coudenhove. *Japanische Jahreszeiten.* Zürich, Manesse Verlag, 1963. p.135

MARUOKA Akira　丸岡　明　1907–1968

Bara iro no kiri　薔薇いろの霧

'Rose-coloured mist'　Tr. by Warren Carlisle. *Japan P.E.N. News*, no.17, Feb. 1966. p.14–22

MARUOKA Katsura　丸岡　桂　1878–1919

Tanka　短歌

'1 tanka'　Tr. by V. H. Viglielmo. *Japanese literature in the Meiji era*. Tokyo, Obunsha, 1955. p.378

MARUYAMA Kaoru　丸山　薫　1899–1974

Poems　詩

'Voile, lampe et mouettes; Le chant des mouettes; Le chant de la lampe; Le port; Le mensonge' Tr. par Kuni Matsuo et Steinilber-Oberlin. *Anthologie des poètes japonais contemporains*. Paris, Mercure de France, 1939. p.244–251

'Conscience of Japan; Mother's umbrella' Tr. by Shigeshi Nishimura. *The Current of the World*, v.29, no.1, 1952. p.42–43, v.29, no.2, 1952. p.34–35

'A distant view of the school; A rhinoceros and a lion'　Tr. by S. Sato and C. Urdang. *Poetry*, May 1956. p.90–91

'A dream; An afternoon; Distant view of the school; The estuary; Fragments; All day long; The wings; Living; Happiness of the snow; Requiem; The anchor; The pain of parting' *An anthology of modern Japanese poetry*, ed. and tr. by Ichiro Kono and Rikutaro Fukuda. Tokyo, Kenkyusha, 1957. p.76–80

'Distant view of school; A gyroscopic lamp' *The poetry of living Japan*, by Takamichi Ninomiya and D. J. Enright. London, John Murray, 1957. p.86

'Rhinocéros et lion' *La poésie japonaise*, par Karl Petit. Paris, Seghers, 1959. p.224

'Bütün gün; Fragman; Yaşamak' Tercüme etmek L. Sami Akalin. *Japon şiiri*. İstanbul, Varlik Yayinevi, 1962. p.267–268

'Sorrow of parting; Gun emplacement; Wings' Tr. by Geoffrey Bownas and Anthony Thwaite. *The Penguin book of Japanese verse*. Harmondsworth, Penguin Books, 1964. p.203

'가바린님 ; 사랑의追憶' 崔一秀訳 「기다리고있네」 서울 韓国政経社　1966. p.65–68

'祈禱歌; 愛日愛花 ; 지붕 ; 저녁노을에 ; 물의精神' 金巣雲訳 「世界의文学大全集 34」 서울　同和出版公社 1970. p.513–514

'물의精神' 金光林訳 「現代詩学」 第4巻3号 1972.

'Spirit of the water' Tr. by James Kirkup. *Poetry Nippon*, no.33 and 34, 1976. p.6–7

'A leve; Dagen lang; Vinger' Til norsk ved Paal Brekke. *Moderne japansk lyrikk*. Oslo, Norske Bokklubben, n.d. p.44–46

MARUYAMA Kenji　丸山健二　1943–

Natsu no nagare　夏の流れ

'夏流' 劉慕沙訳 「純文學」 (台湾版) 第2巻1期 1967.

p.163–210; 「純文學」 (香港版) 第1巻5期　1967.
p.163–210; 「夏流」 台北　純文學出版社　1969.
p.1–74
'夏日的轉變' 劉與堯訳 「現代日本小説選」 台北　雲天出版社　1970. p.99–172

MARUYAMA Manabu　丸山　学　1904–

Bungaku kenkyūhō　文学研究法

「文學研究法」 郭虚中訳　上海　商務印書館　1937. 259p.; 台北　台湾商務印書館　1968. 259p.

MARUYAMA Masaya　円山雅也　1926–

Satsui no ganpeki　殺意の岩壁

「아내는告白한다」 金恩康訳　서울　新世紀文化社 1964. 183p.

MARUYAMA Michio　丸山通郎

Anatahan　アナタハン

Anatahan.　Tr. by Younghill Kang. N. Y. Hermitage, 1954. 206p.
Anatahan.　Tr. from the English by Miro Rajkovič Zagreb, Epoha, 1956. 169p.

MASAMUNE Hakuchō　正宗白鳥　1879–1962

Dokoe　何処へ

'向那裏去' 方光燾訳 「小説月報」 第21巻10号　1930. p.1477–1490;　第21巻11号　1930. p.1639–1654; 第21巻12号　1930. p.1767–1780

Doro ningyō　泥人形

'The mud doll'　Tr. by Gregg M. Sinclair and Kazo Suita. *Tokyo people, three stories from the Japanese*. Tokyo, Keibunkan, 1925. p.119–233

Hisa san　久さん

'Something for nothing'　Tr. by Asataro Miyamori. *Representative tales of Japan*. Tokyo, Sanko Shoten, 1917. p.303–319

Jin'ai　塵埃

'Dust'　Tr. by Robert Rolf. *Monumenta Nipponica*, v.25, no.3–4, 1970. p.407–414

Kokoro no yakeato　心の焼跡

'마음의탄자리' 李柱訓訳 「日本代表作家百人集 2」 서울 希望出版社　1966. p.10–30; 「日本短篇文学全集 2」 서울　新太陽社　1969. p.74–94

Kokyō　故郷

'Home'　*Contemporary Japan*, v.2, no.3, 1933. p.506–513

Reirui　冷涙

Larmes froides.　Paris, 1930. 1v.

MASAMUNE Hakuchō

Zeitaku 贅沢

'Le luxe' Tr. par M. Yoshitomi. *Anthologie de la littérature japonaise contemporaine*. Grenoble, Drevet, 1924. p.126–137

Essay エッセイ

'The guest of one afternoon' *Japan Times*, Dec. 23, 1928.
'Review of Mr. Hosoda's novel "Shinri no haru"' Tr. by Einosuke Omiya. *Eigo Seinen*, v.66, no.4, 1931. p.24; v.66, no.5, 1931. p.164–165

「正宗白鳥集」 方光燾訳 上海 開明書店 1932. 1冊

MASAOKA Shiki 正岡子規 1867–1902

Bokujū itteki 墨汁一滴

'A drop of ink' Tr. by Janine Beichman-Yamamoto. *Monumenta Nipponica*, v.30, no.3, 1975. p.291–315

Botan kuroku 牡丹句録

'The verse record of my peonies' Tr. by Earl Miner. *Japan Quarterly*, v.12, no.2, 1965. p.228–230; *Japanese poetic diaries*. Berkeley, Univ. of California Press, 1969. p.201–203
Peonies kana. Tr. by Harold J. Isaacson. Tokyo, Weatherhill, 1972; London, Allen and Unwin, 1973; N. Y. Theatre Books, 1973. 89p.

Haijin Buson 俳人蕪村

'Die asthetischen Abschnitte aus Masaoka Shikis Haijin Buson' *Oriens Extremus*, Band 3, 1956.

Haiku and Tanka 俳句・短歌

'71 haiku' Tr. by Asataro Miyamori. *Anthology of haiku, ancient and modern*. Tokyo, Maruzen, 1932. p.613–658
'5 haiku' Tr. par Georges Bonneau. *Rythmes japonais*, par. G. Bonneau. Paris, Geuthner, 1933. p.68–71
'Reading the Manyoshu; Summer evening; Scarecrows; At the pool of a Shinto shrine; "Keeping house"; Waiting' Tr. by Harold Gould Henderson. *The bamboo broom*. Tokyo, J. L. Thompson, 1933; London, Kegan Paul, 1933. p.110–112
'8 haiku' Tr. by Harold Gould Henderson. *The bamboo broom*. Tokyo, J. L. Thompson, 1933; London, Kegan Paul, 1933. p.101, 105–108
'10 haiku' *Lyrisme du temps présent*, par Georges Bonneau. Paris, Paul Geuthner, 1935. p.16–21; *Anthologie de la poésie japonaise*. Paris, Paul Geuthner, 1935. p.172–177
'The dews on pine leaves; The milky way; The evening-glories' Tr. by Asataro Miyamori. *Masterpieces of Japanese poetry, ancient and modern*. Tokyo, Maruzen, 1936; Tokyo, Taiseido, 1956; N. Y. Greenwood Press, 1971. p.621–623
'Пжтник; Пладня; Душа; Летна луна' Преведе от франц. Никола Джеров. *Песните на Ямато*. София, Корали, 1937. p.65
'Tanka et haiku' Tr. par Kuni Matsuo et Steinilber-Oberlin. *Anthologie des poètes japonais contemporains*. Paris, Mercure de France, 1939. p.253–255, 288–289
'A ferry-boat; The Mogami River; The soaring sky; The peony; Cherry-blossoms and a pickpocket; The long spring day; Midday skylarks; The spring day; The spring night; Atsumori's tomb; A spider's web; Spring mist; A flower pot; Spring daybreak; The report of a gun; The price of the orchids' Tr. by Asataro Miyamori. *Haiku poems, ancient and modern*. Tokyo, Maruzen, 1940. p.290–302
'Spring in the hills; Waiting; A picture; Scarecrows' Tr. by Harold Gould Henderson. *From the bamboo broom*. N. Y. Japan Reference Library, 1940.
'Caille en cage; Passant; Midi; Réponses; Dernière chanson' *Histoire de la littérature japonaise contemporaine*. Paris, Payot, 1944. p.239–240
'2 haiku' Tr. by Lois J. Erickson. *Songs from the land of dawn*. N. Y. Friendship Press, 1949; Freeport, Books for Libraries Press, 1968. p.63–64
'The butterflies' Tr. by S. G. Brickley. *The writing of idiomatic English*. Tokyo, Kenkyusha, 1951. p.51–56
'10 haiku' Tr. par Conrad Meili. *Cahiers du Sud*, no.305, 1951. p.34–35
'5 хайку' Перевод В. Н. Марковой. *Японская поэзия*. Москва, Гослитиздат, 1954. p.194–198
'9 tanka and 25 haiku' Tr. by V. H. Viglielmo. *Japanese literature in the Meiji era*. Tokyo, Obunsha, 1955. p.394–396, 423–427
'15 haiku' Tr. by Peter Beilenson. *Japanese haiku*. Mount Vernon, Peter Pauper Press, 1955. p.11, 14, 16, 25, 31, 32, 39, 44, 45, 46, 49, 57, 59, 60
'Eight haiku poems' Tr. by H. G. Henderson. *Modern Japanese literature*, ed. by D. Keene. N. Y. Grove Press, 1956; Tokyo, Tuttle, 1957. p.122–132
'2 haiku' Tr. par Roger Bersihand. *La littérature japonaise*. Paris. Presses Universitaires de France, 1956. p.111
'11 tanka' Tr. by H. H. Honda. *The Reeds*, v.3, 1957. p.10, 13, 14, 18, 23; v.5, 1959. p.144
'Ellentát; Rekkenő éjszaka; Feher pillango; Utolsé dal; Tavaszi éjazaka; Hajnalpir; Apám' *Kinai és Japán költők*. Budapest, Szepirodalmi, 1957. p.204–208
'The poetry of Masaoka Shiki' Tr. by H. H. Honda. *The Reeds*, v.4, 1958. p.3–15
'14 haiku' *Haikai and haiku*. Tokyo, Nippon Gakujutsu Shinkokai, 1958. p.80–92
'Tous feux éteints; L'oiseau silencieux; Silence d'hiver; La prisonnière; Dolce far niente; Quiétude monastique; Apparition; Oubli' *La poésie japonaise*, par Karl Petit. Paris, Seghers, 1959. p.181–182
'17 haiku' Tr. by Harold Stewart. *A net of fireflies*. Tokyo, Tuttle, 1960. p.17, 25, 26, 44, 46, 49, 56, 77, 84, 88, 101, 102, 107, 109
'21 haiku' Übers. von Günther Debon. *Im Schnee die Fähre*. München, Piper, 1960. p.9–16
'Fruits' Tr. by Ryozo Matsumoto. *Japanese literature, new and old*. Tokyo, Hokuseido, 1961. p.249–256
'10 haiku und 4 tanka' Übers. von Kuniyo Takayasu und Manfred Hausmann. *Ruf der Regenpfeifer*. München, Bechtle Verlag, 1961. p.73–74, 94–95
'Spring' Tr. by Earl Miner. *Orient West*, v.6,

no.1, Jan. 1961. p.52

'17 haiku' Tr. by Peter Beilenson and Harry Behn. *Haiku harvest*. Mount Vernon, Peter Pauper Press, 1962. p.29, 33, 36, 41, 45, 54, 55, 58, 59, 61

'Haiku' Tercüme etmek L. Sami Akalin. *Japon şiiri*. İstanbul, Varlik Yayinevi, 1962. p.223

'13 haiku' Tr. de Colette de Saint Maurice. *Poésie du Japon*. Paris, Scorpion, 1963. p.11, 30, 35, 46, 47, 64, 67, 86, 87, 90

'130 haiku' Übers. von Gerolf Coudenhove. *Japanische Jahreszeiten*. Zürich, Manesse Verlag, 1963. p.15–374

'2 tanka and 10 haiku' Tr. by Geoffrey Bownas and Anthony Thwaite. *The Penguin book of Japanese verse*. Harmondsworth, Penguin Books, 1964. p.159, 165–166

'Sommer Strom; Auf dem Krankenlager' *Lyrik des Ostens*, hrg. von Wilhelm Gundert usw. München, Carl Hanser, 1965. p.470–471

'2 haiku' Tr. from the French by Unity Evans. *Japanese literature*. N. Y. Walker, 1965. p.94

'15 haiku' Til norsk ved Paal Helge Haugen. *Blad frå ein austleg hage*. Oslo, Det Norske Samlaget, 1965. p.19, 75–82

'12 haiku' Übers. von Erwin Jahn. *Fallende Blüten*. Zürich, Arche, 1968. p.33, 49, 50, 53, 54, 62, 67, 74, 76, 83, 91

'1 haiku' Tr. by Tsutomu Fukuda. *Poetry Nippon*, no.14, 1971. p.16

'5 haiku and 3 tanka' Tr. by Donald Keene. *Landscapes and portraits*. Tokyo, Kodansha International, 1971. p.158, 160, 162, 163, 264

'18 haiku' Tr. by William Howard Cohen. *To walk in seasons*. Tokyo, Tuttle, 1972. p.25, 29, 31, 40, 67–70

'Tavaszi éjszaka' Ford. Kosztolányi Dezsö. *A zene szava*. Budapest, Zenemükiadó, 1973. p.78

'1 haiku' Tr. by Tsutomu Fukuda. *Poetry Nippon*, no.26, 1974. p.3

'8 haiku' Tr. by Takamasa Sasaki. *Eigo Seinen*, v.120, no.10, 1975. p.33

'3 haiku' Przeł. Wiesław Kotański. *Poezja*, no.1, 1975. p.19

'1 haiku' Przeł. Andrzej Szuba. *Poezja*, no.1, 1975. p.45

'1 haiku' Tr. by Akira Kawano. *Poetry Nippon*, no.29 & 30, 1975. p.16

'The mist; The banana-plant; Wild geese; In spring; On the withered plain; Firecrackers; Winter sunset; The crescent moon; Summer moon; The thistle-flowers; The ocean moon; Yellow roses' Tr. by Kenneth Yasuda. *A pepper-pod*. Tokyo, Tuttle, 1976. p.73–76

'20 haiku' *Modern Japanese haiku, an anthology*, comp. and tr. by Makoto Ueda. Tokyo, Univ. of Tokyo Press, 1976. p.26–36

'1 haiku' Tr. by Takamasa Sasaki. *Eigo Seinen*, v.122, no.5, 1976. p.231

'43 haiku' Tr. Vladimir Devide. *Japanska haiku poesija*. Ljubljana, Delo, 1976. p.227–240

MASATOMI Ōyō　正富汪洋　1881–1967

Poems　詩

'Yearnings for Rosa Luxemburg' Tr. by S. Nishimura. *The lyric garland*, ed. by Makoto Sangu. Tokyo, Hokuseido, 1957. p.35–38

'155 tanka' Tr. by Shigeshi Nishimura. *The Shikai*, no.56, 59, 60, 62, 63, 65, 66, 67, 68, 69, 1959–62.

'The Taoist "real man"; Each day a fine day' Tr. by Shigeshi Nishimura. *The Shikai*, no.60, 1960. p.13–15

'April; A mood in spring; Eve of the shrine festival; Three verses on sushi; Visiting Mr. Sangu's home; Seeing Mrs. Sangu; Three verses on Mrs. Hori's visit to me at Aoyama Gakuin College library; Miscellaneous' Tr. by Shigeshi Nishimura. *The Shikai*, no.61, 1690. p.31–34

'The month of May; The atlas; The pond; Different natures' Tr. by Shigeshi Nishimura. *The Shikai*, no.62, 1960. p.30–31

'June; The bright; Light' Tr. by Shigeshi Nishimura. *The Shikai*, no.63, 1961. p.34–37

'July' Tr. by Shigeshi Nishimura. *The Shikai*, no.64, 1961. p.38–40

'To the merry tune of the boat-song; People burdened with selves' Tr. by Shigeshi Nishimura. *The Shikai*, no.65, 1961. p.18–19

'Tantrums; Legs; He comes hustling; A song of a girl; Shinran' Tr. by Haxon Ishii. *The Shikai*, no.66, 1962. p.26–28

'I stand for morality' Tr. by Haxon Ishii. *The Shikai*, no.67, 1962. p.35–37

'Two ditties' Tr. by Haxon Ishii. *The Shikai*, no.68, 1962. p.31

'二張小臉兒'「標準日本名著選讀」孫文斗編 台北 大新書局 1969. p.73–74

MASUDA Hajime　益田　甫

Junkan tōsō　循環闘争

'循環爭闘' 蘇儀貞訳 「小説月報」第16巻10号 1925. p.1–20

MASUDA Misako　益田美佐子

Poems　詩

'To the dear soul of Ken who was killed by the A-bomb' Tr. by Miyao Ohara. *The songs of Hiroshima*. Tokyo, Taihei Shuppansha, 1971. p.103–109

MASUOKA Toshikazu　増岡敏和　1928–

Poems　詩

'В борьбе за мир я сложил эту песню, сестра!' Перевод В. Н. Марковой. *Японская поэзия*. Москва, Гослитиздат, 1954. p.319–323

MATSUBARA Hisako　松原久子

Taketori monogatari　たけとりものがたり

The tale of the shining princess. Tokyo, Japan Publications Trading Co. 1966. 1v.; Tokyo, Kodansha International, 1966. 1v.

Die Geschichte vom Bambussammler und dem Mädchen Kaguya. München, Langewiesche Brandt, 1968. 1v.

MATSUBARA Shin'ichi 松原新一 1940–

Criticism 評論

'A survey of literature in 1975' *Japanese Literature Today*, no.1, March, 1976. p.1–4

MATSUDA Tokiko 松田解子 1905–

Chitei no hitobito 地底の人々

「地底下的人們」 金芷等訳 上海 泥土社 1954. 390p.

Orin kuden おりん口伝

'礦坑姑娘' 張資平訳「資平譯品集」上海 現代書局 192?.

Poems 詩

'Радиоволны; Не допустим убийства, Джамилы!' Перевод А. Мамонова. *Иностранная Литература*, апрель 1960. p.76–79
'Радиотолкундар' Которгон Ж. Алыбаев. *Хиросима кектери*. Фрунзе, Кыргызстан, 1969. p.29–31

MATSUI Shōō 松居松翁 1870–1933

Ningyōshi 人形師

'Der Figurenschnitzer' Übers. von Maria Piper. *Die Schaukunst der Japaner*. Berlin, de Gruyter, 1927. p.132–138

MATSUI Tadashi 松居 直 1926–

Daiku to Oniroku だいくとおにろく

Oniroku and the carpenter. Tr. by Masako Matsuno. Englewood Cliffs, N.J. Prentice-Hall, 1963. 28p.

Pika kun ピカくん

Peeka the traffic light. N.Y. Walker, 1970. 28p.

MATSUI Tōru 松居とおる 1910–

Satoko en haar voddenrapers. Tr. Uyttendaele & Gabriel Smit. Brugge, Desclee de Brouwer, 1960. 211p.

MATSUMOTO Masao 松本正雄 1901–1976

Essay エッセイ

"松川事件"与広津先生' 蔡子民訳 「世界文学」 1964年6月 p.113–116

MATSUMOTO Seichō 松本清張 1909–

Amagi goe 天城越え

'時効' 文滌訳 「大男 3」 서울 三韓文化社 1976. p.304–342

Aru shōkanryō no massatsu ある小官僚の抹殺

'小官僚의抹殺' 文滌訳 「大男 1」 서울 三韓文化社 1976. p.178–219

Aru Kokura nikki den 或る「小倉日記」伝

'어느고꾸라日記伝' 李元壽訳 「芥川賞小説集」 서울 新丘文化社 1960. p.91–121;「깊은江」 서울 三耕社 1971. p.91–121

Atsui kūki 熱い空気

'뜨지운空気' 文滌訳 「大男 3」 서울 三韓文化社 1976. p.7–151

Bankei 晩景

'晩景' 文滌訳 「大男 8」 서울 三韓文化社 1976. p.313–360

Beirūto jōhō ベイルート情報

'베이루트情報' 文滌訳 「大男 8」 서울 三韓文化社 1976. p.399–466

Chihōshi o kau onna 地方紙を買う女

'地方紙를사는女子' 文滌訳 「大男 4」 서울 三韓文化社 1976. p.289–327

Chiisana ryokan 小さな旅館

'投資殺人' 文滌訳 「大男 8」 서울 三韓文化社 1976. p.228–258

Chi no hone 地の骨

「暗黒大学」 洪性裕訳 서울 三耕社 1968. 2冊
「빌래먹은象牙塔」 洪性裕訳 서울 三耕社 1972. 518p.

Dansen 断線

'断線' 文滌訳 「大男 7」 서울 三韓文化社 1976. p.7–135

Ekiro 駅路

'蒸発' 文滌訳 「大男 8」 서울 三韓文化社 1976. p.53–76

Fusai no kan 怖妻の棺

'懼内之棺' 徐白訳 「日本短篇譯集 3」 台北 晩蟬書店 1969. p.41–75

Futari no shinhannin 二人の真犯人

'두사람의真犯' 文滌訳 「大男 8」 서울 三韓文化社 1976. p.136–226

Gosa 誤差

'誤差' 文滌訳 「大男 2」 서울 三韓文化社 1976. p.198–228

Hakone shinjū 箱根心中

'人間密林' 文滌訳 「大男 1」 서울 三韓文化社 1976. p.156–176

Hitai to ha 額と歯

'토막' 文滌訳 「大男 5」 서울 三韓文化社 1976. p.367–412

Himo 紐

'끈' 文滌訳 「大男 1」 서울 三韓文化社 1976. p.7–133

Hossa　発作

　'強止反応'　文潔訳　「大男 7」　서울　三韓文化社　1976.
　p.137-157

Ichinen han mate　一年半待て

　'Just eighteen months'　Tr. by John Bester. *Japan Quarterly*, v.9, no.1, 1962.　p.57-73
　'一年半기다려세요'　表文台訳　「日本代表作家百人集 4」　서울　希望出版社　1966.　p.130-146;「日本短篇文学全集 5」　서울　新太陽社　1969. p.10-26
　'一事不再理'　文潔訳　「大男 4」　서울　三韓文化社　1976.
　p.378-405

Jiko　事故

　'事故'　文潔訳　「大男 4」　서울　三韓文化社　1976.
　p.7-187

Kage　影

　'숨쉬는그림자'　文潔訳　「大男 5」　서울　三韓文化社
　1976. p.322-365

Kaitaikō　拐帯行

　'逃避行'　文潔訳　「大男 2」　서울　三韓文化社　1976.
　p.230-258

Kami no kiba　紙の牙

　'종이덫'　文潔訳　「大男 7」　서울　三韓文化社　1976.
　p.408-461

Kanryū　寒流

　'寒流'　文潔訳　「大男 5」　서울　三韓文化社　1976.
　p.154-289

Kao　顔

　'얼굴'　文潔訳　「大男 5」　서울　三韓文化社　1976.
　p.414-469

Karuneadesu no funaita　カルネアデスの舟板

　'카르네아데스의舟板'　文潔訳　「大男 3」　서울　三韓出版社　1976. p.397-451

Katachi　形

　'定石法'　文潔訳　「大男 1」　서울　三韓文化社　1976.
　p.431-468

Kiken na shamen　危険な斜面

　'危険한斜面'　文潔訳　「大男 2」　서울　三韓文化社　1976.
　p.133-196

Kichiku　鬼畜

　'怪畜'　文潔訳　「大男 4」　서울　三韓文化社　1976.
　p.329-376

Kimyō na hikoku　奇妙な被告

　'The cooperative defendant' *Japanese golden dozen*, ed. by Ellery Queen. Tokyo, Tuttle, 1978. p.39-67

Koe　声

　'목소리'　文潔訳　「大男 4」　서울　三韓文化社　1976.
　p.189-260

Kōkōsei satsujin jiken　高校生殺人事件

　「高校生살인사건」　李圭植訳　서울　지소림文庫　1976.
　264p.

Kūhaku no ishō　空白の意匠

　'空白의意匠'　文潔訳　「大男 8」　서울　三韓文化社　1976.
　p.78-134

Kuroi fukuin　黒い福音

　Черное Евангелие. Перевод П. Петрова. Москва, Молодая Гвардия, 1967. 284p.
　Juedeji evanelija.　Tr. J. Baishnoras. Vilnius, Vaga, 1969. 270p.

Kusa　草

　'麻薬病棟'　文潔訳　「大男 2」　서울　三韓文化社　1976.
　p.338-473

Kyōhansha　共犯者

　「共犯者」　李英朝訳　서울　豊林出版社　1974. 338p.
　'共犯者'　文潔訳　「大男 4」　서울　三韓文化社　1976.
　p.262-287

Kyōki　凶器

　'凶器'　文潔訳　「大男 4」　서울　三韓文化社　1976.
　p.430-472

Me no kabe　眼の壁

　「눈의壁」　李敏載訳　서울　豊林出版社　1975. 372p.
　'首'　文潔訳　「大男 6」　서울　三韓文化社　1976.　p.1-451

Mokusei gō sōnan jiken　「もく星」号遭難事件

　"木星"号遇难记'　文活若訳　「世界文学」　1964年6月
　p.85-101

Nami no tō　波の塔

　「波濤의塔」　玄雲　尹甲鐘訳　서울　弘益文化社　1966.
　2冊

Nejiki　寝敷き

　'주름잡기'　文潔訳　「大男 8」　서울　三韓文化社　1976.
　p.7-51

Nigotta hi　濁った陽

　'灰色太陽'　文潔訳　「大男 3」　서울　三韓文化社　1976.
　p.153-302

Nihon no kuroi kiri　日本の黒い霧

　「日本的黒霧」　文活若訳　北京　作家出版社　1965. 1冊

Nikai　二階

　'二層의天國'　文潔訳　「大男 1」　서울　三韓文化社　1976.
　p.399-429

Nikunabe o kuu onna　肉鍋を食う女

　'人肉譚'　文潔訳　「大男 7」　서울　三韓文化社　1976.
　p.363-406

Renkan　連環

　'活字의함정'　文潔訳　「大男 9」　서울　三韓文化社　1976.
　p.1-466

Rikukō suikō　陸行水行

　'陸行水路'　文潔訳　「大男 7」　서울　三韓文化社　1976.
　p.292-361

Rōshun　老春

　'老衰期'　文潔訳　「大男 8」　서울　三韓文化社　1976.
　p.362-397

MATSUMOTO Seichō

Sakamichi no ie 坂道の家

'언덕길의집' 文湊訳 「大男 1」 서울 三韓文化社 1976. p.221–397

Satsui no dansō 殺意の断層

「殺意의断層」 李英朝訳 서울 豊林文化社 1974. 292p.

Sebirofuku no henshisha 背広服の変死者

'生의迷路' 文湊訳 「大男 2」 서울 三韓文化社 1976. p.457–475

Shiharai sugita endan 支払いすぎた縁談

'二重幸運' 文湊訳 「大男 7」 서울 三韓文化社 1976. p.159–175

Shinsō kairyū 深層海流

Подводное течение. Перевод С. Гутермана. Москва, Прогресс, 1965. 270p.
Подводное течение, на армянском языке. Перевод М. Сафарьян. Ереван, Аыастан, 1968. 340p.

Shiroi yami 白い闇

'白闇' 文湊訳 「大男 3」 서울 三韓文化社 1976. p.344–395

Shito gyōden 使徒行伝

'使徒行傳' 文湊訳 「大男 4」 서울 三韓文化社 1976. p.407–428

Shōgen 証言

'Evidence' Tr. by John Bester. *Japan Quarterly,* v.9, no.1, 1962. p.74–85

Shuzoku dōmei 種族同盟

'種族同盟' 文湊訳 「大男 8」 서울 三韓文化社 1976. p.260–311

Sōnan 遭難

'Neštěstí' Přel. I. Krouský. *Světová Literatura,* no.4, 1962. p.235–256
'遭難' 文湊訳 「大男 2」 서울 三韓文化社 1976. p.7–131

Sōsa kengai no jōken 捜査圏外の条件

'捜査圏' 文湊訳 「大男 5」 서울 三韓文化社 1976. p.291–320

Sōshitsu 喪失

'喪失' 文湊訳 「大男 1」 서울 三韓文化社 1976. p.135–154

Tazutazushi たづたづし

'愛憎의迷路' 文湊訳 「大男 2」 서울 三韓文化社 1976. p.260–301

Teigin jiken no nazo 帝銀事件の謎

"帝国銀行事件"之謎' 文浩若訳 「世界文学」 1966年 1月 p.61–93

Ten 点

'Точка' Перевод П. Смирнова. *Японская новелла.* Москва, Изд. Иност. Лит. 1961. p.133–150
'Хокат' Орусшадан аударган Нурахмет Телеупов. *Хиросима касрети.* Алма-Ата, Жазушы, 1969. p.17–34

Ten to sen 点と線

Body a prímka. Přel. Ivan Krouský. Praha, Mladá Fonta, 1964. 106p.
Spiel mit dem Fahrplan. Aus dem Japanischen von Buccie Kim und Edith Shimomura. Berlin, Volk und Welt, 1969. 192p.
Points and lines. Tr. by Makiko Yamamoto and Paul C. Blum. Tokyo, Kodansha International, 1970. 159p.
Точки и линии, на армянском языке. Перевод М. Сафарьян. Ереван, Аыастан, 1973. 151p.
Junaongelma. Kääntää Kristiina Kivivuori. Porvoo, Werner Söderström, 1973. 153p.
「點과線」 李文賢訳 서울 弘益出版社 1974. 280p.
Mäng sõiduplaaniga. Jaapani keelest tõlkinud Agu Sisask. Tallinn, Eesti Raamat, 1974. 110p.
'點과線' 姜龍俊訳 「世界推理文学全集 3」 서울 河西出版社 1974. p.309–475
'點과線' 文湊訳 「大男 5」 서울 三韓文化社 1976. p.7–152
「點與綫」 晏洲訳 香港 天地圖書 1977. 149p.

Yami ni kakeru ryōjū 闇に駆ける猟銃

'어둠을달린猟銃'文湊訳 「大男 7」 서울 三韓文化社 1976. p.177–290

Zero no shōten 零の焦点

「제로의焦点」 李圭稙訳 서울 自由舎 1961. 230p.
「零的焦点」 邱素臻訳 台北 林白出版社 1969. 306p.
「0의焦点」 李英朝訳 서울 豊林出版社 1974. 356p.
'0의焦点' 姜龍俊訳 「世界推理文学全集 3」 서울 河西出版社 1974. p.11–305
'失踪된男子' 文湊訳 「大男10」 서울 三韓文化社 1976. p.1–437

'까마귀' 文湊訳 「大男 2」 서울 三韓文化社 1976. p.303–336

MATSUMOTO Takashi 松本たかし 1906–1956

Haiku 俳句

'4 haiku' Tr. by Geoffrey Bownas and Anthony Thwaite. *The Penguin book of Japanese verse.* Harmondsworth, Penguin Books, 1964. p.172–173

MATSUMURA Eiichi 松村英一 1889–

Tanka 短歌

'Herons; Insects' voices; A toy' Tr. by Asataro Miyamori. *Masterpieces of Japanese poetry, ancient and modern.* Tokyo, Maruzen, 1936; Tokyo, Taiseido, 1956; N. Y. Greenwood Press, 1971. p.764–765

MATSUMURA Takeo 松村武雄 1883–1969

Criticism 評論

'精神分析學與文藝' 「文學週報」 第57巻71期
「文藝與性愛」 謝六逸訳 上海 開明書店 n.d. 1冊
「童話與兒童の研究」 鐘子岩訳 上海 開明書店 n.d. 1冊
「歐州的傳説」 鐘子岩訳 上海 開明書店 n.d. 1冊

「日本童話集」 許達年訳 上海 中華書局 n.d. 1冊

MATSUMURA Tatsuo 松村達雄 1911–

「당신의아기는송아지가아니다」 洪潤基訳 서울 明書苑 1973. 204p.

MATSUNAGA Shin'ichi 松永信一 1908–1970

Poems 詩

'Моей жене' Перевод Анатолия Мамонова. *Иностранная Литература*, август 1959. p.170–171; *Вкус хризантемы*. Москва, Восточная Литература, 1976. p.60
'To my wife' Tr. by Miyao Ohara. *The songs of Hiroshima*. Tokyo, Taihei Shuppansha, 1971. p.64–67

MATSUNE Tōyōjō 松根東洋城 1878–1964

Haiku 俳句

'2 haiku' Tr. by Asataro Miyamori. *Anthology of haiku, ancient and modern*. Tokyo, Maruzen, 1932. p.789–790
'The balmy spring day' Tr. by Asataro Miyamori. *Haiku poems, ancient and modern*. Tokyo, Maruzen, 1940. p.344
'2 haiku' Tr. by V. H. Viglielmo. *Japanese literature in the Meiji era*. Tokyo, Obunsha, 1955. p.444
'6 haiku' *A history of haiku v.2*, by R. H. Blyth. Tokyo, Hokuseido, 1964. p.138–140
'The balmy spring day; At sunset' Tr. by Kenneth Yasuda. *A pepper-pod*. Tokyo, Tuttle, 1976. p.92

MATSUNO Masako 松野正子

Fushigi na takenoko ふしぎなたけのこ

Taro and the bamboo shoot. Adapted by Alice Low. N. Y. Pantheon Books, 1964. 1v.; N. Y. Pinwheel Book, 1974. 1v.
Taro og det vidunderlige bambusskud. Tr. from the English by Viggo Vorgaard-Jepsen. København, Høst, 1967. 28p.

MATSUOKA Kyōko 松岡享子 1935–

Kanta sama no ibiki かん太さまのいびき

'Jak Kanta chrápal' Přel. Ivan Krouský a Z. K. Slabý. *Modré vánoce*. Parha, Albatros, 1975.

Kushami kushami ten no megumi くしゃみくしゃみ天のめぐみ

'Kýchání je dar boží' Přel. Ivan Krouský a Z. K. Slabý. *Modré vánoce*. Praha, Albatros, 1975.

MATSUOKA Yōko 松岡洋子 1916–

「귀리부인」 權東淑訳 서울 電波科学社 1973. 250p.

MATSUSE Seisei 松瀬青々 1869–1937

Haiku 俳句

'5 haiku' Tr. by Asataro Miyamori. *Anthology of haiku, ancient and modern*. Tokyo, Maruzen, 1932. p.714–717
'The uguisu; The autumn moon; The autumn wind; The autumn sky' Tr. by Asataro Miyamori. *Haiku poems, ancient and modern*. Tokyo, Maruzen, 1940. p.312–314
'1 haiku' Tr. by R. H. Blyth. *Haiku v.4*. Tokyo, Hokuseido, 1952. p.222
'2 haiku' Tr. by V. H. Viglielmo. *Japanese literature in the Meiji era*. Tokyo, Obunsha, 1955. p.432
'1 haiku' Übers. von Gerolf Coudenhove. *Japanische Jahreszeiten*. Zürich, Manesse Verlag, 1963. p.333
'5 haiku' *A history of haiku v.2*, by R. H. Blyth. Tokyo, Hokuseido, 1964. p.115–116
'1 haiku' Til norsk ved Paal-Helge Haugen. *Blad frå ein austleg hage*. Oslo, Det Norske Samlaget, 1965. p.83

MATSUSHIMA Keisui 松島渓水

Haiku 俳句

'The harvest moon' Tr. by Asataro Miyamori. *Anthology of haiku, ancient and modern*. Tokyo, Maruzen, 1932. p.831

MATSUTANI Miyoko 松谷みよ子 1926–

Chiisai Momochan ちいさいももちゃん

'Momočan a strašidla' Přel. Ivan Krouský a Z. K. Slabý. *Modré vánoce*. Parha, Albatros, 1975.

Hanasaka jijii はなさかじじい

How the withered trees blossomed. Philadelphia, Lippincott, 1971. 40p.

Kintarō きんたろう

「桃太郎跟金太郎」 洪炎秋訳 台北 國語日報出版部 1973. 1冊

Kitsune no yomeiri きつねのよめいり

The fox wedding. Tr. by Masako Matsuno. Englewood Cliffs, Prentice-Hall, 1963. 28p.; London, Encyclopaedia Britannica, 1963. 1v.
'Dračí nevěsta' Přel. I. Krouský a Z. K. Slabý. *Zlatý maj*, v.18, no.4, 1974. p.282–284

Koinu no shiro 小犬のしろ

Щенок Сиро, на украинском языке. Перевод И. Дзюб. Киев, Вешерка, 1973. 32p.

MATSUTANI Miyoko

Mokichi no neko　茂吉のねこ

'Mokiči a kočka' Přel. Ivan Krouský a Z. K. Slabý. *Modré vánoce.* Praha, Albatros, 1975.

Momotarō　ももたろう

「桃太郎跟金太郎」　洪炎秋訳　台北　國語日報出版部　1973. 1冊

Tatsunoko Tarō　龍の子太郎

Taro the dragon boy. Tr. by Donald Boone. Tokyo, Kodansha International, 1967. 127p.
Taro, das Drachenkind. Übers. vom Engl. Inge M. Artl. Freiburg, Alsatia Verlag, 1968. 127p.
Приключения Таро в стране гор. Перевод Г. Ронской. Москва, Дет. Лит. 1970. 94p.
Приключения Таро в стране гор. Перевод М. Жяпаридзе. Тбилиси, Накадули, 1973. 78p.
Приключения Таро в стране гор, на азербайжанском языке. Перевод А. Ибрагимов. Баку, Гянжилик, 1973. 94p.
Приключения Таро в стране гор, на мордавском языке. Перевод Е. Керекелуватамас. Кишинев, Румина, 1973. 92p.

Ten ni nobotta Gengorō　てんにのぼったげんごろう

The little man and his drum. London, Hamlyn, 1969. 1v.
Gengoroh and the thunder god. N. Y. Parents' Magazine Press, 1970. 1v.

'Jak se z bubínku stala hvězda' Přel. Ivan Krouský a Z. K. Slabý. *Modré vánoce.* Praha, Albatros, 1975.

Tsuru no ongaeshi　つるのおんがえし

The crane maiden. English version by Alvin Tresselt. N. Y. Parents' Magazine Press, 1968. 32p.

Urashima Tarō　うらしまたろう

The fisherman under the sea. N. Y. Parents' Magazine Press, 1969. 1v.

Yamanba no nishiki　やまんばのにしき

Witch's magic cloth. Tr. by Alvin Tresselt. N. Y. Parents' Magazine Press, 1969. 1v.

MATSUURA Masao　まつうら・まさお　1931–

Poems　詩

'Билдинги' Перевод Анатолия Мамонова. *Бкус хризантемы.* Москва, Восточная Литература, 1976. p.62

MAYAMA Miho　真山美保　1922–

Aa bara no hana wa izuko ni saku　ああ薔薇の花は何処に咲く

「薔薇何処开」　陳北鷗訳　北京　中国戯劇　1958. 88p.

Ichikawa Umagorō ichiza tenmatsuki　市川馬五郎一座顛末記

'馬五郎劇団'　陳北鷗　梁夢廻訳　「劇本」　1962年4月号　p.53–96

MAYUMURA Taku　眉村 卓　1934–

'Приказ о прекращения работ' Перевод З. Рахима. *Продается Япония.* Москва, Мир, 1969. p.80–99

MEIJI Tennō　明治天皇　1852–1912

Tanka　短歌

'10 tanka' Tr. by Suematsu, Arthur Lloyd, Wadagaki, and Yone Noguchi. *Eigo Seinen,* v.13, no.14, 1905. p.277; v.13, no.15, 1905. p.289–290
Imperial songs. Tr. by Arthur Lloyd. Tokyo, Kinkodo, 1905. 159p.
'The heart of the Mikado, 16 poems' Tr. by Kencho Suematsu. *Nineteenth Century and After,* v.57, 1905. p.566–572
'Poems by Emperor Meiji and his Empress' Tr. by Kenzo Wadagaki. *Stray Leaves.* Tokyo, 1908.
'La poésie de l'Empereur' Tr. par Michel Revon. *Anthologie de la littérature japonaise.* Paris, Delagrave, 1910. p.450
'4 tanka' *The master singers of Japan,* by Clara A. Walsh. London, John Murray, 1910. p.116–117
'Eine Auswahl von Gedichten des Kaisers von Japan' Übers. von Rudolf Lange. *Mitteilungen des Seminars für orientalische Sprachen an der Königl. Friedrich Wilhelm-Universität,* Bd.13, Teil 1, 1910. p.306–338
'Imperial songs of Japan' Tr. by Arthur Lloyd. *Open Court,* v.25, 1911. p.532–539, 747–752
'His Majesty the late Emperor as a poet' Tr. by John Thomas Ingram Bryan. *Japan Magazine,* v.3, 1912. p.289–296
A voice out of the serene. Tr. by Hidesaburo Saito. Tokyo, 1912. 136p.
Petals. Tr. by Medora Adam. Tokyo, Japan Gazette, 1913. 48p.
Imperial Japanese poems of the Meiji era. Tr. by Frank Alanson Lombard. Tokyo, Keiseisha Shoten, 1915. 1v.
'Odes by the Emperor Meiji' Tr. by Kenzo Wadagaki. *Gleanings from Japanese literature.* Tokyo, Nampokusha, 1919. p.2–12
'8 tanka' *Japanese poetry, an historical essay,* by Curtis Hidden Page. Boston, Houghton Mifflin, 1923; Folcroft, Folcroft Library, 1976. p.162, 164, 165, 166
'Imperial song' Tr. by Kanesumi Suematsu. *Nineteenth Century,* no.105, 1929. p.566–572
'40 tanka' Tr. by Asataro Miyamori. *Masterpieces of Japanese poetry, ancient and modern.* Tokyo, Maruzen, 1936; Tokyo, Taiseido, 1956; N. Y. Greenwood Press, 1971. p.535–573
'Kaiser Meiji als Dichter' Übers. von Hermann Heuvers. *Monumenta Nipponica,* v.2, 1939. p.1–16
Kaiserliche Verse von Meiji Tenno. Übers. von Waldemar Oehlke. Berlin, Herbig, 1940. 47p.
'Kaiserliche Verse' Übers. von Waldemar Oehlke. *Japan: Tradition und Gegenwart.* Stuttgart, Deutsche Volksbücher, 1942. p.117–118
Ausgewählte Gedichte von Meiji Tenno. Übers. von Reikichi Kita. Tokyo, Tonan Shobo, 1944. 145p.

'1 tanka' Tr. par Roger Bersihand. *La littérature japonaise*. Paris, Presses Universitaires de France, 1956. p.105
'1 tanka' Tr. by H. H. Honda. *The Reeds*, v.3, 1957. p.23
'Vis' *Kínai és Japán koltëk*. Budapest, Szepiro-dalmi, 1957. p.204
'2 tankas' Übers. von Manfred Hausmann. *Lyrik der Welt*. Berlin, Safari Verlag, 1960. p.145–147
'Tanka' Tercüme etmek L. Sami Akalin. *Japon şiiri*. İstanbul, Varlik Yayinevi, 1962. p.222
'19 tanka' Übers. von Gerolf Coudenhove. *Japanische Jahreszeiten*. Zürich, Manesse Verlag, 1963.
Waka poetry of the Emperor Meiji and Empress Shoken. Tokyo, Meiji Jingu, 1964. 5p.
'Tanka' Tr. by Geoffrey Bownas and Anthony Thwaite. *The Penguin book of Japanese verse*. Harmondsworth, Penguin Books, 1964. p.157
'1 tanka' Tr. from the French by Unity Evans. *Japanese literature*. N. Y. Walker, 1965. p.89
'17 haiku' Übers. von Paul Adler. *Japanische Literatur*. Frankfurt am Main, Frankfurter Verlags Anstalt, n.d. p.408–411

MICHIKO Hi 美智子妃 1934–

Poems 詩

'1 tanka' Tr. by Shigeshi Nishimura. *The Current of the World*, v.38, no.3, 1961. p.48
'The silk tree's lullaby' Tr. by Marie Philomene. *Poetry Nippon*, no.37 & 38, 1977. p.19

MIDORIKAWA Eiko 緑川英子 1912–

Koneko no shi 小猫の死

'小猫的死' 「日本短篇小説選」 香港 藝美圖書公司 1959. p.83–87

MIHARA Makoto 三原 誠

Tatakai たたかい

'爭戰' 劉慕沙訳 「日本現代小説選 1」 台北 聯經出版事業公司 1976. p.221–254

MIKI Eiji 三木英治

Poems 詩

'22 層의 回転라운지에서 바라본黃昏에대한会話' 「現代詩学」 第84巻3号 1976. p.76–78

MIKI Kiyoshi 三木 清 1897–1945

Jinseiron nōto 人生論ノート

'利己主義에대하여 ; 娛楽에대하여 ; 旅行에대하여' 鄭成煥 金泳杓訳 「世界에세이文学全集 8」 서울 東西出版社 1974. p.81–100 ; 「世界随筆文学全集 8」 서울 世進出版社 1976. p.81–100
「人生論ノート」 張炅龍訳 서울 文芸出版社 1975. 185p.

Criticism 評論

'藝術價值與政治價值哲學的考察' 馮憲章訳 「拓荒者」 第1巻3期 1930. p.1043–1060
'사랑의情念에대하여 ; 教養에대하여 ; 德에대하여' 鄭成煥 金泳杓訳 「世界에세이文学全集 8」 서울 東西出版社 1974. p.42–79 ; 「世界随筆文学全集 8」 서울 世進出版社 1976. p.42–79

MIKI Rofū 三木露風 1889–1964

Poems 詩

'Снежна ношь' Преведе Никола Джеров. *Песните на Ямато*. София, Корали, 1937. p.81
'La chanson du jour blanc est morte; Le chant de la pluie; Amour perdu; Mes doigts; Les souvenirs; La neige nocturne; D'une fenêtre de la maison sur la colline; Chant nocturne; La neige et la lune; Le soupir' Tr. par Kuni Matsuo et Steinilber-Oberlin. *Anthologie des poètes japonais contemporains*. Paris, Mercure de France, 1939. p.132–140
'From winter poems; Conversation with Anko' *An anthology of modern Japanese poetry*, ed. and tr. by Ichiro Kono and Rikutaro Fukuda. Tokyo, Kenkyusha, 1957. p.80–81
'Native place; After the kiss; Bell across the snow; Song of departing May' *The poetry of living Japan*, by Takamichi Ninomiya and D. J. Enright. London, John Murray, 1957. p.33–36
'Après le baiser; Cloche à travers la neige' *La poésie japonaise*, par Karl Petit. Paris, Seghers, 1959. p.210–211
'Home; After the kiss' Tr. by Geoffrey Bownas and Anthony Thwaite. *The Penguin book of Japanese verse*. Harmondsworth, Penguin Books, 1964. p.187
'Boschetto; Segreto; La canzone della pioggia; Lamento; Un filare di alberi nel pomeriggio; Fede e prigione' Tr. di R. Beviglia. *Antologia della letteratura coreana e giapponese*. Milano, Fratelli Fabbri, 1969. p.275–277
'Immagne ; Boschetto; Verso la regione delle tenebre; La casa sulla riva; Segreto; La canzone della pioggia; La barca; Lamento; Un filare di alberi nel pomeriggio; La fiamma del gas; Tempo di singhiozzi; Fede e prigione' *Il simbolismo nella poesia giapponese dell'era Meiji*, di Rosaria Beviglia. Roma, Istituto Italiano per il Medio ed Estremo Oriente, 1971. p.151–159, 161
'흘러가는배 ; 가고있는오월의시 ; 가을 ; 흐느껴울고있다 ; 구름' 「永遠한世界名詩全集 2」 黃錦燦編 서울 翰林出版社 1969. p.61, 62, 96, 201, 236 ; 「永遠한世界名詩全集 5」 黃錦燦編 서울 翰林出版社 1973. p.61, 62, 96, 201, 236
'Ave Maria; Home-sailing' Tr. by Hideo Yamaguchi. *Kobe Jogakuin Daigaku Ronshu*, v.18, no.3, 1972. p.31–33
'입맞춤뒤에' 金禧宝訳 「世界名詩選」 서울 一麦社 1974. p.197
'După sărut; Clopot străbătind nămeţii; Iubirea pierdută' Traducerea Dan Constantinescu. *Din lirica japoneză*. Bucureşti, Editura Univers, n.d. p.161–162

MIKI Taku 三木 卓 1935–

Hiwa 鶸

'검은방울새' 金后蘭訳 「70年代芥川賞小説集」 서울 玄岩社 1976. p.9–51; 「新鋭世界文学選集20世紀 9」 서울 玄岩社 1977. p.9–53

Poems 詩

'Idee bambine' *La protesta poetica del Giappone*, a cura di Dacia Maraini e Michiko Nojiri. Roma, Officina Edizioni, 1968. p. 147–149
'The howling man; Escape from the city; Adolescent thought; Managed days; Genealogy; Calculation' Tr. by Whang Insu. *The poetry of postwar Japan*. Iowa City, Univ. of Iowa Press, 1975. p.214–221

MINAKAMI Tsutomu 水上 勉 1919–

Nishijin no chō 西陣の蝶

'풀밭의나비처럼' 金東史訳 「日本代表作家百人集 5」 서울 希望出版社 1966 p.10–38; 「日本短篇文学全集 5」 서울 新太陽社 1969. p.306–334

Shiroi kusari 白いくさり

'白色鉄索' 陳濤訳 「世界文学」 1964年6月 p.66–84
'白色鐵索' 「白色鐵索」 香港 上海書局 1970. p.1–34

Umi no koto 湖の琴

「湖畔琴絃」 荷書訳 台北 蘭開書局 1968. 2冊

Essay エッセイ

'Oyashirazu' *This is Japan*, v.14, 1967. p.218–219

'Záliv tajemných světel' Přel. M. Jelinková. *Nový Orient*, 1968, no.7, 8, 9, 10; 1969. no.1
'黃金牙的秘密' 文良出版社訳 「推理小説 日本偵探名著」 台南 文良出版社 1969. p.137–210

MINAMI Kiichi 南 喜一 1893–1967

Gama no seidan ガマの聖談

「두꺼비의聖談」 李端宗訳 서울 栄信文化社 1969. 284p.

MINAMIKAWA Jun 南川 潤 1913–1955

Haru no furyo 春の俘虜

'Vom Frühling gefangen' Übers. von Kurt Meissner. *Der Tanzfächer*, von K. Meissner. Tokyo, 1943. p.69–87

MINATONO Kiyoko 港野喜代子 1913–

Poems 詩

'母親的發言' 適夷訳 「譯文」 1955年8月 p.66–68
'Пейзаж' Перевод Анатолия Мамонова. *Вкус*

хризантемы. Москва, Восточная Литература, 1976. p.67

MISHIMA Shōdō 三島章道 1897–1965

Kaigan de kiita fue 海岸できいた笛

'Kaigan de kiita fue' Tr. by Yaichiro Isobe. *Chugai Eigo*, Sept. 1922.

MISHIMA Sōsen 三島霜川 1876–1934

Kaibōshitsu 解剖室

'The dissecting-room' Tr. by Asataro Miyamori. *Representative tales of Japan*. Tokyo, Sanko Shoten, 1917. p.333–363

MISHIMA Yukio 三島由紀夫 1925–1970

Ai no kawaki 愛の渇き

Thirst for love. Tr. by Alfred H. Marks. N. Y. Knopf, 1969; London, Secker and Warburg, 1969; Tokyo, Tuttle, 1970. 200p.; N. Y. Berkley Pub. 1970. 178p.
「愛的飢渇」 邱素臻訳 台北 水牛出版社 1970. 200p.
「愛的飢渇」 金淏若訳 台北 志文出版社 1971. 225p.; 1974. 218p.

Akatsuki no tera 暁の寺

The temple of dawn. Tr. by E. Dale Saunders and Cecilia Segawa Seigle. N. Y. Knopf, 1973. 334p.; London, Secker and Warburg, 1974; Tokyo, Tuttle, 1974; N. Y. Pocket Books, 1974. 334p.

Akinai bito 商ひ人

'生意' 余阿勲訳 「三島由紀夫短編傑作選」 彰化 現代潮出版社 1970. p.51–62

Ame no naka no funsui 雨のなかの噴水

'빗속의噴水' 具滋雲訳 「現代日本代表文学全集 6」 서울 平和出版社 1973. p.285–290

Asa no jun'ai 朝の純愛

'Love in the morning' Tr. by Leon Zolbrod. *The East*, v.2, no.2, 1965. p.32–36

Bishin 美神

'美神' 奔煬訳 「三島由紀夫短篇傑作選」 彰化 現代潮出版社 1970. p.88–95

Bitoku no yoromeki 美徳のよろめき

'비틀거리는美徳' 洪性裕訳 「日本文学選集 1」 서울 青雲閣 1964. p.321–433; 서울 知文閣 1966. p.321–433
'美徳的動揺' 劉慕沙訳 台北 巨人出版社 1971. 164p.
'비틀거리는美徳' 朴尚均訳 「日本文学大全集 6」 서울 東西文化院 1975. p.86–169

Budō pan 葡萄パン

'Rosinenbrot' Übers. von Margarete Donath. *Japan erzählt*. Hamburg, Fischer, 1969. p.112–124
'葡萄빵' 具滋雲訳 「現代日本代表文学全集 6」 서울 平和出版社 1973. p.270–283

Fudōtoku kyōiku kōza 不道徳教育講座

「남에페를끼치고죽어라」洪二培訳 서울 徽文出版社
1970. 1冊
「不道徳教育講座」李時哲訳 서울 世紀出版社 1971.
164p.

Fukushū 復讐

'Revenge' Tr. by Grace Suzuki. *Ukiyo*. Tokyo,
Phoenix Books, 1954. p.3–10; *Ukiyo*, ed. by
J. Gluck. N. Y. Vanguard Press, 1963.
p.43–47; London, Universal Library, 1964.
p.43–47
'復仇' 傅寶齡訳 「勲章」台北 文壇社 1960. p.176–
188
'復仇' 余阿勲訳 「三島由紀夫短篇傑作選」彰化 現代潮
出版社 1970. p.31–42

Fune no aisatsu 船の挨拶

'Pozdrav lodi' Přel. M. Novák. *Světová Literatura*, no.4, 1962. p.190–193

Gogo no eikō 午後の曳航

The sailor who fell from grace with the sea. Tr. by
John Nathan. N. Y. Knopf, 1965. 181p.;
London, Secker and Warburg, 1966. 150p.;
Tokyo, Tuttle, 1967; Harmondsworth, Pen-
guin Books, 1970. 143p.; N. Y. Berkley Pub.
1971. 1v.
Sjømannen som falt i undde hos havet. Oversette
Knut Johansen. Oslo, Gyldendal Norsk For-
lag, 1966. 159p.
Il sapore della gloria. Tr. di Mario Teti. Milano,
Mondadori, 1967. 183p.
Sjömannen som föll i onåd hos havet. Översätta B.
Edlund och M. Edlund. Stockholm, Bonniers,
1967. 177p.
Le marin rejeté par la mer. Tr. par Gaston Re-
nondeau. Paris, Gallimard, 1968. 225p.;
Lausanne, La Guilde du Livre, 1977. 229p.
Sømanden der padrog sig hařjets vrede. Oversaette
Ralph Oppenheim. København, Gyldendal,
1968. 151p.
Der Seemann, der die See verriet. Übers. von
Sachiko Yatsushiro. Reinbek, Rowohlt,
1970. 191p.
Een zeeman door de zee verstoten. Oversetting
door Eugen Tedeau. Amsterdam, Meulen-
hoff, 1969. 160p.
Kunnia on katkera juoma. Kääntää Eeva-Liisa
Manner. Helsinki, Otava, 1971. 153p.
Mornar koji je izneverio more. Tr. Andreja Gros-
berger. Novi Sad, Matica Srpska, 1971. 180p.
'Na uwięzi' Przeł. Ariadna Demkowska-Boh-
dziewicz. *Na uwięzi, Ballada o miłości.* Wars-
zawa, Państwowy Instytut Wydawniczy, 1972.
Denizi yitiren denizci. Türkçesi Seçkin Selvi.
İstanbul, Hilâl Matbaacilik Koll, 1973. 158p.

Hagakure nyūmon 葉隠入門

On Hagakure. Tr. by Kathryn Sparling. N. Y.
Basic Books, 1977. 166p.; London, Souvenir
Press, 1977. 166p.

Haru no yuki 春の雪

「春雪」余阿勲訳 台北 青年出版社 1969. 365p.; 台
北 星光出版社 1974. 356p.
Spring snow. Tr. by Michael Gallagher. N. Y.
Knopf, 1971. 392p.; London, Secker and Warburg, 1973. 392p.; Tokyo, Tuttle, 1972.
389p.; N. Y. Pocket Books, 1973. 376p.

Nieve de primavera. Tr. de Domingo Manfredi.
Barcelona, L. de Caralt, 1974. 381p.

Hashi zukushi 橋づくし

'The seven bridges' Tr. by Donald Keene. *Death
in midsummer, and other stories.* N. Y. New
Directions, 1966. p.76–92; London, Secker
and Warburg, 1967. p.101–120; Harmondsworth, Penguin Books, 1971.
'踏橋' 閔丙山訳 「日本代表作家百人選 5」서울 希望出
版社 1966. p.176–188; 「日本短篇文学全集 6」서
울 新太陽社 1969. p.88–100; 「世界代表短篇文
学全集 21」서울 正韓出版社 1976. p.327–346
'橋愿' 劉慕沙訳 「仲夏之死」台北 皇冠出版社 1970.
p.57–79
'Die sieben Brücken' Aus dem Amerikanischen
übersetzt von Ulla Hengst. *Yukio Mishima,
Gesammelte Erzählungen.* Reinbek, Rowohlt,
1971. p.83–98
'I sette ponti' Tr. di Marco Amante. *Morte di
mezza estate.* Milano, Longanesi, 1971.
'다리돌이' 韓栄珣訳 「世界短篇文学全集 9」서울 三珍
社 1971. p.354–367; 「世界代表短編文学全集 9」
서울 三熙社 1976. p.354–367; 「世界短篇文学全
集 9」서울 新韓出版社 1976. p.220–246

Honba 奔馬

Runaway horses. Tr. by Michael Gallagher. N. Y.
Knopf, 1973. 421p.; Tokyo, Tuttle, 1973;
London, Secker and Warburg, 1973. 421p.;
N. Y. Pocket Books, 1975. 1v.

Hyakuman'en senbei 百万円煎餅

'Three million yen' Tr. by Edward Seidensticker.
Japan Quarterly, v.9, no.2, 1962. p.190–200;
Death in midsummer, and other stories. N. Y.
New Directions, 1966. p.30–42; London,
Secker and Warburg, 1967. p.45–60; Har-
mondsworth, Penguin Books, 1971; *Asian
P.E.N. anthology*, ed. by F. S. Jose. N. Y.
Taplinger, 1966. p.58–67
'Drei Millionen Yen' Aus dem Amerikanischen
übersetzt von Ulla Hengst. *Yukio Mishima,
Gesammelte Erzählungen.* Reinbek, Rowohlt,
1971. p.37–49
'Tre milioni di yen' Tr. di Marco Amante. *Morte
di mezza estate.* Milano, Longanesi, 1971.

Junkyō 殉教

'殉教' 金深温訳 「日本研究」第19巻12号 1974. p.78–
87

Kaibutsu 怪物

'The monster' Tr. by David O. Mills. *Occasional
Papers* (Univ. of Michigan, Center for Japanese Studies), no.11, 1969. p.198–211

Kajitsu 果実

'果實' 余阿勲訳 「純文學」(香港版) 第11巻1期 1972.
p.60–66

Kamen no kokuhaku 仮面の告白

'Omi' Tr. by Meredith Weatherby. *Modern
Japanese literature*, ed. by Donald Keene.
N. Y. Grove Press, 1956; Tokyo, Tuttle,
1957. p.429–438
Confessions of a mask. Tr. by Meredith Weather-
by. N. Y. New Directions, 1958. 255p.;
London, Secker and Warburg, 1960. 255p.;
London, World Distributors, 1965. 1v.;

MISHIMA Yukio

London, Sphere Books, 1967. 192p.; Tokyo, Tuttle, 1970. 255p.; London, Panther, 1972. 206p.

Geständnis einer Maske. Übers. von Helmut Hilzheimer. Reinbek, Rowohlt, 1964. 151p.

Bir maskenin itiraflari. Almancasindan çeviren Zeyyat Selimoğlu. İstanbul, Hüsnü Tabiat Matbaasi, 1966. 207p.

Bekentenissen van een gemaskerde. Vertaling Jef Last. Amsterdam, Bezige Bij, 1967. 221p.

Confessioni di una maschera. Tr. di Ufficio Grafieo Feltrinelli e Marcella Bonsanti. Milano, Feltrinelli, 1969. 219p.

'假面的告白' 張良澤訳 「假面的告白」 台北 晨鐘出版社 1970. p.1–175

'仮面의告白' 申東漢訳 「藝術界」 第2巻4号 1970.

Confessions d'un masque. Tr. par Renée Villoteau. Paris, Gallimard, 1971. 250p.

Ken 剣

'剣' 具滋雲訳 「現代日本代表文学全集 6」 서울 平和出版社 1973. p.227–268

Kindai nōgaku shū 近代能楽集

'Noh-Spiele' *Oriens Extremus*, Band 3, 1956.

'Hanjo' Tr. by Donald Keene. *Encounter*, v.8, no.1, 1957. p.45–51

'A modern noh play: Sotoba komachi' Tr. by Donald Keene. *Virginia Quarterly Review*, Spring 1957.

Five modern noh plays. Tr. by Donald Keene. N. Y. Knopf, 1957. 198p.; London, Secker and Warburg, 1957; Tokyo, Tuttle, 1957. 198p.; N. Y. Vintage Books, 1973. 1v.

'El tambor de damasco' Tr. por Kazuya Sakai. *Sur*, no. 249, Nov.-Dec. 1957. p.101–118

Fünf moderne Nô-Spiele. Übers. von Gerda von Uslar. Reinbek, Rowohlt, 1958. 166p.

La mujer del abanico: seis piezas de teatro Noh moderne. Tr. de Kazuya Sakai. Buenos Aires, La Mandragora, 1959. 135p.

'Hanjo' Tr. par Gaston Renondeau. *France-Asie*, Nouvelle série, v.17, no.170, 1961. p.2781–2794

Sechs moderne Nô-Spiele. Übers. von Gerda von Uslar. Reinbek, Rowohlt, 1962. 141p.

Fem moderna no-spel. Översättning från engelskan av Erik Wahlund. Stockholm, Bonniers, 1963. 153p.

Fem moderne no-spil. Oversaette Asta Hoff-Jøegensen. København, Gyldendal, 1964. 132p.

'Arc a tükörben' Ford. Söveny Aladár. *Nagyvilág*, no.6, 1964. p.1011–1021

Vijf moderne noh-spelen. Vertaald door Jef Last. Amsterdam, Bezige Bij, 1966. 167p.

'Dojoji' Tr. by Donald Keene. *Death in midsummer, and other stories.* N. Y. New Directions, 1966. p.119–138; London, Secker and Warburg, 1967. p.152–172; Harmondsworth, Penguin Books, 1971.

Hanjo. Ford. Radish Juditt. Budapest, 1966. 1v.

'A játszma vége' Ford. Gergely Erzsébet. *Modern one-act plays v.2*, ed. by Osztovics Levente. Budapest, Európa, 1969. p.75–91

Cinq nôs modernes. Tr. par Georges Bonmarchand. Paris, Gallimard, 1970. 168p.

'Dojoji' Tr. di Marco Amante. *Morte di mezza estate.* Milano, Longanesi, 1971.

Seis piezas Nô. Tr. por Vicente Ribera Cueto. Barcelona, Seix y Barral, 1973. 165p.

'Pani Aoi' Przeł. Henryk Lipszyc. *Dialog*, no.9, 1974. p.38–45

Kinjiki 禁色

Forbidden colors. Tr. by Alfred H. Marks. N. Y. Knopf, 1968. 403p; London, Secker and Warburg, 1968; Tokyo, Tuttle, 1969. 403p.; N. Y. Avon Books, 1970. 408p.; Harmondsworth, Penguin Books, 1971. 429p.

Kinkakuji 金閣寺

The temple of the golden pavilion. Tr. by Ivan Morris. N. Y. Knopf, 1959. 262p.; London, Secker and Warburg, 1959; Tokyo, Tuttle, 1959. 262p.; N. Y. Avon Books, 1959. 272p.; N. Y. Berkley Pub. 1971. 285p.

Le pavillon d'or. Tr. par Marc Mécréant. Paris, Gallimard, 1961. 265p.

Kultainen temppeli. Kääntää Sirppa Kauppinen. Helsinki, Otava, 1961. 265p.

'Il racconto di Uiko (da Il padiglione d'oro)' Tr. di Romano Vulpitta. *Il Giappone*, anno 1, 1961. p.42–46

Der Tempelbrand. Übers. von Walter Donat. München, List, 1961. 297p.

Den gyllene paviljongens tempel. Övers. från engelskan av Torsten Blomkvist. Stockholm, Bonniers, 1962. 235p.

El pabellón de oro. Tr. de Juan Marsé. Barcelona, Seix y Barral, 1963. 244p.

Il padiglione d'oro. Tr. di Mario Teti. Milano, Feltrinelli, 1962. 250p.; Milano, Garzanti, 1971. 247p.

Den gylne paviljongs tempel. Oversette Hans Braarvig. Oslo, Gyldendal, 1963. 203p.

Det gyldne tempel Oversaette Ida Elisabeth Hammerich. København, Gyldendal, 1965. 252p.

Het gouden paviljoen. Vertaald door C. Ouwehand. Amsterdam, Meulenhoff, 1966. 233p.

'金閣寺' 辛東門訳 「現代世界文学全集 12」 서울 新丘文化社 1968. p.9–175

'Il padiglione d'oro' Tr. di R. Vulpitta. *Antologia della letteratura coreana e giapponese.* Milano, Fratelli Fabbri, 1969. p.333–339

'The temple of the golden pavilion' Tr. by Ivan Morris. *The Mentor book of modern Asian literature*, ed. by D. B. Shimer. N. Y. New American Library, 1969. p.297–320

「金閣寺」 鐘肇政 張良澤訳 台北 晩蟬書店 1969. 238p.; 台北 大地出版社 1976. 246p.

'金閣寺' 楊明文訳「오늘의世界文学 10」 서울 民衆書館 1969. p.141–326

「金閣寺」 陳孟鴻訳 台北 志文出版社 1970. 240p.

'金閣寺' 李東柱訳 「世界의文学大全集 8」 서울 同和出版公社 1970. p.353–511

「金閣寺」 李東柱訳 서울 同和出版公社 1972. 308p.

「金閣寺」 郭宇鍾訳 서울 高麗文化社 1973. 320p.

'金閣寺' 朴敬勛訳 「日本文学大全集 6」 서울 東西文化院 1975. p.286–433

「悲戀의金閣寺」 郭宇鍾訳 서울 集賢閣 1975. 320p.

'金閣寺' 金永壽訳 「金閣寺外」 서울 主婦生活社 1976. p.11–159

'金閣寺' 金鎮郁訳 「新選世界文学全集 19」 서울 三珍社 1976. p.175–337

Kōdōgaku nyūmon 行動学入門

'Yang-ming thought as revolutionary philosophy' Tr. by Harris I. Martin. *Japan Interpreter*, v.7, no.1, 1971. p.80–87

'行動学入門' 権五雄訳 「行動과죽음의美学」 서울 人文出版社 1971. p.15–91

Kujaku 孔雀

'The peacock' Tr. by David O. Mills. *Occasional Papers* (Univ. of Michigan, Center for Japanese Studies) no.11, 1969. p.213–225
'孔雀' 鐘肇政訳 「戦後日本短篇小説選」 台北 商務印書館 1968. p.55–75

Mahōbin 魔法瓶

'Thermos bottles' Tr. by Edward Seidensticker. *Japan Quarterly*, v.9, no.2, 1962. p.201–214; *Death in midsummer, and other stories*. N. Y. New Directions, 1966. p.43–58; London, Secker and Warburg, 1967. p.61–80; Harmondsworth, Penguin Books, 1971.
'暖水瓶' 劉慕沙訳 「三島由紀夫短篇傑作集」 彰化 現代潮出版社 1970. p.63–87; 「仲夏之死」 台北 皇冠出版社 1970. p.89–113
'Thermosflaschen' Aus dem Amerikanischen übersetzt von Ulla Hengst. *Yukio Mishima, Gesammelte Erzählungen*. Reinbek, Rowohlt, 1971. p.50–66
'La paura dei thermos' Tr. di Marco Amante. *Morte di mezza estate*. Milano, Longanesi, 1971.

Manatsu no shi 真夏の死

'Death in midsummer' Tr. by Edward G. Seidensticker. *Japan Quarterly*, v.4, no.3, 1956. p.315–340; *Modern Japanese short stories*. Tokyo, Japan Publications Trading Co. 1960. p.201–235; Rev. ed. Tokyo, Japan Publications Trading Co. 1970. p.160–187; *Death in midsummer, and other stories*. N. Y. New Directions, 1966. p.1–29; London, Secker and Warburg, 1967. p.9–44; Harmondsworth, Penguin Books, 1971.
'Tod im Hochsommer' Übers. von Tatsuji Iwabuchi. *Eine Glocke in Fukagawa*. Tübingen, Erdmann, 1969. p.313–358
'한여름의죽음' 楊明文訳 「오늘의世界文学 10」 서울 民衆書館 1969. p.327–369
Tod im Hochsommer. Übers. von Sachiko Yatsushiro. Reinbek, Rowohlt, 1970. 1v.
'仲夏之死' 劉慕沙訳 「仲夏之死」 台北 皇冠出版社 1970. p.114–171
'Morte di mezza estate' Tr. di Marco Amante. *Morte di mezza estate*. Milano, Longanesi, 1971.
'Tod im Hochsommer' Aus dem Amerikanischen von Ulla Hengst. *Yukio Mishima, Gesammelte Erzählungen*. Reinbek, Rowohlt, 1971. p. 7–36
'仲夏之死' 江上訳 「日本名家小説選」 高雄 大舞台書苑 1976. p.147–202

Nagasugita haru 永すぎた春

'기루했던봄' 朴尚均訳 「日本文学大全集 6」 서울 東西文化院 1975. p.172–284

Nettaiju 熱帯樹

'Tropical tree' Tr. by Kenneth Strong. *Japan Quarterly*, v.11, no.2, 1964. p.174–210

Nikutai no gakkō 肉体の学校

「愛憎의나무」 金相黙訳 서울 栄豊文化社 1976. 263p.

Onnagata 女方

'Onnagata' Tr. by Donald Keene. *Death in midsummer, and other stories*. N. Y. New Directions, 1966. p.139–161; London, Secker and Warburg, 1967. p.173–200; Harmondsworth, Penguin Books, 1971.
'Der Onnagata' Aus dem Amerikanischen von Ulla Hengst. *Yukio Mishima, Gesammelte Erzählungen*. Reinbek, Rowohlt, 1971. p.122–142
'Onnagata' Tr. di Marco Amante. *Morte di mezza estate*. Milano, Longanesi, 1971.

Ranryōō 蘭陵王

'蘭陵王' 余阿勲訳 「三島由紀夫短篇傑作選」 彰化 現代潮出版社 1970. p.43–50
'蘭陵王' 李浩哲訳 「月刊文学」 第3巻12号 1970.

Sado kōshaku fujin サド侯爵夫人

Madame de Sade. Tr. by Donald Keene. N. Y. Grove Press, 1967. 107p.; London, Peter Owen, 1968. 108p.; Tokyo, Tuttle, 1971. 108p.
Madame de Sade. Version française d'André Pieyre de Mandiargues. Paris, Gallimard, 1976. 133p.

San genshoku 三原色

'Three primary colors' Tr. by Miles K. McElrath. *Occasional Papers* (Univ. of Michigan, Center for Japanese Studies), no.11, 1969. p. 175–194

Shigadera shōnin no koi 志賀寺上人の恋

'The priest and his love' Tr. by Ivan Morris. *Modern Japanese stories*, ed. by I. Morris. London, Spottiswoode, 1961; Tokyo, Tuttle, 1962. p.484–501
'Pěndeta kuil Shiga děngan kěběrahian-nya' Děngan kata pěngantar oleh James Kirkup. *Shoji*. Kuala Lumpur, Oxford Univ. Press, 1961. p.114–138
'L'amore dell'abate di Shiga' Tr. di Atsuko Ricca Suga. *Narratori giapponesi moderni*. Milano, Bompiani, 1965. p.583–602
'Der Priester des Shiga-Tempels und seine Liebe' Deutsch von Monique Humbert. *Nippon*. Zürich, Diogenes, 1965. p.509–522; *Yukio Mishima, Gesammelte Erzählungen*. Reinbek, Rowohlt, 1971. p.67–82
'The priest of Shiga temple and his love' Tr. by Ivan Morris. *Death in midsummer, and other stories*. N. Y. New Directions, 1966. p.59–75; London, Secker and Warburg, 1967. p.81–100; Harmondsworth, Penguin Books, 1971; *The world of Japanese fiction*. N. Y. Dutton, 1973. p.291–307
'L'amore del sacerdote del Tempio di Shiga' Tr. di Marco Amante. *Morte di mezza estate*. Milano, Longanesi, 1971.

Shinbungami 新聞紙

'Swaddling clothes' Tr. by Ivan Morris. *Today's Japan*, v.5, Jan.-Feb. 1960. p.67–70; *The Japanese image*, ed. by M. Schneps and A. D. Coox. Tokyo, Orient West, 1965. p.212–216; *Death in midsummer, and other stories*. N. Y. New Directions, 1966. p.175–181; London, Secker and Warburg, 1967. p.217–224; Harmondsworth, Penguin Books, 1971.
'新聞紙' 崔貞熙訳 「世界戦後文学全集 7」 서울 新丘文化社 1962. p.211–215
'新聞紙' 劉慕沙訳 「仲夏之死」 台北 皇冠出版社 1970. p.80–88
'Windeln' Aus dem Amerikanischen von Ulla Hengst. *Yukio Mishima, Gesammelte Erzählungen*. Reinbek, Rowohlt, 1971. p.155–160

MISHIMA Yukio

Shinju 真珠

'The pearl' Tr. by Geoffrey W. Sargent. *Death in midsummer, and other stories.* N. Y. New Directions, 1966. p. 162–174; London, Secker and Warburg, 1967. p.201–216; Harmondsworth, Penguin Books, 1971.

'Die Perle' Aus dem Amerikanischen von Ulla Hengst. *Yukio Mishima, Gesammelte Erzählungen.* Reinbek, Rowohlt, 1971. p.143–154

'La perla' Tr. di Marco Amante. *Morte di mezza estate.* Milano, Longanesi, 1971.

Shi o kaku shōnen 詩を書く少年

'詩言쓰는少年' 宋相玉訳 「文学春秋」 第3巻7号 1966.

'寫詩的少年' 余阿勲訳 「三島由紀夫短篇傑作選」 彰化 現代潮出版社 1970. p.16–30

'The boy who wrote poetry' Tr. by Ian H. Levy. *Contemporary Japanese literature,* ed. by Howard Hibbett. N. Y. Knopf, 1977. p. 283–291

Shiosai 潮騒

The sound of waves. Tr. by Meredith Weatherby. N. Y. Knopf, 1956.; Tokyo, Tuttle, 1956; London, Secker and Warburg, 1957. 182p.; N. Y. Berkley Pub. 1961. 141p.

Kipenje morja. Tr. Ivan Slamming. Zagreb, Zora, 1958. 162p.

Die Brandung. Übertragen von Gerda von Uslar und Oscar Benl. Reinbek, Rowohlt, 1959. 145p. 3. Aufl. 1962; Berlin, Volk und Welt, 1966. 298p.

Aaltojen pauhu. Kääntää Irmeli Nykänen. Helsinki, Otava, 1960. 221p.

Broesems over Uta-jima. Vertaald door Ank van Haaren. Amsterdam, Meulenhoff, 1960. 140p.

La voce delle onde. Tr. di Liliana Frassati Sommavilla. Milano, Feltrinelli, 1961. 180p.

Kipenje morja. Tr. Edvard Kockbek. Ljubljana, Durzba, 1961. 134p.

「波濤소리」 金潤成訳 서울 新太陽社 1962. 298p.

Bruset av vågor. Översättning från amerikanskan av Sonja Bergvall. Stockholm, Bonniers, 1965. 176p.

Bølgeslag. Pa dansk ved Ida Elisabeth Hammerich. København, Gyldendal, 1967. 163p.

Al-hubb al-awwal. Tr. Jamal-al-Din al-Ramadi. al-Qahirah, Dar al-Katib al-'Arabi, 1968. 141p.

Le tumulte des flots. Tr. par Gaston Renondeau. Paris, Gallimard, 1969. 236p.

「潮騒」 劉慕沙訳 台北 阿波羅出版社 1970. 167p.

'Die Brandung' Übers. von Gerda von Uslar und Oscar Benl. *Yukio Mishima, Gesammelte Erzählungen.* Reinbek, Rowohlt, 1971. p.161–290

'Ballada o miłości' Przeł. Ariadna Demkowska-Bohdziewicz. *Na uwięiz, Ballada o miłości.* Warszawa, Państwowy Instytut Wydawniczy, 1972.

Dalgalarin sesi. Çeviren Zeyyat Selimoğlu. İstanbul, Dizerkonca Matbaasi, 1972. 183p.

Tumultul valurilor. În românește de Ana Maria Năvodaru. Bucureşti, Editura Univers, 1975. 151p.

'潮騒' 朴尚均訳 「日本文学大全集 6」 서울 東西文化院 1975. p.2–84

Tabako 煙草

'Cigarette' Tr. by Tadao Katayama. *The Reeds,* v.13, 1972. p.89–106

Taiyō to tetsu 太陽と鉄

Sun and steel. Tr. by John Bester. Tokyo, Kodansha International, 1970. 104p.; N. Y., Grove Press, 1970. 107p.; London, Secker and Warburg, 1971. 104p.

「太陽與鐵」 鐘肇政訳 台北 林白出版社 1972. 104p.

'Le soleil et l'acier' Tr. par Tanguy Kenec'hdu. *Le soleil et l'acier.* Paris, Gallimard, 1973. p.7–121

Tennin gosui 天人五衰

「天人五衰」 余阿勲訳 台北 晨鐘出版社 1971. 263p.

The decay of the angel. Tr. by Edward G. Seidensticker. N. Y. Knopf, 1974. 236p.; Tokyo, Tuttle, 1974. 238p.; London, Secker and Warburg, 1975. 236p.; N. Y. Pocket Books, 1975. 1v.

Umi to yūyake 海と夕焼

'海與晩霞' 劉慕沙訳 「仲夏之死」 台北 皇冠出版社 1970. p.44–56

Utage no ato 宴のあと

After the banquet. Tr. by Donald Keene. N. Y. Knopf, 1963. 271p.; London, Secker and Warburg, 1963; Tokyo, Tuttle, 1963. 271p.; N. Y. Avon Books, 1967. 176p.; N. Y. Berkley Pub. 1971. 1v.

Dopo il banchetto. Tr. dall'inglese di Livio Livi. Milano, Feltrinelli, 1964. 250p.

Efter festen. Oversaette Ida Elizabeth Hammerich. København, Gyldendal, 1964. 210p.

Après le banquet. Tr. par Gaston Renondeau. Paris, Gallimard, 1965. 252p.

Na het banket. Uit het Japans vertaald door Jef Last. Amsterdam, Meulenhoff, 1966. 175p.

Juhlan jälkeen. Suomentanut Helvi Vasara. Helsinki, Otava, 1966. 228p.

Nach dem Bankett. Übers. von Sachiko Yatsushiro. Reinbek, Rowohlt, 1967. 220p.; Frankfurt am Main, Suhrkamp Verlag, 1976. 220p.

Poslije banketa. Tr. Ivan Slamming. Zagreb, Zora, 1967. 166p.

Efter banketten. Översätta Vanja Lantz. Stockholm, Bonniers, 1969. 193p.

Posle banketa, na estonskom iazyke. Tallin, Eesti Raamat, 1969. 183p.

Po banketu. Prevesti Katarina Bogataj. Ljubljana, Drzavna Zalozba Slovenije, 1971. 184p.

Utsukushii hoshi 美しい星

Den vackra stjärnam. Översätta Erik Sundström. Stockholm, Bonniers, 1970. 248p.

Waga tomo Hittorā わが友ヒットラー

'My friend Hitler' Tr. by Hiroaki Sato. *St. Andrews Review,* v.4, no.3 & 4, 1977. p.23–70

Yorobōshi 弱法師

'The blind young man' Tr. by Ted T. Takaya. *Anthology of modern Japanese drama.* N. Y. Columbia Univ. Press, forthcoming.

Yoru no himawari 夜の日向葵

Twilight sunflower Tr. by Sigeho Sinozaki and Virgil A. Warren. Tokyo, Hokuseido, 1958. 143p.

Yūkoku 憂国

'Patriotism' Tr. by Geoffrey W. Sargent. *Death in midsummer, and other stories*. N. Y. New Directions, 1966. p.93–118; London, Secker and Warburg, 1967. p.121–151; Harmondsworth, Penguin Books, 1971; *New writing in Japan*. London, Penguin Books, 1972. p.152–181

「憂國」張良澤訳 「假面的告白」台北 晨鐘出版社 1970. p.177–236

「憂國」劉慕沙訳 「三島由紀夫短篇傑作選」彰化 現代潮出版社 1970. p.96–125;「仲夏之死」台北 皇冠出版社 1970. p.15–43

「憂國」陳千武訳 台北 巨人出版社 1970. 45p.

'Patriotismus' Aus dem Amerikanischen von Ulla Hengst. *Yukio Mishima, Gesammelte Erzählungen*. Reinbek, Rowohlt, 1971. p. 99–121

'Patriottismo' Tr. di Marco Amante. *Morte di mezza estate*. Milano, Longanesi, 1971.

「憂国」権五爽訳 「行動과죽음의美学」서울 人文出版社 1971. p.269–307

'Miłość i smierć' Przeł. Henryk Lipszyc. *Literatura na świecie*. Warszawa, Pazdziernik, 1976. p.144–177

Poems 詩

'Farewell poems of Yukio Mishima' Tr. by Alan Ireland. *Poetry Nippon*, no.14, 1971. p.1

'A bright oak tree' Tr. by Junko Ohmagari. *Poetry Nippon*, no.35 & 36, 1976. p. 9–10

Criticism and Essays 評論・エッセイ

'Party of one' Tr. by Donald Keene. *Holiday*, v. 30, Oct. 1961.

「거꾸로본人生」高啓栄訳 서울 正信社 1962. 248p.

「구멍뚫린人間真理」尹尚根訳 서울 徽文出版社 1962. 358p.

'Famous Japanese judges the U. S. giant' Tr. by Donald Keene. *Life*, v.57, no.11, Sept. 11, 1964. p.81–84

'An ideology for an age of languid peace' *Journal of Social and Political Ideas in Japan*, v.2, no.2, 1964. p.42–43; *Solidarity*, August 1971. p.36–37; *Japan Interpreter*, v.7, no.1, 1971. p.79–80

"美" 에게夏하는것' 金賢珠訳 「바이바이바다」서울 三韓出版社 1966. p.192–194

「印度書簡」司馬長風訳 「明報」第2巻12期 1967. p.40–42;「三島由紀夫短篇傑作集」彰化 現代潮出版社 1970. p.129–135

「美麗的悲哀評」金淏若訳「美麗的悲哀」台北 志文出版社 1969. p.232–240

'The Shield Society' Tr. by Ivan Morris. *Queen*, Jan. 7–20, 1970.

「電燈的觀念」朱佩蘭訳 「三島由紀夫短篇傑作選」彰化 現代潮出版社 1970. p.126–128

'Tate no kai' Tr. by Andrew Horvat. *Solidarity*, August 1971. p.36–37; *Japan Interpreter*, v.7, no.1, 1971. p.77–78

'An appeal' Tr. by Harris I. Martin. *Japan Interpreter*, v.7, no.1, 1971. p. 73–77; *Solidarity*, August 1971. p.32–35

'Testament of a samurai' Tr. by Michael Gallagher. *Sports Illustrated*, Jan. 1971. p. 24–27

「永遠의旅人 川端康成其人及作品」鄭清文訳 「水月」高雄 文皇出版社 1971. p.178–188

「끝의美学」革命哲学으로서의陽明学」権五爽訳 「行動과죽음의美学」서울 人文出版社 1971. p.93–267

'Icare' Tr. par Tanguy Kenec'hdu. *Le soleil et l'acier*. Paris, Gallimard, 1973. p. 143–145

'Défense de la culture (extraits)' *Esprit*, février 1973. p.344–354

'Long after love' 「다리」第4巻4号 1973.

'Four song-dramas from the Kojiki' Tr. by D. L. Philippi. *Today's Japan*, v.5, no.1, 1960.

'F104' 余阿勲訳 「三島由紀夫短篇傑作選」彰化 現代潮出版社 1970. p.1–15

'Fasce pen bambini' Tr. di Marco Amante. *Morte di mezza estate*. Milano, Longanesi, 1971.

'Epilogue, F 104' Tr. par Tanguy Kenec'hdu. *Le soleil et l'acier*. Paris, Gallimard, 1973. p.123–141

Mneputen. Overs. fra tysk. av Knut Johansen. Oslo, Norsk Rikskringkasting, 1975.

MISUMI Kan 三角 寛 1903–1971

Essay エッセイ

'Flag over the ruins' *This is Japan*, v.11, 1964. p.225–227

MITA Hanako 三田華子

Awa danuki retsuden 阿波狸列伝

'The badger of Awa' Tr. by Tadayuki Tsukasa. *Info*, Sept.-Oct. Dec. 1965, Jan.-Dec. 1966, Jan.-Nov. 1967 in 22 parts.

MITA Masahiro 三田誠広 1948–

Bokutte nani 僕って何

'나는뭐냐' 洪東菩訳 「에게海에바찬다外」서울 世代文庫社 1977. p.53–218

MITARAI Tokie 御手洗ときえ

Shiroi hige no ojisan 白いひげのおじさん

'Дед с белой бородой' Перевод Г. Ронской. *Лети, журавлик!* Москва, Дет. Лит. 1966. p.87–95

MITOBE Mono 水戸部茂野

Nankō fushi ketsubetsu 楠公父子訣別

The loyal Kusunoki, a historical play. Tokyo, Daito-kaku, 1919. 122p.

MITOMI Kyūyō 三富朽葉 1889–1917

Poems 詩

'L'oiseau de nuit; Pétales et pollens; Hypocondrie; Images coupées' Tr. par Kuni Matsuo et Steinilber-Oberlin. *Anthologie des poètes japonais contemporains*. Paris, Mercure de France, 1939. p.147–154

MITSUHASHI Takajo　三橋鷹女　1899-1972

Haiku　俳句

'2 haiku' *The burning heart*, tr. and ed. by Kenneth Rexroth and Ikuko Atsumi. N. Y. Seabury Press, 1977. p.80

MITSUI Futabako　三井ふたばこ　1918-

Poems　詩

'Poésie; Landscape' *An anthology of modern Japanese poetry*, ed. and tr. by Ichiro Kono and Rikutaro Fukuda. Tokyo, Kenkyusha, 1957. p.83

'Sourire' Tr. par Kazouko Yanagisawa. *The lyric garland*, ed. by Makoto Sangu. Tokyo, Hokuseido, 1957. p.39

'뽀에지 ; 발자국' 辛東門訳 「世界戦後文学全集 9」서울 新丘文化社 1962. p.260

'Poesia; Paisaje' Tr. por Kikuya Ionesawa. *Poesia japonesa contemporanea*. Bogotá, Colombia Editoriales de Librería, 1965.

'Poesia' *La protesta poetica del Giappone*, a cura di Dacia Maraini e Michiko Nojiri. Roma, Officina Edizioni, 1968. p.61

'Grazing' *The burning heart,* tr. and ed. by Kenneth Rexroth and Ikuko Atsumi. N. Y. Seabury Press, 1977. p.95

MITSUSE Ryū　光瀬　龍　1928-

Yūsha kaeru　勇者還る

'Возвращение героев' Перевод З. Рахима. *Времена Хокусая*. Москва, Мир, 1967. p.48-88

'Didvyriu grizimas' *Hokusajaus laikai*. Vilnius, Vaizdo, 1969. p.32-64

MIURA Ayako　三浦綾子　1922-

Ai ni tōku aredo　愛に遠くあれど

「太陽永在雲層上」 許璀槙訳 台北 源成文化圖書供應社 1976. 212p.

Hitsuji ga oka　ひつじが丘

「사랑이흘러간곳」 安東民訳 서울 新亜出版社 1966. 302p.
「羊치는언덕」 李英朝訳 서울 鐘文閣 1966. 299p.
「羊치는언덕」 李容豊訳 서울 春秋閣 1966. 342p.
「언덕위의羊떼들」 南九訳 서울 文耕社 1966. 287p.
「原罪」 曺貞植訳 서울 児童文化社 1966. 332p.
「羊치는언덕」 玄相杰訳 서울 不二出版社 1966. 361p.; 서울 東根文化社 1975. 2冊
「原罪」 姜慧姸訳 서울 韓一出版社 1966. 2冊; 서울 世宗閣 1974. 2冊; 서울 英一文化社 1974. 466p.
「原罪」 玄相杰訳 서울 不二出版社 1970. 2冊; 서울 平和出版社 1971. 2冊; 서울 旺文社 1972. 509p.
「綿羊山」 秋田訳 台北 聯合圖書公司 1973. 1冊
「綿羊山」 朱佩蘭訳 台北 道聲出版社 1973. 345p.; 香港 基督教文藝出版社 1973. 280p.
「羊치는언덕」 曺貞植外訳 서울 東昌出版社 1973. 412p.
「양치는언덕」 金素影訳 서울 雪友社 1976. 2冊

Hyōten　氷点

「氷点」 李時哲訳 서울 韓国政経社 1965. 430p.
「氷点」 孫玟訳 서울 春秋閣 1965. 2冊; 서울 豊成閣 1972. 2冊
「冰點」 徐白訳 台北 徴信新聞報 1966. 581p.; 香港 藝聯書店 1977. 581p.

「冰點」 朱佩蘭訳 台北 聯合報社 1966. 419p.; 香港 基督教文藝出版社 1970. 492p.; 台北 三民書局 1974. 492p.
「氷點」 権雄達訳 서울 松仁出版社 1968. 518p.; 서울 新文出版社 1972. 2冊
「氷點」 玄相杰訳 서울 不二出版社 1970. 689p.; 서울 五倫出版社 1972. 689p.; 서울 大一出版社 1972. 2冊
「氷点」 鄭成煥訳 서울 主婦生活社 1975. 2冊
「빙점」 서울 西東社 1975. 2冊
Jäätymispiste. Suomentanut Martti Turunen. Helsinki, Otava, 1972. 508p.

Hyōten zoku　氷点　続

「冰點續集」 朱佩蘭訳 台北 聯合報社 1971. 472p.; 香港 基督教文藝出版社 1972. 566p.

Jiga no kōzu　自我の構図

「自我構圖」 朱佩蘭訳 台北 道聲出版社 1974. 224p.

Kaerikonu kaze　帰りこぬ風

「愛の日記」 朱佩蘭訳 台北 道聲出版社 1973. 243p.
「돌아오지않는바람」 申洙澈訳 서울 旺文社 1973. 295p.
「돌아오지않는木馬」 李英淑訳 서울 光学社 1974. 317p.

Kono tsuchi no utsuwa omo　この土の器をも

「我的結婚生活」 朱佩蘭訳 台南 台湾教會公報社 1974. 226p.

Michi ariki　道ありき

「尋道記」 劉蕚沙訳 香港 基督教文藝出版社 1971. 291p.
「길은여기에」 李鐘恒訳 서울 雪友社 1971. 291p.
'The Church of Christ' Tr. by David Reid. *Japan Christian Quarterly*, v.38, no.4, 1972. p.225-231
「여기에길은있다」 韓用雨訳 서울 興文図書 1972. 301p.
「길은여기에」 陳雄基訳 서울 汎友社 1976. 318p.

Sabaki no ie　裁きの家

「家」 朱佩蘭訳 台北 道聲出版社 1974. 339p.

Shi no kanata mademo　死の彼方までも

'撒旦的玩笑' 朱佩蘭訳 「撒旦的玩笑」 台南 豊生出版社 1975. p.7-73

Shiokari tōge　塩狩峠

「雁狩嶺」 朱佩蘭訳 香港 基督教文藝出版社 1970. 330p.
Shiokari Pass. Tr. by Bill and Sheila Fearnehough. London, OMF Books, 1974. 272p.

Tsumiki no hako　積木の箱

「運命의길」 朴在姫訳 서울 上智社 1967. 304p.
「집짓개箱子」 姜慧姸訳 서울 三年出版社 1967. 194p.
「運命」 姜慧姸訳 서울 韓一出版社 1967. 2冊; 서울 世宗閣 1973. 2冊; 서울 東根文化社 1975. 2冊

Yameru tokimo　病める時も

「五個故事」 朱佩蘭訳 台南 台湾教會公報社 1972. 265p.

Zanzō　残像

「残像」 朱佩蘭訳 台北 道聲出版社 1975. 442p.

「告白」 朱蓮姫訳 서울 弘益出版社 1967. 145p.
「原点」 南紋訳 서울 上智社 1967. 303p.
'우물' 金菊子訳 「20世紀女流文学選集 3」 서울 新太陽社 1967. p.191-212
「찾아온山莊」 孫玟訳 서울 五星出版社 1968. 211p.; 서울 現代書林 n.d. 211p.
「사랑한다는것믿는다는것」 朴泰文訳 서울 三友出版社 1968. 279p.; 서울 弘益出版社 1974. 223p.

「旅情」 洪民性訳 서울 平和文化社 1972. 307p.
「빗속에서」 黃必連訳 서울 가톨릭出版社 1972. 203p.
「愛情의언덕길」 申洙澈訳 서울 平和文化社 1973. 367p.
「빛이있는곳에서」 金允玉訳 서울 雪友社 1973. 204p.
「그대는보라빛」 李英淑訳 서울 光学社 1974. 317p.
「순애보」 孫玟訳 서울 文学堂 1975. 150p.
「겨울장미」 李英淑訳 서울 光学社 1975. 913p.
「어떤가을날」 李英淑訳 서울 光学社 1975. 353p.
「살며생각하며」 金允玉訳 雪友社 1975. 258p.
'汚泥不染' 朱佩蘭訳 「撒旦的玩笑」 台南 豊生出版社 1975. p.125–172
「빛과사랑을찾아서」 金容駿訳 서울 泉文閣 1976. 274p.

MIURA Shumon 三浦朱門 1926–

Kizu darake no paipu 傷だらけのパイプ

'His old pipe' Tr. by Hiro Mukai. *Quadrant*, Nov.-Dec. 1970. p.63–77

Semiramisu no sono セミラミスの園

'Semiramisu no sono' Tr. di Francesco Marraro. *Annali della Facoltà di Lingue e Letterature Straniere di Ca' Foscari*, XVII, Serie Orientale, 9, 1978.

Sotsugyō shiki 卒業式

'卒業式' 崔白山訳 「日本代表作家百人集 5」 서울 希望出版社 1966. p.190–207; 「日本短篇文学全集 6」 서울 新太陽社 .969. p.102–119

MIURA Tetsuo 三浦哲郎 1931–

Hatsukoi 初恋

'初戀' 朱佩蘭訳 「伊豆的舞娘」 嘉義 明山書店 1969. p.131–152

Ibo kyōdai 異母姉妹

'異母姉妹' 劉與堯訳 「現代日本小説選」 台北 雲天出版社 1970. p.1–23

Kenjū 拳銃

'Pistol' Tr. by John Bester. *Japanese Literature Today*, no.3, March 1978. p.4–9

Kikyō 帰郷

'歸郷' 朱佩蘭訳 「撒旦的玩笑」 台南 豊生出版社 1975. p.173–211

Niji no mieru fūkei 虹の見える風景

'虹' 朱佩蘭訳 「夏流」 台北 純文學出版社 1969. p.103–124

Shinobu gawa 忍ぶ川

'Река терпения' Перевод А. Додина. *Иностранная Литература*, январь 1975. p.103–120.

'Река терпения' Перевод Т. Григорьевой. *И была любовь, и была ненависть.* Москва, Наука, 1975. p.221–248

Shoya 初夜

'初夜' 朱佩蘭訳 「純文學」(台湾版) 第4巻3期 1968. p.138–152; 「夏流」 台北 純文學出版社 1969. p.79–102

MIYA Shūji 宮 柊二 1912–

Tanka 短歌

'1 tanka' *Modern Japanese poetry*, by Donald Keene. Ann Arbor, Mich. Center for Japanese Studies, 1964. p.37; *Landscapes and portraits.* Tokyo, Kodansha International, 1971. p.154

MIYAGAWA Yasue 宮川やすえ

Nise bikko no usagi don にせびっこのうさぎどん

The hare and the bear. English version by Alvin Tresselt. N. Y. Parents' Magazine Press, 1971. 32p.

MIYAJIMA Shinzaburō 宮島新三郎 1892–1934

Bungei hihyō shi 文芸批評史

「世界文藝批評史」 美子訳 廈門 國際學術書社 1928. 1冊
「文藝批評史」 黃清幗訳 上海 現代書局 1929. 1冊
「文藝批評史」 高明訳 開明書局 1930. 1冊

Ōshū saikin no bungei shichō 欧州最近の文芸思潮

「歐州最近文藝思潮」 高明訳 上海 現代書局 1931. 1冊

Criticism 評論

'日本文壇之現状' 李達訳 「小説月報」 第12巻4号 1921. p.5–15
'英國新興文學概論' 陳勺水訳 「楽羣月刊」 第1巻4期 1929
'文藝批評的新基準' 錢歌川訳 「北新半月刊」 第4巻3期 1930.
「現代日本文學評論」 張我軍訳 上海 開明書局 1930. 1冊
'蕭百納訪問記' 高明訳 「讀書月刊」 第2巻2期 1931. p 201–206
'美國文學概觀' 森堡訳 「當代文藝」 第2巻4期 1931. p.655–661
'英美的新文學理論' 白河訳 「徵音月刊」 第2巻2期 3期 1932.
'志賀氏的藝術的特色' 謝六逸訳 「志賀直哉集」 上海 中華書局 1935. p.13–19
「小説研究十六講」 高明訳 上海 北新書局 193?. 1冊
'逝了的哈代翁' 「當代」 第2巻

'劉易士' 錢歌川訳 「青年界」 第1巻1期 1931.

MIYAKE Kaho 三宅花圃 1868–1943

Akebono zome 曙ぞめ

'A cloth dyed in rainbow colours' Tr. by Tei Fujiu. *Hanakatsura.* Tokyo, Ikuseikai, 1903. p.16–36

MIYAKE Tsuyako 三宅艶子 1912–

Hibari 雲雀

'雲雀' 傅寶齡訳 「勲章」 台北 文壇社 1960. p.128–145

Poems 詩

'寄月' 錢稻孫訳 「世界文学」 1963年11月 p.28–29

MIYAKE Tsuyako

Essays エッセイ

'斗争到底一定能夠贏得最后胜利' 「世界文学」1963年8月 p.33–37

'开罗归来' 王效賢訳 「世界文学」1964年6月 p.117–119

MIYAKE Yasuko 三宅やす子 1890–1932

Kuroneko no ensoku 黒猫の遠足

'Kuroneko no ensoku' Tr. by Yasutaro Kanzaki. *Eisakubun Zasshi*, June 1922.

MIYAMORI Asatarō 宮森麻太郎 1869–1952

Haiku 俳句

'1 haiku' Tr. by Lois J. Erickson. *Songs from the land of dawn.* N. Y. Friendship Press, 1949; Freeport, Books for Libraries Press, 1968. p.74

Criticism 評論

'近代劇大觀' 周健侯 龔漱溟訳 「戯劇」第2巻1期 2期 1921.

'近代劇和世界思潮' 周健侯訳 「戯劇」第2巻2期 1921.

MIYAMOTO Ken 宮本 研 1926–

Za pairotto ザ・パイロット

'Der Pilot' Übers. von Jürgen Berndt. *Japanische Dramen.* Berlin, Volk und Welt, 1968. p.169–260

MIYAMOTO Kenji 宮本顕治 1908–

Criticism 評論

'宮本百合子的發展道路' 李芒訳 「譯文」 1956年3月 p.137–153

'回忆小林多喜二' 刘仲平訳 「譯文」 1958年2月 p.113–115

'十二年書簡' 李統汶訳 「世界文学」1959年7月 p.99–107

'二十年前一回忆宮本百合子' 陈九仁訳 「世界文学」1961 年1月 p.63–71

MIYAMOTO Masao 宮本正男

Geijutsu to shi ni tsuite 芸術と死について

Da arte e da morte. Tr. por Manuel de Seabra. Lisboa, Editorial Futura, 1973. 1v.

MIYAMOTO Shichirō 宮本七郎 1906–

Okorinbō no tonosama おこりんぼうのとのさま

The mighty prince. Retold by Yasoo Takeichi. London, Oxford Univ. Press, 1970. 1v.; N. Y. Crown Publishers, 1971. 1v.

MIYAMOTO Yasuko 宮本泰子

Kingyo きんぎょ

'Золотые рыбки' Перевод Г. Ронской. *Лети, журавлик!* Москва, Дет. Лит. 1966. p.47–52

MIYAMOTO Yuriko 宮本百合子 1899–1951

Banshū heiya 播州平野

'Rovina Banšú' Přel. M. Novák. *Nový Orient*, v.9, no.5, 1954. p.70–91

'Равнина Бансю' Перевод В. Логуновой. *Миямото Юрико, повести.* Москва, Гослитиздат, 1958. p.250–376

'播州平野' 叔昌訳 「宮本百合子選集 3」北京 人民文学 出版社 1959. p.1–158

'Die Banshu-Ebene' Übers. von Jürgen Berndt. *Die Banshu-Ebene, drei Erzählungen.* Berlin, Aufbau Verlag, 1960. p.71–267

'Banshu Plain' Tr. by Yukiko Sakaguchi and Jay Gluck. *Ukiyo*, ed. by J. Gluck. N. Y. Vanguard Press, 1963. p.73–80; London, Universal Library, 1964. p.73–80

Chibusa 乳房

'Грудь' Перевод А. Рябкина. *Миямото Юрико, повести.* Москва, Гослитиздат, 1958. p.211–249

'乳房' 蕭蕭訳 「宮本百合子選集 1」北京 人民文学出版 社 1959. p.281–321

'Die Brust' Übers. von Jürgen Berndt. *Die Banshu-Ebene, drei Erzählungen.* Berlin, Aufbau Verlag, 1960. p.19–70

Fūchisō 風知草

'知風草' 張夢麟訳 「譯文」 1956年1月 p.90–138; 「宮 本百合子選集 3」 北京 人民文学出版社 1959. p.159–221

'Футисо' Перевод А. Пашковского. *Японские повести.* Москва, Молодая Гвардия, 1957. p.123–324; *Миямото Юрико, повести.* Москва, Гослитиздат, 1958. p.377–430

'Fuchiso' Übers. von Jürgen Berndt. *Die Banshu-Ebene, drei Erzählungen.* Berlin, Aufbau Verlag, 1960. p.268–347

'Футисо' Торжимаси Ф. Ранихужаев. *Япон повестрали.* Тошкент, Бадиий Адабиёт, 1960. p.117–308

'Футисо' Прев. от русс. Манол Наков. *Трябва да живея.* София, Народ. Култура, 1964.

Futatsu no niwa 二つの庭

'两个院子' 儲元熹訳 「宮本百合子選集 4」北京 人民文 学出版社 1959. p.1–255

Hiroba 広場

'广場' 蕭蕭訳 「宮本百合子選集 1」北京 人民文学出版 社 1959. p.335–356

Ippon no hana 一本の花

'一朵花' 蕭蕭訳 「宮本百合子選集 1」北京 人民文学出 版社 1959. p.123–166

Kaze ni notte kuru koropokkuru 風に乗って来るコロポックル

'乗風而来的可洛波茨克尔' 蕭蕭訳 「宮本百合子選集 1」 北京 人民文学出版社 1959. p.83–110

Koiwai no ikka　小祝の一家

'小祝的一家' 蕭蕭訳 「宮本百合子選集 1」 北京　人民文学出版社　1959. p.259–280

Kokkoku　刻々

'За часом час' Перевод В. Константинова. *Миямото Юрико, повести.* Москва, Гослитиздат, 1958. p.153–210

'时时刻刻' 蕭蕭訳 「宮本百合子選集 1」 北京　人民文学出版社　1959. p.200–258

Kokoro no kawa　心の河

'心河' 曼堅訳 「世界文学」 1961年1月　p.41–62

Mazushiki hitobito no mure　貧しき人々の群

'Бедные люди' Перевод В. Логуновой. *Миямото Юрико, повести.* Москва, Гослитиздат, 1958. p.11–79

'貧穷的人們' 蕭蕭訳 「宮本百合子選集 1」 北京　人民文学出版社　1959. p.1–82

Negi sama Miyata　禰宜様宮田

'Блаженный Мияда' Перевод А. Стругацкого. *Миямото Юрико, повести.* Москва, Гослитиздат, 1958. p.80–120

Nobuko　伸子

'伸子' 馮淑兰　石堅白訳 「宮本百合子選集 2」 北京　人民文学出版社　1959. p.1–334

Omokage　おもかげ

'面貌' 蕭蕭訳 「宮本百合子選集 1」 北京　人民文学出版社　1959. p.322–334

1932 nen no haru　一九三二年の春

'Весна 1932 года' Перевод В. Константинова. *Миямото Юрико, повести.* Москва, Гослитиздат, 1958. p.121–152

'一九三二年的春天' 蕭蕭訳 「宮本百合子選集 1」 北京　人民文学出版社　1959. p.167–199

Umaichi　午市

'午市' 蕭蕭訳 「宮本百合子選集 1」 北京　人民文学出版社　1959. p.111–122

Criticism　評論

'蘇俄劇場的實際' 歐陽予情訳 「戲劇」 第2巻6期 1931.

MIYAZAKI Hiroshi　宮崎博史　1900–

「酷海姻縁」 陳秋帆訳　台北　鸚鵡譯粹社　1957. 120p.

MIYAZAWA Kenji　宮沢賢治　1896–1933

Chūmon no ōi ryōriten　注文の多い料理店

'The restaurant of many orders' Tr. by John Bester. *Winds and wildcat places.* Tokyo, Kodansha International, 1967; London, Ward Lock, 1967. p.25–37; *Winds from afar.* Tokyo, Kodansha International, 1972. p.57–64

'The restaurant that asked so many favors' Tr. by Fumio Morizuka and Junior class of 1969. *The Reeds,* v.14, 1976. p.41–52

Donguri to yamaneko　どんぐりと山猫

'Wildcat and the acorns' Tr. by John Bester. *Japan Quarterly,* v.5, no.1, 1958. p.63–69; *Winds and wildcat places.* Tokyo, Kodansha International, 1967; London, Ward Lock, 1967. p.11–24; *Winds from afar.* Tokyo, Kodansha International, 1972. p.93–99

'Glanoj kaj linko' Tr. Yasutaro Nozima. *El Japana literaturo.* Tokyo, Japana Esperanto Instituto, 1965. p.117–125

Haru to shura　春と修羅

'Wiosna i demony' Preł. M. Melanowicz. *Przegląd Orientalistyczny,* 34, 1960. p.175–188

'Spring and the Ashura' Tr. by Gary Snyder. *Orient West,* v.9, no.1, 1964. p.62–63; *The Japanese image,* ed. by M. Schneps and A. D. Coox. Tokyo, Orient West, 1965. p. 365–367

Spring and Asura. Tr. by Hiroaki Sato. Chicago, Chicago Review Press, 1973. 104p.

Horaguma gakkō o sotsugyō shita sannin　ほら熊学校を卒業した三人

'The spider, the flag, and the racoon' Tr. by John Bester. *Winds from afar.* Tokyo, Kodansha International, 1972. p.41–52

Kai no hi　貝の火

'The fire stone' Tr. by John Bester. *Winds from afar.* Tokyo, Kodansha International, 1972. p.103–118

Kenjū kōen rin　虔十公園林

Kenzyuu Parko-arbaro. Tr. S. Matsuda. (privata eldono), 1964.

'The Kenju wood' Tr. by John Bester. *Winds from afar.* Tokyo, Kodansha International, 1972. p.153–158

Manazuru to dariya　まなづるとダリヤ

'The dahlias and the crane' Tr. by John Bester. *Winds from afar.* Tokyo, Kodansha International, 1972. p.11–14

Matsuri no ban　祭の晩

'Night of the festival' Tr. by John Bester. *Winds from afar.* Tokyo, Kodansha International, 1972. p.119–123

Nametoko yama no kuma　なめとこ山の熊

'The bears of Mt. Nametoko' Tr. by Masako Ohnuki. *Chicago Review,* v.20, June 1968. p.24–31

'The bears of Mt. Nametoko' Tr. by John Bester. *Winds from afar.* Tokyo, Kodansha International, 1972. p.29–37

Ohōtsuku banka　オホーツク挽歌

'Okhotsk elegy' *Chicago Review,* v.25, no.2, 1973. p.21–23

Oinomori to Zarumori, Nusutomori　狼森と笊森, 盗森

'Wolf-Forest and Basket-Forest and Thief-Forest' Tr. by Kerstin Vidaeus. *The Journal of Intercultural Studies* (Kansai Gaikokugo Daigaku), no.4, 1977. p.65–72

MIYAZAWA Kenji

Opperu to zō オッペルと象

'Oppel and the elephant' Tr. by Masako Ohnuki. *Chicago Review*, v.20, no.21, May 1969. p.77–82

Sannin kyōdai no isha to Kitamori shōgun 三人兄弟の医者と北守将軍

'Northguard General Son Ba Yu and the three doctor brothers' Tr. by Masako Ohnuki. *Chicago Review*, v.20, June 1968. p.42–53
'General Son Ba-yu and three physicians' Tr. by John Bester. *Winds from afar*. Tokyo, Kodansha International, 1972. p.65–80

Sero hiki no Gōshu セロひきのゴーシュ

Gauche la ĉelisto. Tr. Y. Nozima. Tokyo, Japana Esperanto Librokooperativo, 1955. 41p
'Gorsh, the cellist' Tr. by John Bester. *Winds from afar*. Tokyo, Kodansha International, 1972. p.137–150

Shika odori no hajimari 鹿踊りのはじまり

'The first deer dance' Tr. by John Bester. *Winds and wildcat places*. Tokyo, Kodansha International, 1967; London, Ward Lock, 1967. p.50–63; *Winds from afar*. Tokyo, Kodansha International, 1972. p.127–136

Shokubutsu ishi 植物医師

'Plant doctor' Tr. by Shoichi Sato. *Eigo Eibungaku* (Iwate Univ.), no.101, 1959. p.38–48

Suisenzuki no yokka 水仙月の四日

'The red blanket' Tr. by John Bester. *Winds and wildcat places*. Tokyo, Kodansha International, 1967; London, Ward Lock, 1967. p.84–95; *Winds from afar*. Tokyo, Kodansha International, 1972. p.150–164

Tegami 手紙

'An unaddressed letter' Tr. by Shohei Shimada. *The Reeds*, v.5, 1959. p.14–15

Tsuchigami to kitsune 土神と狐

'The Earth-God and the fox' Tr. by John Bester. *Winds and wildcat places*. Tokyo, Kodansha International, 1967; London, Ward Lock, 1967. p.64–83
'Earth-God and the fox' Tr. by John Bester. *Winds from afar*. Tokyo, Kodansha International, 1972. p.17–27

Tsue nezumi ツエネズミ

'The ungrateful rat' Tr. by John Bester. *Winds from afar*. Tokyo, Kodansha International, 1972. p.81–85

Yamanashi やまなし

'In the bottom of a brook' Tr. by George Saito. *Art around Town*, v.6, no.7, Feb. 1968.
'Wild pear' Tr. by Burton Watson. *East-West Review*, 2, Spring-Summer 1965. p.62–66

Yodaka no hoshi よだかの星

'The nighthawk star' Tr. by Shohei Shimada. *The Reeds*, v.5, 1959. p.5–13

'Nighthawk and the stars' Tr. by John Bester. *Winds and wildcat places*. Tokyo, Kodansha International, 1967; London, Ward Lock, 1967. p.38–49; *Winds from afar*. Tokyo, Kodansha International, 1972. p.87–92

Yotsumata no yuri 四又の百合

'A stem of lilies' Tr. by John Bester. *Winds from afar*. Tokyo, Kodansha International, 1972. p.53–56

Poems 詩

'Never marred by rain' Tr. by Shigeshi Nishimura. *Eigo Seinen*, v.101, no.12, 1955. p.561
'Composition 1063' Tr. by Donald Keene. *Modern Japanese literature*, ed. by D. Keene. N. Y. Grove Press, 1956; Tokyo, Tuttle, 1957. p.377
'Tema 1063' *Sur*, no.249, Nov.-Dec. 1957. p.95
'Unyielding to rain' *An anthology of modern Japanese poetry*, ed. and tr. by Ichiro Kono and Rikutaro Fukuda. Tokyo, Kenkyusha, 1957. p.84
'Sapporo city; Orchard; Fantasia under the clear silent wail' *The poetry of living Japan*, by Takamichi Ninomiya and D. J. Enright. London, John Murray, 1957. p.57–60
'Shadow from a future sphere; Petals of Karma; The dance of a snake' Tr. by J. G. Mills and Rikutaro Fukuda. *Japan Quarterly*, v.5, no.1, 1958. p.69–70
'Das Signal der Wolke' Übertragen von Shin Aizu. *Der schwermütige Ladekran*. St. Gallen, Tschudy verlag, 1960. p.10
'Dem Regen Trotz bieten' Übers. von Kuniyo Takayasu und Manfred Hausmann. *Ruf der Regenpfeifer*. München, Bechtle Verlag, 1961. p.89
'Three poems' Tr. by Gary Snyder. *East-West Review*, v.1, no.1, 1964. p.38–41
'November third' Tr. by Geoffrey Bownas and Anthony Thwaite. *The Penguin book of Japanese verse*. Harmondsworth, Penguin Books, 1964. p.201
'Il corvo' *La protesta poetica del Giappone*, a cura di Dacia Maraini e Michiko Nojiri. Roma, Officina Edizioni, 1968. p.37
'作品第1063番；作品第1090番；비에도지지말고' 金巣雲 訳 「世界의文学大全集 34」 서울 同和出版公社 1971. p.526–528
'The sword-dancers' troupe of Haratai-a mental picture' Tr. by Hideo Yamaguchi. *Kobe Jogakuin Daigaku Ronshu*, v.18, no.3, 1972. p.43, 45, 47
'Spring; The carbide warehouse; A young land cultivation department; The last farewell; The master of the field; The prefectural engineer's statement' Tr. by Hiroaki Sato. *Ten Japanese poets*. Hanover, N. H. Granite Publications, 1973. p.126–136
'Politicians; Ukiyo-e; Spring in kitaguni mountains, part l' Tr. by Joshua Goldberg. *Poetry Nippon*, no.29 & 30, 1975. p.29
'Dawn' Tr. by Joshua Goldberg. *Poetry Nippon*, no.35 & 36, 1976. p.14
'Conpoziţie 1063; 3 noviembrie' Traducerea Virgil Teodorescu. *Din lirica japoneză*. Bucureşti, Editura Univers, n.d. p.183–184

MIYAZAWA Shōji　宮沢章二　1919–

Yamata no orochi　やまたのおろち

Le dragon dans la rizière.　Tr. par Reiko Kurashige. Paris, Casterman, 1969. 32p.

MIYAZONO Maki　宮園マキ

Poems　詩

'Chikyu (The earth)'　Tr. by Onsey Nakagawa. *Poetry Nippon*, no.28, 1974. p.3

MIYOSHI Sekiya　三好碩也

Dabide no uta　だびでのうた

Singing David.　N. Y. Franklin Watts, 1970. 1v.; London, Methuen, 1971. 25p.

Kāku to Pūku　かーくとぷーく

Pooke and Kark in the ark.　N. Y. Hawthorn Books, 1966. 25p.
Tucniacata Puk a Kak.　Praha, Mláde Leta, 1968. 1v.

Sekai de ichiban hajime no ohanashi　せかいでいちばんはじめのおはなし

The oldest story in the world.　Valley Forge, Judson Press, 1969. 1v.
When the world began.　London, Methuen, 1971. 24p.

MIYOSHI Tatsuji　三好達治　1900–1964

Poems　詩

'The pearls of names of heroes nine' Tr. by Shigeshi Nishimura. *The Current of the World*, v.19, no.5, 1942. p.133
'Crickets'　Tr. by Shigeshi Nishimura. *Eigo Seinen*, v.92, no.11, 1946. p.337
'Greyish sea-gulls' Tr. by Shigeshi Nishimura. *Eigo Kenkyu*, v.42, no.8, 1953. p.2–3
'The bygone days' Tr. by Shigeshi Nishimura. *The Current of the World*, v.30, no.8, 1953. p.45
'Seagulls'　Tr. by D. J. Enright. *Bulletin of the Japan Society of London*, no.20, 1955. p.11
'A boy; Sea-gull' Tr. by Shonosuke Ishii. *Japan Quarterly*, v.3, no.1, 1956. p.89–90
'Nostalgia'　Tr. by S. Sato and C. Urdang. *Poetry*, May 1956. p.79
'1 tanka'　Tr. par Roger Bersihand. *La littérature japonaise*. Paris, Presses Universitaires de France, 1956. p.119
'Souvenir of winter; Spring; The ground; A book; The snow' *An anthology of modern Japanese poetry*, ed. and tr. by Ichiro Kono and Rikutaro Fukuda. Tokyo, Kenkyusha, 1957. p.85–87
'Snow; Nostalgia; Sea-gulls; The deer' *The poetry of living Japan*, by Takamichi Ninomiya and D. J. Enright. London, John Murray, 1957. p.77–80

'Mouettes'　*La poésie japonaise*, par Karl Petit. Paris, Seghers, 1959. p.227–228
'Im Gras' Übertragen von Shin Aizu. *Der schwermütige Ladekran*. St. Gallen, Tschudy Verlag, 1960. p.14
'Schnee'　Übers. von Kuniyo Takayasu und Manfred Hausmann. *Ruf der Regenpfeifer*. München, Bechtle Verlag, 1961. p.86
'Toprakta; Kar'　Tercüme etmek L. Sami Akalin. *Japon şiiri*. İstanbul, Varlik Yayinevi, 1962. p.269
'二重の眺望；駱駝의혹에절터앉아서'　鄭漢模訳 「世界戦後文学全集 9」 서울 新丘文化社 1962. p.223–224
'Lake; Thunder moth: On the grass'　Tr. by Geoffrey Bownas and Anthony Thwaite. *The Penguin book of Japanese verse*. Harmondsworth, Penguin Books, 1964. p. 204–205
'Hagiwara Sakutaro—teacher'　*Modern Japanese poetry*, by Donald Keene. Ann Arbor, Mich. Center for Japanese Studies, 1964. p.29
'Perambulator; On the pavement; Young boy; Village; Spring; Breakfast beside a pond; Enfance finie; Crow; Quiet night; Stonebeating birds; Losing a friend; Break of day; I desire; Frail flowers; Flag' Tr. by James Kirkup and Rikutaro Fukuda. *Japan Quarterly*, v.12, no.3, 1965. p.370–378
'1 tanka'　Tr. from the French by Unity Evans. *Japanese literature*. N. Y. Walker, 1965. p.101
'My cat'　Tr. by Makoto Ueda. *East-West Review*, v.2, no.1, 1965. p.56
'Sull'erba; Il lago'　*La protesta poetica del Giappone*, a cura di Dacia Maraini e Michiko Nojiri. Roma, Officina Edizioni, 1968. p.41–42
'눈' 「永遠한世界名詩全集 2」 黄錦燦編 서울 翰林出版社 1969. p.34; 「永遠한世界名詩全集 5」 黄錦燦編 서울 翰林出版社 1973. p.34
'Faint gleam the waters'　Tr. by Masao Handa. *Poetry Nippon*, no.11, 1970. p.16
'喪友' 徐和隣訳 「現代詩解説」 台北 葡萄園詩刊社 1970. p.22–23
'Hagiwara Sakutaro—teacher'　Tr. by Donald Keene. *Landscapes and portraits*. Tokyo, Kodansha International, 1971. p.147
'아베마리아；까마귀' 金巣雲訳 「世界의文学大全集 34」 서울 同和出版公社 1971. p.510–512
'Lake water; A boy; Snow bunting; Golden Venus; Great Aso; Over the paving stones; The deer'　*Anthology of modern Japanese poetry*, tr. and comp. by Edith Marcombe Shiffert and Yuki Sawa. Tokyo, Tuttle, 1972. p.79–83
'A story'　Tr. by Makiko Morisawa and Marie Philomene. *Poetry Nippon*, no.21, 1972. p.13
'郷愁' 金光林訳 「現代詩学」 第4巻3号 1972.
'The feeble flower'　Tr. by Makiko Morisawa and Marie Philomene. *Poetry Nippon*, no.22, 1973. p.19
'My dream having vanished; Amidst grasses; By the waterside'　Tr. by Kazuko Ishigaki. *Poetry Nippon*, no.27, 1974. p.23–24
'Soon after we had lost the war'　Tr. by Keiko Sasaki. *Poetry Nippon*, no.27, 1974. p.20–21
'The bare woods; Thistle seeds'　Tr. by Keiko Sasaki and Kazuko Ishigaki. *Poetry Nippon*, no.28, 1974. p.20
'아베마리아' 金禧宝訳 「世界名詩選」 서울 一麦社 1974. p.197
'The eagle; Grandmother; The perambulator; In the islet at the offing; A bunting; A gull; Sea gulls; My poem; At the skirts of a mountain'　Tr. by Makiko Ichikawa, Keiko Sasaki, Ikuko Masada, Kazuko Kato and Shonosuke

MIYOSHI Tatsuji

Ishii. *Poetry Nippon*, no.31 & 32, 1975. p.31–35
'Grandmother; The perambulator; My own cat; Upon the rugged stones; A boy; At the skirts of a mountain; Gadfly; A tulip; A bunting; Thistle seeds; The bare woods; My poem; One red flower; Waves; Sea-gulls of long ago; The gulls; Gray gulls; Chattering in early spring; Reality as a dream; The feeble flower; Dandelion; The thatched cottage; By the waterside; In the islet at the offing; The *Miyako wasure*; Thinking of someone; Call my name; Touching grief; My life-goal; Amidst grasses; My dream having vanished; Soon after we had lost the war; Chirp, pond snails; Sea gulls; The eagle; A story' Tr. by Keiko Sasaki and others. *Japanese songs of innocence and experience*. Tokyo, Hokuseido Press, 1975. p.9–31
'Муравей; Аве Мария' Перевод Анатолир Мамонова. *Вкус хризантемы*. Москва, Восточная Литература, 1976. p.64
'Over gresset' Til norsk ved Paal Brekke. *Moderne japansk lyrikk*. Oslo, Norske Bokklubben, n.d. p.50

Essay エッセイ

'The new world of Hachiko' *This is Japan*, v.11, 1964. p.222–223

MIYOSHI Tōru 三好 徹 1931–

Shisha no tayori 死者の便り

'A letter from the dead' *Japanese golden dozen*, ed. by Ellery Queen. Tokyo, Tuttle, 1978. p.69–94

MIYOSHI Toyoichirō 三好豊一郎 1920–

Poems 詩

'A prisoner' *An anthology of modern Japanese poetry*, ed. and tr. by Ichiro Kono and Rikutaro Fukuda. Tokyo, Kenkyusha, 1957. p.87
'나는陽달속에서있다' 金龍済訳 「日本詩集」 서울 青雲社 1960. p.122–126
'囚人；손；우리들의五月의밤의노래에서' 辛東門訳 「世界戦後文学全集 9」 서울 新丘文化社 1962. p.257–258
'愛情' 崔一秀訳 「기다리고있네」 서울 韓国政経社 1966. p.207–210
'Il prigioniero; L'ombra' *La protesta poetica del Giappone*, a cura di Dacia Maraini e Michiko Nojiri. Roma, Officina Edizioni, 1968. p.79–80
'The prisoner; Poetry; A newer hell' Tr. by Harry and Lynn Guest and Shozo Kajima. *Post-war Japanese poetry*. London, Penguin Books, 1972. p.69–76
'Sleepless night; Prisoner; Soft death by water' Tr. by Thomas Fitzsimmons. *Japanese poetry now*. London, André Deutsch, 1972. p.78–80; *Japanese poetry today*. N. Y. Schocken Books, 1972. p.80–82
'Узник' Перевод Анатолия Мамонова. *Вкус хризантемы*. Москва, Восточная Литература, 1976. p.66

Criticism 評論

'이메지와리듬' 金龍済訳 「日本詩集」 서울 青雲社 1960. p.199–216

MIZUHARA Shūōshi 水原秋桜子 1892–

Haiku 俳句

'2 haiku' Tr. by R. H. Blyth. *Haiku*. Tokyo, Hokuseido, 1950. v.1, p.295, v.3, p.359
'One haiku' Tr. by Donald Keene. *Modern Japanese literature*, ed. by D. Keene. N. Y. Grove Press, 1956; Tokyo, Tuttle, 1957. p.381
'1 haiku' Übers. von Kuniyo Takayasu und Manfred Hausmann. *Ruf der Regenpfeifer*. München, Bechtle Verlag, 1961. p.104
'5 haiku' Tr. by Geoffrey Bownas and Anthony Thwaite. *The Penguin book of Japanese verse*. Harmondsworth, Penguin Books, 1964. p.170
'10 haiku' *A history of haiku v.2*. by R. H. Blyth. Tokyo, Hokuseido, 1964. p.254–257
'1 haiku' Tr. by Donald Keene. *The Mentor book of modern Asian literature*, ed. by D. B. Shimer. N. Y. New American Library, 1969. p.124
'4 haiku' *Anthology of modern Japanese poetry*, tr. and comp. by Edith Marcombe Shiffert and Yuki Sawa. Tokyo, Tuttle, 1972. p.167
'20 haiku' *Modern Japanese haiku, an anthology*, comp. and tr. by Makoto Ueda. Tokyo, Univ. of Tokyo Press, 1976. p.147–156
'Nightingales' Tr. by Kenneth Yasuda. *A pepperpod*. Tokyo, Tuttle, 1976. p.100
'1 haiku' Traducere Virgil Teodorescu. *Din lirica japoneză*. Bucureşti, Editura Univers, n.d. p.176

MIZUKI Kyōta 水木京太 1894–1948

Criticism 評論

'論獨幕劇' 國喬訳 「北平晨報劇刊」 1931年7月
'日本戯劇概況' 楚橋訳 「北平晨報劇刊」 1931年9月

MIZUKI Yōko 水木洋子 1910–

'Please not a word to anybody' Tr. by Grace Suzuki and Jay Gluck. *Orient Digest*, 1955; *Ukiyo*, ed. by J. Gluck. N. Y. Vanguard Press, 1963. p.149–151; London, Universal Library, 1964. p.149–151

MIZUMACHI Kyōko 水町京子 1891–1974

Tanka 短歌

'A bird in the sun's ray' Tr. by Asataro Miyamori. *Masterpieces of Japanese poetry, ancient and modern*. Tokyo, Maruzen, 1936; Tokyo, Taiseido, 1956; N. Y. Greenwood Press, 1971. p.781–782

MIZUMORI Kamenosuke 水守亀之助 1886–1958

Kaigyōi 開業医

'開業醫師' 「標準日本名著選讀」 孫文斗編 台北 大新書局 1969. p.75–80

MIZUMURA Kazue　水村かずえ

If I build a village.　N. Y. Crowell, 1971. 32p.

MIZUNO Hironori　水野広徳　1875–1945

Kono issen　此一戦

This one battle.　Tr. by C. H. Heill James. Tokyo, Daitoa Shuppan, 1944. 218p.

MIZUNO Yōshū　水野葉舟　1883–1947

Tanka　短歌

'Insects'　Tr. by Asataro Miyamori. *Masterpieces of Japanese poetry, ancient and modern.* Tokyo, Maruzen, 1936; Tokyo, Taiseido, 1956; N. Y. Greenwood Press, 1971. p.690
'1 tanka'　Übers. von Gerolf Coudenhove. *Japanische Jahreszeiten.* Zürich, Manesse Verlag, 1963. p.203

Essays　エッセイ

'Mimizuku to kaeru'　Tr. by Yasutaro Kanzaki. *Eisakubun Zasshi,* Nov. and Dec. 1922.
'Oshaberi no Matsuko'　Tr. by Yasutaro Jinbo. *Eigo Kenkyu,* Oct. 1923.

MIZUOCHI Roseki　水落露石　1872–1919

Haiku　俳句

'2 haiku'　Tr. by Asataro Miyamori. *Anthology of haiku, ancient and modern.* Tokyo, Maruzen, 1932. p.694–695
'The winter moon'　Tr. by Asataro Miyamori. *Haiku poems, ancient and modern.* Tokyo. Maruzen, 1940. p.317
'1 haiku'　Tr. by R. H. Blyth. *Haiku v.4.* Tokyo, Hokuseido, 1952. p.204
'Haiku'　Tercüme etmek L. Sami Akalin. *Japon şiiri.* İstanbul, Varlik Yayinevi, 1962. p.235
'2 haiku'　*A history of haiku v.2,* by R. H. Blyth. Tokyo, Hokuseido, 1964. p. 143–144

MIZUSHIMA Hatsu　水嶋波津　1896–

Haiku　俳句

'24 haiku'　Tr. by Geoffrey Bownas. *New writing in Japan.* Harmondsworth, Penguin Books, 1972. p.243–246

MIZUTANI Masaru　水谷まさる　1894–1950

Poems　詩

'不響的笛子'　謝六逸訳　「文學週報」　第147期
'A flute'　*An anthology of modern Japanese poetry,* ed. and tr. by Ichiro Kono and Rikutaro Fukuda. Tokyo, Kenkyusha, 1957. p.88

'Kaval'　Tercüme etmek L. Sami Akalin. *Japon şiiri.* İstanbul, Varlik Yayinevi, 1962. p.302

MOCHIDA Mineko　持田美根子　1924–

Wakare　別れ

'分道揚鑣'　劉慕沙訳　「日本現代小説選 1」　台北　聯経出版事業公司　1976. p.125–161

MOCHIMARU Yoshio　持丸良雄　1913–

'夢之碎片'　徐雲濤訳　「當代日本小説選」　台南　經緯書局　1954. p.164–182；「當代日本創作小説」　台南　經緯書局　1961. p.164–182；「當代日本短篇小説選」　台南　大行出版社　1973. p.164–182

MOCHIZUKI Kazuhiro　望月一宏　1924–

Hankōki　反抗期

「反抗期」　金潤成訳　서울　新太陽社　1960. 294p.
「反抗하는季節」　金潤成訳　서울　聖峰閣　1962. 294p.

MOGI Akihiro　茂木昭洋

Fushigi na mori no naka no Roro　ふしぎな森のなかのロロ

Lollo i urskogen.　Övers. av Oddmund Ljone. Oslo, Gyldendal, 1974. 1v.
Juhlat viidakossa.　Suomentanut Lea Pennänen. Helsinki, 1974. 24p.

Roro to ryū　ロロとりゅう

Lollo och draken.　Övers. av Helen L. Lilja, Bromma, Opal, 1975. 249p.

MOMIYAMA Shigetsu　籾山梓月　1878–1958

Haiku　俳句

'2 haiku'　Tr. by Asataro Miyamori. *Anthology of haiku, ancient and modern.* Tokyo, Maruzen, 1932. p.792–793

MOMOTA Sōji　百田宗治　1893–1955

Poems　詩

'L'enfance; Ombres; Comme une fleur s'épanouit en hiver; Coeur adouci; Neige; Vers le ciel très haut'　Tr. par Kuni Matsuo et Steinilber-Oberlin. *Anthologie des poètes japonais contemporains.* Paris, Mercure de France, 1939. p.213–217
'The monument of the heroic spirits'　Tr. by Kyohei Hagiwara. *Eigo Seinen,* v.87, no.6, 1942. p.182
'Tree climbing'　*An anthology of modern Japanese poetry,* ed. and tr. by Ichiro Kono and Riku-

taro Fukuda. Tokyo, Kenkyusha, 1957. p.89

'Ağaçlarin tepesinde' Tercüme etmek L. Sami Akalin. *Japon şiiri.* İstanbul, Varlik Yayinevi, 1962. p.260

'Весна' Перевод Веры Марковой. *Восточный альманах 6.* Москва, Худож. Лит. 1963. p.328–329

'Утренний холод' Перевод Веры Марковой. *Птица, птица красная.* Москва, Дет. Лит. 1967.

'О Россия, ты птица тройка!' Перевод Анатолия Мамонова. *Вкус хризантемы.* Москва, Восточная Литература, 1976. p.68

'Zăpada' Traducerea Virgil Teodorescu. *Din lirica japoneză.* Bucureşti, Editura Univers, n.d. p.177

MORI Haruki 森 治樹 1900–

Poems 詩

'Пальцы' Перевод Анатолия Мамонова. *Вкус хризантемы.* Москва, Восточная Литература, 1976. p.70

MORI Kazuo 森 一歩 1928–

Koropokkuru no hashi コロポックルの橋

Мост коропоккуру. Перевод Б. Бейко и К. Черевко. Москва, Дет. Лит. 1963. 143p.

MORI Kosen 森 古泉 1879–

Haiku 俳句

'A moonlight night' Tr. by Asataro Miyamori. *Haiku poems, ancient and modern.* Tokyo, Maruzen, 1940. p.345–346

MORI Michiyo 森 三千代 1901–1977

Shinjuku ni ame furu 新宿に雨降る

'新宿夜雨' 徐白訳 「日本短篇譯集 3」 台北 晚蟬書店 1969. p.1–39

Poems 詩

'보헤미안의哀情' 崔一秀訳 「기다리고있네」 서울 韓国政経社 1966. p.219–228

MŌRI Motonori 毛利元徳 1840–1896

Tanka 短歌

'Falling snow' Tr. by Asataro Miyamori. *Masterpieces of Japanese poetry, ancient and modern.* Tokyo, Maruzen, 1936; Tokyo, Taiseido, 1956; N. Y. Greenwood Press, 1971. p.609–610

MORI Ōgai 森 鷗外 1862–1922

Abe ichizoku 阿部一族

'Das Geschlecht der Abe' Übers. von Kenji Koike. *Das Geschlecht der Abe, Sanshodayu.* Tokyo, Japanisch-Deutsche Gesellschaft, 1960. p.3–60

'Der Untergang des Hauses Abe' Übers. von Walter Donat. *Die fünfstöckige Pagode.* Düsseldorf, Diederichs, 1960. p.113–153; Regensburg, Pustet, n.d. p.113–153

'La familianoj de Abe' Tr. Yasutaro Nozima. *Oriento-Okcidento*, no.2, 1962; *Rakontoj de Oogai.* Tokyo, Japana Esperanto Instituto, 1962. p.63–100

'Az Abe ház' Ford. Sz. Holti Mária. *Modern Japán elbeszélök.* Budapest, Euröpa Könyvkiadó, 1967. p.39–43

'阿部一族' 黄憲燁訳 「世界代表短篇文学全集 21」 서울 正韓出版社 1976. p.150–188

'The Abe family' Tr. by David Dilworth. *The incident at Sakai, and other stories.* Honolulu, Univ. Press of Hawaii, 1977. p.37–69

Asobi あそび

'遊戯' 魯迅訳 「現代日本小説集」 上海 商務印書館 1923; 「日本現代小説集 1」 上海 商務印書館 1930; 「魯迅全集 11」 上海 魯迅全集出版社 1938. 作家書屋 1946. 大連 光華書店 1948. 北京 人民文学出版社 1973. p.411–431; 「魯迅譯文集 1」 北京 人民文学出版社 1958. p.446–461

Chinmoku no tō 沈黙の塔

'沈黙之塔' 魯迅訳 「現代日本小説集」 上海 商務印書館 1923; 「日本現代小説集 1」 上海 商務印書館 1930; 「魯迅全集 11」 上海 魯迅全集出版社 1938. 作家書屋 1946. 大連 光華書店 1948. 北京 人民文学出版社 1973. p.432–445; 「魯迅譯文集 1」 北京 人民文学出版社 1958. p.462–471

Doitsu nikki 独逸日記

'Mori Ogai in Germany' Tr. by Karen Brazell. *Monumenta Nipponica*, v.26, no.1–2, 1971. p.77–100

Fumi zukai 文づかい

Der geheime Briefträger. Übers. von K. Koike. Tokyo, Nankodo, 1920. 117p.

'La mesagô kimisiita' Tr. Kikunobu Matuba. *Oriento-Okcidento*, no.2, 1962; *Rakontoj de Oogai.* Tokyo, Japana Esperanto Instituto, 1962. p.45–62

'The courier' Tr. by Karen Brazell. *Monumenta Nipponica*, v.26, no.102, 1971. p.101–114

Fushinchū 普請中

'Under reconstruction' Tr. by Ivan Morris. *Modern Japanese stories*, ed. by I. Morris. London, Spottiswoode, 1961; Tokyo, Tuttle, 1962. p.37–44; *The Japanese image*, ed. by M. Schneps and A. D. Coox. Tokyo, Orient West 1965. p.190–196

'Dalam pĕmbangunan kĕmbali' Dĕngan kata pĕngantar oleh James Kirkup. *Shoji.* Kuala Lumpur, Oxford Univ. Press, 1961. p.1–9

'Im Wiederaufbau' Deutsch von Monique Humbert. *Nippon.* Zürich, Diogenes, 1965. p. 45–52

Gan 雁

'The wild goose' Tr. by S. G. Brickley. *The writing of idiomatic English.* Tokyo, Kenkyusha, 1951. p.57–62

'The wild goose' Tr. by Burton Watson. *Modern Japanese literature*, ed. by D. Keene. N. Y.

Grove Press, 1956; Tokyo, Tuttle, 1957. p.232–241

The wild geese. Tr. by Kingo Ochiai and Sanford Goldstein. Tokyo, Tuttle, 1959. 119p.

Die Wildgans. Übertragen von Fritz Vogelsang. Frankfurt am Main, Insel Verlag, 1962. 139p.

'The wild geese' Tr. by Kingo Ochiai and Sanford Goldstein. *The world of Japanese fiction.* N. Y. Dutton, 1973. p.89–179

Gojiingahara no katakiuchi　護持院原の敵討

'La vengo sur la kampo Goziingahara' Tr. Masao Miyamoto. *El Japana literaturo.* Tokyo, Japana Esperanto Instituto, 1965. p.126–157

'The vendetta at Gojiingahara' Tr. by David Dilworth. *The incident at Sakai, and other stories.* Honolulu, Univ. Press of Hawaii, 1977. p.71–98

Gyogenki　魚玄機

'魚玄機' 江珠訳 「人魚的悲戀」 台中　中央書局　1955. p.52–62

'Gyogenki' Tr. by David Dilworth. *The incident at Sakai, and other stories.* Honolulu, Univ. Press of Hawaii, 1977. p.155–168

Hanako　花子

'Hanako' Tr. by Yonejiro Noguchi. *Chugai Eigo,* Nov. and Dec. 1918.

'花子' 畫室訳 「莽原」 第1巻11期　1926. p.445–456; 「妄想」 上海　人間書店　192?.

'Hanako' Tr. by Torao Taketomo. *Paulownia, seven stories from contemporary Japanese writers.* N. Y. Duffield, 1918. p.35–51

Hannichi　半日

'Hannichi' Tr. by Darcy Murray. *Monumenta Nipponica,* v.28, no.3, 1973. p.347–362

Hebi　蛇

'Snake' Tr. by John W. Dower. *Monumenta Nipponica,* v.26, no. 1–2, 1971. p.120–132

Ishida Jisaku　石田治作

'Ishida Jisaku' Tr. by Shigeshi Nishimura. *The Current of the World,* v.21, no.5, 1944. p.56–58

Jiisan baasan　ぢいさんばあさん

'The old man and the old woman' Tr. by David Dilworth and J. Thomas Rimer. *The incident at Sakai, and other stories.* Honolulu, Univ. Press of Hawaii, 1977. p.169–177

Kamen　仮面

'Maske' Übers. von K. Koike. *Maske, und Studienreise nach Tokyo.* Tokyo, Nankodo, 1918. p.1–150

Kano yō ni　かのように

'As if' Tr. by G. M. Sinclair and Kazo Suita. *Tokyo people, three stories from the Japanese.* Tokyo, Keibunkan, 1925. p.61–117

Kanzan Jittoku　寒山拾得

'Han Shan and Shih-te' Tr. by D. A. Dilworth and J. T. Rimer. *Monumenta Nipponica,* v.26, no.1–2, 1971. p.159–167

'Han-shan and Shih-te' Tr. by Hiroaki Sato. *Literature East and West,* v.15, no.2, 1971. p.260–268

'Kanzan Jittoku' Tr. by David Dilworth and J. Thomas Rimer. *The incident at Sakai, and other stories.* Honolulu, Univ. Press of Hawaii, 1977. p.205–214

Kuriyama Daizen　栗山大膳

'Kuriyama Daizen' Tr. by J. Thomas Rimer. *Saiki Kōi, and other stories.* Honolulu, Univ, Press of Hawaii, 1977. p.91–116

Maihime　舞姫

My lady of the dance. Tr. by F. W. Eastlake. Tokyo, Saiunkaku, 1906. 47p.

'Die Tänzerin' *Die Tänzerin, und Der London Tower.* Tokyo, Nankodo, 1917.

「舞姫」 林雪清訳　上海　文化生活出版社　1937. 1冊

'舞姫' 郭夏信訳 「世界文学全集　94」 서울　乙酉文化社　1962. p.53–73

'The girl who danced' Tr. by Leon Zolbrod. *The language of love.* N. Y. Bantam Books, 1964. p.1–14

'Maihime (The dancing girl)' Tr. by Richard Bowring. *Monumenta Nipponica,* v.30, no.2, 1975. p.151–166

Mōsō　妄想

'妄想' 畫室訳 「妄想」 上海　人間書店　192?.

'Delusion' Tr. by John W. Dower. *Monumenta Nipponica,* v.25, no.3–4, 1970. p.415–430

Nogi shōgun　乃木将軍

'Nogi Shogun' Tr. by Shigeshi Nishimura. *The Current of the World,* v.13, 1936.

Okitsu Yagoemon no isho　興津弥五右衛門の遺書

'The last testament of Okitsu Yogoemon' Tr. by William Ritchie Wilson. *Monumenta Nipponica,* v.26, no.1–2, 1971. p.143–158

'The last testament of Okitsu Yagoemon' Tr. by Richard Bowring and William Ritchie Wilson. *The incident at Sakai, and other stories.* Honolulu, Univ. Press of Hawaii, 1977. p.15–33

Rekishi sono mama to rekishi banare　歴史其儘と歴史離れ

'History as it is and history ignored' Tr. by Darcy Murray. *The incident at Sakai, and other stories.* Honolulu, Univ. Press of Hawaii, 1977. p.149–154

Ru Parunasu Anbyuran　ル・パルナス・アンビュラン

'拉・巴爾納斯・阿姆菩蘭' S. F. 訳 「小説月報」 第19巻6号　1928. p.740–748; 「妄想」 上海　人間書店　192?.

Sahashi Jingorō　佐橋甚五郎

'Sahashi Jingoro' Tr. by J. Thomas Rimer. *Saiki Kōi, and other stories.* Honolulu, Univ. Press of Hawaii, 1977. p.35–44

Saigo no ikku　最後の一句

'最後的一句' 「標準日本名著選讀」 孫文斗編　台北　大新書局　1969. p.163–192

'마지막한마디' 黄憲樺訳 「世界代表短篇文学全集　21」 서울　正韓出版社　1976. p.103–114

'The last phrase' Tr. by David Dilworth and J. Thomas Rimer. *The incident at Sakai, and other stories.* Honolulu, Univ. Press of Hawaii, 1977. p.179–191

Saiki Kōi　細木香以

'Saiki Kōi' Tr. by William R. Wilson. *Saiki Kōi, and other stories.* Honolulu, Univ. Press of Hawaii, 1977. p.141–174

Sakai jiken　堺事件

'L'incidente di Sakai' Tr. di Franco Corsi. *Il Giappone*, anno 6, 1966. p.177–203

'The incident at Sakai' Tr. by David Dilworth. *The incident at Sakai, and other stories.* Honolulu, Univ. Press of Hawaii, 1977. p.99–121

Sakazuki　杯

'Cups' Tr. by Asataro Miyamori. *Representative tales of Japan.* Tokyo, Sanseido, 1914. p.423–430

'Cups' Tr. by John W. Dower. *Monumenta Nipponica*, v.26, no.1–2, 1971. p.139–142

'杯' 黄憲燁訳 「世界代表短篇文学全集 21」 서울 正韓出版社 1976. p.116–120

Sanbashi　棧橋

'The pier' Tr. by Torao Taketomo. *Paulownia, seven stories from contemporary Japanese writers.* N. Y. Duffield, 1918. p.55–68; *Treasury of world literature*, ed. by D. D. Runes. N. Y. Philosophical Library, 1956. p.910–914

Sanshō dayū　山椒大夫

'Sansho-Dayu' Tr. by Tsutomu Fukuda. *Eigo Seinen*, v.97, no.6, 1951. p.258–260

'Sansho Dayu' Tr. by Tsutomu Fukuda. *Sansho Dayu, and other stories.* Tokyo, Hokuseido, 1952. p.1–48

Sansho-Dayu. Tr. by Tsutomu Fukuda. South Pasadena, P. D. Perkins, 1953. 83p.

'Sansho Dayu' Tr. by Masaki Seikai. *Asia Scene*, v.1, no.4, 5, 6, 1956.

'Sanshodayu' Übers. von Kenji Koike. *Das Geschlecht der Abe, Sanshodayu.* Tokyo, Japanisch-Deutsche Gesellschaft, 1960. p.63–106

'Sansho-dayu' Tr. Masao Miyamoto. *Orient-Okcidento*, no.2, 1962; *Rakontoj de Oogai.* Tokyo, Japana Esperanto Instituto, 1962. p.16–44

'산쵸大夫' 金龍済訳 「日本代表作家百人集 1」 서울 希望出版社 1966. p.9–30; 「日本短篇文学全集 1」 서울 新太陽社 1969. p.10–30

'山椒大夫' 黄憲燁訳 「世界代表短篇文学全集 21」 서울 正韓出版社 1976. p.73–101

'Sanshō the steward' Tr. by J. Thomas Rimer. *The incident at Sakai, and other stories.* Honolulu, Univ. Press of Hawaii, 1977. p.123–148

Suginohara Shina　椙原品

'Suginohara Shina' Tr. by David A. Dilworth. *Monumenta Nipponica*, v.26, no.1–2, 1971. p.169–179; *Saiki Kōi, and other stories.* Honolulu, Univ. Press of Hawaii, 1977. p.117–128

Takasebune　高瀬舟

'Takase-bune' Tr. by Torao Taketomo. *Paulownia, seven stories from contemporary Japanese writers.* N. Y. Duffield, 1918. p.3–31

'Le Takasebune' Tr. par Moise Charles Haguenauer. *Japon et Extrême-Orient*, no.11 et 12, Nov.-Dec. 1924. p.294–309

'高瀬舟' 畫室訳 「妄想」 上海 人間書店 192?.

'Takasebune' Tr. by K. Takahashi. *Yamato*, Jahrgang 4, 1932. p.2–11

'Takase River boat' Tr. by G. Ogura. *Japan Times*, July 15, 16, 1934.

'Takasebune' Tr. by W. J. Whitehouse. *Eigo no kenkyu to kyoju*, June 1936.

'Takase-bune' Tr. by Tosiyosi. *Travel Bulletin*, 1940.

'Takasebune' Tr. by Akira Ota. *New World*, June 1946.

'The Takase-boat' Tr. by Tsutomu Fukuda. *Sansho Dayu, and other stories.* Tokyo, Hokuseido, 1952. p.49–65

'Łódź Takase' *Przegląd Orientalistyczny*, no.3, 1954. p.267–274

'The Takase boat' Tr. by Eiichi Hayashi. *The Reeds*, v.2, 1956. p.65–84

'Takasebune' Tr. by Garland W. Paschal. *The heart is alone*, ed. by Richard McKinnon. Tokyo, Hokuseido, 1957. p.37–48

Takasebune, oder, Takase-Kahn. Übers. von Kenji Koike. Tokyo, Japanisch-Deutsche Gesellschaft, 1958. 34p.

'Однажды в лодке' Перевод В. Костеревой. *Восточный альманах 4.* Москва, Худож. Лит. 1961. p.343–350

'Takase-barko' Tr. Teruo Mikami. *Orient-Okcidento*, no.2, 1962; *Rakontoj de Oogai.* Tokyo, Japana Esperanto Instituto, 1962. p.5–15

'Der Takase-Kahn' Aus dem Japanischen von Kenji Koike. *Japan, Geistige Begegnung.* Tübingen, Erdmann, 1964. p.295–306; *Eine Glocke in Fukagawa.* Tübingen, Erdmann, 1969. p.295–306

'Takasebune' Tr. di Atsuko Ricca Suga. *Narratori giapponesi moderni.* Milano, Bompiani, 1965. p.39–52

'The Takase boat' Tr. by Edmund R. Skrzypczak. *Monumenta Nipponica*, v.26, no.1–2, 1971. p.181–189

'高瀬舟' 黄憲燁訳 「世界代表短篇文学全集 21」 서울 正韓出版社 1976. p.137–148

'The boat on the river Takase' Tr. by Edmund R. Skrzypczak. *The incident at Sakai, and other stories.* Honolulu, Univ. Press of Hawaii, 1977. p.193–204

'Ruetakase' Tr. Wallapa Banchongmanee. *Rueng sun yeepun 1.* Bangkok, Uksornsasna, 1977. p.21–42

Tokō Tahei　都甲太兵衛

'Tokō Tahei' Tr. by J. Thomas Rimer. *Saiki Kōi, and other stories.* Honolulu, Univ. Press of Hawaii, 1977. p.129–140

Tsuge Shirōzaemon　津下四郎左衛門

'Tsuge Shirōzaemon' Tr. by Edmund R. Skrzypczak. *Saiki Kōi, and other stories.* Honolulu, Univ. Press of Hawaii, 1977. p.61–89

Tsuina 追儺

'Exorcising demons' Tr. by John W. Dower. *Monumenta Nipponica*, v.26, no.1–2, 1971. p.133–138

Utakata no ki うたかたの記

'Utakata no ki' Tr. by Richard Bowring. *Monumenta Nipponica*, v.29, no.3, 1974. p.247–262

Vita sekusuarisu ヰタ・セクスアリス

'Vita sexualis' 豈明訳 「北新半月刊」第2巻14号 1927. p.1535–1541, 第2巻21号 1927. p.53–60
Vita sexualis. Tr. by Kazuji Ninomiya and Sanford Goldstein. Tokyo, Tuttle, 1972. 153p.

Yasui fujin 安井夫人

'Yasui fujin' Tr. by David Dilworth and J. Thomas Rimer. *Saiki Kōi, and other stories.* Honolulu, Univ. Press of Hawaii, 1977. p.45–60

Poems 詩

'Vigorous feet' Tr. by Asataro Miyamori. *Masterpieces of Japanese poetry, ancient and modern.* Tokyo, Maruzen, 1936; Tokyo, Taiseido, 1956; N. Y. Greenwood Press, 1971. p.612
'In Mitsukoshi's store' Tr. by Shigeshi Nishimura. *The Current of the World*, v.29, no.12, 1952. p.32

'Il triunfo della mòrte' Tr. di Harukichi Shimoi e Attilio Colucci. *Sakura*, 1, 1920. p.22–24
'두 親旧' 黄憲燁訳 「世界代表短篇文学全集 21」 서울 正韓出版社 1976. p.121–135

MORI Reiko 森 礼子 1928–

Usugurai basho 薄暗い場所

'A twilight place' Tr. by Miriam L. Olson. *Japan Christian Quarterly*, v.38, no.4, 1973. p.232–240

MORIMOTO Kaoru 森本 薫 1912–1946

Onna no isshō 女の一生

'Жизнь женщины' Перевод А. Глаткова. *Современная Драматургия 10.* Москва, Искусство, 1959. p.247–293
Жизнь женщины. Перевод А. Глаткова. Москва, ВУОАП, 1959. 66p.
'A woman's life' Tr. by Koji Oi. *The Reeds*, v.7, 1961. p.109–144; v.8, 1962. p.99–154

MORIMURA Seiichi 森村誠一 1933–

Akumu no dezainā 悪夢の設計者

「그늘의 目撃者」 李英朝訳 서울 豊林出版社 1974. 330p.

Mashōnen 魔少年

'Devil of a boy' *Japanese golden dozen*, ed. by Ellery Queen. Tokyo, Tuttle, 1978. p.95–121

MORISHITA Hiroshi 森下 弘 1931–

Poems 詩

'The first aid station; This year again' Tr. by Miyao Ohara. *The songs of Hiroshima.* Tokyo, Taihei Shuppansha, 1971. p.78–85

MORITA Shiken 森田思軒 1861–1897

Jūgo shōnen 十五少年

「十五小豪傑」 北京 新民報社 1904. 1冊

Tetsu sekai 鉄世界

「鐵世界」 天笠生重訳 北京 文明書局 1903. 1冊

MORITA Sōhei 森田草平 1881–1949

Natori deshi 名取弟子

'L'élève diplômée' Tr. par Serge Elisséev. *Le jardin des pivoines.* Paris, Au Sans Pareil, 1927. p.101–116

Suishi 水死

'O-Suma's mysterious suicide' Tr. by Asataro Miyamori. *Representative tales of Japan.* Tokyo, Sanko Shoin, 1917. p.504–543

Criticism 評論

'On "Botchan"' *Essays on Natsume Soseki's works.* Tokyo, Japan Society for the Promotion of Science, 1972. p.33–48

MORITA Tama 森田たま 1894–1970

Poems 詩

'봄은왔어도；嘆息' 崔一秀訳 「기다리고있네」 서울 韓国政経社 1966. p.58, 64

MORIYA Tadashi 守屋 正 1909–

Raguna ko no kita ラグナ湖の北

No requiem. Tr. by Geoffrey S. Kishimoto. Tokyo, Hokuseido, 1968. 374p.

MORIYAMA Kei 森山 啓 1904–

Poems 詩

'Песня об умершей дочери' Перевод А. Глускиной. *Японская поэзия.* Москва, Гослитиздат, 1954. p.297–299; изд. 2. 1956. p.418–420

MORIYAMA Kei

'Рабочий из района Нанкацу' Перевод Ю. Хазанова и Б. Раскина. *Поэты Азии.* Москва, Гослитиздат, 1957. p.849–850
'Кез жумган кызым кошонун' Которгон Т. Байзаков. *Хиросима кектери.* Фрунзе, Кыргызстан, 1969. p.36–38

Criticism 評論

「唯物史観的文學論」 廖芰光訳 上海 上海雜誌公司 1936. 1冊

MOTOORI Toyokai 本居豊頴 1838–1913

Tanka 短歌

'1 tanka' Tr. by Hidesaburo Saito. *Eigo Seinen*, v.28, no.1, 1912. p.25

MOZUME Takami 物集高見 1847–1928

Essay エッセイ

'Rengeso' Tr. by Yaichiro Isobe. *Chugai Eigo*, April 1922.

MUCHAKU Seikyō 無着成恭 1927–

Yamabiko gakkō 山びこ学校

'Compositions of school children of Yamamoto' *Occasional Papers* (Univ. of Michigan, Center for Japanese Studies), no.2, 1952. p.73–87
Echoes from a mountain school. Tr. by Geneviève Caulfield and Michiko Kimura. Tokyo, Kenkyusha, 1953. 70p.
Kinderstimmen aus einer japanischen Gebirgsschule. Übers. aus dem Engl. von Marie Morgenstern. Köln, Schaffstein, 1956. 46p.
'Echoes from a mountain school' Tr. by Michiko Kimura and Geneviève Caulfield. *Ukiyo*, ed. by J. Gluck. N. Y. Vanguard Press, 1963. p.174–180

MUKU Hatojū 椋 鳩十 1905–

Kin'iro no ashiato 金色の足跡

The golden footprints. Tr. by Taro Yashima. Cleveland, World Publishing Co. 1960. 50p.
De gyldene fodspor. Oversaette Ellen Kirk. København, Munksgaard, 1966. 63p.

MURAI Gensai 村井弦斎 1863–1927

Hanako 花子

Hana, a daughter of Japan. Tokyo, Hochi Shinbunsha, 1904. 297p.

Kibun daijin 紀文大尽

Kibun daijin, or, From sharkboy to merchant prince. Tr. by Masao Yoshida. Tokyo, Yurakusha, 1906. 138p.

'Кибун дейзин' Перевод с англ. Ю. Н. Щербацкой. *Семия и школа*, 1906. p.1–92

Ōmi seijin 近江聖人

The sage of Omi. Tr. by T. Takayanagi. Tokyo, Eigaku Shinpo, 1902. 129p.

Sakura no gosho 桜の御所

「血襲衣」 商務編譯所編 上海 商務印書館 1943. 1冊

「賣國奴」 上海 商務印書館 1926. 1冊

MURAKAMI Akio 村上昭夫 1927–1968

Poems 詩

'動物哀歌抄' 金光林訳 「現代詩学」 第2巻3号 1970.
'The call of the wild goose' Tr. by Wesley Richard. *Poetry Nippon*, no.16, 1971. p.6
'The rat' Tr. by Wesley Richard. *Poetry Nippon*, no.17, 1971. p.13
'The crane' Tr. by Wesley Richard. *Poetry Nippon*, no.19, 1972. p.19

MURAKAMI Genzō 村上元三 1910–

Oni ga itaka inaika to yū hanashi 鬼がいたか居ないかという話

'Gibt es den Teufel oder gibt es ihn nicht?' *Mitteilungen* (Institut für Auslandsbeziehungen) Nr.7, Jan.-Mar. 1957. p. 28–31

MURAKAMI Hiroshi 村上 尋 1917–

Dangai 断崖

'斷崖' 廖清秀訳 「投水自殺營教業」 台北 蘭開書局 1968. p.80–100

MURAKAMI Kijō 村上鬼城 1865–1938

Haiku 俳句

'8 haiku' Tr. by Asataro Miyamori. *Anthology of haiku, ancient and modern.* Tokyo, Maruzen, 1932. p.717–722
'Haiku' Tr. par Kuni Matsuo et Steinilber-Oberlin. *Anthologie des poètes japonais contemporains.* Paris, Mercure de France, 1939. p.283–284
'Crows; To-night's moon; Autumn's voices' Tr. by Asataro Miyamori. *Haiku poems, ancient and modern.* Tokyo, Maruzen, 1940. p.317–319
'1 haiku' Tr. by Lois J. Erickson. *Songs from the land of dawn.* N. Y. Friendship Press, 1949; Freeport, Books for Libraries Press, 1968. p.71
'Blick zurück in mich selbst' Übertragen von Shin Aizu. *Der schwermütige Ladekran.* St. Gallen, Tschudy Verlag, 1960. p.42
'1 haiku' Übers. von Gerolf Coudenhove. *Japanische Jahreszeiten.* Zürich, Manesse Verlag, 1963. p.163

'13 haiku' *A history of haiku v.2*, by R. H. Blyth. Tokyo, Hokuseido, 1964. p.262–267
'1 haiku' Til norsk ved Paal-Helge Haugen. *Blad frå ein austleg hage*. Oslo, Det Norske Samlaget, 1965. p.89
'1 haiku' Übers. von Erwin Jahn. *Fallende Blüten*. Zürich, Arche, 1968. p.51
'20 haiku' *Modern Japanese haiku, an anthology*, comp. and tr. by Makoto Ueda. Tokyo, Univ. of Tokyo Press, 1976. p.86–95
'2 haiku' Tr. by Takamasa Sasaki. *Eigo Seinen*, v.122, no.5, 1976. p.231
'Harvest moon' Tr. by Kenneth Yasuda. *A pepper-pod*. Tokyo, Tuttle, 1976. p.81

MURAKAMI Namiroku 村上浪六 1865–1944

Mikazuki 三日月

Falce di luna. Tr. di H. Shimoi e G. Marone. Lanciano, Carabba, 1930. 1v.

MURAKAMI Ryū 村上 龍 1952–

Kagirinaku tōmei ni chikai burū 限りなく透明に近いブルー

Almost transparent blue. Tr. by Nancy Andrew. Tokyo, Kodansha International, 1977. 126p.
「半透明藍」 黄也白訳 台北 年鑑出版社 1977. 189p.

MURAKAMI Seigetsu 村上霽月 1869–1946

Haiku 俳句

'2 haiku' Tr. by Asataro Miyamori. *Anthology of haiku, ancient and modern*. Tokyo, Maruzen, 1932. p. 812–813
'The samisen' Tr. by Asataro Miyamori. *Haiku poems, ancient and modern*. Tokyo, Maruzen, 1940. p.332

MURAKAMI Yukio 村上幸雄 1914–

Kodomo no chie o nobasu nenne no hanashi 子どもの知恵をのばすねんねの話

「媽媽的故事」 黄澄輝訳 台南 台湾教會公報社 1974. 288p.

MURAMATSU Masatoshi 村松正俊 1895–

Criticism 評論

'意國文學家鄧南遮' 海鏡訳 「小説月報」 第12巻12号 1921. p.1–8

MURAMATSU Shōfū 村松梢風 1889–1961

Hana no Kōdōkan 花の講道館

'Young blood' Tr. by Hiroo Mukai. *The Yomiuri*, Jan. 3-Jan. 20, 1960.

Hon'inbō monogatari 本因坊物語

'The titans, a story of Go' Tr. by Hiroo Mukai. *The Yomiuri*, Feb. 2-April 9, 1960.

Essay エッセイ

'Onore no sugata' Tr. by Koh Masuda. *Eigo to Eibungaku*, 1938.

MURAMATSU Takeshi 村松 剛 1929–

Criticism 評論

'Die Modernisierung Japans und die Nichiren-sekte' Übers. von Hartmut O. Rotermund. *Kagami*, Bd. 3, Heft 2, 1965. p.34–47

MURANO Jirō 村野次郎 1894–

Tanka 短歌

'The spring rain; Misty streets' Tr. by Asataro Miyamori. *Masterpieces of Japanese poetry, ancient and modern*. Tokyo, Maruzen, 1936; Tokyo, Taiseido, 1956; N. Y. Greenwood Press, 1971. p.785–786

MURANO Shirō 村野四郎 1901–1975

Gendaishi dokuhon 現代詩読本

「現代詩的探求」 陳千武訳 台北 田園出版社 1969. 164p.

Gendaishi o motomete 現代詩を求めて

「現代詩的研究」 洪順隆訳 台北 大江出版社 1969. 142p.

Poems 詩

'Physique' Tr. by Katue Kitasono. *New world writing*, 6th, 1954. p.59–60
'An autumn dog; A beggar' Tr. by Ichiro Ando. *Japan Quarterly*, v.3, no.1, 1956. p.92–94
'Pole vault' Tr. by S. Sato and C. Urdang. *Poetry*, May 1956. p.78
'Winter of our own time' *United Asia*, v.8, no.3, 1956. p.268
'The faint-hearted; Hammer throwing; An old village; Beggar; Diving; Spring drifting; An autumn dog; The flesh; In the dead grass' *An anthology of modern Japanese poetry*, ed. and tr. by Ichiro Kono and Rikutaro Fukuda. Tokyo, Kenkyusha, 1957. p.89–94
'Un mendiant' *La poésie japonaise*, par Karl Petit. Paris, Seghers, 1959. p.229
'Koldus' Ford. Illyés Gyula. *Nagyvilág*, 1960. no. 10
'Зеленый камень; Человек, у которого были цветы' Перевод Веры Марковой. *Иностранная Литература*, сентябрь 1969. p.152
'盲導犬' 金龍済訳 「日本詩集」 서울 青雲社 1960. p.133–134
'Eski bir köy' Tercüme etmek L. Sami Akalin. *Japon şiiri*. İstanbul, Varlik Yayinevi, 1962. p.272
'自殺考；無神論；가을의개' 辛東門訳 「世界戦後文学全集 9」 서울 新丘文化社 1962. p.225–226
'A statue of the poet' Tr. by Haruo Shibuya and

MURANO Shirō

James Kirkup. *Japan Quarterly*, v.11, no.3, 1964. p.360

'My pale journey, and other poems' Tr. by Hiroshi Takamine. *Orient West*, v.9, no.3, 1964. p.51–54

'Black song; The flesh; Present winter; Beggar' Tr. by Geoffrey Bownas and Anthony Thwaite. *The Penguin book of modern Japanese verse*. Harmondsworth, Penguin Books, 1964. p.210–212

'Fish' Tr. by Makoto Ueda. *East-West Review*, v.2, no.1, 1965. p.57

'The blind man's god; Death; A wintry journey; Spring; Springtime of life' Tr. by Rikutaro Fukuda and Hiroshi Takamine. *The Japanese image*, ed. by M. Schneps and A. D. Coox. Tokyo, Orient West, 1965. p.355–357

'La accion del martillo; La carne' Tr. por Kikuya Ionesawa. *Poesia japonesa contemporanea*. Bogotá, Colombia Editoriales de Librería, 1965.

'A deer' Tr. by William L. Clark. *Jiji Eigo Kenkyu*, v.21, no.4, 1966. p.15

'女人의房' 崔一秀訳 「기다리고있네」 서울 韓国政経社 1966. p.35–36

'On suicide' Tr. by Edith Shiffert and Yuki Sawa. *Mondus Artium*, v.2, no.2, 1969. p.39

'가을' 「永遠한世界名詩全集 2」 黄錦燦編 서울 翰林出版社 1969. p.38;「永遠한世界名詩全集 5」 黄錦燦編 서울 翰林出版社 1973. p.38

'體操; 水上跳舞; 歌; 黄昏的田園' 陳千武 徐和隣訳 「現代詩解説」 台北 葡萄園詩刊社 1970. p.43–49

'乞人; 검은노래; 봄의漂流; 담장저편; 가을' 金巣雲訳 「世界의文学大全集 34」 서울 同和出版社 1971. p.519–521

'Diving; Grave visiting; Horse on a city street; On suicide; A small bird's sky; Night storm; A deer; The bridge; The canal at night; The ox' *Anthology of modern Japanese poetry*, tr. and comp. by Edith Marcombe Shiffert and Yuki Sawa. Tokyo, Tuttle, 1972. p.87–96

'体操' 金光林訳 「現代詩学」 第4巻3号 1972.

'Hammer throw' Tr. by James Kirkup and Shozo Tokunaga. *Listening to Japan*, ed. by Jackson H. Bailey. N. Y. Praeger, 1973. p.86

'Олень' Перевод Анатолия Мамонова. *Новый Мир*, август 1973; *Вкус хризантемы*. Москва, Восточная Литература, 1976. p.71

'Cerşetorul; Cîntec negru' Traducerea Virgil Teodorescu. *Din lirica japoneză*. Bucureşti, Editura Univers, n.d. p.191

Criticism 評論

'論詩的内容' 葉泥訳 「大學生活」 第3巻9期 1958. p.21–24

'詩에있어서言語란무엇인가' 金光林訳 「現代詩学」 第4巻2号 1972.

Essays エッセイ

'A boy and a bird, and other sketches' *Today's Japan*, v.5, March-April 1960. p.11–17

'An appointed time, and other sketches' *Today's Japan*, v.6, Jan. 1961. p.67–69

MURAOKA Hanako 村岡花子 1893–1968

Burēmen no ongakutai ブレーメンのおんがくたい

The donkey's band. Retold by Jane Carruth. London, Hamlyn, 1969. 1v.

MURATA Chikako 村田ちか子

Tanka 短歌

'1 tanka' Tr. by Shigeshi Nishimura. *Eigo Seinen*, v.91, no.3, 1946. p.81

MURAYAMA Kaita 村山槐多 1896–1919

Poems 詩

'어스름햇빛; 사랑의피; 아베크' 崔一秀訳 「기다리고있네」 서울 韓国政経社 1966. p.47–48, 88–89, 202–203

MURAYAMA Kazuko 村山籌子 1903–1946

Tarō no odekake たろうのおでかけ

Stop, Taro. English version by Kenneth Williams. Tokyo, Labo-Teaching Information Center, 1970. 27p.

MURAYAMA Tomoyoshi 村山知義 1901–1977

Ahen sensō 鴉片戦争

「最初的歐羅巴之旗」 袁殊訳 上海 湖風 1932. 1冊

Guretsu na chūgakkō 愚劣な中学校

'愚劣的中學校' 秦覺訳 「小説月報」 第21巻8号 1930. p.1219–1222

Yappari dorei da やっぱり奴隷だ

'畢竟是奴隷罷了' 陶晶孫訳 「洪水」 復刊第3巻10期 1926.

Criticism 評論

'新興藝術解説' 呉承均訳 「微音月刊」 第9巻10号 1939.

「西戰無戰事劇本」 梅君訳 上海 拔提 193?. 1冊

MURŌ Saisei 室生犀星 1889–1962

Ani imōto あにいもうと

'Brother and sister' Tr. by Edward Seidensticker. *Modern Japanese stories*, ed. by I. Morris. London, Spottiswoode, 1961; Tokyo, Tuttle, 1962. p.145–161

'Bruder und Schwester' Deutsche von Monique Humbert. Zürich, Diogenes, 1965. p.167–190

Aojiroki sōkutsu 蒼白き巣窟

'蒼白한巢窟' 崔行淑訳 「사랑에눈뜰무렵」 서울 新潮文化社 1962. p.92–155

Oshibana 押し花

'A pressed flower' Tr. by Max Bickerton. *Eigo Seinen*, v.66, no.7–v.68, no.6, 1932.

Sei ni mezameru koro 性に眼覚める頃

'性에눈뜰무렵' 崔行淑訳 「사랑에눈뜰무렵」 서울 新潮文化社 1962. p.13–89

Shita o kamikitta onna　舌を嚙み切った女

'혀를불어끊은女人'　金龍済訳　「日本代表作家百人集 2」서울　希望出版社　1966.　p.246-257；「日本短篇文学全集 2」서울　新太陽社　1969. p.310-321

Utsukushiki hyōga　美しき氷河

'아름다운氷河'崔行淑訳「사랑에눈뜰무렵」서울　新潮文化社　1962. p.157-191

Yasashiki toki mo arishi ga　優しきときもありしが

'Ternuras que fenecem' Tr. de Yoshihiro Watanabe. *Maravilhas do conto japonês*. São Paulo, Editora Cultrix, 1962. p.241-251

Poems　詩

'1 haiku' Tr. by Asataro Miyamori. *Anthology of haiku, ancient and modern*. Tokyo, Maruzen, 1932. p.804

'Poem' Tr. by Kyohei Hagiwara. *Kairyu*, 1938.

'Comme une émotion fraternelle; Dans les poussières; Printemps dans la banlieue; Les Dieux; Beau temps momentané; Le printemps; Les péchés; La mouette; Le printemps solitaire' Tr. par Kuni Matsuo et Steinilber-Oberlin. *Anthologie des poètes japonais contemporains*. Paris, Mercure de France, 1939. p.141-146

'Winter grass' Tr. by S. Sato and C. Urdang. *Poetry*, May 1956. p.95

'Evening; Jelly-fish; Customs-house' *An anthology of modern Japanese poetry*, ed. and tr. by Ichiro Kono and Rikutaro Fukuda. Tokyo, Kenkyusha, 1957. p.94-95

'Lonely spring; Susaki waterfront' *The poetry of living Japan*, by Takamichi Ninomiya and D. J. Enright. London, John Murray, 1957. p.52-53

'어서와주십시요；눈離別'　金龍済訳　「日本詩集」　서울　青雲社　1960. p.49-53

'Die Schlange auf dem Baum; Weisse Wolken' Übers. von Kuniyo Takayasu und Manfred Hausmann. *Ruf der Regenpfeifer*. München, Bechtle Verlag, 1961. p.86

'Akşam; Gümrük' Tercüme etmek L. Sami Akalin. *Japon şiiri*. İstanbul, Varlik Yayinevi, 1962. p.247-248

'室生犀星詩選'崔行淑訳「사랑에눈뜰무렵」서울　新潮文化社　1962. p.193-210

'남의夫人'崔一秀訳「기다리고있네」서울　韓国政経社 1966. p.142-143

'Muddy thought; Double vision; Glass' Tr. by Graeme Wilson. *Japan Quarterly*, v.14, no.3, 1967. p.357, 369, 375

'Summer flower; Snake; Bairn; Camel; Custom house; Railway train; In the dust; Rain on the sandhills; Asakusa sunset; Evening; A pair of socks; Glass; Lonely spring; Elephant; Who is it; Snapping turtle; Homesickness; Frost; Red moon; Seaside; Nunnery by the sea; For a dead friend; Early November; King in a dreary field; Blue coolness; Sword; Summer morning' Tr. by Ikuko Atsumi and Graeme Wilson. *Japan Quarterly*, v.18, no.3, 1971. p.307-315

'Muddy thoughts, and other poems' Tr. by Graeme Wilson. *Solidarity*, August 1971. p.56

'A sparrow' Tr. by Masao Handa. *Poetry Nippon*, no.13, 1970. p.7

'在郊外；一個陶器；泡菜' 徐和隣訳 「現代詩解説」台北 葡萄園詩刊社 1970. p.4-7

'Bairn; Railway train' Tr. by Graeme Wilson and Ikuko Atsumi. *Times Literary Supple-

ment*, August 20, 1971. p.1006

'After a music concert; Trout shadows; A camel; A baby-tending song; City river; Inside a deep isolation; An unfinished poem' *Anthology of modern Japanese poetry*, tr. and comp. by Edith Marcombe Shiffert and Yuki Sawa. Tokyo, Tuttle, 1972. p.52-56

'The tender leaves aflame' Tr. by Hideo Yamaguchi. *Kobe Jogakuin Daigaku Ronshu*, v.18, no.3, 1972. p.49

'Память' Перевод А. Мамонова. *Новый Мир*, август 1973.

'Song of an eagle' Tr. by Machiko Tanase. *Poetry Nippon*, no.33 & 34, 1976. p.8-9

'Dawn' Tr. by Machiko Tanase. *Poetry Nippon*, no.35 & 36, 1976. p.13

'Колыбельная песня; Иней; Медузы; Чайки; Март' Перевод Анатолия Мамонова. *Вкус хризантемы*. Москва, Восточная Литература, 1976. p.72-73

'Primăvară tristă' Traducerea Virgil Teodorescu. *Din lirica japoneză*. Bucureşti, Editura Univers, n.d. p.163

Essay　エッセイ

'My neighbor Kokei' *Japan Quarterly*, v.4, no.4, 1957. p. 466-471

MUROBUSE Kōshin　室伏高信　1892-1970

Criticism　評論

'請看這個時代' 陳慶雄訳 「北新半月刊」 第3巻11号 1929. p.25-41

MUROZUMI Soshun　室積徂春　1886-1956

Haiku　俳句

'1 haiku' Tr. by V. H. Viglielmo. *Japanese literature in the Meiji era*. Tokyo, Obunsha, 1955. p.438

MUSHANOKŌJI Saneatsu　武者小路実篤
1885-1976

Ai to shi　愛と死

「愛與死」 藍婉秋訳 台北　寶島文藝月刊社　1950. 71p.
Love and death. Tr. by William F. Marquardt. N. Y. Twayne Publishers, 1958. 101p.
Love and death. Tr. by Saburo Yamamura. Tokyo, Hokuseido, 1967. 98p.
「愛與死」 藍詳雲訳 台北　台湾商務印書館　1971. 91p.
「愛與死」 江柏峰訳 台北　鴻文出版社　1973. 1冊

Aiyoku　愛慾

'愛慾' 章克標訳 「東方雑誌」 第23巻14期　15期　16期 17期 1926.
「愛慾」 章克標訳 上海　金屋書店　192?. 1冊
'The passion' Tr. by Noboru Hidaka. *The passion, and three other Japanese plays*. Honolulu, Oriental Literature Society, 1933. p.87-178; N. Y. Greenwood Press, 1971. p.87-178

Akatsuki　暁

Dawn. Tr. by Takehide Kikuchi. Tokyo, Information Publishing, 1972. 45p.

Aru fūfu　ある夫婦

　'某夫婦'　周作人訳　「小説月報」　第14巻11号　1923.
　　p.1–8;「武者小路實篤集」上海　商務實書館　1926;
　　「兩條血痕」上海　開明書店　192?.

Aru gaka to sonchō　ある画家と村長

　'某畫家與村長'　陳碬訳　「小説月報」　第15巻7号　1924.
　　p.1–9

Aru gashitsu no nushi　ある画室の主

　'畫室主人'　楊雲飛訳　「武者小路實篤戯曲集」上海　中華
　　書局　1929. p.135–219

Aru hi no Ikkyū　或る日の一休

　'一日裏的一休和尚'　周作人訳　「小説月報」　第13巻4号
　　1922. p.1–12;「現代日本小説集」上海　商務印書
　　館　1923;「武者小路實篤集」上海　商務印書館
　　1926;「兩條血痕」上海　開明書店　192?.
　'Ein Tag aus Ikkyus Leben'　Übers. von Alexan-
　　der Spann. *Das Junge Japan*, Bd. 1, 1924. p.9–19
　'The day's episode in Ikkyu's life'　Tr. by Fumi-
　　kazu Tanaka. *Osaka Mainichi*, June 8–11, 1929.
　'一日裏的一休和尚'　「一休和尚」　台北　台湾啓明書局
　　1958. p.1–19
　'Monk Ikkyu'　Tr. by Umeyo Hirano. *Buddhist
　　plays from Japanese literature*. Tokyo, CIIB
　　Press, 1962. p.28–37

Aru hi no koto　或る日の事

　'某日的事'　仲雲訳　「小説月報」　第15巻8号　1924. p.1–
　　17

Aru kazoku　或る家族

　'A family affair'　Tr. by Yozan T. Iwasaki and
　　Glenn Hughes. *New plays from Japan*. Lon-
　　don, Ernest Benn, 1930. p.73–108; *Treasury of
　　world literature*, ed. by D. D. Runes. N. Y.
　　Philosophical Library, 1956. p.938–946

Aru seinen no yume　或る青年の夢

　'一個青年的夢'　魯迅訳　「新青年」　第7巻2期　3期　4期
　　5期 1920;「魯迅全集 12」上海　魯迅全集出版社
　　1938. 作家書屋　1946. 大連　光華書店　1948. 北
　　京　人民文学出版社　1973. p.7–286;「魯迅譯文集
　　2」北京　人民文学出版社　1958. p.9–200
　'一個青年的夢'　魯迅訳　上海　商務印書館　1922. 1冊;
　　上海　北新書局　192?. 1冊; 香港　今代圖書公司
　　1966. 284p.

Atarashiki mura　新しき村

　「新村」　孫百剛訳　上海　光華書局　1927. 1冊

Chichi to musume　父と娘

　'父與女'　崔萬秋訳　「武者小路實篤戯曲集」上海　中華書
　　局　1929. p.1–74

Daini no haha　第二の母

　'第二的母親'　周作人訳　「現代日本小説集」上海　商務印
　　書館　1923;「日本現代小説 1」上海　商務印書
　　館　1930.
　'第二的母親'　「少年的悲哀」　郁達夫等訳　台北　啓明書
　　局　1956. p.26–48

Daruma　だるま

　'Daruma'　Tr. by G. Ogura. *Japan Times*, Oct. 28,
　　1928.
　'Daruma'　Tr. by J. M. Shinshiro. *Aoba no fue*.
　　Honolulu, Univ. of Hawaii, 1937. n.p.
　'Bodhidharma'　Tr. by Umeyo Hirano. *Buddhist
　　plays from Japanese literature*. Tokyo, CIIB
　　Press, 1962. p.108
　'Daruma'　Tr. Saipin Meksakul. *Rueng sun yee-
　　pun 1*. Bangkok, Ukrornsasna, 1977. p.73–
　　84.

Eiji satsuriku chū no ichi shō dekigoto　嬰児殺戮中の一
小出来事

　'嬰児屠殺中的一件小事'　周作人訳　「語絲」　第77期
　　1926. p.1–4;「兩條血痕」上海　開明書店　192?.

Ei no tegami mittsu　Aの手紙三つ

　'三封遺書'　湯鶴逸訳　「東方雑誌」　第23巻4期　1926.
　　p.119–126

Gonen mae no koto　五年前の事

　'五年前에있었던일'　表文台訳　「日本代表作家百人集 2」
　　서울　希望出版社　1966.　p.66–82;「日本短篇文学
　　全集 2」서울　新太陽社　1969. p.130–146

Fukō na otoko　不幸な男

　'不幸的男子'　張資平訳　「東方雑誌」　第22巻13期　1925.
　　p.122–142,　第22巻14期　1925.　p.118–132;「資
　　平譯品集」上海　現代書局　192?.

Haha to ko　母と子

　'母與子'　崔萬秋訳　「真美善」　第1巻7期　8期　9期　10
　　期 11期 1928.
　「母與子」　崔萬秋訳　上海　真美善書店　192?. 1冊

Hanasaka jijii　花咲爺

　The man of the flowers.　Tr. by Junichi Natori.
　　Tokyo, Hokuseido, 1955. 54p.
　'The man of the flowers'　Tr. by Junichi Natori.
　　Two fables of Japan. Tokyo, Hokuseido, 1957.
　　p.7–54

Jinsei ronshū　人生論集

　「幸福的人生」　劉焜輝訳　台北　漢文書店　1972. 244p.
　「人生論」　陳冠學訳　高雄　北辰印行　1974. 158p.
　「人生小品」　王祥琳訳　台北　常春樹書房　1975. 179p

Kachi kachi yama　かちかち山

　'The rabbit's revenge'　Tr. by Junichi Natori.
　　Two fables of Japan. Tokyo, Hokuseido, 1957.
　　p.55–115

Kodoku no tamashii　孤独の魂

　「孤獨之魂」　崔萬秋訳　上海　中華書局　1929. 1冊

Kōfuku na kazoku　幸福な家族

　'A happy family'　Tr. by Takehide Kikuchi.
　　Info.　Sept.-Oct. Nov. Dec. 1961, Jan.
　　Feb.—March 1962, May 1962.

Kugi o utsu oto　釘を打つ音

　'The driving of nails'　Tr. by Takehide Kikuchi.
　　Eigo Kenkyu, v.42, no.9, 1953.　p.60–63

Kume no sennin　久米仙人

　'久米仙人'　韜玉訳　「東方雑誌」　第18巻13期　1921.
　　p.93–95;「近代日本小説集」上海　商務印書館　192?.
　'久米仙人'　周作人訳　「日本現代小説集 1」上海　商務印
　　書館　1930.
　'久米仙人'　新興書局編輯部訳　「日本短篇小説選」　台北
　　新興書局　1958. p.42–44; 台南　鳴宇出版社 1972.
　　p.42–44
　'久米仙人'　「日本作家十二人集」香港　新學書店　1959.
　　p.73–77

Minōryokusha no nakama 未能力者の仲間

'没有能力者' 仲雲訳 「東方雑誌」 第21巻11号 1924. p.125–142

Miyamoto Musashi 宮本武蔵

'Miyamoto Musashi' Tr. by S. G. Brickley. *The writing of idiomatic English*. Tokyo, Kenkyusha, 1951. p.63–71

Momoiro no heya 桃色の室

'桃色女郎' 樊仲雲訳 「小説月報」 第15巻6号 1924. p.1–13;「武者小路實篤集」上海 商務印書館 1926. '桃色女郎' 「一休和尚」台北 啓明書局 1958. p.21–56

Nihiki no nezumi 二疋の鼠

'Two mice' Tr. by Richard Foster. *Eigo Kenkyu*, v.55, no.11, 1966. p.19–23; no.12, 1966. p.33–35

Niji 虹

'A rainbow' Tr. by Takehide Kikuchi. *Info*, Dec. 1962. Jan. Feb.-March, April, May 1963 in four parts.

Ningen banzai 人間万才

'Three cheers for man' Tr. by Kenneth Strong. *Japan Quarterly*, v.10, no.1, 1963. p.52–94

Nojima sensei no yume 野島先生の夢

'野島先生之夢' 崔萬秋訳 「武者小路實篤戯曲集」上海 中華書局 1929. p.75–133

Ryōkan 良寛

'Ryokan' Übers. von Oscar Benl. *Flüchtiges Leben, moderne japanische Erzählungen*. Berlin, Landsmann, 1942.

Shaka 釈迦

'迦留夷陀' 湯鶴逸訳 「東方雑誌」 第21巻24期 1924. p.99–108

Shoka Taizan no yume 書家泰山の夢

'Счастливый каллиграф Тайдзан' Перевод З. Рахима. *Японская новелла 1960–1970*. Москва, Прогресс, 1972. p.162–172

Sono imōto その妹

'Seine Schwester' Übers. von Alexander Spann. *Das Junge Japan*, Bd. 1, 1925. p.259–278, 350–368, 415–430
「妹妹」 周白棣訳 上海 中華書局 1932. 1冊
The sister. Tr. by Kiichi Nishi. Tokyo, Kairyudo, 1936. 162p.

Toge made uruwashi 棘まで美し

'Even thorns are beautiful' Tr. by Takehide Kikuchi. *Info*, June, July, Aug.-Sept. Oct. Nov. 1962 in 5 parts.

Washi mo shiranai わしも知らない

'I don't know either' Tr. by Umeyo Hirano. *Young East*, no.19, Autumn, 1956. p.23–32; *Buddhist plays from Japanese literature*. Tokyo, CIIB Press, 1962. p.9–27

Yonin 四人

'四人' 王古魯 恆祖正訳 「四人及其他」 上海 南京書店 1931.

Yuda no benkai hoka ユダの弁解(他)

'Judas' explanation; John, on hearing Judas' explanation' Tr. by Richard McKinnon. *The heart is alone*, ed. by R. McKinnon. Tokyo, Hokuseido, 1957. p.86–98

Yūjō 友情

Friendship. Tr. by Ryozo Matsumoto. Tokyo, Hokuseido, 1958. 162p.
'Amicizia' Tr. di R. Vulpitta. *Antologia della letteratura coreana e giapponese*. Milano, Fratelli Fabbri, 1969. p. 246–252

Poems 詩

'1 poem' 周作人訳 「新青年」 第9巻4期 1921. p.35
'The closed door' Tr. by Shigeshi Nishimura. *The Current of the World*, v.26, no.11, 1949. p.45
'Scene of peace' Tr. by Shigeshi Nishimura. *The Current of the World*, v.28, no.1, 1951. p.41
'Loneliness' *An anthology of modern Japanese Poetry*, ed. and tr. by Ichiro Kono and Rikutaro Fukuda. Tokyo, Kenkyusha, 1957. p.95
'1 poem' Übers. von Kuniyo Takayasu und Manfred Hausmann. *Ruf der Regenpfeifer*. München, Bechtle Verlag, 1961. p.83

Criticism and Essays 評論・エッセイ

'Kokoro no utsukushisa' Tr. by Yokichi Okuma. *Chugai Eigo*, April 1920.
'與支那未知的友人' 周作人訳 「新青年」 第7巻3期 1920. p.47–52
'論詩' 魯迅訳 「莽原」 第12期 1926. p.496–499;「壁下譯叢」 上海 北新書局 1929;「魯迅全集 16」上海 魯迅全集出版社 1938. 作家書屋 1946. 大連 光華書店 1948. 北京 人民文学出版社 1973. p.179–182;「魯迅譯文集 5」北京 人民文学出版社 1958. p.268–270
'在一切藝術' 魯迅訳 「莽原」 第16期 1926. p.652–655;「壁下譯叢」 上海 北新書局 1929;「魯迅全集 16」 上海 魯迅全集出版社 1938. 作家書屋 1946. 大連 光華書店 1948. 北京 人民文学出版社 1973. p.164–167;「魯迅譯文集 5」北京 人民文学出版社 1958. p.255–258
'凡有藝術品' 魯迅訳 「莽原」 第17期 1926. p.685–687;「壁下譯叢」 上海 北新書局 1929. p.253–254;「魯迅全集 16」 上海 魯迅全集出版社 1938. 作家書屋 1946. 大連 光華書店 1948. 北京 人民文学出版社 1973. p.162–163;「魯迅譯文集 5」 北京 人民文学出版社 1958. p.253–254
'文學者の一生' 魯迅訳 「莽原」 第2巻3期 1927. p.83–94;「壁下譯叢」 上海 北新書局 1929;「魯迅全集 16」 上海 魯迅全集出版社 1938. 作家書屋 1946. 大連 光華書店 1948. 北京 人民文学出版社 1973. p.168–178;「魯迅譯文集 5」北京 人民文学出版社 1958. p.259–267
'藝術家の使命' 湯鶴逸訳 「世界日報付刊」 1927年6月
'創作家の資格' 張我軍訳 「華北日報副刊」 1929年7月
'随想録' 沈思訳 「讀書月刊」 第2巻1期 1931. p.297–311
「戯劇研究」 沈宰白訳 上海 良友圖書 193?. 1冊
'給志於文學者' 羅伯建訳 「藝文雑誌」 第1巻2期 1943. p.50–52
'論語雑感' 陳淑女訳 「書和人」 第48期 1966. p.1–3
'Return to nature' *Chanoyu Quarterly*, v.1, no.2, 1970. p.1–4
'友情に関해서 ; 人生과나에관해서' 鄭成煥 金泳杓訳 「世界에세이文学全集 8」 서울 東西出版社 1974. p.10–31;「世界随筆文学全集 8」서울 世進出版社 1976. p.10–31

MUSHANOKŌJI Saneatsu

'B 的自述'　倫叟訳　「東方雑誌」　第18巻14期　1921.
p.95–105
'His birth—one act Kyogen' *Japan Times*, Sept.
15, 1929.
'忠厚老實人'　崔萬秋訳　「眞美善」　第6巻 1931.
「人的生活」　毛詠棠　李宗武訳　上海　中華書局　193?.
1冊
「조용한暴風」　朴敬勛訳　서울　玄岩社 1964. 294p.
「이야기의八相録」　朴敬勛訳　서울　玄岩社 1970. 377p.

N

NADA Inada　なだ・いなだ　1920–

Essays　エッセイ

'Just a little difference' Tr. by Ronald Toby.
Japan Quarterly, v.24, no.3, 1977. p.314–316
'An age of useless information' Tr. by Nina Raj.
Japan Quarterly, v.24, no.4, 1977. p.432–434

NAGAE Michitarō　長江道太郎　1905–

Poems　詩

'사랑하는時間'崔一秀訳　「기다리고있네」　서울　韓国政
経社 1966. p.166–168
'고백'　「永遠한世界名詩全集 2」 黄錦燦編　서울　翰林
出版社 1969. p.66;「永遠한世界名詩全集 5」黄
錦燦編 서울　翰林出版社 1973. p.66

NAGAI Kafū　永井荷風　1879–1959

Ajisai　あぢさゐ

'Hydrangea' Tr. by Edward Seidensticker. *Mo-
dern Japanese stories*, ed. by Ivan Morris.
London, Spottiswoode, 1961; Tokyo, Tuttle,
1962. p.66–80
'Hortensie' Deutsch von Monique Humbert.
Nippon. Zürich, Diogenes, 1965.

Aki no onna　秋の女

'秋女'　鐘肇政訳　「戰後日本短篇小説選」　台北　台湾商
務印書館 1968. p.77–82

Ame shōshō　雨瀟瀟

'Quiet rain' Tr. by Edward Seidensticker. *Japan
Quarterly*, v.11, no.1, 1964. p.46–63; *Kafu the
scribbler*. Stanford, Stanford Univ. Press,
1965. p.253–277; *A strange tale from East of
the River, and other stories*. Tokyo, Tuttle,
1971. p.81–105
'Pioggia a cateratte' Tr. di R. Vulpitta. *Antologia della letteratura coreana e giapponese*.
Milano, Fratelli Fabbri, 1969. p.257–262

Azumabashi　あづま橋

'吾妻橋'　傅寶齡訳　「勲章」　台北　文壇社 1960. p.107–
118

Bokutō kitan　濹東綺譚

'A strange tale from East of the River' Tr. by
Edward Seidensticker. *Japan Quarterly*, v.5,
no.2, 1958. p.195–222; *Kafu the scribbler*.
Stanford, Stanford Univ. Press, 1965. p.278–
328; *A strange tale from East of theRiver, and
other stories*. Tokyo, Tuttle, 1971. p.106–156

Botan no kyaku　牡丹の客

'Le jardin des pivoines' Tr. par Serge Elisséev.
Le jardin des pivoines. Paris, Au Sans Pareil,
1927. p.1–16
'A bazsarózsák kertje' Ford. Thein Alfréd. *Mai
Japán dekameron*. Budapest, Nyugat, 1935.
p.187–198
'The peony garden' Tr. by Edward Seidensticker.
Kafu the scribbler. Stanford, Stanford Univ.
Press, 1965. p.219–225; *A strange tale from
East of the River, and other stories*. Tokyo,
Tuttle, 1971. p.47–53
'모란꽃을찾는손'李柱訓訳　「日本代表作家百人集 2」서
울　希望出版社 1966. p.32–37;「日本短篇文学全
集 2」서울　新太陽社 1969. p.96–101

Futari zuma　二人妻

'The two wives' Tr. by S. G. Brickley. *The Writing
of idiomatic English*. Tokyo, Kenkyusha, 1951.
p.72–77

Geisha no haha　芸者の母

'A gésa snyja' Ford. Sz. Holti Mária. *Modern
Japán elbeszélők*. Budapest, Európa Könyvkiadó, 1967. p.25–31

Irootoko　色男

'Ihr Geliebter' Übers. von Kurt Meissner. *Der
Tanzfächer*, von K. Meissner. Tokyo, 1943.
p.197–220
'Ihr Geliebter' Übers. von Oscar Benl. *Japan,
Geistige Begegnung*. Tübingen, Erdmann,
1964. p.114–130; *Eine Glocke in Fukagawa*.
Tübingen, Erdmann, 1969. p. 114–130

Kaketori　掛取り

'The bill-collecting' Tr. by Torao Taketomo.
*Paulownia, seven stories from contemporary
Japanese writers*. N. Y. Duffield, 1918. p.71–
102; *Treasury of world literature*, ed. by D. D.
Runes. N. Y. Philosophical Library, 1956.
p. 674–684
'Bill collecting' Tr. by Roland A. Lange. *Journal-
Newsletter of the Association of Teachers of
Japanese*, v.5, no.2, 1968. p.32–41

Kanraku　歓楽

'Pleasure' Tr. by Ryozo Matsumoto. *Japanese
literature, new and old*. Tokyo, Hokuseido,
1961. p.31–74
'Nautinto' Suomentanut Kari Jalonen. *Kiusaus
ja Nautinto*. Hämeenlinnä, 1973.

Katsushika miyage　葛飾みやげ

'The scavengers' Tr. by Edward Seidensticker.
Kafu the scribbler. Stanford, Stanford Univ.
Press, 1965. p.339–344; *A strange tale from
East of the River, and other stories*. Tokyo,
Tuttle, 1971. p.167–172

Kazagokochi 風邪ごこち

'Coming down with a cold' Tr. by Edward Seidensticker. *Kafu the scribbler.* Stanford, Stanford Univ. Press, 1965. p.226–236; *A strange tale from East of the River, and other stories.* Tokyo, Tuttle, 1971. p.54–64

Kitsune 狐

'The fox' Tr. by Asataro Miyamori. *Representative tales of Japan.* Tokyo, Sanko Shoin, 1917. p.126–150

'Le renard' Tr. par Serge Elisséev. *Japon et Extrême-Orient,* no.3, Feb. 1924. p.194–216; *Neuf nouvelles japonaises.* Paris, G. van Œst, 1924. p.31–53

Kunshō 勲章

'The decoration' Tr. by Edward Seidensticker. *Kafu the scribbler.* Stanford, Stanford Univ. Press, 1965. p.329–335; *A strange tale from East of the River, and other stories.* Tokyo, Tuttle, 1971. p.157–163

Kyūkon 旧恨

「舊恨」方光燾訳 「東方雜誌」 第28巻6期 1931. p.107–114

Nichiyōbi 日曜日

「星期日」傅寶齡訳 「勲章」 台北 文壇社 1960. p.119–127

Nigirimeshi にぎり飯

'Рисовые шарики' Перевод Т. Чегодарь. *Японская новелла.* Москва, Изд. Иност. Лит. 1961. p.151–159

'Аемдестик' Аударган Ж. Мухамеджанов. *Жапон енгимелери.* Алма-Ата, Жазушы, 1965. p.59–68

Odoriko 踊子

'The dancing girl' Tr. by Edward Seidensticker. *Kafu the scribbler.* Stanford, Stanford Univ. Press, 1965. p.336–338; *A strange tale from East of the River, and other stories.* Tokyo, Tuttle, 1971. p.164–166

Ōkubo dayori 大窪だより

'Tidings from Okubo' Tr. by Edward Seidensticker. *Kafu the scribbler.* Stanford, Stanford Univ. Press, 1965. p.237–243; *A strange tale from East of the River, and other stories.* Tokyo Tuttle, 1971. p.65–71

Omokage おもかげ

'Geliebtes Gesicht' Übers. von Oscar Benl. *Flüchtiges Leben, moderne japanische Erzählungen.* Berlin, Landsmann, 1942; *Der Kirschblütenzweig.* München, Nymphenburger, 1965. p.382–400

Pari no wakare 巴里のわかれ

'Adiau Parizo!' Tr. Yutaka Waseda. *El Japana literaturo.* Tokyo, Japana Esperanto Instituto, 1965. p.158–168

Sumida gawa すみだ川

'The River Sumida' Tr. by Donald Keene. *Modern Japanese literature,* ed. by D. Keene. N. Y. Grove Press, 1956; Tokyo, Tuttle, 1957. p.159–200

'The River Sumida' Tr. by Edward Seidensticker. *Kafu the scribbler.* Stanford, Stanford Univ. Press, 1965. p.181–218; *A strange tale from East of the River, and other stories.* Tokyo, Tuttle, 1971. p.9–46

Ude kurabe 腕くらべ

Geisha in rivalry. Tr. by Kurt Meissner, with the collaboration of Ralph Friedrich. Tokyo, Tuttle, 1963. 206p.

'Rivalry (from chapter 12)' Tr. by Edward Seidensticker. *Kafu the scribbler.* Stanford, Stanford Univ. Press, 1965. p.244–252; *A strange tale from East of the River, and other stories.* Tokyo, Tuttle, 1971. p.72–80

Ukiyoe 浮世絵

'Ukiyoe' Tr. by Torao Taketomo. *Paulownia, seven stories from contemporary Japanese writers.* N. Y. Duffield, 1918. p.105–114

NAGAI Michiko 永井路子 1925–

Rekishi o sawagaseta onna tachi 歴史をさわがせた女たち

「世界史上名女人」 王家成訳 台北 四季出版社 1976. 1冊

NAGAI Takashi 永井 隆 1908–1951

Horobinu mono o 亡びぬものを

Notizen auf einem Sterbebett. Übers. von Olaf Graf Osb. St. Ottilien, Eos, 1953. 299p.

Kono ko o nokoshite この子を残して

Lasciando questi ragazzi. Tr. di S. Bosniak. Milano, Nuova Massimo, 1952. 292p.

Nagasaki no kane 長崎の鐘

We of Nagasaki. Tr. by Ichiro Shirato and Herbert B. L. Silverman. N. Y. Sloan and Pearce, 1951. 189p.

Le campane di Nagasaki. Tr. di Mièga Maria Pia. Milano, Garzanti, 1952. 140p.

Les cloches de Nagasaki. Adapté en français par K. et M. Yoshida, M. Suzuki et J. Masson. Paris, Castermann, 1954. 255p.; Tournai, Castermann, 1954, 196p.

Die Glocken von Nagasaki. Übers. von Friedrich Seizaburo Nohara. München, Rex Verlag, 1955. 170p.

Dzwony Nagasaki. Tłumaczyc Maria Szwykowska. Warszawa, Pax, 1955. 165p.

La campana de Nagasaki. Tr. por Namio Sakai. Buenos Aires, Oberon, 1956. 1v.

Zvony Nagasaki. Přel. Jitka Křesálková. Praha, Lidova Demokratie, 1958. 132p.; Praha, Vysehrad, 1969. 133p.

Dingen die niet vergaan. Vertaald door Uytten-

NAGAI Takashi

daele. Kasterlee, De Vroente, 1960. 135p.
Anubōmbu vinappāl. Tr. into Malayalam by A.
Atappur. Kottayam, S. C. P. S. 1962. 180p.

Rozario no kusari ロザリオの鎖

'The chain of rosary' Tr. by Tamako Matsumoto. *Missionary Bulletin*, v.2, no.4, 1948.
p.85–86
La chaine du rosaire. Tr. par Masao Yoshida et
J. Masson. Louvain, Revue de l'Aucam,
1951. 79p.; Paris, Castermann, 1951. 69p.
Nel deserto dell'atomica. Parma, Edizioni Mis-
sionarie, 1963. 1v.

「永遠한것을」李承雨訳 서울 聖바오로出版社 1965.
354p.
「묵주알」李承雨訳 서울 聖바오로出版社 1970. 217p.

NAGAI Tatsuo 永井龍男 1904–

Aibiki あいびき

'Brief encounter' Tr. by Edward Seidensticker.
Japan Quarterly, v.7, no.2, 1960. p.200–211;
Asian P.E.N. anthology, ed. by F. S. Jose.
N. Y. Taplinger 1966. p.19–29; *Contempo-
rary Japanese literature*, ed. by Howard
Hibbett. N. Y. Knopf, 1977. p.390–399

Aotsuyu 青梅雨

'За пеленой дождя' Перевод С. Гутермана.
Японская новелла 1960–1970. Москва, Прогресс, 1972. p.173–185

Asagiri 朝霧

'Morning mist' Tr. by Edward Seidensticker.
Modern Japanese stories, ed. by Ivan Morris.
London, Spottiswoode, 1961; Tokyo, Tuttle,
1962. p.302–319
'아침안개' 崔白山訳 「日本代表作家百人集 3」 서울 希
望出版社 1966. p.318–332;「日本短編文学全集 4」
서울 新太陽社 1969. p.78–92

Ikko 一個

'One' Tr. by E. G. Seidensticker. *Japan Quarterly*,
v.7, no.2, 1960. p.211–217
'Ein Stück' Deutsch von Jürgen Berndt. *Träume
aus zehn Nächten*. Berlin, Aufbau Verlag,
1975. p.580–590

Kochabanba yuki コチャバンバ行き

'Bound for Cochabamba' Tr. by David W.
Plath. *Japan Interpreter*, v.8, no.4, 1974.
p.510–524

Mikan 蜜柑

'Oranges' Tr. by John Bester. *Japan P.E.N.
News*, no.16, Jan. 1966. p.1–4

Shiroi saku 白い柵

'The white fence' Tr. by William L. Clark.
Jiji Eigo Kenkyu, v.11, no.12, 1956. p.38–42,
v.12, no.1, 1957. p.38; *Various kinds of bugs,
and other stories from present-day Japan.*
Tokyo, Kenkyusha, 1958. p.55–71

Shō bijutsukan de 小美術館で

'Quadri di una esposizione' Tr. de Enrico Ci-
cogna. *Novelle giapponesi*. Milano, Martello, 1969. p.225–231

Yui Mahoko 由比 真帆子

'Mahoko Yui' Tr. by Kazutomo Takahashi.
Eigo Kenkyu, v.23, no.9, 1930. p.826–831

NAGAMATSU Kazu 永松かず

Kono kora o misute rarenai この子らを見すてられない

「이 땅에 저 별빛을」 黄順必訳 서울 創文社 1965. 289p.

NAGAMI Tokutarō 永見德太郎 1890–1950

Criticism 評論

'芥川龍之介氏與河童' 黎烈文訳 「河童」 上海 商務印書
館 193?.

NAGASAWA Tetsuo 長沢哲夫 1942–

Poems 詩

'From "Au I Lu Mahara"' Tr. by Gary Snyder.
Japanese poetry now. London, André Deutsch,
1972. p.46; *Japanese poetry today*. N.Y.
Schocken Books, 1972. p.48

NAGASE Kiyoko 永瀬清子 1906–

Poems 詩

'At the foot of the mountain' *An anthology of
modern Japanese poetry*, ed. and tr. by Ichiro
Kono and Rikutaro Fukuda. Tokyo, Ken-
kyusha, 1957. p.96
'속삭여요살며시; 薔薇' 崔一秀訳 「기다리고있네」 서울
韓国政経社 1966. p.25–27, 139–141
'Европада карлан журет; Кулаган кайын; Гурме'
Которгон Ж. Садыков. *Хиросима кектери*.
Фрунзе, Кыргызстан, 1969. p.40–42
'The ruins have not yet grown cold' Tr. by
Miyao Ohara. *The songs of Hiroshima*, Tokyo,
Taihei Shuppansha, 1971. p.36–37
'Mother' *The burning heart*, tr. and ed. by Kenneth
Rexroth and Ikuko Atsumi. N. Y. Seabury
Press, 1977. p.90

NAGASHIMA Toyotarō 長島豊太郎 1888–

Tanka 短歌

'A lion performer' Tr. by Asataro Miyamori.
*Masterpieces of Japanese poetry, ancient and
modern*. Tokyo, Maruzen, 1936; Tokyo,
Taiseido, 1956; N. Y. Greenwood Press,
1971. p.761–762

NAGATA Hideo 長田秀雄 1885–1949

Shigai no kōshō 死骸の哄笑

'死骸的哄笑' 楊騒訳 「語絲」 第4巻41期 1928. p.61–90

Poems 詩

'The beggars' Tr. by Shigeshi Nishimura. *The Current of the World*, v.15, no.8, 1938. p.98–99

'接生院' 楊騒訳 「北新半月刊」 第3巻1号 1929. p.195–224

NAGATA Mikihiko 長田幹彦 1887–1964

Haha no te 母の手

'His mother's arm' Tr. by G. M. Sinclair and Kazo Suita. *Tokyo people, three stories from the Japanese*. Tokyo, Keibunkan, 1925. p.1–60

Mai ōgi 舞扇

'Der Tanzfächer' Übers. von Kurt Meissner. *Der Tanzfächer*, von K. Meissner. Tokyo, 1943. p.17–59

NAGATA Seiran 永田青嵐 1876–1943

Haiku 俳句

'3 haiku' Tr. by Asataro Miyamori. *Anthology of haiku, ancient and modern*. Tokyo, Maruzen, 1932. p.822–824
'The River Tama; An uguisu; Mosquitoes' Tr. by Asataro Miyamori. *Haiku poems, ancient and modern*. Tokyo, Maruzen, 1940. p.341–342
'1 haiku' Übers. von Gerolf Coudenhove. *Japanische Jahreszeiten*. Zürich, Manesse Verlag, 1963. p.286
'Insect symphony; Spring hills' Tr. by Kenneth Yasuda. *A pepper-pod*. Tokyo, Tuttle, 1976. p.93

Essay エッセイ

'On angling' Tr. by Shigeshi Nishimura. *Eigo kenkyu*, v.26, no.7, 1933. p.618–620

NAGATANI Kunio 長谷邦夫

Poems 詩

'Haniwa' Tr. by William L. Clark. *Jiji Eigo Kenkyu*, v.21, no.3, 1966. p.69

NAGATSUKA Takashi 長塚 節 1879–1915

Ofusa おふさ

'오후사' 郭夏信訳 「世界文学全集 94」 서울 乙酉文化社 1962. p.133–145

Otsugi no ko おつぎの子

'媒母御次' 「標準日本名著選讀」 孫文斗編 台北 大新書局 1969. p.65–72

Tanka 短歌

'The moonbeams; Written during illness' Tr. by Asataro Miyamori. *Masterpieces of Japanese poetry, ancient and modern*. Tokyo, Maruzen, 1936; Tokyo, Taiseido, 1956; N. Y. Greenwood Press, 1971. p.687–688
'5 tanka' Tr. by V. H. Viglielmo. *Japanese literature in the Meiji era*. Tokyo, Obunsha, 1955. p.396–398
'6 tanka' Tr. by H. H. Honda. *The Reeds*, v.3, 1957. p.8, 11, 16, 17
'4 tanka' Übers. von Kuniyo Takayasu und Manfred Hausmann. *Ruf der Regenpfeifer*. München, Bechtle Verlag, 1961. p.96

NAGAYO Yoshirō 長与善郎 1888–1961

Naki ane ni 亡き姉に

'亡姉' 周作人訳 「現代日本小説集」 上海 商務印書館 1923; 「日本現代小説集 2」 上海 商務印書館 1930. p.182–197

Saigyō 西行

'西行法師' 周作人訳 「東方雑誌」 第20巻13期 1923. p.111–116; 「兩條血痕」 上海 開明書店 192?.

Seidō no Kirisuto 青銅の基督

Der Bronze-Christus. Übers. von Karl Weidinger. München, Weidinger, 1934. 120p.
Le Christ de bronze. Tr. par Kikou Yamata. Tokyo, Kokusai Bunka Shinkokai, 1941. 153p.
A imagem de bronze. Tr. por Zenaide Andrea. Rio de Janeiro, Pongetti, 1941. 170p.
Il Cristo di bronzo. Tr. di Aldo Alberti. Milano, A. Corticelli, 1942. 1v.
The bronze Christ. Tr. by Kenzoh Yada and Henry P. Ward. N. Y. Taplinger, 1959. 159p.; N. Y. Asia Publishing House, 1962. 159p.
Bronzestoberen frå Nagasaki. Overs frå engel. per Gunnar Juel Jorgensen. København, Credo, 1959. 159p.
De bronzen Christus. Vertaald door J. Verstraeten. Bilthoven, Neilssen, 1960. 158p.
Il Christo di bronzo. Tr. Maria Gallone. Milano, Rizzoli, 1961. 147p.
Kristo el bronzo. Tr. Masao Ueyama. Osaka, Pirato-sha, 1970. 108p.

Yama no ue no kannon 山の上の観音

'山上的觀音' 周作人訳 「現代日本小説集」 上海 商務印書館 1923; 「日本現代小説集 2」 上海 商務印書館 1930. p.198–205
'山上的觀音' 新興書局編集部訳 「日本短篇小説選」 台北 新興書局 1958. p.115–119; 台南 鳴字出版社 1972. p.115–119

Essay エッセイ

'我為什麽創作呢' 謝六逸訳 「文学週報」 第32期

NAITŌ Meisetsu 内藤鳴雪 1847–1926

Haiku 俳句

'16 haiku' Tr. by Asataro Miyamori. *Anthology of haiku, ancient and modern*. Tokyo, Maruzen, 1932. p.658–668

'Wreaths; A rainbow; A woman and a priest; A plum-tree in the field; A kite; The autumn tempest; An angry stream and smiling mountains' Tr. by Asataro Miyamori. *Haiku poems, ancient and modern*. Tokyo, Maruzen, 1940. p.298–300

'2 haiku' Tr. by Harold Gould Henderson. *The bamboo broom*. Tokyo, J. L. Thompson, 1933; London, Kegan Paul, 1933. p.115, 117

'Haiku' Tr. par Kuni Matsuo et Steinilber-Oberlin. *Anthologie des poètes japonais contemporains*. Paris, Mercure de France, 1939. p.281–282

'5 haiku' Tr. by V. H. Viglielmo. *Japanese literature in the Meiji era*. Tokyo, Obunsha, 1955. p.428

'The only trace; Samsara's wheel' Tr. by Harold Stewart. *A net of fireflies*. Tokyo, Tuttle, 1960. p.97, 102

'4 haiku' Übers. von Günther Debon. *Im Schnee die Fähre*. München, Piper, 1960. p.9–16

'Haiku' Tercüme etmek L. Sami Akalin. *Japon şiiri*. İstanbul, Varlik Yayinevi, 1962. p.222

'3 haiku' Tr. by Peter Beilenson and Harry Behn. *Haiku harvest*. Mount Vernon, Peter Pauper Press, 1962. p.51, 53, 54

'2 haiku' Übers. von Gerolf Coudenhove. *Japanische Jahreszeiten*. Zürich, Manesse Verlag, 1963. p.11, 333

'22 haiku' *A history of haiku v.2*, by R. H. Blyth. Tokyo, Hokuseido, 1964. p.108–115

'4 haiku' Tr. by Geoffrey Bownas and Anthony Thwaite. *The Penguin book of Japanese verse*. Harmondsworth, Penguin Books, 1964. p.164

'1 haiku' Til norsk ved Paal-Helge Haugen. *Blad frå ein austleg hage*. Oslo, Det Norske Samlaget, 1965. p.83

'Golden maple-spray; New year's day; A butterfly' Tr. by Kenneth Yasuda. *A pepper-pod*. Tokyo, Tuttle, 1976. p.77

'1 haiku' Tr. by Takamasa Sasaki. *Eigo Seinen*, v.122, no.5, 1976. p.231

'Frunze de arţar; Pitpalaci' Traducerea Virgil Teodorescu. *Din lirica japoneză*. Bucureşti, Editura Univers, n.d. p.125

Criticism 評論

'俳句之來歷及特色' 周豊一訳 「藝文雜誌」 第1卷1期 1943. p.61–67

NAKA Kansuke 中 勘助 1885–1965

Gin no saji 銀の匙

'Sanctuary' Tr. by Howard Hibbett. *Modern Japanese literature*, ed. by D. Keene. N. Y. Grove Press, 1956; Tokyo, Tuttle, 1957. p.254–260

'The silver spoon' Tr. by James Kirkup and Michio Nakano. *Japan Quarterly*, v.20, no.3, 1973. p.294–307

The silver spoon. Tr. by Etsuko Terasaki. Chicago, Chicago Review Press, 1976. 188p.

NAKA Tarō 那珂太郎 1922–

Poems 詩

'Castles; Fautrier's birds' *Post-war Japanese poetry*, ed. and tr. by Harry and Lynn Guest and Kajima Shozo. London, Penguin Books, 1972. p.87–89

NAKADA Chūtarō 中田忠太郎

Poems 詩

'Rain' *An anthology of modern Japanese poetry*, ed. and tr. by Ichiro Kono and Rikutaro Fukuda. Tokyo, Kenkyusha, 1957. p.97

'Yağmur' Tercüme etmek L. Sami Akalin. *Japon şiiri*. İstanbul, Varlik Yayinevi, 1962. p.303–304

NAKAE Toshio 中江俊夫 1933–

Poems 詩

'아버지의故鄕' 金龍済訳 「日本詩集」 서울 青雲社 1960. p.89–91

'Parole; Perdere se stessi' *La protesta poetica del Giappone*, a cura di Dacia Maraini e Michiko Nojiri. Roma, Officina Edizioni, 1968. p.143–145

'Night; Moon' Tr. by Thomas Fitzsimmons. *Japanese poetry now*. London, André Deutsch, 1972. p.58–61; *Japanese poetry today*. N. Y. Schocken Books, 1972. p.60–63

'Gutnacht' Übers. von Helmut Gross. *Internationales Jahrbuch für Literatur*, Ensemble 8, 1977. p.102

NAKAGAMI Kenji 中上健次 1946–

Misaki 岬

'꽃' 李元燮訳 「70年代芥川賞小説集」 서울 玄岩社 1976. p.299–372; 「新鋭世界文学選集20世紀 9」 서울 玄岩社 1977. p.299–397

NAKAGAWA Kazumasa 中川一政 1893–

Poems 詩

'Anemone' *An anthology of modern Japanese poetry*, ed. and tr. by Ichiro Kono and Rikutaro Fukuda. Tokyo, Kenkyusha, 1957. p.97

'1 poem' Übers. von Kuniyo Takayasu und Manfred Hausmann. *Ruf der Regenpfeifer*. München, Bechtle Verlag, 1961. p.84

'Gelincik' Tercüme etmek L. Sami Akalin. *Japon şiiri*. İstanbul, Varlik Yayinevi, 1962. p.259

NAKAGAWA Mikiko 中河幹子 1897–

Tanka 短歌

'3 tanka' *Anthology of modern Japanese poetry*, tr. and comp. by Edith Marcombe Shiffert and Yuki Sawa. Tokyo, Tuttle, 1972. p.149

NAKAGAWA Rieko 中川李枝子 1935–

Guri to Gura グリとグラ

Guri and Gura. London, Richard Sadler and Brown, 1966. 1v.
Gumle og Gimle. Oversaette Ib Permin. København, Høst, 1969. 27p.

Guri to Gura no okyakusama グリとグラのおきゃくさま

A surprise visitor. English version by Kenneth Williams. Tokyo, Labo-Teaching Information Center, 1970. 27p.

Iya iya en いやいやえん

Детский сад Тюльпан. Перевод А. Коломиец. Москва, Дет. Лит. 1967. 1v.
Der nein-nein Kindergarten. Übers. von Siegfried Schaarschmidt. Berlin C. Dressler, 1968. 144p.
Bernudarzs «Tulpe». Tr. from the Russian by. Velta Kapteine. Riga, Liesma, 1971. 39p.

Sorairo no tane そらいろのたね

A blue seed. London, Richard Sadler and Brown, 1965. 1v; N. Y. Hastings House, 1967. 1v.
The sky blue seed. Tokyo, Labo-Teaching Information Center, 1972. 26p.

NAKAGAWA Yoichi 中河与一 1897–

Hige 鬚

'The moustache' Tr. by Chieko Morozumi. *Asian and Pacific short stories.* Seoul, Cultural and Social Centre for the Asian and Pacific Region, 1974; Tokyo, Tuttle, 1974. p.84–95

Kōru butōjō 氷る舞踏場

'歡盡悲来' 新興書局編集部訳 「日本短篇小説選」 台北 新興書局 1958. p.6–20; 台南 鳴宇出版社 1972. p.6–20
'冰結的跳舞場' 高汝鴻訳 「日本短篇小説集」 台北 台湾 商務印書館 1969. p.247–279

Senkyō kitan 泉郷奇譚

'A strange story of hot-spring resort' *Cultural Nippon*, v.6, no.2, July 1938. p.107–115

Shitsuraku no niwa 失楽の庭

The garden of lost joy. Tr. by Yoshitaro Negishi. Tokyo, Hokuseido, 1953. 109p.

Son Issen no tomo 孫逸仙の友

'孫逸仙的朋友' 吶吶鷗訳 「色情文化」 上海 水洙書店 1929.

Ten no yūgao 天の夕顔

A moonflower in heaven. Tr. by Akira Ota. Tokyo, Hokuseido, 1949. 96p.
Les longues années. Tr. par Rikutaro Fukuda et Poporsky Leger. Paris, Denöel, 1952. 157p.
Duge godine. Tr. from the French by Milica Grabovac. Ljubljana, Prosvetni Servis, 1957. 220p.; Sarajevo, Svjetlost, 1957. 112p.
'Die Yugao-Blüte am Himmel' Übers. von Oscar Benl. *Der Kirschblütenzweig.* München, Nymphenburger, 1965. p.274–345
Năm dài tình yên. Tr. Pham Quŏc Báo. Saigon, Hŏng-Linh, 1969. 159p.
Tenno yugao. Tr. by Jeremy Ingalls. N. Y. Twayne Publishers, 1975. 176p.

「天上人間」 方紀生訳 大阪 綿城出版社 1929. 1冊
'天上人間' 紀生訳 「藝文雑誌」 第1巻1期 1943. p.79–88

NAKAGIRI Masao 中桐雅夫 1919–

Poems 詩

'A chorus' *An anthology of modern Japanese poetry*, ed. and tr. by Ichiro Kono and Rikutaro Fukuda. Tokyo, Kenkyusha, 1957. p.97
'어느 국회의원의 장례' 金龍済訳 「日本詩集」 서울 青雲社 1960. p.23–26
'Poem for New Year's eve' Tr. by Makoto Ueda. *Literary Review*, v.6, no.1, 1962. p.108
'Kuzey denizi; Bir kiş günü anisi' Tercüme etmek L. Sami Akalin. *Japon şiiri.* İstanbul, Varlik Yayinevi, 1962. p.288–289
'Birdie' 辛東門訳 「世界戦後文学全集 9」 서울 新丘文化社 1962. p.254–255
'The electric train' *Anthology of modern Japanese poetry*, tr. and comp. by Edith Marcombe Shiffert and Yuki Sawa. Tokyo, Tuttle, 1972. p.120
'Seventy nonsensical lines' Tr. by Thomas Fitzsimmons. *Japanese poetry now.* London, André Deutsch, 1972. p.69; *Japanese poetry today.* N. Y. Schocken Books, 1972. p.71
'This bloody-awful country' Tr. by Harry and Lynn Guest and Shozo Kajima. *Postwar Japanese poetry.* Harmondsworth, Penguin Books, 1972. p.59
'Seventy nonsensical lines; A poem for New Year's eve; Spring pilgrimage' Tr. by Thomas Fitzsimmons and Hiroaki Sato. *The poetry of postwar Japan.* Iowa City, Univ. of Iowa Press, 1975. p.49–55

NAKAHARA Ayako 中原綾子 1898–1969

Tanka 短歌

'My heart; Gentle women; Swords; The rose' Tr. by Asataro Miyamori. *Masterpieces of Japanese poetry, ancient and modern.* Tokyo, Maruzen, 1936; Tokyo, Taiseido, 1956; N. Y. Greenwood Press, 1971. p.796–798
'Vanities; Contraries; The diamond' Tr. by Makoto Sangu. *The lyric garland.* Tokyo, Hokuseido, 1957. p.40

NAKAHARA Chūya 中原中也 1907–1937

Poems 詩

'Morning song; The hour of death' Tr. by Donald Keene. *Modern Japanese literature*, ed. by D. Keene. N. Y. Grove Press, 1956; Tokyo, Tuttle, 1957. p.379–380

'Memory of a winter day; The north sea; A cold night' *An anthology of modern Japanese poetry*, ed. and tr. by Ichiro Kono and Rikutaro Fukuda. Tokyo, Kenkyusha, 1957. p.99–100

'La hora de la muerte' *Sur*, no.249, Nov.-Dec. 1957. p.96

'Two poems by Chuya Nakahara' Tr. by Donald Keene. *Today's Japan*, v.5, no.1, 1960. p.41

'Der Zirkus' Übertragen von Shin Aizu. *Der schwermütige Ladekran*. St. Gallen, Tschudy Verlag, 1960. p.28–29

'Leaves of the fig-tree; Cold night; The Marunouchi Building' Tr. by Geoffrey Bownas and Anthony Thwaite. *The Penguin book of Japanese verse*. Harmondsworth, Penguin Books, 1964. p.222–223

'To a dragonfly' *Modern Japanese poetry*, by Donald Keene. Ann Arbor, Center for Japanese Studies, Univ. of Michigan, 1964. p.29–30

'Spring will come again; Bones' Tr. by Donald Keene. *The Japanese image*, ed. by M. Schneps and A. D. Coox. Tokyo, Orient West, 1965. p.347–348

'The hour of death' Tr. by Donald Keene. *The Mentor book of modern Asian literature*, ed. by D. B. Shimer. N. Y. New American Library, 1969. p.128

'正午；大陸風景；馬戯' 徐和隣訳 「現代詩解説」 台北 葡萄園詩刊社 1970. p.71–74

'To a dragonfly' Tr. by Donald Keene. *Landscapes and portraits*. Tokyo, Kodansha International, 1971. p.148

'때묻어버린슬픔에；자장가；겨울날의追憶' 金巣雲訳 「世界의文学大全集 34」 서울 同和出版公社 1971. p.536–537

'In my boyhood; L'espoir abandonné; A song of my life' Tr. by Hideo Yamaguchi. *Kobe Jogakuin Daigaku Ronshu*, v.18, no.3, 1972. p.39–43

'Snowy evening' Tr. by Hideo Naito. *Poetry Nippon*, no.33 & 34, 1976. p.7–8

'Chomon ravine in winter' Tr. by M. Yamaguchi. *Poetry Nippon*, no.35 & 36, 1976. p.11

'Листья с моковницы' Перевод Анатолия Мамонова. *Вкус хризантемы*. Москва, Восточная Литература, 1976. p.79

'North sea' Tr. by Hideo Naito. *Poetry Nippon*, no.37 & 38, 1977. p.24

'Cînted în zori; Cerul morţii' Traducerea Virgil Teodorescu. *Din lirica Japoneză*. Bucureşti, Editura Univers, n.d. p.207–208

'Half my life' Tr. by Yoshiko Nozaki. *Poetry Nippon*, no.41 & 42, 1978. p.13–14

NAKAJIMA Atsushi 中島 敦 1909–1942

Fūfu 夫婦

'Husband and wife' Tr. by Sakuko Matsui. *Solidarity*, June 1970. p.54–60

Gojō shusse 悟浄出世

'Wu Ching's quest' Tr. by Gretchen Evans and Akira Mitsuhashi. *Monumenta Nipponica*, v.27, no.2, 1972. p.191–210

Hikari to kaze to yume 光と風と夢

Light, wind, and dreams. Tr. by Akira Miwa. Tokyo, Hokuseido, 1962. 183p. 1969. 152p

Kitsune tsuki 狐憑

'The possessed' Tr. by Sakuko Matsui. *Solidarity*, June 1970. p.60–64

Meijin den 名人伝

'The expert' Tr. by Ivan Morris. *Encounter*, v.10, no.5, 1958. p.49–53

'Mistrz' Przeł. Anna Gostyńska. *Irys, opowiadania japońskie*. Warszawa, Pánstwowy Instytut Wydawniczy, 1960. p.29–42

'La vivo de arkomajstro' Tr. Masao Miyamoto. *La obstino*. Osaka, Librejo Pirato, 1964. p. 13–26

'Il virtuoso' Tr. di Atsuko Ricca Suga. *Narratori giapponesi moderni*. Milano, Bompiani, 1965. p.735–744

Riryō 李陵

'Li Ling' Tr. Masao Miyamoto. *La obstino*. Osaka, Librejo Pirato, 1964. p.27–86

Sangetsu ki 山月記

'The wild beast' Tr. by Ivan Morris. *Japan Quarterly*, v.6, no.3, 1959. p.342–350; *Modern Japanese short stories*. Tokyo, Japan Publications Trading Co. 1960. p.178–189; Rev. ed. Tokyo, Japan Publications Trading Co. 1970. p.141–150

'Tiger-poet' Tr. by Ivan Morris. *Modern Japanese stories*, ed. by I. Morris. London, Spottiswoode, 1961; Tokyo, Tuttle, 1962. p.453–463

'La luno supermonto' Tr. Masao Miyamoto. *La obstino*. Osaka, Librejo Pirato, 1964. p.1–12

'Das wilde Tier' Deutsch von Monique Humbert. *Nippon*. Zürich, Diogenes, 1965. p.473–485

'Sangetsu-ki' Tr. by Kenji Miki. *The Azaleas*, no.3, 1969.

NAKAJIMA Kawatarō 中島河太郎 1917–

Criticism 評論

'Detective fiction in Japan' *Japan Quarterly*, v.9, no.1, 1962. p.50–56

NAKAJIMA Kenzō 中島健蔵 1903–

Criticism 評論

'Modern Japanese literature' *Atlantic Monthly*, no.195, Jan. 1955. p.165–169

'Miyazawa Kenji, the man and his works' *Japan Quarterly*, v.5, no.1, 1958. p.59–62

'中国现代文学在日本' 李芒訳 「世界文学」 1959年9月 p.89–92

NAKAJIMA Toshi　中島兎士　1884–

Haiku　俳句

'2 haiku'　Tr. by Asataro Miyamori. *Anthology of haiku, ancient and modern*. Tokyo, Maruzen, 1932. p.829–830
'Goldfish'　Tr. by Asataro Miyamori. *Haiku poems, ancient and modern*. Tokyo, Maruzen, 1940. p.350
'Ellentet'　*Kinai és Japán Költök*. Budapest, Szépirodalmi, 1957. p.209
'1 haiku'　Übers. von Günther Debon. *Im Schnee die Fähre*. München, Piper, 1960. p.49
'The notice-board'　Tr. by Harold Stewart. *A net of fireflies*. Tokyo, Tuttle, 1960. p.108

NAKAMOTO Takako　中本たか子　1903–

Bikko no kobae　跛の小蠅

'瘤腿的小蒼蠅'　肖肖訳　「世界文学」1959年5月　p.24–40;「當代亜非拉小説選」香港　中流出版社　1977. p.373–398

Haha　母

Мать. Перевод　В. М. Константинова. Москва, Наука, 1964. 60p.

Kassōro　滑走路

Взлетная полоса. Перевод В. Проникова и М. Прососовой. Москва, Изд. Иност. Лит. 1962. 263p.
「跑道」金福訳　上海　上海文芸　1962. 284p.

Kichi no onna　基地の女

'The only one'　Tr. by Grace Suzuki. *Preview*, no. 195; *Ukiyo*. Tokyo, Phoenix Books, 1954. p.11–35; *Ukiyo*. N. Y. Vanguard Press, 1963. p.159–173; London, Universal Library, 1964. p.159–173

Essays　エッセイ

'日本民族的雄壮气概'　李芒訳　「世界文学」1962年12月　p.45–48
「日本人民的英雄气概」　李芒等訳　北京　作家出版社　1965. 76p
'我的反対安全条約斗争日記（选譯）'「世界文学」1964年7月　p.106–112

NAKAMURA Chio　中村千尾　1913–

Poems　詩

'A diary without dates'　*The burning heart*, tr. and ed. by Kenneth Rexroth and Ikuko Atsumi. N. Y. Seabury Press, 1977. p.91

NAKAMURA Katsutomo　中村かつとも

Poems　詩

'A death reverie'　Tr. by Kinussa and Charlotte M. A. Peake. *Lotus and chrysanthemum*. N. Y. Liveright, 1928. p.155

NAKAMURA Keiu　中村敬宇　1832–1891

Poems　詩

'Progress'　Tr. by Tetsuzo Okada. *Chinese and Sino-Japanese poems*. Tokyo, Seikanso, 1937. p.97

NAKAMURA Kenkichi　中村憲吉　1889–1934

Tanka　短歌

'On Mount Hi-ei'　Tr. by Asataro Miyamori. *Masterpieces of Japanese poetry, ancient and modern*. Tokyo, Maruzen, 1936; Tokyo, Taiseido, 1956; N. Y. Greenwood Press, 1971. p.762
'5 tanka'　Tr. by Shigeshi Nishimura. *The Current of the World*, v.15, no.4, 1938. p.101
'1 tanka'　Tr. by V. H. Viglielmo. *Japanese literature in the Meiji era*. Tokyo, Obunsha, 1955. p.411
'3 tanka'　Übers. von Kuniyo Takayasu und Manfred Hausmann. *Ruf der Regenpfeifer*. München, Bechtle Verlag, 1961. p.101–102
'3 tanka'　*Anthology of modern Japanese poetry*, tr. and comp. by Edith Marcombe Shiffert and Yuki Sawa. Tokyo, Tuttle, 1972. p.147

NAKAMURA Kichizō　中村吉蔵　1877–1941

Hoshi Tōru　星亨

'星享'　章克標訳　「日本戯曲集」上海　中華書局　1934. p.45–152

Ii Tairō no shi　井伊大老の死

The death of Ii Tairo.　Tr. by Mock Joya. Tokyo, Japan Times, 1927. 247p.

Kamisori　剃刀

'The razor'　Tr. by Yozan Iwasaki and Glenn Hughes. *Three modern Japanese plays*. Cincinnati, Stewart Kidd, 1923. p.13–56
'剃刀'　顧仲彝訳　「文藝月刊」第2巻第4期　1931. p.85–106

Mushukumono　無宿者

'無籍者'　田漢訳　「日本現代劇三種」　上海　東南書局　193?.

Ori no naka　檻の中

'檻之中'　楊騒訳　「語絲」第4巻40期　1928. p.19–41

'The slave ship'　*Japan Times*, March 31, 1929.

NAKAMURA Kōsuke　中村孝助　1901–

Tsuchi no uta　土の歌

'Из сборника《Крестиянские песни》; Из других глав'　Перевод В. Н. Марковой. *Японская поэзия*. Москва, Гослитиздат, 1954. p.303–316; Изд. 2. 1956. p.424–433
'Сыргган келген куруч' Которгон С. Фмурбаев.

NAKAMURA Kōsuke

Хиросима кектери. Фрунзе, Кыргызстан, 1969. p.43–44

Tanka 短歌

'Cocoons' Tr. by Asataro Miyamori. *Masterpieces of Japanese poetry, ancient and modern.* Tokyo, Maruzen, 1936; Tokyo, Taiseido, 1956; N. Y. Greenwood Press, 1971. p.799

NAKAMURA Kusatao 中村草田男 1901–

Haiku 俳句

'Three haiku poems' Tr. by Donald Keene. *Modern Japanese literature,* ed. by D. Keene. N. Y. Grove Press, 1956; Tokyo, Tuttle, 1957. p.382
'3 haiku' Übers. von Kuniyo Takayasu und Manfred Hausmann. *Ruf der Regenpfeifer.* München, Bechtle Verlag, 1961. p.105
'5 haiku' Tr. by Geoffrey Bownas and Anthony Thwaite. *The Penguin book of Japanese verse.* Harmondsworth, Penguin Books, 1964. p.171–172
'1 haiku' Tr. by Donald Keene. *The Mentor book of modern Asian literature,* ed. by D. B. Shimer. N. Y. New American Library, 1969. p.124
'4 haiku' *Anthology of modern Japanese poetry,* tr. and comp. by Edith Marcombe Shiffert and Yuki Sawa. Tokyo, Tuttle, 1972. p.172
'20 haiku' *Modern Japanese haiku, an anthology,* comp. and tr. by Makoto Ueda. Tokyo, Univ. of Tokyo Press, 1976. p.195–204
'1 haiku' Tr. by Takamasa Sasaki. *Eigo Seinen,* v.122, no.5, 1976. p.231
'Meiji era' Tr. by Kenneth Yasuda. *A pepper-pod.* Tokyo, Tuttle, 1976. p.99
'4 haiku' Traducerea Dan Constantinescu. *Din lirica japoneză.* Bucureşti, Editura Univers, n.d. p. 190–191

NAKAMURA Minoru 中村 稔 1927–

Poems 詩

'연 ; 밤 ; 겨울' 辛東門訳 「世界戦後文学全集 9」 서울 新丘文化社 1962. p.256–257
'Night; Castle' Tr. by Thomas Fitzsimmons. *Japanese poetry now.* London, André Deutsch, 1972. p.108–110; *Japanese poetry today.* N. Y. Schocken Books, 1972. p.110–112

NAKAMURA Mitsuo 中村光夫 1911–

Nihon no gendai shōsetsu 日本の現代小説

Contemporary Japanese fiction 1926–1968. Tokyo, Kokusai Bunka Shinkokai, 1969. 185p.
Novela japonesa contemporanea 1926–1968. Tokyo, Kokusai Bunka Shinkokai, 1970. 169p.

Nihon no kindai shōsetsu 日本の近代小説

Japanese fiction in the Meiji era. Tokyo, Kokusai Bunka Shinkokai, 1966. 119p.
Japanese fiction in the Taisho era. Tokyo, Kokusai Bunka Shinkokai, 1968. 61p.

Modern Japanese fiction 1868–1926. Tokyo, Kokusai Bunka Shinkokai, 1968. 180p.

Shōsetsu nyūmon 小説入門

「文學論」 江上訳 高雄 大舞台書苑 1976. 164p.

Criticism 評論

'The French influence in modern Japanese literature' *Japan Quarterly,* v.7, no.1, 1960. p.57–65
'The intellectual class' *Journal of Social and Political Ideas in Japan,* v.2, no.1, 1964. p.17–20
'川端康成與雪郷' 李映荻訳 「文壇」 第117期 1970. p.32–35

'心事重重' 金仲達訳 「純文學」 (台湾版) 第9巻2期 1971. p.86–105

NAKAMURA Rakuten 中村楽天 1865–1939

Haiku 俳句

'1 haiku' Tr. by Lois J. Erickson. *Songs from the land of dawn.* N. Y. Friendship Press, 1949; Freeport, Books for Libraries Press, 1968. p.70

NAKAMURA Shin'ichirō 中村真一郎 1918–

Ikinokotta kyōfu 生き残った恐怖

'Оживший страх' Перевод Л. Ермаковой. *Японская новелла 1960–1970.* Москва, Прогресс, 1972. p.186–205

Tōi mukashi 遠い昔

'Далекое прошлое' Перевод Г. Максимовой. *Красная лягушка.* Москва, Наука, 1973. p.118–137

Poems 詩

'불꽃 ; 微笑' 崔一秀訳 「기다리고있네」 서울 韓国政経社 1966. p.74–75, 173–174

Essay エッセイ

'The unending nightmare' Tr. by Robert Wargo. *Japan Interpreter,* v.8, no.4, 1974. p.525–531

NAKAMURA Shun'u 中村春雨 1877–1941

Nozomi no hoshi 望みの星

Sterne der Hoffnung. Übers. von A. Wendt. Halle a S. Gebauer Schwetschke, 1904. 210p.

NAKAMURA Teijo 中村汀女 1900–

Haiku 俳句

'3 haiku' *A history of haiku v.2,* by R. H. Blyth. Tokyo, Hokuseido, 1964. p.238–239
'Falling cherry-flowers' Tr. by Kenneth Yasuda. *A pepper-pod.* Tokyo, Tuttle, 1976. p.104

'Трехстишия' Перевод Анатолия Мамонова. *Вкус хризантемы.* Москва, Восточная Литература, 1976. p.74
'1 haiku' *The burning heart,* tr. and ed. by Kenneth Rexroth and Ikuko Atsumi. N. Y. Seabury Press, 1977. p.82

NAKAMURA Toshiaki 中村俊亮 1939–

Poems 詩

'悪童' 金龍済訳 「日本詩集」 서울 青雲社 1960. p.146–150

NAKANE Hiroshi 中根 弘

Criticism 評論

'盲詩人最近時的踪迹' 魯迅訳 「晨報副刊」 1921年10月 ; 「魯迅譯文集 10」 北京 人民文学出版社 1958. p.459–461

NAKANISHI Godō 中西悟堂 1895–

Poems 詩

'Here we are on the table-land' Tr. by Makoto Sangu. *The lyric garland.* Tokyo, Hokuseido, 1957. p.41

NAKANISHI Inosuke 中西伊之助 1893–1958

Akatsuchi ni megumu mono 赭土に芽ぐむもの

'В стране красной грины' Перевод Н. Фельдман. *Интернациональная Литература,* 1939, No. 11. p.114–162
Произрастающие на красной глине. Перевод Н. Фельдман. Москва, Гослитиздат, 1940. 487p.

Densaku no yōnen jidai 伝作の幼年時代

'Детство Дэнсаку' Перевод Н. Фельдман. *Борьба Миров,* 1931, No.6. p.13–26
Детство Дэнсаку. Перевод Н. И. Фельдман. Москва, Молодая Гвардия, 1931. 70p.

Haha no kokoro 母の心

'Сердце матери' Перевод Н. Фельдман. *Красная Панорама,* 1928, No.32. p.5

Manshū 満州

Маньчжурия. Перевод Н. Гребова и А. Успенской. Москва, Гослитиздат, 1936. 310p.

Nanjira no haigo yori 汝等の背後より

「汝等의背後에서」 李益相訳 京城 建設社 1930. 268p.

Nōfu Kihei no shi 農夫喜兵衛の死

Смерть Кихея. Перевод Н. И. Фельдман. Ленинград, Прибой, 1927. 164p.; Москва, Гослитиздат, 1963. 169p.

Osaki おさき

'Осаки, дочь Сэйроку' Перевод А. А. Лейферта, *Вестник иностранной литературы,* 1928. No.9. p.17–42

NAKANO Hirotaka 中野弘隆

Zōkun no sanpo ぞうくんのさんぽ

The elephant Happy. Indianapolis, Bobbs-Merrill, 1968. 1v.
En dejlig elefantdag. Oversaette Ib Permin. København, Høst, 1969. 27p.
The elephant blue. Indianapolis, Bobbs-Merrill, 1970. 31p.

NAKANO Kōji 中野孝次 1925–

Criticism 評論

'In pursuit of a mystery, Minakami Tsutomu's "Ikkyu" *Japanese Literature Today,* no.1, March 1976. p.11–12

NAKANO Minoru 中野 実 1901–1973

Hanayome sekkeizu 花嫁設計図

「新婚設計図」 韓龍得訳 서울 永和出版社 1961. 377p.

Kiso Yoshinaka 木曾義仲

'Kiso Yoshinaka' Übers. von Maria Piper. *Das japanische Theater.* Berlin, Societäts Verlag, 1937. p.128–133

'遺落了東西的乗客' 林鐘隆訳 「譯文選粋 1」 三重市 大立書店 1971. p.67–78

NAKANO San'in 中野三允 1879–1955

Haiku 俳句

'A scarecrow' Tr. by Asataro Miyamori. *Anthology of haiku, ancient and modern.* Tokyo, Maruzen, 1932. p.832
'1 haiku' Tr. by V. H. Viglielmo. *Japanese literature in the Meiji era.* Tokyo, Obunsha, 1955. p.444
'1 haiku' Tr. by Peter Beilenson. *Japanese haiku.* Mount Vernon, Peter Pauper Press, 1955. p.23
'1 haiku' Übers. von Gerolf Coudenhove. *Japanische Jahreszeiten.* Zürich, Manesse Verlag, 1963. p.244

NAKANO Shigeharu 中野重治 1902–

Harusaki no kaze 春さきの風

'初春的風' 沈端先訳 「初春的風」 上海 大江書舗 1929.
'La vento en frua printempo' Tr. Kei Kurisu. *El japana literaturo.* Tokyo, Japana Esperanto Instituto, 1965. p.169–177

NAKANO Shigeharu

'A tabasz széle' Ford. Sz. Holti Mária. *Modern Japán elbeszélők*. Budapest, Európa Könyvkiadó, 1967. p.132–139

'Весенний ветер' Перевод А. А. Бабинцева. *Пляшущий мужчина*. Москва, Наука, 1970. p.54–61

Odoru otoko 踊る男

'The dancing man' Tr. by William L. Clark. *Jiji Eigo Kenkyu*. v.12, no.10, 1957. p.37–42; *Various kinds of bugs, and other stories from present-day Japan*. Tokyo, Kenkyusha, 1958. p.41–53

'Tančici muž' Přel. M. Novák. *Nový Orient*, v.14, no.3, 1959. p.46–48

'Пляшущий мужчина' Перевод З. Рахима. *Пляшущий мужчина*. Москва, Наука, 1970. p.62–66

'Der tanzende Mann' Deutsch von Jürgen Berndt. *Träume aus zehn Nächten*. Berlin, Aufbau Verlag, 1975. p.436–443

Satō no hanashi 砂糖の話

'Сахар' Перевод Г. Г. Иммермана. *Пляшущий мужчина*. Москва, Наука, 1970. p.27–43

Tetsu no hanashi 鉄の話

'Tecu történetei' Ford. Sz. Holti Mária. *Modern Japán elbeszélők*. Budapest, Európa Könyvkiadó, 1967. p.140–151

'Рассказ Тэцу' Перевод Г. Г. Иммермана. *Пляшущий мужчина*. Москва, Наука, 1970. p.44–53

Uta no wakare 歌のわかれ

'Юность, прощай!' Перевод Л. Л. Громковской и О. К. Войнюш. *Пляшущий мужчина*. Москва, Наука, 1970. p.67–131

Poems 詩

'Песня' Перевод А. Е. Глускиной. *Японская поэзия*. Москва, Гослитиздат, 1954. p.292; Изд. 2. 1956. p.413

'Song' Tr. by Donald Keene. *Modern Japanese literature*, ed. by D. Keene. N. Y. Grove Press, 1956; Tokyo, Tuttle, 1957. p.378

'Good-bye before dawn' Tr. by S. Sato and C. Urdang. *Poetry*, May 1956. p.80–81

'这些人們；雨中的品川車站；歌' 李芒 黎波訳 「譯文」 1956年12月 p.112–115

'Canción' *Sur*, no.249, Nov.–Dec. 1957. p.97

'The rearmost carriage' *An anthology of modern Japanese poetry*, ed. and tr. by Ichiro Kono and Rikutaro Fukuda. Tokyo, Kenkyusha, 1957. p.101

'Locomotive; Tokyo Imperial University students' *The poetry of living Japan*, by Takamichi Ninomiya and D. J. Enright. London, John Murray, 1957. p.63–64

'Chanson, Locomotive' *La poésie japonaise*, par Karl Petit. Paris, Seghers, 1959. p.231–232

'Lokomotive; Studenten der Kaiserlichen Universität Tokyo' Übertragen von Shin Aizu. *Der schwermütige Ladekran*. St. Gallen, Tschudy Verlag, 1960. p.30

'Mozdony; Dal' Ford. Illyés Gyula. *Nagyvilág*, no.10, 1960.

'Die Fremde' Übers. von Kuniyo Takayasu und Manfred Hausmann. *Ruf der Regenpfeifer*. München, Bechtle Verlag, 1961. p.90

'The Imperial Hotel; Song; Farewell before dawn; Tokyo Imperial University students' Tr. by Geoffrey Bownas and Anthony Thwaite. *The Penguin book of Japanese verse*. Harmondsworth, Penguin Books, 1964. p.213–215

Волны Японии. Перевод А. Мамонова. Москва, Правда, 1964. 31p.

'Canzone; Un saluto prima che faccia giorno' *La protesta poetica del Giappone*, a cura di Dacia Maraini e Michiko Nojiri. Roma, Officina Edizioni, 1968. p.45–47

'Song' Tr. by Donald Keene. *The Mentor book of modern Asian literature*, ed. by D. B. Shimer. N. Y. New American Library, 1969. p.128–129

'Чыныгы адамдар; Кезунен; Ажырашуу; Токиого жаны келген елчи женунде; Губернатор' Которгон Т. Арыков, С. Маймулов. *Хиросима кектери*. Фрунзе, Кыргызстан, 1969. p.59–63

'명랑한소녀들' 「永遠한世界名詩集 2」 黄錦燦編 서울 翰林出版社 1969. p.243; 「永遠한世界名詩集 5」 黄錦燦編 서울 翰林出版社 1973. p.243

'Расставание; Белые волны; Уборка' Перевод Анатолия Мамонова. *Вкус хризантемы*. Москва, Восточная Литература, 1976. p.76–77

'Hotel Imperial; Locomotiva, et al' Traducerea Virgil Teodorescu. *Din lirica japoneză*. Bucureşti, Editura Univers, n.d. p.196–198

'Imperial Hotel; Sang; Farvel for daggry' Til norsk ved Paal Brekke. *Moderne japansk lyrikk*. Oslo, Norske Bokklubben, n.d. p.53–55

「中野重治集」 尹庚訳 上海 現代書局 1934. 1冊

NAKANO Suzuko 中野鈴子 1906–1958

Poems 詩

'袂別' 金龍済訳 「日本詩集」 서울 青雲社 1960. p.151–153

NAKANO Yoshio 中野好夫 1903–

Criticism and Essay 評論・エッセイ

'Youth and the "modern classics"' *Japan Quarterly*, v.6, no.1, 1959. p.120–124

'English literature in Japan' *Japan Quarterly*, v.6, no.2, 1959. p.165–174

'現実의이라고하는것' 金賢珠訳 「바이 바이 바다」 서울 三韓出版社 1966. p.290–294

NAKAO Kiyoaki 中尾清秋 1916–

Poems 詩

'A flower's name; A doctor?; Rambling through the woods' *The lyric garland*, ed. by Makoto Sangu. Tokyo, Hokuseido, 1957. p.42–44

NAKATA Nobuko 中田信子 1902–

Muma 夢魔

Inkubo. Tr. Yukichi Yasuda. Kyoto, Kaniya, 1924. 16p.

NAKATANI Chiyoko 中谷千代子 1930–

Boku no uchi no dōbutsuen ぼくのうちのどうぶつえん

The zoo in my garden. N. Y. Crowell, 1973. 31p.; London, Bodley Head, 1973. 1v.
Dyr jeg kender. Oversaette Eva Glistrup. København, Høst, 1973. 31p.

Fumio to iruka ふみおといるか

Fumio and the dolphins. London, Bodley Head, 1970. 32p.: N. Y. World Publishing Co. 1971. 32p.
Fumio und die Delphine. Übers. von Bettina Hürlimann. Freiburg, Atlantis Verlag, 1970. 16p.

Maigo no Chiro まいごのチロ

The day Chiro was lost. London, Bodley Head, 1969. 1v.
Chiro. Zürich, Atlantis Verlag, 1969. 1v.
Da flip blev vaek. Oversaette Ib Permin. København, Høst, 1973. 1v.

NAKATSUKA Ippekirō 中塚一碧楼 1887–1946

Haiku 俳句

'6 haiku' Tr. by V. H. Viglielmo. Japanese literature in the Meiji era. Tokyo, Obunsha, 1955. p.449, 450, 453
'Haiku' Tercüme etmek L. Sami Akalin. Japon şiiri. İstanbul, Varlik Yayinevi, 1962. p.246
'5 haiku' A history of haiku v.2, by R. H. Blyth. Tokyo, Hokuseido, 1964. p.202–204

NAKATSUKA Kyōya 中塚響也 1888–1945

Haiku 俳句

'1 haiku' Tr. by V. H. Viglielmo. Japanese literature in the Meiji era. Tokyo, Obunsha, 1955. p.450

NAKAUCHI Chōji 中内蝶二 1875–1937

Inaka musume 田舎娘

'Ein Mädchen vom Lande' Übers. von Kurt Meissner. Der Tanzfächer, von K. Meissner. Tokyo, 1943. p.162

Haiku 俳句

'2 haiku' Tr. by Asataro Miyamori. Anthology of haiku, ancient and modern. Tokyo, Maruzen, 1932. p.800–801
'O-Ev' Kinai és Japán költök. Budapest, Szépirodalmi, 1957. p.208
'1 haiku' Übers. von Gerolf Coudenhove. Japa-

nische Jahreszeiten. Zürich, Manesse Verlag, 1963. p.378

NAKAYAMA Gishū 中山義秀 1900–1969

Essay エッセイ

'照像機' 傅寶齡訳 「勲章」 台北 文壇社 1960. p.296–298

NAKAYAMA Tadanao 中山忠直

Poems 詩

An elegy on the earth, and eight other poems. Tr. by Asataro Miyamori. Tokyo, Maruzen, 1941. 77p.

NAKAZATO Kaizan 中里介山 1885–1944

Daibosatsu tōge 大菩薩峠

Dai-Bosatsu toge, Great Boddhisattva Pass. Tr. by C. S. Bavier. Tokyo, Shunju-sha, 1929. 383p.
「盲人劍士」 金日秀訳 서울 大湖出版文化社 1974. 3冊

NAKAZATO Kishō 中里喜昭 1936–

Nokori yama のこりやま

Шахта в море. Перевод О. Морошкиной. Москва, Прогресс, 1975. 191p.

Essay エッセイ

'沉重的海' 文洁若節訳 「人民文学」 1965年2月 p.6–8

NAKAZATO Satarō 中里左太郎

Hanagoyomi hasshōjin 花暦八笑人

The eight laughters. Tr. by Sataro Nakazato. Tokyo, Kochokaku, 1886. 58p.

NAKAZAWA Keiji 中沢啓治 1939–

Hadashi no Gen はだしのゲン

'Barefoot Gen' Tr. by Lora Sharnoff. Japan Quarterly, v.25, no.4, 1978. p.484–495

NAKAZAWA Rinsen 中沢臨川 1878–1920

Criticism 評論

'羅曼羅蘭的眞勇主義' 魯迅訳 「莽原」 第7・8期 1926; 「魯迅全集 16」 上海 魯迅全集出版社 1938. 作家書屋 1946. 大連 光華書店 1948. 北京 人民

MAKAZAWA Rinsen

文学出版社 1973. p.293–323;「魯迅譯文集 10」北京 人民文学出版社 1958. p 95–118

NAKAZONO Eisuke　中薗英助　1920–

Honoo no naka no namari　炎の中の鉛

'Свинец в пламени' Перевод С. Гутермана. *Зарубежный детектив*. Москва, Молодая Гвардия, 1970. p.123–226

Matsuri no shinu hi　祭りの死ぬ日

Koniec święta. Przeł. Krystyna Okazaki. Warszawa, Państwowy Instytut Wydawniczy, 1977. 175p.

Mikkō teikibin　密航定期便

Тайный рейс. Перевод С. Гутермана. Москва, Прогресс, 1967. 207p.

Yoru no baiyōsha　夜の培養者

Сеятели ночи. Перевод С. Гутермана. Москва, Прогресс, 1971. 158p.

Essays　エッセイ

'Lotus prize' *Japan Quarterly*, v.20, no.3, 1973. p.319–323
'Доброволец корпуса мира' Перевод З. Рахима. *Иностранная Литература*, август 1965. p.72–76

NAN'E Jirō　南江治郎　1902–

Poems　詩

'Quiet anger; Sands' Tr. by Harumi Haru. *Japan P.E.N. News*, no.20, Sept. 1967. p.6

Essay　エッセイ

'Appreciation of Bunraku' *KBS Bulletin*, no.36, 1959. p.5–8

NANJŌ Norio　南条範夫　1908–

Bibō no otto　美貌の良人

「美貌的丈夫」 邱素臻訳　台北　水牛出版社　1969. 219p.

Ishigaki no naka no futari　石垣の中の二人

'돌담속의두사람' 金龍済訳 「日本代表作家百人集 4」 서울 希望出版社 1966. p.68–82;「日本短篇文学全集 4」 서울 新太陽社 1969. p.294–308

Shisha no warai　死者の笑い

'死者的笑' 廖清秀節訳 「自由談」 第24巻5期 1973.

Tōdai ki　燈台鬼

'Lamp devil' Tr. by G. W. Sargent. *Eigo Seinen*, v.103, no.7–no.12, 1957 in 6 parts.

NARUCHI Hideo　鳴地秀雄

Kattō　葛藤

「葛藤」 정수웅訳 서울 三正文化社 1967. 332p.

NARUSE Mukyoku　成瀬無極　1884–1958

Criticism　評論

「現代世界文學小史」 胡雪訳 上海 光華書局 1932. 1冊

NATSUKI Shizuko　夏樹静子　1938–

Dangai kara no koe　断崖からの声

'Cry from the cliff' *Japanese golden dozen*, ed. by Ellery Queen. Tokyo, Tuttle, 1978. p.123–146

Muhyō　霧氷

「霧冰」 林玲玉訳 台北 成文出版社 1977. 249p.

NATSUME Sōseki　夏目漱石　1867–1916

Bokusetsu roku　木屑錄

'Record of chips and shavings (excerpts)' Tr. by Burton Watson. *Japanese literature in Chinese v.2*. N. Y. Columbia Univ. Press, 1976. p.174–183

Botchan　坊ちゃん

Botchan, master darling. Tr. by Yasotaro Morri. Tokyo. Ogawa Seibundo, 1918. 271p.
'Botchan' Tr. by Umeji Sasaki. *Chugai Eigo*, 1919.
Botchan. Tr. by Umeji Sasaki. Tokyo, Shunyodo, 1922. 457p.; 1968. 188p.
Botchan, ou, jeune homme irréfléchi. Tr. par Naota Ogata. Tokyo, Maruzen, 1923. 179p.
Botchan, ein reiner Tor. Übers. von Alexander Spann. Osaka, Kyodo Shuppansha, 1924. 238p.
'哥兒' 章克標訳 「小説月報」 第21巻7号 1930. p.1029–1046, 8号 1930. p.1229–1252, 9号 1930. p.1373–1391
Bôtčan, mazlíček staré Kijo. Přel. L. Vesecký. Praha, Pavel Prokop, 1942. 157p.
Барчук. Перевод М. П. Григориева. Дальний, Южно-Маньчж. Ж. Д. 1943. 246p.
'Botchan' Tr. by Burton Watson. *Modern Japanese literature*, ed. by D. Keene. N. Y. Grove Press, 1956; Tokyo, Tuttle, 1957. p.124–133
Мальчуган. Перевод Р. Карлиной. Москва, Гослитиздат, 1956. 153p.
Nije kriva samo Madona. Tr. from the Russian by Dušan Stojiljkivić. Beograd, Narodna Knjiga, 1957. 208p.
'哥儿' 開西訳 北京 人民文学出版社 1958. 76p.
'버챵' 金聲翰訳 「나는고양이다, 버챵」 서울 乙酉文化社 1962. p.322–425
'봇쟝' 金聲翰訳 「世界文学全集 33」 서울 乙酉文化社 1962. p.291–377
Botchan. Tr. by Yasotaro Mori. Tokyo, Kinshodo, 1963. 271p.
'Il signorino' Tr. di Atsuko Ricca Suga. *Narratori giapponesi moderni*. Milano, Bompiani,

1965. p.25–38

Der Tor aus Tokio. Übers. von Jürgen Berndt und Seiei Shinohara. Berlin, Aufbau Veralg, 1965. 178p.

'도령님' 李鐘烈訳 「日本文学選集 1」 서울 青雲社 1964. p.203–315; 서울 知文閣 1966. p.201–315

'哥兒' 張克明訳 「夏目漱石選集」 台南 開山書店 1967 p.11–132

Botchan, el joven mimado. Tr. por Jesús González Valles. Tokyo, Sociedad Latino Americana, 1969. 253p.

「少爺」 金仲達訳 台北 純文學出版社 1970. 230p.

Botchan. Tr. by Alan Turney. Tokyo, Kodansha International, 1972. 173p.; London, Peter Owen, 1973. 176p.

Bunchō 文鳥

'Buncho' Tr. by Umeji Sasaki. *Chugai Eigo*, 1923; *Kusamakura, and Buncho.* Tokyo, Iwanami Shoten, 1927. p.1–33

'The paddy bird' Tr. by S. G. Brickley. *The writing of idiomatic English.* Tokyo, Kenkyusha, 1951. p.79–84

'文鳥' 「少年的悲哀」 郁達夫等訳 台北 啓明書局 1956. p.14–25

'文鳥' 「文鳥・夢十夜」 英紹唐編 台北 n.d. p.3–35

Bungaku hyōron 文学評論

「文學評論」 哲人訳 厦門 國際學術書社 1928. 1冊

Bungaku ron 文学論

「文學論」 張我軍訳 上海 神州書局 1931. 1冊

Garasudo no naka 硝子戸の中

'The master' Tr. by Iwao Matsubara. *Osaka Mainichi*, April 26, 1928.

'Natsume Soseki's childhood' Tr. by Shigeo Inoue. *Eigo Kenkyu*, v.22, no.5, 1929. p.522–523, v.22, no.6, 1929. p.618–619

Within my glass doors. Tr. by Iwao Matsubara and E. T. Iglehart. Tokyo, Shinseido, 1928. 154p.

'玻璃門裏' 方紀生訳 「朔風」 第1期 1938. p.40–43

'玻璃門裏' 金仲達訳 「純文學」（台湾版） 第7巻2期 1970. p.55–89

Gubijinsō 虞美人草

'Red poppy' Tr. by Kazutomo Takahashi. *Japan Magazine*, v.8, 1918. p.577–581, 644–646, 691–694, p.745–748. v.9, 1918. 103–106, 150–152

Hibachi 火鉢

'火鉢' 謝六逸訳 「小説月報」 第19巻1号 1928. p.187–188

Hitoyo 一夜

'一夜' 郭夏信訳 「世界文学全集 94」 서울 乙酉文化社 1962. p.75–82; 「日本短篇文学選」 서울 乙酉文化社 1976. p.9–25

Kakemono 懸物

'掛幅' 魯迅訳 「現代日本小説集」 上海 商務印書館 1923; 「日本現代小説集 1」上海 商務印書館 1930; 「魯迅全集 11」 上海 魯迅全集出版社 1938. 作家書屋 1946. 大連 光華書店 1948. 北京 人民文学出版社 1973. p.397–399; 「魯迅譯文集 1」 北京 人民文学出版社 1958. p.435–437

Kēberu sensei ケーベル先生

'Professor Raphael Koeber' Übers. von S. Yuasa. *Nippon*, Jahrgang 2, 1936. p.16–20

Keitōjo 鶏頭序

'鶏頭序' 張克明訳 「夏目漱石選集」 台南 開山書店 1967. p.155–163

Kōjin 行人

'Mon camarade' Tr. par Serge Elisséev. *Japon et Extrême-Orient*, no.4, 1924. p.347–363, no.5, 1924. p.101–119, no.7–8, 1924. p. 69–85, no.9, 1924. p.164–182

The wayfarer. Tr. by Beongcheon Yu. Detroit, Wayne State Univ. Press, 1967; Tokyo, Tuttle, 1969. 326p.

Kokoro こゝろ

Сердце. Перевод Н. И. Конрад. Ленинград, Гослитиздат, 1935. 295р.; Токио, Наука, 1973. 295р.

Le pauvre coeur des hommes. Tr. par Daigaku Horiguchi et Georges Bonneau. Paris, Institut International de Coopération Intellectuelle, 1939. 369p.; Paris, Gallimard, 1957. 308p.

Kokoro. Tr. by Ineko Sato. Tokyo, Hokuseido, 1941. 288p.

Kokoro. Tr. by Ineko Kondo. Tokyo, Kenkyusha 1948. 287p.

Kokoro. Tr. Mirko Paut. Zagreb. Zora, 1953. 240p.

Kokkōrō. Tr. into Tamil. Coimbatore, Kalaikkathir Veliyidu. 1959. 128p.

Kokoro. Tr. by Edwin McClellan. Chicago, Henry Regnery, 1957. 248p.; London, Peter Owen, 1967; Tokyo, Tuttle, 1969. 248p.

Kokkoro. Tr. from the English into Malayan by M. R. Chandrashekharan. Trichur, Current Books, 1960. 117p.

Sedno rzeczy. Przeł. Mikołaj Melanowicz. Warszawa, Państwowy Instytut Wydawniczy, 1973. 222p.

Kokoro. Übers. von Oscar Benl. Zürich, Manesse Verlag, 1976. 379p.

Kokoro. Tr. into Kannada by D. V. Raghavendra. Mysore, Newspaper House, n.d. 108p.

Koto no sorane 琴のそら音

'琴音幻聴' 金仲達訳 「純文學」（台湾版） 第6巻3期 1969. p.35–61

'Hearing things' Tr. by Aiko Ito and Graeme Wilson. *Japan Quarterly*, v.19, no.3, 1972. p.317–335; *Ten nights of dream, Hearing things, The heredity of taste.* Tokyo, Tuttle, 1974. p.65–115

Kureigu sensei クレイグ先生

'Herr Craig' Übers. von K. Koike. *Zwei Skizzen von S. Natsume.* Tokyo, Nankodo, 1917. p.1–39

'克萊喀先生' 魯迅訳 「現代日本小説集」 上海 商務印書館 1923; 「日本現代小説集 1」 上海 商務印書館 1930; 「魯迅全集 11」 上海 魯迅全集出版社 1938. 作家書屋 1946. 大連 光華書店 1948. 北京 人民文学出版社 1973. p.401–410; 「魯迅譯文集 1」 北京 人民文学出版社 1958. p.438–445

Kusamakura 草枕

'Kusamakura' Tr. by Umeji Sasaki. *Juken Eigo*, 1924; *Kusamakura and Buncho.* Tokyo, Iwanami Shoten, 1927. p.34–276

Unhuman tour. Tr. by Kazutomo Takahashi. Tokyo, Japan Times, 1927. 193p.

「草枕」 崔萬秋訳 上海 眞美善書店 1929. 1冊

NATSUME Sōseki

「草枕」 郭沫若訳 北京 華麗書店 1930. 1冊
'Kusamakura, unhuman tour' Tr. by Kazutomo Takahashi. *Treasury of Japanese literature*, ed. by Takichi Watanabe. Tokyo, Jippoh-kaku, 1933. p.352–361
'Polštář z trávy' Přel. V. Hilská. *Milenci z Jeda*. Praha, Melantrich, 1942.
Polštář z trávy. Přel. V. Hilská. Praha, SNKHLU, 1958. 213p.
'Grass pillow' Tr. by Alan Turney. *Orient West*, v.9, no.1, 1964. p.39; *The Japanese image*, v.2 ed. by M. Schneps and A. D. Coox. Tokyo, Orient West, 1966. p.208–217
The three-cornered world. Tr. by Alan Turney. London, Peter Owen, 1965. 184p.; Tokyo, Tuttle, 1966; Chicago, Henry Regnery, 1967. 184p.
'草枕' 表文台訳 「日本代表作家百人集 1」 서울 希望出版社 1966. p.32–118
「조짐」 表文泰訳 서울 希望出版社 1966. 255p.
'草枕' 方基煥 表文台訳 「日本短篇文学全集 1」 서울 新太陽社 1969. p.32–118
「草枕」 台北 鷲聲文物供応股份 1973. 1冊

Meian 明暗

Light and darkness. Tr. by V. H. Viglielmo. Honolulu, Univ. of Hawaii Press, 1971; London, Peter Owen, 1971; Tokyo, Tuttle, 1971. 397p.

Michikusa 道草

Grass on the wayside. Tr. by Edwin McClellan. Chicago, Univ. of Chicago Press, 1969; Tokyo, Tuttle, 1971. 169p.

Mon 門

La porte. Tr. par R. Martinie. Paris, Rieder, 1925. 343p.
A kapu. Ford. Kolumbán Mózes. Budapest, Európa Könyvkiadó, 1962. 249p.
Mon. Tr. by Francis Mathy. London, Peter Owen, 1972; Tokyo, Tuttle, 1972. 217p.
'Врата' Перевод А. Рябкина. *Сансиро, Затем, Врата*. Москва, Худож. Лит. 1973. p.353–478

Neko no haka 猫の墓

'猫的墓' 謝六逸訳 「小説月報」 第19巻1号 1928. p.185–186
'Our cat's grave' Tr. by Sankichi Hata and Dofu Shirai. *Ten nights' dreams, and Our cat's grave*. Tokyo, Seito Shoin, 1934. p.99–112; *Treasury of world literature*, ed. by D. D. Runes. N.Y. Philosophical Library, 1956. p.950–953
'The grave of our cat' Tr. by Tadakuni Mizutani. *Aries* (Kwansai Gakuin Univ.), 1938.

Nihyaku tōka 二百十日

'Nihyakutoka' Tr. by T. Johnes and H. Tomabechi. *Eigo Seinen*, v.36, no. 1, 1916– v.36, no. 12, 1917, v.37, no.1–no.12, 1917, v.38, no.1–no.12, 1971–1918, v.39, no.4–no.8, 1918.

Rondon tō 倫敦塔

'Der London Tower' Übers. von Kenji Koike. *Zwei Skizzen von S. Natsume*. Tokyo, Nankodo, 1917. p.1–115
La turo de Londono. Tr. Seiho Nishi. Tokyo, Japana Esperanto Instituto, 1928. 28p.; 1960. 55p.
'倫敦塔' 張克明訳 「夏目漱石選集」 台南 開山書店 1967. p.133–154

Sanshiro 三四郎

'Sanshiro' Übers. von C. Schaarschmidt. *Der Neue Orient*, Bd.1, 1917–18. p.97–100
「三四郎」 崔萬秋訳 上海 中華書局 1925. 1冊; 台南 開山書店 1969. 280p.
'Mount Fuji' Tr. by Shigeshi Nishimura. *Eigo Kenkyu*, v.26, no.3, 1933. p.226–228
'Sanshiro' Tr. by W. J. Whitehouse. *Eigo no kenkyu to kyoju*. Tokyo, 1939.
Сансиро. Перевод. А. Рябкина. *Сансиро, Затем, Врата*. Москва, Худож. Лит. 1973. p.23–187
Sanshiro. Tr. by Jay Rubin. Tokyo, Univ. of Tokyo Press, 1977. 248p.; Seattle, Univ. of Washington Press, 1977. 248p.

Shumi no iden 趣味の遺伝

'The heredity of taste' Tr. by Aiko Ito and Graeme Wilson. *Japan Quarterly*, v.20, no.1, 1973. p.46–77; *Ten nights of dream, Hearing things, The heredity of taste*. Tokyo, Tuttle, 1974. p.117–203

Sorekara それから

'Затем' Перевод А. Рябкина. *Сансиро, Затем, Врата*. Москва, Худож. Лит. 1973. p.189–351
And then. Tr. by Norma Moore Field. Baton Rouge, Louisiana State Univ. Press, 1978. 304p.

Wagahai wa neko de aru 吾輩は猫である

I am a cat. Tr. by Kanichi Ando. Tokyo, Hattori Shoten, and Okura, 1906–9. 2v.
I am a cat. Committed to writing by Elford Eddy. San Francisco, Japan-American News, 1921. 304p.
'猫' 出雲訳 「東方雑誌」 第31巻15期 1934. p.9–16
「我是猫」 程伯軒 羅芷訳 東京 鳳文書院 1936. 1冊
Ваш покорный слуга кот. Перевод Л. Коршкова и А. Стругацкого. Москва, Гослитиздат, 1960. 431p.
I am a cat. Tr. by Katsue Shibata and Motonari Kai. Tokyo, Kenkyusha, 1961. 431p.; London, Peter Owen, 1971. 431p.
'나는고양이다' 金聲翰訳 「나는고양이다, 버창」 서울 乙酉文化社 1962. p.1–321; 「世界文学全集 33」 서울 乙酉文化社 1962. p.5–289
'Io sono un gatto' Tr. di R. Vulpitta. *Antologia della letteratura coreana e giapponese*. Milano, Fratelli Fabbri, 1969. p.297–302
'I am a cat' Tr. by Aiko Ito and Graeme Wilson. *Japan Quarterly*, v.17, no.4, 1970. p.421–432, v.18, no.1, 1971. p.39–75. v.18, no.2, 1971. p.177–206, v.21, no.4, 1974. p.365–386
'I am a cat' Tr. by Katsue Shibata and Motonari Kai. *Asian laughter*. Tokyo, Weatherhill, 1971. p.378–408
I am a cat. Tr. by Aiko Ito and Graeme Wilson. Tokyo, Tuttle, 1972. 218p.
Ваш покирний слуга кит. Переклав Иван Дзюб Киев, Днепро, 1973. 454p.
Yo soy un gato. Tr. por Jesús González Valles. Tokyo, Universidad Soisen, 1974. 453p.
Montanul are cuvîntul. În românește de Mihai Matei. Bucureşti, Editura Univers, 1975. 436p.
'나는고양이다' 閔丙山訳 「世界文学全集 20」 서울 三省出版社 1975. p.15–334
Jestem kotem. Przeł. Mikołaj Melanowicz. Warszawa, Książka i Wiedza, 1977. 500p.

Yume jūya 夢十夜

'Dreams' Tr. by Asataro Miyamori. *Representative tales of Japan*. Tokyo, Sanko Shoten, 1917. p.57–71

'Ten dreams' *Japan Magazine*, v.13, 1922. p.209–213, 235–282

'夢' 陳箸訳 「小説月報」 第16巻2号 1925. p.10–11

'Ten nights' dreams' Tr. by Sankichi Hata and Dofu Shirai. *Ten nights' dreams, and Our cat's grave*. Tokyo, Seito Shorin, 1934. p.1–98

'Träume der zehn Nächte' *Geschichten und Erzählungen aus Japan*, herausgegeben von B. Matsuoka. Leipzig, Firkentscher Verlag, 1950. p.197–229

Deset snù. Přel. Vlasta Hilská. Praha, Malá Knižnice Orientu, 1955. 51p.

'Ten nights of dreams' Tr. by Earl Miner and Yukio Oura. *Orient-West*, v.6, no.2, 1961. p.25–37; *The Japanese image*, ed. by M. Schneps and A. D. Coox. Tokyo, Orient West, 1965. p.144–162

'Um sonho' Tr. de Antonio Nojiri. *Marvilhas do conto japonês*. São Paulo, Editôra Cultrix, 1962. p.71–73

'열흘밤의꿈' 金潤成訳 「世界短篇文学全集 7」 서울 啓蒙社 1966. p.158–178; 「世界短篇文学全集 9」 서울 三珍社 1971. p.6–26; 「世界代表短篇文学全集 9」 서울 三熙社 1976. p.6–27; 「世界短篇文学全集 9」 서울 新韓出版社 1976. p.14–50

'Tiz éjszaka tíz álma' Ford. Sz. Holti Mária. *Modern Japán elbeszélők* Budapest, Európa Könyvkiadó, 1967. p.5–24

'Ten nights of dream' Tr. by Aiko Ito and Graeme Wilson. *Japan Quarterly*, v.16, no.3, 1969. p.314–329; *Ten nights of dream, Hearing things, The heredity of taste*. Tokyo, Tuttle, 1974. p.27–63

'Träume aus zehn Nächten' Deutsch von Jürgen Berndt. *Träume aus zehn Nächten*. Berlin, Aufbau Verlag, 1975. p.71–96

夢十夜(第一、第七、第十夜) 「文鳥・夢十夜」 英紹唐編 台北 n.d. p.36–54

Chinese poems 漢詩

'Sixteen Chinese poems by Natsume Soseki' Tr. by Burton Watson. *Essays on Natsume Soseki's works*, comp. by Japanese National Commission for Unesco. Tokyo, Japan Society for the Promotion of Science, 1972. p.119–124

'6 poems untitled' Tr. by Burton Watson. *Japanese literature in Chinese v.2*. N. Y. Columbia Univ. Press, 1976. p.184–189

Haiku 俳句

'26 haiku' Tr. by Asataro Miyamori. *Anthology of haiku, ancient and modern*. Tokyo, Maruzen, 1932. p.673–690; Tokyo, Taiseido, 1947.

'4 haiku' Tr. by Harold Gould Henderson. *The bamboo broom*. Tokyo, J. L. Thompson, 1933; London, Kegan Paul, 1933. p.118, 125, 126

'The Bay of Waka-no-Ura; Clear water; On the death of Madame Otsuka; A camellia flower; Scarlet maple leaves; Since your death; The wind and leaves; Gods Ni-O; A butterfly; A snowstorm' Tr. by Asataro Miyamori. *Haiku poems, ancient and modern*. Tokyo, Maruzen, 1940. p.303–308

'1 haiku' Tr. by Lois J. Erickson. *Songs from the land of dawn*. N. Y. Friendship Press, 1949; Freeport, Books for Libraries Press, 1968. p.78

'3 haiku' Tr. by R. H. Blyth. *Haiku*. Tokyo, Hokuseido, 1952. v.3, p.88, v.4, p.52, 152

'Two poems' *Atlantic Monthly*, no.195, 1955. p.164

'7 haiku' Tr. by V. H. Viglielmo. *Japanese literature in the Meiji era*. Tokyo, Obunsha, 1955. p.432–433

'One haiku' Tr. by H. G. Henderson. *Modern Japanese literature*, ed. by D. Keene. N. Y. Grove Press, 1956; Tokyo, Tuttle, 1957. p.123

'Trois haiku; Meditation' *La poésie japonaise*. Tr. par Karl Petit. Paris, Seghers, 1959. p.179–180

'3 haiku' Übers. von Günther Debon. *Im Schnee die Fähre*. München, Piper, 1960. p.28

'10 haiku' Tr. by Peter Beilenson and Harry Behn. *Haiku harvest*. Mount Vernon, Peter Pauper Press, 1962. p.36, 37, 50, 51, 52

'Haiku' Tercüme etmek L. Sami Akalin. *Japon şiiri*. İstanbul, Varlik Yayinevi, 1962. p.223

'5 haiku' Übers. von Gerolf Coudenhove. *Ja panische Jahreszeiten*. Zürich, Manesse Verlag, 1963. p.184, 293, 309, 332

'Haiku' *Lyrik des Ostens*, hrg. von Wilhelm Gundert usw. München, Carl Hanser, 1965. p.471

'2 haiku' Til norsk ved Paal Helge Haugen. *Blad frå ein austleg hage*. Oslo, Det Norske Samlaget, 1965. p.85

'1 haiku' Übers. von Erwin Jahn. *Fallende Blüten*. Zürich, Arche, 1968. p.53

'20 haiku' Tr. by Makoto Ueda. *Modern Japanese haiku, an anthology*. Tokyo, Univ. of Tokyo Press, 1976. p.38–47

'1 haiku' *Japanese love poems*, ed. by Jean Bennett. Garden City, Doubleday, 1976. p.26

'Leaves; Train; Snowy morning; On death of Madame Otsuka; Spring day' Tr. by Kenneth Yasuda. *A pepper-pod*. Tokyo, Tuttle, 1976. p.78–80

Criticism 評論

'Stevenson and Meredith' Tr. by Yaichiro Isobe. *Chugai Eigo*, July 1923.

「夏目漱石集」 章克標訳 北京 開明書局 1932. 1冊
「夏目漱石選集」 胡雪 豊子愷其他訳 北京 人民文学出版社 1958. 2冊

NII Itaru 新居 格 1888–1951

Criticism 評論

'機械與藝術' 薛仁訳 「流露月刊」 第1巻5期 193?.

NIIKUNI Seiichi 新国誠一 1925–

Poems 詩

Poèmes franco-japonais. Tr. par Seiichi Niikuni et Pierre Garner. Paris, Silvaire, 1966. 16p.

'River of sandbank; Rain; Prisoner; Cloud and sky; Anti-war; The sea has already been reduced to pass' Tr. by Harry and Lynn Guest and Shozo Kajima. *Post-war Japanese poetry*. Harmondsworth, Penguin Books, 1972. p.95–100

NIIMI Nankichi 新美南吉 1913–1943

Poems 詩

'A spring; Hedges; Lyric of an early summer' Tr. by Crown Princess Michiko. *Poetry Nippon*, no.37 & 38, 1977. p.20–22
'Fallen leaves' Tr. by Crown Princess Michiko. *Poetry Nippon*, no.39 & 40, 1977. p.17
'In the morning; Funeral' Tr. by Crown Princess Michiko. *Poetry Nippon*, no.41 & 42, 1978. p.16–18

NIKI Etsuko 仁木悦子 1928–

Neko wa shitte ita 猫は知っていた

「貓影踪謎」 許振江訳 台南 文良出版社 1960. 188p.
「貓影謀殺案」 振江訳 台南 文良出版社 1966. 184p.
「고양이는알고있다」 李文賢訳 서울 弘益出版社 1974. 301p.

NISHI Junko にし・じゅんこ

Poems 詩

'Revolution; Remorse came slowly' *The burning heart*, tr. and ed. by Kenneth Rexroth and Ikuko Atsumi. N. Y. Seabury Press, 1977. p.132–133

NISHIDE Shinzaburō 西出新三郎

Poems 詩

'За спиной' Перевод Анатолия Мамонова. *Вкус хризантемы*. Москва, Восточная Литература, 1976. p.81

NISHIGORI Kurako 錦織くら子 1899–

Tanka 短歌

'Voiceless voices; The doors of life' Tr. by Asataro Miyamori. *Masterpieces of Japanese poetry, ancient and modern*. Tokyo, Maruzen, 1936; Tokyo, Taiseido, 1956; N. Y. Greenwood Press, 1971. p.766–767

NISHIJIMA Bakunan 西島麦南 1895–

Haiku 俳句

'1 haiku' *A history of haiku v.2*, by R. H. Blyth. Tokyo, Hokuseido, 1964. p.250

NISHIKAWA Mitsuru 西川 満 1908–

Chūgoku bijo tan 中国美女譚

「殘忍的呂后」 曙光訳 台北 龍門出版社 1960. 35p.
「中國美女譚」 李俊凡訳 서울 世宗出版社 1962. 312p.

'我要話下去' 景唐 明偉訳 「純文學」 (台湾版) 第3巻1期 1968. p.93–114; 「純文學」 (香港版) 第2巻2期 1968. p.93–114

NISHIKAWA Sumiko 西川澄子

Watakushi 私

「綠色의手帖」 李丙永訳 서울 隆文社 1965. 264p.

NISHIKAWA Tsutomu 西川 勉 1894–1934

Criticism 評論

'我國的童話文學' 夏丏尊訳 「小説月報」 第12巻増刊号 1921.

NISHIMURA Kyōtarō 西村京太郎 1930–

Yasashii kyōhakusha 優しい脅迫者

'The kind blackmailer' *Japanese golden dozen*, ed. by Ellery Queen. Tokyo, Tuttle, 1978. p.147–165

NISHIMURA Yōkichi 西村陽吉 1892–1959

Tanka 短歌

'中産階級' 周作人訳 「新青年」 第9巻4期 1921. p.39–40; 「陀螺」 192?.
'My dwelling-place; Plane-trees; A packhorse; Sunday' Tr. by Asataro Miyamori. *Masterpieces of Japanese poetry, ancient and modern*. Tokyo, Maruzen, 1936; Tokyo, Taiseido, 1956; N. Y. Greenwood Press, 1971. p.790–792

NISHIMURA Tenshū 西村天囚 1865–1924

Poems 詩

'Bushido' Tr. by S. Uchida. *The mastersingers of Japan*, by Clara A. Walsh. London, John Murray, 1910. p.112–115

NISHINO Tatsukichi 西野辰吉 1916–

Beikei Nichijin 米系日人

'Дети смешанной крови' Перевод Е. М. Пинус. *Звезда*, 1957, No.5. p.80–87
'Дети смешанной крови' Перевод Л. Бабкиной. *Японская новелла*. Москва, Изд. Иност. Лит. 1961. p.175–186
'Japaner amerikanischen Blutes' Deutsch von Jürgen Berndt und Ursula-Eleonore Winkler. *Träume aus zehn Nächten*. Berlin, Aufbau Verlag, 1975. p.490–505

Umenai　産めない

'Горести Кэндзо'　Перевод Е. Пинус. *Новый Мир*, 1958, No.6. p.185–191; *Рассказы писателей Востока*. Ленинград, Лениздат, 1958. p.347–357

NISHIUCHI Minami　西内ミナミ

Gurunpa no yōchien　グルンパのようちえん

Grumpa's børnehabe. Oversaette Viggio Nørgaard-Jepsen. København, Høst, 1967. 28p.
The happiest elephant in the world. London, Evans Brothers, 1969. 30p.
The kindergarten elephant. English version by Kenneth Williams. Tokyo, Labo-Teaching Information Center, 1969. 1v.

NISHIWAKI Junzaburō　西脇順三郎　1894–

Shigaku　詩学

'詩學' 洪順隆訳　「自由青年」　第47–48巻 1961–62.
「詩學」 林國清訳　台北　田園出版社　1969. 174p.; 台北　華新出版有限公司　1976. 1冊
「西詩探源」 洪順隆訳　台北　台湾商務印書館 1975. 272p.

Poems　詩

'Journal ayant une profondeur intérieure'　Tr. par Kuni Matsuo et Steinilber-Oberlin. *Anthologie des poètes japonais contemporains.* Paris, Mercure de France, 1939. p.233–234
'January in Kyoto'　*Japan Quarterly*, v.3, no.1, 1956. p.81–83
'Rain; The sun'　*Poetry*, May 1956.　p.75
'Inverted graces; Mutability; Past; Fall'　*United Asia*, v.8, no.4, 1956. p.265–266
'The sun; The traveller; Roman de la rose; Rain; A dish; An eye; Weather'　*An anthology of modern Japanese poetry*, ed. and tr. by Ichiro Kono and Rikutaro Fukuda. Tokyo, Kenkyusha, 1957. p.101–105
'Rain; Let the traveller pause'　*The poetry of living Japan*, by Takamichi Ninomiya and D. J. Enright. London, John Murray, 1957. p.79–80
'La pluie; Le soleil'　*La poésie japonaise*, par Karl Petit. Paris, Seghers, 1959. p.219
'無果花' 金龍済訳　「日本詩集」　서울　青雲社　1960. p.30–34
'Rain; Weather; Eye'　Tr. by Geoffrey Bownas and Anthony Thwaite. *The Penguin book of Japanese verse.* Harmondsworth, Penguin Books, 1964. p.200–201
'Hava'　Tercüme etmek L. Sami Akalin. *Japon şiiri.* İstanbul, Varlik Yayinevi, 1962. p.261
'永遠히가까히서' 崔一秀訳　「기다리고있네」 서울　韓国政経社　1966. p.241–243
'사시나무열매 ; 나그네돌아오지않다 ; 명아주' 鄭漢模訳 「世界戦後文学全集 9」 서울　新丘文化社 1962. p.208–209
'Il viaggiatore; Il sole'　*La protesta poetica del Giappone*, a cura di Dacia Maraini e Michiko Nojiri. Roma Officina Edizioni, 1968. p.33–34
'Rain; The hand'　Tr. by Tsutomu Fukuda. *Poetry Nippon*, no.9 & 10, 1970. p.23
'One winter day'　Tr. by Tsutomu Fukuda. *Poetry Nippon*, no.11, 1970. p.24–25

'豊饒의女神; 近代의寓話; 哀' 金巣雲訳　「世界의文学大全集 34」 서울　同和出版公社　1971. p.523–525
'날씨' 金光林訳　「現代詩学」　第4巻3号 1972.
'Katherine; Autumn; Bitterness of the plum; Winter day; Porcelain; January; Loquat; Winter conversation; Esthetique foraine'　Tr. by Hiroaki Sato. *Ten Japanese poets.* Hanover, N. H. Granite Publications, 1973. p. 56–67
'Дождь'　Перевод Анатолия Мамонова. *Вкус хризантемы.* Москва, Восточная Литература, 1976. p.80
'Ochii; Ploaia'　Traducerea Virgil Teodorescu. *Din lirica japoneză.* Bucureşti, Editura Univers, n.d. p.185–186
'Regn; Vaer; Øyet; Solen; Stans reisende'　Til norsk ved Paal Brekke. *Modern Japansk lyrikk.* Oslo, Norske Bokklubben, n.d. p.39–43

Criticism　評論

'詩의内容論' 金光林訳　「現代詩学」　第4巻2号 1972.

NISHIYAMA Hakuun　西山泊雲　1877–1944

Haiku　俳句

'2 haiku'　Tr. by Asataro Miyamori. *Anthology of haiku, ancient and modern.* Tokyo, Maruzen, 1932. p.766–767
'Dewdrops'　Tr. by Asataro Miyamori. *Haiku poems, ancient and modern.* Tokyo, Maruzen, 1940. p.342
'Clear spring'　Tr. by Kenneth Yasuda. *A pepperpod.* Tokyo, Tuttle, 1976. p.90

NITOBE Inazō　新渡戸稲造　1862–1933

Essays　エッセイ

'On the unification of the spoken and written languages'　*Seinen*, v.5, no.19, 1901. p.7. no. 20, 1901. p.9–10
'East and West in contact'　Tr. by C. G. Elder and S. Suga . *Eigo Seinen*, v.64, no.10, 1931. p.347–348

NITTA Jirō　新田次郎　1912–

Fuyuta no tsuru　冬田の鶴

'겨울논의鶴' 金潤成訳　「日本代表作家百人集 4」 서울　希望出版社　1966. p.298–309; 「日本短篇文学全集 5」 서울　新太陽社　1969. p.138–149

Kuroi yuki no yume　黒い雪の夢

'黒雪夢' 廖清秀訳　「投水自殺営救業」　台北　蘭開書局 1968. p.10–32

Shinigami ni owareru otoko　死神に追われる男

'死神的追逐' 劉慕沙訳　「狐鶏」　台北　林白出版社 1969. p.140–168

NIWA Akiko　丹羽安喜子　1890–

Tanka　短歌

'The great-tit; The October sea'　Tr. by Asataro Miyamori. *Masterpieces of Japanese poetry, ancient and modern.* Tokyo, Maruzen, 1936; Tokyo, Taiseido, 1956; N. Y. Greenwood Press, 1971. p.773–775

NIWA Fumio　丹羽文雄　1904–

Aijin　愛人

「愛人」　方虎振訳　서울　理智社　1961. 335p.
「戀人」　良乙平訳　서울　誠和文化社　1961. 335p.

Bodaiju　菩提樹

The Buddha tree.　Tr. by Kenneth Strong. London, Peter Owen, 1966. 380p; Tokyo, Tuttle, 1968. 380p.

Hana no nai kajitsu　花のない果実

'無花的果實'　朱佩蘭訳　「伊豆的舞娘」　嘉義　明山書局　1969. p.153–176

Hōchō　庖丁

Les couteaux du cuisinier.　Tr. par Tsuruyo Kohno et Henriette Valot. Paris, Mondiales, 1960. 313p.; Paris, Del Duca, 1960. 313p.

Iyagarase no nenrei　厭がらせの年齢

'The hateful age'　Tr. by Ivan Morris. *Japan Quarterly*, v.3, no.1, 1956. p.54–78; *Modern Japanese stories*, ed. by I. Morris. London, Spottiswoode, 1961; Tokyo, Tuttle, 1962. p.321–348; *The hateful age.* Tokyo, Hara Shobo, 1965. p.7–101
'The hateful years'　Tr. by William L. Clark. *Jiji Eigo Kenkyu*, v.13, no.4–no.11, 1958. v.14, no.2, 1959; *Various kinds of bugs, and other stories from present-day Japan.* Tokyo, Kenkyusha, 1958. p.97–175
'Brzemię starości'　Przeł. Anna Gostyńska. *Irys, opowiadania japońskie.* Warszawa, Państwowy Instytut Wydawniczy, 1960. p.43–87
'Umor yang di-běnchi'　Děngan kata pěngantar oleh James Kirkup. *Shoji.* Kuala Lumpur, Oxford Univ. Press, 1961. p.52–92
'L'eta odiosa'　Tr. di Atsuko Ricca Suga. *Narratori giapponesi moderni.* Milano, Bompiani, 1965. p.435–466

Jokyū　女給

'Служанка из столовой'　Перевод Я. Берлина и З. Рахима. *Японская новелла.* Москва, Изд. Иност. Лит. 1961. p.160–174

Sannin no tsuma　三人の妻

'三主婦'　朱佩蘭訳　「伊豆的舞娘」　嘉義　明山書局　1969. p.177–196

Shūchi　羞恥

'A touch of shyness'　Tr. by E. G. Seidensticker. *Japan Quarterly*, v.2, no.1, 1955. p.76–85; *The hateful age.* Tokyo, Hara Shodo, 1965. p.103–137

Tsuioku　追憶

'追憶'　金洙暎訳　「日本代表作家百人集 3」　서울　希望出版社　1966. p.282–298;「日本短篇文学全集 4」　서울　新太陽社　1969. p.42–58

Zeiniku　贅肉

'Indulgent flesh'　Tr. by Richard Foster. *The hateful age.* Tokyo, Hara Shobo, 1965. p.139–245

'Il progetto della moglie'　*Yamato*, v.1, no.6, 1941. p.178–181
「秘密의門」　李文賢訳　서울　弘益出版社　1974. 323p.

NOBUCHI Bin　野淵　敏

'禿山・月光・卡斯巴'　劉慕沙訳　「日本現代小説選」　台北　聯經出版社　1976. p.59–84

NOBORI Shomu　昇　曙夢　1878–1958

Rokoku gendai no shichō oyobi bungaku　露国現代の思潮及文学

「現代俄國文藝思潮」　陳淑達訳　上海　華通書局　1929. 1冊
「俄國現代思潮及文學」　許亦非訳　上海　現代書局　1933. 1冊

Criticism　評論

'啓發託爾斯泰的両個農夫'　鄒訒訳　「新青年」　第6巻6期　1919. p.603–605
'無産階級詩人和農民詩人'　畫室訳　「莽原」　第1巻21期　1926. p.845–855
「新俄文藝的曙光期」　畫室訳　上海　北新書局　1926. 1冊
「蘇我的二種跳舞劇」　畫室訳　「莽原」　第2巻5期　1927. p.182–188
「新俄的演劇運動與跳舞」　畫室訳　上海　北新書局　1927. 1冊
'最近之高爾基'　李可訳　「小説月報」　第19巻8号　1928. p.925–932
'最近的戈理基'　魯迅訳「壁下譯叢」上海　北新書局　1929;「魯迅全集 16」　上海　魯迅全集出版社　1938. 作家書屋　1946. 大連　光華書店　1948. 北京　人民文学出版社　1973. p.271–290;「魯迅譯文集 5」北京　人民文学出版社　1958. p.341–356

NODA Bettenrō　野田別天楼　1869–1944

Haiku　俳句

'2 haiku'　Tr. by Asataro Miyamori. *Anthology of haiku, ancient and modern.* Tokyo, Maruzen, 1932. p.827–829

NOGAMI Akira　野上　彰　1908–1967

Poems　詩

Preludes.　Tr. by George Saito. Tokyo, Sogensha, 1956. 29p.
'작은꽃다발；愛人이여；받아주신다면'　崔一秀訳　「기다리고있네」　서울　韓国政経社　1966. p.101–103, 183–184, 193–195

'Poems from Preludes' Tr. by George Saito. *Japan P.E.N. News*, no.21, May 1968. p.1–3

NOGAMI Toyoichirō 野上豊一郎 1883–1950

Criticism 評論

Zeami and his theories on Noh. Tr. by Ryozo Matsumoto. Tokyo, Hinoki Shoten, 1955. 89p.

NOGAMI Yaeko 野上弥生子 1885–

Fue 笛

'플루트' 金龍済訳 「日本代表作家百人集 2」 서울 希望出版社 1966. p.84–127; 「日本短篇文学全集 2」 서울 新太陽社 1969. p.148–191
'플루트' 高永絢訳 「日本文学大全集 10」 서울 東西文化院 1975. p.231–272

Fujito 藤戸

'Foujito' Tr. par M. Yoshitomi. *Femmes japonaises et leur littérature.* Paris, Chariot, 1924. p.149–167

Kaijin maru 海神丸

Kaijin-maru. Esperanta traduko de Kazuo Osaki. Tokyo, Japana Esperanto Instituto, 1935. 76p.
'The Neptune' Tr. by Ryozo Matsumoto. *The Neptune, The foxes.* Tokyo, Kenkyusha, 1957. p.1–103; *Japanese literature, new and old.* Tokyo, Hokuseido, 1961. p.119–176
'Шхуна «Кайдзин мару»' Перевод И. Львовой. *Иностранная Литература*, апрель 1961. p.140–162

Kitsune 狐

'The foxes' Tr. by Ryozo Matsumoto. *The Neptune, The foxes.* Tokyo, Kenkyusha, 1957. p.105–226; *Japanese literature, new and old.* Tokyo, Hokuseido, 1961. p.177–242

Meiro 迷路

'Обрыв' отрывок из романа «Лабиринт». Перевод С. Гутермана. *Японская новелла.* Москва, Изд. Иност. Лит. 1961. p.187–207
Лабиринт. Перевод С. Гутермана и Н. Д. Неверовой. Москва, Изд. Иност. Лит. 1963. 2т.

NOGI Maresuke 乃木希典 1849–1912

Chinese poems 漢詩

'Outside the Chin Chou castle' Tr. by Tetsuzo Okada. *Chinese and Sino-Japanese poems.* Tokyo, Seikanso, 1937. p.97

Tanka 短歌

'2 tanka' Tr. by Hidesaburo Saito. *Eigo Seinen*, v.28, no.1, 1912. p.25
'A good name' Tr. by Asataro Miyamori. *Masterpieces of Japanese poetry, ancient and modern.* Tokyo, Maruzen, 1936; Tokyo, Tai-

seido, 1956; N. Y. Greenwood Press, 1971. p 610–611
'1 tanka' Übers. von Gerolf Coudenhove. *Japanische Jahreszeiten.* Zürich, Manesse Verlag, 1963. p.23

NOGI Miki 乃木みき

Poems 詩

'Леса Латинской Америки' Перевод Анатолия Мамонова. *Вкус хризантемы.* Москва, Восточная Литература, 1976. p.82

NOGUCHI Kakuchū 野口赫宙 1905–

Izoku no otto 異俗の夫

'風習이다른남편' 趙能植訳 「日本代表作家百人集 3」 서울 希望出版社 1966. p.388–408; 「日本短篇文学全集 4」 서울 新太陽社 1969. p.148–168

NOGUCHI Takehiko 野口武彦 1937–

Criticism 評論

'Time in the world of Sasameyuki' Tr. by Teruko Craig. *The Journal of Japanese Studies*, v.3, no.1, Winter 1977. p.1–36

NOGUCHI Ujō 野口雨情 1882–1945

Poems 詩

'Soap bubbles; A cage without a firefly' Tr. by Shigeno Hamada and Klara Sugano. *Aoba no fue.* Honolulu, Univ. of Hawaii Press, 1937.
'Port de Habu' *Histoire de la littérature japonaise contemporaine*, par Georges Bonneau. Paris, Payot, 1944. p.249–250

NOGUCHI Yonejirō 野口米次郎 1875–1947

Poems 詩

'The morning-glory' *The spirit of Japanese poetry*, by Yone Noguchi. London, John Murray, 1914. p.68–70
'小曲' 周作人訳 「新青年」 第9巻4期 1921. p.35–36
'Rainbow song; A farmer' Tr. by Sherard Vines. *Osaka Mainichi*, Oct. 17, 31, 1925.
'The sunflower; A lone pine tree; The Korin design; The sea; The morning-glory' Tr. by Yone Noguchi. *Lotus and chrysanthemum.* N. Y. Liveright, 1928. p.149–154
'Bouddhiste zeniste; A Hiroshigué; La neige singulière; Une feuille d'arbre; Le fantôme; Les voyageurs de l'ombre; Batelier' Tr. par Kuni Matsuo et Steinilber-Oberlin. *Anthologie des poètes japonais contemporains.* Paris, Mercure de France, 1939. p.45–52
'Le bonze en méditation; Lignes; Telle une feuille'

NOGUCHI Yonejirō

La poésie japonaise, par Karl Petit. Paris, Seghers, 1959. p.194–195

'I worship the sun' Tr. by Hisakazu Kaneko. *Orient West*, v.8, no.1, 1963. p.50

'I worship the sun; My hands' Tr. by Hisakazu Kaneko. *The Japanaese image*, ed. by M. Schneps and A. D. Coox. Tokyo, Orient West, 1965. p.350–351, 353–354

'My hands' Tr. by Hisakazu Kaneko. *London Magazine*, v.7, no.7, 1967. p.35–36

'Slaughter them; The American and English are our enemies' Tr. by Donald Keene. *Landscapes and portraits*. Tokyo, Kodansha International, 1971. p.317–318

Criticism 評論

'愛蘭蘭文學之回顧' 魯迅訳 「奔流」 第2巻2期 1929; 「魯迅全集 16」 上海 魯迅全集出版社 1938. 作家書屋 1946. 大連 光華書店 1948. 北京 人民文学出版社 1973. p.439–451; 「魯迅譯文集 10」 北京 人民文学出版社 1958. p.210–220

NOMA Hiroshi 野間 宏 1915–

Dai sanjū rokugō 第三十六号

'No.36' Перевод Е. Пинус. *No.36: новеллы японских писателей*. Москва, Наука, 1968. p.31–55

Hōkai kankaku 崩壊感覚

'Az összeomlás érzése' Ford. Sz. Holti Mária. *Modern Japán elbeszélök*. Budapest, Európa Könyvkiadó, 1967. p.309–338

Kao no naka no akai tsuki 顔の中の赤い月

'Красная луна над Филиппинами' Перевод Г. Ронской. *Японская новелла*. Москва, Изд. Иност. Лит. 1964. p.208–228

'A red moon in her face' Tr. by Kinya Tsuruta. *Literary Review*, v.6, no.1, 1962. p.35–37

'Punane kuu Filipinide kohal' *Elada!* Tallinn Eesti Riiklik Kirjastus, 1962. p.163–185

'Филиппин аралындаты кызыл апаи' Аударган Е. Атыгаев. *Жапон енгимелери*. Алма-Ата, Жазушы, 1965. p.69–93

'얼굴속의붉은달' 朴松訳 「日本代表作家百人集 4」 서울 希望出版社 1966. p.356–377; 「日本短篇文学全集 5」 서울 新太陽社 1969. p.196–217

'Červený měsíc ve tváři' Přel. Vlasta Winkelhöferová. *Světová literatura*, v.19, no.2, 1974. p.146–161

'Ein roter Mond in ihrem Gesicht' Deutsch von Jürgen Berndt. *Träume aus zehn Nächten*. Berlin, Aufbau Verlag. 1975. p.273–304

Kuruma no yoru 車の夜

'Noč automobilu' Přel. M. Novák. *Světová Literatura*, no.4, 1962. p.136–143

Shinkū chitai 真空地帯

Zone de vide. Tr. par Translator Group of Tokyo University et Henriette de Boissel. Paris, Sycomore, 1954. 464p.

Zone of emptiness. Tr. from the French by Bernard Frechtman. Cleveland, World Publishing Co. 1956. 319p.

Strefa próżni. Przeł. Jadwiga Dutkiewicz. War-szawa, Wydaiwnictwo Ministerstwa Obrony Narodowej, 1957. 412p.

El gran vaćio. Tr. de francés por Manuel Peyrou. Buenos Aires, Goyanarte, 1958. 306p.

「眞空地帯」 蕭蕭訳 北京 作家出版社 1956. 390p.; 北京 人民文学出版社 1959. 288p.

Зона пустоты. Перевод А. Рябкина и А. Стругацкого. Москва, Гослитиздат, 1960. 375p.

Oblast prázdnoty. Přel. Zdeněk Havlík, Praha, N. Vojsko, 1963. 334p.

Légüres övezet. Ford. Lomb Kató. Budapest, Európa Könyvkiadó, 1964. 366p.

Poems 詩

'Глаза всего мира обращены на нас' Перевод В. Н. Марковой. *Огонек*, 1952, No.18. p.23; *Японская поэзия*. Москва, Гослитиздат, 1954. p.362–363; Изд. 2. 1956. p.464–465

'Взгляды миллионов' Перевод А. Мамонова. *Смена*, 1955, No.17. p.18; *Поэты Азии*. Москва, Гослитиздат, 1957. p.854–855

'三十亿只眼睛' 李芒訳 「詩刊」 第4期 1961. p.58

'그대의눈물' 崔一秀訳 「기다리고있네」 서울 韓国政経社 1966. p.59–63

Essays エッセイ

「我們是日本人」 北京大学東方語言系日本語專業同学集体訳 北京 人民文学出版社 1958. 34p.

'Русская литература в Японии' *Иностранная Литература*, сентябрь 1959. p.173–174

'О Чехове' *Иностранная Литература*, январь 1960. p.190–192

NOMURA Hakugetsu 野村泊月 1882–1961

Haiku 俳句

'From the hill top; Maple-spray' Tr. by Kenneth Yasuda. *A pepper-pod*. Tokyo, Tuttle, 1976. p.94

NOMURA Hideo 野村秀夫

Poems 詩

'少女의노래; 마음속에서; 祈禱; 나의마음속에' 崔一秀訳 「기다리고있네」 서울 韓国政経社 1966. p.97–100, 114–118

NOMURA Kishū 野村喜舟 1886–

Haiku 俳句

'Silent traveller' Tr. by Harold Stewart. *A net of fireflies*. Tokyo, Tuttle, 1960. p.88

NOMURA Mansuke 野村万介

Ireme いれ眼

'A dealer in eyes, a No farce' Tr. by T. Aoki. *Eigo Seinen*, v.53, no.8, 1925. p.239. no.9, 1925. p.267. no.10, 1925. p.305–306

NOMURA Yoshiya 野村吉哉 1903–

Poems 詩

'The economical noon' *An anthology of modern Japanese poetry*, ed. and tr. by Ichiro Kono and Rikutaro Fukuda. Tokyo, Kenkyusha, 1957. p.105

NONAGASE Masao 野長瀬正夫 1906–

Poems 詩

'A favorite' *An anthology of modern Japanese poetry*, ed. and tr. by Ichiro Kono and Rikutaro Fukuda. Tokyo, Kenkyusha, 1957. p.106

NONAKA Kōji 野中晃治

Kiseki no tsuma 奇跡の妻

「奇蹟の妻」鄭成煥訳 서울 青雲出版社 1965. 250p.
「너무나사랑했기에」鄭成煥訳 서울 大韓出版社 1971. 247p.

NORO Kuninobu 野呂邦暢 1937–

Kusa no tsurugi 草のつるぎ

'풀의劍' 玄在勲訳 「70年代芥川賞小説集」서울 玄岩社 1976. p.55–135;「新鋭世界文学選集20世紀 9」서울 玄岩社 1977. p.55–135

NOSAKA Akiyuki 野坂昭如 1930–

Amerika hijiki アメリカひじき

'American hijiki' Tr. by Jay Rubin. *Contemporary Japanese literature*, ed. by Howard Hibbett. N. Y. Knopf, 1977. p.436–468

Erogotoshi tachi エロ事師たち

The pornographers. Tr. by Michael Gallagher. N. Y. Knopf, 1968. 304p.; London, Secker and Warburg, 1969. 304p.; N. Y. Bantam Books, 1969. 234p.; Tokyo, Tuttle, 1970. 305p.; London, Mayflower, 1970. 206p.
Japanische Freuden. Übers. aus dem Amerikanische von Norbert Wolf. München, Droemer Knaur, 1971. 319p.

Hotaru no haka 火垂るの墓

'A grave of fireflies' Tr. by James R. Abrams. *Japan Quarterly*, v.25, no.4, 1978. p.445–463

NUKADA Roppuku 額田六福 1890–1948

Dai Nankō 大楠公

'Dai-Nanko, a historic drama' Tr. by Glenn W. Shaw. *Cultural Nippon*, v.7, 1939. p.95–115

Sakichi no ningyō 佐吉の人形

'Sakichi's doll' Tr. by Takehide Kikuchi. *Info*, June-July, 1961. p.73–78, Aug. 1961. p.74–78

Shinnyo 真如

'Shinnyo, oder, Das Wahre Echte' Übers. von Maria Piper. *Die Schaukunst der Japaner*. Berlin, Walter de Gruyter, 1927. p.106–114

NUNAMI Keion 沼波瓊音 1877–1927

Haiku 俳句

'2 haiku' *A history of haiku v.2*, by R. H. Blyth. Tokyo, Hokuseido, 1964. p.157–158

NUYAMA Hiroshi ぬやま・ひろし 1903–1976

Poems 詩

'Радость' Перевод Ю. Хазанова и Б. Раскина. *Огонек*, 1954, No.14. p.28
'Глаза; В пути састает меня вечер; Полевой колокольчик' Перевод В. Журавлева. *Поэты Азии*. Москва, Гослитиздат, 1957. p.879–883
'桔梗花之歌 ; 斗笠' 李芒訳 「世界文学」 1961年3月 p.40–41
'Барацам желдон кеч кирип; Кездер' Которгон Ж. Алыбаев. *Хиросима кектери*. Фрунзе, Кыргызстан, 1969. p.79

O

ŌBA Hakusuirō 大場白水郎 1890–1962

Haiku 俳句

'Lake Kawaguchi' Tr. by Asataro Miyamori. *Anthology of haiku, ancient and modern*. Tokyo, Maruzen, 1932. p.826

ŌBA Minako 大庭みな子 1930–

Sanbiki no kani 三匹の蟹

'三隻蟹' 朱佩蘭訳 「純文學」(台湾版) 第4卷5期 1968. p.11–38;「夏流」 台北 純文學出版社 1969. p.127–168
'세마리의게' 姜尚求訳 「現代文学」 第14卷9号 1968.
'Три краба' Перевод З. Рахима. *Японская новелла 1960–1970*. Москва, Прогресс, 1972. p.206–237
'The three crabs' Tr. by Stephen Kohl and Toyama Ryōko. *Japan Quarterly*, v.25, no.3, 1978. p.323–339

Essay エッセイ

'Double suicide, a Japanese phenomenon' Tr.

ŌBA Minako

by Manabu Takechi and Wayne Root. *Japan Interpreter*, v.9, no.3, 1975. p.344–350

OBATA Teiichi 小畠貞一 1888–1942

Poems 詩

'A lie' *An anthology of modern Japanese poetry*, ed. and tr. by Ichiro Kono and Rikutaro Fukuda. Tokyo, Kenkyusha, 1957. p.107

ŌBAYASHI Kiyoshi 大林 清 1908–

Yokubō no kawa 慾望の河

「慾望之河」 台北 台湾商務印書館 1969. 346p.

───────────

'熱抱' 徐雲濤訳 「當代日本小説選」 台南 經緯書局 1954. p.49–71；「當代日本創作小説」 台南 經緯書局 1961. p.49–71；「當代日本短篇小説選」 台南 大行出版社 1973. p.49–71

OCHI Harumi 越智春海 1918–

Kyōran no Shingapōru 狂乱のシンガポール

「狂乱의大地」 安東民訳 서울 新亜出版社 1967. 439p.

OCHIAI Naobumi 落合直文 1861–1903

Kōjo Shiragiku no uta 孝女白菊の歌

Japanische Dichtungen Weißaster, ein romantisches Epos. Übers. von Karl Florenz. Tokyo, Hasegawa, 1895; Leipzig, Amelang, 1895, 84p.
White aster. Tr. by Arthur Lloyd. Tokyo, Hasegawa, 1897. 82p.

Tanka 短歌

'Horsetails; Death; My poems; When ill in bed; I am a God; Mount Fuji; Violets and dandelions' Tr. by Asataro Miyamori. *Masterpieces of Japanese poetry, ancient and modern*. Tokyo, Maruzen, 1936; Tokyo, Taiseido, 1956; N. Y. Greenwood Press, 1971. p.613–617
'5 tanka' Tr. by Shigeshi Nishimura. *The Current of the World*, v.15, no.7, 1938. p.105
'4 tanka' Tr. by V. H. Viglielmo. *Japanese literature in the Meiji era*. Tokyo, Obunsha, 1955. p.373
'1 tanka' Tr. by H. H. Honda. *The Reeds*, v.5, 1959. p.86
'2 tanka' Tr. by James Kirkup. *Eigo Seinen*, v.106, no.8, 1960. p.401
'Mein Gedicht; Der Dichter; Auf dem Krankenlager' Übers. von Günther Debon. *Im Schnee die Fähre*. München, Piper, 1960. p.7–9
'2 tanka' Übers. von Gerolf Coudenhove. *Japanische Jahreszeiten*. Zürich, Manesse Verlag, 1963. p.278, 340
'Der Dichter' *Lyrik des Ostens*, hrg. von Wil-

helm Gundert usw. München, Carl Hanser, 1965. p.469

ODA Makoto 小田 実 1932–

Kūkan to jikan no tabi 空間と時間の旅

「벌써가야할時間인가」 李英雨訳 서울 文学社 1964. 490p.

Nandemo mite yarō 何でも見てやろう

「나는이렇게보았다」 印泰星訳 서울 徽文出版社 1962. 350p.

Nihon o kangaeru 日本を考える

「이것이日本이다」 韓致煥訳 서울 徽文出版社 1964. 370p.

Essays エッセイ

'세계無銭旅行후일담' 金賢珠訳 「바이바이바다」 서울 三韓出版社 1966. p.286–289
'Making democracy our own' Tr. by John H. Boyle. *Japan Interpreter*, v.6, no.3, 1970. p.235–254
「무엇이든지봐주리라」 具滋性訳 서울 青山文化社 1974. 344p.

ODA Sakunosuke 織田作之助 1913–1947

Keiba 競馬

'Corrida de cavalos' Tr. de José Yamashiro. *Maravilhas do conto japonês*. São Paulo, Editôra Cultrix, 1962. p.184–199

ODAGIRI Susumu 小田切 進 1924–

Criticism 評論

「日本의名作 近代小説55篇 鑑賞과研究」 李延秀訳 서울 進明文化社 1977. 239p.

ODAKA Yoshio 尾高芳雄

Haisō 敗走

「敗走」 金顕済訳 서울 育生社 1950. 187p.

ŌE Kenzaburō 大江健三郎 1935–

Atomikku eiji no shugojin アトミック・エイジの守護神

'Лесной отшельник ядерного века' Перевод З. Рахима. *Японская новелла 1960–1970*. Москва, Прогресс, 1972. p.278–307; *Кэндзабро Оэ*. Москва, Прогресс, 1978. p.367–394

Fui no oshi 不意の唖

'不意의벙어리' 李鍾烈訳 「日本新鋭文学作家受賞作品選集 5」 서울 青雲社 1964. p.317–329；「戦後日本短篇文学選集 5」 서울 日光出版社 1965. p.317–329；「現代日本代表文学全集 5」 서울 平和出版社 1973. p.317–329

'벙어리들' 許東雲訳 「日本研究」 第19巻12号 1974.
p.114–123
'Und plötzlich stumm' Deutsch von Jürgen
Berndt und Eiko Saito-Berndt. *Träume aus
zehn Nächten*. Berlin, Aufbau Verlag, 1975.
p.563–579

Genshuku na tsunawatari　厳粛な綱渡り

'Из книги «Хождение по канату»' Перевод Б.
Раскина. *Иностранная Литература*, сентябрь 1977. p.224–225

Keirō shūkan　敬老週間

'Неделя почитания старости' Перовод В. Гривнина. *Кэндзабро Оэ.* Москва, Прогресс, 1978.
p.394–408

Kimyō na shigoto　奇妙な仕事

'奇妙한作業' 李鐘烈訳 「日本新鋭文学作家受賞作品選
集 5」 서울 青雲社 1964. p.273–284;「戦後日本
短篇文学全集 5」 서울 日光出版社 1965. p.273–
285;「現代日本代表文学全集 5」 서울 平和出版社
1973. p.273–284
'Чудная работа' Перевод А. Бабинцева. *No. 36:
новеллы японских писателей.* Москва,
Наука, 1968. p.56–66

Kojinteki na taiken　個人的な体験

A personal matter. Tr. by John Nathan. N. Y.
Grove Press, 1968. 214p.; London, Weiden-
feld and Nicolson, 1969. 214p.; Tokyo,
Tuttle, 1969. 211p.
Mardrömmen. Tr. Th. Warburton. Uppsala,
Almqvist & Wiksell, 1969. 208p.
Une affaire personnelle. Tr. de l'americain par
Claude Elsen. Paris, Stock, 1971. 179p.
Un asunto personal. Tr. del inglés de Fernando
Novoa. Buenos Aires, Losada, 1971. 231p.
Eine persönliche Erfahrung. Übers. von Siegfried
Schaarschmidt. Frankfurt am Main, Suhr-
kamp, 1972. 239p.
Sprawa osobista. Przeł. Zofia Uhrynowska.
Warszawa, Państwowy Instytut Wydawniczy,
1974. 189p.

Kōzui wa waga tamashii ni oyobi　洪水はわが魂に及び

'Обьяли меня воды до дчши моей, Перовод В.
Гривнина. *Кэндзабро Оэ.* Москва, Прогресс,
1978. p.25–325

Man'en gannen no futtobōru　万延元年のフットボール

'Футбол 1860 года' Перевод В. Гривнина.
Иностранная Литература, январь 1972.
p.143–208; февраль 1972. p.70–154
'A game of football' Tr. by John Bester. *Japan
Quarterly*, v.20, no.4, 1973. p.414–427; v.21,
no.1, 1974. p.45–57; v.21, no.2, 1974. p.168–
180
The silent cry. Tr. by John Bester. Tokyo, Kodansha International, 1974. 274p.

Mizukara waga namida o nugui tamau hi　みずから我が涙をぬぐいたまう日

'The day he himself shall wipe my tears away' Tr.
by John Nathan. *Teach us to outgrow our
madness.* N. Y. Grove Press, 1977. p.1–110

Ningen no hitsuji　人間の羊

'Birkaemberek' Ford. Vihar Judit. *Nagyvilág*,
no.12, 1968. p.1763–1772
'Sheep' Tr. by Frank Motofuji. *Japan Quarterly*,
v.17, no.2, 1970. p.167–177
'Люди-бараны' Перевод Г. Иммерман. *Красная
лягушка.* Москва, Наука, 1973. p.102–117

Okurete kita seinen　遅れてきた青年

Опоздавшая молодежь. Перевод В. Гривнина.
Москва, Прогресс, 1973. 341p.

Sakebi goe　叫び声

「외침소리」 林炫訳 서울 東南文化社 1976. 224p.

Sebuntein　セブンテイン

'Seventeen' 趙能植 金元基訳「日本代表作家百人集 5」
서울 希望出版社 1966. p.380–419;「日本短篇小
説全集 6」 서울 新太陽社 1969. p.292–331

Shiiku　飼育

'The catch' Tr. by John Bester. *Japan Quarterly*,
v.6, no.1, 1959. p.60–94; *The shadow of sunrise.* Tokyo, Kodansha International, 1966;
London, Ward Lock, 1966. p.15–60; *New
writing in Japan.* Harmondsworth, Penguin
Books, 1972. p.51–98
'飼育' 呉尚源訳 「世界戦後文学全集 7」 서울 新丘文化
社 1962. p.123–153;「世界代表短篇文学全集 21」
서울 正韓出版社 1976. p.403–452
'飼育' 李鐘烈訳 「日本新鋭文学作家受賞作品選集 5」
서울 青雲社 1964. p.228–271;「戦後日本短篇文学
全集 5」 서울 日光出版社 1965. p.229–271;「現
代日本代表文学全集 5」 서울 平和出版社 1973.
p.229–270
'Mint egy állatot' Ford. Kjoko Hani. *Nagyvilág*,
no.9, 1965. p.1291–1310
'Зверь' Переклав И. Дзюб. *Всесвет*, 1967, No.8.
p.116–131
'Der Fang' Aus dem Japanischen von Tatsuji
Iwabuchi. *Japan, Geistige Begegnung.* Tübingen, Erdmann, 1964. p.167–219; *Eine Glocke
in Fukagawa.* Tübingen, Erdmann, 1969.
p.167–219
'Mint egy állatot' Ford. Sz. Holti Mária. *Modern Japán elbeszélők.* Budapest, Európa
Könyvkiadó, 1967. p.459–488
'Zdobycz' Przeł. Mikołaj Melanowicz. *Cień
wschodzącego słońca.* Warszawa, Książka i
Wiedza, 1972.
'Prize stock' Tr. by John Nathan. *Teach us to
outgrow our madness.* N. Y. Grove Press,
1977. p.111–148
'Содержание скотины' Перевод В. Смирнова.
Кэндзабро Оэ. Москва, Прогресс, 1978.
p.329–366

Shisha no ogori　死者の奢り

'死者의奢侈' 李鐘烈訳 「日本新鋭文学作家受賞作品選集
5」 서울 青雲社 1964. p.286–315;「戦後日本短篇文
学全集 5」 서울 日光出版社 1965. p.286–316;
「現代日本代表文学全集 5」 서울 平和出版社 1973.
p.286–315
'Lavish are the dead' Tr. by John Nathan. *Japan
Quarterly*, v.12, no.2, 1965. p.193–211
'Der Stolz der Toten' Übers. von Margarete
Donath. *Japan erzählt.* Hamburg, Fischer,
1969. p.125–152

ŌE Kenzaburō

Sora no kaibutsu Aguī　空の怪物アグイー

'Aghwee the sky monster'　Tr. by John Nathan. *Evergreen Review*, no.54, 1968; *Teach us to outgrow our madness*. N. Y. Grove Press, 1977. p.221–261; *Contemporary Japanese literature*, ed. by Howard Hibbett. N. Y. Knopf, 1977. p.413–434

Tanpen shōsetsu no kanōsei　短篇小説の可能性

'Время «малых жанров»?'　диалог с Кобо Абэ. Перевод И. Львовой. *Иностранная Литература*, август 1965. p.220–229

Warera no kyōki o iki nobiru michi o oshieyo　われらの狂気を生き延びる道を教えよ

'Teach us to outgrow our madness'　Tr. by John Nathan. *Japan Quarterly*, v.19, no.2, 1972. p.182–204; *Teach us to outgrow our madness*. N. Y. Grove Press, 1977. p.169–219

Essay　エッセイ

'내가 "소비에트"의 청년이라면'　金賢珠訳　「바이바이바디」　서울　三韓出版社　1966. p.230–243

'짓밟히는싹들'　金世煥訳　「現代世界文学全集 6」　서울　新丘文化社　1968. p.285–393
Não matem o bébé.　Tr. por Daniel Gonçalves. Porto, Liv. Civilização, 1972. 1v.

ŌE Mitsuo　大江満雄　1906–

Poems　時

'The old weaving room; Rain; I want to be in different eyes'　*An anthology of modern Japanese poetry*, ed. and tr. by Ichiro Kono and Rikutaro Fukuda. Tokyo, Kenkyusha, 1957. p.107–109
'Yağmur'　Tercüme etmek L. Sami Akalin. *Japon şiiri*. İstanbul, Varlik Yayinevi, 1962. p.286
'Японский язык'　Перевод Анатолия Мамонова. *Вкус хризантемы*. Москва, Восточная Литература, 1976. p.100

OGATA Kamenosuke　尾形亀之助　1900–1942

Poems　詩

'Night'　*An anthology of modern Japanese poetry*, ed. and tr. by Ichiro Kono and Rikutaro Fukuda. Tokyo, Kenkyusha, 1957. p.110
'Gece'　Tercüme etmek L. Sami Akalin. *Japon şiiri*. İstanbul, Varlik Yayinevi, 1962. p.268

OGATA Korekiyo　緒方惟精　1909–

Nihon kan bungakushi　日本漢文学史

「日本漢文學史」　丁策訳　台北　正中書局　1968. 248p.

OGAWA Masami　小川正己

Poems　詩

'世界'　金龍済訳　「日本詩集」　서울　青雲社　1960. p.70–72

OGAWA Mimei　小川未明　1882–1961

Akai doku　赤い毒

'Red poison'　Tr. by Myrtle B. McKenney and Seison N. Yoshioka. *Rose and witch, and other stories*. San Francisco, Overland, 1925. p.63–82

Akai rōsoku to ningyo　赤い蠟燭と人魚

'The red candle and the mermaid'　Tr. by Yoshiko Akiyama. *The tipsy star, and other tales*. Tokyo, Hokuseido, 1957. p.85–93
'The red candle and the mermaid'　Tr. by Atsumu Kanayama. *The Reeds*, v.8, 1962. p.159–170

Akai sakana to kodomo　赤い魚と子ども

'赤魚小孩'　姜景苦訳　「文學週報」　第167期

Akai yubi　赤い指

'The rosy finger'　Tr. by Myrtle B. McKenney and Seison N. Yoshioka. *Rose and witch, and other stories*. San Francisco, Overland, 1925. p.23–44

Aozora ni egaku　青空に描く

'描在青空'　吶鷗訳　「莽原」　第2巻24期　1927. p.898–924;「色情文化」　上海　水沫書店　1929.

Aru natsu no hi no koto　ある夏の日のこと

'On a summer day'　Tr. by Yoshiko Akiyama. *The tipsy star, and other tales*. Tokyo, Hokuseido, 1957. p.10–12

Arukenu hi　歩けぬ日

'The day he could not walk'　Tr. by Myrtle B. McKenney and Seison N. Yoshioka. *Rose and witch, and other stories*. San Francisco, Overland, 1925. p.45–62

Bara to miko　薔薇と巫女

'Rose and witch'　Tr. by Myrtle B. McKenney and Seison N. Yoshioka. *Rose and witch, and other stories*. San Francisco, Overland, 1925. p.3–22

Beni suzume　紅すずめ

'紅雀'　張曉天訳　「小川未明童話集本」　上海　新中國書局　n.d.

Bikko no ouma　びっこのお馬

'The lame horse'　Tr. by Yoshiko Akiyama. *The tipsy star, and other tales*. Tokyo, Hokuseido, 1957. p.24–28

Chiisana akai hana　小さな赤い花

'小的紅花'　張曉天訳　「小説月報」　第16巻11号　1925. p.1–2

Echigo no fuyu　越後の冬

'A winter night's episode in Echigo'　Tr. by

Asataro Miyamori. *Representative tales of Japan.* Tokyo, Sanko Shoten, 1917. p.431–450

Fubuki 吹雪

'暴風雪' 張資平訳 「資平譯品集」 上海 現代書局 192?.

Futatsu no koto to futari no musume 二つの琴と二人の娘

'The story of two kotos and two girls' Tr. by Yoshiko Akiyama. *The tipsy star, and other tales.* Tokyo, Hokuseido, 1957. p.32–37

Ii ojiisan no hanashi いいおじいさんの話

'The story of a good old man' Tr. by Yoshiko Akiyama. *The tipsy star, and other tales.* Tokyo, Hokuseido, 1957. p.80–84

Ippon no kaki no ki 一本の柿の木

'The persimmon tree' Tr. by Yoshiko Akiyama. *The tipsy star, and other tales.* Tokyo, Hokuseido, 1957. p.49–51

Iroiro na hana いろいろな花

'種種的花' 張暁天訳 「小説月報」 第15巻6号 1924. p.1–2

Kimagure no ningyōshi きまぐれの人形師

'The whimsical doll-maker' Tr. by Yoshiko Akiyama. *The tipsy star, and other tales.* Tokyo, Hokuseido, 1957. p.18–23

Kisha no naka no kuma to niwatori 汽車の中の熊と鶏

'Kisha no naka no kuma to niwatori' Tr. by Yasutaro Kanzaki. *Eisakubun Zasshi*, May 1923.

Kita no fuyu 北の冬

'北國之冬' 「日本作家十二人集」 香港 新學書店 1959. p.147–158

Komadori to sake 駒鳥と酒

'The robin and the sake' Tr. by Yoshiko Akiyama. *The tipsy star, and other tales.* Tokyo, Hokuseido, 1957. p.57–63

Kūchū no geitō 空中の芸当

'The handstand' Tr. by Ivan Morris. *Modern Japanese stories,* ed. by I. Morris. London, Spottiswoode, 1962; Tokyo, Tuttle, 1962. p.186–203; *The Mentor book of modern Asian literature,* ed. by D. B. Shimer. N. Y. New American Library, 1969. p.409–423
'Wager in midair' Tr. by Ivan Morris. *The Japanese image,* ed. by M. Schneps and A. D. Coox. Tokyo, Orient West, 1965. p.163–176
'Wette im Äther' Deutsch von Monique Humbert. *Nippon.* Zürich, Diogenes, 1965. p.215–238

Kuroi hito to akai sori 黒い人と赤いそり

'黒人和紅雪車' 張暁天訳 「小川未明童話集本」 上海 新中國書局 n.d.

Kumo to kusa 蜘蛛と草

'蜘蛛與草花' 張暁天訳 「小説月報」 第15巻2号 1924. p.3–4

Kyōshi to kodomo 教師と子供

'教師與兒童' 張暁天訳 「小説月報」 第15巻1号 1925. p.10–11

Machi no tenshi 町の天使

'The angel in the town' Tr. by Yoshiko Akiyama. *The tipsy star, and other tales.* Tokyo, Hokuseido, 1957. p.13–17

Monogusa jijii no raise ものぐさじじいの来世

'懶惰老人的來世' 張暁天訳 「小説月報」 第16巻6期 1924. p.3–4

Mozu to sugi no ki もずと杉の木

'The shrike and the cryptomeria' Tr. by Yoshiko Akiyama. *The tipsy star, and other tales.* Tokyo, Hokuseido, 1957. p.29–31

Musan kaikyūsha 無産階級者

'無産階級者' 張資平訳 「別宴」 武昌 時中合作社 1926; 「襯衣」 上海 光華書局 1928.

Nakunatta ningyō なくなった人形

'The doll stolen' Tr. by Yoshiko Akiyama. *The tipsy star, and other tales.* Tokyo, Hokuseido, 1957. p.6–9

Natsukashimareta hito なつかしまれた人

'Should auld acquaintance be forgot . . .' Tr. by Yoshiko Akiyama. *The tipsy star, and other tales.* Tokyo, Hokuseido, 1957. p.94–99

Nibanme no musume 二番目の娘

'The second daughter' Tr. by Yoshiko Akiyama. *The tipsy star, and other tales.* Tokyo, Hokuseido, 1957. p.64–72

Nobara 野薔薇

'The wild rose' Tr. by Atsumu Kanayama. *The Reeds,* v.8, 1962. p.171–175
Laukinês rožês. Tr. Arvydas Alisăuskas. Vilnjius, Vaga, 1971. 86p.

Ōkina kani 大きな蟹

'The huge crab' Tr. by Yoshiko Akiyama. *The tipsy star, and other tales.* Tokyo, Hokuseido, 1957. p.73–79

Roji ura 路地裏

'街路裏' 張資平訳 「資平譯品集」 上海 現代書局 192?.

Sakana to hakuchō 魚と白鳥

'魚與天鵝' 暁天訳 「小説月報」 第16巻12号 1925. p.1–4

Shiroi kuma 白い熊

'The polar bear' Tr. by Yoshiko Akiyama. *The tipsy star, and other tales.* Tokyo, Hokuseido, 1957. p.52–56

Sono hi kara shōjiki ni natta hanashi その日から正直になった話

'The story of a boy who became honest' Tr. by Yoshiko Akiyama. *The tipsy star, and other tales.* Tokyo, Hokuseido, 1957. p.38–41

OGAWA Mimei

Umi kara kita tsukai 海から来た使

'The messenger from the sea' Tr. by Yoshiko Akiyama. *The tipsy star, and other tales.* Tokyo, Hokuseido, 1957. p.42–48

Ushi onna 牛女

'The ox woman' Tr. by John Bester. *Japan P.E.N. News*, no.12, Feb. 1964. p.9–12

Yuki no ue no ojiisan 雪の上のおじいさん

'雪上老人' 張暁天訳 「小川未明童話集本」 上海 新中國書局 n.d.

Yopparai boshi よっぱらい星

'The tipsy star' Tr. by Yoshiko Akiyama. *The tipsy star, and other tales.* Tokyo, Hokuseido, 1957. p.1–5

Criticism 評論

'少年主人公的文學' 高明訳 「文學週報」 第7巻14期
'小川未明童話文學論' 張暁天訳「開明」 第2巻1期 1929.

'他們的悲哀和自負' 竹舟訳 「三民半月刊」

OGAWA Shinkichi 小川真吉

「闘魂」 金顕弘訳 서울 博文書館 1945. 178p.

OGAWA Usen 小川芋銭 1868–1938

Haiku 俳句

'Falling chestnuts' Tr. by Asataro Miyamori. *Anthology of haiku, ancient and modern.* Tokyo, Maruzen, 1932. p.817

OGIWARA Seisensui 荻原井泉水 1884–1976

Haiku 俳句

'5 haiku' Tr. by Asataro Miyamori. *Anthology of haiku, ancient and modern.* Tokyo, Maruzen, 1932. p.757–760

'Haiku' Tr. par Kuni Matsuo et Steinilber-Oberlin. *Anthologie des poètes japonais contemporains.* Paris, Mercure de France, 1939. p.293–294

'We parted; Winter night' Tr. by Asataro Miyamori. *Haiku poems, ancient and modern.* Tokyo, Maruzen, 1940. p.349–350

'3 haiku' Tr. by V. H. Viglielmo. *Japanese literature in the Meiji era.* Tokyo, Obunsha, 1955. p.452–453

'2 haiku' Tr. by R. H. Blyth. *Haiku v.1.* Tokyo, Hokuseido, 1956. p.370, 376

'3 haiku' Übers. von Günther Debon. *Im Schnee die Fähre.* München, Piper, 1960. p.42

'20 haiku' *A history of haiku v.2*, by R. H. Blyth. Tokyo, Hokuseido, 1964. p.193–200

'4 haiku' *Anthology of modern Japanese poetry*, tr. and comp. by Edith Marcombe Shiffert and Yuki Sawa. Tokyo, Tuttle, 1972. p.165

'20 haiku' Tr. by Makoto Ueda. *Modern Japanese haiku, an anthology.* Tokyo, Univ. of Tokyo Press, 1976. p.74–83

'1 haiku' Tr. by Takamasa Sasaki. *Eigo Seinen*, v.122, no.5, 1976. p.231

Essay エッセイ

'芭蕉雜記' 周豊一訳 「譯文」 第1巻5期 1943. p.38–41

'Ryojin Basho sho' Tr. by Shigeshi Nishimura. *The Current of the World*, v.30, no.4,5,7,8,11, v.31, no.2, 1953–54.

ŌGIYA Shōzō 扇谷正造 1913–

Criticism 評論

'Yoshikawa Eiji' *Japan Quarterly*, v.13, no.4, 1965. p.498–500

ŌGUCHI Taiji 大口鯛二 1864–1920

Tanka 短歌

'Filial piety; A young bird' Tr. by Asataro Miyamori. *Masterpieces of Japanese poetry, ancient and modern.* Tokyo, Maruzen, 1936; Tokyo, Taiseido, 1956; N. Y. Greenwood Press, 1971. p.617–618

OGUMA Hideo 小熊秀雄 1901–1940

Poems 詩

'Песни мои поручаю ветру; Песня кузнеца' Перевод Веры Марковой. *Иностранная Литература*, сентябрь 1960. p.143–144

'Песня выезжающей коляски; Волга-река' Перевод Анатолия Мамонова. *Восточный альманах 6.* Москва, Худож. Лит. 1963. p.322–325

'Стихи на коне' Перевод Анатолия Мамонова. *Из современной японской поэзии.* Москва, Прогресс, 1971. p.9–168

'Мешок пчелей' Перевод А. И. Мамоновой. *Свободний стих в японской поэзии.* Москва, Наука, 1971. p.182–188

'Беременный камень; Дерево в лучах заката; Конский назов; Тротуар в большом городе; Черный зонт; Политика моя возлюбленная' Перевод Анатолия Мамонова. *Вкус хризантемы.* Москва, Восточная Литература, 1976. p.84–89

OGURA Seitarō 小倉清太郎 1895–

Onna no shippo 女の尻っぽ

「四分의一処女」 李鐘仁訳 서울 隆文社 1960. 173p.

OGURI Fūyō 小栗風葉 1875–1926

Oni shikan 鬼士官

「鬼士官」 商務編譯所訳 上海 商務印書館 1907. 1冊

Renbo nagashi 恋慕ながし

'Renboryu' Tr. by Heisaku Udaka. *Eigo no Nippon*, 1917.

Ryōen 涼炎

'Silence gives consent' Tr. by Asataro Miyamori. *Representative tales of Japan*. Tokyo, Sanko Shoten, 1917. p.364–391

Sekenshi 世間師

'떠돌이処士' 郭夏信訳 「世界文学全集 94」 서울 乙酉文化社 1962 p.171–191; 「日本短篇文学選」 서울 乙酉文化社 1976. p.119–158

ŌHARA Miyao 大原三八雄 1905–

Poems 詩

The songs of Hiroshima. Hiroshima, YMCA Service Center, 1955. 78p.
'Elegy; The divine wind; Humanity; Genbaku no hana; The man in meditation; The candle-light held aloft by a keloided hand; The Strangled-Hiroshima; Christmas in the atom city; To the citizens of Coventry; It thaws; The season of the fallen hydrangea; At the season of wild madness; The composition of partiality; Because the earth is green' *The songs of Hiroshima*. Tokyo, Taihei Shuppansha, 1971. p.115–117
'Цветок атомной бомбы' Перевод Анатолия Мамонова. *Песни Хиросимы.* Москва, Худож. Лит. 1964. p.23–24; *Вкус хризантемы.* Москва, Восточная Литература, 1976. p.98

ŌHARA Tomie 大原富枝 1912–

En to yū onna 婉という女

'Её звали о Эн' Перевод И. Львовой. *Иностранная Литература*, 1970, No.2. p.64–135
Её звали о-Эн. Перевод И. Львовой. Москва, Худож. Лит. 1973. 173p.
Её ввали о-Эн, на казахском языке. Алма-Ата, Жазушы, 1973. 190p.

ŌISHI Makoto 大石 真 1925–

Hoshi eno yakusoku 星へのやくそく

'Slib hvězdám' *Modré vánoce*. Přel. Ivan Kroyský a Z. K. Slabý. Praha, Albatros, 1975.

OKA Fumoto 岡 麓 1877–1951

Tanka 短歌

'My grandchild; A mountain and a ricefield; The Kiso River' Tr. by Asataro Miyamori. *Masterpieces of Japanese poetry, ancient and modern*. Tokyo, Maruzen, 1936; Tokyo, Taiseido, 1956; N. Y. Greenwood Press, 1971. p.674–676

OKA Kiyoshi 岡 潔 1901–1978

Essay エッセイ

'The second mind' *Chanoyu Quarterly*, v.1, no.2, 1970. p.5–7

OKA Masamichi 岡 正路 1916–

Janguru no koi ジャングルの恋

'Love in the Annam jungle' Tr. by Grace Suzuki. *Ukiyo*. Tokyo, Phoenix Books, 1954. p.146–171; *Ukiyo*, ed. by J. Gluck. N. Y. Vanguard Press, 1963. p.95–109; London, Universal Library, 1964. p.95–109

OKA Sōtarō 岡 荘太郎 1920–

Kamen no yoru 仮面の夜

'假面之夜' 徐雲濤訳 「當代日本小説選」 台南 經緯書局 1954. p.21–48; 「當代日本創作小説」 台南 經緯書局 1961. p.21–48; 「當代日本短篇小説選」 台南 大行出版社 1973. p.21–48

OKADA Kaname 岡田 要

「암컷과수컷」 정부당訳 서울 青雲出版社 1962. 218p.

OKADA Saburō 岡田三郎 1890–1954

Kake 賭

'賭' 章克標訳 「當代文藝」 第1巻2期 1931. p.339–349

OKADA Shachihiko 岡田鯱彦 1907–

Mō hitori no watashi もう一人の私

'另一個我' 徐白訳 「日本短篇譯集 1」 台北 晩蟬書店 1969. p.165–189

OKADA Takahiko 岡田隆彦 1939–

Poems 詩

'Sono un cavallo' *La protesta poetica del Giappone*, a cura di Dacia Maraini e Michiko Nojiri. Roma, Officina Edizioni, 1968. p.163–164

OKADA Teiko 岡田禎子 1902–

Muma 夢魔

'The night mare' *Japan Times*. Feb. 1929.

OKADA Tetsuzō 岡田哲蔵 1869–1945

Poems 詩

'詩匠' 周作人訳 「新青年」 第9巻4期 1921. p.36;「陀螺」192?.

OKADA Yachiyo 岡田八千代 1883–1962

Fumiko no ningyō 文子の人形

'Fumiko no ningyo' Tr. by Yasutaro Kanzaki. *Eisakubun zasshi*, Feb. 1922.

Mikka 三日

'Les trois jours' Tr. par Serge Elisséev. *Japon et Extrême-Orient*, no.5, 1924. p.405–419; *Neuf nouvelles japonaises.* Paris, G. van Œst, 1924. p.74–88

OKAKURA Tenshin 岡倉天心 1862–1913

Cha no hon 茶の本

The book of tea. N. Y. Duffield, 1906. 160p.; Sydney, Angus and Robertson, 1932. 102p.; Tokyo, Tuttle, 1963. 133p.; Tokyo, Kenkyusha, n.d. 117p.
Boken om té. Tr. Fanny v. Wilamowitz-Moellendorff. Stockholm, Wahlstom & Widstrang, 1921. 183p.
Das Buch vom Tee. Übers. von Horst Hammitzsch. Wiesbaden, Insel Verlag, 1949. 77p.
Le livre du thé. Tr. de l'anglais par Gabriel Mourey. Paris, Delpeuch, 1927. 159p.; Paris, Derain, 1958. 124p.; Paris, Club des Libres de France, 1960. 247p.; Paris, Libraires Associés, 1964. 119p.
El libro del té. Buenos Aires, Instituto Cultural Argentino-Japonés, 1938. 154p.
La libro de teo. Tr. T. Nakamura. Osaka, Kosumo-sha, 1965. 132p.
Das Buch vom Tee. Aus dem Englischen von Marguerite und Ulrich Seindorff übersetzt. Leipzig, Insel Verlag, n.d. 83p.
Cartes ceaiulu. În românește de Emanoil Bucuta. București, Col. Enciclopedia, n.d. 90p.

Nihon no mezame 日本の覚醒

The awaking of Japan. N. Y. Century, 1904. 1v.; London, 1905. 1v.; N. Y. Japan Society, 1921. 223p.; London, John Murray, 1922. 182p.; Tokyo, Sanseido, 1939. 172p.; Tokyo, Kenkyusha, 1948. 180p.

Tōyō no risō 東洋の理想

The ideals of the East. London, John Murray, 1903. 244p.; London, John Murray, 1920. 227p.; Tokyo, Kenkyusha, 1941. 307p.
Les idéaux de l'Orient. Tr. de Jenny Serruys. Paris, Payot, 1917. 360p.
Die Ideale des Ostens. Leipzig, Insel Verlag, 1922. 214p.
Österlandets ideal. Oversätt av Fanny v. Wilamowitz-Moellendorff. Stockholm, Wahlstrom & Widstrand, 1925. 249p.

Letters 書翰

'3 letters' Tr. by Taizo Nonaka. *Eigo Seinen*, v.87, no.12, 1942. p.367

The heart of heaven. Tokyo, Nippon Bijutsuin, 1922. 252p.

OKAMATSU Kazuo 岡松和夫 1931–

Shigano shima 志賀島

'志賀島' 李元燮訳 「70年代芥川賞小説集」 서울 玄岩社 1976. p.375–427; 「新鋭世界文学選集20世紀 9」 서울 玄岩社 1977. p.375–398

OKAMOTO Jun 岡本 潤 1901–

Poems 詩

'一九五二年五月一日的血' 楊鉄襲訳 「人民文学」 第36期 1952. p.90
'Under the cloudy sky in the flower season; A wind-swept bridge; A vanished bridge; A bridge' *An anthology of modern Japanese poetry*, ed. and tr. by Ichiro Kono and Rikutaro Fukuda. Tokyo, Kenkyusha, 1957. p.110–112
'Песенка министра' Перевод Веры Марковой. *Иностранная Литература*, сентябрь 1960. p.149
'Under the hazy, blossom-laden sky; Battlefield of dreams' Tr. by Geoffrey Bownas and Anthony Thwaite. *The Penguin book of Japanese verse.* Harmondsworth, Penguin Books, 1964. p.207–208
'Cîmpul de bătălie al viselor' Traducerea Virgil Teodorescu. *Din lirica japoneză.* București, Editura Univers, n.d. p.192

OKAMOTO Hekisansui 岡本癖三酔 1878–1942

Haiku 俳句

'2 haiku' Tr. by V. H. Viglielmo. *Japanese literature in the Meiji era.* Tokyo, Obunsha, 1955. p.444

OKAMOTO Kanoko 岡本かの子 1889–1939

Hana wa tsuyoshi 花は勁し

'Scarlet flower' Tr. by Edward Seidensticker. *Japan Quarterly*, v.10, no.3, 1963. p.331–348

Kōmori 蝙蝠

'Komori, the bat' *Nippon*, v.28, 1940. p.39–44

Konton mibun 渾沌未分

'渾沌未分' 郭夏信訳 「世界文学全集 94」 서울 乙酉文化社 1962. p.383–403

Tanka 短歌

'The sound of waves; At the foot of Mount Fuji;

The golden bee' Tr. by Asataro Miyamori. *Masterpieces of Japanese poetry, ancient and modern.* Tokyo, Maruzen, 1936; Tokyo, Taiseido, 1956; N. Y. Greenwood Press, 1971. p.782–784
'1 tanka' *The moment of wonder*, ed. by Richard Lewis. N. Y. Dial Press, 1964. p.16
'1 tanka' *The burning heart*, tr. and ed. by Kenneth Rexroth and Ikuko Atsumi. N. Y. Seabury Press, 1977. p.70

OKAMOTO Kidō　岡本綺堂　1872–1939

Amerika no tsukai　亜米利加の使

The American envoy, Townsend Harris. Tr. by Masanao Inouye. Kobe, Thompson, 1931. 56p.

Hosokawa Tadaoki no tsuma　細川忠興の妻

'Lady Hosokawa' Tr. by Asataro Miyamori. *Tales of the samurai, and Lady Hosokawa.* Yokohama, Kelly and Walsh, 1922.

Kirishitan yashiki　切支丹屋敷

'Prison de Chrétiens' Tr. par Kuninosuke Matsuo et Émile Steinilber-Oberlin. *Drames d'amour.* Paris, 1929. p.137–195

Ōsaka jō　大阪城

'Osaka Schloß' Übers. von Hermann Bohner. *Deutsche Gesellschaft für Natur- und Völkerkunde Ostasiens Jubiläumsband.* Teil 1. p.14–49

Shuzenji monogatari　修禅寺物語

The mask maker. Adapted by Zoë Kincaid, tr. by Hanso Tarao. N. Y. French, 1928. 28p.
'Une histoire de Shuzenji' Tr. par Kuninosuke Matsuo et Émile Steinilber-Oberlin. *Drames d'amour.* Paris, 1929. p.77–135
Epizodo en Suzenĵi. Tr. Ŝ. Mijake. Tokyo, Esperanto Kenkyusha, 1931. 46p.
'修禪寺物語' 章克標訳 「日本戯曲集」 上海　中華書局 1934. p.247–274

Toribeyama shinjū　鳥辺山心中

'Le double suicide de Toribeyama' Tr. par Kuninosuke Matsuo et Émile Steinilber-Oberlin. *Drames d'amour.* Paris, 1929. p.77–135

Haiku　俳句

'4 haiku' Tr. by Asataro Miyamori. *Anthology of haiku, ancient and modern.* Tokyo, Maruzen, 1932. p.771–773
'Issa the poet' Tr. by Asataro Miyamori. *Haiku poems, ancient and modern.* Tokyo, Maruzen, 1940. p.319–320

OKAMOTO Ruka　岡本ルカ

Poems　詩

'Пустота' Перевод Анатолия Мамонова. *Вкус хризантемы.* Москва, Восточная Литература, 1976. p.91

OKANO Chijū　岡野知十　1860–1932

Haiku　俳句

'The bright moon' Tr. by Asataro Miyamori. *Anthology of haiku, ancient and modern.* Tokyo, Maruzen, 1932. p.702; *Haiku poems, ancient and modern.* Tokyo, Maruzen, 1940. p.303
'2 haiku' Tr. by V. H. Viglielmo. *Japanese literature in the Meiji era.* Tokyo, Obunsha, 1955. p.437–438
'1 haiku' Übers. von Gerolf Coudenhove. *Japanische Jahreszeiten.* Zürich, Manesse Verlag, 1963. p.265

OKAZAKI Seiichirō　岡崎清一郎　1900–

Poems　詩

'剣豪伝' 金龍済訳 「日本詩集」 서울 青雲社 1960. p.57–61
'벗꽃' 崔一秀訳 「기다리고있네」 서울 韓国政経社 1966. p.231–232

OKAZAKI Yoshie　岡崎義恵　1892–

Meiji bunkashi bungei hen　明治文化史文芸編

Japanese literature in the Meiji era, comp. and ed. by Yoshie Okazaki. Tr. and adapted by V. H. Viglielmo. Tokyo, Obunsha, 1955. 673p.; Tokyo, Toyo Bunko, 1974. 673p.

OKAZAWA Hidetora　岡沢秀虎　1902–1973

Criticism　評論

'蘇我十年間的文學論研究' 陳雪帆訳 「小説月報」 第20巻3号, 5号–9号, 1929. 第21巻8号 1930.
'以理論為中心的俄國無産階級文學發達史' 魯迅訳 「文藝政策」 上海　水沫書店 1930;「魯迅譯文集 6」 北京　人民文学出版社 1958. p.445–466
「郭果爾研究」 韓侍桁訳 上海　中華書局 192?. 1冊
「蘇俄文學理論」 陳雪帆訳 上海　大江書舗 1930. 1冊

ŌKI Atsuo　大木惇夫　1895–

Poems　詩

'В пощьта' Преведе оф франц. Никола Джеров. *Песните на Ямато.* София, Корали, 1937. p.79–80
'Destination; Ces gens-là . . .; Poésie de décembre; Paroles adressées aux étoiles; Cailloux lancés; Bruit de marée; La nuit, je chemine' Tr. par Kuni Matsuo et Steinilber-Oberlin. *Anthologie des poètes japonais contemporains.* Paris, Mercure de France, 1939. p.237–243
'They' Tr. by Shigeshi Nishimura. *The Current of the World*, v.31, no.9, 1954. p.27
'Bread and a song; They' *An anthology of modern Japanese poetry*, ed. and tr. by Ichiro Kono and Rikutaro Fukuda. Tokyo, Kenkyusha, 1957. p.112

ŌKI Atsuo

'The Buddha' Tr. by Umeyo Hirano. *Buddhist Plays from Japanese literature*. Tokyo, CIIB Press, 1963. p.101–103
'Wind, light and a leaf' Tr. by Hisakazu Kaneko. *London Magazine*, v.6, no.9, Dec. 1966. p.23–24
'Drumul' Traducerea Virgil Teodorescu. *Din lirica japoneză*. Bucureşti, Editura Univers, n.d. p.181

ŌKI Minoru 大木 実 1913–

Poems 詩

'Young child' *An anthology of modern Japanese poetry*, ed. and tr. by Ichiro Kono and Rikutaro Fukuda. Tokyo, Kenkyusha, 1957. p.113
'門' 金龍済訳 「日本詩集」 서울 青雲社 1960. p.135–136
'Das Kind' Übers. von Kuniyo Takayasu und Manfred Hausmann. *Ruf der Regenpfeifer*. München, Bechtle Verlag, 1961. p.90–91
'Minik yavru' Tercüme etmek L. Sami Akalin. *Japon şiiri*. İstanbul, Varlik Yayinevi, 1962. p.295
'Coughing at night' Tr. by Greg Campbell. *TransPacific*, no.5, 1970. p.23
'鉈；三輪車' 徐和隣訳 「現代詩解説」 台北 葡萄園詩刊社 1970. p.7–10

ŌKŌCHI Kazuo 大河内一男 1905–

Essay エッセイ

「나의人間像」 尹亮模訳 서울 交友社 1969. 272p.

ŌKŌCHI Tsunehira 大河内常平 1925–

Haji o kaku 恥をかく

'沉冤記' 劉慕沙訳 「狐鶏」 台北 林白出版社 1969. p.85–138

OKU Eiichi 奥 栄一 1891–1969

Poems 詩

'鴒子；寫信問母親索錢的晩' 周作人訳 「新青年」 第9巻4期 1921. p.39；「陀螺」 上海 192?.

ŌKUNI Takamasa 大国隆正 1792–1871

Tanka 短歌

'Aim in life' Tr. by Asataro Miyamori. *Masterpieces of Japanese poetry, ancient and modern*. Tokyo, Maruzen, 1936; Tokyo, Taiseido, 1956; N. Y. Greenwood Press, 1971. p.589–590

OKUNO Miki 奥野みき

Tanka 短歌

'3 tanka' Tr. by Onsey Nakagawa. *Poetry Nippon*, no.28, 1974. p.5

OKUNO Takeo 奥野健男 1926–

Criticism 評論

'日本文學家的自我追尋' 祖威訳 「純文學」（香港版） 第10巻6期 1972. p.22–24

ŌMACHI Keigetsu 大町桂月 1869–1925

Poems 詩

'Rasthaus am Paß' Übers. von Kurt Meissner. *Der Tanzfächer*, von K. Meissner. Tokyo, 1943. p.68

ŌMORI Chisetsu 大森痴雪 1877–1936

Akinari no ie 秋成の家

'Das Haus des Akinari' Übers. von Maria Piper. *Die Schaukunst der Japaner*. Berlin, Walter de Gruyter, 1927. p.192–203

ŌMORI Ritsuō 大森栗翁 1821–1905

Haiku 俳句

'The Bon-dance' Tr. by Asataro Miyamori. *Anthology of haiku, ancient and modern*. Tokyo, Maruzen, 1932. p.690–691

ŌMURA Kayoko 大村嘉代子 1884–1953

Ofune お舟

'La fille du passeur' Tr. par Raymond Martinie et Claude Gevel. *Japon et Extrême-Orient*, no.3, 1924. p.217–288

ŌMURA Kimiko 大村きみ子

Geysa'nin hatira defteri. Tercüme etmek Meral Gaspirali. İstanbul, Türkiye Yayinevi, 1963. 112p.

ONCHI Kōshirō 恩地孝四郎 1891–1955

Poems 詩

'The face' Tr. by S. Sato and C. Urdang. *Poetry*, May 1956. p.69
'Moth; Spider; Jelly-fish; Horn shell' *An anthol-*

ogy of modern Japanese poetry, ed. and tr. by Ichiro Kono and Rikutaro Fukuda. Tokyo, Kenkyusha, 1957. p.114–115

'Örümcek' Tercüme etmek L. Sami Akalin. *Japon şiiri.* İstanbul, Varlik Yayinevi, 1962. p.252

ŌNISHI Hajime 大西 祝 1864–1900

Tanka 短歌

'The tempest' Tr. by Asataro Miyamori. *Master-pieces of Japanese poetry, ancient and modern.* Tokyo, Maruzen, 1936; Tokyo, Taiseido, 1956; N. Y. Greenwood Press, 1971. p.618–619

ONO Bushi 小野蕪子 1888–1943

Haiku 俳句

'5 haiku' Tr. by Asataro Miyamori. *Anthology of haiku, ancient and modern.* Tokyo, Maruzen, 1932. p.778–781

'A street scene at Tsinan, China; In the Indian Ocean' Tr. by Asataro Miyamori. *Haiku poems, ancient and modern.* Tokyo, Maruzen, 1940. p.352

'Macska, napraforgoval' *Kinai es Japán koltok.* Budapest, Szépirodalmi, 1957. p.209

'Scenă pe o stradă din Taivan; Pisica; Peninsula Malaya' Traducerea Virgil Teodorescu. *Din lirica japoneză.* Bucureşti, Editura Univers, n.d. p.157–158

ONO Kaoru 小野かおる 1930–

Harukaze to puu はるかぜとぷう

Spring breezes huff and puff. English version by Anita M. Teeter. Tokyo, Labo Teaching Information Center, 1970. 27p.

Yubikko ゆびっこ

Five little fingers. Tokyo, Tuttle, 1969. 28p.

ŌNO Masashige 大野正重

Aruka goya アルカ小屋

'阿爾加小屋' 鐘肇政訳 「戰後日本短篇小説選」 台北 台湾商務印書館 1968. p.179–217

ŌNO Mitsuko 大野允子 1931–

Kappa かっぱ

'Каппа умер' Перевод Г. Ронской. *Лети, жу-равлик!* Москва, Дет. Лит. 1966. p.19–26

Midori no jidōsha みどりのじどうしゃ

'Зеленая машина' Перевод Г. Ронской *Лети, журавлик!* Москва, Дет. Лит. 1966. p.27–40

Tsuru yo tobe ツルよとべ

'Лети, журавлик!' Перевод Г. Ронской. *Лети, журавлик!* Москва, Дет. Лит. 1966. p. 53–60

ŌNO Rinka 大野林火 1904–

Haiku 俳句

'5 haiku' *A history of haiku v.2,* by R. H. Blyth. Tokyo, Hokuseido, 1964. p.260–262

ŌNO Shachiku 大野酒竹 1872–1913

Haiku 俳句

'5 haiku' *A history of haiku v.2,* by R. H. Blyth. Tokyo, Hokuseido, 1964. p.148–150

'2 haiku' Tr. by V. H. Viglielmo. *Japanese literature in the Meiji era.* Tokyo, Obunsha, 1955. p.434

ONO Tosaburō 小野十三郎 1903–

Poems 詩

'Country of reeds' *An anthology of modern Japanese poetry,* ed. and tr. by Ichiro Kono and Rikutaro Fukuda. Tokyo, Kenkyusha, 1957. p.115

'Winter; Nature-hater' *The poetry of living Japan,* by Takamichi Ninomiya and D. J. Enright. London, John Murray, 1957. p.65–66

'Conte féerique' *La poésie japonaise,* par Karl Petit. Paris, Seghers, 1959. p.234

'Der Naturfeind' Übertragen von Shin Aizu. *Der schwermütige Ladekran.* St. Gallen, Tschudy Verlag, 1960. p.16

'Руки сына пустыни' Перевод Веры Марковой. *Иностранная Литература,* сентябрь 1960. p.150

'사과의피' 金龍済訳 「日本詩集」 서울 青馬社 1960. p.144–145

'Подводное землетрясение' Перевод Анатолия Мамонова. *Иностранная Литература,* июнь 1966. p.104

'Газеталар; Жарылган кезде бучуплер' Которгон Т. Байзаков. *Хиросима кектери.* Фрунзе, Кыргызстан, 1969. p.55–56

'A monster fish' Tr. by Tsutomu Fukuda *Poetry Nippon,* no.11, 1970. p.4

'工業；明天；有盧葦的地方；關於砲塔旋盤；廢墟；某種荒漠；接近来；地殼變動' 徐和隣訳 「現代詩解説」 台北 葡萄園詩刊社 1970. p.91–101

'내일；未知의世界；土民의손；不当하게物質이否定되었을때' 金巢雲訳 「世界의文学大全集 34」 서울 同和出版公社 1971. p.530–532

'Подсолнухи' Перевод Анатолия Мамонова. *Новый Мир,* август 1973. p.34

'Folk tale' Tr. by Graeme Wilson. *Japan Quarter-ly,* v.20, no.3, 1973. p.307

'Native's hands; The burning coop; At the foot of Turquino; The enormous fish; From the

ONO Tosaburō

winter ocean; Ogre thistle; A flock of sparrows' Tr. by Hajime Kijima and Fukuko Kobayashi. *The poetry of postwar Japan.* Iowa City, Univ. of Iowa Press, 1975. p.6–11

'Man who hates nature' Tr. by Graeme Wilson. *Japan Quarterly*, v.22, no.2, 1975. p.107

'Подсолнухи; Подводное землетрясение; Мания коллекционирования новых слов' Перевод Анатолия Мамонова. *Вкус хризантемы.* Москва, Восточная Литература, 1976. p.92–94

'Basm feeric; Iarnă' Traducerea Dan Constantinescu. *Din lirica japoneză.* Bucureşti, Editura Univers, n.d. p.200–201

Criticism 評論

'詩論' 金光林訳 「現代詩学」 第4巻2号 1972.

ONOE Saishū 尾上柴舟 1876–1957

Tanka 短歌

'4 tanka' Tr. by Kaisen Odoi. *Mizugame*, 1918.

'A small bird; The evening haze; The same trees; The dale in springtime; Peony flowers; Frogs; Early summer; Early spring; Old and new leaves; Trifling words; The morning sun' Tr. by Asataro Miyamori. *Masterpieces of Japanese poetry, ancient and modern.* Tokyo, Maruzen, 1936; Tokyo, Taiseido, 1956; N. Y. Greenwood Press, 1971. p.659–665

'Tanka' Tr. by Shigeshi Nishimura. *The Current of the World*, v.13, 1936.

'6 tanka' Tr. by V. H. Viglielmo. *Japanese literature in the Meiji era.* Tokyo, Obunsha, 1955. p.389–390

'Die nahmlichen Bäume; Frösche' Übers. von Günther Debon. *Im Schnee die Fähre.* München, Piper, 1960. p.34–35

'3 tanka' Übers. von Gerolf Coudenhove. *Japanische Jahreszeiten.* Zürich, Manesse Verlag, 1963. p.74, 75, 305

'1 tanka' Tr. by Kenneth Rexroth. *One hundred more poems from the Japanese.* N. Y. New Directions, 1976. p.50

ŌNUKI Tetsuyoshi 大貫哲義 1928–

Shichinin no keiji 七人の刑事

'黒色的幻惑' 振江訳 「黒色幻惑」 台南 文良出版社 1966. p.1–39

ŌOKA Makoto 大岡 信 1931–

Poems 詩

'神話는오는속에밖에없다; 가련한이웃들; 1951年降誕祭前後' 柳呈訳 「世界戦後文学全集 9」 서울 新丘文化社 1962. p.245–246

'Toccare' *La protesta poetica del Giappone*, a cura di Dacia Maraini e Michiko Nojiri. Roma, Officina Edizioni, 1968. p.135–136

'Childhood' Tr. by T. Niikura. *TransPacific*, no. 5, 1970. p.18

'For spring; The return; Attempt at a poetic sketch

of death; Marylin; The colonel and I' Tr. by Thomas Fitzsimmons. *Japanese poetry now.* London, André Deutsch, 1972. p.22–31; *Japanese poetry today.* N. Y. Schocken Books, 1972. p.24–33

'Touch; Boyhood; Without sentimentality' Tr. by Harry and Lynn Guest and Shozo Kajima. *Post-war Japanese poetry.* Harmondsworth, Penguin Books, 1972. p.133–136

'Coral island; A man without a grain of sentiment; To live; Family' Tr. by Hiroaki Sato. *The poetry of postwar Japan.* Iowa City, Univ. of Iowa Press, 1975. p.159–163

'Жизнь' Перевод Анатолия Мамонова. *Вкус хризантемы.* Москва, Восточная Литература, 1976. p.96

ŌOKA Shōhei 大岡昇平 1909–

Chichi 父

'아버지' 朴在森訳 「世界短篇文学全集 7」 서울 啓蒙社 1966. p.401–418; 「世界短篇文学全集 9」 서울 三珍社 1971. p.291–307; 「世界代表短篇文学全集 9」 서울 三熙社 1976. p.291–305; 「世界短篇文学全集 9」 서울 新韓出版社 1976. p.122–151

Furyoki 俘虜記

'俘虜記' 安壽吉訳 「世界戦後文学全集 7」 서울 新丘文化社 1962. p.184–208

'Memoire di un prigioniero di guerra' Tr. di Atsuko Ricca Suga. *Narratori giapponesi moderni.* Milano, Bompiani, 1965. p.535–582

'Prisoner of war' Tr. by Sakuko Matsui. *Solidarity*, v.2, no.7, 1967. p.54–84

Gaka 雅歌

'雅歌' 金洙暎訳 「日本代表作家百人集 4」 서울 希望出版社 1966. p.84–103; 「日本短篇文学全集 4」 서울 新太陽社 1969. p.310–329

'Недопетая песня' Перевод З. Рахима. *Японская новелла 1960–1970.* Москва, Прогресс, 1972. p.238–264

Nobi 野火

Les feux. Tr. par Seiichi Motono. Paris, Seuil, 1957. 189p.

Fires on the plain. Tr. by Ivan Morris. N. Y. Knopf, 1957. 246p.; London, Secker and Warburg, 1957. 212p.; Tokyo, Tuttle, 1967. 246p.; London, Transworld, 1959. 191p.; London, Panther, 1968. 204p.; Harmondsworth, Penguin Books, 1969. 240p.

La guerra del soldato Tamura. Tr. di Giuseppe Morichini. Torino, Einaudi, 1957. 214p.

'I proiettori (da La guerra del soldato Tamura)' Tr. di G. Morichini. *Il Giappone*, v.2, no.1–2, 1958. p.48–53

Vuren op de vlakte. Vertaalt door Age Bergman. Baarn, Hollandia, 1958. 193p.

Feuer im Grasland. Übers. von Oscar Benl und G. S. Dombrady. Stuttgart, Henry Goverts, 1959. 221p.

Esh ba-amakim. Tr. from the English by G. Aryokh. Tel-Aviv, Am Oved, 1959. 189p.

Hogueras en la llanura. Tr. de inglés por Roberto E. Bixio. Buenos Aires, Sudamericana, 1959. 150p.

Ognie polne. Przeł. Antoni Slosarczyk. Warszawa, Pax, 1959. 212p.

「野火」 徐雲濤訳 台南 經緯書局 1959. 143p.
Tulia tasangolla. Suomentanut Kyllikki Härkäpää. Helsinki, Weilin ja Goos, 1964. 232p.
'野火' 李東桂訳 「現代世界文学全集 6」 서울 新丘文化社 1968. p.179–281
'La guerra del soldato Tamura' Tr. di G. Morichini. *Antologia della letteratura coreana e giapponese.* Milano, Fratelli Fabbri, 1969. p.315–318

Essays エッセイ

'비평가의 "딘렘머"' 金賢珠訳 「바이바이바디」 서울 三韓出版社 1966. p.311–314
'World view of Japanese literature' *Japan Quarterly*, v.14, no.1, 1969. p.61–63

ŌOKA Tatsuo 大岡龍男 1892–1972

Essay エッセイ

'The hundredth memorial day' Tr. by Fumiko Yamazaki. *Japan Times*, Jan. 3, 1929.

ORIKUCHI Shinobu 折口信夫 1887–1953

Criticism 評論

'The Susa-no-wo trilogy' Tr. by D. L. Philippi. *Today's Japan*, v.5, no.6, June 1960. p.31–35
'A study of life in ancient days' *Traditions*, v.1, no.4, 1977. p.29–54

OSADA Arata 長田 新 1887–1961

Genbaku no ko 原爆の子

Infanoj de l'atombombo. Tr. Kansai-Ligo de Esperantaj Grupoj. Osaka, Japana Esperanta Librokooperativo, 1951. 71p.
Children of the A-bomb, comp. by Dr. Arata Osada. Tr. by Jean Dan and Ruth Sieben-Morgen. Tokyo, Uchida Rokakuho, 1959. 448p.
Kinder von Hiroshima. Übers. von Edith Rau. Berlin, Volk und Welt, 1965. 286p.
Atom bombasi çocuklari. Çeviren Alaattin Bilgi. Ankara, Başnur Matbaasi, 1965. 88p.

OSADA Hiroshi 長田 弘 1939–

Poems 詩

'A un impiccato' *La protesta poetica del Giappone*, a cura di Dacia Maraini e Michiko Nojiri. Roma, Officina Edizioni, 1968. p.167–168
'My poetry; The phantom class; On love; Nowhere; I shouted; A life of fighting; Jailhouse rock; Blue blues to remember not to remember; Refusal to tell; What the young Canadian Indian said; A poem for a lullaby; I must pay my debt' Tr. by Takako Uchino Lento. *The poetry of postwar Japan.* Iowa City, Univ. of Iowa Press, 1975. p.234–248

OSADA Tsuneo 長田恒雄 1902–1977

Poems 詩

'The earrings; A lily; Sweet pea; Lion; The sheep' *An anthology of modern Japanese poetry*, ed. and tr. by Ichiro Kono and Rikutaro Fukuda. Tokyo, Kenkyusha, 1957. p.116–117
'Tokio' *La poésie japonaise*, par Karl Petit. Paris, Seghers, 1959. p.230
'Küpeler' Tercüme etmek L. Sami Akalin. *Japon şiiri.* İstanbul, Varlik Yayinevi, 1962. p.273

OSANAI Kaoru 小山内 薫 1881–1928

Byōyū 病友

'Chums in ill-health' Tr. by Asataro Miyamori. *Representative tales of Japan.* Tokyo, Sanko Shoten, 1917. p.473–490

Daiichi no sekai 第一の世界

'第一的世界' 章克標訳 「日本戯曲集」 上海 中華書局 1934. p.275–317
'The first world' Tr. by Tadao Katayama. *The Reeds*, v.5, 1959. p.111–143

Entaku no hiai 円タクの悲哀

'Taxicab 的悲哀' 楊騒訳 「北新半月刊」 第2巻24号 1927. p.61–74

Iro no sameta onna 色の褪めた女

'Das bleiche Mädchen' Übers. von Alexander Spann. *Die Brücke*, Jahrgang 3, no.31–32, 1927. p.258

Musuko 息子

'Der Sohn' Übers. von S. Yuasa. *Nippon*, Jahrgang 3, 1937. p.29–41
'The son' Tr. by Takeshi Terajima. *Language and Literature*, no.2, 1956. p.97–109

Teishu 亭主

'男人' 田漢訳 「日本現代劇三種」 上海 東南書局 193?.

Criticism 評論

'一封談無形劇場的信' 徐半梅訳 「戯劇」 第1巻2期 1921. p.1–5
'自由劇場第一次試演談' 徐半梅訳 「戯劇」 第1巻5期 1921. p.1–2
'先得新土地' 徐半梅訳 「戯劇」 第2巻1期 1922. p.75–78
'日本戯劇運動的經過' 予倩訳 「戯劇」 第1巻3期 1929. p.91–116

OSARAGI Jirō 大佛次郎 1897–1973

Dorefyusu jiken ドレフュス事件

'드레퓌스事件' 趙白羽訳 「世界記録文学全集 4」 서울 良書閣 1968.

Gin kanzashi 銀簪

'銀빗치개' 金龍済訳 「日本代表作家百人集 3」 서울 希望出版社 1966. p.50–65; 「日本短篇文学全集 3」 서울 新太陽社 1969. p.198–213
'은빗치개' 張文平訳 「日本文学大全集 1」 서울 東西文化院 1975. p.434–448

OSARAGI Jirō

Kaiketsu Kurama Tengu　怪傑鞍馬天狗

「怪傑鞍馬天狗」 영암조訳 서울 青雲社 1963. 541p.

Kikyō　帰郷

Homecoming. Tr. by Brewster Horwitz. N. Y. Knopf, 1954. 303p.; London, Secker and Warburg, 1955. 273p.; Tokyo, Tuttle, 1955. 303p.; N. Y. Berkley Publications, 1961. 223p.

'From "Homecoming"' Tr. by Brewster Horwitz. *Treasury of world literature*, ed. by D. D. Runes. N. Y. Philosophical Library, 1956. p.963–967

Chi alzara la regina di quadri? Tr. dall'inglese di Bruno Tasso. Milano, Corriere della Sera, 1956. 256p.

Hermkomsten. Översätta Christina Strandberg. Stockholm, Tidens Förlag, 1958. 254p.

Timantti. Suomentanut Auli Tarkka. Helsinki, Otava, 1960. 294p.

Retour au pays. Tr. par Kikou Yamata. Paris, Albin Michel, 1962. 296p.

'帰郷' 李鐘烈訳 「日本文学選集 4」 서울 知文閣 1966. p.7–261

'帰郷' 張文平訳 「日本文学大全集 1」 서울 東西文化院 1975. p.240–432

Tabiji　旅路

The journey. Tr. by Ivan Morris. N. Y. Knopf, 1960. 342p.; London, Secker and Warburg, 1961. 342p.; Tokyo, Tuttle, 1967. 342p.

Resan. Tr. from the English by Christina Strandberg. Stockholm, Tiden-Barnangen, 1961. 343p.

Essays　エッセイ

'Cats and Kabuki' *Japan Quarterly*, v.7, no.2, 1960. p.231–232

'Murders every night' *This is Japan*, v.11, 1964. p.230–232

OSE Keishi　尾瀬敬止　1889–1952

Criticism　評論

'浮士徳與城　作者小傳' 魯迅訳 「浮士徳與城」 上海 神州國光社 1930; 「魯迅譯文集 10」 北京 人民文学出版社 1958. p.355–362

OSEKI Kōichi　小関こういち

Poems　詩

'О синева безмятежного неба!' Перевод Анатолия Мамонова. *Вкус хризантемы*. Москва, Восточная Литература, 1976. p.97

ŌSHIKA Taku　大鹿　卓　1898–1959

Poems　詩

'Soldiers' Tr. by S. Sato and C. Urdang. *Poetry*, May 1956. p.98

'Fishermen' Tr. by Hisakazu Kaneko. *London*

Magazine, v.7, no.7, 1967. p.30–31

OSHIKAWA Shunrō　押川春浪　1876–1914

Kūchū hikōtei　空中飛行艇

「空中飛艇」 海天獨 嘯子訳 上海 商務印書館 1926. 2冊

'怪僧蹤' 懺紅訳 「小説時報」 第20期 1913. p.1–16

「新舞臺」 東海覺我訳 小説林 1905. 1冊

「秘密電光艇」 金石 褚嘉猷訳 上海 商務印書館 1906. 1冊

「俠女郎」 上海 商務印書館 1926. 1冊

ŌSHIMA Hiromitsu　大島博光　1910–

Poems　詩

'富士之歌' 趙迺梓訳 「譯文」 1956年6月 p.65–66

'在草丛中' 李芒訳 「詩刊」 第4期 1961. p.56–57

'献給我們的野坂同志' 梅韜訳 「世界文学」 1962年5月 p.45–46

'Еки жуз слуу' Которгон Ж. Алыбаев. *Хиросима кектери*. Фрунзе, Кыргызстан, 1969. p.77–78

'비가' 「永遠한世界名詩全集 2」 黃錦燦編 서울 翰林出版社 1969. p.128; 「永遠한世界名詩全集 5」 黃錦燦編 서울 翰林出版社 1973. p.128

ŌSHIMA Hōsui　大島宝水　1880–1971

Haiku　俳句

'1 haiku' Tr. by V. H. Viglielmo. *Japanese literature in the Meiji era*. Tokyo, Obunsha, 1955. p.438

ŌSHIMA Nagisa　大島　渚　1932–

Seishun zankoku monogatari　青春残酷物語

'青春은惨酷하다' 李明遠訳 「世界戦後文学全集 10」 서울 新丘文化社 1962. p.307–341

ŌSHIMA Ryōkichi　大島亮吉　1899–1928

Ashiato　足跡

'Footprints' Tr. by S. G. Brickley. *The writing of idiomatic English*. Tokyo, Kenkyusha, 1951. p.85–90

ŌSHIMA Yō　大島　洋　1935–

Poems　詩

'To Abbey Lincoln' Tr. by Miyao Ohara. *The songs of Hiroshima*. Tokyo, Taihei Shuppansha, 1971. p.110–115

ŌSHIRO Tatsuhiro　大城立裕　1925–

Kakuteru pātei　カクテル・パーティ

'Приглашение на коктейль'　Перевод Л. Левина. *Японская новелла 1960–1970*. Москва, Прогресс, 1972. p.265–277

ŌSUGA Otsuji　大須賀乙字　1881–1920

Haiku　俳句

'2 haiku'　Tr. by Asataro Miyamori. *Anthology of haiku, ancient and modern*. Tokyo, Maruzen, 1932. p.696–697

'My voice'　Tr. by Asataro Miyamori. *Haiku poems, ancient and modern*. Tokyo, Maruzen, 1940. p.323–324

'3 haiku'　Tr. by R. H. Blyth. *Haiku*. Tokyo, Hokuseido, 1950. v.1, p.124, v.2, p.104, v.4, p.152

'7 haiku'　Tr. by V. H. Viglielmo. *Japanese literature in the Meiji era*. Tokyo, Obunsha, 1955. p.443, 447, 448

'Haiku'　Tercüme etmek L. Sami Akalin. *Japon şiiri*. İstanbul, Varlik Yayinevi, 1962. p.239

'2 haiku'　Tr. by Peter Beilenson and Harry Behn. *Haiku harvest*. Mount Vernon, Peter Pauper Press, 1962. p.49

'8 haiku'　*A history of haiku v.2*, by R. H. Blyth. Tokyo, Hokuseido, 1964. p.140–143

'1 haiku'　Übers. von Erwin Jahn. *Fallende Blüten*. Zürich, Arche, 1968. p.37

'2 haiku'　Tr. by William Howard Cohen. *To walk in seasons*. Tokyo, Tuttle, 1972. p.29, 90

'Old fort'　Tr. by Kenneth Yasuda. *A pepper-pod*. Tokyo, Tuttle, 1976. p.80

ŌSUGI Sakae　大杉　栄　1885–1923

Criticism　評論

'民衆藝術的技巧'　楚橋訳　「北平華北日報副刊」　1930年11月

ŌTA Chizuo　太田千鶴夫　1906–1968

'跨過死屍'　陳勺水訳　「日本新寫實派代表傑作集」　上海　楽羣雜誌社　1929.

ŌTA Daihachi　太田大八　1918–

Ametarō　あめたろう

Raintaro.　Tr. by Ann Herring. Tokyo, Gakken, 1972. 23p.

ŌTA Gyokumei　太田玉茗　1871–1927

Poems　詩

'The stream at night; Old woman at the doll's festival'　Tr. by James R. Morita. *Journal of the Association of Teachers of Japanese*, v.10, no.2 & 3, 1975. p.199–200

ŌTA Mizuho　太田水穂　1876–1955

Tanka　短歌

'At my old home; The camellia bud; A wreath of cloud; A pond in the night'　Tr. by Asataro Miyamori. *Masterpieces of Japanese poetry, ancient and modern*. Tokyo, Maruzen, 1936; Tokyo, Taiseido, 1956; N. Y. Greenwood Press, 1971. p.665–668

'2 tanka'　Tr. by V. H. Viglielmo. *Japanese literature in the Meiji era*. Tokyo, Obunsha, 1955. p.392

'Verselets'　Tr. by H. H. Honda. *The Reeds*, v.5, 1969. p.16, 88

'1 tanka'　Übers.　von Gerolf Coudenhove. *Japanische Jahreszeiten*. Zürich, Manesse Verlag, 1963. p.147

'2 tanka'　*Anthology of modern Japanese poetry*, tr. and comp. by Edith Marcombe Shiffert and Yuki Sawa. Tokyo, Tuttle, 1972. p.141

ŌTA Saburō　太田三郎　1909–1976

Criticism　評論

'川端康成「水晶幻想」論'　林文月訳　「中外文學」　第1巻3期　1972. p.138–156

ŌTA Tenpei　おおた・てんぺい

Poems　詩

'След самолета; Извещение о переезде'　Перевод Е. Винокурова. *Иностранная Литература*, июнь 1964. p.151–158

'Бака; Баыкауиге кечуу кабары'　Которгон Т. Байзаков. *Хиросима кектери*. Фрунзе, Кыргызстан, 1969. p.53–54

ŌTA Yōko　大田洋子　1903–1963

Doko made　どこまで

'До каких пор?'　Перевод И. Львовой и Б. Бейко. *Иностранная Литература*, сентябрь 1955. p.185–196

'Pina cind?'　În româneste de Gheorghe Voropanov si Jaques Costin. *Cintecul porcului*. Bucureşti, ESPLA, 1956. p.49–85

Shikabane no machi　屍の街

「廣島的一家」　周豊一訳　北京　新文艺　1957. 172p.

ŌTAGAKI Rengetsu　大田垣蓮月　1791–1875

Tanka　短歌

'The uguisu; Beneath cherry blossoms; The voices of pine trees'　Tr. by Asataro Miyamori. *Masterpieces of Japanese poetry, ancient and modern*. Tokyo, Maruzen, 1936; Tokyo, Taiseido, 1956; N. Y. Greenwood Press, 1971. p.587–589

ŌTAKI Yasukichi 大滝安吉

Poems 詩

'In the museum' Tr. by William L. Clark. *Jiji Eigo Kenkyu*, v.21, no.2, 1966. p.72

ŌTANI Chūichirō 大谷忠一郎 1902–1963

Poems 詩

'A village' *An anthology of modern Japanese poetry*, ed. and tr. by Ichiro Kono and Rikutaro Fukuda. Tokyo, Kenkyusha, 1957. p.117

ŌTANI Kubutsu 大谷句仏 1875–1943

Haiku 俳句

'11 haiku' Tr. by Asataro Miyamori. *Anthology of haiku, ancient and modern.* Tokyo, Maruzen, 1932. p.735–743
'A baby; At the prison in Kurume; The harvest moon; The founder of our sect' Tr. by Asataro Miyamori. *Haiku poems, ancient and modern.* Tokyo, Maruzen, 1940. p.337–340
'1 haiku' Tr. by R. H. Blyth. *Haiku v.2.* Tokyo, Hokuseido, 1950. p.333
'2 haiku' Übers. von Günther Debon. *Im Schnee die Fähre.* München, Piper, 1960. p.36
'1 haiku' Tr. by Peter Beilenson and Harry Behn. *Haiku harvest.* Mount Vernon, Peter Pauper Press, 1962. p.25
'1 haiku' Til norsk ved Paal-Helge Haugen. *Blad frå ein austleg hage.* Oslo, Det Norske Samlaget, 1965. p.87
'Haiku' *Lyrik des Ostens,* hrg. von Wilhelm Gundert usw. München, Carl Hanser, 1965. p.472
'Winter moon; The Karasaki's pine' Tr. by Kenneth Yasuda. *A pepper-pod.* Tokyo, Tuttle, 1976. p.88

Essay エッセイ

'Shinso shiroku' Tr. by C. G. Elder and S. Sugai. *The Current of the World,* v. 8, no. 2, 1931.

ŌTE Takuji 大手拓次 1887–1934

Poems 詩

'Blue fox' Tr. by S. Sato and C. Urdang. *Poetry,* May 1956. p.96
'Man walking from a bud to another' Tr. by Makoto Ueda. *East-West Review,* v.2, no.1, 1965. p.56

ŌTSUKA Naoko 大塚楠緒子 1875–1910

Kyakuma 客間

'Souls in peril' Tr. by Asataro Miyamori. *Representative tales of Japan.* Tokyo, Sanko Shoten, 1917. p.491–503

Shinobine しのび音

'Shinobine' Tr. by Tei Fujiu. *Hanakatsura.* Tokyo, Ikuseikai, 1903. p.94–117

Tanka 短歌

'A hundred prayers' Tr. by Yohei Iitsuka. *Eigo Seinen,* v.45, no.1, 1921. p.9, 11
'Tanka' Tr. by Shigeshi Nishimura. *The Current of the World,* v. 13, 1936.

ŌTSUKA Yūzō 大塚勇三 1935–

Ōkina kanū おおきなカヌー

Rota's great canoe. Tokyo, Weatherhill, 1970. 1v.; N. Y. Walker, 1970. 26p.

Sūho no shiroi uma スーホの白い馬

Suho and the white horse. Tr. by Yasuko Hirawa. Indianapolis, Bobbs-Merrill, 1969. 47p.

Umi no ongakutai うみのおんがくたい

The ocean-going orchestra. Tokyo, Labo Teaching Information Center, 1972. 26p.
'Morska kapela' Přel. Ivan Krouský. *Třicet stribrnych klicu.* Praha, Prace, 1971. p.49–51

ŌYA Sōichi 大宅壮一 1900–1970

Bungakuteki senjutsu ron 文学的戦術論

「文學的戰術論」 毛合戈訳 上海 聯合書舍 1930. 1冊

Essay エッセイ

'사랑도비즈니스도특급전화로' 金賢珠訳 「바이바이바디」 서울 三韓出版社 1966. p.61–64

OYAMA Tokujirō 尾山篤二郎 1889–1963

Tanka 短歌

'A wild garden; The voices of strangers' Tr. by Asataro Miyamori. *Masterpieces of Japanese poetry, ancient and modern.* Tokyo, Maruzen, 1936; Tokyo, Taiseido, 1956; N. Y. Greenwood Press, 1971. p.758–759

OZAKI Hirotsugu 尾崎宏次 1914–1970

Shingeki no ashioto 新劇の足音

Новый японский театр. Перевод Л. З. Левина и Б. В. Раскина. Москва, Изд. Иност. Лит. 1960. 198p.

OZAKI Hōsai 尾崎放哉 1885–1926

Haiku 俳句

'12 haiku' *A history of haiku v.2,* by R. H. Blyth. Tokyo, Hokuseido, 1964. p.158–161

'20 haiku' *Modern Japanese haiku, an anthology*, comp. and tr. by Makoto Ueda. Tokyo, Univ. of Tokyo Press, 1976. p.122–131

OZAKI Kazuo　尾崎一雄　1899–

Kashoku no hi　華燭の日

'華燭을밝히는날' 金東史訳 「日本代表作家百人集 3」서울 希望出版社 1966. p.162–170;「日本短篇文学全集 3」서울 新太陽社 1969. p.310–318

'The day of wedding' Tr. by Hiro Mukai. *Hemisphere*, v.11, Jan. 1967. p.7–12

Mushi no iroiro　虫のいろいろ

'Insects of various kinds' Tr. by Hiroo Mukai. *Pacific Spectator*, v.5, Autumn, 1951. p.426–434

'Various kinds of bugs' Tr. by William L. Clark. *Jiji Eigo Kenkyu*, v.12, no.11, no.12, 1957; *Various kinds of bugs, and other stories.* Tokyo, Kenkyusha, 1958. p.73–96

Yaseta ondori　痩せた雄鶏

'The thin rooster' Tr. by E. G. Seidensticker. *Japan Quarterly*, v.2, no.2, 1955. p.184–201; *Modern Japanese short stories.* Tokyo, Japan Publications Trading Co. 1960. p.263–286; Rev. ed. Tokyo, Japan Publications Trading Co. 1970. p.209–226

OZAKI Kihachi　尾崎喜八　1892–1974

Poems　詩

'Mittagsstunde im Sommer' Übers. von Kuniyo Takayasu und Manfred Hausmann. *Ruf der Regenpfeifer.* München, Bechtle Verlag, 1961. p.87–88

'November; Footprints' Tr. by Hisakazu Kaneko. *London Magazine*, v.6, no.9, 1966. p.27–29

'Winter field' Tr. by Yuki Sawa and Edith Shiffert. *The Southern Review*, v.5, no.4, 1969. p.1172–1173

'A word; Winter field; Being' *Anthology of modern Japanese poetry*, tr. and comp. by Edith Marcombe Shiffert and Yuki Sawa. Tokyo, Tuttle, 1972. p.57–59

'Little field-streams' Tr. by James A. O'Brien. *Poetry Nippon*, no.19, 1972. p.20

'Izvorul din munte' Traducerea Virgil Teodorescu. *Din lirica japoneză.* Bucureşti, Editura Univers, n.d. p.176

OZAKI Kōko　尾崎孝子　1897–1970

Tanka　短歌

'Беш кайрыктар' Которгон Т. Байзаков. *Хиросима кектери.* Фрунзе, Кыргызстан, 1969. p.52

OZAKI Kōyō　尾崎紅葉　1867–1903

Fumi nagashi　文ながし

'A wonderful legacy' Tr. by Asataro Miyamori. *Representative tales of Japan.* Tokyo, Sanko Shoten, 1917. p.151–162

Futari nyōbō　二人女房

Zwei Frauen. Übers. von Yujiro Yoshino und Karl Mischke. Shanghai, Ostasiatische Lloyd, 1905. 1v.

'Две женщины' *Вестник японской литературы*, 1905, No.5. p.15–36

Higashi nishi tanryo no yaiba　東西短慮之刃

The Japanese Desdemona. Tr. by T. Kimoto. Tokyo, Shunyodo, 1902. 28p.

Kan botan　寒牡丹

「寒牡丹」呉檮訳　上海　商務印書館　1906. 2冊

Koi no yamai　恋の病

'Болезнь от любви' Перевод В. Айваз-Огру. *Гамаюн.* Петербург, 1911. p.281–334

Konjiki yasha　金色夜叉

The golden demon. Rewritten in English by Arthur Lloyd and Mary Lloyd. Tokyo, Seibundo, 1905. 562p.

'The golden demon' Tr. by A. and M. Lloyd. *The treasury of Japanese literature*, ed. by Tokichi Watanabe. Tokyo, Jippohkaku, 1933. p.324–331

Le démon doré. Tr. par Miti Van Hecke-Kataoka. Paris, Club Bibliophile de France, 1952. 306p.

「金色夜叉」徐雲濤訳　台北　新興書局　1956. 374p.

「金色夜叉」李元珏編　李守一·沈順愛訳　서울　永和出版社　1961. 219p.

'Sulla spiaggia di Atami' Tr. di R. Vulpitta. *Antologia della letteratura coreana e giapponese.* Milano, Fratelli Fabbri, 1969. p.221–224

'The demon of gold and love' Tr. by Arthur Lloyd. *Info.* Feb.—Dec. 1968, Jan.—Sept. Nov.—Dec. 1969, Jan.—Feb. Apr.—Dec. 1970, Jan.—June, 1971 in 40 parts.

Poslaćenje demona. Preveo s francuskog Vlastimir Djaković. Beograd, Minerva, 1976. 319p.

Kyōkokuji　侠黒児

'侠黒奴' 呉檮訳　「東方雑誌」第3巻1期—3期 1906.

「侠黒奴」上海　商務印書館　1926. 1冊

Ninin bikuni iro zange　二人比丘尼色懺悔

'두比丘尼의愛欲懺悔' 郭夏信訳 「世界文学全集 94」서울 乙酉文化社　1962. p.17–51

Shichijū ni mon inochi no yasuuri　七十二文命安売

'За 72 копейки' *Первый художественно-литературный сборник.* Токио, 1909. p.17–23

Shiobara　塩原

'Shiobara (part)' Tr. by F. J. Daniels. *Japanese prose.* London, Lund Humphries, 1944. p.80–85

OZAKI Kōyō

Tori kaji 取舵

'Larboard' Tr. by T. Kimoto. *The Orient*, v.14, 1899.

Haiku and Tanka 俳句・短歌

'4 haiku' Tr. by Asataro Miyamori. *Anthology of haiku, ancient and modern*. Tokyo, Maruzen, 1932. p.670–672

'1 haiku' Tr. by Harold Gould Henderson. *The bamboo broom*. Tokyo, J. L. Thompson, 1933; London, Kegan Paul, 1933. p.122

'Perfection' Tr. by Harold Gould Henderson. *From the bamboo broom*. N. Y. Japan Reference Library, 1940.

'The harvest moon; A pilgrim in spring' Tr. by Asataro Miyamori. *Haiku poems, ancient and modern*. Tokyo, Maruzen, 1940. p.309–310

'3 haiku' Tr. by V. H. Viglielmo. *Japanese literature in the Meiji era*. Tokyo, Obunsha, 1955. p.436–437

'1 haiku' Tr. by Peter Beilenson. *Japanese haiku*. Mount Vernon, Peter Pauper Press, 1955. p.28

'The neighbour' Tr. by Harold Stewart. *A net of fireflies*. Tokyo, Tuttle, 1960. p.82

'1 haiku' Tr. by Peter Beilenson and Harry Behn. *Haiku harvest*. Mount Vernon, Peter Pauper Press, 1962. p.53

'1 tanka' Übers. von Gerolf Coudenhove. *Japanische Jahreszeiten*. Zürich, Manesse Verlag, 1963. p.28

'11 haiku' *A history of haiku v.2*, by R. H. Blyth. Tokyo, Hokuseido, 1964. p.145–148

'Harvest moon' Tr. by Kenneth Yasuda. *A pepper-pod*. Tokyo, Tuttle, 1976. p.78

「美人煙草」 呉檮訳 上海 商務印書館 1906. 1冊

OZAKI Shirō 尾崎士郎 1898–1964

Mikan no kawa 蜜柑の皮

'밀감껍질' 李炯基訳 「世界短篇文学全集 7」 서울 啓蒙社 1966. p.322–332; 「世界短篇文学全集 9」 서울 三珍社 1971. p.191–202; 「世界代表短篇文学全集 9」 서울 三熙社 1976. p.191–201; 「世界短篇文学全集 9」 서울 新韓出版社 1976. p.318–336

Nagasugiru koinaka 長すぎる恋仲

'文士와妓女의恋情' 金龍済訳 「日本代表作家百人集 2」 서울 希望出版社 1966. p.376–386; 「日本短篇文学全集 3」 서울 新太陽社 1969. p.62–72

OZAWA Hekidō 小沢碧童 1881–1941

Haiku 俳句

'2 haiku' Tr. by V. H. Viglielmo. *Japanese literature in the Meiji era*. Tokyo, Obunsha, 1955. p.442–443

OZAWA Ryōkichi 小沢良吉

Jingo no hanashi じんごのはなし

Jingo. Pittsburgh, Tundra Books, 1977. 1v.

Tokomasa no hanashi とこまさのはなし

Toko. Pittsburgh, Tundra Books, 1977. 1v.

OZAWA Tadashi 小沢 正 1937–

Me o samase Toragorō 目をさませトラゴロウ

'Pohádka o tygrovi' *Modré vánoce*. Přel. Ivan Krouský a Z. K. Slabý. Praha, Albatros, 1975.

OZU Seizaemon 小津清左衛門

Tanka 短歌

'1 tanka' Tr. by Shigeshi Nishimura. *Eigo Seinen*, v.92, no.3, 1946. p.81

OZU Yasujirō 小津安二郎 1903–1963

Tōkyō monogatari 東京物語 (with Kogo Noda)

'Tokyo story' Tr. by Donald Richie and Eric Klestadt. *Contemporary Japanese literature*, ed. by Howard Hibbett. N. Y. Knopf, 1977. p.189–237

R

RI Kaisei 李 恢成 1935–

Kinuta o utsu onna 砧をうつ女

'다듬이질하는女人' 李浩哲訳 「다듬이질하는女人」 서울 正音社 1972; 「現代日本代表文学全集 6」 서울 平和出版社 1973. p.307–334

S

SAEKI Hiroko 佐伯浩子

Waga ai o hoshi ni inorite わが愛を星に祈りて

「내사랑별에빌며」 尹尚峽訳 서울 韓一出版社 1968. 257p.; 1972. 259p.

「내사랑별과같이」 裵秀貞訳 서울 無等出版社 1968. 289p.

SAEKI Shōichi 佐伯彰一 1922–

Criticism 評論

'日本小説的時代' 鐘肇政訳 「文壇」 第194期 1965.
p.22–26

SAGA Nobuyuki 嵯峨信之 1902–

Poems 詩

'雨期到来' 金龍済訳 「日本詩集」 서울 青雲社 1960.
p.38–40
'Fire; On loving women; The myth of Hiroshima;
Bone' Tr. by Hajime Kijima and John
Bean. *The poetry of postwar Japan.* Iowa
City, Univ. of Iowa Press, 1975. p.3–5

SAIJŌ Yaso 西条八十 1892–1970

Poems 詩

'L'étoile du soir; Le cerf-volant rouge; Hanneton;
Les prisonniers; Le moulin qui chante; Le
printemps enseveli' Tr. par Georges Bon-
neau. *Rythmes japonais,* par G. Bonneau.
Paris, Paul Geuthner, 1933. p.94–103; *Ly-
risme du temps présent,* par G. Bonneau. Paris,
Paul Geuthner, 1935. p.84–93; *Anthologie de
la poésie japonaise.* Paris, Paul Geuthner,
1935. p.218–229
'Mother and the reeds' Tr. by Haxon Ishii.
Japan Advertiser, June 2, 1935.
'Майскиат брембар; Вечерницата' Преведе от
франц. Никола Джеров. *Песните на Ямато.*
София, Корали, 1937. p.76–77
'The canary' Tr. by Tatsue Fujita. *Aoba no fue.*
Honolulu, Univ. of Hawaii, 1937.
'Le canari; Les cinq doigts; Devant la mer; Ma
mère sur la montagne; Ne pleurez pas . . .;
Chant secret' Tr. par Kuni Matsuo et
Steinilber-Oberlin. *Anthologie des poètes
japonais contemporains.* Paris, Mercure de
France, 1939. p.192–196
'Le moulin qui chante; Le printemps enseveli'
*Histoire de la littérature japonaise contem-
poraine,* par Georges Bonneau. Paris, Payot,
1944. p.246–248
'Balançoire dans un matin d'hiver; Le canari;
The canary' Tr. par Nico D. Horiguchi.
The lyric garland, ed. by Makoto Sangu.
Tokyo, Hokuseido, 1957. p.47–49
'Cards and love; By the sea; A mask; Some-
body' *An anthology of modern Japanese
poetry,* ed. and tr. by Ichiro Kono and Ri-
kutaro Fukuda. Tokyo, Kenkyusha, 1957.
p.118–119
'J'ai vu ma mère sur la montagne' *La poésie
japonaise,* par Karl Petit. Paris, Seghers,
1959. p.209
'Der rote Drachen' Übers. von Günther Debon.
Im Schnee die Fähre. München, Piper, 1960.
p.44
'Maske; Adamin biri' Tercüme etmek L. Sami
Akalin. *Japon şiiri.* İstanbul, Varlik Yayinevi, 1962. p.258–259
'Письмо от лесных птиц; Две песенки о карандаше; Горное эхо' Перевод Веры Марковой. *Восточный альманах 6.* Москва, Ху-

дож. Лит. 1963. p.329–330
'The crow's letter' Tr. by Geoffrey Bownas and
Anthony Thwaite. *The Penguin book of Jap-
anese verse.* Harmondsworth, Penguin Books,
1964. p.194
'Junto al mar' Tr. por Kikuya Ionesawa. *Poesia
japonesa contemporanea.* Bogotá, Colombia
Editoriales de Librería, 1965.
'At sea; Tomb; Face' Tr. by Graeme Wilson.
Japan Quarterly, v.13, no.2, 1966. p.220, 230,
243
'Две песни о карандаше' Перевод В. Марковой.
Птица, птица красная. Москва, Дет. Лит.
1967.
'La canzone del mulino' Tr. di R. Beviglia.
*Antologia della letteratura coreana e giap-
ponese.* Milano, Fratelli Fabbri, 1969. p.281
'老人與帆' 「標準日本名著選讀」 孫文斗編 台北 大新
書局 1969. p.81–85
'앵무새' 「永遠한世界名詩全集 2」 黃錦燦編 서울 翰
林出版社 1969. p.222; 「永遠한世界名詩全集 5」
黃錦燦編 서울 翰林出版社 1973. p.222
'By the deep, one; and other poems' Tr. by
Graeme Wilson. *Solidarity,* August 1971. p.57
'Mi-am vazut mana pe culmea muntelui; Canarul;
Vis ciudat; Scrisoarea corbului' Traducerea
Ion Ascan. *Din lirica japoneză.* Bucureşti,
Editura Univers. n.d. p.168–169

SAIONJI Kinmochi 西園寺公望 1849–1940

Tanka 短歌

'Primavara' Traducerea Virgil Teodorescu. *Din
lirica japoneză.* Bucureşti, Editura Univers,
n.d. p.125

SAISHO Atsuko 税所敦子 1825–1900

Tanka 短歌

'Uguisu; Spring rain; Young green shoots; The
fragrance of chrysanthemums; Falling flowers;
The shadows of pine-trees' Tr. by Asataro
Miyamori. *Masterpieces of Japanese poetry,
ancient and modern.* Tokyo, Maruzen, 1936;
Tokyo, Taiseido, 1956; N. Y. Greenwood
Press, 1971. p.589–601

SAITŌ Fumi 斎藤 史 1909–

Tanka 短歌

'1 tanka' Tr. by H. H. Honda. *The Reeds,* v.5,
1959. p.87
'6 tanka' Tr. by Edith Shiffert. *Literary Review,*
v.6, no.1, 1962. p.104
'12 tanka' *Anthology of modern Japanese poetry,*
tr. and comp. by Edith Marcombe Shiffert
and Yuki Sawa. Tokyo, Tuttle, 1972. p.150–153

SAITŌ Hiroshi 斎藤広志

Poems 詩

'消失点으로' 金龍済訳 「日本詩集」 서울 青雲社 1960.
p.62–63

SAITŌ Jakushi 斎藤雀志 1851–1908

Haiku 俳句

'Love and snow' Tr. by Asataro Miyamori. *Anthology of haiku, ancient and modern.* Tokyo, Maruzen, 1932. p.669

'Afterwords' Tr. by Harold Stewart. *A net of fireflies.* Tokyo, Tuttle, 1960. p.98

'1 haiku' Tr. by Peter Beilenson and Harry Behn. *Haiku harvest.* Mount Vernon, Peter Pauper Press, 1962. p.12

SAITŌ Mokichi 斎藤茂吉 1882–1952

Shi ni tamau haha 死にたまふ母

'My mother is dying' Tr. by Amy Vladeck Heinrich. *Monumenta Nipponica*, v.33, no.4, 1978. p.413–423

Tanka 短歌

'The frogs in distant ricefields: A lunatic; A dirge; Old age; A baby; Evening birds; My mother's cremation; In a tram-car' Tr. by Asataro Miyamori. *Masterpieces of Japanese poetry, ancient and modern.* Tokyo, Maruzen, 1936; Tokyo, Taiseido, 1956; N. Y. Greenwood Press, 1971. p.690–695

'Mother at death' Tr. by Haxon Ishii. *Eigo Seinen*, v.81, no.5, 1939. p.141–142, no.6, 1939. p.174–175, no.7, 1939. p.201, no.8, 1939. p.234

'Tanka' Tr. par Kuni Matsuo et Steinilber-Oberlin. *Anthologie des poètes japonais contemporains.* Paris, Mercure de France, 1939. p.268–269

'1 tanka' Tr. by Shigeshi Nishimura. *The Current of the World*, v.17, no.2, 1940. p.131

'1 tanka' Tr. by Shigeshi Nishimura. *Eigo Seinen*, v.93, no.3, 1947. p.120

'Dawn of new Japan' Tr. by Shigeshi Nishimura. *The Current of the World*, v.29, no.6, 1952. p.33

'5 tanka' Tr. by V. H. Viglielmo. *Japanese literature in the Meiji era.* Tokyo, Obunsha, 1955. p.412–413

'Four waka poems' Tr. by Howard Hibbett. *Modern Japanese literature*, ed. by Donald Keene. N. Y. Grove Press, 1956; Tokyo, Tuttle, 1957. p.209–210

'1 tanka' Tr. by H. H. Honda. *The Reeds*, v.3, 1957. p.21

'Ode mélancolique' *La poésie japonaise*, par Karl Petit. Paris, Seghers, 1959. p.199

'In der Straßenbahn' Übers. von Günther Debon. *Im Schnee die Fähre.* München, Piper, 1960. p.38

'11 tanka' Übers. von Kuniyo Takayasu und Manfred Hausmann. *Ruf der Regenpfeifer.* München, Bechtle Verlag, 1961. p.98–100

'5 tanka' Tr. by Geoffrey Bownas and Anthony Thwaite. *The Penguin book of Japanese verse.* Harmondsworth, Penguin Books, 1964. p.160–161

'In der Straßenbahn; An der Isar 1923; Bocken 1923' *Lyrik des Ostens*, hrg. von Wilhelm Gundert usw. München, Carl Hanser, 1965. p.472–473

'1 tanka' Tr. by Mayumi Hara. *Poetry Nippon*,

no.5 & 6, 1969. p.17

'13 tanka' *Anthology of modern Japanese poetry*, tr. and comp. by Edith Marcombe Shiffert and Yuki Sawa. Tokyo, Tuttle, 1972. p.143–146

'Mt. Zao; Mortal life; Contrition' Tr. by Hideo Yamaguchi. *Kobe Jogakuin Daigaku Ronshu* v.18, no.3, 1972. p.25–31

SAITŌ Ren 斎藤憐

Akame 赤目

'Red eyes' Tr. by David Goodman. *Concerned Theatre Japan*, v.2, no.1–2, 1971. p.46–109

SAITŌ Ryū 斎藤瀏 1879–1953

Tanka 短歌

'A lark; My field-glasses' Tr. by Asataro Miyamori. *Masterpieces of Japanese poetry, ancient and modern.* Tokyo, Maruzen, 1936; Tokyo, Taiseido, 1956; N. Y. Greenwood Press, 1971. p.688–689

'1 tanka' Übers. von Gerolf Coudenhove. *Japanische Jahreszeiten.* Zürich, Manesse Verlag, 1963. p.85

'2 tanka' Tr. by Donald Keene. *Landscapes and portraits.* Tokyo, Kodansha International, 1971. p.305

SAITŌ Ryūsuke 斎藤隆介 1917–

Hibari no ya ひばりの矢

'Skřivánčí šípy' *Modré vánoce.* Přel. Ivan Krouský a Z. K. Slabý. Praha, Albatros, 1975.

Midori no uma 緑の馬

'Zelený kůň' *Modré vánoce.* Přel. Ivan Krouský a Z. K. Slabý. Praha, Albatros, 1975.

Sanko ミコ

'Sanko' *Modré vánoce.* Přel. Ivan Krouský a Z. K. Slabý. Praha, Albatros, 1975.

Someko to oni ソメコとオニ

'Someko a čert' *Modré vánoce.* Přel. Ivan Krouský a Z. K. Slabý. Praha, Albatros, 1975.

SAITŌ Sanki 西東三鬼 1900–1962

Haiku 俳句

'2 haiku' *Anthology of modern Japanese poetry*, tr. and comp. by Edith Marcombe Shiffert and Yuki Sawa. Tokyo, Tuttle, 1972. p.170

'20 haiku' *Modern Japanese haiku, an anthology*, comp. and tr. by Makoto Ueda. Tokyo, Univ. of Tokyo Press, 1976. p.230–239

SAITŌ Sen 斎藤 千

Poems 詩

'媽媽, 勝利就在眼前！' 李芒訳 「世界文学」 1955年
　　10月 p.65–67

SAITŌ Takeshi 斎藤 勇 1887–

Bungaku no sekai 文学の世界

「文学에의招待」 李哲範訳 서울 京西出版社 1974. 303p.

SAKAGAMI Hiroshi 坂上 弘 1936–

Aru aki no dekigoto ある秋の出来事

'어느가을에일어난일' 金鐘仁訳 「戦後日本新人受賞作品
　　選」 서울 隆文社 1960. p.113–152

SAKAGAWA Mitsuo 酒川蜜男

Poems 詩

'담배' 金龍済訳 「日本詩集」 서울 青雲社 1960.
　　p.81–83

SAKAGUCHI Ango 坂口安吾 1906–1955

Hakuchi 白痴

'The idiot' Tr. by George Saito. *Modern Japanese
stories*, ed. by Ivan Morris. London, Spottiswoode, 1961; Tokyo, Tuttle, 1962. p.384–415;
The world of Japanese fiction. N. Y. Dutton,
1973. p.232–264

Kaze hakase 風博士

'Professor Vento' Tr. de Katsunori Wakisaka.
Maravilhas do conto japonês. São Paulo, Editôra
Cultrix, 1962. p.163–169

SAKAI Tokuzō 坂井徳三 1901–1973

Poems 詩

'胸腔' 方紀生訳 「世界文学」 1964年6月 p.128–129
'Пейзаж репрессии; Идет годовщина!' Перевод
Анатолия Мамонова. *Вкус хризантемы*.
Москва, Восточная Литература, 1976.
p.102–103

Criticism 評論

'請接受吧, 我悄聲的細語' 梅韜訳 「人民文学」 1953年
　　6月 p.92

SAKAKI Nanao さかき・ななお 1922–

Poems 詩

'Bellyfulls IV; Bellyfulls no.101' Tr. by Neale
Hunter and Nanao Sakaki. *Japanese poetry
now*. London, André Deutsch, 1972. p.44–46;

Japanese poetry today. N. Y. Schocken Books,
1972. p.46–48

SAKAKIYAMA Jun 榊山 潤 1900–

Gisō kekkon 偽装結婚

'偽装結婚' 徐雲濤訳 「當代日本小説選」 台南 經緯書局
　　1954. p.1–20; 「當代日本創作小説」 台南 經緯書
　　局 1961. p.1–20; 「當代日本短篇小説選」 台南
　　大行出版社 1973. p.1–20

'奇怪的觸手' 徐雲濤訳 「當代日本小説選」 台南 經緯書
　　局 1954. p.134–163; 「當代日本創作小説」 台南
　　經緯書局 1961. p.134–163; 「當代日本短篇小説選」
　　台南 大行出版社 1973. p.134–163

SAKAMOTO Etsurō 阪本越郎 1906–1969

Poems 詩

'A white bud; Subway; Rain of death' *An antho-
logy of modern Japanese poetry*, ed. and tr. by
Ichiro Kono and Rikutaro Fukuda. Tokyo,
Kenkyusha, 1957. p.119–120
'The musical instruments of Pompei' Tr. by J.
G. Mills and Rikutaro Fukuda. *Japan
Quarterly*, v.7, no.1, 1960. p.23
'Ak tomurcuk; Metro' Tercüme etmek L.
Sami Akalin. *Japon şiiri*. İstanbul, Varlik
Yayinevi, 1962. p.287–288
'Subway' Tr. por Kikuya Ionesawa. *Poesia
japonesa contemporanea*. Bogotá, Colom-
bia Editoriales de Librería, 1965. n.p.

SAKAMOTO Ryō 坂本 遼 1904–1970

Poems 詩

'My beloved' *An anthology of modern Japanese
poetry*, ed. and tr. by Ichiro Kono and Rikutaro Fukuda. Tokyo, Kenkyusha, 1957.
p.120
'恋人' 崔一秀訳 「기다리고있네」 서울 韓国政経社
　　1966. p.20–22

SAKAMURA Shinmin 坂村真民 1909–

Poems 詩

'Everything white looks like bones' Tr. by Mo-
kuo Nagayama. *Poetry Nippon*, no.15, 1971.
p.4

SAKATA Hiroo 阪田寛夫 1925–

Tsuchi no utsuwa 土の器

'瓦器' 劉慕沙訳 「祭場」 台北 皇冠出版社 1975.
　　p.137–211
'土器' 安東林訳 「70年代芥川賞小説集」 서울 玄岩社
　　1976. p.137–195;「新鋭世界文学選集20世紀 9」 서
　　울 玄岩社 1977. p.137–194

SAKO Jun'ichirō

SAKO Jun'ichirō 佐古純一郎 1919–

Criticism 評論

'Christianity and Japanese literature' *Japan Christian Quarterly*, v.22, April 1956. p.124–129

'The problem of Rinzo Shiina' Tr. by Peyton Palmore. *Japan Christian Quarterly*, v.39, no.4, 1973. p.185–189

SAKUMA Takeshi 佐久間　彪

Hoeru raion ほえるライオン

Lion's nose. English version by Kiyoko Ishizuka Tucker. N. Y. Hawthorn, 1966. 1v.

SAKURAI Ōson 桜井鷗村 1872–1929

Hatsu kōkai 初航海

「航海少年」　商務編譯所訳　上海　商務印書館 1907. 1冊

Kuchiki no fune 朽木の舟

「朽木舟」　商務編譯所訳　上海　商務印書館 1907. 1冊

Ōshū kenbutsu 欧洲見物

「澳洲歷險記」　金石　褚嘉猷訳　上海　商務印書館 1906. 1冊

「橘英雄」　上海　商務印書館 1926. 1冊

SAKURAI Tadayoshi 桜井忠温 1879–1965

Jūgo 銃後

Jugo, Dietro i fuili. Tr. di Bartolomeo Balbi. Napoli, Casa Editrice Italo-Cino-Giapponese, 1917. 2v.

Ken to inku 剣とインク

'The sword and ink' Tr. by Kazutomo Takahashi. *Eigo Kenkyu*, v.23, no.10, 1931. p.930–931, v.23, no.11, 1931. p.1029–1031

Nikudan 肉弾

Human bullets. Tr. by Masujiro Honda and Alice M. Bacon. Tokyo, Teibi Pub. 1907. 250p.; Boston, 1907. 270p.

Живые ядра. С английского перевод Ю. Романовский и А. фон Шварц. Петербург, Комиссия Военно-Учебн. Заведения, 1909. 248p.

「旅順實戰記」　黄……訳　北京　武學編譯社 1909. 1冊

Niku-dan, Menschenopfer. Übers. von A. Schinzinger. Tokyo, Seibundo, 1911. 206p.; Freiburg, 1911. 1v.

Mitraille humaine. Tr. par Corvisart. Paris, A. Challamel, 1913. 375p.

Haiku 俳句

'Long ago' Tr. by Asataro Miyamori. *Anthology of haiku, ancient and modern.* Tokyo, Maruzen, 1932. p.774

'Long ago' Tr. Kenneth Yasuda. *A pepper-pod.* Tokyo, Tuttle, 1976. p.91

SANGŪ Makoto 山宮　允 1892–1967

Poems 詩

'Adoration of life' Tr. by Shigeshi Nishimura. *The Current of the World*, v.31, no.10, 1954. p.48

'Silence; Dusk; Green hill poems' *The lyric garland*, ed. by Makoto Sangu. Tokyo, Hokuseido, 1957. p.50–52

'Sea-urchin; At Takaragawa; Autumn song' Tr. by Makoto Sangu. *The Shikai*, no.59, 1959. p.16

SANO Yō 佐野　洋 1928–

Naibu no teki 内部の敵

'内部의敵' 張壽哲訳 「日本代表作家百人集 5」 서울 希望出版社 1966. p.278–304; 「日本短篇文学全集 6」 서울 新太陽社 1969. p.190–216

Shōko nashi 証拠なし

'No proof' *Japanese golden dozen*, ed. by Ellery Queen. Tokyo, Tuttle, 1978. p.167–189

'討厭警官的女人' 文良出版社訳 「推理小説　日本偵探名著」 台南　文良出版社 1969. p.53–96

SANUMA Heisuke 佐沼平助

Poems 詩

'끝없는彷徨' 崔一秀訳 「기다리고있네」 서울 韓国政経社 1966. p.196–199

SANYŪTEI Enchō 三遊亭円朝 1839–1900

Kaidan botan dōrō 怪談牡丹燈籠

Пионовый фонарь. Перевод А. Стругацкого. Москва, Худож. Лит. 1964. 235p.

SAOTOME Katsumoto 早乙女勝元 1932–

Shitamachi no seishun 下町の青春

'Из переулка' Г. Ронской. *Встреча.* Москва, Дет. Лит. 1970. p.182–190

Дети из предместия. Перевод Г. Ронской. Москва, Детгиз, 1973. 159p.

SASAGAWA Rinpū 笹川臨風 1870-1949

Haiku 俳句

'Nichiren Shonin Tatsu no Kuchi' Tr. by Sakuji-ro Kamikawa. *Jitsuyo Eigo*, Oct. 1921.
'3 haiku' Tr. by Asataro Miyamori. *Anthology of haiku, ancient and modern.* Tokyo, Maruzen, 1932. p.775-776
'2 haiku' Tr. by V. H. Viglielmo. *Japanese literature in the Meiji era.* Tokyo, Obunsha, 1955. p.434
'The pavilion on the lake' Tr. by Harold Stewart. *A net of fireflies.* Tokyo, Tuttle, 1960. p.39
'Cuckoo' Tr. by Kenneth Yasuda. *A pepper-pod.* Tokyo, Tuttle, 1976. p.91

Criticism 評論

「帝國文學史」 范迪吉等訳 北京 會文學社 1903. 1冊

SASAKI Chiyo 佐佐木千代

Poems 詩

'A reggel; Hajszál' Ford. Jobbágy Károly. *Nagyvilág*, no.8, 1964. p.1275

SASAKI Hirotsuna 佐佐木弘綱 1828-1891

Tanka 短歌

'When seriously ill' Tr. by Asataro Miyamori. *Masterpieces of Japanese poetry, ancient and modern.* Tokyo, Maruzen, 1936; Tokyo, Taiseido, 1956; N. Y. Greenwood Press, 1971. p.602-603
'1 tanka' Übers. von Gerolf Coudenhove. *Japanische Jahreszeiten.* Zürich, Manesse Verlag, 1963. p.178

SASAKI Kiichi 佐々木基一 1914-

Essay エッセイ

'孤独한권력' 金賢珠訳 「바이바이바디」 서울 三韓出版社 1966. p.218-220

SASAKI Kuni 佐々木 邦 1883-1964

Akachan 赤ちゃん

'Aka-chan, baby' Tr. by Kuni Sasaki. *The Yomiuri*, July 17-Sept. 9, 1959.

Ekidan to yūrei 易断と幽霊

'Wahrsager und Gespenster' Übers. von Kurt Meissner. *Der Tanzfächer*, von K. Meissner. Tokyo, 1943. p.163-180

Kokoro no rekishi 心の歴史

The reluctant bachelor. Tr. by Kuni Sasaki and Jiro Araki. N. Y. Vantage Press, 1962. 229p.

SASAKI Nobutsuna 佐佐木信綱 1872-1963

Tanka 短歌

'The sound of the water; The true I; My mind; A flute; Lake Tung-ting; Pampas grass leaves; When climbing Mount Fuji; The mountain village; My verses; My eyes; My chosen way; The morning breeze of spring; The spring breeze; Under the flowers' Tr. by Asataro Miyamori. *Masterpieces of Japanese poetry, ancient and modern.* Tokyo, Maruzen, 1936; Tokyo, Taiseido, 1956; N. Y. Greenwood Press, 1971. p.627-635
'Tanka' Tr. par Kuni Matsuo et Steinilber-Oberlin. *Anthologie des poètes japonais contemporains.* Paris, Mercure de France, 1939. p.256-257
'1 tanka' Tr. by Shigeshi Nishimura. *Eigo Seinen*, v.93, no.3, 1947. p.120
'6 tanka' Tr. by V. H. Viglielmo. *Japanese literature in the Meiji era.* Tokyo, Obunsha, 1955. p.375, 376
'Mein Lied; Das wahre Ich; Mein Weg' Übers. von Günther Debon. *Im Schnee die Fähre.* München, Piper, 1960. p.17-18
'Tanka' Tercüme etmek L. Sami Akalin. *Japon şiiri.* İstanbul, Varlik Yayinevi, 1962. p.236
'6 tanka' Übers. von Gerolf Coudenhove. *Japanische Jahreszeiten.* Zürich, Manesse Verlag, 1963. p.39, 55, 248, 274, 340, 350
'Standesehre; Der Evangelist; Das wahre Ich' *Lyrik des Ostens*, hrg. von Wilhelm Gundert usw. München, Carl Hanser. 1965. p.470

Essay エッセイ

'Mimitsu' Tr. by Haxon Ishii. *Eigo Seinen.* v.84, no.8, 1941. p.238, no.9, 1941. p.269, no. 10, 1941. p.301

SASAKI Tazu 佐々木たづ 1932-

Shiroi bōshi no oka 白い帽子の丘

The golden thread, Japanese stories for children. Tr. by Fanny Hagin Mayer. Tokyo, Tuttle, 1968. 64p.; Englewood Cliffs, Prentice-Hall, 1968. 64p.

SASAZAWA Saho 笹沢佐保 1930-

Umi kara no shōtaijō 海からの招待状

'Invitation from the sea' *Japanese golden dozen*, ed. by Ellery Queen. Tokyo, Tuttle, 1978. p.191-210

Yūrei no shi 幽霊の死

'幽靈之死' 劉奧堯訳 「現代日本小說選」 台北 雲天出版社 1970. p.24-54

'失效的偽証' 振江訳 「黑色幻惑」 台南 文良出版社 1966. p.112-140
'晩虹' 純音節訳 「知識分子」 第53期 1970. p.28-32, 第54期 1970. p.28-32

SASAZAWA Yoshiaki 笹沢美明 1898–

Poems 詩

'An invitation; Ten zelkova trees; Organ melody'
An anthology of modern Japanese poetry, ed.
and tr. by Ichiro Kono and Rikutaro Fukuda.
Tokyo, Kenkyusha, 1957. p.121–122

'Organ melody' Tr. por Kikuya Ionesawa.
Poesia japonesa contemporanea. Bogotá,
Colombia Editoriales de Librería, 1957.

'A white bank; Primitive' Tr. by Ikuko Atsumi.
Prism International, Winter 1965. p.13–15

'Flowers of June; The tower' *Anthology of
modern Japanese poetry*, comp. by Edith
Marcombe Shiffert and Yuki Sawa. Tokyo,
Tuttle, 1972. p.75–76

'離別의노래 ; 記憶 ; 菊花' 崔仁秀訳 「기다리고있네」 서
울 韓国政経社 1966. p.53–54, 86–87, 200–201

SASSA Seisetsu 佐々醒雪 1872–1917

Haiku 俳句

'1 haiku' Tr. by Harold Gould Henderson. *The
bamboo broom*. Tokyo, J. L. Thompson, 1933;
London, Kegan Paul, 1933. p.123

'2 haiku' Tr. by V. H. Viglielmo. *Japanese
literature in the Meiji era*. Tokyo, Obunsha,
1955. p.434

'2 haiku' *A history of haiku v.2*, by R. H. Blyth.
Tokyo, Hokuseido, 1964. p.262

'1 haiku' Tr. by Takamasa Sasaki. *Eigo Seinen*,
v.122, no.5, 1976. p.231

SATA Ineko 佐多稲子 1904–

Doro ningyō 泥人形

'Clay doll' Tr. by John Bester. *Japan P.E.N.
News*, no.9, July 1962. p.1–9; *Asian P.E.N.
anthology*, ed. by F. Sionil Jose. N. Y. Taplinger, 1966. p.77–89

Kawaita kaze 乾いた風

'Сухой ветер' Перевод Г. Иммерман. *Пока не
угаснет пламя, рассказы*. Москва, Гослитиздат, 1960. p.194–206

Kyarameru kōjō kara キャラメル工場から

'V tovarne na karamely' Přel. Z. Vasiljevová.
Světová Literatura, no.4, 1962. p.129–135

'Chakrong-ngantam look-kwao' Tr. Unchalee
Sarabunchong. *Rueng sun yeepun 1*. Bangkok,
Uksornsasna, 1977. p. 207–232

Moyuru kagiri 燃ゆる限り

'Пока не угаснет пламя' Перевод Г. Иммерман.
Пока не угаснет пламя, рассказы. Москва,
Гослитиздат, 1960. p.11–170

Puroretaria joyū プロレタリア女優

'Пролетарская актриса' Перевод К. Осга. *На
рубеже*, 1936, No.1. p.89–93

Nakama 仲間

'Подруги' Перевод Г. Иммерман. *Пока не угаснет пламя, рассказы*. Москва, Гослитиздат,
1960. p.207–217

Shōjo tachi 少女たち

'Девочки' Перевод Г. Иммерман. *Пока не угаснет пламя, рассказы*. Москва, Гослитиздат, 1960. p.173–183

Shukuji 祝辞

'Свадебный тост' Перевод Г. Иммерман. *Пока
не угаснет пламя, рассказы*. Москва, Гослитиздат, 1960. p.184–193

Toki ni tatsu 時に佇つ

'Standing still in time' Tr. by Charles S. Terry.
Japanese Literature Today, no.2, March 1977.
p.4–11

Toshiyori to wakamono 年寄と若者

'Старики и молодежь' Перевод Г. Иммерман.
No. 36, новеллы японских писателей. Москва, Наука, 1968. p.98–108

Essay エッセイ

'談花' 銭稲孫訳 「世界文学」 1961年3月 p.36–39

────────────

'Сорванная демонстрация' Перевод К. Осга.
На рубеже, 1935, No.11–12. p.36–42

SATŌ Aiko 佐藤愛子 1923–

Futari no onna 二人の女

'両個女人' 劉慕沙訳 「日本現代小説選」 台北 聯經出版
1976. p.143–201

Sokuratesu no tsuma ソクラテスの妻

'蘇格拉底的妻子' 劉慕沙訳 「日本現代小説選 1」 台北
聯經出版 1976. p.1–59

'蘇格拉底之妻' 江上訳 「日本名家小説選」 高雄 大舞台
書苑 1976. p.89–146

Tatakai sunde hi ga kurete 戦いすんで日が暮れて

「戰闘完了己黄昏」 喬遷訳 台北 幼獅文化事業公司
1971. 49p.

'Банкротство' Перевод О. Морошкиной. *Японская новелла 1960–1970*. Москва, Прогресс,
1972. p.308–338

────────────

'狗國春秋' 喬遷訳 「純文學」(台湾版) 第8巻4期 1970.
p.21–28

SATŌ Hachirō サトウ・ハチロー 1903–1973

Poems 詩

'The apple song' Tr. by Henry H. Armstrong.
Jiji Eigo Kenkyu, v.2, no.6, 1947. p.25

SATŌ Hajime　佐藤 ―　1921–

Poems　詩

'謝謝你們'　李芒訳　「世界文学」　1955年10月　p.63–65
'Путь жизни' Перевод Анатолия Мамонова. *Вкус хризантемы.* Москва, Восточная Литература, 1976. p.105

SATŌ Haruo　佐藤春夫　1892–1964

Aru onna no gensō　或る女の幻想

'某女之幻想'　査士元訳　「新月月刊」　第2巻2期　1929. p.1–19

Den'en no yūutsu　田園の憂鬱

'田園之憂鬱'　李漱泉訳　「田園之憂鬱」　上海　中華書局　1934.

Hoshi　星

'星'　江珠訳　「人魚の悲戀」　台中　中央書局　1955. p.29–51

Ichiya no yadori　一夜の宿

'一夜之宿'　査士元訳　「東方雑誌」　第28巻10期　1931. p.101–108

Jokaisen kitan　女誡扇綺譚

'The tale of the bridal fan' Tr. by Edward Seidensticker. *Japan Quarterly*, v.9, no.3, 1962. p.309–336

Nyonin funshi　女人焚死

'女人焚死'　金洙暎訳　「日本代表作家百人集 2」　서울　希望出版社　1966. p.324–356;「日本短篇文学全集 3」　서울　新太陽社　1969. p.10–42
'或女之死'　鐘肇政訳　「戰後日本短篇小説選」　台北　台湾商務印書館　1968. p.134–177
'女人焚死'　申庚林訳「日本文学大全集 10」　서울　東西文化院　1975. p.309–340

Keiei mondō　形影問答

'形影問答'　周作人訳　「現代日本小説集」　上海　商務印書館　1923;「日本現代小説集 3」　上海　商務印書館　1930. p.345–349

Kiji no aburiniku　雉子の炙肉

'雉鶏的焼烤'　周作人訳　「現代日本小説集」　上海　商務印書館　1923;「日本現代小説集 3」　上海　商務印書館　1930. p.350–355

Kōseiki　更生記

「更生記」　査士驤訳　上海　中華書局　1935. 1冊

Okinu to sono kyōdai　お絹とその兄弟

'阿絹和她的兄弟'　李漱泉訳　「田園之憂鬱」　上海　中華書局　1934.

Shimon　指紋

'指紋'　金溟若訳　「小説月報」　第21巻3号　1930. p.521–546

Supein ken no ie　西班牙犬の家

'The house of a Spanish dog' Tr. by George Saito. *Modern Japanese stories*, ed. by Ivan Morris.

London, Spottiswoode, 1961; Tokyo, Tuttle, 1962. p.163–172
'Das Haus eines Neufundländers' Deutsch von Monique Humbert. *Nippon.* Zürich, Diogenes, 1965. p.191–202

Taikutsu mondō　退屈問答

'逍遺的對話'　張資平訳　「別宴」　武昌　時中合作社　1926;「襯衣」　上海　光華書局　192?.
'逍遺的對話'　「少年的悲哀」　郁達夫等訳　台北　啓明書局　1956. p.65–81

Tasogare no ningen　たそがれの人間

'黄昏的人'　周作人訳　「現代日本小説集」　上海　商務印書館　1923;「日本現代小説集 3」　上海　商務印書館　1930. p.338–344

Tokai no yūutsu　都会の憂鬱

「都會的憂鬱」　査士元訳　上海　華通書局　1931. 1冊

Watashi no chichi to chichi no tsuru tono hanashi　私の父と父の鶴との話

'我的父親與父親的鶴的故事'　周作人訳　「現代日本小説集」　上海　商務印書館　1923;「日本現代小説集 3」　上海　商務印書館　1930. p.329–337;「世界著名作家散文選」　香港　上海書局　1977. p.437–445

Yameru sōbi　病める薔薇

'啊啊薔薇你病了'　謝六逸訳　「大江月刊」　第1巻2期

Yoki tomo　好き友

'Good friends' Tr. by S. G. Brickley. *The writing of idiomatic English.* Tokyo, Kenkyusha, 1951. p.91–95

Poems　詩

'海邊的戀愛'　張定璜訳　「語絲」　第6期　1924.
'殉情詩集'　李漱泉訳　「田園之憂鬱」　上海　中華書局　1934.
'Nuit d'automne; L'amour au bord de la mer; Herbe d'automne; Chanson du bord de l'eau et de la nuit de lune' Tr. par Georges Bonneau. *Lyrisme du temps présent,* par G. Bonneau. Paris, Geuthner, 1935. p.58–63; *Anthologie de la poésie japonais.* Paris, Paul Guethner, 1935. p.190–195
'Есенна нощб' Преведе от франц. Никола Джеров. *Песните на Ямато.* София, Корали, 1937. p.68
'The warriors eat of the maple leaf' Tr. by Haxon Ishii. *The Current of the World,* v.16, no.8, 1939. p.132
'Soupirs; Chanson des fleurs de poirier sous la clarté de la lune vague et blanche; Le feu d'artifice lointain; Pigeon' Tr. par Kuni Matsuo et Steinilber-Oberlin. *Anthologie des poètes japonais contemporains.* Paris, Mercure de France, 1939. p.207–212
'2 poemes' *Histoire de la littérature japonaise contemporaine,* par Georges Bonneau. Paris, Payot, 1944. p.244
'Lines sent my younger brother with a music box' Tr. by Shigeshi Nishimura. *The Current of the World,* v.30, no.12, 1953. p.54
'The cold night' Tr. by Shigeshi Nishimura. *The Current of the World,* v.31, no.3, 1954. p.48
'1 poem' Tr. par Roger Bersihand. *La littérature*

SATŌ Haruo

japonaise. Paris, Presses Universitaires de France, 1956. p.116–117

'La mort d'un imbécile; Incompréhension; Lune diurne' Tr. par Nico D. Horiguchi. *The lyric garland*, ed. by Makoto Sangu. Tokyo, Hokuseido, 1957. p.53–54

'Song of samma; To a person; A wish' *The poetry of living Japan*, by Takamichi Ninomiya and D. J. Enright. London, John Murray, 1957. p.54–56

'Liebe am Meeresstrand' Übers. von Kuniyo Takayasu und Manfred Hausmann. *Ruf der Regenpfeifer*. München, Bechtle Verlag, 1961. p.85

'Song of the pike' Tr. by Geoffrey Bownas and Anthony Thwaite. *The Penguin book of Japanese verse*. Harmondsworth, Penguin Books, 1964. p.194

'1 poem' Tr. from the French by Unity Evans. *Japanese literature*. N. Y. Walker, 1965. p.99–100

'Gold dust miners' Tr. by Graeme Wilson. *Japan Quarterly*, v.13, no.1, 1966. p.35

'어느女人에게; 그리운님에게; 東京哀歌' 崔一秀訳 「기다리고있네」 서울 韓国政経社 1966. p.125, 147, 244–247

'Notte d'autunno' Tr. di R. Beviglia. *Anthologia della letteratura coreana e giapponese*. Milano, Fratelli Fabbri, 1969. p.279

'바닷가사랑' 「永遠한世界의名詩全集 2」 黄錦燦編 서울 翰林出版社 1969. p.144; 「永遠한世界의名詩全集 5」 黄錦燦編 서울 翰林出版社 1973. p.144

Choix de poésies de Sato Haruo. Tr. par Mikiko Ishimura. Tokyo, Privately pub. n.d. 41p.

'Dragostea pe ţărmul mării; Cuiva; Cîntecul florilor de păr sub palida lumină-a lunii' Traducerea Virgil Teodorescu. *Din lirica japoneză*. Bucureşti, Editura Univers, n.d. p.174–175

Essays エッセイ

'嫩治閣録' 張佐文 蕭保德訳 「北新半月刊」 第3巻14号 1929. p.61–85

'論描寫' 謝六逸訳 「中學生」 第9期

「佐藤春夫集」 高明訳 上海 現代書局 1933. 1冊

SATŌ Hiroshi 佐藤 博 1924–

Tanka 短歌

'1 tanka' Tr. by Shigeshi Nishimura. *Eigo Seinen*, v.93, no.3, 1947. p.120

SATŌ Ichiei 佐藤一英 1899–

Poems 詩

'Die Perlen' Übers. von Kuniyo Takayasu und Manfred Hausmann. *Ruf der Regenpfeifer*. München, Bechtle Verlag, 1961. p.87

SATŌ Kōjin 佐藤弘人 1897–1962

Hadaka zuihitsu はだか随筆

「裸裸随筆」 邱思敏訳 台北 友聯書局 1969. 221p.
「生之苦悶」 邱思敏訳 台北 裕川出版社 1970. 211p.

SATŌ Kōroku 佐藤紅緑 1874–1949

Hannin hanjū 半人半獣

「人獣之間」 張資平訳 上海 商務印書館 1936. 1冊

Haiku 俳句

'The hood of Jizo image' Tr. by Asataro Miyamori. *Anthology of haiku, ancient and modern*. Tokyo, Maruzen, 1932. p.800

'3 haiku' Tr. by V. H. Viglielmo. *Japanese literature in the Meiji era*. Tokyo, Obunsha, 1955. p.432

SATŌ Makoto 佐藤 信 1943–

Atashi no Bītoruzu あたしのビートルズ

'My Beatles' Tr. by David Goodman. *Concerned Theatre Japan*, v.2, no.3–4, 1973. p.306–336

'Moi Beatelsi' Przeł. Henryk Lipszyc. *Dialog*, no. 9, 1974. p.46–65

Nezumi kozō Jirokichi 鼠小僧次郎吉

'Nezumi Kozo, the Rat' Tr. by David Goodman. *Concerned Theatre Japan*, v.1, no.1, 1970. p.76–133

Tsubasa o moyasu tenshi tachi no butō 翼を燃やす天使たちの舞踏

'The dance of angels who burnt their own wings' by Makoto Sato and others. Tr. by David Goodman. *Concerned Theatre Japan*, v.1, no. 4, 1971. p.54–118

SATŌ Rokkotsu 佐藤肋骨 1871–1944

Haiku 俳句

'2 haiku' Tr. by Asataro Miyamori. *Anthology of haiku, ancient and modern*. Tokyo, Maruzen, 1932. p.808–809

SATŌ Sanpei サトウ・サンペイ 1929–

Sukatan kanpanii スカタン Co.

Nonsense Co. Tr. by Tommy Uematsu. Tokyo, Hyoronsha, 1971–72. 3v.

SATŌ Satarō 佐藤佐太郎 1909–

Poems 詩

'Selected poems' Tr. by George Saito. *Japan*

Times Literary Supplement, no.1, Sept.1, 1957. p.14

SATŌ Satoru 佐藤さとる 1928–

Obaasan no hikōki おばあさんのひこうき

El avion de la abuera. Alcoy, Marfil, 1970. 30p.
Die fliegende Großmutter. Übers. von Siegfried Schaarschmidt. Berlin, Dressler, 1970. 95p.

SATŌ Satoru 佐藤 覚

Poems 詩

'On the bridge; Japan that sank under the sea' *Poetry*, May 1956. p.105–107

SATŌ Shiroji 佐藤四郎次

Poems 詩

'Творчество' Перевод Анатолия Мамонова. *Вкус хризантемы.* Москва, Восточная Литература, 1976. p.104

SATŌ Sōnosuke 佐藤惣之助 1890–1942

Poems 詩

'Mousoumé; Repentir; La lune; Elégie du Sud' Tr. par Kuni Matsuo et Steinilber-Oberlin. *Anthologie des poètes japonais contemporains.* Paris, Mercure de France, 1939. p.173–178
'The moon; Our maid-servant' Tr. by S. Sato and C. Urdang. *Poetry*, May 1956. p.92–93
'The son' Tr. by Hisakazu Kaneko. *London Magazine*, v.6, no.9, 1966. p.26–27
'Luna' Traducerea Virgil Teodorescu. *Din lirica japoneză.* Bucureşti, Editura Univers, n.d. p.165

SATOMI Ton 里見 弴 1888–

Chichioya 父親

'父親' 表文台訳 「日本代表作家百人集 2」 서울 希望出版社 1966. p.230–243; 「日本短篇文学全集 2」 서울 新太陽社 1969. p.294–307

Ginjirō no kataude 銀二郎の片腕

'Unu brado de Ginzirô' Tr. Kikunobu Matuba. *El japana literaturo.* Tokyo, Japana Esperanto Instituto, 1965. p.178–193

Kawanami no oto 川波の音

'Le bruit des vagues de la rivière' Tr. par Serge Elisséev. *Japon et Extrême-Orient*, no.10, Oct. 1924. p.205–227; *Neuf nouvelles japonaises*, par Serge Elisséev. Paris, G. van Œst, 1924. p.171–193
'Morajlo hullámck' Ford. Thein Alfréd. *Mai*

Japán dekameron. Budapest, Nyugat, 1935. p.203–224

Shitto 嫉妬

'Eifersucht' Übers. von Alexander Spann. *Das Junge Japan*, Bd.1, 1924. p.193–202

Tsubaki 椿

'The camellia' Tr. by Edward Seidensticker. *Modern Japanese stories*, ed. by I. Morris. London, Spottiswoode, 1961; Tokyo, Tuttle, 1962. p.138–143

Yuki no yobanashi 雪の夜話

'雪的夜話' 高汝鴻訳 「日本短篇小説集」 台北 台湾商務印書館 1969. p.45–65

SAWADA Bushō 沢田撫松 1871–1927

'Confession of a tattooed woman' Tr. by Kanichi Ando. *Eibun Osaka Mainichi*, Aug. 2–14, 1923.

SAWAKI Takako 沢木隆子 1907–

Poems 詩

'Winter' *An anthology of modern Japanese poetry*, ed. and tr. by Ichiro Kono and Rikutaro Fukuda. Tokyo, Kenkyusha, 1957. p.123

SAWANO Hisao 沢野久雄 1912–

Kokyaku 孤客

'Misanthrope' *Japan P.E.N. News*, no.23, Oct. 1970. p.4–15

Kyō no kage 京の影

'The roof-tile maker' *Chanoyu Quarterly*, v.2, no.3, 1971. p.55–68
'Twilight at Koetsuji Temple' *Chanoyu Quarterly*, v.2, no.4, 1971. p.68–78

Yoru no kawa 夜の河

'The river at night' Tr. by E. G. Seidensticker. *Japan Quarterly*, v.4, no.3, 1957. p.339–357

'遙遠的音楽' 朱佩蘭訳 「伊豆の踊子」 嘉義 明山書局 1969. p.197–219

SEKI Keigo 関 敬吾 1899–

Nihon no mukashi banashi 日本の昔話

Folktales of Japan, ed. by Keigo Seki. Tr. by Robert J. Adams. London, Routledge and Kegan Paul, 1963. 221p.

SEKINE Hiroshi 関根 弘 1920–

Poems 詩

'무엇이고第一 ; 女子의自尊心을이렇게이진다' 辛東門訳
「世界戰後文学全集 9」 서울 新丘文化社 1962.
p.248–249

'A fellow traveller' Tr. by Hisakazu Kaneko.
London Magazine, v.7, no.7, 1967. p.31–32

'The aquarium; The isle of dreams' Tr. by Harry
and Lynn Guest and Shozo Kajima. *Post-
war Japanese poetry*. Harmondsworth, Penguin Books, 1972. p.77–79

'Me and trains; Civilization at night' Tr. by
Thomas Fitzsimmons. *Japanese poetry now*.
London, André Deutsch, 1972. p.34–36;
Japanese poetry today. N. Y. Schocken Books,
1972. p.36–38

'Заданный рисунок; Туман; Горящий дом; Солдат; Дерево' Перевод А. Долина. *Иностранная Литература*, февраль 1973. p.84–89

'Squid and handkerchief; One's fate; Enemy; In
front of a bank' Tr. by Gregory Campbell,
Shigenori Nagatomo and Hajime Kijima. *The
poetry of postwar Japan*. Iowa City, Univ. of
Iowa Press, 1975. p.74–78

'Abe Sada; The Golden Pavilion; Dream Island'
Tr. by Christopher Drake. *Contemporary
Japanese literature*, ed. by Howard Hibbett.
N. Y. Knopf, 1977. p.319–334

SENA Keiko せな・けいこ

Nenaiko dareda ねないこだれだ

Kiu ne estas en la lito. Tokyo, Infana Verdajo,
1975. 1v.

SENGE Motomaro 千家元麿 1888–1948

Bara no hana ばらの花

'薔薇花' 周作人訳 「新潮」 第3巻1期 1921. p.115–
119; 「現代日本小説集」 上海 商務印書館 1923;
「日本現代小説集 2」 上海 商務印書館 1930.
p.239–244

'薔薇花' 新興書局編集部訳 「日本短篇小説選」 台北 新
興書局 1958. p.45–48; 台南 鳴宇出版社 1972.
p.45–48

Nekkyō shitaru kodomora 熱狂したる子供等

'熱狂的小孩們' 周作人訳 「新潮」 第3巻1期 1921.
p.120–124

Shin'ya no rappa 深夜のラッパ

'深夜的喇叭' 周作人訳「新青年」 第8巻4期 1920. p.565–
572; 「現代日本小説集」 上海 商務印書館 1923;
「日本現代小説集 2」 上海 商務印書館 1930.
p.228–238

Poems 詩

'蒼蠅; 軍隊; 草葉; 賣納豆的女人; 他; 小詩' 周作人訳
「新青年」 第9巻4期 1921. p.32–34; 「陀螺」 上
海 192?

'Canard sauvage; Cerisier; Le secret; Mon enfant
marche' Tr. par Kuni Matsuo et Steinilber-
Oberlin. *Anthologie des poètes japonais contemporains*. Paris, Mercure de France, 1939.
p.108–113

'My child walks' Tr. by Shigeshi Nishimura. *The
Current of the World*, v.26, no.4, 1949. p.36–
39

'Arashi' Tr. by Shigeshi Nishimura. *The Current
of the World*, v.26, no.9, 1949.

'The evening sea' Tr. by Shigeshi Nishimura. *The
Current of the World*, v.30, no.9, 1953. p.51

'Secret' Tr. by S. Sato and C. Urdang. *Poetry*,
May 1956. p.76

'Rain; Daffodils; Paulownia blossoms' *An anthology of modern Japanese poetry*, ed. and
tr. by Ichiro Kono and Rikutaro Fukuda.
Tokyo, Kenkyusha, 1957. p.123–124

'Le secret' *La poésie japonaise*, par Karl Petit.
Paris, Seghers, 1959. p.216

'Sah ich selbst' Übertragen von Shin Aizu. *Der
schwermütige Ladekran*. St. Gallen, Tschudy
Verlag, 1960. p.25

'1 poem' Übers. von Kuniyo Takayasu und
Manfred Hausmann. *Ruf der Regenpfeifer*.
München, Bechtle Verlag, 1961. p.84

'Zerrinler' Tercüme etmek L. Sami Akalin. *Japon
şiiri*. İstanbul, Varlik Yayinevi, 1962. p.246

'A snow garden' Tr. by Hisakazu Kaneko. *Orient
West*, v.8, no.1, 1963. p.51; *The Japanese image*,
ed. by M. Schneps and A. D. Coox. Tokyo,
Orient West, 1965. p.351–352

'桐花; 海的驚異; 春' 徐和隣訳 「現代詩解説」 台北 葡
萄園詩刊社 1970. p.1–3

'아기는걷는다' 金巣雲訳 「世界의文学大全集 34」 서울
同和出版公社 1971. p.505–507

'Wild geese' Tr. by James Kirkup. *Poetry Nippon*,
no.35 & 36, 1976. p.6–7

SENUMA Shigeki 瀬沼茂樹 1904–

Criticism 評論

'The influence of Russian literature in Japan'
Japan Quarterly, v.7, no.3, 1960. p.343–349

'Der Stammbaum der Literatur der Nachkriegs-
gruppe' Übers. von Wolfram Naumann.
Kagami, Bd.3, Heft 1, 1965. p.79–90

'Wagahai wa neko de aru (I am a cat)' *Essays on
Natsume Soseki's works*. Tokyo, Japan
Society for the Promotion of Science, 1972.
p.19–31

SEO Fumiko 瀬尾文子

Poems 詩

'人事' 「時調文學」 第35巻6号 1975. p.53–54

SERITA Hōsha 芹田鳳車 1885–1954

Haiku 俳句

'5 haiku' *A history of haiku v.2*, by R. H. Blyth.
Tokyo, Hokuseido, 1964. p.200–202

'1 haiku' Tr. by R. H. Blyth. *Haiku v.1*. Tokyo,
Hokuseido, 1950. p.384

SERIZAWA Kōjirō 芹沢光治良 1897–

Hitotsu no sekai 一つの世界

'One world' Tr. by Grace Suzuki. *Ukiyo*, Tokyo, Phoenix Books, 1954. p.36–57; *Ukiyo*. N. Y. Vanguard Press, 1963. p.230–243; London, Universal Library, 1964. p.230–243

Kowai onnatachi こわい女達

'무서운女子들' 金龍済訳 「日本代表作家百人集 3」 서울 希望出版社 1966. p.68–79;「日本短篇文学全集 3」서울 新太陽社 1969. p.216–227

Onna no umi 女の海

'Die Frau des Meeres' Übers. von Kurt Meissner. *Der Tanzfächer*, von K. Meissner. Tokyo, 1943. p.240–262

Ōwashi 大鷲

'A rich poor father' Tr. by Hatsu Imajo. *Young forever, and five other novelettes*, ed. by Japan Writers' Society, Tokyo, Hokuseido, 1941. p.45–70

Pari fujin パリ夫人

Madame Aida. Tr. par Armand Pierhal. Paris, Robert Laffont, 1958. 254p.

Pari ni shisu 巴里に死す

J'irai mourir à Paris. Tr. par Armand Pierhal. Paris, Robert Laffont, 1954. 260p.
「魂断巴黎」 黄凡訳 台北 林白出版社 1969. 172p.

Samurai no matsuei サムライの末裔

La fin du samourai. Tr. par Armand Pierhal. Paris, Robert Laffont, 1955. 306p.
Koniec samuraja. Przeł. Daniela Kolendo. Warszawa, Pax, 1957. 274p.

SETA Teiji 瀬田貞二 1916–

Furuya no mori ふるやのもり

The dreadful drops. Tokyo, Labo Teaching Information Center, 1972. 26p.

SETO Eiichi 瀬戸英一 1892–1934

Futasuji michi 二筋道

'Zwei Wege' Übers. von Maria Piper. *Das japanische Theater*. Frankfurt am Main, Societäts Verlag, 1937. p.55–69

Oka o koete 丘を越えて

'Über den Berg' Übers. von Maria Piper. *Das japanische Theater*. Frankfurt am Main, Societäts Verlag, 1937. p.43–47

Urabon no yo no satsujin 盂蘭盆の夜の殺人

'Der Mord in der Nacht vom Bon-Fest' Übers. von Maria Piper. *Das japanische Theater*. Frankfurt am Main, Societäts Verlag, 1937. p.48–54

SETO Hanmin 瀬戸半眠

Okurimono 贈物

'Подарок' Перевод П. Чечина. *Вестник Иностранной Литературы*, 1910, No.6. p.68–70; *Миниатюра и юмористка*, выпуск 2.

SETOUCHI Harumi 瀬戸内晴美 1922–

Asana asana 朝な朝な

「迷路」 金蓮姫訳 서울 東西出版社 1967. 358p.
「早朝」 金芝郷訳 「日本文学大全集 7」서울 東西文化院 1975. p.2–182

Moenagara 燃えながら

「情炎」 尹尚峽訳 서울 三午出版社 1967. 265p.
「第三の恋人」 姜慧妍訳 서울 韓一出版社 1969. 265p.
「사랑과이별의恋情」 任承彬訳 서울 興文図書 1972. 251p.

Shunjin 春塵

'春塵' 李東植訳 「日本代表作家百人集 5」서울 希望出版社 1966. p.68–80;「日本短篇文学全集 5」서울 新太陽社 1969. p.364–376

「運命의勝利者」 琴鏞振 楊鐘泰訳 서울 相一文化社 1973. 370p.

SHAKU no Chōkū 釈 迢空 1887–1953
(ORIKUCHI Shinobu)

Tanka 短歌

'Tanka' Tr. by Shigeshi Nishimura. *The Current of the World*, v.13, 1936.
'Take care to do my soul no harm' Tr. by Shigeshi Nishimura. *Eigo Seinen*, v. 92, no. 7, 1946. p.198
'Searching the hills' Tr. by Shigeshi Nishimura. *The Current of the World*, v.31, no.4, 1954. p.31
'22 tanka selected from Umi-yama no aida' Tr. by Donald Philippi. *Today's Japan*, v.11, no.1, Jan. 1961. p.67–69
'1 tanka' Übers. von Kuniyo Takayasu und Manfred Hausmann. *Ruf der Regenpfeifer*. München, Bechtle Verlag, 1961. p.102
'사랑' 崔一秀訳 「기다리고있네」 서울 韓国政経社 1966. p.182

SHIBA Fukio 芝 不器男 1903–1930

Haiku 俳句

'6 haiku' *A history of haiku v.2*, by R. H. Blyth. Tokyo, Hokuseido, 1964. p.227–229
'1 haiku' Tr. by Takamasa Sasaki. *Eigo Seinen*, v.122, no.5, 1976. p.231

SHIBA Ryōtarō 司馬遼太郎 1923–

Kokyō bōjigataku sōrō 故郷忘じがたく候

'故郷을어이잊으리까' 金巣雲訳 「文学思想」 第49号

SHIBA Ryōtarō

1976. p.104–136; 「故郷을어이잇으리까」 서울 文
学思想出版部 1977. p.6–72

Kunitori monogatari 国盗り物語

「実録大河小説 大志 1–6」 安東民訳 서울 大河出版社
1973. 6冊

Ryōma ga yuku 龍馬がゆく

「大河実録 国運 1–5」 元應瑞訳 서울 河西出版社 1973.
5冊
「大河小説 大望 21–26」 朴在姫訳 서울 東西文化社
1974. 6冊

Saka no ue no kumo 坂の上の雲

「大河小説 大望 30–35」 朴在姫訳 서울 東西文化社
1974. 6冊
「大河実録 国運 6–10」 元應瑞訳 서울 河西出版社
1975. 5冊

Tōge 峠

「大河小説 大望 27–29」 朴在姫訳 서울 東西文化社
1974. 3冊

「雙金刀」 宋文訳 서울 大興出版社 1974. 3冊

SHIBA Shirō 斯波四郎 1910–

Santō 山塔

'山塔' 李浩哲訳 「芥川賞小説集」 서울 新丘文化社
1960. p.217–251; 「깊은江」 서울 三耕社 1971.
p.217–251
'山塔' 朴敬勘訳 「日本文学大全集 10」 서울 東西文化
院 1975. p.421–450

SHIBAKI Yoshiko 芝木好子 1914–

Fuchin 浮沈

'Ups and downs' Tr. by Grace Suzuki. *Ukiyo.*
Tokyo, Phoenix Books, 1954. p.100–111;
Ukiyo, ed. by J. Gluck. N. Y. Vanguard Press,
1963. p.152–158; London, Universal Library,
1964. p.152–158

Fuyu no tsubaki 冬の椿

「冬天裡的茶花」 朱佩蘭訳 台北 七十年代出版公司 1970.
260p.

Musume no yukue 娘の行方

'両幅畫' 廖清秀訳 「投水自殺営救業」 台北 蘭開書局
1968. p.129–151
'女兒的歸宿' 朱佩蘭訳 「伊豆的舞娘」 嘉義 明山書局
1969. p.71–90

Otoko to onna 男と女

'男與女' 朱佩蘭訳 「伊豆的舞娘」 嘉義 明山書局 1969.
p.25–47

Seishun no yukue 青春の行方

'青春遠逝' 朱佩蘭訳 「伊豆的舞娘」 嘉義 明山書局 1969.
p.49–70

'彩虹' 朱佩蘭訳 「伊豆的舞娘」 嘉義 明山書局 1969.
p.5–24

SHIBATA Michiko 柴田道子 1934–1975

Hitosuji no hikari ひとすじの光

'A ray of light' Tr. by Lora Sharnoff. *Japan
Quarterly,* v.24, no.4, 1977. p.435–462

SHIBATA Renzaburō 柴田錬三郎 1917–1978

Chansu wa sando aru チャンスは三度ある

「機會」 徐白訳 台中 中台書局 1959. 517p.
「追求」 徐白訳 台北 中台書局 1961. 517p.; 台北 文
化圖書 1963. 317p.

Haiboku 敗北

'敗北' 權純萬訳 「日本代表作家百人集 4」 서울 希望出
版社 1966. p.418–428; 「日本短篇小説全集 5」 서
울 新太陽社 1969. p.258–268
'敗北' 朴敬勘訳 「日本文学大全集 10」 서울 1975.
p.273–284

Kettōsha 決闘者

「決闘者宮本武蔵」 王家成訳 台北 四季出版社 1976.
2冊

Korega fukushū da これが復讐だ

'復讐' 徐白訳 「日本短篇譯集 2」 台北 晩蟬書店 1969.
p.61–86

Onna no teki 女の敵

「無宿女」 金企宇訳 서울 藝文館 1968. 274p.
「春愁點點」 朱佩蘭訳 台北 皇冠雑誌社 1969. 425p.
「七顛八起」 康曙海訳 「経営大望 8」 서울 鮮京図書
1975. p.1–457
「無宿女」 成杰訳 서울 芸苑社 1972; 서울 普京出
版社 1975. 2冊

Sannin no onna 三人の女

「紅色藍色茶色」 李學熙訳 台北 希代書版公司 1975.
308p.

Wakakute warukute sugoi koitsura 若くて，悪くて，
凄いこいつら

「這一羣」 徐白訳 台北 文星書店 1963. 293p.
「一網兜収」 徐白訳 台北 文星書店 1964. 307p.

Yume ni tsumi ari 夢に罪あり

「三姉妹」 徐白訳 台北 文星書店 1965. 484p.

Zūzūshii yatsu 図々しい奴

「出世街道」 李永秀訳 서울 志成社 1961. 296p.
'快男大成' 康曙海訳 「経営大望 6」 서울 鮮京図書
1975. 446p.

'構想' 徐白訳 「日本短篇譯集 1」 台北 晩蟬書店 1969.
p.77–101
「人間経営 45–46」 李京南訳 서울 平和文化社 1976.
2冊
「大物人間 15–16」 李京南訳 서울 韓音社 1976. 2冊

SHIBUYA Teisuke 渋谷定輔 1905–

Poems 詩

'Мои стихи' Перевод Анатолия Мамонова.
Вкус хризантемы. Москва, Восточная Литература, 1976. p.107

SHIGA Mitsuko 四賀光子 1885–1976

Tanka 短歌

'Domestic animals; My old home' Tr. Asataro Miyamori. *Masterpieces of Japanese poetry, ancient and modern.* Tokyo, Maruzen, 1936; Tokyo, Taiseido, 1956; N. Y. Greenwood Press, 1971. p.721–722

SHIGA Naoya 志賀直哉 1883–1971

Abashiri made 網走まで

'到網走去' 周作人訳 「小説月報」 第12巻4号 1921. p.1–6;「現代日本小説集」上海 商務印書館 1923; 「日本現代小説集 2」 上海 商務印書館 1930. p.206–219;「日本小説集」上海 商務印書館 193?.
'Abashiri made' Tr. by C. S. Bavier. *The Pen*, 1932.
'到網走去' 楼適夷訳 「志賀直哉小説集」 北京 作家出版社 1956. p.36–51
'Até Abashiri' Tr. de Shinobu Saiki. *Maravilhas do conto japonês.* São Paulo, Editôra Cultrix, 1962. p.74–82

Akanishi Kakita 赤西蠣太

'Akanishi Kakita' Übers. von Kenji Takahashi. *Nippon*, Jahrgang 2, 1936. p.20–37
'Liebesbriefe eines Spions' *Geschichten und Erzählungen aus Japan*, hrg. von B. Matsuoka. Leipzig, Fikentscher Verlag, 1950. p.229–251
'Akanishi Kakita' Tr. by Saburo Haneda. *The Reeds*, v.2, 1956. p.104–125
'赤西蠣太' 楼適夷訳 「志賀直哉小説集」 北京 作家出版社 1956. p.36–51
'Le samourai' Tr. par Marc Mécréant. *Le samourai.* Paris, Marabout, 1970. p.143–166

Akikaze 秋風

'Autumn wind' Tr. by Michihiro Niijima. *Eigo Kenkyu*, v.41, no.8–no.11, 1952. v.44, no.5, 1955.

Amagaeru 雨蛙

'Les rainettes' Tr. par Marc Mécréant. *Le samourai.* Paris, Marabout, 1970. p.197–213

An'ya kōro 暗夜行路

'暗夜行路' 朴栄濬訳 「世界文学全集 後期 17」 서울 正音社 1962. p.235–378
A dark night's passing. Tr. by Edwin McClellan. Tokyo, Kodansha International, 1976. 408p.

Araginu 荒絹

'Araginu' Tr. by Eric S. Bell and Eiji Ukai. *Eminent authors of contemporary Japan. v.1.* Tokyo, Kaitakusha, 1930. p.149–157
'荒絹' 謝六逸訳 「志賀直哉集」 上海 中華書局 1935. p.21–28
'Fil d'aragne' Tr. par Marc Mécréant. *Le samourai.* Paris, Marabout, 1970. p.5–11
'荒絹' 黄錦堂訳 「荒絹」 台北 大明王氏出版公司 1972. p.231–236

Aru otoko sono ane no shi 或る男其姉の死

'一個人' 謝六逸訳 「志賀直哉集」 上海 中華書局 1935. p.51–176;「志賀直哉小説集」 北京 作家出版社 1956. p.158–230

Asagao 朝顔

'Les belles-de-jour' Tr. par Marc Mécréant. *Le samourai.* Paris, Marabout, 1970. p.313–316

Ban 鴇

'A moorhen' Tr. by Eric S. Bell and Eiji Ukai. *Eminent authors of contemporary Japan v.2.* Tokyo, Kaitakusha, 1930. p.147–153

Chijō 痴情

'Rage d'amour' Tr. par Marc Mécréant. *Le samourai.* Paris, Marabout, 1970. p. 233–245

Fūfu 夫婦

'Couples' Tr. par Marc Mécréant. *Le samourai.* Paris, Marabout, 1970. p.373–375

Haha no shi to atarashii haha 母の死と新しい母

'死母與新母' 謝六逸訳 「志賀直哉集」 上海 中華書局 1935. p.177–191

Haiiro no tsuki 灰色の月

'The gray moon' Tr. by Ineko Sato. *Eigo Seinen*, v.92, no.8, 1946. p.239–241
'A gray moon' Tr. by Saburo Haneda. *The Reeds*, v.2, 1956. p.92–96
'灰色的月亮' 楼適夷訳 「譯文」 1956年5月 p.66–68;「志賀直哉小説集」 北京 作家出版社 1956. p.247–250
'灰色的月亮' 彭澤周訳 「明報」 第8巻8期 1973. p.96–98
'The ashen moon' Tr. by Stephen W. Kohl. *Monumenta Nipponica*, v.32, no.2, 1977. p.222–224

Han no hanzai 范の犯罪

'Le crime du jongleur' Tr. par Serge Elisséev. *Japon et Extrême-Orient*, no.1, Dec. 1923; *Neuf nouvelles japonaises*, par S. Elisséev. Paris, G. van Œst, 1924. p.1–16
Krimo de Fan. Tr. Machiko Kaji. Tokyo, Esperanto Kenkyusha, 1926. 31p.
'The murder' Tr. by Eiji Ukai and Eric S. Bell. *Japan Times*, Aug. 28, 1927.
'范某的犯罪' 謝六逸訳 「范某的犯罪」 上海 現代書局 1929;「志賀直哉集」 上海 中華書局 1935. p.29–49
'A murder case' Tr. by Eric S. Bell and Eiji Ukai. *Eminent authors of contemporary Japan v.2.* Tokyo, Kaitakusha, 1930. p.131–147
'A zsonglör büne' Ford. Thein Alfréd. *Mai Japán dekameron.* Budapest, Nyugat, 1935. p.229–244
'Han's crime' Tr. by Ivan Morris. *Japan Quarterly*, v.2, no.4, 1955. p.460–469; *Modern Japanese literature*, ed. by D. Keene. N. Y. Grove Press, 1956; Tokyo, Tuttle, 1957. p.261–271; *Modern Japanese short stories.* Tokyo, Japan Publications Trading Co. 1960. p.1–14; Rev. ed. Tokyo, Japan Publications Trading Co. 1970.
'El crimen de Han' Tr. por Carla Viola Soto. *Sur*, no.249, Nov.-Dec. 1957. p.33–42
'Zbrodnia Hana' Przeł. Anna Gostyńska. *Irys, opowiadania japońskie.* Warszawa, Państwowy Instytut Wydawniczy, 1960. p.14–28
'Han's crime' Tr. by Ryozo Matsumoto. *Japanese literature, new and old.* Tokyo, Hokuseido, 1961. p.89–104
'Il delitto di Han' Tr. di Atsuko Ricca Suga.

Narratori giapponesi moderni. Milano, Bompiani, 1965. p.171–184

'Das Verbrechen des Han' Übers. von Margarete Donath. *Japan erzählt.* Hamburg, Fischer, 1969. p.67–76

'Le crime de Han' Tr. par Marc Mécréant. *Le samourai.* Paris, Marabout, 1970. p.53–67

'Das Verbrechen des Han' Deutsch von Oscar Benl. *Träume aus zehn Nächten.* Berlin, Aufbau Verlag, 1975. p.97–109

'Zbrodnia Chana' Przeł. Zdzisław Reszelewski. *Tygodnik Demokratyczny,* no.43, 1975. p.21, no.44, 1975. p.20

'Преступление Хана' Перевод Т. Григорьевой. *Иностранная Литература,* январь 1975. p.121–126; *И была любовь, и была ненависть.* Москва, Наука, 1975. p.205–214

Horibata no sumai 濠端の住まい

'城濠居' 錢稻孫訳 「藝文雜誌」 第1巻5期 1943. p.7–9

'Dwelling by the moat' Tr. by Edward Fowler. *Monumenta Nipponica,* v.32, no.2, 1977. p.225–229

Itazura いたづら

'Une farce' Tr. par Marc Mécréant. *Le samourai.* Paris, Marabout, 1970. p.372

Jūichigatsu mikka gogo no koto 十一月三日午後の事

'An incident on the afternoon of November third' Tr. by Iwao Matsubara. *Osaka Mainichi,* Nov. 29, 1925.

'十一月三日午後的事' 適夷訳 「譯文」 1956年5月 p.68–73

'十一月三日午后的事' 楼適夷訳 「志賀直哉小説集」 北京 作家出版社 1956. p.122–128

'十一月三日午後的事' 「日本作家十二人集」 香港 新學書店 1959. p.127–134

'В полдень третьего ноября' Перевод Т. Григорьевой. *И была любовь, и была ненависть.* Москва, Наука, 1975. p.199–204

Kamisori 剃刀

'The razor' Tr. by Eric S. Bell and Eiji Ukai. *Eminent authors of contemporary Japan v.1.* Tokyo, Kaitakusha, 1930. p.131–146

'The razor' Tr. by Francis H. Mathy. *Monumenta Nipponica,* v.13, no.3–4, 1957. p.165–176

'The razor' Tr. by Nobuyuki Honna. *Kinjo Gakuin Daigaku Ronshu,* no.36, 1968. p.94–104

'Le rasoir' Tr. par Marc Mécréant. *Le samourai.* Paris, Marabout, 1970. p.13–25

Kinosaki nite 城の崎にて

'At Kinosaki' Tr. by Ineko Sato. *Eigo Seinen,* v. 90, no.5, 1944. p.107–110, no.6, 1944. p.147–150

'In Kinosaki' Übers. von Oscar Benl. *In Kinosaki, Der Herbst.* Wolfenbüttel, Kallmeyer, 1951.

'At Kinosaki' Tr. by Saburo Haneda. *The Reeds,* v.1, 1955. p.115–141

'At Kinosaki' Tr. by Edward Seidensticker. *Modern Japanese literature,* ed. by D. Keene. N. Y. Grove Press, 1956; Tokyo, Tuttle, 1957. p.272–277

'In Kinosaki' Aus dem Japanischen von Oscar Benl. *Japan, Geistige Begegnung.* Tübingen, Erdmann, 1964. p.131–136

'En Kinosaki' Tr. Kyuzo Ito. *El japana literaturo.* Tokyo, Japana Esperanto Instituto, 1965.

p.194–200

'Soggiorno a Kinosaki' Tr. di R. Vulpitta. *Antologia della letteratura coreana e giapponese.* Milano, Fratelli Fabbri, 1969. p.253–257

'A Kinosaki' Tr. par Marc Mécréant. *Le samourai.* Paris, Marabout, 1970. p.97–106

'在城崎的時候' 黄玉燕訳 「純文學」(香港版) 第10巻6期 1972. p.36–39

'На водах в Киносаки' Перевод В. Скальника. *И была любовь, и была ненависть.* Москва, Наука, 1975. p.215–220

Kōjinbutsu no fūfu 好人物の夫婦

'The man and wife' Tr. by Nobuyuki Honna. *Kinjo Gakuin Daigaku Ronshu,* no.36, 1968. p.105–119

'Mari et femme' Tr. par Marc Mécréant. *Le samourai.* Paris, Marabout, 1970. p.125–142

Ko o nusumu hanashi 児を盗む話

'Le voleur d'enfant' Tr. par Marc Mécréant. *Le samourai.* Paris, Marabout, 1970. p.69–96

Kozō no kamisama 小僧の神様

'Die Gottheit des Burschen Senkichi' Übers. von Heinz Brasch. *Yamato,* Jahrgang 2, 1930. p.278–287

'The patron saint of a shop-boy' Tr. by Eric S. Bell and Eiji Ukai. *Eminent authors of contemporary Japan v.2.* Tokyo, Kaitakusha, 1930. p.113–129

'The shop-boy's god' *Selections from modern Japanese writers,* by A. L. Sadler. Sydney, Australian Medical Publications, 1943. p.63–71

'The guardian god of an apprentice' Tr. by Saburo Haneda. *The Reeds,* v.1, 1955. p.115–128

'The apprentice's patron God' Tr. by Shigeru Tadokoro. *Wakayama Daigaku Gakugei Gakubu Kiyo, Jinbun kagaku hen,* no.6, 1956. p.17–26

'学徒の菩薩' 楼適夷訳 「志賀直哉小説集」 北京 作家出版社 1956. p.148–157

'The patron saint' Tr. by Michael Y. Matsudaira. *The heart is alone,* ed. by Richard McKinnon. Tokyo, Hokuseido, 1957. p.74–85; *The Mentor book of modern Asian literature,* ed. by D. B. Shimer. N. Y. New American Library, 1969. p.423–432

'Dio de subkomizo' Tr. Manzaua Maki. *El japana literaturo.* Tokyo, Japana Esperanto Instituto, 1965. p.201–210

'Le petit commis et son Dieu' Tr. par Marc Mécréant. *Le samourai.* Paris, Marabout, 1970. p.167–180

'小徒弟的天使' 余直夫訳 「純文學」(香港版) 第10巻5期 1972. p.35–42

'Бог мальчугана' Перевод Т. Григорьевой. *И была любовь, и была ненависть.* Москва, Наука, 1975. p.190–198

'Theppachaokhongnunoi' Tr. Marasri Saengnikorn. *Rueng sun yeepun 1.* Bangkok, Uksornsasna. 1977. p.55–72

Kuma クマ

'Kuma' Tr. par Marc Mécréant. *Le samourai.* Paris, Marabout, 1970. p.293–307

Kuniko 邦子

'Kuniko' Übers. von Oscar Benl. *Flüchtiges Leben, moderne japanische Erzählungen.* Berlin, Landsmann, 1942.
'구니꼬' 李柱訓訳 「日本代表作家百人集 2」 서울 希望出版社 1966. p.40–64; 「日本短篇文学全集 2」 서울 新太陽社 1969. p.104–128
'Kuniko' Tr. par Marc Mécréant. *Le samourai.* Paris, Marabout, 1970. p.247–291
'邦子' 李喜春訳 「日本文学大全集 10」 서울 東西文化院 1975. p.165–190

Kurōdiasu no nikki クローディアスの日記

'En marge de «Hamlet», journal de Claudius' Tr. par Marc Mécréant. *Le samourai.* Paris, Marabout, 1970. p.33–52

Manazuru 真鶴

'Manazuru' Übers. von Oscar Benl. *In Kinosaki, Der Herbst.* Wolfenbüttel, Kallmeyer, 1951.
'眞鶴' 楼適夷訳 「志賀直哉小説集」 北京 作家出版社 1956. p.242–246
'眞鶴' 「日本短篇小説選」 香港 藝美圖書公司 1959. p.18–23
'眞鶴' 高汝鴻訳 「日本短篇小説集」 台北 台湾商務印書館 1969. p.27–34
'Manazuru' Přel. Vlasta Winkelhöferová. *Nový Orient*, v.28, no.10, 1973. p.1–2
'Manazuru' Tr. by Stephen W. Kohl. *Monumenta Nipponica*, v.32, no.2, 1977. p.218–221

Nanohana to komusume 菜の花と小娘

'A little girl and a flowering colza' Tr. by Michihiro Niijima. *Eigo Kenkyu*, v.44, no.9, 1955. p.28–32

Nijūdai ichimen 廿代一面

'20代의一面' 金潤成訳 「世界短篇文学全集 7」 서울 啓蒙社 1966. p.192–228; 「世界短篇文学全集 9」 서울 三珍社 1971. p.40–76; 「世界代表短篇文学全集 9」 서울 三熙社 1976. p.40–76; 「世界短篇文学全集 9」 서울 新韓出版社 1976. p.72–135

Rōjin 老人

'老人' 湯鶴逸訳 「東方雑誌」 第23巻22期 1926. p.107–110
'老人' 馮厚生訳 「小説月報」 第22巻3号 1931. p.465–467
'An old man' Tr. by Arthur L. Sadler. *Selections from modern Japanese writers*, ed. by A. L. Sadler. Sydney, Australian Medical Publications, 1943. p.40–44
'老人' 楼適夷訳 「志賀直哉小説集」 北京 作家出版社 1956. p.9–12
'老人' 「日本作家十二人集」 香港 新學書店 1959. p.87–92
'老人' 金仲達訳 「純文學」(台湾版) 第4巻6期 1968. p.74–78
'Le vieil homme' Tr. par Marc Mécréant. *Le samourai.* Paris, Marabout, 1970. p.27–32
'老人' 「世界著名作家小説選」 香港 上海書局 1977. p.393–398

Ryūkō kanbō 流行感冒

'流行性感冒' 侍玗訳 「志賀直哉小説集」 北京 作家出版社 1956. p.129–147
'流行性感冒' 「日本作家十二人集」 香港 新學書店 1959. p.105–126

Sasaki no baai 佐々木の場合

'佐佐木的遭遇' 楼適夷訳 「志賀直哉小説集」 北京 作家出版社 1956. p.25–35
'佐佐木的遭遇' 「日本作家十二人集」 香港 新學書店 1959. p.93–104
'Le cas Sasaki' Tr. par Marc Mécréant. *Le samourai.* Paris, Marabout, 1970. p.107–124

Seibei to hyōtan 清兵衛と瓢箪

'Seibei and hyotan' Tr. by Taro Ito. *Jokyu Eigo*, Dec. 1929–March 1930.
'清兵衛與壺蘆' 周作人訳 「現代日本小説集」 上海 商務印書館 1923; 「日本現代小説集 2」 上海 商務印書館 1930. p.220–227
'Seibei and the gourd' *Selections from modern Japanese writers*, by A. L. Sadler. Sydney, Australian Medical Publications, 1943. p.44–48
'The artist' Tr. by Ivan Morris. *Japan Quarterly*, v.2, no.4, 1955. p.456–460
'Seibei and his gourds' Tr. by Saburo Haneda. *The Reeds*, v.2, 1956. p.97–103
'清兵衛與胡蘆' 楼適夷訳 「志賀直哉小説集」 北京 作家出版社 1956. p.20–24
'清兵衛和胡蘆' 新興書局編集部訳 「日本短篇小説選」 台北 新興書局 1958. p.103–107; 台南 鳴宇出版社 1972. p.103–107
'Seibei i tykwy' Przeł. Anna Gostyńska. *Irys, opowiadania japońskie.* Warszawa, Państwowy Instytut Wydawniczy, 1960. p.5–13
'Seibei's gourds' Tr. by Ivan Morris. *Modern Japanese stories*, ed. by I. Morris. London, Spottiswoode, 1961; Tokyo, Tuttle, 1962. p.83–89
'Sěniman' Děngan kata pěngantar oleh James Kirkup. *Shoji.* Kuala Lumpur, Oxford Univ. Press, 1961. p.10–16
'Seibei und seine Flaschenkürbisse' Aus dem Japanischen von Fumio Hashimoto. *Japan, Geistige Begegnung.* Tübingen, Erdmann, 1964. p.307–312; *Eine Glocke in Fukagawa.* Tübingen, Erdmann, 1969. p.307–312
'Der Künstler' Deutsch von Monique Humbert. *Nippon.* Zürich, Diogenes, 1965. p.97–104
'Szébé es a dísztök' Ford. Sz. Holti Mária. *Modern Japán elbeszélők.* Budapest, Európa Könyvkiadó, 1967. p.39–43
'清兵衛與葫蘆' 金仲達訳 「純文學」(台湾版) 第4巻6期 1968. p.74–78
'A dísztök' Ford. Sz. Holti Mária. *Nagyvilág*, 1976; *Törtenetek as öt világrész gyerekeiről.* Budapest, Móra, 1976. p.80–84
'Der Flaschenkürbis' Übers. von Oscar Benl. *Der Flaschenkürbis.* München, Nymphenburger, n.d.

Seigiha 正義派

'The righteous' Tr. by Kenji Takahashi. *Contemporary Japan*, v.3, Dec. 1937. p.486–491
'正义派' 楼適夷訳 「志賀直哉小説集」 北京 作家出版社 1956. p.13–19
'正義派' 「日本短篇小説選」 香港 藝美圖書公司 1959. p.24–30
'正義派' 高汝鴻訳 「日本短篇小説集」 台北 台湾商務印書館 1969. p.35–44
'Kabuankarnyuttitham' Tr. Malee Suriyamongkol. *Rueng sun yeepun 1.* Bangkok, Uksornsasna, 1977. p.43–54

Taifū 台風

'Taijfun' Přel. M. Novák. *Nový Orient*, no.4, 1965.

SHIGA Naoya

Takibi 焚火

'Les feux' Tr. par Serge Elisséev. *Le jardin des pivoines*. Paris, Au Sans Pareil, 1927. p.47–64
'焚火' 謝六逸訳 「志賀直哉集」 上海 中華書局 1935. p.193–212
'焚火' 葉素訳 「焚火」 上海 天馬書店 1935.
'篝火' 楼適夷訳 「志賀直哉小説集」 北京 作家出版社 1956. p.231–241
'Feux' Tr. par R. P. Sauveur Candau. *Feux, et Le pluvier*. Tokyo, Daigaku Syorin, 1961. p.1–32
'La flambée au bord du lac' Tr. par Marc Mécréant. *Le samourai*. Paris, Marabout, 1970. p.181–196
'Fires' Tr. by S. F. Richards. *Literature East and West*, v.15, no.4, v.16, no.1 & 2, 1972. p.791–802
'The bonfire' Tr. by Dennis Keene. *Japan Quarterly*, v.22, no.2, 1975. p.144–150

Tenshō 転生

'Tensho' Übers. von Oscar Benl. *In Kinosaki, Der Herbst*. Wolfenbüttel, Kallmeyer, 1951.
'Reincarnation' Tr. by Shigeru Tadokoro. *Wakayama Daigaku Gakugei Gakubu Kiyo*, no.7, 1957. p.20–25
'Die Wiedergeburt' Aus dem Japanischen von Oscar Benl. *Japan, Geistige Begegnung*. Tübingen, Erdmann, 1964. p.278–281; *Eine Glocke in Fukagawa*. Tübingen, Erdmann, 1969. p.278–381
'Métempsycoses' Tr. par Marc Mécréant *Le samourai*. Paris, Marabout, 1970. p.215–222
'Tensho' Tr. by Wen-kai Kung. *The East*, v.13, no.1 & 2, Nov. 1976. p.71–72, 79

Wakai 和解

'和解' 張資平訳 「東方雑誌」 第24巻7期 1927. p.78–94. 8期 1927. p.86–100. 9期 1927. p.77–98; 「襯衣」 上海 光華書店 1928.
'和解' 張夢麟訳 「志賀直哉小説集」 北京 作家出版社 1956. p.52–121
「和解」 北京 人民文学出版社 1960. 1冊
「和解」 香港 上海書局 1960. 108p.

Yamabato 山鳩

'Les palombes' Tr. par Marc Mécréant. *Le samourai*. Paris, Marabout, 1970. p.309–311

Yamashina no kioku 山科の記憶

'Naguère à Yamashina' Tr. par Marc Mécréant. *Le samourai*. Paris, Marabout, 1970. p.223–231

Yadokari no shi 宿かりの死

'Death of a hermit crab' Tr. by S. G. Brickley. *The writing of idiomatic English*. Tokyo, Kenkyusha, 1951. p.96–101

Yoru no hikari 夜の光

'Un vieillard' Tr. par Moise Charles Haguenauer. *Japon et Extrême-Orient*, no.3, 1924. p.229–234

Yuki no hi 雪の日

'雪之日' 謝六逸訳 「志賀直哉集」 上海 中華書局 1935. p.213–223

SHIINA Rinzō 椎名麟三 1911–1973

Ai no shōgen 愛の証言

The flowers are fallen. Tr. by Sydney Gifford. London, Heinemann, 1961. 208p.

Aru fukō na hōkokusho ある不幸な報告書

'어떤不幸한報告書' 朴在森訳 「世界短篇文学全集 7」 서울 啓蒙社 1966. p.379–391; 「世界短篇文学全集 9」 서울 三珍社 1971. p.253–266; 「世界代表短篇文学全集 9」 서울 三熙社 1976. p.253–266; 「世界短篇文学全集 9」 서울 新韓出版社 1976. p.58–80

Baishaku nin 媒灼人

'The go-between' Tr. by Noah S. Brannen. *The go-between, and other stories*. Valley Forge, Judson Press, 1970. p.61–106

Daisan no shōgen 第三の証言

'A third witness' Tr. by Noah S. Brannen. *Japan Christian Quarterly*, v.39, no.4, 1973. p.238–247

Eien naru joshō 永遠なる序章

'永遠한序章' 鮮于輝訳 「世界戦後文学全集 7」 서울 新丘文化社 1962. p.294–377

Hanpamono no hankō 半端者の反抗

'The lukewarm one' Tr. by Noah S. Brannen. *The go-between, and other stories*. Valley Forge, Judson Press, 1970. p.107–128

Jiyū no kanata de 自由の彼方で

'自由의저쪽에서' 洪性裕訳 「現代世界文学全集 12」 서울 新丘文化社 1968. p.311–414
Приговор, не приведенный в исполнение, на узбекском языке. Тошкент, Гослитиздат, 1971. 144p.

Nimotsu 荷物

'가방' 閔暎訳 「日本研究」 第19巻12号 1974. p.59–64

Omoki nagare no naka ni 重き流れのなかに

'混濁한흐름속에' 金元基訳 「日本代表作家百人集 4」 서울 希望出版社 1966. p.148–186; 「日本短篇文学全集 4」 서울 新太陽社 1969. p.356–394
'From "In the sluggish stream"' *Tri-Quarterly*, no.31, 1974. p.46–57

Shin'ya no shuen 深夜の酒宴

'Midnight banquet' Tr. by Noah S. Brannen. *The go-between, and other stories*. Valley Forge, Judson Press, 1970. p.17–60

Yoru no tansaku 夜の探索

'Night search' Tr. by John O. Barksdale. *Japan Christian Quarterly*, v.42, no.1, 1976. p.33–44

Essays エッセイ

'The mix-up' Tr. by Noah S. Brannen. *Japan Christian Quarterly*, v.38, no.4, 1972. p.241–252
'Dostoyevsky and I' Tr. by Robert Epp. *Japan Christian Quarterly*, v.39, no.4, 1973. p.220–222
'The lie detector' Tr. by Noah S. Brannen. *Japan Christian Quarterly*, v.39, no.4, 1973. p.231–234

'My pin-up' Tr. by Noah S. Brannen. *Japan Christian Quarterly*, v.39, no.4, 1973. p.235–237

'On suicide' Tr. by Robert Epp. *Japan Christian Quarterly*, v.39, no.4, 1973. p.223–230

'Sprawozdanie' Przeł. Blanka Yonekawa. *Przekrój*, no.1542, 1974. p.15–17

SHIMA Shōsuke 島 匠介 1913–

Poems 詩

'Плывущий букет' Перевод Анатолия Мамонова. *Песни Хиросимы.* Москва, Худож. Лит. 1964. p.21–22; *Вкус хризантемы.* Москва, Восточная Литература, 1976. p.108

'To a drifting bouquet' Tr. by Miyao Ohara. *The songs of Hiroshima.* Tokyo, Taihei Shuppansha, 1971. p.62–64

SHIMADA Kazuo 島田一男 1909–

Shinigami no chizu 死神の地図

「死神的地圖」 何年訳 台北 交通出版社 n.d. 3冊

SHIMADA Seihō 島田青峰 1882–1944

Haiku 俳句

'8 haiku' Tr. by Asataro Miyamori. *Anthology of haiku, ancient and modern.* Tokyo, Maruzen, 1932. p.751–756

'The parasol' Tr. by Harold Gould Henderson; *The bamboo broom.* Tokyo, J. L. Thompson, 1933; London, Kegan Paul, 1933. p.126; *From the bamboo broom.* N. Y. Japan Reference Library, 1940.

'New Year's day in snow; Rape flowers' Tr. by Asataro Miyamori. *Haiku poems, ancient and modern.* Tokyo, Maruzen, 1940. p.348

'1 haiku' Übers. von Günther Debon. *Im Schnee die Fähre.* München, Piper, 1960. p.52

'1 haiku' *A history of haiku v.2,* by R. H. Blyth. Tokyo, Hokuseido, 1964. p.243–244

'Summer heat; New Year's day' Tr. by Kenneth Yasuda. *A pepper-pod.* Tokyo, Tuttle, 1976. p.89

SHIMAKI Akahiko 島木赤彦 1876–1926

Tanka 短歌

'A marsh-tit; At the hot spring of Kami-Kochi; My soul; The hill covered with green leaves; The voices of my children; My sorrow; Mount Fuji' Tr. by Asataro Miyamori. *Masterpieces of Japanese poetry, ancient and modern.* Tokyo, Maruzen, 1936; Tokyo, Taiseido, 1956; N. Y. Greenwood Press, 1971. p.651–654

'10 tanka' Tr. by Shigeshi Nishimura. *The Current of the World,* v.16, no.11, 12, 1939.

'Tanka' Tr. par Kuni Matsuo et Steinilber-Oberlin. *Anthologie des poètes japonais contemporains.* Paris, Mercure de France, 1939. p.261–263

'2 tanka' Tr. by V. H. Viglielmo. *Japanese literature in the Meiji era.* Tokyo, Obunsha, 1955. p.411

'Nuit d'hiver' *La poésie japonaise,* par Karl Petit. Paris, Seghers, 1959. p.196

'Kinderstimmen' Übers. von Günther Debon. *Im Schnee die Fähre.* München, Piper, 1960. p.21

'2 tanka' Übers. von Kuniyo Takayasu und Manfred Hausmann. *Ruf der Regenpfeifer.* München, Bechtle Verlag, 1961. p.98

SHIMAKI Kensaku 島木健作 1903–1945

Aka gaeru 赤蛙

'The red frog' Tr. by Tadao Katayama. *The Reeds,* v.3, 1957. p.61–69

'The frog' Tr. by John Bester. *Japan P.E.N. News,* no.10, Dec. 1962. p.1–5

'Красная лягушка' Перевод Д. Бугаевой. *Красная лягушка.* Москва, Наука, 1973. p. 80–87; *Современная Восточная новелла.* Москва, Наука, 1975. p.128–134

'赤蛙' 江上訳 「日本名家小説選」 高雄 大舞台書苑 1976. p.47–57

Kunō 苦悩

'Suferado' Tr. T. Hattori. *Karcero.* Kyoto, Kaniya, 1937. p.55–94

Kuroneko 黒猫

'A fekete macska' Ford. Sz. Holti Mária. *Modern Japán elbeszélők.* Budapest, Európa Könyvkiadó, 1967. p.234–239

'Черный кот' Перевод Д. Бугаевой. *No.36; новеллы японских писателей.* Москва, Наука, 1968. p.132–139

Mōmoku 盲目

'Слепой' *Интернациональная Литература,* 1935, No.4. p.54–61

'Blindigo' Tr. T. Hattori. *Karcero.* Kyoto, Kaniya, 1937. p.124–163

Rai 癩

'麻瘋' 陸少懿訳 「譯文」 新1巻5期 1936. p.927–950, 1178–1206

'Lepro' Tr. T. Hattori. *Karcero.* Kyoto, Kaniya, 1937. p.1–54

Tenraku 転落

'Falo' Tr. T. Hattori. *Karcero.* Kyoto, Kaniya, 1937. p.95–123

SHIMAMURA Hōgetsu 島村抱月 1871–1918

Criticism 評論

'文藝上的自然主義' 曉風訳 「小説月報」 第12巻12号 1921.

SHIMAMURA Tamizō

SHIMAMURA Tamizō　島村民蔵　1888–1970

Criticism　評論

'德國的民衆劇場' 柯 訳 「北平晨報劇刊」 第18期 1931.

SHIMAOKA Shin　嶋岡　晨　1932–

Poems　詩

'Story of a lonely elephant'　Tr. by Makoto Ueda. *Literary Review*, v.6, no.1, 1962.　p.118
'青春；遺書' 辛東門訳 「世界戦後文学全集 9」 서울 新丘文化社 1962. p.247
'Looking at a child's face; Palmways'　Tr. by Thomas Fitzsimmons. *Japanese poetry now*. London, André Deutsch, 1972. p.99–100; *Japanese poetry today*. N. Y. Schocken Books, 1972.　p.101–102

SHIMAZAKI Tōson　島崎藤村　1872–1943

Arashi　嵐

'Storm'　Tr. by Ineko Sato. *Eigo Seinen*, v.90, no.11, 1944.　p.324–326, v.90, no.12, 1944. p.352–353, v.91, no.2, 1945.　p.23, v.91, no.3, 1945.　p.38–39
'暴風雨' 金龍済訳 「日本代表作家百人集 1」 서울 希望出版社 1966. p.332–364; 「日本短篇文学全集 1」 서울 新太陽社 1969. p.332–364
'暴風雨' 申基宣訳 「日本文学大全集 1」 서울 東西文化院 1975. p.205–237

Asakusa dayori　浅草だより

'從淺草来' 魯迅摘訳 「壁下譯叢」 上海 北新書局 1929; 「魯迅全集 16」 上海 魯迅全集出版社 1938. 作家書屋 1946. 大連 光華書店 1948. 北京 人民文学出版社 1973. p.94–109; 「魯迅譯文集 5」 北京 人民文学出版社 1958. p.199–210; 「世界著名作家散文選」 香港 上海書局 1977. p.247–256

Asameshi　朝飯

'The breakfast'　Tr. by Osamu Nakamura and H. P. Holt. *Eigo Seinen*, v.31, no.10, 1914. p.298, v.31, no.11, 1914.　p.329, v.31, no.12 1914.　p.361
'Breakfast'　Tr. by Kanichi Ando. *Osaka Mainichi*, Nov. 1 and 2, 1923.

Bunpai　分配

'分配' 郭夏信訳 「世界文学全集 94」 서울 乙酉文化社 1962. p.437–455

Haha　母

'Should she have told him?'　Tr. by Asataro Miyamori. *Representative tales of Japan*. Tokyo, Sanko Shoten, 1917. p.451–472

Hakai　破戒

Нарушенный завет. Перевод Н. И. Фельдман. Москва, Гослитиздат, 1931. 318p.; Москва, Гослитиздат, 1955. 255p.
「破戒」 白雲訳 上海 上海文藝聯合 1955. 314p.
'The broken commandment'　Tr. by Edward Seidensticker. *Modern Japanese literature*, ed. by Donald Keene. N. Y. Grove Press, 1956; Tokyo, Tuttle, 1957. p.134–141
「破戒」 平白訳 北京 新文艺 1957. 1冊
「破戒」 由其訳 北京 人民文学出版社 1958. 1冊
Орынаалмаган фсвет. Которгон Б. Исабекова. Алма-Ата, Казгослитиздат, 1962. 259p.
'破戒' 金東里訳 「世界文学全集 後期 17」 서울 正音社 1962. p.15–231
Legămîntul călcat. În româneste de Ion Caraion şi Vladimir Vasiliev. Bucureşti, Editura pentru Literatura Universălă, 1966. 335p.
'L'ingiunzione violata'　Tr. di R. Vulpitta. *Antologia della letteratura coreana e giapponese*. Milano, Fratelli Fabbri, 1969. p.235–239
The broken commandment.　Tr. by Kenneth Strong. Tokyo, Univ. of Tokyo Press, 1974. 249p.
'破戒' 申基宣訳 「日本文学大全集 1」 서울 東西文化院 1975. p.2–203

Haru　春

「春」 雲山訳 台北 新興出版社 1963. 284p.

Hatsutabi　初旅

'First journey'　Tr. by S. G. Brickley. *The writing of idiomatic English*. Tokyo, Kenkyusha, 1951. p.102–108

Ie　家

Семья. Перевод Б. Поспелова и А. Рябкина. Москва, Худож. Лит. 1966. 361p.
An integral translation with an introduction of Ie. Tr. by Cecilia Segawa Seigle. Ann Arbor, University Microfilm, 1971. 659p.
The family.　Tr. by Cecilia Segawa Seigle. Tokyo, Univ. of Tokyo Press, 1976. 311p.

Kachiku　家畜

'A domestic animal'　Tr. by Torao Taketomo. *Paulownia, seven stories from contemporary writers*. N. Y. Duffield, 1918. p.117–131

Nobi jitaku　伸び支度

'Awakening'　Tr. by Eric S. Bell and Eiji Ukai. *Eminent authors of contemporary Japan v.1*. Tokyo, Kaitakusha, 1930. p.81–91

Orokana uma no hanashi　愚かな馬の話

'Ryokan Sho-nin, or Saint Ryokan'　Tr. by Yoshitaro Takenobu. *Eigo Kenkyu*, v.18, no.7, 1925. p.816–821

Osanaki mono ni　幼きものに

'給兒童' 黎烈文訳 「文學週報」 第5卷9期 1927. p.305–310

Shinsei　新生

「新生」 徐祖正訳 上海 北新書局 1927. 2冊

Tsugaru kaikyō　津軽海峡

'Tsugaru Strait'　Tr. by Torao Taketomo. *Paulownia, seven stories from contemporary Japan*. N. Y. Duffield, 1918. p.135–165

Yoake mae　夜明け前

'Aus "Yoake mae: Vor Tagesanbruch" *Nippon*, Jahrgang 2, 1936.　p.155–164

Poems 詩

'Mountain spirit; Tree spirit' *The spirit of Japanese poetry*, by Yone Noguchi. London, John Murray, 1914. p.94–95

'Junrei no uta' Tr. by Kyohei Yamamoto. *Eigo to Eibungaku*, July 1928.

'Drunken song, Tr. by Shigeshi Nishimura. *The Current of the World*, v.15, no.6, 1938. p.102–103

'Printemps, où es-tu?; Le connais-tu?; Petit poème; La mouette; Tatonnant de pensée à pensée...; Rayons de lune' Tr. par Georges Bonneau. *Lyrisme du temps present*, par G. Bonneau. Paris, Paul Geuthner, 1935. p.48–57; *Anthologie de la poésie japonaise*. Paris, Paul Geuthner, 1935. p.180–189

'Chant du vent d'automne; Mademoiselle Okumé; Sous le même parapluie; Chant nostalgique du voyage à la rivière Chikuma-gawa; Le saviez-vous?; Votre coeur; Où es-tu, printemps' Tr. par Kuni Matsuo et Steinilber-Oberlin. *Anthologie des poètes japonais contemporains*. Paris, Mercure de France, 1939. p.28–38

'Le connais-tu?' *Histoire de la littérature japonaise contemporaine*, par Georges Bonneau. Paris, Payot, 1944. p.240

'Wakanashu, Collection of young names' *Introduction to classic Japanese literature*. Tokyo, Kokusai Bunka Shinkokai, 1948. p.425–430

'Kani no kodomo' Tr. by Howard Norman. *The Youth's Companion*. v.3, no.3, 1948.

'At Komoro's old castle; Beside the Chikuma River' Tr. by Shigeshi Nishimura. *The Current of the World*, v.28, no.3, 4, 1951.

'On the carved vines and squirrel at the Zuiganji Temple of Matsushima' Tr. by Shigeshi Nishimura. *The Current of the World*, v.28, no.12, 1951. p.44

'Songs of labour' Tr. dy Shigeshi Nishimura. *Eibungaku Shicho* (Aoyama Gakuin Univ.), v.24, no.2, 1952. p.47–52

'The six maidens' Tr. by Shigeshi Nishimura. *Eibungaku Shicho* (Aoyama Gakuin Univ.), v.25, no.1, 1952. p.42–51

'In a birdless land' Tr. by Shigeshi Nishimura. *The Current of the World*, v.30, no.7, 1953. p.46

'Кокоровый орех; Утро; Придорожная слива; От сердца к сердцу' Перевод В. Н. Марковой. *Японская поэзия*. Москва, Гослитиздат, 1954. p.200–209; Изд. 2. 1956. p.286–289, 291

'Otsuta' Tr. by D. J. Enright. *Bulletin of the Japan Society of London*, no.20, Oct. 1955. p.7

'First love; By the ancient castle at Komoro' Tr. by S. Sato and C. Urdang. *Poetry*, May 1956. p.73–74

'Song on travelling the Chikuma River' Tr. by Donald Keene. *Modern Japanese literature*, ed. by D. Keene. N. Y. Grove Press, 1956; Tokyo, Tuttle, 1957. p.201–202

'2 poèmes' Tr. par Roger Bersihand. *La littérature japonaise*. Paris, Presses Universitaires de France, 1956. p.112–113

'Весна пришла; Проказы лисички' Перевод В. Марковой. *Японская поэзия*. Изд. 2. Москва, Гослитиздат, 1957. p.284, 290

'Like a fox; A coconut' *An anthology of modern Japanese poetry*, ed. and tr. by Ichiro Kono and Rikutaro Fukuda. Tokyo, Kenkyusha, 1957. p.125

'Otsuta; In the birdless country; Crafty fox; First love; A coconut' *The poetry of living Japan*, by Takamichi Ninomiya and D. J. Enright. London, John Murray, 1957. p.13–18

'Из «Песен труда»' Перевод В. Марковой. *Восточный альманах 2*. Москва, Худож. Лит. 1958. p.390–394

'Premier amour; Otsuta; Chant du voyage à la rivière Chikuma' *La poésie japonaise*, par Karl Petit. Paris, Seghers, 1959. p.183–196

'Kleines Lied; Die Möwe' Übers. von Günther Debon. *Im Schnee die Fähre*. München, Piper, 1960. p.22–23

'Die alte Burg von Komoro; Am Grunde dieses Herzens; Abendlied' Übers. von Kuniyo Takayasu und Manfred Hausmann. *Ruf der Regenpfeifer*. München, Bechtle Verlag, 1961. p.74–77

'By the old castle at Komoro; Song of travel on the Chikuma River; Coconut' Tr. by Geoffrey Bownas and Anthony Thwaite. *The Penguin book of Japanese verse*. Harmondsworth, Penguin Books, 1964. p.178

'By the old castle of Komoro (part)' *Modern Japanese poetry*, by Donald Keene. Ann Arbor, Center for Japanese Studies, Univ. of Michigan, 1964. p.18

'Die Möwe' *Lyrik des Ostens*, hrg. von Wilhelm Gundert usw. München, Carl Hanser, 1965. p.471

'2 poems' Tr. from the French by Unity Evans. *Japanese literature*. N. Y. Walker, 1965. p.95–96

'첫사랑' 崔一秀訳 「기다리고있네」 서울 韓国政経社 1966. p.93–94

'Lungo il fiume Chikuma' *La protesta poetica del Giappone*, a cura di Dacia Maraini e Michiko Nojiri. Roma, Officina Edizioni, 1968. p.21

'구름이가는곳; 가을의노래; 소시' 「永遠한世界名詩全集 2」 黄錦燦編 서울 翰林出版社 1969. p.156, 166, 170; 「永遠한世界名詩全集 5」 서울 翰林出版社 1973. p.156, 166, 170

'Shimazaki Toson's four collections of poems' Tr. by James R. Morita. *Monumenta Nipponica*, v.25, no.3–4, 1970. p.325–369

'Песня о путешествии вдоль берегов реки Тикума; Листья ловкость' Перевод Анатолия Мамонова. *Вкус хризантемы*. Москва, Восточная Литература, 1976. p.109

'A coconut' Tr. by Hisayuki Idemaru. *Poetry Nippon*, no.37 & 38, 1977. p.24–25

'Otsuta; Over Komoros gamle borg' Til norsk ved Paal Brekke. *Moderne japansk lyrikk*. Oslo, Norske Bokklubben, n.d. p.15–18

Essays エッセイ

'給志在文學者' 孫明訳 「北平晨報學園」 第93期 193?.

'The art of writing' Tr. by Takamasa Sasaki. *Eigo no kenkyu to kyoju*. Tokyo, 1940.

SHIMIZU Ikkō 清水一行 1931–

Kōshoku zanmai 好色三昧

'人生三昧' 康曙海訳 「経営大望 12」 서울 鮮京図書 1975. p.1–402

SHIMIZU Ikkō

Kyogyō shūdan　虚業集団

'虚業集団'　康曙海訳　「経営大望 20」　서울　鮮京図書
1975. p.1–455

Saikō kimitsu　最高機密

'最高機密'　康曙海訳　「経営大望 2」　서울　鮮京図書
1975.

Tōki chitai　投機地帯

'投機大業'　康曙海訳　「経営大望 17」　서울　鮮京図書
1975. p.1–422

Tokumei shōsha　匿名商社

'仮名会社'　康曙海訳　「経営大望 15」　서울　鮮京図書
1975. p.1–401

'計略達道'　康曙海訳　「経営大望 4」　서울　鮮京図書
1975. p.1–438
'雄将大器'　康曙海訳　「経営大望 10」　서울　鮮京図書
1975. p.1–453
'快速突破'　康曙海訳　「経営大望 7」　서울　鮮京図書
1975. p.1–441

SHIMIZU Ikutarō　清水幾太郎　1907–

Kichi no ko　基地の子

La infanoj de militbazoj. Tokyo, Nihon Esperanto Tosho Kankokai, 1954. 80p.
「基地兒童」　汪向榮等訳　北京　中国青年出版社　1954.
84p.

SHIMIZU Mioko　清水深生子

Poems　詩

'遠雪'　金龍済訳　「日本詩集」　서울　青雲社　1960.
p.94–99

SHIMIZU Ryōjin　清水寥人　1920–

Kikanshi Naporeon no taishoku　機関士ナポレオンの退
職

'可機拿破崙'　劉慕沙訳　「日本現代小説選 1」　台北　聯經
出版　1976. p.61–124

SHIMIZU Takanori　清水高範　1917–

Poems　詩

'Людям всего мира'　Перевод Анатолия Мамонова. *Иностранная Литература*, август
1959. p.165–166
'Людям всего мира; Жизнь'　Перевод Анатолия
Мамонова. *Песни Хиросимы*. Москва, Худож. Лит. 1964. p.17–20; *Вкус хризантемы*. Москва, Восточная Литература, 1976.
p. 111–112
'To people; Light'　Tr. by Miyao Ohara. *The
songs of Hiroshima*. Tokyo, Taihei Shuppansha, 1971. p.12–17

SHIMODA Utako　下田歌子　1854–1937

Mikuni buri　皇国不李

A Japanese poetess. Tr. by Arthur Lloyd and Hajime Matsuura. Tokyo, Shunyodo, 1907.
215p.

SHIMOMURA Chiaki　下村千秋　1893–1955

Shōjo no tamashii　少女の魂

'Eines kleinen Mädchens Seele'　Übers. von Kurt
Meissner. *Der Tanzfächer*, von K. Meissner.
Tokyo, 1943. p.127–143

SHIMOMURA Izan　下村為山　1865–1949

Haiku　俳句

'2 haiku'　Tr. by Asataro Miyamori. *Anthology
of haiku, ancient and modern*. Tokyo, Maruzen, 1932. p.802–803
'Mount Fuji'　Tr. by Asataro Miyamori. *Haiku
poems, ancient and modern*. Tokyo, Maruzen,
1940. p.330
'1 haiku'　Tr. by Lois J. Erickson. *Songs from the
land of dawn*. N. Y. Friendship Press, 1949;
Freeport, Books for Libraries Press, 1968.
p.72
'With mindless skill'　Tr. by Harold Stewart. *A
net of fireflies*. Tokyo, Tuttle, 1960. p.55

SHIMOMURA Kojin　下村湖人　1884–1955

Rongo monogatari　論語物語

A book of heaven and the earth.　Tr. by Nobuyoshi Okumura. Tokyo, Univ. of Tokyo Press,
1973. 191p.
「論語平話」　李君奭訳　彰化　專心企業公司　1976. 242p.

SHIMOTA Seiji　霜多正次　1913–

Gun sagyo　軍作業

'軍工'　南冠訳　「譯文」　1955年12月　p.103–125

Nihon hei　日本兵

Японский солдат. Перевод Г. Ронской. Москва,
Прогресс, 1975. 188p.

Okinawa jima　沖縄島

'Остров Окинава'　Перевод В. Логуновой, В.
Константинова и К. Попова. *Иностранная
Литература*, сентябрь 1958. p.121–176.
октябрь 1958. p.89–157
'Окинава'　Перевод Д. Бугаевой. *Рассказы писателей Востока*. Ленинград, Лениздат,
1958. p.303–318
Insula Okinawa. În românește de Ion Timus și
Pericle Martinescu. București, Editura pentru Literatura Universală, 1961. 260p.
'沖縄島'　金福訳　上海　上海文芸　1963. 204p.; 上海
作家出版社　1964. 314p.

Senseisho 宣誓書

'宜誓书' 陳九仁訳 「世界文学」 1963年5月 p.13–27

Shurei no tami 守礼の民

「守礼之民」 迟叔昌訳 上海 作家出版社 1965. 278p.

Criticism 評論

'黒色的跑道' 卞立強訳 「世界文学」1962年12月 p.48–51

SHINBA Eiji 榛葉英治 1912–

Akai yuki 赤い雪

「아까이유끼」 李俊汎訳 서울 新興出版社 1961. 286p.

SHINDŌ Chie 新藤千恵 1920–

Poems 詩

'속삭임；빛나는恋情' 崔一秀訳 「기다리고있네」 서울 韓国政経社 1966. p.82–83, 148–150
'Space' *The burning heart*, tr. and ed. by Kenneth Rexroth and Ikuko Atsumi. N. Y. Seabury Press, 1977. p.99

SHINJŌ Yoshiakira 新庄嘉章 1904–

Essay エッセイ

'学生의 "에티케트' 金賢珠訳 「바이바이바더」 서울 三韓出版社 1966. p.283–285

SHINKAWA Kazue 新川和江 1929–

Poems 詩

'An event which makes no news' *The burning heart*, tr. and ed. by Kenneth Rexroth and Ikuko Atsumi. N. Y. Seabury Press, 1977. p.105

SHINODA Hajime 篠田一士 1927–

Criticism 評論

'Über Tanizaki Junichiro' Übers. von Annelotte Piper. *Kagami*, Bd, 5. Heft 1, 1966. p.48–66

SHINOHARA Bon 篠原 梵 1910–1975

Haiku 俳句

'1 haiku' *A history of haiku v.2*, by R. H. Blyth. Tokyo, Hokuseido, 1964. p.249

SHINOHARA Ontei 篠原温亭 1872–1926

Haiku 俳句

'2 haiku' Tr. by Asataro Miyamori. *Anthology of haiku, ancient and modern*. Tokyo, Maruzen, 1932. p.698–700
'Viewpoint' Tr. by Harold Stewart. *A net of fireflies*. Tokyo, Tuttle, 1960. p.19
'1 haiku' Tr. by Peter Beilenson and Harry Behn. *Haiku harvest*. Mount Verson, Peter Pauper Press, 1962. p.48

SHIOI Ukō 塩井雨江 1869–1913

Poems 詩

'The bamboo flute by the shore' Tr. by William G. Aston. *A history of Japanese literature*. N. Y. D. Appleton, 1899; Tokyo, Tuttle, 1972; *Japanese love poems*, ed. by Jean Bennett. Garden City, Doubleday, 1976. p.94–95
'The bamboo flute' *The master singers of Japan*, by Clara A. Walsh. London, John Murray, 1910. p.109–112
'La flûte de bambou près du rivage' Tr. par Henry D. Davray. *Littérature japonaise*. Paris, Armand Colin, 1921. p.388–389

SHIOSE Nobuko 塩瀬信子 1941–

Inochi aru hi ni 生命ある日に

「사랑해」 尹吉仁訳 서울 弘益出版社 1971. 287p.

SHIOZAWA Sadamu 塩沢 定

Tanka 短歌

'1 tanka' Tr. by Shigeshi Nishimura. *Eigo Seinen*, v.93, no.3, 1947. p.120

SHIOJIRI Kōmei 塩尻公明 1901–1969

Essay エッセイ

'人生의즐거움' 金賢珠訳 「바이바이바더」 서울 三韓出版社 1966. p.42–45

SHIRAFUJI Shigeru 白藤 茂

'心獄' 徐白訳 「日本短篇譯集 2」 台北 晚蟬書店 1969. p.191–220

SHIRAISHI Kazuko 白石かずこ 1931–

Poems 詩

'Pond' Tr. by Ikuko Atsumi and Graeme Wilson. *Quadrant*, Nov.-Dec. 1970. p.60
'Lion's humming; The town where eggs are falling; Egg of fire; Cold meat; Non stop; All day

SHIRAISHI Kazuko

long a tiger; Street; Pond' Tr. by Graeme Wilson and Ikuko Atsumi. *Three contemporary Japanese poets*. London, Magazine Editions, 1972. p.39–50

'Phallic root, for Sumiko, on her birthday; The man with the sky on' Tr. by Thomas Fitzsimmons. *Japanese poetry now*. London, André Deutsch, 1972. p.37–40; *Japanese poetry today*. N. Y. Schocken Books, 1972. p.39–42

'Street; Nick and Muriel; Lake; Memory of Joe; My Tokyo' Tr. by Geoffrey Bownas. *New writing in Japan*. Harmondsworth, Penguin Books, 1972. p.220–229

'The season of the sacred lecher, part I, II, VI' Tr. by Hiroaki Sato. *Ten Japanese poets*. Hanover, N. H. Granite Publications, 1973. p. 30–38

'My Tokyo; Phallus for Sumiko's birthday; The lion's humming; Non-stop; My America' Tr. by John Bean and Ikuko Atsumi. *The poetry of postwar Japan*. Iowa City, Univ. of Iowa Press, 1975. p.184–198

'The anniversary of Samansa's death; I fire at the face of the country where I was born; A Chinese Ulysses; The man root' *The burning heart*, tr. and ed. by Kenneth Rexroth and Ikuko Atsumi. N. Y. Seabury Press, 1977. p.108–117

'Der Teich' Übers. von Helmut Gross. *Internationales Jahrbuch für Literatur*, Ensemble 8, 1977. p.100

SHIRAKAWA Atsushi　白川　渥　1907–

'紅藍襯領' 徐雲濤訳 「當代日本小説選」 台南 經緯書局 1954. p.111–133; 「當代日本創作小説」 台南 經緯書局 1961. p.111–133; 「當代日本短篇小説選」 台南 大行出版社 1973. p.111–133

SHIROTORI Seigo　白鳥省吾　1890–1973

Poems　詩

'幸福；自由' 勞人訳 「文學週報」 第31期

'Mon grand-père campagnard' Tr. par Nico D. Horiguchi. *The lyric garland*, ed. by Makoto Sangu. Tokyo, Hokuseido, 1957. p.55

'The day when they lose their land' Tr. by Hisakazu Kaneko. *Orient West*, v.9, no.3, 1964. p.62–63

Criticism　評論

'俄國的詩壇' 夏丐尊訳 「小説月報」 第12巻 増刊号 1921.

SHIROYAMA Saburō　城山三郎　1927–

Hyakusen hyakushō　百戦百勝

'百戦百勝' 康曙海訳 「経営大望 1」 서울 鮮京図書 1975. p.1–446

Jinmu kuzure　神武崩れ

'Крах' Перевод Г. Каспарова. *Японская новелла*. Москва, Изд. Иност. Лит. 1961. p.229–260

Mōjin jūyaku　盲人重役

'盲人重役' 康曙海訳 「経営大望 11」 서울 鮮京図書 1975. p.1–421

Rakujitsu moyu　落日燃ゆ

War criminal, the life and death of Hirota Koki. Tr. by John Bester. Tokyo, Kodansha International, 1977. 301p.

Shinsan　辛酸

「辛酸」 王敦旭訳 北京 作家出版社 1965. 101p.

'黒字経営' 康曙海訳 「経営大望 3」 서울 鮮京図書 1975. p.1–449

'悪人設計' 康曙海訳 「経営大望 14」 서울 鮮京図書 1975. p.1–439

'上流人生' 康曙海訳 「経営大望 19」 서울 鮮京図書 1975. p.1–441

'商略達人' 康曙海訳 「経営大望 16」 서울 鮮京図書 1975. p.1–431

SHISHI Bunroku　獅子文六　1893–1969

Jiyū gakkō　自由学校

'Jiyū gakkō' *The Youth's Companion*, v.7, no.7, 1952.

Kaigun　海軍

'Kaigun' by Toyoo Iwata. Tr. by Kumiko Takagi. *Nippon Times*, Jan. 10, 17, 20, 31, 1944. Feb. 7, 14, 21, 28, 1944.

Kare mainichi yokujōsu　彼女毎日欲情す

'그는날마다発情한다' 金東史訳 「日本代表作家百人集 3」 서울 希望出版社 1966. p.10–20; 「日本短篇文学全集 3」 서울 新太陽社 1969. p.158–168

Musume to watashi　娘と私

Meine Tochter und Ich. Übers. von Hirao Konami und Wilhelm Schiffer. Tokyo, Japanisch-Deutsche Gesellschaft, 1967. 2v.

Seishun kaidan　青春怪談

'The young know best' Tr. by Hiroo Mukai. *The Yomiuri*, March 2—July 15, 1959.

'青春怪談' 李剛緑訳 「日本文学選集 7」 서울 知文閣 1966. p.237–512; 서울 韓国読書文化院 1973. p.233–512

'青春怪談' 李浩哲訳 「現代日本代表文学全集 7」 서울 平和出版社 1973. p.181–329

Essays　エッセイ

'Memories of a Meiji boyhood' *This is Japan*, v.14, 1967. p.87–91

'Shoes in the tokonoma' *This is Japan*, v.16, 1969. p.148–149

SHŌDA Shinoe　正田篠枝　1910–1965

Haiku　俳句

'1 haiku' *A history of haiku v.2*, by R. H. Blyth. Tokyo, Hokuseido, 1964. p.249

SHŌGENJI Haruko 生源寺美子 1914–

The rainbow deer. Tr. by Ann Herring. Tokyo, Gakken, 1973. 23p.

SHŌJI Sadao 東海林さだお 1937–

Kochira sonota ka コチラその他課

Rank and file. Tr. by Tommy Uematsu. Tokyo, Hyoronsha, 1972. 127p.

SHŌJI Sensui 庄司浅水 1903–

Sekai no kidan 世界の奇談

「세계의수수께끼」 金一英訳 서울 大一出版社 1973. 292p.

SHŌKEN Kōtaigō 昭憲皇太后 1849–1914

Tanka 短歌

'2 tanka' Tr. by Arthur Lloyd. *Eigo Seinen*, v.13, no.7, 1905. p.133–134
Imperial songs. Tr. by Arthur Lloyd. Tokyo, 1905. 159p.
'Poems by Emperor Meiji and his Empress' Tr. by Kenzo Wadagaki. *Stray leaves.* Tokyo, 1908.
'The shrine; The river; In spring' *The master singers of Japan*, by Clara A. Walsh. London, John Murray, 1910. p.117–118
'La poésie de l'Impératrice' Tr. par Michel Revon. *Anthologie de la littérature japonaise.* Paris, Delagrave, 1910. p.451
'Odes by the Empress Dowager Shoken' Tr. by K. Wadagaki. *Gleanings from Japanese literature.* Tokyo, Nampokusha, 1919. p.14
'3 tanka' *Japanese poetry, an historical essay*, by Curtis Hidden Page. Boston, Houghton Mifflin, 1923; Folcroft, Folcroft Library, 1976. p.163
'20 tanka' Tr. by Asataro Miyamori. *Masterpieces of Japanese poetry, ancient and modern.* Tokyo, Maruzen, 1936; Tokyo, Taiseido, 1956; N. Y. Greenwood Press, 1971. p.574–587
Waka poetry of the Emperor Meiji and Empress Shoken, Tr. by Harold P. Wright. Tokyo, Meiji Jingu, 1964. 5p.
'1 tanka' Tr. par Roger Bersihand. *La littérature japonaise.* Paris, Presses Universitaires de France, 1956. p.106
'1 tanka' Übers. von Gerolf Coudenhove. *Japanische Jahreszeiten.* Zürich, Manesse Verlag, 1963. p.18
'1 tanka' Tr. from the French by Unity Evans. *Japanese literature.* N. Y. Walker, 1965. p.89

SHŌNO Eiji 庄野英二 1915–

Himaraya no ryū ヒマラヤの竜

'Himálajský drak' *Modré vánoce.* Přel. Ivan Krou-

ský a Z. K. Slabý. Praha, Albatros, 1975.

Hoshi no makiba 星の牧場

The meadow of stars. Tr. by Yoko Sugiyama, Roy E. Teele and Nick Teele. Tokyo, Rironsha, 1970. 207p.

Kangarū no ojiisan カンガルーのおじいさん

'Dědeček klokan' *Modré vánoce.* Přel. Ivan Krouský a Z. K. Slabý. Praha, Albatros, 1975.

Risu リス

'Veverky' *Modré vánoce.* Přel. Ivan Krouský a Z. K. Slabý. Praha, Albatros, 1975.

SHŌNO Junzō 庄野潤三 1921–

Kekkon 結婚

'Marriage' Tr. by Saburo Haneda. *The Reeds*, v.5, 1959. p.66–85

Michi 道

'La strada' Tr. di Atsuko Ricca Suga. *Narratori giapponesi moderni.* Milano, Bompiani, 1965. p.699–734

Pūru saido shōkei プールサイド小景

'Near the swimming pool' Tr. by Saburo Haneda. *The Reeds*, v.4, 1958. p.134–163
'푸울싸이드小景' 鄭漢模訳 「芥川賞小説集」 서울 新丘文化社 1960. p.39–57; 「깊은江」 서울 三耕社 1971. p.39–57
'Poolside vignette' Tr. by George Saito. *Literary Review*, v.6, no.1, 1962. p.86–102
'池畔小景' 劉慕沙訳 「芥川獎作品選集 1」 台北 晚蟬書店 1969. p.121–147; 「芥川賞作品選集 2」 台北 大地出版社 1974. p.123–150
'푸울싸이드小景' 河在麒訳 「日本文学大全集 10」 서울 東西文化院 1975. p.381–396
'Vignetten vom Schwimmbeckenrand' Deutsch von Jürgen Berndt und Ursula Eleonore Winkler. *Träume aus zehn Nächten.* Berlin, Aufbau Verlag, 1975. p.541–562

Seibutsu 静物

'Still life (extract)' Tr. by Ted Takaya. *Japan P.E.N. News*, no.17, Feb. 1966. p.22–25

Yūbe no kumo タベの雲

Nuvole di sera. Tr. di Atsuko Ricca Suga. Milano, Ferro Edizioni, 1966. 245p.

Criticism 評論

'The international symposium on the short story III' *Kenyon Review*, v.31, no.4, 1969. p.492–497

SŌ Sakon 宗 左近 1919–

Poems 詩

'Dedication; The demon; Epitaph for a Kappa; The tomb of a Kappa' Tr. by Ann Herring. *The poetry of postwar Japan.* Iowa City, Univ. of Iowa Press, 1975. p.41–44

SODA Kōichi 祖田浩一 1935–

Criticism 評論

'Minakami Tsutomu's "Ikkyu"' *Japanese Literature Today*, no.1, March, 1976. p.8–10

SŌMA Gyofū 相馬御風 1883–1950

Tanka and Poems 短歌・詩

'White clouds; Flowers in a small vase; Footprints; Lies; Hail; White peonies' Tr. by Asataro Miyamori. *Masterpieces of Japanese poetry, ancient and modern.* Tokyo, Maruzen, 1936; Tokyo, Taiseido, 1956; N. Y. Greenwood Press, 1971. p.700–703

'Footprints' Tr. by Shigeshi Nishimura. *The Current of the World*, v.31, no.8, 1954. p.49

'1 tanka' Tr. by V. H. Viglielmo. *Japanese literature in the Meiji era.* Tokyo, Obunsha, 1955. p.387

'2 tanka' Übers. von Gerolf Coudenhove. *Japanische Jahreszeiten.* Zürich, Manesse Verlag, 1963. p.248, 324

Criticism 評論

「近代歐州文藝思潮」楊啓瑞訳 上海 中華書局 1915. 1冊

'法國自然主義的文藝' 汪馥泉訳 「小説月報」

Essays エッセイ

'Hato to roba' Tr. by Koh Masuda. *Eigo to Eibungaku*, Oct. 1928.

'The cuttlefish fleet' Tr. by Iwao Matsuhara. *Eigo Kenkyu*, v.26, no.1, 1933. p.30–32

'From summer to autumn' Tr. by Iwao Matsuhara. *Eigo Kenkyu*, v.25, no.12, 1933. p.1136–1137

'Ryokan' Tr. by Mamine Ishii. *Eigo Seinen*, v.82, no.5, 1939. p.135

'The fencing master' Tr. by Iwao Matsuhara. *Eigo Seinen*, v.75, no.5, 1936. p.153

SONO Ayako 曾野綾子 1931–

Aozameta nichiyōbi 蒼ざめた日曜日

'蒼白的星期日' 劉慕沙訳 「曾野綾子短篇選」 台北 蘭開書局 1969. p.142–158

Dangai 断崖

'断崖' 劉慕沙訳 「曾野綾子短篇選」 台北 蘭開書局 1969. p.63–87

Dare no tameni aisuru ka 誰のために愛するか

「為誰而愛」余阿勲訳 台北 晨鐘出版社 1973. 162p.
「為誰而愛」柳麗華訳 台北 天人出版社 1973. 1冊
「續為誰而愛」朱佩蘭訳 台南 台湾教会公報社 1974. 173p.

Enrai no kyaku tachi 遠来の客たち

'멀리서온손님들' 金龍済訳 「日本新鋭文学作家受賞作品選集 1」 서울 青雲社 1964. p.331–365
'멀리서온손님들' 李蓉姫訳 「戦後日本短篇文学全集 1」 서울 日光出版社 1965. p.331–365; 「現代日本代表文学全集 1」 서울 平和出版社 1973. p.331–334

Fūdo 風土

「누구를위해사랑하느냐노」 李俊凡訳 서울 学友社 1973. 226p.

Hajimete no tabi 初めての旅

'初旅' 劉慕沙訳 「曾野綾子短篇選」 台北 蘭開書局 1969. p.7–39

Hanataba to hōyō 花束と抱擁

'花束與擁抱' 廖清秀訳 「投水自殺營救業」 台北 蘭開書局 1968. p.152–171

Hanayaka na te 華やかな手

'華貴的手' 劉慕沙訳 「曾野綾子短篇選」 台北 蘭開書局 1969. p.88–111

Hi to yūhi 火と夕陽

'火與夕陽' 劉慕沙訳 「曾野綾子短篇選」 台北 蘭開書局 1969. p.40–62

Kyokō no ie 虚構の家

「虚構的家」 朱佩蘭訳 台北 道聲出版社 1977. 316p.

Nijūissai no chichi 二十一才の父

「二十一歳的父親」 林耀川訳 台北 徳昌出版社 1976. 276p.

Ningyo hime にんぎょひめ

The little mermaid. Retold by Jane Carruth. London, Hamlyn, 1969. 1v.

Nyoshin shuppon 女神出奔

「女神出奔」 李学熙訳 台北 希代書版公司 1974. 250p.

Seiganji fūkei 青巌寺風景

'The environs of Seiganji Temple' Tr. by Kazue Kuma. *Today's Japan*, v.5, Jan.-Feb. 1960. p.33–40; *The Japanese image* v.2, ed. by M. Schneps and A. D. Coox. Tokyo, Orient West, 1966. p.145–154

Shisha no umi 死者の海

'死者의바다' 金龍済訳 「日本新鋭文学作家受賞作品選集 1」 서울 青雲社 1964. p.223–330
'死者의바다' 李蓉姫訳 「戦後日本短篇文学全集 1」 서울 日光出版社 1965. p.223–330 「現代日本代表文学全集 1」 서울 平和出版社 1973. p.223–328

Suiren no odori 睡蓮の踊り

'睡蓮花의춤' 表文台訳 「日本代表作家百人集 5」 서울 希望出版社 1966. p.328–342; 「日本短篇文学全集 6」 서울 新太陽社 1969. p.240–254

Tōzakaru ashioto 遠ざかる足音

「遠離的脚歩聲」 黄季媛訳 台北 道聲出版社 1975. 273p.

Uchū ni fuyū suru 宇宙に浮游する

'Drifting in outer space' Tr. by Robert Epp. *Japan Christian Quarterly*, v.38, no.4, 1972. p.206–215

Umi no mieru shibafu de 海の見える芝生で

'臨海的草坪上' 劉慕沙訳 「曾野綾子短篇選」 台北 蘭開書局 1969. p.112–141

Umi no ohaka 海の御墓

'바다의墓' 方基煥訳 「20世紀女流文学選集 3」 서울 新

太陽社　1967. p.168–190

Zetsubō kara no shuppatsu　絶望からの出発

「從絶望出發」朱佩蘭訳　台南　豊生出版社　1975. 238p.

Essays　エッセイ

'I am glad we lost the war'　*This is Japan*, v.11, 1964. p.79–80

「我所看到的中國大陸」蘇琨煌訳　高雄　文皇出版社 1975. 95p.

———————

'替身聖母' 劉慕沙訳　「曾野綾子短篇選」台北　蘭開書局 1969. p.159–172

'大空飛碟' 劉慕沙訳　「曾野綾子短篇選」台北　蘭開書局 1969. p.173–185

「幸福의샘」呉在仁訳　서울　大韓出版社　1972. 258p.

「죽음과바굴사랑」蔡鎮淑訳　서울　大光出版社　1973. 244p.；서울　東根文化社　1974. 244p.

「누구를위해사랑하는가」洪允淑訳　서울　가톨릭出版社 1973. 2冊

「누구를위해사랑하느냐」李俊凡訳　서울　学友社　1973. 2冊

「누구를위하여사랑하느냐」慎一晟訳　서울　玄文社 1974. 190p.

「사랑과幸福의対話」朴在姫訳　서울　中央文化社　1975. 235p.

SŌNO Tadao　草野唯雄　1917–

Fukugan　復顔

'Facial restoration' *Japanese golden dozen*, ed. by Ellery Queen. Tokyo, Tuttle, 1978. p.211–231

SONOYAMA Shunji　園山俊二　1935–

Karejji neechan　カレッヂねえちゃん

Here is Gewako. Tr. by Tommy Uematsu. Tokyo, Hyoronsha, 1973. 127p.

Mai pēsu ikka　マイペース一家

To each his own. Tr. by Tommy Uematsu. Tokyo, Hyoronsha, 1972. 127p.

SUDŌ Gojō　数藤五城　1871–1915

Haiku　俳句

'1 haiku' Tr. by R. H. Blyth. *Haiku v.2.* Tokyo, Hokuseido, 1952. p.xi

SUEMATSU Kenchō　末松謙澄　1855–1920

Tanka　短歌

'The sound of a waterfall' Tr. by Asataro Miyamori. *Masterpieces of Japanese poetry, ancient and modern.* Tokyo, Maruzen, 1936; Tokyo, Taiseido, 1956; N. Y. Greenwood Press, 1971. p.611–612

SUETAKE Masaaki　末武正明　1933–

Sekai musekinin ryokō　世界無責任旅行

「世界無責任旅行」安應杓訳　서울　王子出版社　1963. 234p.

SUGANO Yoshikatsu　菅野喜勝　1915–

Neko　ねこ

The kitten's adventure. N. Y. McGraw-Hill, 1971. 1v.

SUGAWARA Katsumi　菅原克己　1911–

Poems　詩

'Два вечерних стихотворения' Перевод А. И. Мамонова. *Свободный стих в японской поэзий.* Москва, Наука, 1971. p.179–180

'Our residence; I am alone, but we are all; Mitsuko; Poet's mourning; Hands' Tr. by Hajime Kijima and Takako Ayusawa. *The poetry of postwar Japan.* Iowa City, Univ. of Iowa Press, 1975. p.19–25

'Воскресная Золушка' Перевод Анатолия Мамонова. *Вкус хризантемы.* Москва, Восточная Литература, 1976. p.114

SUGAWARA Shichiku　菅原師竹　1863–1919

Haiku　俳句

'3 haiku' Tr. by V. H. Viglielmo. *Japanese literature in the Meiji era.* Tokyo, Obunsha, 1955. p.442, 448

'The executioners' Tr. by Harold Stewart. *A net of fireflies.* Tokyo, Tuttle, 1960. p.20

SUGIMOTO Etsuko　杉本鉞子　1873–

Samurai no musume　武士の娘

A daughter of the samurai. N. Y. Doubleday Page, 1926. 314p.; N. Y. Doubleday, Doran, 1930. 314p.; London, Hutchinson, 1960. 175p.

Etsu, fille de Samurai. Tr. de l'anglais par René de Cérenville. Paris, Victor Attinger, 1930. 327p.

Eine Tochter des Samurai. Übertragen von Richard Küas. Berlin, Wolfgang Krüger, 1935. 348p.; Hamburg, Krüger, 1952. 293p.; Reinbek, Rowohlt, 1962. 197p.

En samurais datter. Oversat fra engelsk af Fredrik Nygaard. København, Jespersen og Pios, 1937. 296p.

Samurain tytär. Englänninkielestä suomentanut Katri Vuorisalo. Helsinki, Werner Söderström Ösakeyhtiö, 1937. 278p.

Corka samuraja. Przeł. Tomira Zori. Warszawa, Renaissance, 1938. 319p.

O fata de samurai. Craiova, Scrisul Romanesc, n. d. 267p.

———————

SUGIMOTO Etsuko

A daughter of the narikin. Garden City, Doubleday, Doran, 1932. 325p.
A daughter of the nohfu. Garden City, Doubleday, Doran, 1935. 340p.

SUGIMOTO Ryōkichi 杉本良吉 1907–1939

Essay エッセイ

'瑪耶闊夫司基的葬式' 毛翰哥訳 「現代文學」 第1巻4期
1930.

SUGIMURA Sojinkan 杉村楚人冠 1872–1945

Tokiko 時子

'Tokiko, the story of a Tokyo geisha' Tr. by Arthur Lloyd. *Eigo Seinen*, v.23, no.11, 1910.
p.252. v.23, no.23, 1910. p.277. v.24, no.2,
1910. p.37. no.3, 1910. p.63. no.4, 1910. p.83.
no.5, 1910. p.111. no.6, 1910. p.132–133
'For love's sweet sake' Tr. by Asataro Miyamori.
Representative tales of Japan. Tokyo, Sanko
Shoten, 1917. p.544–569

SUGITA Hisajo 杉田久女 1890–1946

Haiku 俳句

'2 haiku' *The burning heart*, tr. and ed. by Kenneth
Rexroth and Ikuko Atsumi. N. Y. Seabury
Press, 1977. p.79

SUGITA Yutaka 杉田 豊 1930–

Minna no onegai みんなのおねがい

Wake up, little three. Camden, N. J. Nelson,
1970. 32p.
Kul med siffror. Övers. av Britt G. Hallqvist.
Örebri, I.P.C. 1973. 28p.

SUGIURA Satoko 杉浦里子

'悲魔' 劉慕沙訳 「日本現代小説選」 台北 聯經出版
1976. p.37–58

SUGIURA Suiko 杉浦翠子 1891–1960

Tanka 短歌

'Plantains; My soul' Tr. by Asataro Miyamori.
*Masterpieces of Japanese poetry, ancient and
modern*. Tokyo, Maruzen, 1936; Tokyo,
Taiseido, 1956; N. Y. Greenwood Press,
1971. p.778–779

SUGIYAMA Heiichi 杉山平一 1914–

Poems 詩

'Running' *An anthology of modern Japanese*

poetry, ed. and tr. by Ichiro Kono and Rikutaro Fukuda. Tokyo, Kenkyusha, 1957. p.126
'Koşu' Tercüme etmek L. Sami Akalin. *Japon
şiiri*. İstanbul, Varlik Yayinevi, 1962. p.296

SUMIDA Chikurei 角田竹冷 1856–1919

Haiku 俳句

'4 haiku' *A history of haiku v.2*, by R. H. Blyth.
Tokyo, Hokuseido, 1964. p.144–145

SUNADA Hiroshi 砂田 弘 1933–

Saraba haiuei さらばハイウェイ

Прощай, дорога. Перевод Г. Ронской. Москва,
Дет. Лит. 1974. 137p.

SUSUKIDA Kyūkin 薄田泣菫 1877–1945

Poems 詩

'Ode to the broken pitcher' Tr. by Shigeshi Nishimura. *The Current of the World*, v.15, no.4,
1938. p.100
'Au carrefour; Fille de village; Le baiser; Indem-
nité du temps; Poème sur Hototogisou' Tr.
par Kuni Matsuo et Steinilber-Oberlin.
Anthologie des poètes japonais contemporains.
Paris, Mercure de France, 1939. p.61–66
'The spring eve' Tr. by Shigeshi Nishimura. *The
Current of the World*, v.30, no.5, 1953. p.42
'Were I in the province of Yamato; In the heat of
the day; Home thoughts' *The poetry of living Japan*, by Takamichi Ninomiya and D. J.
Enright. London, John Murray, 1957. p.22–
26
'희망' 「永遠한世界名詩全集 2」 黃錦燦編 서울 翰林
出版社 1969. p.117; 「永遠한世界名詩全集 5」 黃
錦燦編 서울 翰林出版社 1973. p.117
'Would that I were in Yamato' Tr. by Hideo
Yamaguchi. *Kobe Jogakuin Daigaku Ronshu*,
v.18, no.3, 1972. p.23–25

Essays エッセイ

'嗅妻房的男人' 謝六逸訳 「小説月報」 第18巻11期
1927. p.70–71
'A faint sigh' Tr. by Kazuo Yamada. *Eigo
Kenkyu*, v.26, no.6, 1933. p.521–522

SUYAMA Hisayo 寿山久代 1882–1977

Poems 詩

'Autumn rain' Tr. by Akiko Takemoto. *Poetry Nippon*, no.16, 1971. p.12

SUZAKI Katsuya 須崎勝弥 1922–

Korega seishun da これが青春だ

「이것이青春이다」 李文壽訳 서울 無等出版社 1969.
364p.

「너도나도高校열등생」 高起雲訳 서울 無等出版社
1970. 366p.

SUZUKI Akira 鈴木 章

Poems 詩

'노부코' 金禧宝編訳 「世界名詩選」 서울 一麦社 1974.
p.199

SUZUKI Hanamino 鈴木花蓑 1881–1942

Haiku 俳句

'The river of heaven' Tr. by Kenneth Yasuda. *A
pepper-pod*. Tokyo, Tuttle, 1976. p.93

SUZUKI Miekichi 鈴木三重吉 1882–1936

Chidori 千鳥

'Le pluvier' Tr. par R. P. Sauveur Candau.
Feux, et Le pluvier. Tokyo, Daigaku Syorin,
1961. p.41–133
'도요새' 尹鼓鐘訳 「日本代表作家百人集 1」 서울 希望
出版社 1966. p.294–314; 「日本短篇文学全集 1」
서울 新太陽社 1969. p.294–314

Kingyo 金魚

'金魚' 周作人訳 「東方雑誌」 第18巻24期 1921. p.91–
95; 「現代日本小説集」 上海 商務印書館 1923;
「日本現代小説集 1」 上海 商務印書館 1930.
'Goldfische' Übers. von S. Yuasa. *Nippon*, Jahrgang 3, 1937. p.211–215
'金魚' 新興書局編集部訳 「日本短篇小説選」 台北 新興
書局 1958. p.98–102; 台南 鳴宇出版社 1972.
p.98–102
'金魚' 「散文欣賞」 台北 大学書局 1977. p.97–102

Koneko 小猫

'새끼고양이' 郭夏信訳 「世界文学全集 94」 서울 乙酉文
化社 1962. p.285–308

Kurokami 黒髪

'A tress of black hair' Tr. by Asataro Miyamori.
Representative tales of Japan. Tokyo, Sanko
Shoten, 1917. p.110–125
'Die Locke' Übers. von Heinz Brasch. *Yamato*,
Jahrgang 3, 1931. p.69–75

Oshaberi baasan お喋り婆さん

'Oshaberi baasan' Tr. by Masuji Ishihara. *Eigakusei no tomo*, March 1922.

Shashin 写真

'照相' 周作人訳 「現代日本小説集」 上海 商務印書館
1923; 「日本現代小説集 1」 上海 商務印書館 1930.

Tasogare たそがれ

'黄昏' 周作人訳 「現代日本小説集」 上海 商務印書館
1923; 「日本現代小説集 1」 上海 商務印書館 1930.

SUZUKI Senzaburō 鈴木泉三郎 1893–1924

Futari no mibōjin 二人の未亡人

'Die beiden Witwen' Übers. von Hermann Bohner. *Nippon*, Jahrgang 2, 1936. p.219–236

Hiaburi 火あぶり

'Burning her alive' Tr. by Yozan T. Iwasaki and
Glenn Hughes. *New plays from Japan*. London, Ernest Benn, 1930. p.109–125

Ikiteiru Koheiji 生きてゐる小平次

'Living Koheiji' Tr. by Noboru Hidaka. *The
passion, and three other Japanese plays*. Honolulu, Oriental Literature Society, 1933; N.
Y. Greenwood Press, 1971. p.23–54

SUZUKI Shiroyasu 鈴木志郎康 1935–

Poems 詩

'In the wall' Tr. by Harry and Lynn Guest and
Shozo Kajima. *Post-war Japanese poetry*.
Harmondsworth, Penguin Books, 1972. p.145

SUZUKI Yasubumi 鈴木康文 1896–

Tanka 短歌

'Farming; On a bull's back' Tr. by Asataro Miyamori. *Masterpieces of Japanese poetry,
ancient and modern*. Tokyo, Maruzen, 1936;
Tokyo, Taiseido, 1956; N. Y. Greenwood
Press, 1971. p.788–789

T

TACHIBANA Jun'ichi 橘 純一 1884–

Tanka 短歌

'Two brothers; The Sumida River' Tr. by Asataro Miyamori. *Masterpieces of Japanese poetry, ancient and modern*. Tokyo, Maruzen,
1936; Tokyo, Taiseido, 1956; N. Y. Greenwood Press, 1971. p.710–711

TACHIHARA Erika 立原えりか 1937–

Hana kui raion 花くいライオン

'O lvu, který žral květiny' Přel. Ivan Krouský

TACHIHARA Erika

a Z. K. Slabý. *Modré vánoce*. Praha, Albatros, 1975.

Ohimesama o tabeta ōotoko お姫さまをたべた大男

Jak obr spolky princeznu. Přel. Ivan Krouský. Praha, Lidové Nakladatelstvi, 1970. 30p.
'Jak obr spolky princeznu' Přel. Ivan Krouský a Z. K. Slabý. *Modré vánoce*. Praha, Albatros, 1975.

Omatsuri お祭り

'Svátek panenek' Přel. Ivan Krouský a Z. K. Slabý. *Modré vánoce*. Praha, Albatros, 1975.

Yōsei to obake 妖精とお化け

Skritkove a strasidla. Přel. Ivan Krouský. Praha, Lidové Nakladatelství, 1970. 30p.

TACHIHARA Masaaki　立原正秋　1926–

Koibito tachi 恋人たち

「誘惑者」林貞姫訳 서울 新思潮社 1966. 290p.

Yamahada 山肌

'山肌' 劉與堯訳 「現代日本小説選」 台北 雲天出版社 1970. p.235–270

Essay エッセイ

'The path to the tearoom' *Chanoyu Quarterly*, no.18, 1977. p.47–58

TACHIHARA Michizō　立原道造　1914–1939

Poems 詩

'For a later dream' *An anthology of modern Japanese poetry*, ed. and tr. by Ichiro Kono and Rikutaro Fukuda. Tokyo, Kenkyusha, 1957. p.126
'Preface' *The poetry of living Japan*, by Takamichi Ninomiya and D. J. Enright. London, John Murray, 1957. p.93
'Pensamientos' *Sur*, no.249, 1957. p.98
'Nachimittag' Übertragen von Shin Aizu. *Der schwermütige Ladekran*. St. Gallen, Tschudy Verlag, 1960. p.11
'Afterthoughts; Night song of a traveller' Tr. by Geoffrey Bownas and Anthony Thwaite. *The Penguin book of Japanese verse*. Harmondsworth, Penguin Books, 1964. p.224–225
'For future remembrance' *Modern Japanese poetry*, by Donald Keene. Ann Arbor, Center for Japanese Studies, Univ. of Michigan, 1964. p.30; *Landscapes and portraits*, by Donald Keene. Tokyo, Kodansha International, 1971. p.148–149
'꿈속의사랑' 崔一秀訳 「기다리고있네」 서울 韓国政経社 1966. p.170–172
'시골살이 ; 故郷의밤에' 金巣雲訳 「世界의文学大全集 34」 서울 同和出版社 1971. p.537–538
'To the thoughts of later days' Tr. by Katsuko Sayama. *Poetry Nippon*, no.28, 1974. p.19
'Song of summer flowers; To the thoughts of later days; It will soon be autumn; Invitation to sleep; Prologue to *Gentle songs*; Fields of

loneliness; In the morning; At noontime, too; In the afternoon; In the shadow of the trees; At the autumn woods again; What I dreamed; White butterfly; Birds in the motor of my brain; The shadow cast by the moonlight; Blue lamp in my brain; A pastoral; Cricket in my chest; I'm tall' Tr. by Katsuko Sayama. *Japanese songs of innocence and experience*. Tokyo, Hokuseido, 1975. p.75–93
'At the autumn woods again' Tr. by Katsuko Sayama. *Poetry Nippon*, no.31 & 32, 1975. p.39–40
'Quatrains; Along the fence; Blue lamp in my brain; The road before me' Tr. by Katsuko Sayama. *Poetry Nippon*, no.33 & 34, 1976. p.9–10
'Gînduri trîzii' Traducerea Virgil Teodorescu. *Din lirica japoneză*. Bucureşti, Editura Univers, n.d. p.210

TADA Chimako　多田智満子　1930–

Poems 詩

'Mirror' *The burning heart*, tr. and ed. by Kenneth Rexroth and Ikuko Atsumi. N. Y. Seabury Press, 1977. p.107

TAISHŌ Tennō　大正天皇　1879–1926

Tanka 短歌

'3 tanka' *Japanese poetry, an historical essay*, by Curtis Hidden Page. Boston, Houghton Mifflin, 1923; Folcroft, Folcroft Library, 1976. p.167, 168

TAKADA Chōi　高田蝶衣　1886–1930

Haiku 俳句

'Haiku' Tr. par Kuni Matsuo et Steinilber-Oberlin. *Anthologie des poètes japonais contemporains*. Paris, Mercure de France, 1939. p.295–296
'2 haiku' Tr. by V. H. Viglielmo. *Japanese literature in the Meiji era*. Tokyo, Obunsha, 1955. p.444
'Haiku' Tercüme etmek L. Sami Akalin. *Japon şiiri*. İstanbul, Varlik Yayinevi, 1962. p.244
'1 haiku' Übers. von Erwin Jahn. *Fallende Blüten*. Zürich, Arche, 1968. p.69

TAKADA Eiichi　高田栄一　1925–

Poems 詩

'Tortoise' Tr. by William L. Clark. *Jiji Eigo Kenkyu*, v.20, no.12, 1966.

TAKADA Toshiko　高田敏子　1914–

Poems 詩

'Качели' Перевод Анатолия Мамонова. *Вкус*

хризантемы. Москва, Восточная Литература, 1976. p.116
'The seacoast at Mera' *The burning heart*, tr. and ed. by Kenneth Rexroth and Ikuko Atsumi. N. Y. Seabury Press, 1977. p.92
'A peony; The color of clouds; On a rainy day; The tangerine blossoms; Side face; The winter garden' Tr. by Akiko Kitagawa and others. *Poetry Nippon*, no.41 & 42, 1978. p.7–12
'Silver thaw' Tr. by Akio Chida. *Poetry Nippon*, no.43 & 44, 1978. p.40–41

TAKAGI Toshirō　高木俊朗　1908–

Inpāru sakusen　インパール作戦

「인팔作戰」金潤成訳　서울　良書閣　1968. 1冊

TAKADO Kaname　たかど・かなめ

Criticism　評論

'Postwar Japanese Christian writers' Tr. by Esther L. Hibbard. *Japan Christian Quarterly*, v.38, no.4, 1972. p.185–192

TAKAGI Akimitsu　高木彬光　1920–

Madan no shashu　魔弾の射手

「魔彈的射手」何年訳　台北　交通出版社　1963. 4冊

Mikkokusha　密告者

The informer. Tr. by Sadako Mizuguchi. Queensland, Anthos Publishing, 1971. 260p.
De zaak kgawa. Overzetten door N. Brink-Wessels. Utrecht, Het Spectrum, 1973. 190p.
Ilmiantaja. Suomentanut Marjukka Iizuka et al. Helsinki, 1974. 259p.

Mokugekisha　目撃者

'目撃者' 徐白訳　「日本短篇譯集 2」台北　晩蟬書店　1969. p.87–129

Shinpi no tobira　神秘の扉

「神秘之門」摩斯訳　台中　藝聲出版社　1968. 136p.

'儥情的男女' 振江訳　「黑色幻惑」台南　文良出版社　1966. p.77–111

TAKAGI Kyōzō　高木恭造　1903–

Poems　詩

'The winter moon' Tr. by James Kirkup. *Japan Quarterly*, v.17, no.3, 1970. p.301–307
'Early spring at Gappo Park; Hamanasu; Wedding night; Stones; Mother' Tr. by Michio Nakano and James Kirkup. *TransPacific*, no.5, 1970. p.54–57
'Stones' Tr. by Michio Nakano and James Kirkup. *Listening to Japan*, ed. by Jackson H.

Bailey. N. Y. Praeger, 1973. p.86
Selected poems of Takagi Kyozo. Tr. by James Kirkup and Michio Nakano. Cheadle, Carcanet Press, 1973. 51p.
'The old women's hut' Tr. by James Kirkup and Michio Nakano. *Japan Quarterly*, v.21, no.3, 1974. p.284–290

TAKAGI Shūkichi　高木秀吉　1902–

Poems　詩

'A winter night' *An anthology of modern Japanese poetry*, ed. and tr. by Ichiro Kono and Rikutaro Fukuda. Tokyo, Kenkyusha, 1957. p.127
'Kiş gecesi' Tercüme etmek L. Sami Akalin. *Japon şiiri*. İstanbul, Varlik Yayinevi, 1962. p.273

TAKAHAMA Kyoshi　高浜虚子　1874–1959

Fūryū senpō　風流懺法

'Ichinen' Tr. by John Bester. *Japan P.E.N. News*, no.11, August 1963. p.1–8

Ikaruga monogatari　斑鳩物語

'Ikaruga monogatari' Übers. von Oscar Benl. *Der Kirschblütenzweig*. München, Nymphenburger, 1965. p.256–273

Jūgodai shōgun　十五代将軍

'Der 15. Shogun' Übers. von K. Koike. *Der geheime Briefträger*. Tokyo, Nankodo, 1920. p.121–185

Kaki futatsu　柿二つ

'The two persimmons' Tr. by S. G. Brickley. *The writing of idiomatic English*. Tokyo, Kenkyusha, 1951. p.109–117

Haiku　俳句

'10 haiku' Tr. by Asataro Miyamori. *Anthology of haiku, ancient and modern*. Tokyo, Maruzen, 1932. p.722–728
'1 haiku' Tr. by Harold Gould Henderson. *The bamboo broom*. Tokyo, J.L. Thompson, 1933; London, Kegan Paul, 1933. p.115
'Haiku' Tr. par Kuni Matsuo et Steinilber-Oberlin. *Anthologie des poètes japonais contemporains*. Paris, Mercure de France, 1939. p.290–292
'The white lilies; My heart; Spring; The snake; The spring moon; The butterfly; The autumn wind: A scarecrow's hat; The glove' Tr. by Asataro Miyamori. *Haiku poems, ancient and modern*. Tokyo, Maruzen, 1940. p.333–337
'Freshness' Tr. by Harold Gould Henderson. *From the bamboo broom*. N. Y. Japan Reference Library, 1940.
'1 haiku' Tr. by Lois J. Erickson. *Songs from the land of dawn*. N. Y. Friendship Press, 1949; Freeport, Books for Libraries Press, 1968. p.70
'10 haiku' Tr. by R. H. Blyth. *Haiku*. Tokyo, Hokuseido, 1950–52. v.1, p.220, 285. v.2, p.60.

TAKAHAMA Kyoshi

v.3, p.299, v.4, p.19, 74, 146, 152, 260, 312
'17 haiku' Tr. par Conrad Meili. *Cahiers du Sud*, no.305, 1951. p.36–38
'14 haiku' Tr. by V. H. Viglielmo. *Japanese literature in the Meiji era*. Tokyo, Obunsha, 1955. p.430–431, 443–444
'1 haiku' Tr. by Peter Beilenson. *Japanese haiku*. Mount Vernon, Peter Pauper Press, 1955. p.28
'Three haiku poems' Tr. by H. G. Henderson. *Modern Japanese literature*, ed. by Donald Keene. N. Y. Grove Press, 1956; Tokyo, Tuttle, 1957. p.123
'1 haiku' Tr. par Roger Bersihand. *La littérature japonaise*. Paris, Presses Universitaires de France, 1956. p.112
Neuzeitliche Haiku-Gedichte. Übers. von Tomio Tezuka. Tokyo, Japanisch-Deutsche Gesellschaft, 1958. 68p.
'Distraction; La comète' *La poésie japonaise*, par Karl Petit. Paris, Seghers, 1959. p.193
'2 haiku' Übers. von Günther Debon. *Im Schnee die Fähre*. München, Piper, 1960. p.37
'Sunflower; Fear; Inspiration' Tr. by Harold Stewart. *A net of fireflies*. Tokyo, Tuttle, 1960. p.31, 52, 84
'5 haiku' Übers. von Kuniyo Takayasu und Manfred Hausmann. *Ruf der Regenpfeifer*. München, Bechtle Verlag, 1961. p.103–104
'Poèmes de Kyoshi Takahama' *France-Asie* t.17, no.165, 1961. p.1708–1710
'2 haiku' Tr. by Peter Beilenson and Harry Behn. *Haiku harvest*. Mount Vernon, Peter Pauper Press, 1962. p.13, 46
'Haiku' Tercüme etmek L. Sami Akalin. *Japon şiiri*. İstanbul, Varlik Yayinevi, 1962. p.236
'10 haiku' Tr. by Geoffrey Bownas and Anthony Thwaite. *The Penguin book of Japanese verse*. Harmondsworth, Penguin Books, 1964. p.166–167
'46 haiku' *A history of haiku v.2*, by R. H. Blyth. Tokyo, Hokuseido, 1964. p.116–132
'2 haiku' Til norsk ved Paal Helge Haugen. *Blad frå ein austleg hage*. Oslo, Det Norske Samlaget, 1965. p.88
'1 haiku' Tr. from the French by Unity Evans. *Japanese literature*. N. Y. Walker, 1965. p.95
'11 haiku' *Anthology of modern Japanese poetry*, tr. and comp. by Edith Marcombe Shiffert and Yuki Sawa. Tokyo, Tuttle, 1972. p.162–164
'1 haiku' Tr. by William Howard Cohen. *To walk in seasons*. Tokyo, Tuttle, 1972. p.90
'20 haiku' *Modern Japanese haiku, an anthology*, comp. and tr. by Makoto Ueda. Tokyo, Univ. of Tokyo Press, 1976. p.50–59
'4 haiku' Tr. by Takamasa Sasaki. *Eigo Seinen*, v.122, no.5, 1976. p.231
'Chilly night; Autumn wind; The withering moor; Artesian well; Cherry-flowers; Summer moon; Summer night; On the death of Shiki; Spring night; Violet; The crisp spring air; The fallen leaves' Tr. by Kenneth Yasuda. *A pepperpod*. Tokyo, Tuttle, 1976. p.82–85

'Eiko' Tr. by Kanichi Ando. *Osaka Mainichi*, June 26–29, 1924.

TAKAHASHI Kazumi 高橋和巳 1931–1971

Sange 散華

Sangué-blomsterdryss. Overs. av Finn Havrevold. Oslo, Norsk Rikskringkasting, 1972. 33p.

TAKAHASHI Kenji 高橋健二 1902–

Criticism 評論

'Die moderne Literatur und ihre Schulen' Übers. von Takuichi Nomura. *Mitteilungen* (Institut für Auslandsbeziehungen) Bd. 7, Heft 1, 1957. p.24–31
'German literature in Japan' *Japan Quarterly*, v.7, no.2, 1960. p.193–199

TAKAHASHI Mitsuko 高橋光子 1928–

Chō no kisetsu 蝶の季節

'Сезон бабочек' Перевод З. Рахима. *Японская новелла 1960–1970*. Москва, Прогресс, 1972. p.339–376

TAKAHASHI Mutsuo 高橋睦郎 1937–

Poems 詩

'Christ of the thieves in memory of Mr. M.' Tr. by James Kirkup. *Poetry Nippon*, no.13, 1970. p.5–6
'A tableau for sunset; Winter 1955' Tr. by Harry and Lynn Guest and Shozo Kajima. *Post-war Japanese poetry*. Harmondsworth, Penguin Books, 1972. p.155–156
'Sleeping wrestler; A negro before he sings; From slumber and sin and fall; End of summer; Boys; Rose love; Dead boy' Tr. by James Kirkup, Fumiko Miura, and Geoffrey Bownas. *New writing in Japan*. Harmondsworth, Penguin Books, 1972. p.230–240
'Dove; Mino; Mother and son; The rose tree; The god statue I love; Dream of Barcelona: my ancient world; End of summer' Tr. by Hiroaki Sato. *Ten Japanese poets*. Hanover, N. H. Granite Publications, 1973. p.114–123
'비둘기' 「世界名詩選」 金穂宝編訳 서울 一麦社 1974. p.198
Poems of a penisist. Tr. by Hiroaki Sato. Chicago, Chicago Review Press, 1975. 108p.

TAKAHASHI Shigeyoshi 高橋重義 1944–

Poems 詩

'Сады' Перевод Анатолия Мамонова. *Вкус хризантемы*. Москва, Восточная Литература, 1976. p.119

238

TAKAHASHI Shin'ichi 高橋磌一

Reportage ルポルタージュ

'九月十三日的砂川' 劉仲平訳 「譯文」 1956年8月 p.82–97

TAKAHASHI Shinkichi 高橋新吉 1901–

Zanzō 残像

Afterimages, Zen poems. Tr. by Lucien Stryk and Takashi Ikemoto. Chicago, Swallow Press, 1970. 127p.

Poems 詩

'Birth' Tr. by S. Sato and C. Urdang. *Poetry*, May 1956. p.89

'Rainbow on the seashore; The ache of life; A butterfly; The eastern sky; Endless; Dishes; Fish' *An anthology of modern Japanese poetry*, ed. and tr. by Ichiro Kono and Rikutaro Fukuda. Tokyo, Kenkyusha, 1957. p.127–130

'The raven; The fine rain' *The poetry of living Japan*, by Takamichi Ninomiya and D. J. Enright. London, John Murray, 1957. p.61–62

'바위' 金龍済訳 「日本詩集」 서울 青雲社 1960. p.35–37

'Nebelrieseln' Übertragen von Shin Aizu. *Der schwermütige Ladekran*. St. Gallen, Tschudy Verlag, 1960. p.39

'Balik' Tercüme etmek L. Sami Akalin *Japon şiiri* İstanbul, Varlik Yayinevi, 1962. p.272

'Three Zen poems; Horse; Quails; The peach' Tr. by Takashi Ikemoto and Lucien Stryk. *Orient West*, v.8, no.1, 1963. p.60–71; *The Japanese image*, ed. by M. Schneps and A. D. Coox. Tokyo, Orient West, 1965. p.362–364

'Beach rainbow; Birth' Tr. by Geoffrey Bownas and Anthony Thwaite. *The Penguin book of Japanese verse*. Harmondsworth, Penguin Books, 1964. p.205–206

'Strange thing' Tr. by Makoto Ueda. *East West Review*, v.2, no.1, 1965. p.57

'Zen poems' Tr. by Takashi Ikemoto and Lucien Stryk. *Tri Quarterly*, no.5, 1966. p.111–116

'Calm' Tr. by Graeme Wilson. *Japan Quarterly*, v.14, no.1, 1967. p.81

'Dreams; Bottom of the sea' Tr. by Graeme Wilson. *Japan Quarterly*, v.14, no.2, 1967. p.150, 174

'Three poems' Tr. by Lucien Stryk and Takashi Ikemoto. *Chicago Review*, no.20–21, May 1969. p.22–24

'Crab; Ants; Cock; Man; Here; Sun and flowers; Wind among the pines; Wind 1; Wind 2; Immutability' Tr. by Lucien stryk and Takashi Ikemoto. *Literature East and West*, v.13, no. 3 & 4, 1969. p.416–422

'Four poems by Takahashi Shinkichi' Tr. by Lucien Stryk and Takashi Ikemoto. *Poetry*, August-Sept. 1970. p.364–367

'Ivies' Tr. by Lucien Stryk and Takashi Ikemoto. *Michigan Quarterly Review*, v.9, no.4, 1970. p.238

'海；寒風；物；眞理的大海；心的瓦礫；心；杜撰' 徐和隣訳 「現代詩解説」 台北 葡萄園詩刊社 1970. p.101–107

'Broken glasses; The fly; The ocean' *Anthology of modern Japanese poetry*, tr. and comp. by Edith Marcombe Shiffert and Yuki Sawa. Tokyo, Tuttle, 1972. p.97–99

'倦怠' 金光林訳 「現代詩学」 第4巻3号 1972.

'White cloud' Tr. by Harold P. Wright. *Chelsea*, no.30–31, June 1972; *Listening to Japan*, ed. by Jackson H. Bailey. N. Y. Praeger, 1973. p.85

'Corbul' Traducerea Dan Constantinescu. *Din lirica japoneză*. Bucureşti, Editura Univers, n.d. p.195

'Uten slutt; Tallerkener' Til norsk ved Paal Brekke. *Moderne japansk lyrikk*. Oslo, Norske Bokklubben, n.d. p.51–52

TAKAHASHI Teiji 高橋禎二 1891–1953

Criticism 評論

'文學研究法' 張我軍訳 「小説月報」 第21巻6号 1930. p.887–899

TAKAHASHI Yasukuni 高橋泰邦 1925–

Fukai umi no uta 深い海の歌

'Песня морских глубин' Перевод З. Рахима. *Времена Хокусая*. Москва, Мир, 1967. p.155–183

'Jures gelmiu daina' *Hokusajaus laikai*. Vilnius, Vaizdo, 1969. p.117–138

TAKAHASHI Yoshitaka 高橋義孝 1913–

Criticism 評論

'Basho' *Mitteilungen* (Deutsche Gesellschaft für Natur- und Völkerkunde Ostasiens), Bd.44, 1964. p.27–32

TAKAI Yūichi 高井有一 1932–

Chiisana hama nite 小さな浜にて

'在小海濱' 廖清秀訳 「投水自殺營救業」 台北 蘭開書局 1968. p.112–128

Kiri no waku tani 霧の湧く谷

'湧霧谷' 路家訳 「純文學」（香港版） 第1巻1期 1967. p.88–111

'湧霧谷' 鐘肇政訳 「戰後日本短篇小説選」 台北 台湾商務印書館 1968. p.101–133

TAKAKURA Hisako 高倉壽子

Tanka 短歌

'1 tanka' Tr. by Arthur Lloyd. *Eigo Seinen*, v.13, no.7, 1905. p.134

TAKAKURA Teru 高倉 輝 1891–

Buta no uta ぶたのうた

'猪的歌' 蕭蕭訳 「人民文学」 第5巻1期 1951. p.82–94

'Песенка свиньи' Перевод В. Логуновой. *Новый Мир*, 1953, No.2. p.125–137; *Японская новелла*. Москва, Изд. Иност. Лит. 1961. p.261–278

Песенка свиньи. Перевод В. Логуновой. Москва, Правда, 1953. 24p.

Kiaulès dainelè. Vertè St. Rudzevičius. Vilnius, Valstybinè Grožinès Literatŭros Leidykla, 1954. 30p.

Cîntecul porcului. În românește de Gheorghe Voropanov și Jacqueș Costin. București, ESPLA, 1956. 88p.

Дойзын айдымжыгы. Тбилиси, Гослитиздат, 1957. 23p.

A disznó dala. Ford. Wessely László. Budapest, Európa Könyvkiadó, 1958. 44p.

Чочконун ыры. Фрунзе, Киргиз. Гос. Изд. 1958. 32p.

Дуньзунь аидымжыгы. Перевод от русс. А. Мухадов. Ашхабад, Туркмен. Гос. Изд. 1958. 29p.

'Sea lauluka' *Elada*. Tallinn, Eesti Riiklik Kirjastus, 1962. p.126–145

'Виионин енели' Орусшадан аударган Нурахмет Телеупов. *Хиросима касирети*. Алма-Ата, Жазушы, 1969. p.81–100

Hakone yōsui 箱根用水

Воды Хаконе. Перевод И. Львовой. Москва, Изд. Иност. Лит. 1954. 280p.

Воды Хаконе, на украинском языке. Перевод П. Воловьева. Киев, Гос. Украин. Изд. 1955. 271p.

Apele Hakonei. În românește de Tatiana Malița și Rose Hefter. București, ESPLA, 1956. 323p.

Хаконе суулары. Перевод от русс. К. Ариев. Фрунзе, Гос. Изд. 1958. 315p.

「箱根風雲録」 蕭蕭訳 上海 文化生活出版社 1953. 432p.; 北京 作家出版社 1958. 280p.

Vody Hakone. Přel. Imrich Zalupsky. Bratislava, 1959. 260p.

Hyakushō no uta 百姓の唄

「農民之歌」 金福訳 北京 新文芸出版社 1956. 184p.

Ōkami 狼

「狼」 金福訳 北京 新文芸出版社 1956. 1冊

Волк. Перевод Г. Ронской. Москва, Молодая Гвардия, 1959. 139p.

Lupul. În românește de E. Naum și N. Andronescu. București, Editura pentru Literatura Universală, 1962. 176p.

Essay エッセイ

'Новые пути японской литературы' *Иностранная Литература*, июль 1960. p.211–213

TAKAMATSU Fumiki 高松文樹 1926–

Poems 詩

'A setting sun; A collapse' Tr. by Onsey Naka-gawa. *Poetry Nippon*, no.18, 1972. p.19

TAKAMATSU no Miya 高松宮 1905–

Tanka 短歌

'1 tanka' Tr. par Roger Bersihand. *La littérature japonaise*. Paris, Presses Universitaires de France, 1956. p.107

'1 tanka' Tr. from the French by Unity Evans. *Japanese literature*. N. Y. Walker, 1965. p.91

TAKAMI Jun 高見 順 1907–1965

Jumokuha 樹木派

'Из книги «Школа деревьев»' Перевод И. Мотобрывцевой. *Дзюн Таками, избранная лирика*. Москва, Молодая Гвардия, 1976. p.11–44

Jūryō sōshitsu 重量喪失

'Из книги «Потеря веса»' Перевод И. Мотобрывцевой. *Дзюн Таками, избранная лирика*. Москва, Молодая Гвардия, 1976. p.74–76

Mobire モビレ

'Mobile' Tr. by John Bester. *Japan Quarterly*, v.9, no.4, 1962. p.454–466

Ningen 人間

'人間' 金龍済訳 「日本代表作家百人集 2」 서울 希望出版社 1966. p.450–469; 「日本短篇文学全集 3」 서울 新太陽社 1969. p.136–155

Shi no fuchi yori 死の淵より

'By the abyss of death' Tr. by Harold P. Wright. *Japan P.E.N. News*, no.15, July 1965. p.1–7

'Из книги «Из бездны смерти»' Перевод И. Мотобрывцевой. *Дзюн Таками, избранная лирика*. Москва, Молодая Гвардия, 1976. p.52–73

Tosatsu 屠殺

'Slaughter' Tr. by John Bester. *Japan Quarterly*, v.9, no.4, 1962. p.444–453

Waga maisō わが埋葬

'Из книги «Мои похороны»' Перевод И. Мотобрывцевой. *Дзюн Таками, избранная лирика*. Москва, Молодая Гвардия, 1976. p.45–51

Poems 詩

'Jack's bean stalk' Tr. by Shigeshi Nishimura. *The Current of the World*, v.28, no.8, 1951. p.36–37

'Agony; Glass; Heaven; As the grapes have seeds' *An anthology of modern Japanese poetry*, ed. and tr. by Ichiro Kono and Rikutaro Fukuda. Tokyo, Kenkyusha, 1957. p.130–131

'Небо' Перевод Веры Марковой. *Иностранная Литература*, сентябрь 1960. p.153

'Der Himmel' Übers. von Kuniyo Takayasu und Manfred Hausmann. *Ruf der Regenpfeifer*. München, Bechtle Verlag, 1961. p.92

'Cam' Tercüme etmek L. Sami Akalin. *Japon şiiri*. İstanbul, Varlik Yayinevi, 1962. p.291

'Fingernails of the dead; The stupid tear; Song of praise; A gaze; Dream boat' Tr. by Graeme Wilson. *Japan Quarterly*, v.12, no.1, 1965. p.38, 45, 86, 92, 98

'Mind's room' Tr. by Graeme Wilson. *Japan Quarterly*, v.13, no.1, 1966. p.96

'Здоровье молодости; У меня есть кораблик; На границе жизни и смерти; Классная доска; Как Энку резал изваянье Будды; Орган; Потерянный барсук; Ночная вода; Голый берег' Перевод И. Мотобрывцевой. *Иностранная Литература*, август 1968. p.28–32

'At the boundary of life and death; Fingernails of the dead' *Anthology of modern Japanese poetry*, tr. and comp. by Edith Marcombe Shiffert and Yuki Sawa. Tokyo, Tuttle, 1972. p.107–108

'Red fruit/patient; Blackboard; Train that will never come again; Pebble; Wheel; Something terrifying; Lost badger; Dancing demons; Poppies; Garden' Tr. by Thomas Fitzsimmons. *Japanese poetry now*. London, André Deutsch, 1972. p.91–97; *Japanese poetry today*. N. Y. Schocken Books, 1972. p.93–99.

'Поезд, который никогда не вернется' Перевод Анатолия Мамонова. *Вкус хризантемы*. Москва, Восточная Литература, 1976. p.117

Essay エッセイ

'Days of the wild geese' *This is Japan*, v.11, 1964. p.228–230

'Трус' Перевод З. Рахима. *Японская новелла*. Москва, Изд. Иност. Лит. 1961. p.279–294

'Argpuks' *Elada*. Tallinn, Eeste Riiklik Kirjastus, 1962. p.146–162

'Коркак' Аударган Е. Атыгаев. *Жапон Энгимелери*. Алма-Ата, Жазушы, 1965. p.94–111

TAKAMORI Fumio 高森文夫

Poems 詩

'Winter; The moon' *An anthology of modern Japanese poetry*, ed. and tr. by Ichiro Kono and Rikutaro Fukuda. Tokyo, Kenkyusha, 1957. p.132–133

TAKAMURA Kōtarō 高村光太郎 1883–1956

Chieko shō 智恵子抄

'Takamura Mitsutaro, Chieko-sho' Übers. von Suematsu Daiguji. *Monumenta Nipponica*, v.14, no.1–2, 1958. p.204–225

Chieko's sky. Tr. by Soichi Furuta. Tokyo, Kodansha International, 1978. 68p.

Poems 詩

'On the sea; The ocean' Tr. by Asataro Miyamori. *Masterpieces of Japanese poetry, ancient and modern*. Tokyo, Maruzen, 1936;

Tokyo, Taiseido, 1956; N. Y. Greenwood Press, 1971. p.707–708

'Histoire innocente; Ceux qui se ressemblent vivent ensemble; Connaissance par le toucher; Mars est là, dans le ciel!; Divertissements dans les rues; Sous les fleurs, je rencontrais un ermite' Tr. par Kuni Matsuo et Steinilber-Oberlin. *Anthologie des poètes japonais contemporains*. Paris, Mercure de France, 1939. p.74–80

'A young girl' Tr. by Shigeshi Nishimura. *The Current of the World*, v.29, no.7, 1952. p.40

'3 tanka' Tr. by V. H. Viglielmo. *Japanese literature in the Meiji era*. Tokyo, Obunsha, 1955. p.386

'The land of netsuke; Winter has come' Tr. by Donald Keene. *Modern Japanese literature*, ed. by D. Keene. N. Y. Grove Press, 1956; Tokyo, Tuttle, 1957. p.206

'Winter has come' Tr. by S. Sato and C. Urdang. *Poetry*, May 1956. p.94

'A night at atelier' *An anthology of modern Japanese poetry*, ed. and tr. by Ichiro Kono and Rikutaro Fukuda. Tokyo, Kenkyusha, 1957. p.133

'My poetry; Taciturn sea captain; The rain-beaten cathedral' *The poetry of living Japan*, by Takamichi Ninomiya and D. J. Enright. London, John Murray, 1957. p.39–44

'La tierra de Netsuke' *Sur*, no.249, 1957. p.98

'A cock horse; Pearl Harbor day; Paris' Tr. by Ryozo Matsumoto. *Japanese literature, new and old*. Tokyo, Hokuseido, 1961. p.243–248

'Chieko fliegt mit dem Winde' Übers. von Kuniyo Takayasu und Manfred Hausmann. *Ruf der Regenpfeifer*. München, Bechtle Verlag, 1961. p.81

'Bedraggled ostrich; Artless talk; Chieko mounting on the wind' Tr. by Geoffrey Bownas and Anthony Thwaite. *The Penguin book of Japanese verse*. Harmondsworth, Penguin Books, 1964. p.181–182

'My poetry' Tr. by T. Ninomiya and D. J. Enright. *Modern Japanese poetry*, by D. Keene. Ann Arbor, Center for Japanese Studies, Univ. of Michigan, 1964. p.39

'A ragged ostrich' Tr. by William L. Clark. *Jiji Eigo Kenkyu*, v.21, no.6, 1966. p.12–13

'기다리고있네 ; 사랑하라 ; 알몸과심장 ; 사라진모나리자' 崔一秀訳 「사랑의詩 日本篇」 서울 韓國政経社 1966. p.13–16, 30–34, 189–192, 236–238

'Mani bagnate di luna; La strada' *La protesta poetica del Giappone*, a cura di Dacia Maraini e Michiko Nojiri. Roma, Officina Edizioni, 1968. p.23–24

'My poetry' Tr. by Takamichi Ninomiya and D. J. Enright. *The Mentor book of modern Asian literature*, ed. by D. B. Shimer. N. Y. New American Library, 1969. p.131

'Voce' Tr. di R. Beviglia. *Antologia della letteratura coreana e giapponese*. Milano, Fratelli Fabbri, 1969. p.278–279

'에게' 「永遠한世界名詩全集 2」 黄錦燦編 서울 翰林出版社 1969. p.118;「永遠한世界名詩全集 5」黄錦燦編 서울 翰林出版社 1973. p.118

'December 8th' Tr. by Donald Keene. *Landscapes and portraits*. Tokyo, Kodansha International, 1971. p.304

'레몬哀歌 ; 첯없는애기 ; 花下仙人 ; 어머니를그리며' 金巣雲訳 「世界의文学大全集 34」 서울 同和出版公社 1971. p.501–503

'A lonely road; The mountain; Chieko and the plovers' Tr. by Hideo Yamaguchi. *Kobe*

Jogakuin Daigaku Ronshu, v.18, no.3, 1972. p.33–37
'A man sharpening a knife; Mars is out; Plum wine; Another rotating thing; The itinerary; Winter has come; Difficult Chieko' *Anthology of modern Japanese poetry*, tr. and comp. by Edith Marcombe Shiffert and Yuki Sawa. Tokyo, Tuttle, 1972. p.41–47
'To someone; Late night snow; Dinner; Two under the tree; Cattle on a mad run; Two at night; Child's talk; Chieko riding the wind; Chieko playing with plover; Invaluable Chieko; Two at the foot of the mountain; Lemon elegy; Barren homecoming; Metropolis; Dream; Soliloquy on a night of blizzard' Tr. by Hiroaki Sato. *Ten Japanese poets*. Hanover, N. H. Granite Publications, 1973. p.8–28
'Cathedral beaten by rain' Tr. by Takuro Ikeda and John Needham. *Poetry Nippon*, *no.24*, 1973. p.14–17
'The bath is brimful; Winter comes' Tr. by Takuro Ikeda, John Needham, and Keiko Kikuchi. *Poetry Nippon*, no.25, 1973. p.15–16
'Father's face; Rodin in the railway carriage; Chieko climbs the wind; Jottings; Winter has come; A long bead drawn on life; Lemon elegy; At a café; You grow more beautiful; Chieko who no longer fits; Person who delivers beauty to imprisonment; The day of Pearl Harbor; Six edgy epigrams; Central Park zoo; Seven impromptu pieces' Tr. by Ikuko Atsumi and Graeme Wilson. *Japan Quarterly*, v.20, no.3, 1973. p.312–318
'Csieko-versek; Szél virága; Csieko játszik; Malagabor' *Válogatott szerelem*. Budapest, Magvető, 1973. p.175–177
'You and I' Tr. by Kyoko Yamasaki. *Poetry Nippon*, no.26, 1974. p.5–6
'A sultry day' Tr. by Keiko Kikuchi. *Poetry Nippon*, no.27, 1974. p.22–23
'Chieko soaring on the wind; Autumn prayer' Tr. by Kyoko Yamasaki and Keiko Kikuchi. *Poetry Nippon*, no.28, 1974. p.17–18
'Long journey' Tr. by Naoshi Koriyama. *Poetry Nippon*, no.28, 1974. p.16
'Night in a studio; Wind; Summer; A sultry day; Winter comes; Night; Mountain; Winter has come; The soil in May; Autumn prayer; You and I; You and I under a tree; You are becoming increasingly lovelier; Chieko soaring on the wind; Chieko plays with plovers; Unattainable Chieko; Alone with you at the mountain; An elegy on lemons; A lost homecoming' Tr. by Keiko Kikuchi and Kyoko Yukawa. *Japanese songs of innocence and experience*. Tokyo, Hokuseido, 1975. p.33–57
'You and I under a tree; Night in a studio; Winter poem' Tr. by Kyoko Yukawa, Keiko Kikuchi, Takuro Ikeda and John Needham. *Poetry Nippon*, no.29 & 30, 1975. p.19–27
'Chieko plays with plovers; Mountain' Tr. by Kyoko Yukawa and Keiko Kikuchi. *Poetry Nippon*, no.31 & 32, 1975. p.37–39
'You are becoming increasingly lovelier' Tr. by Kyoko Yamasaki. *Poetry Nippon*, no.33 & 34, 1976. p.10–11
'Наивный лепет' Перевод Анатолия Мамонова. *Вкус хризантемы*. Москва, Восточная Литература, 1976. p.118
'3 tanka' Tr. by Kikuchi Keiko. *Poetry Nippon*, no.35 & 36, 1976. p.14–15
'Den regnpiskede katedralen' Til norsk ved Paal

Brekke. *Moderne japansk lyrikk*. Oslo, Norske Bokklubben, n.d. p.18–21

Criticism 評論

'日本詩歌的特徵' 傅寶齡訳 「勲章」 台北 文壇社 1960. p.320–327

TAKANO Kikuo 高野喜久雄 1927–

Poems 詩

'Mirror; Like a disk' Tr. by Makoto Ueda. *Literary Review*, v.6, no.1, 1962. p.109
'팽이 ; 부엉이 ; 당신에게 ; 하늘' 辛東門訳 「世界戦後文学全集 9」 서울 新丘文化社 1962. p.249–250
'When I say' Tr. by Hisakazu Kaneko. *London Magazine*, v.7, no.7, 1967. p.34
'Being; I'm; Days' Tr. by Harry and Lynn Guest and Shozo Kajima. *Post-war Japanese poetry*. Harmondsworth, Penguin Books, 1972. p.113–115
'Top; River; A boy and his mother; For you' Tr. by Thomas Fitzsimmons. *Japanese poetry now*. London, André Deutsch, 1972. p.110–112; *Japanese poetry today*. N. Y. Schocken Books, 1972. p.112–114

TAKANO Sujū 高野素十 1893–1976

Haiku 俳句

'8 haiku' *A history of haiku v.2*, by R. H. Blyth. Tokyo, Hokuseido, 1964. p.208–211
'4 haiku' *Anthology of modern Japanese poetry*, tr. and comp. by Edith Marcombe Shiffert and Yuki Sawa. Tokyo, Tuttle, 1972. p.168
'Autumn evening' Tr. by Kenneth Yasuda. *A pepper-pod*. Tokyo, Tuttle, 1976. p.103

TAKANO Tsugi 鷹野つぎ 1890–1943

'Toute seule sous le soleil' Tr. par M. Yoshitomi. *Femmes japonaises et leur littérature*. Paris, Chariot, 1924. p.94–148

TAKAORI Taeko 高折妙子 1912–

Tanka 短歌

'8 tanka' *Anthology of modern Japanese poetry*, tr. and comp. by Edith Marcombe Shiffert and Yuki Sawa. Tokyo, Tuttle, 1972. p.154–156

TAKASAKI Masakaze 高崎正風 1836–1912

Tanka 短歌

'2 tanka' Tr. by Arthur Lloyd. *Eigo Seinen*, v.13, no.7, 1905. p.134
'The poet laureate of Japan' Tr. by Arthur Lloyd. *Open Court*, v.26, 1912. p.694–698
'Love; The generosity of General Kenshin; The

moon above pine trees' Tr. by Asataro Miyamori. *Masterpieces of Japanese poetry, ancient and modern.* Tokyo, Maruzen, 1936; Tokyo, Taiseido, 1956; N. Y. Greenwood Press, 1971. p.605–608

TAKASHIO Haizan　高塩背山　1882–1956

Tanka　短歌

'A white dove' Tr. by Asataro Miyamori. *Masterpieces of Japanese poetry, ancient and modern.* Tokyo, Maruzen, 1936; Tokyo, Taiseido, 1956; N. Y. Greenwood Press, 1971. p.699–700

TAKAYAMA Chogyū　高山樗牛　1871–1902

Jishō no aki　治承の秋

'Der Jisho Aera' Übers von Maria Piper. *Das japanische Theater.* Frankfurt am Main, Societäts Verlag, 1937. p.114–127

Takiguchi Nyūdō　滝口入道

'Takigoutchi Nyoudô' Tr. par Michel Revon. *Anthologie de la littérature japonaise.* Paris, Delagrave, 1910. p.446–448

Tsukiyo no bikan　月夜の美感

'月夜的美感' 丐尊訳　「東方雑誌」　第19巻16号　1922. p.111–120
'Tsukiyo no bikan' Tr. by Kazutomo Takahashi. *Eigo Seinen*, v.60, no.11, 1929. p.402. no.12, 1929. p.440

Criticism　評論

'詩人與批評家' 侍桁訳　「北新半月刊」　第2巻9期　1927.

TAKAYANAGI Katsuhei　高柳勝平

Tanka　短歌

'1 tanka' Tr. by Shigeshi Nishimura. *Eigo Seinen*, v.93, no.3, 1947. p.120

TAKAYANAGI Shigenobu　高柳重信　1923–

Haiku　俳句

'6 haiku' Tr. by Edith Shiffert. *Literary Review*, v.6, no.1, 1962. p.105
'6 haiku' *Anthology of modern Japanese poetry*, tr. and comp. by Edith Marcombe Shiffert and Yuki Sawa. Tokyo, Tuttle, 1972. p.175–176

TAKAYASU Gekkō　高安月郊　1869–1944

Sakura shigure　桜時雨

'The cherry shower' Tr. by A. L. Sadler. *Japanese plays.* Sydney, Angus and Robertson, 1934. p.155–192

TAKAYASU Kuniyo　高安国世　1913–

Tanka　短歌

Herbstmond. Gesetzt aus der Boris Palatino und der Korpus Post-Kursiv. Esslingen, Bechtle Verlag, 1959. 48p.
'2 tanka' *Anthology of modern Japanese poetry*, tr. and comp. by Edith Marcombe Shiffert and Yuki Sawa. Tokyo, Tuttle, 1972. p.157–158

TAKEBAYASHI Musōan　武林無想庵　1880–1962

Ryu do riiru 28 banchi maɖe　リュ・ド・リイル廿八番地まで

'28 Rue de Lille' Tr. by Kanesada Hanazono. *Osaka Mainichi*, Jan. 13–17, 1926.

TAKEDA Kōichi　武田幸一　1908–

Poems　詩

'Ворота' Перевод Веры Марковой. *Восточный альманах 6.* Москва, Худож. Лит. 1963. p.331

TAKEDA Naoko　武田尚子　1931–

Poems　詩

'Розарии дружбы' Перевод А. И. Мамонова. *Свободный стих в японской поэзии.* Москва, Наука, 1971. p.181–182

TAKEDA Ōtō　武田鶯塘　1871–1935

Haiku　俳句

'Whitebait' Tr. by Asataro Miyamori. *Anthology of haiku, ancient and modern.* Tokyo, Maruzen, 1932. p.777; *Haiku poems, ancient and modern.* Tokyo, Maruzen, 1940. p.319
'1 haiku' Tr. by Lois J. Erickson. *Songs from the land of dawn.* N. Y. Friendship Press, 1949; Freeport, Books for Libraries Press, 1968. p.77
'The catch' Tr. by Harold Stewart. *A net of fireflies.* Tokyo, Tuttle, 1960. p.29

TAKEDA Rintarō　武田麟太郎　1904–1946

Arappoi mura　あらっぽい村

'Raubirska vesnice' Přel. A. Pultr. *Nový Orient*, v.2, no.2–3, 1947. p.8–10. no.4, 1947. p.17–20. no.5, 1947. p.27–28. no.8, 1947. p.22–23. no.9–10, 1947. p.4–5

TAKEDA Rintarō

Daburyū machi no teisō W町の貞操

'W鎮的貞操' 査士驤訳 「東方雑誌」 第27巻24期 1930. p.115–120

Nihon sanmon opera 日本三文オペラ

'日本三文오페라' 金龍済訳 「日本代表作家百人集 1」 서울 希望出版社 1966. p.366–381;「日本短篇文学全集 2」 서울 新太陽社 1969. p.10–25

Shikisai 色彩

'色彩' 高汝鴻訳 「日本短篇小説集」 台北 台湾商務印書館 1969. p.169–181

Udon うどん

'Vermacelo' Tr. Kojiro Nakagaki. *El japana literaturo.* Tokyo, Japana Esperanto Instituto, 1965. p.211–222

─────────

'Stato d'animo' *Yamato*, v.1, no.4, 1941.

TAKEDA Taijun 武田泰淳 1912–1976

Hashi o kizuku 橋を築く

'The bridge' Tr. by Warren Carlisle. *Literary Review*, v.6, no.1, 1962. p.68–69
'To build a bridge' Tr. by Edward Seidensticker. *Contemporary Japanese literature*, ed. by Howard Hibbett. N. Y. Knopf, 1977. p.239–246

Hikari goke ひかりごけ

'Светящийся мох' Перевод Л. Бабкиной. *Японская новелла*. Москва, Изд. Иност. Лит. 1961. p.295–324
'Světélkujici mech' Přel. V. Winkelhöferová. *Světová Literatura*, 1964, no.5. p.82–104
'Luminous moss' Tr. by Yusaburo Shibuya and Sanford Goldstein. *This outcast generation, and Luminous moss*. Tokyo, Tuttle, 1967. p.93–145

Igyō no mono 異形の者

'The misshapen ones' Tr. by E. G. Seidensticker. *Japan Quarterly*, v.4, no.4, 1957. p.472–498; *Modern Japanese short stories*. Tokyo, Japan Publications Trading Co. 1960. p.52–89; Rev. ed. Tokyo, Japan Publications Trading Co. 1970. p.42–71

Jōbu na nyōbō wa arigatai 丈夫な女房はありがたい

'Precious is a healthy wife' Tr. by Tsutomu Shiga. *Tezukayama Tanki Daigaku Kiyo*, no.7, 1970. p.33–36

Mamushi no sue 蝮の裔

'This outcast generation' Tr. by Yusaburo Shibuya and Sanford Goldstein. *This outcast generation, and Luminous moss*. Tokyo, Tuttle, 1967. p.21–89

Mono kuu onna もの食う女

'The eatingest girl' Tr. by John Nathan. *Japan Quarterly*, v.12, no.4, 1965. p.483–490

Saishi kajin 才子佳人

'才士佳人' 崔白山訳 「日本代表作家百人集 4」 서울 希望出版社 1966. p.260–284;「日本短篇文学全集 5」 서울 新太陽社 1969. p.100–123

TAKEDA Tetsuzō 竹田鉄三 1901–

Haiku 俳句

'24 haiku' Tr. by Gene Lehman. *Japan Christian Quarterly*, v.41, no.4, 1975. p.222–229

TAKEDA Tomoju 武田友寿 1931–

Bungaku to jinsei 文学と人生

「문학과인생」 李錫鉉訳 서울 聖바오로社 1974. 190p.

TAKEMURA Toshio 竹村俊郎 1896–1944

Poems 詩

'Blonde hair' Tr. by Hisakazu Kaneko. *London Magazine*, v.6, no.9, 1966. p.22

TAKENAKA Iku 竹中 郁 1904–

Poems 詩

'At Lyons' Tr. by S. Sato and C. Urdang. *Poetry*, May 1956. p.77
'Swallows; A thinking stone; At a hotel in Cairo; My reflection; Tourists' Japan; Crumbling sand' *An anthology of modern Japanese poetry*, ed. and tr. by Ichiro Kono and Rikutaro Fukuda. Tokyo, Kenkyusha, 1957. p.134–137
'Japan for sightseeing; At the close of day; Memory of a witch' *The poetry of living Japan*, by Takamichi Ninomiya and D. J. Enright. London, John Murray, 1957. p.72–84
'Al caer del dia' *Sur*, no.249, 1957. p.99
'Nachruf auf eine Taschenspielerin' Übertragen von Shin Aizu. *Der schwermütige Ladekran*. St. Gallen, Tschudy Verlag, 1960. p.26–27
'Kirlangiçlar; Düşünen taş; Turistlerin Japonyasi' Tercüme etmek L. Sami Akalin. *Japon şiiri*. İstanbul, Varlik Yayinevi, 1962. p.278–280
'Story; Thinking stone; Stars; Tourist Japan' Tr. by Geoffrey Bownas and Anthony Thwaite. *The Penguin book of Japanese verse*. Harmondsworth, Penguin Books, 1964. p.218–220
'심장처럼빨갛게' 崔一秀訳 「기다리고있네」 서울 韓国政経社 1966. p.104–109
'Stelle; Giappone per turisti' *La protesta poetica del Giappone*, a cura di Dacia Maraini e Michiko Nojiri. Roma, Officina Edizioni, 1968. p.53–54
'地圖；片斷；鴿糞；起程' 陳千武 徐和隣訳 「現代詩解説」 台北 葡萄園詩刊社 1970. p.28–33
'Stars at night; Despair' *Anthology of modern Japanese poetry*, tr. and comp. by Edith Marcombe Shiffert and Yuki Sawa. Tokyo, Tuttle, 1972. p.100–101
'Ночные звезды; Япония для туристов; Отчаяние' Перевод Анатолия Мамонова. *Вкус*

хризантемы. Москва, Восточная Литература, 1976. p.124–125
'Japan for turistene; Mitt speilbilde; Stjerner' Til norsk ved Paal Brekke. *Modern Japansk lyrikk.* Oslo, Norske Bokklubben, n.d. p.58–60
'Piatra gînditoare; Stele; Japonia pentru turisti' Traducerea Ion Ascan. *Din lirica japoneză.* Bucureşti, Editura Univers, n.d. p.203–205

TAKESHIMA Hagoromo　武島羽衣　1872–1967

Tanka　短歌

'A stone; To-day; Poetry; Shiobara' Tr. by Asataro Miyamori. *Masterpieces of Japanese poetry, ancient and modern.* Tokyo, Maruzen, 1936; Tokyo, Taiseido, 1956; N. Y. Greenwood Press, 1971. p.643–646
'2 tanka' Übers. von Gerolf Coudenhove. *Japanische Jahreszeiten.* Zürich, Manesse Verlag, 1963. p.168, 278

TAKETOMO Sōfū　竹友藻風　1891–1954

Criticism　評論

'文學的意義之新解釋' 張資平訳 「當代文藝」 第1卷5期 1931. p.1033–1044

TAKEUCHI Katsutarō　竹内勝太郎　1894–1935

Poems　詩

'Himmel und Erde' Übers. von Kuniyo Takayasu und Manfred Hausmann. *Ruf der Regenpfeifer.* München, Bechtle Verlag, 1961. p.88
'The moon and the echo' Tr. by Naotomi Kurata. *Poetry Nippon,* no.11, 1970. p.17

TAKEUCHI Teruyo　竹内てるよ　1904–

Poems　詩

'我, 活着' 徐和隣訳 「現代詩解説」 台北 葡萄園詩刊社 1970. p.10–13

TAKEYAMA Michio　竹山道雄　1903–

Biruma no tategoto　ビルマの竪琴

The harp of Burma. Tr. by Kinichi Ishikawa. Tokyo, Chuo Koronsha, 1950. 199p.
De harp van Birma. Tr. Frans Uyttendaele. Leuven, Davidsfonds, 1964. 215p.
Harp of Burma. Tr. by Howard Hibbett. Tokyo, Tuttle, 1966. 132p.; London, Prentice-Hall, 1966. 132p.

Essays　エッセイ

'The secularization of feudal Japan' *Japan Quarterly,* v.6, no.1, 1959. p.13–22

'Tradition and Japanese youth' *Japan Quarterly,* v.7, no.3, 1960. p.274–280
'Schuldbarkeit' Übers. von Josef Roggendorf. *Kagami,* Bd. 3, Heft 1, 1965. p.69–74

TAKI Kazuo　多岐一雄　1931–

Rikon　離婚

'離婚' 劉慕沙訳 「日本現代小説選 1」 台北 聯經出版 1976. p.163–219

TAKIGAWA Kyō　多岐川　恭　1920–

Akuma no kake　悪魔の賭け

'悪魔的賭博' 文良出版社訳 「推理小説日本偵探名著」 台南 文良出版社 1969. p.1–52

Aru kyōhaku　或る脅迫

'어떤脅迫' 張壽哲訳 「日本代表作家百人集 5」 서울 希望出版社 1966. p.52–66; 「日本短篇文学全集 5」 서울 新太陽社 1969. p.348–362

Shukumei to raiu　宿命と雷雨

「預言」 朱佩蘭訳 嘉義 明山書局 1968. 266p.

'流浪人' 劉慕沙訳 「狐鶏」 台北 林白出版社 1969. p.39–83

TAKIGUCHI Masako　滝口雅子　1918–

Poems　詩

'Poems' Tr. by Shonosuke Ishii. *Tenggara,* v.2, no.1, 1968. p.13–15
'About men' Tr. by Greg Campbell. *Trans-Pacific,* no.5, 1970. p.20
'On man; Future; Blue horse; Just one; Flame' Tr. by Hajime Kijima, John Bean and Fukuko Kobayashi. *The poetry of postwar Japan.* Iowa City, Univ. of Iowa Press, 1975. p.45–48
'Синяя лошадь; О мужчинах' Перевод Анатолия Мамонова. *Вкус хризантемы.* Москва, Восточная Литература, 1976. p.121–122
'Slaughterhouse; Blue horse' *The burning heart,* tr. and ed. by Kenneth Rexroth and Ikuko Atsumi. N. Y. Seabury Press, 1977. p.93–94

TAKIGUCHI Shūzō　滝口修造　1903–

Poems　詩

'Etamines narratives; Amphibia; Basse élégie; The Sphinx of May; Salvador Dali; Max Ernst; René Magritte; Joan Miro; Pablo Picasso; Man Ray; Yves Tanguy' Tr. by Hiroaki Sato. *Ten Japanese poets.* Hanover, N. H. Granite Publications, 1973. p.40–55

TAKIYA Sueko

TAKIYA Sueko　滝谷末子

'茫茫地獄道' 徐雲濤訳 「當代日本小説選」 台南　經緯書局　1954. p.95–110; 「當代日本創作小説」 台南　經緯書局　1961. p.95–110; 「當代日本短篇小説選」 台南　大行出版社　1973. p.95–110

TAKUBO Hideo　田久保英夫　1928–

Fukai kawa　深い河

'깊은江' 金潤成訳 「깊은江」 서울　三耕社　1971. p.371–421

TAMAI Michiko　玉井美知子

Kōkan nikki　交換日記

「니지꼬와게이스께의交換日記」 申東燁訳 서울　隆文社 1965. 1冊
「오고간対話」 申東燁訳 서울　美林出版社 1969. 202p.

TAMIYA Torahiko　田宮虎彦　1911–

Aijō ni tsuite　愛情について

「내가슴에그가산다」 朴巨影訳　서울　人間社　1964. 200p.

Ashizuri misaki　足摺岬

'The promontory' Tr. by Kazuji Ninomiya and Sanford Goldstein. *The Archives* (Duke Univ.) Dec. 1960; *The Japanese image*, v.2, ed. by M. Schneps and A. D. Coox. Tokyo, Orient West, 1966. p.190–207

Chōsen daría　朝鮮ダリア

'韓国달리아' 表文台訳 「日本代表作家百人集 4」 서울　希望出版社　1966. p.188–211; 「日本短篇文学全集 5」 서울　新太陽社　1969. p.28–51
'韓国의다알리아' 河在麒訳 「日本文学全集 10」 서울　東西文化院　1975. p.285–308

Ehon　絵本

'The picture book' Tr. by Charles S. Terry. *Japan Quarterly*, v.4, no.1, 1957. p.40–56

Kaki no ki　柿の木

'The persimmon tree' Tr. by Takashi Kojima. *Eigo Kenkyu*, v.43, no.7, 1953.

Wakarete ikiru toki mo　別れて生きる時も

「이별없이살았으면」 朴巨影訳　서울　五倫出版社 1972. 200p.

Yōjo no koe　幼女の声

'The voice of a little girl' Tr. by Takashi Kojima. *Eigo Kenkyu*, v.41, no.1, 1952. p.26–29. no.2, 1952. p.26–29. no.3, 1952. p.61–64. no.4, 1952. p.40–43. no.5, 1952. p.32–35. no.6, 1952. p.16–20

TAMURA Ryūichi　田村隆一　1923–

Poems　詩

'A poem of October' Tr. by Shigehisa Narita. *Japan Quarterly*, v.3, no.1, 1956. p.87
'The emperor' *An anthology of modern Japanese poetry*, ed. and tr. by Ichiro Kono and Rikutaro Fukuda. Tokyo, Kenkyusha, 1957. p.139
'Un poème d'octobre' *La poésie japonaise*, par Karl Petit. Paris, Seghers, 1959. p.239
'天使' 金龍済訳 「日本詩集」 서울　青雲社　1960. p.92–93
'幻想을보는사람; 鈍한마음; 四千의날과밤' 辛東門訳 「世界戦後文学全集 9」 서울　新丘文化社 1962. p.253
'October poem; Three voices; Four thousand days and nights' Tr. by Geoffrey Bownas and Anthony Thwaite. *The Penguin book of Japanese verse*. Harmondsworth, Penguin Books, 1964. p.226–230
'1 poem' Tr. by Donald Keene. *Modern Japanese poetry*, by D. Keene. Ann Arbor, Center for Japanese Studies, Univ. of Michigan, 1964. p.32–33; *Landscapes and portraits*. Tokyo, Kodansha International, 1971. p.150–151
'Poema de Octobre' Tr. por Kikuya Ionesawa. *Poesia japonesa contemporanea*. Bogotá, Colombia Editoriales de Librería, 1965. n.p.
'Invisible tree' Tr. by Rikutaro Fukuda. *Asian PEN anthology*, ed. by F. Sionil Jose. N. Y. Taplinger, 1966. p.333
'다시만나면' 崔一秀訳 「기다리고있네」 서울　韓国政経社　1966. p.71–73
'Quattro milla giorni e quattro milla notti; Strada di ritorno; L'angelo; Poesia di ottobre' *La protesta poetica del Giappone*, a cura di Dacia Maraini e Michiko Nojiri. Roma, Officina Edizioni, 1968. p.87–90
'The three voices; The world without words' Tr. by Sam and Yuriko Grolmes. *Literature East and West*, v.13, no.3 & 4, 1969. p.404–415
'Four thousand days and nights' *Anthology of modern Japanese poetry*, tr. and comp. by Edith Marcombe Shiffert and Yuki Sawa. Tokyo, Tuttle, 1971. p.125–126
'A far country; Unseen trees; A man who writes a poem' Tr. by Harry and Lynn Guest and Shozo Kajima. *Post-war Japanese poetry*. Harmondsworth, Penguin Books, 1972. p.90–93
'Far-off; Four thousand days and nights' Tr. by Geoffrey Bownas. *New writing in Japan*. Harmondsworth, Penguin Books, 1972. p.208–209
'Seer; The three voices; Invisible tree; Four thousand days and nights; Meet again' Tr. by Thomas Fitzsimmons. *Japanese poetry now*. London, André Deutsch, 1972. p.120–125; *Japanese poetry today*. N. Y. Schocken Books, 1972. p.122–127
'A study in terror' *Chicago Review*, v.25, no.2, 1973. p.120–125
「田村隆一詩文集」 陳千武訳 台北　幼獅文藝社　1974. 223p.
'The man who sees the phantom; Four thousand days and nights; October poem; Narrow line; Hoshino's hint; Angels; On my way back; World without words' Tr. by Takako Uchino Lento. *The poetry of postwar Japan*. Iowa City, Univ. of Iowa Press, 1975. p.79–91
'Четыре тысячи дней и ночей' Перевод Анатолия Мамонова. *Вкус хризантемы*. Москва,

Восточная Литература, 1976. p.126
'The man with a green face; Human house' Tr. by Christopher Drake. *Contemporary Japanese literature*, ed. by Howard Hibbett. N. Y. Knopf, 1977. p.335–337
'Unsichtbare Bäume' Übers. von Helmut Gross. *Internationales Jahrbuch für Literatur*, Ensemble 8, 1977. p.98–99
'Poem de octombrie' Traducerea Virgil Teodorescu. *Din lirica japoneză*. Bucureşti, Editura Univers, n.d. p.212
'Tre stemmer stemmer; Fire tusen dager og netter' Til norsk ved Paal Brekke. *Moderne japansk lyrikk*. Oslo, Norske Bokklubben, n.d. p.70–73

Criticism 評論

'地獄的發現・乾燥的眼―西脇順三郎與金子光晴' 陳千武訳 「笠」 第57期 1962. p.43–51
「田村隆一詩文集」 陳千武訳 台北 幼獅文藝社 1974. 223p.

TAMURA Tadaya 田村忠也 1926–

Poems 詩

'Go back home' *An anthology of modern Japanese poetry*, ed. and tr. by Ichiro Kono and Rikutaro Fukuda. Tokyo, Kenkyusha, 1957. p.138

TAMURA Taijirō 田村泰次郎 1911–

Nigeta sakana 逃げた魚

'漏網之魚' 傅寳齡訳 「勲章」 台北 文壇社 1960. p.198–205

Nikutai no akuma 肉体の悪魔

'肉体의悪魔' 金洙暎訳 「日本代表作家百人集 4」 서울 希望出版社 1966. p.214–244;「日本短篇文学全集 5」 서울 新太陽社 1969. p.54–84
'肉体의悪魔' 李喜春訳 「日本文学全集 10」 서울 東西文化院 1975. p.81–110

Nikutai no mon 肉体の門

'The gateway of flesh' Tr. by Alan Masaru Suzuki. *Preview*, v.7, no.4, 5, 1955.

TAMURA Toshiko 田村俊子 1884–1945

'壓迫' 張資平訳 「壓迫」 上海 新宇宙書局 1929;「資平譯品集」 上海 現代書局 192?.

TANABE Kiichi 田辺機一 1856–1933

Haiku 俳句

'3 haiku' Tr. by Asataro Miyamori. *Anthology of haiku, ancient and modern*. Tokyo, Maruzen, 1932. p.704–706
'The cuckoo' Tr. by Asataro Miyamori. *Haiku poems, ancient and modern*. Tokyo, Maruzen, 1940. p.302–303
'1 haiku' Übers. von Erwin Jahn. *Fallende Blüten*. Zürich, Arche, 1968. p.61

TANABE Moichi 田辺茂一 1905–

Yoru no shichō 夜の市長

Mayor of the night. Tr. by Paul T. Konya. Tokyo, Yohan Publications, 1968. 233p.

TANAKA Chikao 田中千禾夫 1905–

Hizen fudoki 肥前風土記

'Historia de Hizen' Tr. por Josefina Keiko Ezaki. *Teatro japonés contemporaneo*. Madrid, Aguilar, 1964. p.25–94

TANAKA Fuyuji 田中冬二 1894–

Poems 詩

'Native village; A small mountain town; Evening landscape; One day in winter; By the marsh; The village; The cold glass door; Wooddocks returning north-ward' Tr. by S. Sato and C. Urdang. *Poetry*, May 1956. p.63–66
'A chilly moonrise; Autumn in Japan; A cold glazed door' *An anthology of modern Japanese poetry*, ed. and tr. by Ichiro Kono and Rikutaro Fukuda. Tokyo, Kenkyusha, 1957. p.140–141
'Mosquito net; Stone staircase overlooking the sea' *The poetry of living Japan*, by Takamichi Ninomiya and D. J. Enright. London, John Murray, 1957. p.87–88
'Près des marais; Bécasses retournant vers le nord; Mon village natal' *La poésie japonaise*, par Karl Petit. Paris, Seghers, 1959. p.220–221
'南亜聯邦銀行의花氷' 金龍済訳 「日本詩集」 서울 青雲社 1960. p.100–102
'Japonya'da sonbahar' Tercüme etmek L· Sami Akalin. *Japon şiiri*. İstanbul, Varlik Yayinevi, 1962. p.262
'Mosquito-net; Early summer in Izu' Tr. by Hisakazu Kaneko. *Orient West*, v.8, no.1, 1963. p.49, 51
'Lakeside hotel; Autumn night; Blue night road' Tr. by Geoffrey Bownas and Anthony Thwaite. *The Penguin book of Japanese verse*. Harmondsworth, Penguin Books, 1964. p.195–196
'En la cienaga' Tr. por Kikuya Ionesawa. *Poesia japonesa contemporanea*. Bogotá, Colombia Editoriales de Librería, 1965. n.p.
'Mosquito-net; Early summer in Izu' Tr. by Hisakazu Kaneko. *The Japanese image*, ed. by M. Schneps and A. D. Coox. Tokyo, Orient West, 1965. p.349–351
'Kawagushi village; Autumn night' Tr. by Hisakazu Kaneko. *London Magazine*, v.6, no.9, 1966. p.24–26
'바다가보이는; 浪漫의그림자' 崔一秀訳 「기다리고있네」 서울 韓国政経社 1966. p.177–178, 229–230
'Early summer in Izu' Tr. by Hisakazu Kaneko. *London Magazine*, v.7, no.7, 1967. p.35
'바다가보이는돌층계' 「永遠한世界의名詩全集 2」 黄錦燦編 서울 翰林出版社 1969. p.93;「永遠한世界의名詩全集 5」 黄錦燦編 서울 翰林出版社 1973. p. 93
'접시' 金光林訳 「現代詩学」 第4巻3号 1972.
'Hanul de linga lac; Satul meu' Traducerea Virgil Teodorescu. *Din lirica japoneză*. Bucureşti, Editura Univers, n.d. p.180–181

TANAKA Hidemitsu

TANAKA Hidemitsu 田中英光 1913–1949

Orinposu no kajitsu オリンポスの果実

'The fruit of *Olympos*' Tr. by Atsumu Kanayama. *The Reeds*, v.14, 1976. p.1–18

TANAKA Kametarō 田中亀太郎

Poems 詩

'Реальное видение' Перевод Анатолия Мамонова. *Песни Хиросимы.* Москва, Худож. Лит. 1964. p. 25; *Вкус хризантемы.* Москва, Восточная Литература, 1976. p.128

TANAKA Katsumi 田中克己 1911–

Chūgoku kōhi den 中国后妃伝

「五人의女傑―中国史話」 鄭秀重訳 서울 三正文化社 1967. 345p.

Poems 詩

'Chance encounter and wilderness' Tr. by D. J. Enright. *Bulletin of the Japan Society of London*, no.20, Oct. 1955. p.10
'Chance encounter; Wilderness' *The poetry of living Japan*, by Takamichi Ninomiya and D. J. Enright. London, John Murray, 1957. p.91–92
'Encuentro casual' *Sur*, no.249, Nov.-Dec. 1957. p.99
'Suicide unattained' *An anthology of modern Japanese poetry*, ed. and tr. by Ichiro Kono and Rikutaro Fukuda. Tokyo, Kenkyusha, 1957. p.141
'Gerçekleşmiyen harakiri' Tercüme etmek L. Sami Akalin. *Japon şiiri.* İstanbul, Varlik Yayinevi, 1962. p.294
'Intilniri neintimplate' Traducerea Dan Constantinescu. *Din lirica japoneză*. Bucureşti, Editura Univers, n.d. p.209

TANAKA Kishirō 田中喜四郎 1900–

Poems 詩

'Холм; Закат' Перевод Анатолия Мамонова. *Песни Хиросимы.* Москва, Худож. Лит. 1964. p.15–16; *Вкус хризантемы.* Москва, Восточная Литература, 1976. p.129
'The mound; The setting sun; The night of autumn rain' Tr. by Miyao Ohara. *The songs of Hiroshima.* Tokyo, Taihei Shuppansha, 1971. p.38–47
'Uliul gigant' Traducerea Dan Constantinescu. *Din lirica japoneză*. Bucureşti, Editura Univers, n.d. p.165

TANAKA Kishō 田中奇笑 1890–

Haiku 俳句

'A great kite' Tr. by Asataro Miyamori. *Antho-*

logy of haiku, ancient and modern. Tokyo, Maruzen, 1932. p.822
'1 haiku' Übers. von Gerolf Coudenhove. *Japanische Jahreszeiten.* Zürich, Manesse Verlag, 1963. p.283

TANAKA Kogetsu 田中湖月

Criticism 評論

「文藝鑑賞論」 孫俍工訳 上海 中華書局 1935. 1冊

TANAKA Sumie 田中澄江 1908–

Tsuzumi no onna つづみの女

'La mujer del tambor' Tr. por Josefina Keiko Ezaki. *Teatro japonés contemporaneo.* Madrid, Aguilar, 1964. p.229–284

Essay エッセイ

「少女的生活藝術」 張秀英訳 三重市 大立書店 1969. 202p.

TANAMI Mishiro 田波御白 1885–1913

Tanka 短歌

'Tanka' Tr. by Shigeshi Nishimura. *The Current of the World*, v.13, 1936.
'The death-verse' Tr. by Asataro Miyamori. *Masterpieces of Japanese poetry, ancient and modern.* Tokyo, Maruzen, 1936; Tokyo, Taiseido, 1956; N. Y. Greenwood Press 1971. p.779–780

TANEDA Santōka 種田山頭火 1882–1940

Haiku 俳句

'36 haiku' *A history of haiku v.2*, by R. H. Blyth. Tokyo, Hokuseido, 1964. p.173–188
'Hail in the begging bowl: the Odyssey and poetry of Santoka (167 haiku)' by James Abrams. *Monumenta Nipponica*, v.32, no.3, 1977. p.269–302

TANI Shinsuke 谷 真介 1935–

Jūnanasai no kisetsu 十七歳の季節

「푸른계절」 郭漢哲訳 서울 隆文社 1964. 218p.

Ushinawarenu kisetsu 失われぬ季節

Дети из дома No. 300. Перевод Г. Ронской. Москва, Дет. Гиз. 1976. 96p.

TANIGAWA Gan 谷川 雁 1923–

Poems 詩

'Non andare a Tokyo; Hongo' *La protesta poe-*

tica del Giappone, a cura di Dacia Maraini e Michiko Nojiri. Roma, Officina Edizioni, 1958. p.93–94

'Merchant; Shipwrecked' Tr. by Makoto Ueda. *Literary Review*, v.6, no.1, 1962. p.110–111

'나의墓標의옥타아브 ; 구름이여' 辛東門訳 「世界戦後文学全集 9」 서울 新丘文化社 1962. p.250–251

'Don't go to Tokyo' Tr. by Thomas Fitzsimmons. *Japanese poetry now*. London. André Deutsch, 1972. p.106; *Japanese poetry today*. N. Y. Schocken Books, 1972. p.108

'Mao Tse-tung' Tr. by Harry and Lynn Guest and Shozo Kajima. *Post-war Japanese poetry*. Harmondsworth, Penguin Books, 1972. p.94

TANIGUCHI Kisaku 谷口喜作 1902–1948

Haiku 俳句

'1 haiku' Tr. by Harold Gould Henderson. *The bamboo broom*. Tokyo, J. L. Thompson, 1933; London, Kegan Paul, 1933. p.119

TANIGUCHI Masaru 谷口 勝 1916–

Seiya senri 征野千里

The soldier's log. Tr. by R. Toombs Fincher and Yoshi Okada. Tokyo, Hokuseido, 1940. 176p.

TANIGUCHI Zentarō 谷口善太郎 1899–

Men 綿

'Gyapot' Ford. Sz. Holti Mária. *Modern Japán elbeszélők*. Budapest, Európa Könyvkiadó, 1967. p.169–202

TANIKAWA Shuntarō 谷川俊太郎 1931–

Ken wa hetchara ケンはへっちゃら

Ken im Glück. Übers. von Siegfried Schaarschmidt. Berlin, Dressler, 1971. 59p.

Ki き

My tree. Retold by Karen Stenback Stark. Minneapolis, Lerner, 1969. 1v.

Poems 詩

'Museum' Tr. by S. Sato and C. Urdang. *Poetry*, May 1956. p.70

'Museum' *An anthology of modern Japanese poetry*, ed. and tr. by Ichiro Kono and Rikutaro Fukuda. Tokyo, Kenkyusha, 1957. p.141

'Musée' *La poésie japonaise*, par Karl Petit. Paris, Seghers, 1959. p.240

'Múzeum' Ford. Illyés Gyula. *Nagyvilág*, no.10, 1960.

'부탁' 金龍済訳 「日本詩集」 서울 青雲社 1960. p.84–88

'Three sonnets' Tr. by Akira Ueda. *Literary Review*, v.6, no.1, 1962. p.119–120

'베로 ; 슬픔 ; 쏘베트' 辛東門訳 「世界戦後文学全集 9」 서울 新丘文化社 1962. p.251–252

'When the wind is strong; The isolation of two milliard light years; Growing up; Family' Tr. by Geoffrey Bownas and Anthony Thwaite. *The Penguin book of modern Japanese verse*. Harmondsworth, Penguin Books, 1964. p.230–233

'Poem' *Asian PEN anthology*, ed. by F. Sionil Jose. N. Y. Taplinger, 1966. p.323

'At a museum; Nero' Tr. by Hisakazu Kaneko. *London Magazine*, v.7, no.7, 1967. p.37

'Le cose che non parlano; Quando le parole; Sonetto 57; Sonetto 30; Dai tre ai diciotto anni' *La protesta poetica del Giappone*, a cura di Dacia Maraini e Michiko Nojiri. Roma, Officina Edizioni, 1968. p.123–127

'Sonnet' Tr. by Makoto Ueda. *The Mentor book of modern Asian literature*, ed. by D. B. Shimer. N. Y. New American Library, 1969. p.130

'Унум; Сунуу' Которгон Ж. Садыков. *Хиросима кектери*. Фрунзе, Кыргызстан, 1969. p.72–73

'August' Tr. by Greg Campbell. *TransPacific*, no.5, 1970. p.22

'From a syllabary of seeing; Studies of womankind; The first syllable' Tr. by Ikuko Atsumi and Graeme Wilson. *Quadrant*, Nov.-Dec. 1970. p.59

'Cycle of the months' Tr. by Harold P. Wright. *Sumac*, v.4, no.1, 1971.

'A syllabary of seeing' Tr. by Atsumi Ikuko and Graeme Wilson. *Japan Quarterly*, v.18, no.1, 1971. p.80–84

'Growth; The hospital; The kiss; Distress; Picnic to the earth' *Anthology of modern Japanese poetry*, tr. and comp. by Edith Marcombe Shiffert and Yuki Sawa. Tokyo, Tuttle, 1972. p.129–132

'The yellow poet' Tr. by Wesley Richard and Y. Yaguchi. *Poetry Nippon*, no.18, 1972. p.18

'Family portrait; No.62; A child and a railroad; Love to Paul Klee; Little boy's march; Yellow poet; Still life; The sounds for John Cage; Mooncircles/menstruation; Go' Tr. by Thomas Fitzsimmons. *Japanese poetry now*. London, André Deutsch, 1972. p.12–21; *Japanese poetry today*. N. Y. Schocken Books, 1972. p.14–23

'Improvisation on my desk; The silent room; The poem-man I didn't know; The yellow poet' Tr. by Harry and Lynn Guest and Shozo Kajima. *Post-war Japanese poetry*. Harmondsworth, Penguin Books, 1972. p.137–140

'On fate; Jazz at night; Counting; Cycle of the months' Tr. by James Kirkup and Fumiko Miura. *New writing in Japan*. Harmondsworth, Penguin Books, 1972. p.213–217

'Nero' Tr. by Geoffrey Bownas. *New writing in Japan*. Harmondsworth, Penguin Books, 1972. p.218–219

'A syllabary of seeing; Portraits of womankind; Oddly enough; Sea; Moonlover; I too; Ma; TV political debate; Anonym 3; Anonym 6; Travel 1; Travel 3, Arizona; Toba 1; Travel 5' Tr. by Graeme Wilson and Atsumi Ikuko. *Three contemporary Japanese poets*. London, Magazine Editions, 1972. p.62–80

'Cycle of the months; Hands' Tr. by Harold P. Wright. *Listening to Japan*, ed. by Jackson H. Bailey. N. Y. Praeger, 1973. p.84, 87

'Growth; Museum; Picnic to the earth; Cycle of

months (Menstruation); Hands; Billy the Kid; Beggar; Dog; Adherence to apples; Sonnet 41; Oddly enough; Mama; Marijuana; Cool' Tr. by Harold Wright, Hajime Kajima, John Bean, Ikuko Atsumi and Takako Uchino Lento. *The poetry of postwar Japan.* Iowa City, Univ. of Iowa Press, 1975. p.164–178

'Возраст; Поцелуй; Одиночество в два миллиарда световых лет; Гуманизм; Сонет No. 62; Когда штормит' Перевод Анатолия Мамонова. *Вкус хризантемы.* Москва, Восточная Литература, 1976. p.130–133

'Das Fenster; Liebe' Übers. von Helmut Gross. *Internationales Jahrbuch für Literatur*, Ensemble 8, 1977. p.95–97

'Museu; Izolarea celor două miliarde de anilumină' Traducerea Dan Constantinescu & Ion Ascan. *Din lirica japoneză.* Bucureşti, Editura Univers, n.d. p.213

TANIUCHI Kōta　谷内こうた

Densha　でんしゃ

The runaway tram. Retold by Peggy Blakeley. London, Black, 1970. 24p.
Trolly. N. Y. Watts, 1970. 1v.

Natsu no asa　なつのあさ

Boy on a hill top. English version by Peggy Blakeley. London, Black, 1970. 23p.
Up on a hilltop. N. Y. Watts, 1971. 25p.
Pojken på kullen. Övers. av Britt G. Hallqvist. Örebro, I. P. C. 1973. 24p.

Ojiisan no baiorin　おじいさんのバイオリン

The north star man. Tr. by Tamao Fujita. N. Y. Watts, 1970. 25p.

TANIZAKI Jun'ichirō　谷崎潤一郎　1886–1965

Akuma　悪魔

'悪魔' 章克標訳 「東方雑誌」 第25巻19期 1928. p.95–106;「悪魔」 上海 華通書局 1930.

Aoi hana　青い花

'Aguri' Tr. by Howard Hibbett. *Seven Japanese tales.* N. Y. Knopf, 1963; London, Secker and Warburg, 1964; Tokyo, Tuttle, 1967. p.186–204

Aisureba koso　愛すればこそ

Puisque je l'aime. Tr. par Charles Jacob. Paris, Emile Paul Frères, 1925. 166p.

Aru shōnen no osore　或る少年の怯れ

'어느少年의두려움' 張喜汎訳 「世界代表文学全集 9」 서울 高麗出版社 1976. p.499–534

Ashikari　蘆刈

Autumn moon. Tr. by Roy Humpherson and Hajime Okita. Shanghai, 1935. 74p. mimeo.
'Ashikari' Tr. by Roy Humpherson and Hajime Okita. *Ashikari, and The story of Shunkin.* Tokyo, Hokuseido, 1936; N. Y. Stechert,

1936; N. Y. Greenwood Press, 1970. p.1–67
'Ashikari' Tr. by Kikou Yamata. *Deux amours cruelles.* Paris, Stock, 1956. p.91–139
'I canneti' Tr. di Giuseppe Ricca e Atsuko Ricca Suga. *Due amori crudeli.* Milano, Bompiani, 1963. p.99–157; Milano, Garzanti, 1966. p.99–157
'Ashikari' Tr. de inglés por Jesús López Pacheco. *Cuentos crueles.* Barcelona, Seix y Barral, 1968. p.65–99
'Ashikari, czyli Źle mi bez ciebie' Przeł. Mikołaj Melanowicz. *Tanizaki Junichiro, dwie opowieści o miłości okrutnej.* Warszawa, Państwowy Instytut Wydawniczy, 1971. p.7–75

Bushūkō hiwa　武州公秘話

'Vita segreta del Signore di Bushu' Tr. di Atsuko Ricca Suga. *Vita segreta del Signore di Bushu.* Milano, Bompiani, 1970. p.5–182

Byakko no yu　白狐の湯

'The white fox' Tr. by Eric S. Bell and Eiji Ukai. *Eminent authors of contemporary Japan v.1.* Tokyo, Kaitakusha, 1930. p.1–37

Chiisana ōkoku　小さな王国

'小小的王國' 張我軍訳 「東方雑誌」 第27巻4期 1930. p.115–130
'Ein kleines Königreich' Deutsch von Jürgen Berndt und Eiko Saito-Berndt. *Träume aus zehn Nächten.* Berlin, Aufbau Verlag, 1975. p.159–192

Chijin no ai　痴人の愛

「癡人之愛」 楊騒訳 上海 北新書局 1928. 1冊
Любовь глупца. Перевод Г. С. Иммермана. Ленинград, Прибой, 1929. 288p.
'痴人의사랑' 金光稙訳 「世界文学全集 後期17」 서울 正音社 1962. p.381–554
L'amore di uno sciocco. Tr. di Carlo de Dominicis. Milano, Bompiani, 1967. 277p.
Naomi, oder, Eine unersätliche Liebe. Übers. von Oscar Benl. Reinbek, Rowohlt, 1970. 135p.
「痴人的愛」 邱素臻訳 台北 水牛出版社 1972. 277p.

Eien no gūzō　永遠の偶像

'L'éternelle idole' Tr. par Juntaro Maruyama. *Mumyo et Aizen, L'éternelle idole.* Tokyo, Hakusuisha, 1927.

Fumiko no ashi　富美子の足

'富美子的脚' 沈端先訳 「小説月報」 第19巻3号 1928. p.408–423
「富美子的脚」 白鷗訳 上海 曉星 193?. 1冊

Futari no chigo　二人の稚児

'両個幼児' 侍桁訳 「北新半月刊」 第3巻1号 1929. p.165–194

Fūten rōjin nikki　瘋癲老人日記

「狂風老人日記」 方基煥訳 서울 世文社 1963. 250p.
Diario di un vecchio pazzo. Tr. di Atsuko Ricca Suga. Milano, Bompiani, 1964. 193p.
Diary of a mad old man. Tr. by Howard Hibbett. N. Y. Knopf, 1965. 203p.; London, Secker and Warburg, 1966. 203p.; Tokyo, Tuttle, 1967. 177p.
'Journal d'un vieux fou' *Les Temps Modernes*, no.247, Dec. 1966. p.961–1012

Tagebuch eines alten Narren. Deutsch von Oscar Benl. Hamburg, Rowohlt, 1966. 237p.

Journal d'un vieux fou. Tr. par Gaston Renondeau. Paris, Gallimard, 1967. 224p.

Dagboek van een oude dwaas. Tr. from the English by M. & L. Coutinho. Amsterdam, Bezige Bij, 1968. 185p.

'Dziennik szalonego starca' Przeł. Mikołaj Melanowicz. *Dziennik szalonego starca, Niektórzy wolą pokrzywy.* Warszawa, Państwowy Instytut Wydawniczy, 1972. p.7–154

Haha o kouru ki　母を恋ふる記

'The house where I was born' Tr. by S. G. Brickley. *The writing of idiomatic English.* Tokyo, Kenkyusha, 1951. p.118–129

'어머니를그리는마음' 鄭泰鎔訳 「世界短篇文学全集 7」 서울 啓蒙社 1966. p.230–249;「世界短篇文学全集 9」 서울 三珍社 1971. p.99–118;「世界代表短篇文学全集 9」 서울 三煕社 1976. p.99–118;「世界短篇文学全集 9」 서울 新韓出版社 1976. p.170–201

Himitsu　秘密

'Le secret' Tr. par Serge Elisséev. *Le jardin des pivoines.* Paris, Au Sans Pareil, 1927. p.117–146

Hōkan　幇間

'Hokan' Tr. by Edilberto N. Alegre. *Asian Studies* (Univ. of the Philippines), v.4, no.1, 1966. p.59–69

'Шут' Перевод Е. Александровой. *И была любовь, и была ненависть.* Москва, Наука, 1975. p.111–125

In'ei raisan　陰翳礼讃

'Beauty in shadows' *Contemporary Japan*, v.11, no.1, 1942. p.61–83

'In praise of shadows' Tr. by Edward G. Seidensticker. *Atlantic Monthly*, Jan. 1955. p.141–144; *Japan Quarterly*, v.1, no.1, 1955. p.46–52

'En elabanza de las sombras' Tr. por Carla Viola Soto. *Sur*, no.249, Nov.-Dec. 1957. p.18–26

Éloge de l'ombre. Tr. par René Shiffert. Paris, Orientalistes de France, 1977. 104p.

In praise of shadow. Tr. by T. J. Harper and E. G. Seidensticker. Berkeley, Leete's Island Books, 1977. 1v.

Kagi　鍵

「열쇠」 新文苑社訳 서울 新文苑社 1960. 140p.

「열쇠」 南小姫訳 서울 토픽出版社 1960. 198p.

The key. Tr. by Howard Hibbett. N. Y. Knopf, 1961. 183p.; London, Secker and Warburg, 1961. 183p.; Tokyo, Tuttle, 1962. 176p.; N. Y. New American Library, 1962. 125p.; Toronto, New American Library of Canada, 1962. 125p.; N. Y. Berkley Pub. 1971. 1v.

Avain. Englanti. suomentanut Tuomas Anhava. Helsinki, Tammi, 1961. 140p.

Der Schlüssel. Übers. von Sachiko Yatsushiro und Gerhard Knauss. Reinbek, Rowohlt, 1961. 245p.; 1971. 124p.

Nøglen. Oversaette Tom Kristensen. København, Grafisk Forlag, 1962. 157p.

Nyckeln. Översätta Ruth Edlund. Stockholm, Wahlström & Widstrand, 1962. 157p.

De sleutel. Vaataald door M. Coutinho. Amsterdam, Bezige Bij, 1962. 197p.; Amsterdam, Meulenhoff, 1966. 189p.

「鍵夫婦日記」 米津訳 三重市 明志出版社 1962. 168p.

La chiave. Tr. di Satoko Toguchi. Milano, Bompiani, 1963. 181p.

La confession impudique. Tr. par Gaston Renondeau. Paris, Gallimard, 1963. 198p.

「鍵」 米津訳 三重市 明志出版社 1963. 1冊

'열쇠' 李元秀訳 「日本文学選集 2」 서울 青雲社 1964. p.145–273; 서울 知文閣 1966. p.145–273; 서울 韓国読書文化院 1973. p.145–275

「열쇠」 朴鐘禹訳 서울 元文社 1966. 198p.

Ključ. Tr. Ljiljana Čalovska. Beograd, Rad, 1969. 87p.

'La chiave' Tr. di Satoko Toguchi e Atsuko Ricca Suga. *La chiave, La gatta, Shozo e le duo donne.* Milano, Bompiani, 1972.

Kami to ningen tono aida　神と人間との間

'神與人之間' 李漱泉訳 「神與人之間」 上海 中華書局 1934.

Kirin　麒麟

'麒麟' 李漱泉訳 「神與人之間」 上海 中華書局 1934.

'麒麟' 江珠訳 「人魚的悲戀」 台中 中央書局 1955. p.1–11

'麒麟' 閔丙山訳 「世界代表短篇文学全集 22」 서울 正韓出版社 1976. p.39–55

Kyōfu　恐怖

'Terror' Tr. by Howard Hibbett. *Seven Japanese tales.* N. Y. Knopf, 1963; London, Secker and Warburg, 1964; Tokyo, Tuttle, 1967. p.85–94

'Terror' Tr. de inglés por Ángel Crespo. *Cuentos crueles.* Barcelona, Seix y Barral, 1968. p.101–110

Mōmoku monogatari　盲目物語

'A blind man's tale' Tr. by Howard Hibbett. *Seven Japanese tales.* N. Y. Knopf, 1963; London, Secker and Warburg, 1964; Tokyo, Tuttle, 1967. p.205–298

'Un cuento de ciego' Tr. de inglés por Ángel Crespo. *Cuentos crueles.* Barcelona, Seix y Barral, 1968. p.193–272

'Racconto d'un cieco' Tr. di Atsuko Ricca Suga. *Vita segreta del Signore di Bushu.* Milano, Bompiani, 1970. p.183–286

Mumyō to Aizen　無明と愛染

'Mumyo et Aizen' Tr. par Juntaro Maruyama. *Mumyo et Aizen, L'éternelle idole.* Tokyo, Hakusuisha, 1927.

'Mumyo kaj Aizen' Tr. Teruhiko Isiguro. *El la vivo de Syunkin.* Osaka, Librejo Pirato, 1968. p.25–46

Neko to Shōzō to futari no onna　猫と庄造と二人のをんな

'La gatta, Shozo e le duo donne' Tr. di Atsuko Ricca Suga. *Vita segreta del Signore di Bushu.* Milano, Bompiani, 1970. p.287–389; *La chiave, La gatta, Shozo e le due donne.* Milano, Bompiani, 1972.

Ninmensō　人面疽

'人面瘡' 李漱泉訳 「神與人之間」 上海 中華書局 1934.

Ningyo no nageki　人魚の嘆き

'人魚的悲戀' 江珠訳 「人魚的悲戀」 台中 中央書局 1955. p.12–28

TANIZAKI Jun'ichirō

Okuni to Gohei お国と五平

'Okuni and Gohei' Tr. by Isamu Suzuno. *Tokyo Nichinichi*, Sept. 20, 1924.

'Okuni and Gohei' Tr. by Eric S. Bell and Eiji Ukai. *Eminent authors of contemporary Japan* v.2. Tokyo, Kaitakusha, 1931. p.1–29

'御國與五平' 李漱泉訳 「神與人之間」 上海 中華書局 1934.

'Okuni kaj Gohei' Tr. Teruhiko Isiguro. *El la vivo de Syunkin*. Osaka, Librejo Pirato, 1968. p.7–24

Otsuya koroshi お艶殺し

A spring time case. Tr. by Zenchi Iwado. Tokyo, Japan Times, 1927. 154p.

'殺艶' 章克標訳 「殺艶」 上海 水沫書店 1930.

'Milenci z jeda' Přel. V. Hilská. *Milenci z jeda*. Praha, Melantrich, 1942.

'오쓰야殺害' 金龍済訳 「日本代表作家百人集 2」 서울 希望出版社 1966. p.130–170; 「日本短篇文学全集 2」 서울 新太陽社 1969. p.194–234

'오쓰야의죽음' 柳呈 閔丙山訳 「世界代表短篇文学全集 22」 서울 正韓出版社 1976. p.56–115

Radō sensei 蘿洞先生

'蘿洞先生' 章克標訳 「殺艶」 上海 水沫書店 1930.

Sakana no Ri Taihaku 魚の李太白

'The piscatorial Li Tai-po' Tr. by G. W. Shaw. *Eigo Seinen*, v.46, no.2, 1921–v.46, no.9, 1922 in 8 parts.

Sasame yuki 細雪

'The firefly hunt' Tr. by E. G. Seidensticker. *Modern Japanese literature*, ed. by Donald Keene. N. Y. Grove Press, 1956; Tokyo, Tuttle, 1957. p.383–386

The Makioka sisters. Tr. by E. G. Seidensticker. N. Y. Knopf, 1957. 530p.; Tokyo, Tuttle, 1958. 530p.; N. Y. Grosset Press, 1966. 530p.

「細雪」 金龍済 金潤成訳 서울 進明文化社 1960–61. 2冊

Neve sottile. Tr. di Olga Ceretti Borsini e Kisu Hasegawa. Milano, Martello, 1961. 768p.; Milano, Longanesi, 1973. 536p.

Quatre soeurs. Tr. par Gaston Renondeau. Paris, Gallimard, 1964. 614p.

Die Schwestern Makioka. Übertragen von Sachiko Yatsushiro unter Mitarbeit von Ulla Hengst. Hamburg, Rowohlt, 1964. 591p.

Las hermanas Makioka. Versión de M. Menéndez Cuspinera. Barcelona, Seix y Barral, 1966. 509p.

Sestre Makiokove. Vertaald door Alenka Bole-Vrabec. Ljubljana, Cankarjeva Zalozba, 1967. 564p.

Сестре Макиока. Превео са енглеског Александар Петрович. Београд, Просвета, 1972. 696p.

'細雪' 申基宣訳 「日本文学大全集 2」 서울 東西文化院 1975. 486p.

Sestry Makiokovy. Přel. Vlasta Winkelhöferová. Praha, Svoboda, 1977. 622p.

Shinzei 信西

'Shinzei' Tr. by Glenn W. Shaw. *Tokyo Nichinichi*, July 10–13, 1924.

Shisei 刺青

'The young tattooer' Tr. by Asataro Miyamori. *Representative tales of Japan*. Tokyo, Sanko Shoin, 1917. p.1–19

'Tätowierkunst' Übers. von K. Koike. *Zwei Skizzen*. Tokyo, Nankodo, 1917. p.1–49

'Shisei' Tr. by Sumimasa Ijichi. *Herald of Asia*, April 7, 1923.

'La tatouage' Tr. par Serge Elisséev. *Japon et Extrême-Orient*, no.2, 1924. p.116–129; *Neuf nouvelles japonaises*. Paris, G. van Œst, 1924. p.17–30

'Irezumi' Übers. von Heinz Brasch. *Yamato*, Jahrgang 2, 1930. p.8–15; *Geschichten und Erzählungen aus Japan*, hrg. von B. Matsumoto. Leipzig, Fikentscher Verlag, 1950. p.170–178

'A pok' Ford. Thein Alfréd. *Mai Japán dekameron*. Budapest, Nyugat, 1935. p.249–261

'Tatoo' Tr. by Ryozo Matsumoto. *Japanese literature, new and old*. Tokyo, Hokuseido, 1961. p.105–118

'Tattoo' Tr. by Ivan Morris. *Modern Japanese stories*. London, Spottiswoode, 1961; Tokyo, Tuttle, 1962. p.92–100

'Tatuagem' Tr. de Konoske Oseki. *Maravilhas do conto japonês*. São Paulo, Editôra Cultrix, 1962. p.83–90

'The tattooer' Tr. by Howard Hibbett. *Show*, v.3, May 1963. p.70, 106–107; *Seven Japanese tales*. N. Y. Knopf, 1963; London, Secker and Warburg, 1964.; Tokyo, Tuttle, 1967. p.160–169

'Das Opfer' Deutsch von Monique Humbert. *Nippon*. Zürich, Diogenes, 1965. p.105–116

'Il tatuaggio' Tr. di Atsuko Ricca Suga. *Narratori giapponesi moderni*. Milano, Bompiani, 1965. p.227–238

'Tatuo' Tr. Teruhiko Isiguro. *El Japana literaturo*. Tokyo, Japana Esperanto Instituto, 1965. p.223–230

'Tetoválás' Ford. Sz. Holti Mária. *Modern Japán elbeszélők*. Budapest, Európa Könyvkiadó, 1967. p.32–38

'El tatuador' Tr. de inglés por Ángel Crespo. *Cuentos crueles*. Barcelona, Seix y Barral, 1968. p.167–176

'Tätowieung' Übers. von Margarete Donath. *Japan erzählt*. Hamburg, Fischer, 1969. p.32–39

'Татуировка' Перевод А. Долина. *Иностранная Литература*, январь 1975. p.126–131; *И была любовь, и была ненависть*. Москва, Наука, 1975. p.34–42

'文身' 閔丙山訳 「世界代表短篇文学全集 22」 서울 正韓出版社 1976. p.29–32

Shōnen 少年

'少年 査士驥訳 「東方雑誌」 第27巻9期 1930. p.113–120. 第27巻10期 1930. p.121–132

'Knaboj' Tr. Masao Miyamoto. *El la vivo de Syunkin*. Osaka, Librajo Pirato, 1968. p.47–78

Shōshō Shigemoto no haha 少将滋幹の母

'The mother of Captain Shigemoto' Tr. by E. Seidensticker. *Modern Japanese literature*, ed. by Donald Keene. N. Y. Grove Press, 1956; Tokyo, Tuttle, 1957. p.387–397

La madre del Generale Shigemoto. Tr. di Guglielmo Scalise. Milano, Mondadori, 1966. 199p.

'La madre del Generale Shigemoto' Tr. di G.

Scalise. *Antologia della letterature coreana e giapponese*. Milano, Fratelli Fabbri, 1969. p.339–345

'La mère du capitaine palatin Shigémoto' Tr. par Paul Anouilh. *Bulletin de l'Association des Français du Japon*, no.1, été, 1976—no.9, été, 1978.

Shunkin shō 春琴抄

The story of Shunkin. Tr. by Roy Humpherson and Hajime Okita. Shanghai, 1935. 105p. mimeo.

'The story of Shunkin' Tr. by Roy Humpherson and Hajime Okita. *Ashikari, and The story of Shunkin*. Tokyo, Hokuseido, 1936; N. Y. G. E. Stechert, 1936.; N. Y. Greenwood Press, 1970. p.71–169

「春琴抄」 陸少懿訳 上海 文化生活出版社 1936. 1冊

'L'histoire de Shunkin' Tr. par Kikou Yamata. *Deux amours cruelles*. Paris, Stock 1956. p.11–90

'Biographie der Frühlingsharfe' Übers. von Walter Donat. *Die fünfstöckige Pagode*. Düsseldorf, Diederichs, 1960. p.207–256; Regensburg, Pustet, n.d. p.209–256

'A portrait of Shunkin' Tr. by Howard Hibbett. *Seven Japanese tales*. N. Y. Knopf, 1963; London, Secker and Warburg, 1964; Tokyo, Tuttle, 1967. p.3–84

'La storia di Shunkin' Tr. di Giuseppe Ricca e Atsuko Ricca Suga. *Due amori crudeli*. Milano, Bompiani, 1963; Milano, Garzanti, 1966. p.7–96

'春琴抄' 金龍済訳 「春琴抄」 서울 新太陽社 1963.

A portrait of Shunkin. Tr. by Howard S. Hibbett. Tokyo, Hara Shobo, 1965. 203p.

'El la vivo de Syunkin' Tr. Masao Miyamoto. *El la vivo de Syunkin*. Osaka, Librejo Pirato, 1968. p.79–139

'La historia de Shunkin' Tr. de inglés por Jesús López Pacheco. *Cuentos crueles*. Barcelona, Seix y Barral, 1968. p.7–64

'Pokus o životopis Sunkin' Přel. Libuše Boháčková. *5 japonských novel*. Praha, Odeon, 1969. p.149–208

'Shunkinshō, czyli Rozmyślania nad życiem Wiosennej Harfy' Przeł. Mikołaj Melanowicz. *Tanizaki Junichiro, dwie opowieści o miłości okrutnej*. Warszawa, Państwowy Instytut Wydawniczy, 1971. p.77–177

'История Сюнкин' Перевод А. Долина. *И была любовь, и была ненависть*. Москва, Наука, 1975. p.43–110

Tade kuu mushi 蓼喰ふ虫

'Some prefer nettles' Tr. by Edward Seidensticker. *Mademoiselle*, April 1955. p.128–129, 176–186

Some prefer nettles. Tr. by Edward Seidensticker. N. Y. Knopf, 1955; London, Secker and Warburg, 1956; Tokyo, Tuttle, 1956. 202p.; Harmondsworth, Penguin Books, 1970. 155p.

Somliga tycker om nasslor. Översätta Nils Fredricson. Stockholm, Wahlström & Widstrand, 1955. 196p.

'I vermi preferiscono le alghe' Tr. di Mario Teti. *Cipangu*, no.4, 1956. p.12–15

'Some prefer nettles' Tr. by Edward Seidensticker. *Treasury of world literature*, ed. by D. D. Runes. N. Y. Philosophical Library, 1956. p.1288–1291

Insel der Puppen. Aus dem Amerikanischen über-

setzt von Curt Meyer-Clason. Esslingen, Bechtle Verlag, 1957. 304p.; Berlin, Volk und Welt, 1967. 238p.

Le goût des orties. Tr. par Silvie Regnault Gatier et Kazuo Anzai. Paris, Gallimard, 1959. 277p.

Kukin makunsa mukään. Suomentanut Yrjö Kivimies. Helsinki, Tammi, 1959. 206p

Gli insetti preferiscono le ortiche. Tr. di Mario Teti. Milano, Mondadori, 1960. 210p.

Hay quien prefiere las ortigas. Tr. por María Luisa Borrás. Barcelona, Seix y Barral, 1963. 205p.

'나만좋으면' 朴咲里訳 「日本文学選集 2」 서울 青雲社 1964. p.7–139; 「日本文学選集 2」 서울 知文閣 1966. p.7–139

Liever nog op de blaren. Vertaald door M. Coutinho. Amsterdam, Zezige Hij, 1964. 220p.

Ti, kteří radeji kopřivy. Přel. Vlasta Hilská. Praha, Státní nakladatelství Krásne Literatury a Uměni, 1965. 137p.

「食蓼之蟲」 周弦訳 台北 十月出版社 1969. 126p.

Ve konyakla başladi herşey. Çeviren Zihni Küçümen. İstanbul, Kervan Kitapçilik Basin Sanayii ve Ticaret, 1972. 182p.

'Niektórzy wolą pokrzywy' Przeł. Mikołaj Melanowicz. *Dziennik szalonego starca, Niektórzy wolą pokrzywy*. Warszawa, Państwowy Instytut Wydawniczy, 1972. p.157–304

'여뀌머는벌레' 張喜汎訳 「世界代表文学全集 9」 서울 高麗出版社 1976. p.385–497

Tsuki to kyōgenshi 月と狂言師

'Луна и комедианты' Перевод С. Гутермана. *Японская новелла*. Москва, Изд. Иност. Лит. 1961. p.325–351

Watashi 私

'The thief' Tr. by Howard Hibbett. *Seven Japanese tales*. N. Y. Knopf, 1963; London, Secker and Warburg, 1964; Tokyo, Tuttle, 1967. p.170–185

'El ladrón' Tr. de inglés por Ángel Crespo. *Cuentos crueles*. Barcelona, Seix y Barral, 1968. p.177–191

Yume no ukihashi 夢の浮橋

'The bridge of dreams' Tr. by Howard Hibbett. *Seven Japanese tales*. N. Y. Knopf, 1963; London, Secker and Warburg, 1964; Tokyo Tuttle, 1967. p.95–159; *The world of Japanese fiction*. N. Y. Dutton, 1973. p.308–353; *Contemporary Japanese literature*. N. Y. Knopf, 1977. p.355–388

'Il ponte dei songi' Tr. di Atsuko Ricca Suga. *Narratori giapponesi moderni*. Milano, Bompiani, 1965. p.239–292

'El puente de los sueños' Tr. de inglés por Ángel Crespo. *Cuentos crueles*. Barcelona, Seix y Barral, 1968. p.111–165

'Az álmok hídja' Ford. Félix Pál. *Nagyvilág*, no.11, 1973. p.1615–1643

Unien silta. Helsinki, Tammi, n.d.

Zenka mono 前科者

'前科者' 李漱泉訳 「神與人之間」 上海 中華書局 1934.

Essay エッセイ

'Kyoto, her nature, food. . . and women' *This is Japan*, v.12, 1965. p.222–225

TANIZAKI Jun'ichirō

「谷崎潤一郎集」 章克標訳 上海 開明書店 1929. 1冊

TANIZAKI Seiji 谷崎精二 1890–1971

Geisha Eiko 芸者栄子

Гейша Эйко. Перевод А. Лейферт. Ленинград, Прибой, 1929. 223p.

Nusumi 盗み

'Stealing' Tr. by Kanichi Ando. *Eigo Seinen*, v.52, no.1, 1924-v.52, no.6, 1924 in 6 parts.

Shukuen 祝宴

'別宴' 張資平訳 「別宴」 武昌 時中合作社 1926.

TASHIRO Takako 田代たか子 1919–1955

Poems 詩

'An unfinished requiem; Our reminiscences' Tr. by Miyao Ohara. *The songs of Hiroshima.* Tokyo, Taihei Shuppansha, 1971. p.102–107

TATENO Nobuyuki 立野信之 1903–1971

Gōu 豪雨

'豪雨' 陳勺水訳 「日本新寫實派代表傑作集」 上海 楽羣書局 1929.

Criticism 評論

'果戈理私觀' 魯迅訳 「譯文」 第1巻1期 1934;「魯迅全集 16」上海 魯迅全集出版社 1938. 作家書屋 1946. 大連 光華書店 1948. 北京 人民文学出版社 1973. p.566–575;「魯迅譯文集 10」北京 人民文学出版社 1958. p.422–429

TATSUMI Seika 巽 聖歌 1905–1973

Kōri no kuni wa doko こおりのくにはどこ

Mr. Kuma's rocket. Retold by Kiyoko Iizuka Tucker. N. Y. Hawthorn, 1966. 1v.

TATSUNO Yutaka 辰野 隆 1888–1964

Onna no nioi 女の匂い

'Aura of womanhood' Tr. by S. G. Brickley. *The writing of idiomatic English.* Tokyo, Kenkyusha, 1951. p.130–141

TAYAMA Katai 田山花袋 1872–1930

Chiisana kare 小さな「かれ」

'小小的他' 「標準日本名著選讀」 孫文斗編 台北 大新書局 1969. p.133–143

Futon 蒲団

'綿被' 夏丏尊訳 「東方雜誌」 第23巻1期 1926. p.191–208. 第23巻2期 1926. p.117–128;「綿被」上海 商務印書館 1927.
'Futon' Übers. von Oscar Benl. *Flüchtiges Leben, moderne japanische Erzählungen.* Berlin, Landsmann, 1942.
'이불' 郭夏信訳 「世界文学全集 94」 서울 乙酉文化社 1962. p.215–267
'이부자리' 崔泰應訳 「日本代表作家百人集 1」 서울 希望出版社 1966. p.212–259;「日本短篇文学全集 1」 서울 新太陽社 1969. p.212–259

Ippeisotsu 一兵卒

'A mere private' Tr. by Asataro Miyamori. *Representative tales of Japan.* Tokyo, Sanko Shoin, 1917. p.72–109
'One soldier' Tr. by G. W. Sargent. *Modern Japanese literature*, ed. by Donald Keene. N. Y. Grove Press, 1956; Tokyo, Tuttle, 1957. p.142–158
'A soldier' Tr. by William E. Naff. *The heart is alone*, ed. by R. McKinnon. Tokyo, Hokuseido, 1957. p.17–36
'Рядовой' *Восточный альманах 2.* Москва, Худож. Лит. 1958. p.397–408
'Un soldato' Tr. di Atsuko Ricca Suga. *Narratori giapponesi moderni.* Milano, Bompiani, 1965. p.151–170; *Antologia della letteratura coreana e giapponese.* Milano, Fratelli Fabbri, 1969. p.293–296
'小兵' 「標準日本名著選讀」 孫文斗編 台北 大新書局 1969. p.86–132
'Ein Soldat' Deutsch von Edith Shimomura. *Träume aus zehn Nächten.* Berlin, Aufbau Verlag, 1975. p.51–70

Poems 詩

'Die Schwester' Übers. von Kuniyo Takayasu und Manfred Hausmann. *Ruf der Regenpfeifer.* München, Bechtle Verlag, 1961. p.83
'Dark night; A certain night; Tabi ni arikeru yo' Tr. by James R. Morita. *Journal of the Association of Teachers of Japanese*, v.10, no.2 & 3, 1975. p.197–198

'Любовь жены рыбака' *Первый художественно-литературный сборник* Токио, 1909. p.5–11

TAZAKI Hanama 田崎花馬 1913–

Kōdō haruka nari 皇道遥かなり

Long the Imperial Way. Westport, Conn. Greenwood Press, 1949. 372p.
Les montagnes demeurent. Tr. par Roger Allard. Paris, Intercontinentale du Libre, 1957. 349p.
Ha-geysha. Tr. Uri Rapaport. Tel-Aviv, Amihay, 1957. 381p.; Tel-Aviv, M. Newman, 1959. 380p.
Les montanas permanechen. Tr. por Concepción Salvat. Barcelona, Caralt, 1960. 432p.

TEIMEI Kōgō 貞明皇后 1884–1951

Tanka 短歌

'2 tanka' *Japanese poetry, an historical essay*, by

Curtis Hidden Page. Boston, Houghton Mifflin, 1923; Folcroft, Folcroft Library, 1976. p.168, 169
'8 tanka' Tr. by Shigeshi Nishimura. *Eigo Seinen*, v.62, no.11, 1930. p.402. v.64, no.11, 1931. p.366. v.66, no.11, 1932. p.381. v.72, no.12, 1935. p.409. v.74, no.12, 1936. p.413. v.84, no.11, 1941. p.337. v.88, no.11, 1943. v.91, no.3, 1946. p.81

TENNŌ Hirohito 天皇裕仁 1901–

Tanka 短歌

'1 tanka' *Japanese poetry, an historical essay*, by Curtis Hidden Page. Boston, Houghton Mifflin, 1923; Folcroft, Folcroft Library, 1976. p.169
'13 tanka' Tr. by Shigeshi Nishimura. *Eigo Seinen*, v.54, no.11, 1926. p.347; v.62, no.11, 1930. p.402; v.64, no.11, 1931. p.366; v.66, no.11, 1932. p.381; v.72, no.12, 1935. p.409; v.74, no.12, 1936. p.413; v.76, no.11, 1937. p.389; v.84, no.11, 1941. p.337; v.88, no.11, 1943; v.91, no.3, 1946. p.81; v.93, no.3, 1947. p.120; v.99, no.8, 1953. p.368; v.101, no.3, 1955. p.113
'1 tanka' Tr. by Fukujiro Minamiishi. *Eigo Seinen*, v.78, no.11, 1938. p.345
'2 tanka' Tr. par Roger Bersihand. *La littérature japonaise*. Paris, Presses Universitaires de France, 1956. p.106, 107
'7 tanka' Tr. by Shigeshi Nishimura. *The Current of the World*, v.29, no.7, 1952. p.44; v.36, no.3, 1959. p.28; v.38, no.3, 1961. p.48
'1 tanka' Übers. von Gerolf Coudenhove. *Japanische Jahreszeiten*. Zürich, Manesse Verlag, 1963. p.31
'2 tanka' Tr. from the French by Unity Evans. *Japanese literature*. N. Y. Walker, 1965. p.90

TERADA Torahiko 寺田寅彦 1878–1935

Essay エッセイ

'橡木' 周豊一訳 「譯文」 第1巻4期 1943. p.26–27
'The kittens' Tr. by S. G. Brickley. *The writing of idiomatic English*. Tokyo, Kenkyusha, 1951. p.142–148

Haiku 俳句

'3 haiku' Tr. by Asataro Miyamori. *Anthology of haiku, ancient and modern*. Tokyo, Maruzen, 1932. p.794–795
'The lonesome sea' Tr. by Asataro Miyamori. *Haiku poems, ancient and modern*. Tokyo, Maruzen, 1940. p.325
'Das Feuerwerk' Übers. von Gerolf Coudenhove. *Vollmond und Zikadenklänge*. Gütersloh, Sigbert Mohn Verlag, 1955. p.48
'1 haiku' Übers. von Gerolf Coudenhove. *Japanische Jahreszeiten*. Zürich, Manesse Verlag, 1963. p.279
'1 haiku' Til norsk ved Paal Helge Haugen. *Blad frå ein austleg hage*. Oslo, Det Norske Samlaget, 1965. p.87

TERAMURA Teruo 寺村輝夫 1928–

Boku wa ōsama ぼくは王さま

'O králi, který chtěl všechno mít' *Modré vánoce*. Přel. Ivan Krouský a Z. K. Slabý. Praha, Albatros, 1975.

Ki no ue ni beddo 木の上にベッド

'Postel na stromě' *Modré vánoce*. Přel. Ivan Krouský a Z. K. Slabý. Praha, Albatros, 1975.

Ōsama bikkuri 王さまびっくり

'O králi, který na všechno zapomínal' *Modré vánoce*. Přel. Ivan Krouský a Z. K. Slabý. Praha, Albatros, 1975.

Oshaberina tamagoyaki おしゃべりなたまごやき

'Jak vejce promluvilo' *Modré vánoce*. Přel. Ivan Krouský a Z. K. Slabý. Praha, Albatros, 1975.

TERAYAMA Shūji 寺山修司 1936–

Aa kōya あゝ，荒野

vor meinen Augen . . . eine Wildnis. Übersetzung von Manfred Hubricht. Frankfurt am Main, Fischer, 1971. 244p.
Devant mes yeux le désert. Tr. par Alain Colas et Yuriko Kaneda. Paris, Calmann-Lévy, 1973. 291p.

Shisō eno bōkyō 思想への望郷

Theater contra Ideologie. Übers. von Manfred Hubricht. Frankfurt am Main, Fischer, 1971. 99p.

Poems 詩

'Mio Esopo' *La protesta poetica del Giappone*, a cura di Dacia Maraini e Michiko Nojiri. Roma, Officina Edizioni, 1968. p.155–156

────────────

'인력비행기솔로몬' 李泰柱訳 「世界新傾向戲曲選」 서울 成文閣 1976. p. 205–240

TESHIGAHARA Hiroshi 勅使河原 宏 1927–

Suna no onna 砂の女（シナリオ）

Woman in the dunes. N. Y. Phaedra Publishers, 1966. 95p.

TEZUKA Hidetaka 手塚英孝 1906–

Kobayashi Takiji den 小林多喜二伝

「小林多喜二傳」卞立強訳 北京 作家出版社 1963. 194p.

TOGAWA Masako　戸川昌子　1933–

Kiiroi kyūketsuki　黄色い吸血鬼

'The vampire' *Japanese golden dozen*, ed. by Ellery Queen. Tokyo, Tuttle, 1978. p.233–257

Ryōjin nikki　猟人日記

「유랑민」申洙澈訳　서울　旺文社　1973. 271p.

TOGAWA Yukio　戸川幸夫　1912–

Fūka　風花

'風花' 劉慕沙訳 「日本現代小説選」 台北　聯經出版社 1976. p.121–142

Rōjin to taka　老人と鷹

「老人與兀鷹」 劉慕沙訳　台中　光啓出版社　1969. 189p.

'神秘的兇手' 振江訳 「黑色幻惑」 台南 文良出版社 1966. p.141–181

TOGAWA Zanka　戸川残花　1855–1924

Haiku　俳句

'2 haiku' Tr. by V. H. Viglielmo. *Japanese literature in the Meiji era*. Tokyo, Obunsha, 1955. p.436

TŌGE Sankichi　峠　三吉　1917–1953

Genbaku shishū　原爆詩集

'Hiroshima 1945' Tr. by Tsuneo Masaki. *The Reeds*, v.13, 1972. p.29–44
Hiroshima poems. Tr. by Rob Jackaman, Dennis Logan and Tsutomu Shiota. Tokyo, Sanyusha, 1977. 183p.

Poems　詩

'八月六日' 適夷訳 「譯文」 1955年8月 p.64–65
'Рассвет' Перевод Анатолия Мамонова. *Песни Хиросимы*. Москва, Худож. Лит. 1964. p.11–12
'Верните человека; Шестое августа; Рассвет; Призыв' Перевод Анатолия Мамонова. *Иностранная Литература*, октябрь 1967. p.3–7
'Алтынч август' Которгон Ж. Алыбаев. *Хиросима кектери*. Фрунзе, Кыргызстан, 1969. p.57–58
'At a first-aid post' Tr. by James Kirkup and Fumiko Miura. *Poetry Nippon*, no.11, 1970. p.2–3
'Верните человека, и другие поэмы' Перевод Анатолия Мамонова. *Три поэта из Хиросимы*. Москва, Наука, 1970. p.48–83
'Give back the people; August sixth; Death; The blaze; Blindness; At the first-aid stations; Eyes; Notes in the warehouse; The little child; A grave-post; Morning; We call to you' Tr. by Miyao Ohara. *The songs of Hiroshima*. Tokyo, Taihei Shuppansha, 1971. p.178–247

'August six; The eye' Tr. by Akiko Takemoto. *Poetry Nippon*, no.19, 1972. p.3–6
'Верните человека; Смерть; Глаза; Призыв' Перевод Анатолия Мамонова, *Вкус хризантемы*. Москва, Восточная Литература, 1976. p.134–140

TŌKAI Sanshi　東海散士　1852–1922

Kajin no kigū　佳人之奇遇

「佳人之奇遇」 上海　中國書房　1935. 1冊
「政治小説　佳人之奇遇」 上海　商務印書館　193?. 1冊

TOKI Zenmaro　土岐善麿　1885–

Tanka　短歌

'A great temple bell; Graf Zeppelin; The mighty silver bulk; The great Sphinx at Gizeh, Egypt' Tr. by Asataro Miyamori. *Masterpieces of Japanese poetry, ancient and modern*. Tokyo, Maruzen, 1936; Tokyo, Taiseido, 1956; N. Y. Greenwood Press, 1971. p.718–720
'3 tanka' Tr. by V. H. Viglielmo. *Japanese literature in the Meiji era*. Tokyo, Obunsha, 1955. p.404–405
'Подобные мне…' Перевод Анатолия Мамонова. *Вкус хризантемы*. Москва, Восточная Литература, 1976. p.142

TOKUDA Shūsei　徳田秋声　1871–1943

Kawaita kuchibiru　乾いた唇

'Les lèvres sèches' Tr. par M. Yoshitomi. *Anthologie de la littérature japonaise contemporaine*. Grenoble, Xavier Drevet, 1924. p.171–185

Kunshō　勲章

'The white order of the paulownia' *Contemporary Japan*, v.2, 1936. p.267–277
'Order of the white paulownia' Tr. by Ivan Morris. *Modern Japanese stories*. London, Spottiswoode, 1961; Tokyo, Tuttle, 1962. p.46–64
'Der Orden' Deutsch von Monique Humbert. *Nippon*. Zürich, Diogenes, 1965. p.53–76
'A jelvény' Ford. Sz. Holti Mária. *Modern Japán elbeszélők*. Budapest, Európa Könyvkiadó, 1967. p.203–213

Shoiage　背負揚

'The shoiage' Tr. by Asataro Miyamori. *Representative tales of Japan*. Tokyo, Sanko Shoin, 1917. p.320–332

Sōwa　挿話

'挿話' 郭夏信訳 「世界文学全集 94」 서울 乙酉文化社 1962. p.405–436

Tochū　途中

'途中' 韞玉訳 「東方雜誌」 第18巻21期 1921. p.100–110

Wakai 和解

'和解' 柳呈訳 「日本代表作家百人集 1」 서울 希望出版
社 1966. p.316–329;「日本短篇文学全集 1」 서울
新太陽社 1969. p.316–329

'和解' 李文熙訳 「世界短篇文学全集 9」 서울 新韓出版
社 1976. p.318–343

TOKUGAWA Yoshihiro 徳川義寛 1906–

Tanka 短歌

'1 tanka' Tr. by Shigeshi Nishimura. *Eigo Seinen*,
v.91, no.3, 1946. p.81

TOKUNAGA Sunao 徳永 直 1899–1958

Doko e yuku 何処へ行く

「抹殺」不了的情景' 「日本短篇小説選」 香港 藝美圖書
公司 1959. p.47–52

「抹殺」不了的情景' 高汝鴻訳 「日本短篇小説選」 台北
台湾商務印書館 1969. p.149–157

Hataraku ikka はたらく一家

'勤勞的一家' 李芒訳 「譯文」 1955年12月 p.76–102

Hōnen kikin 豊年飢饉

Malsato en riĉa rikolto. Tr. K. Nakagaki. Tokyo,
Teto Shoin, 1932; Tokyo, Toga Shobo, 1949.
42p.

Nōritsu iinkai 能率委員会

'The efficiency committee' *The cannery boat, and
other Japanese short stories*. N. Y. International Publishers, 1933; London, Martin
Lawrence, 1933; N. Y. Greenwood Press,
1968. p.211–243

'Комитет повышения производительности' Перевод Н. Фельдман. *Японская революционная литература*. Москва, Худож. Лит.
1934. p.218–239

Saisho no kioku 最初の記憶

'Первые воспоминания' Перевод В. Цветова.
Дни детства. Москва, Детгиз, 1958. p.9–
32

Shitsugyō toshi Tokyo 失業都市東京

Токио, город безработных. Перевод Н. И.
Фельдман. Ленинград, Гослитиздат, 1934.
320p.; Москва, Гослитиздат, 1935. 383p.

Shizuka naru yamayama 静かなる山々

Тихие горы. Перевод И. Львовой. Москва,
Иност. Лит. 1952. 344p.

Ciche gory. Przeł. Stanisław Tazbir. Warszawa,
Czytelnik, 1953. 324p.

Тихите планини. Переклав Христо Канев. София, Народ. Културa, 1953. 324p.

「静静的羣山」 蕭蕭訳 北京 文化生活出版社 1953.
526p.

In mutii linistiti. În românește de M. Goltz și L.
Soare. București, ESPLA, 1954. 372p.

Stille Berge. Berlin, Volk und Welt, 1954. 476p.

Тихи гори. Переклад Г. Коваленко. Киев, Радя-
нский Письменник, 1954. 311p.

Тихие горы. Перевод И. Львовой, Г. Иммерман
и Е. Пинус. Ленинград, Лениздат, 1958. 695p.

Taiyō no nai machi 太陽のない街

Die Strasse ohne Sonne. Übers. von K. Itow und
A. Raddatz. Leipzig, Internationaler Arbeiter
Verlag, 1930. 308p.

「没有太陽的街」 何鳴心訳 上海 現代書局 1930. 1冊

Улица без солнца. Перевод В. С. Топер. Ленинград, Гос. Изд. Худож. Лит. 1932. 163p.

Улица без солнца, на украинском языке. Одесса, Молодой Большевик, 1932. 232p.

Gaten uten sol. Tr. Just Lippe. Moskva, Forlag for
utenlandske Arbeidere i SSSR, 1932. 243p.

Le quartier sans soleil. Tr. par S. Ohno et F. A.
Orel. Paris, Ed. Sociales Internationales,
1933. 244p.

「没有太陽的街」 馮憲章訳 上海 現代書局 193?. 1冊

Quartiere senza sole. Tr. di Pierre Rancoz. Torino,
Eclettica, 1946. 1v.

Čtvrt bez slunce. Přel. Vlasta Hilská a M. Novak.
Praha, Práce, 1950. 212p.

「没有太陽的街」 李正倫訳 北京 艺术出版社 1956. 142p.

「没有太陽的街」 李芒訳 北京 人民文学出版社 1958.
1冊

Die Strasse ohne Sonne. Berlin, Dietz, 1960. 247p.

A sötét sikátor. Ford. Kemany István. Budapest,
Európa Könyvkiadó, 1962. 210p.

Rruga pa diell. Tr. K. Evangjeli. Tiranë, Naim
Frashëri, 1970. 190p.

Gata utan sol. Overs. fra tysk. Oslo, 1976. 166p.

Tanin no naka 他人の中

'Среди чужих' Перевод М. Ефимова. *Дни детства*. Москва, Детгиз, 1958. p.54–107

'在外人之間' 包容訳 「譯文」 1958年4月 p.23–58

Tasaku 多作

'Тасаку' Перевод М. Ефимова. *Дни детства*.
Москва, Детгиз, 1958. p.108–156

Tsuma yo nemure 妻よねむれ

Spi klidne, žena. Přel. Vlasta Hilská a V. Winkelhöferová. Praha, SNKHLU, 1953. 781p.

「妻呵，安息吧」 周豊一訳 上海 上海文芸 1961. 112p.

Zegnaj, żona. Przeł. Stanisław Gawłowski. Warszawa, Książka i Wiedza, 1964. 221p.

Yōnenki 幼年期

'Ранные годы' Перевод В. Цветова. *Дни детства*. Москва, Детгиз, 1958. p.33–53

Criticism and Essays 評論・エッセイ

'中日両國文學的新的友好関系和聯系' 「人民文学」 第67
期 1955. p.111–113

'眼晴' 肖肖訳 「譯文」 1958年4月 p.8–12

'紅旗会' 馮明訳 「譯文」 1958年4月 p.13–23

'金兵辺老爹' 錢稻孫訳 「世界文学」 1963年3月 p.29–
34

「麦苗」 上海 新創造社 193?. 1冊

「徳永直選集」 李芒 蕭蕭訳 北京 人民文学出版社
1959–60. 4冊

TOKUNŌ Bun　得能　文　1866–1945

Gaku no hanashi　学の話

'A dissertation on scholarship'　Tr. by F. J. Daniels. *Japanese prose*. London, Lund Humphries, 1944. p.50–63

TOKUNŌ Kōichi　徳納晃一　1932–

Poems　詩

'Blood'　Tr. by Miyao Ohara. *The songs of Hiroshima*. Tokyo, Taihei Shuppansha, 1971. p.48–51

TOKUTOMI Roka　徳冨蘆花　1868–1927

Hototogisu　不如帰

'Nami-ko'　Tr. by Sakae Shioya and E. F. Edgett. *The Literary World*, July 1, 1904; *Eigo Seinen*, August 1904. p.1–9

Nami-ko. Tr. by Sakae Shioya and E. F. Edgett. Tokyo, Yurakusha, 1904. 314p.; London, G. P. Putnam, 1904. 313p.

Nami-ko. Tr. por Juan N. Cañizares. Barcelona, Maucci, 1904. 265p.

Hototogisu. Dem Japanischen nacherzählt von Rheinberg Reham. Wolfenbüttel, Heckners Verlag, 1905. 262p.

Kyyneleitä nykyäikäinen. Helsinki, 1906. 1v.

Namiko. Tr. por Couto Nogueira. Lisboa, Guimaraes, 1906. 279p.

Plutôt la mort. Tr. par Olivier le Paladin. Paris, Plon Nourrit, 1911. 302p.

Nami e Takeo. Tr. di Fanny Dalmazzo. Milano, 1909. 1v.; Milano, Fratelli Treves, 1921. 1v.

Хотомогису, трагедия женской души. Перевод Л. Жданова. Петербург, 1913. 279p.

「不如帰」　林緑　魏易訳　上海　商務印書館　1913.　1冊

'Hototoghicou'　Tr. par Michel Revon. *Anthologie de la littérature japonaise*. Paris, Delagrave, 190 . p.436–445

Namiko san. Přel. B. M. Eliasova. Praha, 1922. 208p.

Hototogisu. Tr. di Mauro Janni. Milano, Sonzogno, 1933. 128p.

「不如帰」　林雪清訳　北平　亜東圖書館　1933.　1冊

'The Hototogisu, the heart of Nami-ko'　Tr. by Sakae Shioya and E. Edgett. *The treasury of Japanese literature*, ed. by Tokichi Watanabe. Tokyo, Jippoh-kaku, 1933. p.332–351

'Tuatuwan impanbilay'　Tr. Maria C. Magsano. *Pangasinan Review*, no.211, 1951. p.1–200

Tuatuwan impanbilay. Tr. Maria C. Magsano. Dagupan City, Pangasinan Review, 1951. 221p.

「不如帰」　徐雲濤訳　台南　經緯書局　1963. 251p.

「不如帰」　黄文良訳　台南　綜合出版社　1975. 251p.

Kaijin　灰燼

'Glowing embers'　Tr. by Asataro Miyamori. *Representative tales of Japan*. Tokyo, Sanko Shoten, 1917. p.595–650

「灰燼」　郭夏信訳　「世界文学全集 94」　서울　乙酉文化社　1962. p.53–73

Kokuchō　黒潮

Куросиво. Перевод И. Львовой. Москва, Гослитиздат, 1957. 349p.

「黒潮」　金福訳　上海　上海文芸　1959. 218p.

Omoide no ki　思出の記

Footprints in the snow. Tr. by Kenneth Strong. London, Allen and Unwin, 1970. 442p.; Tokyo, Tuttle, 1971. 371p.

Shizen to jinsei　自然と人生

Nature and man. Tr. by Arthur Lloyd, H. von Fallot and H. Ono. Tokyo, Kogakukan, 1913. 311p.; Tokyo, Kobunsha, 1948. 311p.

'Природа и человек (фрагменты)'　Перевод Е. Пинус. *Восточный альманах 1*. Москва, Худож. Лит. 1957. p.338–348

Essays　エッセイ

'Five minutes' dream'　*Seinen*, v.8, no.7, 1902. p.9–10

'An autumn morning at the Tone'　Tr. by Sumimasa Ijichi. *Eigo Seinen*, v.19, no.7, 1908. p.160–161

'The poor child'　Tr. by Takeo Fujino. *Eigo Seinen*, v.22, no.2, 1909. p.44. v.22, no.3, 1909. p.65–66

'Raiu'　Tr. by Yaichiro Isobe. *Chugai Eigo*, July 1920.

TOKUTOMI Sohō　徳富蘇峰　1863–1957

Haisen gakkō　敗戦学校

「敗戦学校」　朴順来訳　서울　創人社　1950. 130p.

Criticism and Essays　評論・エッセイ

'The mission on educationalists'　*Seinen*, v.6, no.1, 1901. p.9–10

'Inspiration; True friends'　Tr. by Ume Tsuda. *Leaves from Japanese literature*. Tokyo, Eibun Shinshisha, 1906. p.21–23, 89–93

'Pleasure of farming'　Tr. by Yoshitaro Takenobu. *Eigo Seinen*, v.24, no.7, 1911. p.170–171

'The spiritual Japan and the Japanese spirit'　Tr. by Kyohei Hagiwara. *Eigo Seinen*, v.78, no.7, 1933. p.203

「浪漫主義文學」　哲人訳　上海　世界文藝社　n.d.　1冊

TOMI Hayahiko　鳥見迅彦　1910–

Poems　詩

'받자옥있느風景；妖精의빛'　金龍済訳　「日本詩集」　서울　青雲社　1960. p.15–17, 175–176

'한알의乾葡萄'　辛東門訳　「世界戦後文学全集 9」　서울　新丘文化社　1962. p.232–233

'Hearse; Mountain hut'　Tr. by Thomas Fitzsimmons. *Japanese poetry now*. London, André Deutsch, 1972. p.71–73; *Japanese poetry today*. N. Y. Schocken Books, 1972. p.73–75

TOMIOKA Taeko　富岡多恵子　1935–

Poems　詩

'返礼'　金龍済訳　「日本詩集」　서울　青雲社　1960. p.115–121

'Life story' Tr. by Harry and Lynn Guest and Shozo Kajima. *Post-war Japanese poetry*. Harmondsworth, Penguin Books, 1972. p.146–148

'Greetings; Nude drawing; What is your name?; How are you; And then soon; Well then see you tonight; The girlfriend' Tr. by Hiroaki Sato. *Ten Japanese poets*. Hanover, N. H. Granite Publications, 1973. p.92–101

'Between; Let me tell you about myself; Living together; What color was the sky; How are you; Please say something; Marry me please; Chairs; The girlfriend; Greetings' Tr. by Hiroaki Sato. *The poetry of postwar Japan*. Iowa City, Univ. of Iowa Press, 1975. p.222–233

'Between' Tr. by James Kirkup. *Poetry Nippon*, no.39 & 40, 1977. p.13–14

'Girlfriend' *The burning heart*, tr. and ed. by Kenneth Rexroth and Ikuko Atsumi. N. Y. Seabury Press, 1977. p.124–125

TOMISHIMA Takeo 富島健夫 1931–

「다큰계집애」 河在麒訳 서울 大宗出版社 1975. 331p.

TOMITA Saika 富田砕花 1890–

Poems 詩

'Images projetées; Cimetières de fantômes; La prière au crépuscule; Chanson de mai; Les paroles' Tr. par Kuni Matsuo et Steinilber-Oberlin. *Anthologie des poètes japonais contemporains*. Paris, Mercure de France, 1939. p.179–183

TOMITA Takako 富田孝子 1930–

Poems 詩

'The termination of the war and tomatoes' Tr. by Hideo Yamaguchi. *Poetry Nippon*, no.19, 1972. p.1–2

'The end of the war and tomatoes' Tr. by Hideo Yamaguchi. *Kobe Jogakuin Daigaku Ronshu*, v.18, no.3, 1972. p.49–51

TOMITA Tsuneo 富田常雄 1904–1967

「장미의受刑」 李時哲訳 서울 文光社 1963. 384p.

TOMIYASU Fūsei 富安風生 1885–

Haiku 俳句

'5 haiku' *A history of haiku v.2*, by R. H. Blyth. Tokyo, Hokuseido, 1964. p.165–168

'1 haiku' Tr. by Takamasa Sasaki. *Eigo Seinen*, v.122, no.5, 1976. p.231

'20 haiku' *Modern Japanese haiku, an anthology*, comp. and tr. by Makoto Ueda. Tokyo, Univ. of Tokyo Press, 1976. p.171–180

'Nightingale' Tr. by Kenneth Yasuda. *A pepper-pod*. Tokyo, Tuttle, 1976. p.103

TOMIZAWA Kakio 富沢赤黄男 1902–1962

Haiku 俳句

'20 haiku' *Modern Japanese haiku, an anthology*, comp. and tr. by Makoto Ueda. Tokyo, Univ. of Tokyo Press, 1976. p.242–251

TONEGAWA Yutaka 利根川 裕 1927–

Yume no daiyaku 「ゆめ」の代役

'「夢」的替身' 廖清秀訳 「投水自殺営救業」 台北 蘭開 書店 1968. p.46–65

TONOMURA Shigeru 外村 繁 1902–1961

Mugen hōei 夢幻泡影

'夢幻泡影' 金龍済訳 「日本代表作家百人集 2」 서울 希望出版社 1966. p.388–401;「日本短篇文学全集 3」 서울 新太陽社 1969. p.74–87

TORIYAMA Seisen 鳥山星山 1875–

Haiku 俳句

'1 haiku' Tr. by Asataro Miyamori. *Anthology of haiku, ancient and modern*. Tokyo, Maruzen, 1932. p.827

'New Year's day' Tr. by Asataro Miyamori. *Haiku poems, ancient and modern*. Tokyo, Maruzen, 1940. p.340

'1 haiku' Übers. von Gerolf Coudenhove. *Japanische Jahreszeiten*. Zürich, Manesse Verlag, 1963. p.11

TOYAMA Usaburō 外山卯三郎 1903–

Criticism 評論

'超現實主義的作家論' 荘世和訳 「東方雑誌復刊」 第1巻 7期 1968. p.104–110

TOYODA Masako 豊田正子 1922–

Tsuzurikata kyōshitsu 綴方教室

The composition class. Tr. by Z. Tamotsu Iwado. Tokyo, Herald of Asia, 1938. 146p.

TOYOHARA Michiko 豊原路子 1933–

Taiatari dansei ron 体当たり男性論

「男과女」 金文影 林石淵訳 서울 真文出版社 1972. p.9–198

TOYOSAWA Toyoo 豊沢豊雄 1907–

Essay エッセイ

'掌握了人類的味覺' 徐白訳 「日本短篇譯集 3」台北 晩蟬書店 1969. p.41–75

TOYOSHIMA Yoshio 豊島与志雄 1890–1955

Rōdōsha no ko 労働者の子

'工人之子' 「日本短篇小説選」 香港 藝美圖書 1959. p.31–46
'工人之子' 高汝鴻訳 「日本短篇小説集」 台北 台湾商務印書館 1969. p.87–110

Criticism 評論

'創作家的態度' 張我軍訳 「北新半月刊」 第3巻10期 1929. p.37–54

TOYOTAMA Tsuno とよたま・つの

Poems 詩

Gelöstes Haar. Übers. von Manfred Hausmann. Frankfurt am Main, Fischer, 1966. 83p.; Zürich, Verlag der Arche, 1974. 94p.

TSUBOI Sakae 壺井 栄 1899–1967

Kaki no ki no aru ie 柿の木のある家

'Under the persimmon tree' Tr. by Kiyonobu Uno. *The Reeds*, v.10, 1965. p.49–63

Nijūshi no hitomi 二十四の瞳

Twenty-four eyes. Tr. by Akira Miura. Tokyo, Kenkyusha, 1957. 244p.
「스물네개의눈동자」 秋湜訳 서울 韓一出版社 1961. 225p.
Dvadsat'štyri očí. Přel. Viktor Krupa. Bratislava, Mladé Letá, 1961. 191p.
'Vingt-quatre prunelles' Tr. de Maxime Leff. *Les portes de la vie, Japon*. Paris, Éditions du Burin, 1968. p.65–222
「그리운눈동자」 秋湜訳 서울 高麗文化社 1973. 225p.
「잃어버린눈동자」 秋湜訳 서울 集賢社 1975. 225p.

Tabako kai 煙草買ひ

'The cigarette rush' Tr. by Kyohei Hagiwara. *Eigo Seinen*, v.85, no.10, 1941. p.300–301

Wakare わかれ

'Separazione' Tr. di Isaio Yamazaki e Giorgio Prosperi. *Yamato*, anno 1, no.2, 1941. p.56–58

Essay エッセイ

'我的百花故事' 肖肖訳 「世界文学」 1959年6月 p.138–143

「壺井栄小説集」 舒暢 蕭蕭訳 北京 作家出版社 1959. 120p.

TSUBOI Shigeji 壺井繁治 1897–1975

Poems 詩

'The room' Tr. by Shigehisa Narita. *Japan Quarterly*, v.3, no.1, 1956. p.88
'Dvacátý únor' Přel. V. Winkelhöferová. *Nový Orient*, v.11, no.2, 1956. p.21–22
'樹木' 梅韜訳 「譯文」 1956年7月 p.27–28
'Azaleas' Tr. by J. G. Mills and Rikutaro Fukuda. *Japan Quarterly*, v.4, no.2, 1957. p.189
'Входы и выходы' Перевод В. Журавлева. *Поэты Азии*. Москва, Гослитиздат, 1957. p.885–887
'The wind; A pebble; Stars and the dry grass; A path; A stone; The sky; Spring; Autumn; Even if I am silent; The fruit; A beggar in the world; A butterfly' *An anthology of modern Japanese poetry*, ed. and tr. by Ichiro Kono and Rikutaro Fukuda. Tokyo, Kenkyusha, 1957. p.142–147
'Je příliš mnohozívajícízh' Přel. M. Novák a J. Vladislav. *Světová Literatura*, no.6, 1960. p.38–58
'Тема завтрашнего дня; Подсолнечник; Глаза; Осень' Перевод Веры Марковой. *Иностранная Литература*, сентябрь 1960. p.144–149
'迎春' 李芒訳 「詩刊」 第4期 1961. p.54–55
「壺井繁治詩抄」 楼適夷 李芒訳 北京 作家出版社 1962. 40p.
'Gökyüzü; Sesim çikmiyorsa; Taş; Bahar; Çakitaşi; Rüzgâr; Yildizlar ve kurumus cimenler' Tercüme etmek L. Sami Akalin. *Japon şiiri*. İstanbul, Varlik Yayinevi, 1962. p.248–251
Ulice plná pláštů do deště. Přel. Miroslav Novák a Jan Vladislav. Praha, Státní Nakl. Krásné Literatury a Umění, 1963. 112p.
'Autumn in gaol; Star and dead leaves; English-ugh!; Butterfly; Silent, but . . .' Tr. by Geoffrey Bownas and Anthony Thwaite. *The Penguin book of Japanese verse*. Harmondsworth, Penguin Books, 1964. p.188–191
'事件' 林林訳 「世界文学」 1964年6月 p.125–127
'El fruto' Tr. por Kikuya Ionesawa. *Poesia japonesa contemporanea*. Bogotá, Colombia Editoriales de Librería, 1965. n.p.
'River of ice' Tr. by Yuki Sawa and Edith Marcombe Shiffert. *The Southern Review*, v.5, no.4, 1969. p.1171
'Кируучу жана чыгуушу колдор; Кызыл туу' Которгон Ж. Алыбаев. *Хиросима кектери*. Фрунзе, Кыргызстан, 1969. p.82–85
'별과마른풀' 「永遠한世界名詩全集 2」黃錦燦編 서울 翰林出版社 1969. p.150; 「永遠한世界名詩全集 5」黃錦燦編 서울 翰林出版社 1973. p.150
'River of ice; Night skylark; Sunflower; Cable cars; Balloon; Bear; Motionless night' *Anthology of modern Japanese poetry*. Tr. and comp. by Edith Marcombe Shiffert and Yuki Sawa. Tokyo, Tuttle, 1972. p.68–74
'The disinterested sky; The bud; Greeting the dawn; Beggar in the wind' Tr. by Robert Epp. *Japan Christian Quarterly*, v.39, no.1, 1973. p.39–47
'Роза; Песня; Воздушный корабль; Подзорная труба; Звезда и мертвые листья; Скамья в парке' Перевод Анатолия Мамонова. *Вкус хризантемы*. Москва, Восточная Литература, 1976. p.166–170
'En tigger i blåsten; Om himlen; Host i fengslet; Sommerfugl' Til norsk ved Paal Brekke. *Moderne japansk lyrikk*. Oslo, Norske Bok-

klubben, n.d. p.31–34

'Toamna, în temniţă; Stea şi frunze moarte; Fluture' Traducerea Virgil Teodorescu. *Din lirica japoneză.* Bucureşti, Editura Univers, n.d. p.163–164

TSUBOTA Hanako 壺田花子 1905–

Poems 詩

'젊은시절의追憶' 崔一秀訳 「기다리고있네」 서울 韓国政経社 1966. p.135–138

TSUBOTA Jōji 坪田譲治 1890–

Jinshichi rōjin nanga fūkei 甚七老人南画風景

'Der alte Jinschti von einem Liebhaber geschildert' Übers. von Kurt Meissner. *Der Tanzfächer*, von K. Meissner. Tokyo, 1943. p.263–281

Kaki to Jinshichi 柿と甚七

'Der alte Jinshichi' Übers. von Oscar Benl. *Eine Glocke in Fukagawa, und andere japanische Erzählungen.* Tübingen, Erdmann, 1969. p.17–37

Kaze no naka no kodomo 風の中の子供

「風波里的孩子」 聶長振訳 北京 少年兒童 1957. 84p.
La infanoj en vento. Tr. K. Itoo. Fukui, Ĉiama Grupo, 1966. 72p.

Momotarō 桃太郎

'Momotaro' *Nippon*, Bd.4, 1935. p.45–48

Obake no sekai お化けの世界

'The bogeyman world' Tr. by William L. Clark. *Jiji Eigo Kenkyu*, v.13, no.1, 2, 3, 1958; *Various kinds of bugs, and other stories.* Tokyo, Kenkyusha, 1958. p.1–39
'Il mondo dei fantasmi' Tr. di Atsuko Ricca Suga. *Narratori giapponesi moderni.* Milano, Bompiani, 1965. p.367–392

TSUBOUCHI Shōyō 坪内逍遙 1859–1935

En no gyōja 役の行者

L'ermite. Tr. par Takamatsu Yoshie. Paris, Société Littéraire de France, 1920. 86p.

Kiri hitoha 桐一葉

'Kiri-hitoha' Tr. by Arthur Lloyd. *Far East*, v.2, no.7, 1897. p.307–312. v.2, no.8, 1898. p.350–359. v.3, no.25, 1898. p.129–137
'Ein Blatt vom Kiri Baum' Übers. von Maria Piper. *Das japanische Theater.* Frankfurt am Main, Societäts Verlag, 1937. p.150–162

Shinkyoku Urashima 新曲浦島

Ourashima. Tr. du japonais par Takamatou Yoshiye. Paris, Pierre Roger, 1922. 92p.

Urashima. Tr. by Kwanshu M. Furusawa. Urawa, Furusawa, 1936. 92p.

Shōsetsu shinzui 小説神髄

'The essence of the novel' Tr. by Donald Keene. *Modern Japanese literature*, ed. by D. Keene. N. Y. Grove Press, 1956; Tokyo, Tuttle, 1957. p.55–58
'Lo spirito del romanzo' Tr. di R. Vulpitta. *Antologia della letterature coreana e giapponese.* Milano, Fratelli Fabbri, 1969. p.219–220

Criticism 評論

'Chikamatsu and Shakespeare' Tr. by Kazutomo Takahashi. *Eigo Seinen*, v.61, no.1–6, 1929.
History and characteristics of Kabuki. Tr. by Ryozo Matsumoto. Yokohama, Yamagata, 1960. 292p.

TSUCHIDA Kōhei 土田耕平 1895–1940

Tanka 短歌

'Violets; The moon' Tr. by Asataro Miyamori. *Masterpieces of Japanese poetry, ancient and modern.* Tokyo, Maruzen, 1936; Tokyo, Taiseido, 1956; N. Y. Greenwood Press, 1971. p.786–787

TSUCHIDA Kyōson 土田杏村 1891–1934

Criticism 評論

'現代的東洋思想' 王璧如訳 「北新半月刊」 第3巻17号 1929. p.37–45

TSUCHIYA Bunmei 土屋文明 1890–

Tanka 短歌

'A disagreeable man; The first shell' Tr. by Asataro Miyamori. *Masterpieces of Japanese poetry, ancient and modern.* Tokyo, Maruzen, 1936; Tokyo, Taiseido, 1956; N. Y. Greenwood Press, 1971. p.780–781
'1 tanka' Tr. by Shigeshi Nishimura. *The Current of the World*, v.17, no.2, 1940. p.131
'4 tanka' Übers. von Kuniyo Takayasu und Manfred Hausmann. *Ruf der Regenpfeifer.* München, Bechtle Verlag, 1961. p.103
'2 tanka' *Anthology of modern Japanese poetry*, tr. and comp. by Edith Marcombe Shiffert and Yuki Sawa. Tokyo, Tuttle, 1972. p.148

TSUCHIYA Takao 土屋隆夫 1917–

Jōji no haikei 情事の背景

'情事의背景' 申東漢訳 「日本代表作家百人集 4」 서울 希望出版社 1966. p.430–449; 「日本短篇文学全集 5」 서울 新太陽社 1969. p.270–289
'情事의背景' 張文平訳 「日本文学大全集 10」 서울 南西文化院 1975. p.61–80

Kuwaete keshita 加えて、消した

'Write in, rub out' *Japanese golden dozen*, ed. by Ellery Queen. Tokyo, Tuttle, 1978. p.259–274

TSUDA Kiyoko　津田清子　1920–

Haiku　俳句

'2 haiku' *Anthology of modern Japanese poetry*, tr. and comp. by Edith Marcombe Shiffert and Yuki Sawa. Tokyo, Tuttle, 1972. p.174

TSUDA Sōkichi　津田左右吉　1873–1961

Bungaku ni arawaretaru waga kokumin shisō no kenkyū　文学に現はれたる我が国民思想の研究

An inquiry into the Japanese mind as mirrored in literature. Tr. by Fukumatsu Matsuda. Tokyo, Japanese National Commission for Unesco, 1970. 332p.

TSUJI Ryōichi　辻　亮一　1914–

Ihōjin　異邦人

「異邦人」劉慕沙訳　「芥川奨作品選集 1」台北　晩蟬書店　1969.　p.1–76；「芥川賞作品選集 2」台北　大地出版社　1974. p.1–76

TSUJII Takashi　辻井　喬　1927–

Atena no nai tegami　宛名のない手紙

Lieu d'exil. Text français de Jean Clarence Lambert, préséntation par Makoto Ohka. Paris, Seghers, 1964. 71p.

Poems　詩

'Age of disorder; Quiet town' Tr. by Geoffrey Bownas. *New writing in Japan*. Harmondsworth, Penguin Books, 1972. p.210–212

TSUKAHARA Jūshien　塚原渋柿園　1848–1917

Shinbugun　振武軍

'One-sided love' Tr. by Asataro Miyamori. *Representative tales of Japan*. Tokyo, Sanko Shoten, 1917. p.20–56

TSUKAMOTO Kunio　塚本邦雄　1922–

Tanka　短歌

'5 tanka' Tr. by Geoffrey Bownas. *New writing in Japan*. Harmondsworth, Penguin Books, 1972. p.241–242

TSUKAMOTO Yasuhiko　塚本康彦　1933–

Juken bangō 5111　受験番号 5111

「受験番号 5111」沈裁雨訳　서울　徽文出版社　1963. 264p.

TSUMURA Nobuo　津村信夫　1909–1944

Poems　詩

'An old man from the mountain; To the things far away' *An anthology of modern Japanese poetry*, ed. and tr. by Ichiro Kono and Rikutaro Fukuda. Tokyo, Kenkyusha, 1957. p.148

'A las cosas remotas' Tr. por Kikuya Ionesawa. *Poesia japonesa contemporanea*. Bogotá, Colombia Editoriales de Librería, 1965. n.p.

TSUNODA Chikurei　角田竹冷　1856–1919

Haiku　俳句

'4 haiku' Tr. by V. H. Viglielmo. *Japanese literature in the Meiji era*. Tokyo, Obunsha, 1955. p.436

TSUNODA Hirohide　角田ひろひで

Poems　詩

'Прощание в море' Перевод Анатолия Мамонова. *Иностранная Литература*, август 1959. p.168–169; *Песни Хиросимы*. Москва, Худож. Лит. 1964. p.29; *Вкус хризантемы*. Москва, Восточная Литература, 1976. p.171

'A burial at sea' Tr. by Miyao Ohara. *The songs of Hiroshima*. Tokyo, Taihei Shuppansha, 1971. p.60–61

TSUNODA Kikuo　角田喜久雄　1906–

Kiri ni sumu oni　霧に棲む鬼

「霧夜魅影」王全美訳　三重市　明志出版社　1963. 2冊

Zankoku na fukushū　残酷な復讐

「残酷的報復」王全美訳　三重市　明志出版社　1963. 125p.

TSURUMI Yūsuke　鶴見祐輔　1885–1974

Dokusho zanmai　読書三昧

「讀書三昧」李冠禮　蕭品超訳　台北　台湾商務印書館　1967. 201p.

Haha　母

The mother. Tr. by the author. N. Y. Rae D. Henkle, 1932. 287p.

Shisō sansui jinbutsu　思想・山水・人物

「思想 山水 人物」魯迅訳　上海　北新書局　1928. 1冊；香港　今代書局　1966. 272p.

'思想　山水　人物' 魯迅訳　「魯迅全集 13」 上海　魯迅
全集出版社　1938.　作家書屋　1946.　大連　光
華書店　1948.　北京　人民文学出版社　1973.
p.385–648; 「魯迅譯文集 3」 北京　人民文学出版
社　1958.　p.289–493

Essays エッセイ

'所謂懷疑主義者' 魯迅訳　「莽原」　第1巻14期　1926.
p.565–570
'説幽黙' 魯迅訳　「莽原」　第2巻1期　1927. p.23–34
'書斎生活與其危險' 魯迅訳　「莽原」　第2巻12期　1927.
p.443–452
'讀的文章和聽的文字' 魯迅訳　「莽原」　第2巻13期　1927.
p.517–520
'少年之日' 沈思訳　「讀書雜誌」　第1巻　1931年4月
p.1–13
'在異郷發見友人' 兪康德訳　「人間世」　第16期　1934.
p.25–26
'古都的魅力' 周豫才訳　「世界著名作家散文選」 香港　上
海書局　1977. p.457–467

TSURUTA Tomoya　鶴田知也　1902–

Koshamain ki　コシャマイン記

'코샤마인記' 李唯震訳　「新世界」　第2巻9号　p.364–
385

TSUTSUI Yasutaka　筒井康隆　1934–

Kimi tachite nochi　君発ちて後

'自君別後' 劉與堯訳　「現代日本小説選」 台北　雲天出版
社　1970. p.173–201

Nyobosatsu dan　如菩薩団

'Perfectly lovely ladies' *Japanese golden dozen*,
ed. by Ellery Queen. Tokyo, Tuttle, 1978.
p.275–288

TSUTSUI Yoriko　筒井頼子

Hajimete no otsukai　はじめてのおつかい

På egen hånd. København, Høst, 1977. 1v.

TSUTSUMI Sakiko　堤さき子

Tanka　短歌

'2 tanka' Tr. by Haxon Ishii. *Eigo Seinen*, v.81,
no.10, 1939. p.302

TSUYUKI Shigeru　露木　茂

Poems 詩

'Hongkong no hana' Tr. by James Kirkup.
Poetry Nippon, no. 2, 1968. p.10

TSUZUKI Masuyo　都築益世　1898–

Poems 詩

'Fish in the lake' *An anthology of modern Japanese
poetry*, ed. and tr. by Ichiro Kono and Rikutaro Fukuda. Tokyo, Kenkyusha, 1957. p.149
'Göldeki balik' Tercüme etmek L. Sami Akalin.
Japon şiiri. İstanbul, Varlik Yayinevi, 1962.
p. 267

U

UCHIDA Risako　内田利莎子　1928–

Ōkina kabu　おおきなかぶ

Okina kabu. Urdu Bazar, West Pakistan Publishing Co. 1973. 1v.

Suzume no mahō　すずめのまほう

A sparrow's magic. N. Y. Parents' Magazine Press,
1970. 1v.

Usagi no ie　うさぎのいえ

The rabbit's house. London, Evans Brothers, 1970.
30p.

Yuki musume　ゆきむすめ

The snow daughter. English version by Kenneth
Williams. Tokyo, Labo Teaching Information
Center, 1970. 27p.

**UCHIGASAKI Sakusaburō　内ケ崎作三郎
1877–1947**

Criticism 評論

「近代文藝的背景」 王璧如訳　上海　北新書局　1928. 1冊

UEDA Bin　上田　敏　1874–1916

Poems 詩

'Le goflie cadute' Tr. di R. Beviglia. *Antologia
della letteratura coreana e giapponese*. Milano,
Fratelli Fabbri, 1969. p.271

Criticism 評論

'現代的文學' 嬰訳　「貢獻旬刊」　第3巻4期　1928.
「現代藝術十二講」 豊子愷訳　上海　開明書局　192?.

UEDA Chōshū　上田聴秋　1852–1932

Haiku　俳句

'The moon in the water' Tr. by Asataro Miyamori.
Anthology of haiku, ancient and modern.
Tokyo, Maruzen, 1932. p.670; *Haiku poems*,

UEDA Chōshū

ancient and modern. Tokyo, Maruzen, 1940. p.302
'1 haiku' Tr. by Peter Beilenson and Harry Behn. *Haiku harvest*. Mount Vernon, Peter Pauper Press, 1962. p.51
'1 haiku' Übers. von Erwin Jahn. *Fallende Blüten*. Zürich, Arche, 1968. p.71

UEDA Hideo　上田英夫　1894–

Tanka　短歌

'Fine autumn weather' Tr. by Asataro Miyamori. *Masterpieces of Japanese poetry, ancient and modern*. Tokyo, Maruzen, 1936; Tokyo, Taiseido, 1956; N. Y. Greenwood Press, 1971. p.784

UEDA Ryūji　上田龍耳

Haiku　俳句

'1 haiku' Tr. by V. H. Viglielmo. *Japanese literature in the Meiji era*. Tokyo, Obunsha, 1955. p.438

UEDA Shizue　上田静栄　1898–

Poems　詩

'Resistance' *An anthology of modern Japanese poetry*, ed. and tr. by Ichiro Kono and Rikutaro Fukuda. Tokyo, Kenkyusha, 1957. p.149
'Rezistans' Tercüme etmek L. Sami Akalin. *Japon şiiri*. İstanbul, Varlik Yayinevi, 1962. p.266

UEDA Susumu　上田　進　1907–1947

Criticism　評論

'蘇聯文學理論及文學批評的現状' 魯迅訳 「譯文」 第1巻 1期 1934; 「魯迅全集 16」 上海 魯迅全集出版社 1938. 作家書屋 1946. 大連 光華書店 1948. 北京 人民文学出版社 1973. p.524–565; 「魯迅譯文集 10」 北京 人民文学出版社 1958. p.376–402
'偉大的十五周年文學' 適夷訳 「文學月報」 第56期合刊

UEKI Takehiko　植木武彦

Gikyō den　義侠伝

The gikio den, a Japanese romance. Tokyo, Mitsui Chinbei, 1887. 138p.

UEMATSU Hisaki　植松寿樹　1890–1964

Tanka　短歌

'A dirge; The bugles of barracks; A butterfly; A snow-white butterfly' Tr. by Asataro Miyamori. *Masterpieces of Japanese poetry, ancient*

and modern. Tokyo, Maruzen, 1936; Tokyo, Taiseido, 1956; N. Y. Greenwood Press, 1971. p.775–777
'1 tanka' Übers. von Gerolf Coudenhove. *Japanische Jahreszeiten*. Zürich, Manesse Verlag, 1963. p.213

UEMOTO Masao　うえもと・まさお　1922–

Poems　詩

'Пустыня' Перевод Анатолия Мамонова. *Иностранная Литература*, август, 1959. p.170
'A season in the waste-land' Tr. by Miyao Ohara. *The songs of Hiroshima*. Tokyo, Taihei Shuppansha, 1971. p.58–59

UENO Hidenobu　上野英信　1923–

Senburi senji ga waratta　せんぶりせんじが笑った!

「煎黄連笑了」 孫光宇訳　上海　新文芸　1957. 64p.

UENO Noriko　上野紀子　1940–

Zō no botan　ぞうのボタン

Elephant buttons. N. Y. Harper and Row, 1973. 1v.

UMEDA Haruo　梅田晴夫　1920–

Warui Nihonjin　ワルイ日本人

「醜悪한日本人」 裵賢訳　서울　緑文社　1966. 283p.

UMEZAKI Haruo　梅崎春生　1915–1965

Boroya no shunjū　ボロ家の春秋

Occurrences of an old dilapidated house. Tr. by Hisashi Kanekatsu and Takeshi Nakajima. Tokyo, Kobunsha, 1968. 86p.

Eikun no tegami　A君の手紙

'A letter from Mr. A' Tr. by Makoto Ueda. *Literary Review*, v.6, no.1, 1962. p.70–85

Esu no senaka　Sの背中

'The birthmark on S's back' Tr. by Clifton Royston. *Japan Quarterly*, v.16, no.1, 1969. p.78–92
'The secret birth mark on S's back' Tr. by Hisashi Kanekatsu and Takeshi Nakajima. *The secret birth mark on S's back, and four other short stories*. Tokyo, Kobunsha, 1970. p.1–47

Fuku　服

'An antipathy' Tr. by Hisashi Kanekatsu and Takeshi Nakajima. *The secret birth mark on S's back, and four other short stories*. Tokyo, Kobunsha, 1970. p.48–52

Hi no hate 日の果て

Konec dne. Přel. V. Winkelhöferová. Praha, SNKHLU, 1963. 89p.

Kioku 記憶

'Memory' Tr. by Hisashi Kanekatsu and Takeshi Nakajima. *The secret birth mark on S's back, and four other short stories*. Tokyo, Kobunsha, 1970. p.105–130

Megane no hanashi 眼鏡の話

'Про очки' Перевод А. Бабинцева. *No. 36; новеллы японских писателей*. Москва, Наука, 1968. p.88–97

Nise tamago 偽卵

'Falešna násada' Přel. M. Novák. *Světová Literatura*, no.4, 1962. p.108–114
'Falešna násada' Přel. M. Novák a J. Kovandova. *Nový Orient*, v.7, no.2, 1968. p.26–30

Rinshō 輪唱

'A round in three parts' Tr. by Clifton Royston. *Japan Quarterly*, v.15, no.4, 1968. p.481–488

Sakurajima 桜島

'Sakurajima' Aus dem Japanischen von Oscar Benl. *Japan, Geistige Begegnung*. Tübingen, Erdmann, 1964. p.220–277; *Eine Glocke in Fukagawa*. Tübingen, Erdmann, 1969. p.220–277
'Sakurajima' Tr. by D. E. Mills. *The shadow of sunrise*, ed. by Shoichi Saeki. Tokyo, Kodansha International, 1966; London, Ward Lock, 1966. p.63–117
'Cseresznyesziget' Ford. Sz. Holti Mária. *Modern Japán elbeszélők*. Budapest, Európa Könyvkiadó, 1967. p.240–271
'Wiśniowa wyspa' Przeł. Mikołaj Melanowicz. *Cień wschodzącego słońca*. Warszawa, Książka i Wiedza, 1972.
'Sakurajima' Deutsch von Oscar Benl. *Träume aus zehn Nächten*. Berlin, Aufbau Verlag, 1975. p.305–362

Seishun 青春

'青春' 金龍済訳 「日本代表作家百人集 4」 서울 希望出版社 1966. p.330–353;「日本短篇文学全集 5」 서울 新太陽社 1969. p.170–193

Shunjitsu bikō 春日尾行

'An incognito' Tr. by Hisashi Kanekatsu and Takeshi Nakajima. *The secret birth mark on S's back, and four other short stories*. Tokyo, Kobunsha, 1970. p.53–83

Sora no shita 空の下

'Under the sky' Tr. by Sakae Shioya. *Western Humanities Review*, Spring 1952. p.119–128
'Дым' Перевод Я. Берлина и З. Рахима. *Японская новелла*. Москва, Изд. Иност. Лит. 1961. p.352–365

Tottei nite 突堤にて

'At a breakwater' Tr. by Hisashi Kanekatsu and Takeshi Nakajima. *The secret birth mark*

on S's back, and four other short stories. Tokyo, Kobunsha, 1970. p.84–104

UMEZAWA Bokusui 梅沢墨水 1875–1914

Haiku 俳句

'4 haiku' Tr. by Asataro Miyamori. *Anthology of haiku, ancient and modern*. Tokyo, Maruzen, 1932. p.691–693
'The bee; Advertising boards' Tr. by Asataro Miyamori. *Haiku poems, ancient and modern*. Tokyo, Maruzen, 1940. p.320–321
'A bee' Tr. by Kenneth Yasuda. *A pepper-pod*. Tokyo, Tuttle, 1976. p.80

UNO Chiyo 宇野千代 1897–

Garasu no naka no musume ガラスの中の娘

'Shopgirl' Tr. by Mitsugi Teshigawara. *Young forever, and five other novelettes*. Tokyo, Hokuseido, 1941. p.122–139

Ohan おはん

'Ohan' Tr. by Donald Keene. *Three modern Japanese short novels*. N. Y. Viking Press, 1961. p.51–118

UNO Kōichirō 宇能鴻一郎 1934–

Geishin 鯨神

'Бог китов' Перевод Т. Григорьевой. *Иностранная Литература*, июнь 1972. p.76–98; *Японская новелла 1960–1970*. Москва, 1972. p.377–411

UNO Kōji 宇野浩二 1891–1961

Ko o kashi ya 子を貸し屋

'Children for hire' Tr. by Edward Seidensticker. *Japan Quarterly*, v.10, no.2, 1963. p.200–231

Omoi gusa 思い草

'思草' (選訳) 蕭蕭訳 「譯文」 1957年9月 p.107–116

Yaneura no hōgakushi 屋根裏の法学士

'다락방의 법학사' 崔泰應訳 「日本代表作家百人集 2」 서울 希望出版社 1966. p.294–302;「日本短篇文学全集 2」 서울 新太陽社 1969. p.358–366

URIU Yasushi 瓜生 靖

Aru bunshi no shōgai ある文士の生涯

'Autobiographical story through three generations' *Akatsuki, dawn*. Tokyo, Information Publishing, 1972. p.1–44

USAMI Naoki　ウサミ・ナオキ

Poems　詩

'Страшны; Девушка и дерево гингко' Перевод Анатолия Мамонова. *Иностранная Литература*, декабрь 1965. p.68

'Лании мейен бирге; Крудан чекусу; Кайгулуу кезде; Билдар, чеп, гур' Которгон С. Ералиев. Фрунзе, Кыргызстан, 1969.

'Одновременно' Перевод А. И. Мамонова. *Свободный стих в японской поэзии*. Москва, Наука, 1971. p.175

'С Лениным вместе!; Память о дружбе' Перевод Анатолия Мамонова. *Вкус хризантемы*. Москва, Восточная Литература, 1976. p.143–144

USUDA Arō　臼田亜浪　1879–1951

Haiku　俳句

'8 haiku' Tr. by Asataro Miyamori. *Anthology of haiku, ancient and modern*. Tokyo, Maruzen, 1932. p.760–766

'Haiku' Tr. par Kuni Matsuo et Steinilber-Oberlin. *Anthologie des poètes japonais contemporains*. Paris, Mercure de France, 1939. p.297–298

'Snow' Tr. by Asataro Miyamori. *Haiku poems, ancient and modern*. Tokyo, Maruzen, 1940. p.346

'1 haiku' Tr. by R. H. Blyth. *Haiku v.2*. Tokyo, Hokuseido, 1952. p.258

'Haiku' Tercüme etmek L. Sami Akalin. *Japon şiiri*. İstanbul, Varlik Yayinevi, 1962. p.239

'9 haiku' *A history of haiku v.2*, by R. H. Blyth. Tokyo, Hokuseido, 1964. p.257–260

'Mount Fuji' Tr. by Kenneth Yasuda. *A pepper-pod*. Tokyo, Tuttle, 1976. p.90

USUI Taiyoku　臼井大翼　1885–1947

Tanka　短歌

'The snow on New Year's day; A summer day' Tr. by Asataro Miyamori. *Masterpieces of Japanese poetry, ancient and modern*. Tokyo, Maruzen, 1936; Tokyo, Taiseido, 1956; N. Y. Greenwood Press, 1971. p.727–728

'1 tanka' Übers. von Gerolf Coudenhove. *Japanische Jahreszeiten*. Zürich, Manesse Verlag, 1963. p.21

USUI Yoshimi　臼井吉見　1905–

Jiko no tenmatsu　事故のてんまつ

「事故의 顚末」 河龍得訳　서울　経林出版社 1977. 210p.
「川端康成的愛與死」 丁祖威訳　台北　聯合報出版社 1977. 218p.

Criticism　評論

'Shiga and Akutagawa' *Japan Quarterly*, v.2, no.4, 1955. p.447–452

'The young woman novelists today' *Japan Quarterly*, v.4, no.4, 1957. p.519–522

UZAWA Shitei　鵜沢四丁　1869–1944

Haiku　俳句

'6 haiku' Tr. by Asataro Miyamori. *Anthology of haiku, ancient and modern*. Tokyo, Maruzen, 1932. p.728–733

'Through the mosquito-net; Lilies; A mountain village' Tr. by Asataro Miyamori. *Haiku poems, ancient and modern*. Tokyo, Maruzen, 1940. p.330–332

W

WADA Den　和田　伝　1900–

Chikasui　地下水

'Grundwasser' Übers. von Kurt Meissner. *Der Tanzfächer*, von K. Meissner. Tokyo, 1943. p.181–196

Kokuzō mushi　穀象虫

'Rice weevils' Tr. by Grace Suzuki. *Ukiyo*. Tokyo, Phoenix Books, 1954. p.126–145; *Ukiyo*, ed. by J. Gluck. N. Y. Vanguard Press, 1963. p.181–191; London, Universal Library, 1964. p.181–191

Mura no jinan　村の次男

'He who inherits' Tr. by Tadao Kunitomo. *Young forever, and five other novelettes*, ed. by Japan Writers' Society. Tokyo, Hokuseido, 1941. p.98–121

Ōhinata mura　大日向村

'Ohinata-mura' Summary by Den Wada. *Nippon*, v.24, 1940. p.44–49

WAINAI Sadayuki　和井内貞行　1858–1922

Kapacheppo　カパチェッポ

Kapacheppo, a drama. Tr. by Kiichi Nishi. Tokyo, Kyobunkan, 1949. 31p.

WAKAYAMA Bokusui　若山牧水　1885–1928

Tanka　短歌

'Waves; Wild ducks; My friend; The wind rustling through pines; The white bird; Eyeless fish; How many mountains and rivers?; Two clouds; Dandelions; The full moon; How silly!' Tr. by Asataro Miyamori. *Masterpieces of Japanese poetry, ancient and modern*. Tokyo, Maruzen, 1936; Tokyo, Taiseido, 1956; N. Y. Greenwood Press, 1971. p.711–718

266

'7 tanka' Tr. by Shigeshi Nishimura. *The Current of the World*, v.16, no.9, 10, 1939.

'Tanka' Tr. par Kuni Matsuo et Steinilber-Oberlin. *Anthologie des poètes japonais contemporains*. Paris, Mercure de France, 1939. p.274–275

'6 tanka' Tr. by V. H. Viglielmo. *Japanese literature in the Meiji era*. Tokyo, Obunsha, 1955. p.401–402

'16 tanka' Tr. by H. H. Honda. *The Reeds*, v.3, 1957. p.6, 11, 12, 17, 18, 19, 21

The poetry of Wakayama Bokusui. Tr. by Heihachiro Honda. Tokyo, Hokuseido, 1958. 100p.

'2 tanka' Übers. von Kuniyo Takayasu und Manfred Hausmann. *Ruf der Regenpfeifer*. München, Bechtle Verlag, 1961. p.97–98

'1 haiku' Tr. by Peter Beilenson and Harry Behn. *Haiku harvest*. Mount Vernon, Peter Pauper Press, 1962. p.54

'2 haiku' Übers. von Gerolf Coudenhove. *Japanische Jahreszeiten*. Zürich, Manesse Verlag, 1963. p.45, 172

'2 tanka' Übers. von Gerolf Coudenhove. *Japanische Jahreszeiten*. Zürich, Manesse Verlag, 1963. p.29, 148

'5 tanka' Tr. by Geoffrey Bownas and Anthony Thwaite. *The Penguin book of Japanese verse*. Harmondsworth, Penguin Books, 1964. p.163–164

'Пятистишия' Перевод Анатолия Мамонова. *Вкус хризантемы*. Москва, Восточная Литература, 1976. p.24

WAKAYAMA Kishiko　若山喜志子　1888–1968

Tanka　短歌

'The corpse; The cosmos flower; A cooper; A great moon; A silver dragonfly; Lean crows' Tr. by Asataro Miyamori. *Masterpieces of Japanese poetry, ancient and modern*. Tokyo, Maruzen, 1936; Tokyo, Taiseido, 1956; N. Y. Greenwood Press, 1971. p.754–758

WATANABE Jun'ichi　渡辺淳一　1933–

Akan ni hatsu　阿寒に果つ

'雪地之死' 余阿勲訳 「中國時報副刊」 1973.
「雪地之死」 余阿勲訳 台北 道聲出版社 1973. 319p.

Hikari to kage　光と影

'天命' 喬遷訳 「戰闘完了己黃昏」 台北 幼獅文化事業公司 1971. p.49–152

Mueitō　無影燈

「無影燈」 姜佐雄訳 서울 成功文化社 1977. 348p.

Yoru no shuppan　夜の出帆

「午夜揚帆」 台北 精準出版社 1963. 125p.

'體貼與悲哀' 廖清秀節訳 「自由談」 第26巻1期 1975. p.54–57, 2期 1975. p.53–55

WATANABE Junzō　渡辺順三　1894–1972

Poems　詩

'Друзья и товарищи' Перевод В. Н. Марковой. *Японская поэзия*. Москва, Гослитиздат, 1954. p.291

'Sorstarsak' Ford. Sövény Aladár. *Nagyvilág*, no.5, 1958. p.701

'Ненависть' Перевод А. Стругацкого. *Литературная Грузия*, 1958, No.5. p.15

'Тело родины' Перевод М. Дудина. *Нева*, 1958, No.9. p.170

Criticism　評論

'日本普羅短歌運動的陣容' 錦遐訳 「南開」 第99期

WATANABE Katei　渡辺霞亭　1864–1926

Tsuchiya Chikara　土屋主税

'Tsuchiya Chikara' Übers. von Maria Piper. *Die Schaukunst der Japaner*. Berlin, Walter de Gruyter, 1927. p.62–75

WATANABE Kohan　渡辺湖畔　1886–

Tanka　短歌

'Travelling' Tr. by Asataro Miyamori. *Masterpieces of Japanese poetry, ancient and modern*. Tokyo, Maruzen, 1936; Tokyo, Taiseido, 1956; N. Y. Greenwood Press, 1971. p.748

WATANABE Shigeo　渡辺茂男　1928–

Hesomochi　へそもち

The thunder boy. English version by Kenneth Williams. Tokyo, Labo Teaching Information Center, 1970. 1v.

'O silákovi' *Modré vánoce*. Přel. Ivan Krouský a Z. K. Slabý. Praha, Albatros, 1975.

Shōbō jidōsha Jiputa　しょうぼうじどうしゃジプタ

Jeepta, the little fire engine. Tokyo, Labo Teaching Information Center, 1972. 26p.

WATANABE Suiha　渡辺水巴　1882–1946

Haiku　俳句

'1 haiku' Tr. by Asataro Miyamori. *Anthology of haiku, ancient and modern*. Tokyo, Maruzen, 1932. p.813–814

'4 haiku' Tr. by Geoffrey Bownas and Anthony Thwaite. *The Penguin book of Japanese verse*. Harmondsworth, Penguin Books, 1964. p.168

'14 haiku' *A history of haiku v.2*, by R. H. Blyth. Tokyo, Hokuseido, 1964. p.132–137

WATANABE Takenobu 渡辺武信 1938–

Poems 詩

'Nominare' *La protesta poetica del Giappone*,
a cura di Dacia Maraini e Michiko Nojiri.
Roma, Officina Edizioni, 1968. p.159–160

'Wind; Late night show' Tr. by Harry and Lynn
Guest and Shozo Kajima. *Post-war Japanese
poetry*. Harmondsworth, Penguin Books,
1972. p.158–160

WATARI Mutsuko 度 睦子 1946–

Ichigo batake no chiisana obaasan いちごばたけのちいさなおばあさん

The little old lady in the strawberry patch. London,
Bodley Head, 1974. 1v.

WATSUJI Tetsurō 和辻哲郎 1889–1960

Fūdo 風土

A climate. Tr. by Geoffrey Bownas. Tokyo, Japanese Government Printing Bureau, 1961.
235p.

Climate and culture. Tr. by Geoffrey Bownas.
Tokyo, Hokuseido, 1971. 246p.

Criticism 評論

'Japanese ethical thought in the Noh plays of the
Muromachi period' Tr. by David A. Dilworth. *Monumenta Nipponica*, v.24, no.4, 1969.
p.467–498

Y

YADA Sōun 矢田挿雲 1882–1961

Momijiyama daimyō gyōretsu 紅葉山大名行列

'The daimyo procession to Momijiyama' *Selections from modern Japanese prose*, by A. L.
Sadler. Sydney, Australian Medical Publications, 1943. p.59–63

Essay エッセイ

'Emperor Meiji and the Otsu Incident' *Japan
Times*, Feb.17, 1929.

YADA Tsuseko 矢田津世子 1907–1944

Tekona 手古奈

'Tekona' *Nippon*, v.10, 1937. p.34–36

YAGI Jūkichi 八木重吉 1898–1927

Poems 詩

'Native town; An artless harp; Heaven; River of
my home; I sit on the grass' *An anthology of
modern Japanese poetry*, ed. and tr. by Ichiro
Kono and Rikutaro Fukuda. Tokyo, Kenkyusha, 1957. p.150–151

'Ball und Blechkreisel' Übertragen von Shin Aizu.
Der schwermütige Ladekran. St. Gallen,
Tschudy Verlag, 1960. p.23

'Aus den Gedichten eines Armen' Übers. von
Kuniyo Takayasu und Manfred Hausmann.
Ruf der Regenpfeifer. München, Bechtle
Verlag, 1961. p.91

'Yurdumun deresi; Gökler' Tercüme etmek L.
Sami Akalin. *Japon şiiri*. İstanbul, Varlik
Yayinevi, 1962. p.262–263

'I first saw my face in a dream' Tr. by Geoffrey
Bownas and Anthony Thwaite. *The Penguin
book of Japanese verse*. Harmondsworth,
Penguin Books, 1964. p.202

'The sound of the rain' Tr. by Ritsuko Matsumura and Marie Philomene. *Poetry Nippon*,
no.16, 1971. p.13

'The essence of things; Mother' Tr. by Ritsuko
Matsumura and Marie Philomene. *Poetry
Nippon*, no.18, 1972. p.17

'Foreword; The sea of grief; Come into bloom;
The gardener' Tr. by Misao Sato and Tomoko
Suzuki. *Poetry Nippon*, no.28, 1974. p.13–14

'The word' Tr. by Ritsuko Sakamoto and Tomoko Suzuki. *Poetry Nippon*, no.28, 1974.
p.14–15

'Sadness; An artless lyre; My song' Tr. by Hiroko
Kikuta and Mariko Yasukawa. *Poetry Nippon*,
no.28, 1974. p.15

'8 poems' Tr. by Satoko Tasaka. *Japan Christian
Quarterly*, v.41, no.4, 1975. p.215–221

'Foreword; The sea of grief; Seed on the grass;
My heart; Come into bloom!; The gardener;
Red dragonfly; A desire; A lonely garden;
The phoenix; O little field; My wife; Ahchan!; The thing we call a slope; Prayer; The
day when autumn comes; The essence of
things; The sound of the rain; Mother; Light;
An artless lyre; Sadness; Rain; River by
my village home; Morning glories; May it
be possibly true; Since life is so fleeting;
Once, the day I pined for the sea; Even only
for a while; A literary fragment; Wheat;
My song' Tr. by Ritsuko Sakamoto and
others. *Japanese songs of innocence and experience*. Tokyo, Hokuseido, 1975. p.95–106

YAGI Mikajo 八木三日女 1924–

Haiku 俳句

'2 haiku' *The burning heart*, tr. and ed. by Kenneth Rexroth and Ikuko Atsumi. N. Y. Seabury Press, 1977. p.84

YAGI Yasutarō 八木保太郎 1903–

Kome 米（シナリオ）

「米」 陳篤忱訳 北京 中国戏剧 1958. 74p.

YAMADA Bimyō　山田美妙　1868–1910

Poems　詩

'1 poème'　Tr. par Roger Bersihand. *La littérature japonaise*. Paris, Presses Universitaires de France, 1956. p.109
'1 poem'　Tr. from the French by Unity Evans. *Japanese literature*. N. Y. Walker, 1965. p.92–93

YAMADA Haseki　山田葩夕　1887–1957

Tanka　短歌

'A lark'　Tr. by Asataro Miyamori. *Masterpieces of Japanese poetry, ancient and modern*. Tokyo, Maruzen, 1936; Tokyo, Taiseido, 1956; N. Y. Greenwood Press, 1971. p.747–748

YAMADA Imaji　山田今次　1912–

Poems　詩

'Дождь'　Перевод Е. Винокурова. *Иностранная Литература*, июнь 1964. p.155–156
'Мы слышим тебя, Алжир!'　Перевод Анатолия Мамонова. *Вкус хризантемы*. Москва, Восточная Литература, 1976. p.173

YAMADA Katsurō　山田克郎　1910–

Yūreisen　幽霊船

'幽霊船' 黄錦堂訳 「荒絹」 台北　大明王氏出版公司 1972. p.199–230

YAMADA Kazuko　山田数子

Poems　詩

'To the lost ones'　Tr. by Miyao Ohara. *The songs of Hiroshima*. Tokyo, Taihei Shuppansha, 1971. p.86–89

YAMADA Kurō　山田九朗　1902–

Criticism　評論

'法國小説發達史略' 汪馥泉訳 「文藝月刊」 3巻10期

YAMADA Michitaka　山田みちたか　1921–

Poems　詩

'Утренный пейзаж'　Перевод Анатолия Мамонова. *Иностранная Литература*, август 1959. p.169–170; *Песни Хиросимы*. Москва, Худож. Лит. 1964. p.26–28
'Morning anatomy'　Tr. by Miyao Ohara. *The songs of Hiroshima*. Tokyo, Taihei Shuppansha, 1971. p.54–55

YAMADA Seizaburō　山田清三郎　1896–

Tōhō no niji　東方の虹

「天总会亮的」 李统汉訳　上海　新文艺 1958. 212p.

Criticism　評論

'通信員運動與報告文學'　里正訳　「文學月報」　創刊号 1932.

'草叢中' 張資平訳 「日本小説集」 上海　楽羣書局 1928.
'難堪的苦悶' 張資平訳 「資平譯品集」 上海　現代書局 192?.
'別一種被壓迫者' 張資平訳 「資平譯品集」 上海　現代書局 192?.

YAMADA Utako　山田うた子

Ikiru　生きる

「活下去」 文潔若訳　北京　作家出版社 1956. 180p.
'Жить'　Перевод В. В. Логуновой. *Японские повести*. Москва, Молодая Гвардия, 1957. p.325–456
「活下去」 周大勇訳　上海　新文艺 1957. 156p.
'Хаёт!'　Торжимаси Ж. Насриддинова. Тошкент, Бадии Адабиет, 1960. p.309–442
'Elada!'　*Elada!* Tallinn, Eesti Riiklik Kirjastus, 1962. p.5–125
'Трябва да живея'　Прев. от русс. Манол Наков. *Трябва да живея, три японски повести*. София, Нар. Култура, 1964.

YAMAGATA Aritomo　山県有朋　1838–1922

Tanka　短歌

'Maple leaves; A patch of flowers'　Tr. by Asataro Miyamori. *Masterpieces of Japanese poetry, ancient and modern*. Tokyo, Maruzen, 1936; Tokyo, Taiseido, 1956; N. Y. Greenwood Press, 1971. p.608–609

YAMAGISHI Gaishi　山岸外史　1904–

Poems　詩

'Фудзи, гневом гори!'　Перевод В. Н. Марковой. *Японская поэзия*. Москва, Гослитиздат, 1954. p.317–318; Изд. 2. 1956. p.435–436
'Жалында, Фудзи, жалында'　Которгон Ж. Алыбаев. *Хиросима кектери*. Фрунзе, Кыргызстан, 1969. p.97

YAMAGISHI Isshō　山岸一章　1923–

Bohimei　墓碑銘

'墓志銘' 刘和民訳 「世界文学」 1964年6月　p.40–65

'紅娃娃' 「當代亜非拉小説選」 香港　中流出版社 1977. p.345–353

YAMAGISHI Mitsunobu 山岸光宣 1879–1943

Criticism 評論

'德國表現主義的戲曲' 裕青訳 「小説月報」 第12巻8号
1921. p.25–30
'表現主義的諸相' 魯迅訳 「朝花旬刊」 第1巻3期 1929;
「魯迅全集 16」 上海 魯迅全集出版社 1938. 作
家書屋 1946. 大連 光華書店 1948. 北京 人民
文学出版社 1973. p.452–463;「魯迅譯文集 10」
北京 人民文学出版社 1958. p.221–230

YAMAGUCHI Ei 山口 暎

Poems 詩

'The setting sun' *An anthology of modern Japanese poetry*, ed. and tr. by Ichiro Kono and Rikutaro Fukuda. Tokyo, Kenkyusha, 1957. p.151
'Batan güneş' Tercüme etmek L. Sami Akalin. *Japon şiiri*. İstanbul, Varlik Yayinevi, 1962. p.303

YAMAGUCHI Hisayo 山口久代

Ai to shi no katami 愛と死のかたみ

「사랑과죽음이남긴것」 林玉仁訳 서울 新太陽社 1962. 292p.

YAMAGUCHI Seishi 山口誓子 1901–

Haiku 俳句

'Four haiku poems' Tr. by Donald Keene. *Modern Japanese literature*, ed. by D. Keene. N. Y. Grove Press, 1956; Tokyo, Tuttle, 1957. p.382
'1 haiku' Übers. von Kuniyo Takayasu und Manfred Hausmann. *Ruf der Regenpfeifer*. München, Bechtle Verlag, 1961. p.104
'5 haiku' *Anthology of modern Japanese poetry*, tr. and comp. by Edith Marcombe Shiffert and Yuki Sawa. Tokyo, Tuttle, 1972. p.171
'14 haiku' *A history of haiku v.2*, by R. H. Blyth. Tokyo, Hokuseido, 1964. p.223–227
'2 haiku' Tr. by Takamasa Sasaki. *Eigo Seinen*, v.120, no.10, 1975. p.33
'20 haiku' *Modern Japanese haiku, an anthology*, comp. and tr. by Makoto Ueda. Tokyo, Univ. of Tokyo Press, 1976. p.159–168
'Gentian' Tr. by Kenneth Yasuda. *A pepper-pod*. Tokyo, Tuttle, 1976. p.97

YAMAGUCHI Seison 山口青邨 1892–

Haiku 俳句

'2 haiku' *A history of haiku v.2*, by R. H. Blyth. Tokyo, Hokuseido, 1964. p.207
'1 haiku' Übers. von Kuniyo Takayasu und Manfred Hausmann. *Ruf der Regenpfeifer*. München, Bechtle Verlag, 1961. p.105
'Spring night' Tr. by Kenneth Yasuda. *A pepper-pod*. Tokyo, Tuttle, 1976. p.101

YAMAGUCHI Yūko 山口勇子 1916–

Saburō no kyō no dekigoto さぶろうのきょうのできごと

'Сабуро' Перевод Г. Ронской. *Лети, журавлик!* Москва, Дет. Лит. 1966. p.61–70; *Встреча*. Москва, Дет. Лит. 1970. p.176–181

Yōko no hata 洋子の旗

'Флажок Иоко' Перевод Г. Ронской. *Лети, журавлик!* Москва, Дет. Лит. 1966. p.71–86

YAMAJI Hakuu 山地白雨

Haiku 俳句

'1 haiku' Tr. by V. H. Viglielmo. *Japanese literature in the Meiji era*. Tokyo, Obunsha, 1955. p.438

YAMAKAWA Masao 山川方夫 1930–1965

Matteiru onna 待っている女

'The waiting woman' Tr. by John Bester. *Japan P.E.N. News*, no.16, Jan. 1966. p.5–9

Omamori お守り

'The talisman' Tr. by Edward G. Seidensticker. *Life*, v.57, no.11, Sept. 11, 1964. p.94, 97
'Il talismano' *Panorama*, marzo 1965. p.105–106

YAMAKAWA Tomiko 山川登美子 1879–1909

Tanka 短歌

'Fever' Tr. by Asataro Miyamori. *Masterpieces of Japanese poetry, ancient and modern*. Tokyo, Maruzen, 1936; Tokyo, Taiseido, 1956; N. Y. Greenwood Press, 1971. p.686–687
'3 tanka' Tr. by V. H. Viglielmo. *Japanese literature in the Meiji era*. Tokyo, Obunsha, 1955. p.385
'2 tanka' *The burning heart*, tr. and ed. by Kenneth Rexroth and Ikuko Atsumi. N. Y. Seabury Press, 1977. p.67

YAMAMOTO Fujie 山本藤枝 1910–

Hakuchō no mizuumi はくちょうのみずうみ

Swan lake. Retold by Laurence Collinson. London, Hamlyn, 1969. 1v.

YAMAMOTO Hiroshi 山本 洋 1932–

Joshi kōkōsei 女子高校生

「女子高校生」 元鐘睦訳 서울 欧文社 1963. 231p.

YAMAMOTO Kazuo 山本和夫 1907–

Poems 詩

'A red queen trout' *An anthology of modern Japanese poetry*, ed. and tr. by Ichiro Kono and Rikutaro Fukuda. Tokyo, Kenkyusha, 1957. p.152

'Alabalık kıraliçesi' Tercüme etmek L. Sami Akalin. *Japon şiiri*. İstanbul, Varlık Yayinevi, 1962. p.290

YAMAMOTO Kenkichi 山本健吉 1907–

Criticism 評論

'Characteristics of the literature of the Showa period' Tr. by George Saito. *Japan P.E.N. News*, no.5, July 1960. p.1–5

'詩劇の条件' 金龍済訳 「日本詩集」 서울 靑雲社 1960. p.217–228

'Кунио Янагида, жизнь и творчество' Перевод В. Т. Федяинова. *Иностранная Литература*, ноябрь 1976. p.192–199

YAMAMOTO Minoru 山本みのる

Poems 詩

'Ребенок, продающий орехи' Перевод Анатолия Мамонова. *Вкус хризантемы*. Москва, Восточная Литература, 1976. p.175

YAMAMOTO Shūgorō 山本周五郎 1903–1967

Ashi no naka no ichiya 芦の中の一夜

'Ночь в камышах' Перевод Б. Раскина. *Иностранная Литература*, январь 1977. p.73–81

Hana mushiro 花筵

The flower mat. Tr. by Mihoko Inoue and Eileen B. Hennessy. Tokyo, Tuttle, 1977. 172p.

Jizō 地蔵

'Jizo' Tr. by John Bester. *Japan Quarterly*, v.3, no.3, 1961. p.302–355

Machi e yuku densha 街へゆく電車

'Бежит по нашей улице трамвай' Перевод Б. Раскина. *Иностранная Литература*, январь 1977. p.81–88

Mugiwara bōshi 麦藁帽子

'Il cappello di paglia di frumento' Tr. di Giuseppe Morichini. *Il Giappone*, anno 3, no.1–2, 1959. p.41–49

Pūru no aru ie プールのある家

'Дом с бассейном' Перевод Б. Раскина. *Иностранная Литература*, январь 1977. p.88–101

Yojō よじょう

'Yu Rang' Tr. by Minoru Kohda. *The Reeds*, v. 12, 1968. p.27–64

'He who laughs last' Tr. by James Kirkup and Michio Nakano. *Japan Quarterly*, v.23, no.2, 1976. p.165–181

YAMAMOTO Sukeyoshi 山本祐義 1939–

Māchan konnichiwa まあちゃんこんにちは

「하이린이美国」 梁浩増訳 서울 誠和文化社 1963. 256p.

YAMAMOTO Tarō 山本太郎 1925–

Poems 詩

'讃美歌;풋페의노래' 辛東門訳 「世界戦後文学全集 9」 서울 新丘文化社 1962. p.258–259

'Canto delle bambole' *La protesta poetica del Giappone*, a cura di Dacia Maraini e Michiko Nojiri. Roma, Officina Edizioni, 1968. p.99–100

'From journey; In a surgery room' *Anthology of modern Japanese poetry*, tr. and comp. by Edith Marcombe Shiffert and Yuki Sawa. Tokyo, Tuttle, 1972. p.127–128

'Hymn no.1; Hymn no.2' Tr. by Thomas Fitzsimmons. *Japanese poetry now*. London, André Deutsch, 1972. p.126–130; *Japanese poetry today*. N. Y. Schocken Books, 1972. p.128–132

'Lighthouses; Walking song' Tr. by Harry and Lynn Guest and Shozo Kajima. *Post-war Japanese poetry*. Harmondsworth, Penguin Books, 1972. p.101–102

'Hirohito, an elegy; A contract in sunlight; The law; Since I nurture lies; Possession' Tr. by Shigenori Nagatomo and Hajime Kijima. *The poetry of postwar Japan*. Iowa City, Univ. of Iowa Press, 1975. p.102–106

'В хирургическом кабинете' Перевод Анатолия Мамонова. *Вкус хризантемы*. Москва, Восточная Литература, 1976. p.176

YAMAMOTO Yūzō 山本有三 1887–1974

Buji no hito 無事の人

'無事의人' 金潤成訳 「日本代表作家百人集 2」 서울 希望出版社 1966. p.172–227; 「日本短篇文学全集 2」 서울 新太陽社 1969. p.236–291

Dōshi no hitobito 同志の人々

'同志' 章克標訳 「日本戲曲集」 台北 中華書局 1934. p.1–43

'Doshi no hitobito' Tr. by Yoshitaro Negishi. *Philippine's Japan*, no.8, 1939.

Eiji goroshi 嬰児殺し

'A case of child murder' Tr. by Eric S. Bell and Eiji Ukai. *Eminent authors of contemporary Japan v.1*. Tokyo, Kaitakusha, 1930. p.43–76

Infanmurdo. Tr. J. Ŝimomura. Tokyo, Esperanto Kenkyusha, 1930. 47p.

'嬰兒殺戮' 田漢訳 「日本現代劇三種」 上海 東南書局 193?.

YAMAMOTO Yūzō

'Die Kindsmörderin' Übers. von Hisashi Kojima. *Kesa und Morito, Die Kindsmorderin.* Tokyo, Japanisch-Deutsche Gesellschaft, 1959. p.23–51
'嬰兒殺戮'「世界著名作家戲劇選 1」邵穆編選　香港　上海書局　1960. p.625–656
Die Kindsmorderin. Übers. von Hisashi Kojima. Tokyo, Japanisch-Deutsche Gesellschaft, 1960. 35p.

Fushaku shinmyō　不惜身命

'Не щади живота' *Восточное Обозрение*, 1942.

Honzon　本尊

'Buddha' Übers. von Hermann Bohner. *Festgabe K. Florenz.* Osaka, 1935. p.31–42

Jochū no byōki　女中の病気

'The maid's illness' Tr. by Toranosuke Yoshioka. *Toyoda Hakushi Kanreki Kinen Ronshu 1.* Tokyo, 1951.

Kiri no naka　霧の中

En la nabulo. Tr. K. Cujuki. Tokyo, Japana Esperanto Instituto, 1931. 26p.

Koyaku　子役

'Child actor' *Contemporary Japan*, v.7, no.2, Sept. 1938. p.303–313

Kyōdai　兄弟

'Brothers' *Contemporary Japan*, v.6, no.2, Sept. 1937. p.289–292

Nami　波

Wellen. Übers. von Waitsi Sakurai. Stuttgart, J. G. Gotthasche Buchhandlung Nachfolger, 1938. 281p.
Vlny. Praha, 1941. 246p.
'波濤' 金龍済訳 「日本文学選集 1」서울 青雲社 1964. p.5–197; 서울 知文閣 1966. p.5–197; 서울 韓国読書文化院 1973. p.5–200

Nyonin aishi　女人哀詞

'The story of Chink Okichi' Tr. by Glenn W. Shaw. *Three plays of Yamamoto Yuzo.* Tokyo, Hokuseido, 1935; N. Y. Stechert, 1935; London, Allen and Unwin, 1935; Tokyo, Hokuseido, 1957; South Pasadena, Perkins and Hutchins, 1957. p.83–248

Onna no isshō　女の一生

Жизнь женщины. Перевод Н. Гребова и А. Успенской. Ленинград, Гослитиздат, 1936. 404p.; Москва, Худож. Лит. 1956. 376p.; Владивосток, 1958. 376p.

Sakazaki Dewanokami　坂崎出羽守

'Lord Dewa' Tr. by Glenn W. Shaw. *Three plays of Yamamoto Yuzo.* Tokyo, Hokuseido, 1935; N. Y. Stechert, 1935; London, Allen and Unwin, 1935; Tokyo, Hokuseido, 1957; South Pasadena, Perkins and Hutchins, 1957. p.1–82

Seimei no kanmuri　生命の冠

'The crown of life' Tr. by Glenn W. Shaw. *Tokyo*

Nichinichi, Nov.5, 1924—Dec.7, 1924; *Three plays of Yamamoto Yuzo.* Tokyo, Hokuseido, 1935; N. Y. Stechert, 1935; London, Allen and Unwin, 1935; Tokyo, Hokuseido, 1957; South Pasadena, Perkins and Hutchins, 1957. p.249–358

Shinjitsu ichiro　真実一路

Shinjitsu ichiro, der rechte Weg. Übers. von Sinichi Hoshino und John Nertha. Tokyo, Japanisch-Deutsche Gesellschaft, 1960. 330p.

Umihiko Yamahiko　海彦山彦

'Umihiko Yamahiko' Übers. von T. Uchiyama und Alexander Spann. *Das Junge Japan*, Bd.1, 1924.
'海彦山彦' 侍桁訳 「語絲」第4巻48期 1928. p.433–452
'Umihiko and Yamahiko' Tr. by Takashi Kojima. *Eigo Kenkyu*, v.40, no.7, 1951. p.28–31. no.8, 1951. p.42–45. no.9, 1951. p.47–50. no.10, 1951. p.40–42
'Umihiko kaj Yamahiko' Tr. Kikunobu Matuba. *El japana literaturo.* Tokyo, Japana Esperanto Instituto, 1965. p.231–241
'Umihiko and Yamahiko' Tr. by Atsumu Kanayama. *The Reeds*, v.11, 1967. p.59–74

'Der Ausflug an den See Kitaura' Übers. von Waitsi Sakurai. *Japan, Tradition und Gegenwart.* Stuttgart, Deutsche Volksbücher, 1942. p.138–155
'The hidden pioneer' Tr. by U. Uenoda. *Japan Times and Advertiser*, 1942.

YAMAMURA Bochō　山村暮鳥　1884–1924

Poems　詩

'In the blue sky; Headland; A prayer; A spring river; One morning; A name card; Mandala' *An anthoogy of modern Japanese poetry*, ed. and tr. by Ichiro Kono and Rikutaro Fukuda. Tokyo, Kenkyusha, 1957. p.153–155
'Solo; The curve; In the blue sky; An old pond' *The poetry of living Japan*, by Takamichi Ninomiya and D. J. Enright. London, John Murray, 1957. p.45–47
'Im blauen Himmel; Die Kluft; Landschaft: Mosaik reinen Silbers; Das Gedicht über den schwermütigen Ladekran' Übertragen von Shin Aizu. *Der schwermütige Ladekran.* St. Gallen, Tschudy Verlag, 1960. p.7, 12–13, 15, 34–35
'Kartvizit; Dua; Bir sabah; Mavi gökte' Tercüme etmek L. Sami Akalin. *Japon şiiri.* İstanbul, Varlik Yayinevi, 1962. p.240–241
'A song of a fisherman' Tr. by Hisakazu Kaneko. *The Japanese image*, ed. by M. Schneps and A. D. Coox. Tokyo, Orient West, 1965. p.352–353
'Una plegaria; Mandala' Tr. por Kikuya Ionesawa. *Poesia japonesa contemporanea.* Bogotá, Colombia Editoriales de Libreaía, 1965. n.p.
'Fruit; Nightfall' Tr. by Graeme Wilson. *Japan Quarterly*, v.13, no.3, 1966. p.300, 318
'Cat; Lullaby' Tr. by Graeme Wilson. *Japan Quarterly*, v.13, no.4, 1966. p.432, 520
'春河；馬；晨', 徐和隣訳 「現代詩解説」台北　葡萄園詩刊社　1970. p.3–4

'Cat, and other poems' Tr. by Graeme Wilson. *Solidarity*, August 1971. p.56–57
'바람의 방향의 바뀌었다 ; 故郷 ; 어떤때 ; 万物節' 金巣雲 訳 「世界의文学大全集 34」 서울 同和出版公社 1971. p.503–505
'Curves; Fruit; Keeping the commandments; Miracle; Light; On account of sadness; All things day; Mandala; Seed twitter; Sleighs; Impressions on the road; Cornseeds; Clouds; Cat; Nightfall; Love; Once upon a time; Dance; Tautologies; Farmers; Spring; Lullaby; Prayer; On suffering; Landscape; Ecstasy' Tr. by Graeme Wilson and Ikuko Atsumi. *Japan Quarterly*, v.19, no.4, 1972. p.462–466

YAMAMURA Jun 山村 順 1898–

Poems 詩

'Night flight; Dead friend; Confession' *An anthology of modern Japanese poetry*, ed. and tr. by Ichiro Kono and Rikutaro Fukuda. Tokyo, Kenkyusha, 1957. p.155–157
'Gay summertime; The story of a dream' *The poetry of living Japan*, by Takamichi Ninomiya and D. J. Enright. London, John Murray, 1957. p.75–76
'Sommerfrische' Übertragen von Shin Aizu. *Der schwermütige Ladekran*. St. Gallen, Tschudy Verlag, 1960. p.32
'Ölmüş arkadaşlarl; Gece uçuşu' Tercüme etmek L. Sami Akalin. *Japon şiiri*. İstanbul, Varlik Yayinevi, 1962. p.264–265

YAMAMURO Shizuka 山室 静 1906–

Criticism 評論

'Scandinavian literature in Japan' *Japan Quarterly*, v.8, no.1, 1961. p.87–93

YAMANAKA Hisashi 山中 恒 1931–

Pinkiri monogatari ピンキリ物語

'Napůl jakiči a napůl Jaikipte' *Modré vánoce*. Přel. Ivan Krouský a Z. K. Slabý. Praha, Albatros, 1975.

YAMANAKA Minetarō 山中峯太郎 1885–1966

Nogi taishō 乃木大將

「乃木大將傳」 賴耿澤訳 台北 1970. 235p.

YAMANAKA Ryōjirō 山中良次郎 1920–

Poems 詩

'Wind' Tr. by Harry and Lynn Guest and Shozo

Kajima. *Post-war Japanese poetry*. Harmondsworth, Penguin Books, 1972. p.80

YAMANOGUCHI Baku 山之口 獏 1903–1963

Poems 詩

'Marriage; Tatami floor' Tr. by S. Sato and C. Urdang. *Poetry*, May 1956. p.67–68
'The marriage; Scenery in morning; A pattern of life; A letter to my sister; Boston bag' *An anthology of modern Japanese poetry*, ed. and tr. by Ichiro Kono and Rikutaro Fukuda. Tokyo, Kenkyusha, 1957. p.157–160
'Marriage' Tr. par Karl Petit. *La poésie japonaise*. Paris, Seghers, 1959. p.233
'Kizkardeşime mektup; Evlilik' Tercüme etmek L. Sami Akalin. *Japon şiiri*. İstanbul, Varlik Yayinevi, 1962. p.273–275
'処女詩集 ; 無銭取食 ; 玄関 ; 전등 ; 숯 ; 마구로에정어리 ; 世上은갖가지' 辛東門訳 「世界戦後文学全集 9」 서울 新丘文化社 1962. p.226–228
'鼻子的結論 ; 他他米' 徐和隣訳 「現代詩解説」 台北 葡萄園詩刊社 1970. p.76–79
'喪이있는景致' 「現代詩学」 第4巻3号 1972.
'Cununie' Traducerea Dan Constantinescu. *Din lirica japoneză*. Bucureşti, Editura Univers, n.d. p.199

YAMAOKA Sōhachi 山岡荘八 1907–1978

Date Masamune 伊達政宗

「謀計」 安東民訳 서울 語苑閣 1974. 4冊

Haru no sakamichi 春の坂道

「大望 21–25」 朴在姫訳 서울 中央文化社 1973–75. 5冊

Oda Nobunaga 織田信長

「대명청이」 宋蘭庚訳 서울 正友文化社 1971. 3冊

Taiheiyō sensō 太平洋戦争

「太平洋戦争」 朴在姫訳 서울 東西文化社 1973. 8冊

Tokugawa Ieyasu 徳川家康

「大望 1–20」 朴在姫訳 서울 東西文化社 1969–70. 20冊 ; 서울 中央文化社 1973–75. 20冊
「徳川家康」 金家平訳 서울 希文社 1971. 14冊
「大野望」 柳一根訳 서울 書正出版社 1973. 20冊

YAMASHIRO Tomoe 山代 巴 1912–

Niguruma no uta 荷車の歌

'板車之歌' (選訳) 錢稲孫訳 「世界文学」 1959年1月 p.95–124
「板車之歌」 錢稲孫 叔昌訳 北京 作家出版社 1961. 120p.; 北京 人民文学出版社 1962. 1冊
Песня тележки. Перевод Т. Виноградовой. Москва, Изд. Иност. Лит. 1963. 176p.
Арабача садоси. Прев. Ю. Шамшарова. Тошкент, Гос. Тошкент. Изд. 1965. 168p.
Patinu dziesina. Tr. Edgars Katajs. Riga, Liesma, 1966. 244p.

YAMATE Kiichirō 山手樹一郎 1899–1978

Seimei no hi 生命の灯

'生命之燈' 徐白訳 「日本短篇譯集 2」 台北 晩蟬書店 1969. p.131–168

YAMAZAKI Eiji 山崎栄治 1905–

Poems 詩

'Two worlds; Nights; The sod!; Dark blaze' Tr. by Harry and Lynn Guest and Shozo Kajima. *Post-war Japanese poetry*. Harmondsworth, Penguin Books, 1972. p.33–37

YAMAZAKI Masakazu 山崎正和 1934–

Fune wa hobune yo 舟は帆船よ

'The boat is a sailboat' Tr. by Ted T. Takaya. *Anthology of modern Japanese drama*. N. Y. Columbia Univ. Press, forthcoming.

Zeami 世阿弥

'Licht und Schatten' Übers. von Jürgen Berndt. *Japanische Dramen*. Berlin, Volk und Welt, 1968. p.62–144

Poems 詩

'Бросай, топор, лесоруб!' Перевод В. Н. Марковой. *Звезда*, 1952, No.5. p.101–102; *Японская поэзия*. Москва, Гослитиздат, 1954. p.327–329

'Слушайте, десять тысяч студентов Киото' Перевод М. Павловой. *Смена*, 1953, No.21.p.8

Essay エッセイ

'The search for a mirror' *The East*, v.2, no.6, 1966. p.47–49

YAMAZAKI Tomoko 山崎朋子 1932–

Sandakan hachiban shōkan サンダカン八番娼館

'山打根八号妓館' 戴陽訳 「東西風」 第11期 1973. p.26–29; 第12期 1973. p.50–58

YAMAZAKI Toyoko 山崎豊子 1924–

Shibō kiji 死亡記事

'死亡記事' 張壽哲訳 「日本代表作家百人集 5」 서울 希望出版社 1966. p.116–132; 「日本短篇文学全集 6」 서울 新太陽社 1969. p.28–44

YANAGAWA Shun'yō 柳川春葉 1877–1918

Chikai 誓

The vow. Tr. by T. Kihara. Boston, Bruce Humphries, 1934. 536p.

YANAGIHARA Byakuren 柳原白蓮 1885–1967

Tanka 短歌

'White lotus' *Three women poets of modern Japan*, by Glenn Hughes and Yozan Iwasaki. Seattle, Univ. of Washington Book Store, 1932. p.23–34

'Where are the Gods?; When I was lost in thought; Flowers; My soul; My verses; A ship' Tr. by Asataro Miyamori. *Masterpieces of Japanese poetry, ancient and modern*. Tokyo, Maruzen, 1936; Tokyo, Taiseido, 1956; N. Y. Greenwood Press, 1971. p.722–725

'5 tanka' Tr. by Shigeshi Nishimura. *The Current of the World*, v.15, no.5, 1938. p.101

YANAGISAWA Kazuko 柳沢かず子 1921–

Poems 詩

'Paysage d'une montre' *The lyric garland*, ed. by Makoto Sangu. Tokyo, Hokuseido, 1957. p.59

YANAGISAWA Ken 柳沢 健 1889–1953

Poems 詩

'兒童的世界' 周作人訳 「詩」 創刊号 1931.

'Trois poèmes de Ken Yanagisawa' Tr. par Nico D. Horiguchi. *Nippon*, no.8, 1936. p.30–31

'Sur la neige; Perte; L'amour perdu; Sourire; Avenir' Tr. par Kuni Matsuo et Steinilber-Oberlin. *Anthologie des poètes japonais contemporains*. Paris, Mercure de France, 1939. p.169–172

'Juillet; Le navire hollandais; Après l'adieu' Tr. par Kazouko Yanagisawa et Nico D. Horiguchi. *The lyric garland*. Tokyo, Hokuseido, 1957. p.60–62

YANAGITA Kunio 柳田国男 1875–1962

Meiji bunkashi fūzoku hen 明治文化史風俗編

Japanese manners and customs in the Meiji era, comp. and ed. by Kunio Yanagida. Tr. and adapted by Charles S. Terry. Tokyo, Obunsha, 1957. 335p.

Nihon no mukashi banashi 日本の昔話

'Japanese folk tales' Tr. by Fanny Hagin Mayer. *Folklore Studies*, v.11, no.1, 1952. p.1–97

Japanese folk tales. Tr. by Fanny Hagin Mayer and Ishiwara Yasuyo. Tokyo, Tokyo News Service, 1958. 299p.; 1966. 190p.; Tokyo, Japan Society for the Promotion of Science, 1970. 193p.

Japanaj malnovaj rakontoj. Nagoya, Amo-Akademio, 1965. 127p.

Tōno monogatari 遠野物語

'Folklores and tradition of Tono districts' Tr. by Shizuo Toda. *Tohoku Gakuin Daigaku Ronshu, Eigo Eibungaku*, July 1962. p.117–136

The legends of Tono. Tr. by Ronald A. Morse.

Tokyo, Japan Foundation, 1975. 90p.

Sosen no hanashi 祖先の話

About our ancestors. Tr. by Fanny Hagin Mayer and Ishiwara Yasuyo. Tokyo, Japan Society for the Promotion of Science, 1970. 193p.

Poems 詩

'Changed homeland; Parting from love; Aru ori ni' Tr. by James R. Morita. *Journal of the Association of Teachers of Japanese*, v.10, no.2 & 3, 1975. p.196–197

Essay エッセイ

'The Japanese Atlantis' *Contemporary Japan*, v.3, no.1, June 1934. p.34–39

YANATORI Sangi 梁取三義 1912–

Furin no sasoi 不倫の誘い

「흐르는性」 林秋石訳 서울 永和出版社 1961. 367p.

YANO Hōjin 矢野峰人 1893–

Poems 詩

'Autumn wind' Tr. by Shigeshi Nishimura. *The Current of the World*, v.31, no.7, 1954. p.41

YASHIRO Seiichi 矢代静一 1927–

Hokusai manga 北齋漫畫

'Hokusai sketchbooks' Tr. by Ted T. Takaya. *Anthology of modern Japanese drama*. N. Y. Columbia Univ. Press, forthcoming.

YASHIRO Tōson 矢代東村 1889–1952

Tanka 短歌

'The heat; Fans' Tr. by Asataro Miyamori. *Masterpieces of Japanese poetry, ancient and modern*. Tokyo, Maruzen, 1936; Tokyo, Taiseido, 1956; N. Y. Greenwood Press, 1971. p.764–765

YASUDA Yasuo 安田保雄 1914–

Criticism 評論

'Modern poetry' Tr. by Angelus F. Aschoff. *Poetry Nippon*, no.31 & 32, 1975. p.22–26

YASUMIZU Toshikazu 安水稔和 1931–

Poems 詩

'Bird; The identity of love; Bird' Tr. by Thomas

Fitzsimmons. *Japanese poetry now*. London, André Deutsch, 1972. p.74–75; *Japanese poetry today*. N. Y. Schocken Books, 1972. p.76–77

'The flowers of the rock; Fable of the bird; Say you are lovely; Song' Tr. by Fukuko Kobayashi and Hajime Kijima. *The poetry of postwar Japan*. Iowa City, Univ. of Iowa Press, 1975. p.179–183

YASUMOTO Sueko 安本末子

Nianchan にあんちゃん

「구름은흘러도」 柳周鉉訳 서울 新太陽社 1959. 292p.
「在日韓国少女의手記」 大東文化社訳 서울 大東文化社 1959. 185p.
「二哥」 張迅齊訳 台北 成功出版社 1960. 152p.; 台北 宏業出版社 1968. 116p.; 台北 好時年出版 1977. 201p.
「구름은흘러가도」 李文九訳 서울 呂文社 1974. 216p.

YASUOKA Shōtarō 安岡章太郎 1920–

Aigan 愛玩

'Prized possessions' Tr. by Edwin McClellan. *Contemporary Japanese literature*, ed. by Howard Hibbett. N. Y. Knopf, 1977. p.111–118

Ame 雨

'Regen' Übers. von Margarete Donath. *Japan erzählt*. Hamburg, Fischer, 1969. p.103–111

'Дождь' Перевод М. Певзнера. *Красная лягушка*. Москва, Наука, 1973. p.13–20

Garasu no kutsu ガラスの靴

'The glass slipper' Tr. by Edward Seidensticker. *Japan Quarterly*, v.8, no.2, 1961. p.195–206

'Die Glasschuhe' Aus dem Japanischen von Oscar Benl. *Japan, Geistige Begegnung*. Tübingen, Erdmann, 1964. p.373–391; *Eine Glocke in Fukagawa*. Tübingen, Erdmann, 1969. p.378–396

'유리구두' 金龍済訳 「日本新鋭文学作家受賞作品選集 2」 서울 青雲社 1964. p.101–122; 「戦後日本短篇文学全集 2」 서울 日光出版社 1965. p.101–122; 「現代日本代表文学全集 2」 서울 平和出版社 1973. p.103–121

Inki na tanoshimi 陰気な愉しみ

'우울한즐거움' 金龍済訳 「日本新鋭文学作家受賞作品選集 2」 서울 青雲社 1964. p.124–131; 「戦後日本短篇文学全集 2」 서울 日光出版社 1965. p.124–133; 「現代日本代表文学全集 1」 서울 平和出版社 1973. p.124–130

'陰沉的樂趣' 劉蔡沙訳 「芥川賞作品選集 1」 台北 大地出版社 1972. p.171–183

Sākasu no uma サーカスの馬

'Circus horse' Tr. by Leon Zolbrod. *The East*, v.1, no.6, 1965. p.50–51

Shichiya no nyōbō 質屋の女房

'The pawnbroker's wife' Tr. by Edward Seidensticker. *Japan Quarterly*, v.8, no.2, 1961. p.188–195; *New writing in Japan*. Harmondsworth, Penguin Books, 1972. p.123–132

YASUOKA Shōtarō

'典當舗짐아낙네' 權純萬訳 「日本代表作家百人集 4」서울 希望出版社 1966. p.380–387;「日本短篇文学全集 5」서울 新太陽社 1969. p.220–227
'Zastavárníkova žena' Přel. Vlasta Winkelhöferová. *Světová literatura*, v.19, no.2, 1974. p.170–176

Tonsō 遁走

'遁走' 金龍済訳 「日本新鋭文学作家受賞作品選集 2」서울 青雲社 1964. p.3–100;「戦後日本短篇文学全集 2」서울 日光出版社 1965. p.3–100;「現代日本代表文学全集 2」서울 平和出版社 1973. p.3–100

Umibe no kōkei 海辺の光景

'View of the bay' Tr. by Joyce Ackroyd and Mikio Hiramatsu. *Hemisphere*, v.3, no.6, June 1964. p.17–19

Warui nakama 悪い仲間

'悪의季節' 呉尚源訳 「芥川賞小説集」서울 新丘文化社 1960. p.141–162;「깊은江」서울 三耕社 1971. p.141–163
'나쁜친구들' 金龍済訳 「日本新鋭文学作家受賞作品選集 2」서울 青雲社 1964. p.134–155;「戦後日本短篇文学全集 2」서울 日光出版社 1965. p.134–155;「現代日本代表文学全集 2」서울 平和出版社 1973. p.134–153
'壞伙伴' 劉慕沙訳 「芥川賞作品選集 1」台北 大地出版社 1972. p.139–169
'悪의季節' 朴尚均訳 「日本文学大全集 10」서울 東西文化院 1975. p.361–380

Essay エッセイ

'Fuji by any other name' *This is Japan*, v.11, 1964. p.74–76

'懼内講座' 徐白訳 「日本短篇譯集 3」台北 晩蟬書店 1959. p.147–159
'勲章' 傅寶齡訳 「勲章」台北 文壇社 1960. p.25–39

YATABE Ryōkichi 矢田部良吉 1851–1899

Poems 詩

'Elegy in a country orchard; The last rose of summer' Tr. by Donald Keene. *Modern Japanese poetry*, by D. Keene. Ann Arbor, Center for Japanese Studies, Univ. of Michigan, 1964. p.11
'Die vier Jahreszeiten' Übers. von Otto Hauser. *Lyrik der Welt*. Berlin, Safari Verlag, 1960. p.142–143

YODA Jun'ichi 与田準一 1905–

Essay エッセイ

'小公園' 傅寶齡訳 「勲章」台北 文壇社 1960. p.299–300

YODA Shūho 依田秋圃 1885–1943

Tanka 短歌

'A rural scene; Mount Fuji' Tr. by Asataro Miyamori. *Masterpieces of Japanese poetry, ancient and modern*. Tokyo, Maruzen, 1936; Tokyo, Taiseido, 1956; N. Y. Greenwood Press, 1971. p.729–730
'1 tanka' Übers. von Gerolf Coudenhove. *Japanische Jahreszeiten*. Zürich, Manesse Verlag, 1963. p.158

YOKOI Hanzaburō 横井半三郎

Poems 詩

'Севастополь—место былых сражений' Перевод Анатолия Мамонова. *Вкус хризантемы*. Москва, Восточная Литература, 1976. p.32

YOKOI Kunisaburō 横井国三郎

Poems 詩

'小兒' 周作人訳 「新青年」第9巻4期 1921. p.35

YOKOI Tadanao 横井忠直 1857–1928

Poems 詩

'On to Peking' Tr. by Donald Keene. *Landscapes and portraits*. Tokyo, Kodansha International, 1971. p.273

YOKOI Tokio 横井時雄 1857–1927

「模範町村」上海 商務印書館 1926. 1冊

YOKOJIMA Sakurako 横島さくら子 1943–

Yūjō 友情

「友情」楊復周訳 서울 隆文社 1965. 214p.

YOKOMITSU Riichi 横光利一 1898–1947

Aki 秋

'Der Herbst' Übers. von Oscar Benl. *In Kinosaki*. Wolfenbüttel, Kallmeyer, 1951. p.24–53; *Japan, Geistige Begegnung*. Tübingen, Erdmann, 1964. p.354–372; *Eine Glocke in Fukagawa*. Tübingen, Erdmann, 1969. p.359–377

Aoi ishi o hirotte kara 青い石を拾ってから

'After picking up a blue stone' Tr. by Dennis Keene. *Love, and other stories of Yokomitsu Riichi*, Tokyo, Univ. of Tokyo Press, 1974. p.71–95

Aoi taii 青い大尉

'The pale captain' Tr. by Dennis Keene. *Love, and other stories of Yokomitsu Riichi*. Tokyo, Univ. of Tokyo Press, 1974. p.99–108

Baishunfu 売春婦

'賣春婦' 新興書局編集部訳 「日本短篇小説選」台北 新

興書局 1958. p.74–97; 台南 鳴宇出版社 1972. p.74–97

Basha 馬車

'The carriage' Tr. by Dennis Keene. *Love, and other stories of Yokomitsu Riichi.* Tokyo, Univ. of Tokyo Press, 1974. p.183–225

Bishō 微笑

'微笑' 郭夏信訳 「世界文学全集 94」 서울 乙酉文化社 1962. p.485–514;「日本短篇文学選」 서울 乙酉文化社 1976. p.269–323
'Smile' Tr. by Dennis Keene. *Love, and other stories of Yokomitsu Riichi.* Tokyo, Univ. of Tokyo Press, 1974. p.229–264

Ga wa dokoni demo iru 蛾はどこにでもゐる

'到上有的蛾' 章克標訳 「東方雑誌」 第26巻24期 1929. p.119–124

Hae 蠅

'Hae' Tr. by Ken Chikui. *Shin Ei-Bei Bungaku,* 1932.
'The fly' Tr. by John Nathan. *Japan Quarterly,* v.12, no.1, 1965. p.72–77
'Muso' Tr. Hukutaro Okano. *El japana literaturo.* Tokyo, Japana Esperanto Instituto, 1965. p.242–248
'Hae' Tr. by Tsutomu Fukuda. *The Azaleas,* no.3, 1969.
'Moucha' Přel. V. Winkelhöferová. *Nový Orient,* no.8, 1971.
'蠅' 「文島・夢十夜」 英紹唐編 台北 n.d. p.55–69

Hanamuko no kansō 花婿の感想

'新郎的感想' 郭建英訳 「色情文化」 上海 水沫書店 1929.

Hanazono no shisō 花園の思想

'Ideas of a flower garden' Tr. by Dennis Keene. *Japan Quarterly,* v.20, no.2, 1973. p.193–202; *Love, and other stories of Yokomitsu Riichi.* Tokyo, Univ. of Tokyo Press, 1974. p.133–149

Haru wa basha ni notte 春は馬車に乗って

'春天坐了馬車' 章克標訳 「小説月報」 第21巻3号 1930. p.513–520
'Spring came on a horse-drawn cart' Tr. by Mary M. Suzuki. *The heart is alone,* ed. by Richard McKinnon. Tokyo, Hokuseido, 1957. p.99–114
'La primavera arriva su una corrozza' Tr. di Atsuko Ricca Suga. *Narratori Giapponesi moderni.* Milano, Bompiani, 1965. p.339–354
'Spring in a surrey' Tr. by John Nathan. *Japan Quarterly,* v.12, no.1, 1965. p.65–71; *Time, and others.* Tokyo, Hara Shobo, 1965. p.177–217
'Spring riding in a carriage' Tr. by Dennis Keene. *Love, and other stories of Yokomitsu Riichi.* Tokyo, Univ. of Tokyo Press, 1974. p.117–130

Jikan 時間

'Time' Tr. by Donald Keene. *Modern Japanese literature,* ed. by D. Keene. N. Y. Grove Press, 1956; Tokyo, Tuttle, 1957. p.339–356
'Tiempo' Tr. por Carla Viola Soto. *Sur,* no.249, Nov.-Dec. 1957. p.42–57
'Tempo' Tr. de Fuyou Koyama. *Maravilhas do conto japonês.* São Paulo, Editôra Cultrix, 1962. p.145–162

'Time' Tr. by Tadao Katayama. *The Reeds,* v.10, 1965. p.99–119
'Time' Tr. by Richard Foster. *Time, and others.* Tokyo, Hara Shobo, 1965. p.7–68

Kikai 機械

'Machine' Tr. by Edward Seidensticker. *Modern Japanese stories,* ed. by I. Morris. London, Spottiswoode, 1961; Tokyo, Tuttle, 1962. p.223–244; *Time, and others.* Tokyo, Hara Shobo, 1965. p.105–176; *The world of Japanese fiction.* N. Y. Dutton, 1973. p.211–231
'Mechanik' Deutsch von Monique Humbert. *Nippon.* Zürich, Diogenes, 1965. p.245–274
'機械' 金龍済訳 「日本代表作家百人集 1」 서울 希望出版社 1966. p.408–426; 日本短篇文学全集 2」 서울 新太陽社 1969. p.28–46
'기계' 趙演鉉訳 「世界短篇文学全集 7」 서울 啓蒙社 1966. p.299–320;「世界短篇文学全集 9」 서울 三珍社 1971. p.168–189;「世界代表短篇文学全集 9」 서울 新韓出版社 1976. p.282–316
'A gépezet' Ford. Sz. Holti Mária. *Modern Japán elbeszélók.* Budapest, Európa Könyvkiadó, 1967. p.152–168
'Mechanismus' Přel. Jaroslav Pribramsky. *5 japonských novel.* Praha, Odeon, 1969. p.209–228
'The machine' Tr. by Dennis Keene. *Love, and other stories of Yokomitsu Riichi.* Tokyo, Univ. of Tokyo Press, 1974. p.153–180
'Mechanismen' Deutsch von Jürgen Berndt. *Träume aus zehn Nächten.* Berlin, Aufbau Verlag, 1975. p.244–272

Machi no soko 街の底

'The depth of the town' Tr. by Dennis Keene. *Love, and other stories of Yokomitsu Riichi.* Tokyo, Univ. of Tokyo Press, 1974. p.111–114

Maketa otto 負けた良人

'The defeated husband' Tr. by Dennis Keene. *Love, and other stories of Yokomitsu Riichi.* Tokyo, Univ. of Tokyo Press, 1974. p.31–68

Me ni mieta shirami 眼に見えた虱

'現眼的虱子' 高汝鴻訳 「日本短篇小説集」 台北 台湾商務印書館 1969. p.273–312

Nanakai no undō 七階の運動

'七樓的運動' 吶吶鷗訳 「色情文化」 上海 水沫書店 1929.

Naporeon to tamushi ナポレオンと田虫

'拿破崙與輪癬' 黄源訳 「文學」 第1巻1号 1933. p.679–690
'拿破崙與疥癬' 高汝鴻訳 「日本短篇小説集」 台北 台湾商務印書館 1969. p.313–331

Nichirin 日輪

'L'astro solare' Tr. di Maria Teresa Orsi. *Il Giappone,* anno 12, 1972. p.45–84

Onmi 御身

'Love' Tr. by Dennis Keene. *Love, and other stories of Yokomitsu Riichi.* Tokyo, Univ. of Tokyo Press, 1974. p.1–19

Seishun 青春

'Young forever' Tr. by Habuku Kodama. *Young*

forever, and five other novelettes, ed. by Japan Writers' Society. Tokyo, Hokuseido, 1941. p.1–19

Shanhai 上海

'Shanghai' Tr. di R. Vulpitta. *Antologia della letteratura coreana e giapponese.* Milano, Fratelli Fabbri, 1969. p.309–314

Shimaranu kāten 閉らぬカーテン

'The curtain would not draw' Tr. by Kazuo Yamada. *Shin Ei-Bei Bungaku,* 1933; *The roof-garden, and other one-act plays.* Tokyo, Shijo Shobo, 1934. p.71–94

Shin'en 寝園

「寝園」 沈載彦訳 서울 青山書林 1961. 206p.
「寝園」 周弦訳 台北 十月出版社 1969. 152p.

Shizuka naru raretsu 静かなる羅列

'Silent ranks' Tr. by John Bester. *Japan P.E.N. News,* no.12, Feb. 1964. p.1–6; *Time, and others.* Tokyo, Hara Shobo, 1965. p.69–104

Warawareta ko 笑われた子

'The child who was laughed at' Tr. by Dennis Keene. *Love, and other stories of Yokomitsu Riichi.* Tokyo, Univ. of Tokyo Press, 1974. p.21–27

YOKOMIZO Seishi 横溝正史 1902–

Chōchō satsujin jiken 蝶蝶殺人事件

「歌劇女王」 君素訳 香港 環球圖書雜誌出版社 1952. 142p.

YOKOSE Yau 横瀬夜雨 1878–1934

Poems 詩

'O-Sai, a girl's lament' Tr. by Shigeshi Nishimura. *The Current of the World,* v.31, no.5, 1954. p.31

YOKOYAMA Hakukō 横山白虹 1899–

Haiku 俳句

'1 haiku' *A history of haiku v.2,* by R. H. Blyth. Tokyo, Hokuseido, 1964. p.243

YONEDA Eisaku 米田栄作 1910–

Poems 詩

'Песок шестого августа; Будь прекрасной, река, навеки!; В руинах' Перевод Анатолия Мамонова. *Иностранная Литература,* август 1959. p.166–168
'Алтыншы августтагы кум; Сулуу бор, дпира, ар дайым!' Которгон Т. Байваков. *Хиросима кектери.* Фрунзе, Кыргзстан, 1969.

p.89–92
'Standing in the ruins; The family; The sand on August sixth; Be beautiful, river, forever!; To India's Prime Minister J. Nehru' Tr. by Miyao Ohara. *The songs of Hiroshima.* Tokyo, Taihei Shuppansha, 1971. p.18–30
'Песок шестого августа; Новые Офелии; Будь прекрасной, река, навеки!; Тебе; Отсвет на булыжниках мостовой; Ребенку, покинувшему меня навеки; Стихи на памятнике жертвам атомной бомбы' Перевод Анатолия Мамонова. *Вкус хризантемы.* Москва, Восточная Литература, 1976. p.33–37

YONEDA Yūrō 米田雄郎 1891–1959

Tanka 短歌

'Truthfulness; The little child' Tr. by Asataro Miyamori. *Masterpieces of Japanese poetry, ancient and modern.* Tokyo, Maruzen, 1936; Tokyo, Taiseido, 1956; N. Y. Greenwood Press, 1971. p.787–788

YOSANO Akiko 与謝野晶子 1878–1942

Midare gami みだれ髪

Tangled hair. Tr. by Shio Sakanishi. Boston, Marshall Jones, 1935. 87p.
Tangled hair. Tr. by Sanford Goldstein and Seishi Shinoda. Lafayette, Purdue Univ. Press, 1971. 165p.

Poems and Tanka 詩・短歌

'8 tanka' Tr. by Minoru Toyoda. *Toa no Hikari.* 1918.
'Onde del mare azzurro' Tr. di Harukichi Shimoi e Elpidio Jenco. *Sakura,* no.1, 1920. p.4–6
'野草' 周作人訳 「新青年」 第9巻4期 1921. p.32; 「陀螺」 上海 北新書局 1927.
'Thirty poems by Akiko Yosano' Tr. by Glenn Hughes and Y. T. Iwasaki. *New Orient,* v.3, no.3, 1927. p.19–22
'Poems by Akiko Yosano' Tr. by Glenn Hughes and Yozan T. Iwasaki. *Three women poets of modern Japan.* Seattle, Univ. of Washington Book Store, 1932. p.13–22
'1 poem' Tr. by Shigeshi Nishimura. *Eigo Seinen,* v.72, no.10, 1935. p.343
'L'oiseau blanc; Tristesse; A celui qui s'en va; Marches; Le rossignol endormi; Bain d'automne; Papillons mauves; La barque abandonnée; Déception; Lumière; L'exilée; Les nuages; Soupirs de lune; Mon coeur; Fleurs d'étoiles' Tr. par Georges Bonneau. *Lyrisme du temps présent.* Paris, Paul Geuthner, 1935. p.34–45; *Anthologie de la poésie japonaise.* Paris, Geuthner, 1935. p.128–135
'The flowery field; A meteor; The stable; A maiden-hair tree; White lotus-flowers; A rose; The cherry flowers; A little bird; An eye; Love; Spring; The sky of early autumn; The rising sun; A crimson butterfly; The Hanabishiso; A pagoda' Tr. by Asataro Miyamori. *Masterpieces of Japanese poetry, ancient and modern.* Tokyo, Maruzen, 1936; Tokyo, Taiseido, 1956; N. Y. Greenwood Press, 1971. p.677–686

'2 tanka' Tr. by Lily Utsumi. *Aoba no fue*. Honolulu, Univ. of Hawaii, 1937. n.p.

'Бҍлата птица; Печаль; Изоставената лодка; Цветя звезди; На твоя, койко си отива; Светлина; Моего сердце; Облалите; В нлен; Тегло' Переведе от франц. Никола Джеров. *Песните на Ямато*. София, Корали, 1937. p.61–64

'Chanson d'été; Fleur de prunier rose; Forêt de Fontainebleau; Le jong; Abeille; L'écho; Le soleil pointe à l'horizon; Tanka' Tr. par Kuni Matsuo et Steinilber-Oberlin. *Anthologie des poètes japonais contemporains*. Paris, Mercure de France, 1939. p.67–73, 266–267

'Marches; Bain d'automne; L'exilée; Les nuages' *Histoire de la littérature japonaise contemporaine*, par Geroges Bonneau. Paris, Payot, 1944. p.238–239

'Heaven forbid that you shall die!' Tr. by Shigeshi Nishimura. *The Current of the World*, v.28, no.10, 1951. p.44–45

'The typhoon' Tr. by Shigeshi Nishimura. *The Current of the World*, v.29, no.10, 1952. p.33

'The herd of burden beasts' Tr. by Shigeshi Nishimura. *The Current of the World*, v.30, no.2, 1953. p.31–32

'Тайфун; Не отдавай, любимый, жизнь свою!; Чудесный город; В грязном пригороде дождь и мрак; Трусость; Свой собственный путь; Как создается песня; Узы' Перевод В. Н. Марковой. *Японская поэзия*. Москва, Гослитиздат, 1954. p.221–230

'Two poems' Tr. by Kenneth Rexroth. *Atlantic Monthly*, Jan. 1955. p.147

'11 tanka' Tr. by V. H. Viglielmo. *Japanese literature in the Meiji era*. Tokyo, Obunsha, 1955. p.381–383

'The poetry of Akiko Yosano' Tr. by H. H. Honda. *The Reeds*, v.2, 1956. p.3–31

'My songs; One night; A mouse' Tr. by Shio Sakanishi. *Modern Japanese literature*, ed. by D. Keene. N. Y. Grove Press, 1956; Tokyo, Tuttle, 1957. p.202–203

'Two waka poems' Tr. by S. Sakanishi. *Modern Japanese literature*, ed. by D. Keene. N. Y. Grove Press, 1956; Tokyo, Tuttle, 1957. p.207

'2 tanka' Tr. par Roger Bersihand. *La littérature japonaise*. Paris, Presses Universitaires de France, 1956. p.114

'10 tanka' Tr. by H. H. Honda. *The Reeds*, v.3, 1957. p.6, 12, 14, 15, 19, 25

The poetry of Yosano Akiko. Tr. by Heihachiro Honda. Tokyo, Hokuseido, 1957. 104p.

Tanka. Nella interpretazione di Elpidio Jenco. Milano, Ceschina, 1957. 111p.

'Elhagyott bárka' *Kínai es Japán költök*. Budapest, Szépirodalmi, 1957. p.208

'Mis canciones; Una noche; Viniste al fin; De los innumerables escalones' *Sur*, no.249, Nov.-Dec. 1957. p.100–101

'Tu non devi morire, et al' Tr. di Anna Maria Salvagnini Rossi. *Il Giappone*, anno 2, no.3–4, 1958. p.25–40

'Blanche apparition; Le rossignol absent; Couleurs; Offrande; Question indiscrète; La souris' *La poésie japonaise*, par Karl Petit. Paris, Seghers, 1959. p.197–199

'Die Stufen; Ein Vogel; Frühlingszeit; Die Dichterin' Übers. von Günther Debon. *Im Schnee die Fähre*. München, Piper, 1960. p.32–33

'Klage um den in den Krieg gezogenen Bruder, und 4 tanka' Übers. von Kuniyo Takayasu und Manfred Hausmann. *Ruf der Regenpfeifer*. München, Bechtle Verlag, 1961. p.79–81, 93–94

'Tanka' Tercüme etmek L. Sami Akalin. *Japon şiiri*. İstanbul, Varlik Yayinevi, 1962. p.239

'4 tanka' Tr. by Geoffrey Bownas and Anthony Thwaite. *The Penguin book of Japanese verse*. Harmondsworth, Penguin Books, 1964. p.159–160

'Please do not die' Tr. by Hisakazu Kaneko. *Orient West*, v.9, no.3, 1964. p.61–62

'Die Stufen; Die Dichterin' *Lyrik des Ostens*, hrg. von Wilhelm Gundert usw. München, Carl Hanser, 1965. p.472

'2 tanka' Tr. from the French by Unity Evans. *Japanese literature*. N. Y. Walker, 1965. p.97

'A song of May' Tr. by Hisakazu Kaneko. *London Magazine*, v.6, no.9, Dec. 1966. p.21

'9 tanka' Tr. di E. Jenco. *Antologia della letteratura coreana e giapponese*. Milano, Fratelli Fabbri, 1969. p.263–264

'A mouse' Tr. by Shio Sakanishi. *The Mentor book of modern Asian literature*, ed. by D. B. Shimer. N. Y. New American Library, 1969. p.125

'Тайфун' Которгон С. Фмурбаев. *Хиросима кектери*. Фрунзе, Кыргызстан, 1969. p.9–10

'1 tanka' Tr. by Shio Sakanishi. *Landscapes and portraits*, by D. Keene. Tokyo, Kodansha International, 1971. p.152

'1 tanka' Tr. by Eiko Yano and Marie Philomene. *Poetry Nippon*, no.19, 1972. p.21

'4 tanka' Tr. by Mineyo Inai and Marie Philomene. *Poetry Nippon*, no.23, 1973. p.23

'You must not die; Mouse; Killifish; Labor pains; Being unbearably sad; Hair; Inn at Munich; Self declaration; Winter twilight; Window; The sound of autumn; Maiden; The flesh; Priest's tears; Kyoto; Elegy; Confrontation; Blind person; Stairway; Traveler; Hall of fame' Tr. by Ikuko Atsumi and Graeme Wilson. *Japan Quarterly*, v.21, no.2, 1974. p.184–187

'1 tanka' Tr. by Gaku Kojima. *Eigo Kenkyu*, v.63, no.7, 1974.

'4 tanka' Tr. by Mineyo Inai. *Poetry Nippon*, no.27, 1974. p.25

'4 tanka' Tr. by E. Yano and Marie Philomene. *Poetry Nippon*, no.26, 1974. p.3–4

Die Erneuerung der Tanka-Poesie in der Meiji-Zeit und die Lyrik Yosano Akikos, von Katharina May. Wiesbaden, Harrassowitz, 1975. 1v.

'4 tanka' Tr. by Harumi Sugiyama. *Poetry Nippon*, no.29 & 30, 1975. p.17

'16 tanka' Tr. by Kenneth Rexroth. *One hundred more poems from the Japanese*. N. Y. New Directions, 1976. p.5–20

'2 tanka' *Japanese love poems*, ed. by Jean Bennett. Garden City, Doubleday, 1976. p.12, 51

'1 tanka' Tr. by Reiko Tsukimura. *Journal of the Association of Teachers of Japanese*, v.11, no.1, 1976. p.48

'11 tanka, and Labor pains' *The burning heart*, tr. and ed. by Kenneth Rexroth and Ikuko Atsumi. N. Y. Seabury Press, 1977. p.63–66, 87

Essays エッセイ

'貞操論' 周作人訳 「新青年」 第4巻5期 1918. p.386–394

'Issun no ita' Tr. by Yasutaro Kanzaki. *Eisaku-*

YOSANO Akiko

bun Zasshi, Dec. 1921.
'給民國的青年友人' 「新女性」第1卷2期 1926. p.117–120
「與謝野晶子論文集」 張嫻訳 上海 開明書店 1926. 1冊
'創作和批評' 張嫻訳 「眞美善」 女作家号 19

YOSANO Hiroshi 与謝野 寛 1873–1935

Tanka 短歌

'2 tanka' *Japanese poetry, an historical essay*, by Curtis Hidden Page. Boston, Houghton Mifflin, 1923; Folcroft, Folcroft Library, 1976. p.159, 160

'A poet; A meteorite; A rainbow; At the Oigawa; The sea-wind; A butterfly; A dirge; The crossroads; Grasses; A rose; The sun; The rainbow; A sailing ship; My heart' Tr. by Asataro Miyamori. *Masterpieces of Japanese poetry, ancient and modern*. Tokyo, Maruzen, 1936; Tokyo, Taiseido, 1956; N. Y. Greenwood Press, 1971. p.635–643

'Tanka' Tr. par Kuni Matsuo et Steinilber-Oberlin. *Anthologie des poètes japonais contemporains*. Paris, Mercure de France, 1939. p.258–260

'The ego' Tr. by Shigeshi Nishimura. *The Current of the World*, v.30, no.3, 1953. p.44

'The grove' Tr. by Shigeshi Nishimura. *The Current of the World*, v.30, no.4, 1953. p.35

'Майские дожди; Ананасная дыня; Осāй; В пучине; Городская управа; Нищий; Враг; Одна ночь; В руки ее' Перевод В. Н. Марковой. *Японская поэзия*. Москва, Гослитиздат, 1954. p.210–220

'6 tanka' Tr. by V. H. Viglielmo. *Japanese literature in the Meiji era*. Tokyo, Obunsha, 1955. p.374, 383–384

'Éjszaka' Ford. Sövény Aladár. *Nagyvilág*, no.5, 1958. p.701

'Der Meteor; Gräser' Übers. von Günther Debon. *Im Schnee die Fähre*. München, Piper, 1960. p.27–28

'1 tanka' Übers. von Gerolf Coudenhove. *Japanische Jahreszeiten*. Zürich, Manesse Verlag, 1963. p.213

'Der Samurai' *Lyrik des Ostens*, hrg. von Wilhelm Gundert usw. München, Carl Hanser, 1965. p.469

'1 tanka' Tr. by Donald Keene. *Landscapes and portraits*. Tokyo, Kodansha International, 1971. p.263

'1 tanka' *Japanese love poems*, ed. by Jean Bennett. Garden City, Doubleday, 1976. p.12

YOSANO Reigon 与謝野礼厳 1823–1898

Tanka 短歌

'Swallows' Tr. by Asataro Miyamori. *Masterpieces of Japanese poetry, ancient and modern*. Tokyo, Maruzen, 1936; Tokyo, Taiseido, 1956; N. Y. Greenwood Press, 1971. p.595–596

YOSHIDA Genjirō 吉田絃二郎 1886–1956

Den'en shijō 田園詩情

'田園詩情侯樸' 終一訳 「文藝月刊」第2卷5–6号 1931. p.91–96

Fuyugare 冬枯れ

'冬枯' 孫百剛訳 「東方雜誌」第27卷16期 1930. p.91–96

Sakyū nikki 砂丘日記

'砂丘日記' 終一訳 「文藝月刊」第2卷8号 1931. p.29–49

Shūjin no ko 囚人の子

'Das Kind eines Sträflings' *Nippon*, Jahrgang 3, 1937. p.153–169

Criticism and Essays 評論・エッセイ

'太戈爾與音樂教育' 仲雲訳 「小説月報」第14卷9号 1923. p.1–2
'寂靜的夜雨' 青萍訳 「中國公論」第2卷6期 1940. p.157
'靜夜思親' 羅錦堂訳 「人民文学」 1963年3月 p.50–51
「永遠한疑惑」 梁心湖訳 서울 三志社 1977. 320p.

YOSHIDA Issui 吉田一穂 1898–1973

Poems 詩

'Brunnen' Übers. von Kuniyo Takayasu und Manfred Hausmann. *Ruf der Regenpfeifer*. München, Bechtle Verlag, 1961. p.85

'At market' *Japan Quarterly*, v.17, no.2, 1970. p.182

'어머니' 金光林訳 「現代詩学」第4卷3号 1972.

YOSHIDA Mitsuru 吉田 満 1923–

Senkan Yamato no saigo 戦艦大和の最後

'戰艦야마도의最後' 表文台訳 「日本代表作家百人集 5」 서울 希望出版社 1966. p.422–475; 「日本短篇文学全集 6」 서울 新太陽社 1969. p.334–387

YOSHIDA Tomoko 吉田知子 1934–

Mumyō chōya 無明長夜

'The long night of illusion' Tr. by James Kirkup and Harvey Eiko. *Japan Quarterly*, v.24, no.1, 1977. p.57–95

YOSHIDA Toshi 吉田とし 1925–

Biinasu no shiro ヴィナスの城

「비나스의城」 黄明禧訳 서울 青潮社 1977. 228p.

YOSHIDA Tōyō 吉田冬葉 1892–1956

Haiku 俳句

'7 haiku' Tr. by Asataro Miyamori. *Anthology*

of haiku, ancient and modern. Tokyo, Maruzen, 1932. p.784–789
'Angling; The fishing rod' Tr. by Asataro Miyamori. Haiku poems, ancient and modern.
Tokyo, Maruzen, 1940. p.353–354
'1 haiku' Tr. by Lois J. Erickson. Songs from
the land of dawn. N. Y. Friendship Press,
1949; Freeport, Books for Libraries Press,
1968. p.77
'1 haiku' Übers. von Günther Debon. Im Schnee
die Fähre. München, Piper, 1960. p.53
'Podul suspendat' Traducerea Virgil Teodorescu.
Din lirica japoneză. Bucureşti, Editura Univers, n.d. p.170

YOSHIE Takamatsu 吉江喬松 1880–1940

Tsubasa 翼

'Wings' Tr. by S. G. Brickley. The writing of
idiomatic English. Tokyo, Kenkyusha, 1951.
p.158–162

Criticism 評論

「西洋文學概論」 高明訳 上海 現代書局 1933. 1冊

YOSHIHARA Sachiko 吉原幸子 1932–

Poems 詩

'Refuse; Starting' Tr. by Takako Katsumata.
Poetry Nippon, no.35 & 36, 1976. p.8–9
'Candle; Resurrection; Blasphemy; I forget' The
burning heart, tr. and ed. by Kenneth Rexroth
and Ikuko Atsumi. N. Y. Seabury Press,
1977. p.118–122

YOSHII Isamu 吉井 勇 1886–1960

Tanka 短歌

'A chrysoprase; Grief; The footprints of love;
The great sea' Tr. by Asataro Miyamori.
Masterpieces of Japanese poetry, ancient and
modern. Tokyo, Maruzen, 1936; Tokyo, Taiseido, 1956; N. Y. Greenwood Press, 1971.
p.742–744
'1 tanka' Tr. by Lily Utsumi. Aoba no fue. Honolulu, Univ. of Hawaii, 1937. n.p.
'5 tanka' Tr. by V. H. Viglielmo. Japanese literature in the Meiji era. Tokyo, Obunsha, 1955.
p.407–408
'6 tanka' Tr. by H. H. Honda. The Reeds, v.3,
1957. p. 7, 8, 22, 23
'Spur der Liebe' Übers. von Günther Debon.
Im Schnee die Fähre. München, Piper, 1960.
p.47
'The poetry of Yoshii Isamu' Tr. by H. H. Honda.
The Reeds, v. 6, 1960. p.69–83
'6 tanka' Tr. by Shigeshi Nishimura. The Current
of the World, v.38, no.2, 1961. p.40

YOSHIKAWA Eiji 吉川英治 1892–1962

Miyamoto Musashi 宮本武蔵

「宮本武蔵」 鐘進添訳 台北 創譯出版社 1961. 4冊
「宮本武蔵」 柳一根訳 서울 書正出版社 1972. 5冊
「大望 26–32」 朴在姫訳 서울 中央出版社 1973. 7冊

Naruto hichō 鳴門秘帖

「大秘劍」 英文壽訳 서울 大湖出版文化社 1975. 3冊

Sangoku shi 三国志

「三国誌」 李仁光訳 서울 明治書院 1951. 3冊 ; 서울
白潮出版社 1965–66. 10冊 ; 서울 康友出版社
1968. 3冊 ; 서울 韓国読書文化院 1974. 5冊
「三国志」 金海哲訳 서울 不二出版社 1966. 3冊
「三国志」 金志翰訳 서울 呂文社 1974. 816p.

Shin Heike monogatari 新平家物語

The Heike story. Tr. by Fuki Wooyenaka Uramatsu. N. Y. Knopf, 1956; Tokyo, Tuttle,
1956. 627p.
Le chronique de Heike. Tr. de Sylvie Regnault-
Gatier. Paris, Albin Michel, 1956. 491p.

Shinsho Taikōki 新書太閤記

「風雲児」 柳根周訳 서울 三省堂 1970. 8冊

Shōgitai 彰義隊

'The Shogitai' Tr. by Setsuo Uenoda. Nippon
Times, 1943.

Essay エッセイ

'Azumao Sakura' Tr. by Kenichi Otsuka. Japan
Times Advertiser, Nov. 29, 1942.
'굴뚝과책상과나의青春과' 金賢珠訳 「바이 바이 바디」 서
울 三韓出版社 1966. p.49–56

YOSHIMASU Gōzō 吉増剛造 1939–

Poems 詩

'Rivoluzione' La protesta poetica del Giappone,
a cura di Dacia Maraini e Michiko Nojiri.
Roma, Officina Edizioni, 1968. p.171
'Burning' Tr. by Harry and Lynn Guest and Shozo
Kajima. Post-war Japanese poetry. Harmondsworth, Penguin Books, 1972. p.161
'Mad in the morning; Burning; My love, a fire;
The ancient castle in the air; The falling ob-
ject' Tr. by Yuriko Yoshida. The poetry of
postwar Japan. Iowa City, Univ. of Iowa Press,
1975. p.249–263

YOSHIMOTO Haruhiko 吉本晴彦 1923–

KUDUSE okuman chōja KUDUSE 億万長者

「구두쇠 億万長者」 金潤成訳 서울 韓国生産性本部
1971. 272p.

YOSHIMOTO Takaaki 吉本隆明 1924–

Poems 詩

'사람노래 ; 그가을을위하여' 辛東門訳 「世界戰後文学全

YOSHIMOTO Takaaki

集 9」 서울 新丘文化社 1962. p.262–263
'Canto d'amore' *La protesta poetica del Giappone*, a cura di Dacia Maraini e Michiko Nojiri. Roma, Officina Edizioni, 1968. p.97
'Love song' Tr. by Thomas Fitzsimmons. *Japanese poetry now*. London, André Deutsch, 1972. p.49; *Japanese poetry today*. N. Y. Schocken Books, 1972. p.51
'Story of the autumn on fire; Split personality; Tacit understanding; From despair to cruelty; For that autumn' Tr. by Yoshinari Yamada. *The poetry of postwar Japan*. Iowa City, Univ. of Iowa Press, 1975. p.92–101

YOSHIMOTO Takako 吉本隆子

Kuro to Yuki くろとゆき

De to katte. København, Høst, 1968. 27p.

YOSHIMURA Akira 吉村 昭 1927–

Zero shiki sentōki 零式戦闘機

「零式戦闘機」 鄒正訳 台北 天人出版社 1973. 1冊

YOSHINO Hideo 吉野秀雄 1902–1967

Tanka 短歌

'1 tanka' Tr. by Mayumi Hara. *Poetry Nippon*, no.29 & 30, 1975. p.18

YOSHINO Hiroshi 吉野 弘 1926–

Poems 詩

'黄昏' 辛東門訳 「世界戦後文学全集 9」 서울 新丘文化社 1962. p.261
'I was born' *La protesta poetica del Giappone*, a cura di Dacia Maraini e Michiko Nojiri. Roma, Officina Edizioni, 1968. p.107–109
'I was born' Tr. by Thomas Fitzsimmons. *Japanese poetry now*. London, André Deutsch, 1972. p.47; *Japanese poetry today*. N. Y. Schocken Books, 1972. p.49
'To my first child; Sunset colours; Concerning human space' Tr. by Harry and Lynn Guest and Shozo Kajima. *Post-war Japanese poetry*. Harmondsworth, Penguin Books, 1972. p.106–110
'To my first born; Evening glow; A chapter on the breast; Being studied—an embankment suggested; To my wife; Perfume "Good Luck"' Tr. by Kenji Inoue and Hajime Kijima. *The poetry of postwar Japan*. Iowa City, Univ. of Iowa Press, 1975. p.113–119

YOSHIOKA Minoru 吉岡 実 1919–

Poems 詩

'僧侶' 金龍済訳 「日本詩集」 서울 青雲社 1960. p.73–80

'家族' 李永純訳 「詩文学」 第13巻 1960. p.14
'喪服' 辛東門訳 「世界戦後文学全集 9」 서울 新丘文化社 1962. p.260–261
'Natura porta; Il passato' *La protesta poetica del Giappone*, a cura di Dacia Maraini e Michiko Nojiri. Roma, Officina Edizioni, 1968. p.71–73
'Egg; Still life; Funeral piece' *Anthology of modern Japanese poetry*, tr. and comp. by Edith Marcombe Shiffert and Yuki Sawa. Tokyo, Tuttle, 1972. p.112–114
'The past; The holy family' Tr. by Thomas Fitzsimmons. *Japanese poetry now*. London, André Deutsch, 1972. p.41–43; *Japanese poetry today*. N. Y. Schocken Books, 1972. p.43–45
'Still life; Monks' Tr. by Harry and Lynn Guest and Shozo Kajima. Harmondsworth, Penguin Books, 1972. p.60–62
'Still life; Past' Tr. by Geoffrey Bownas. *New writing in Japan*. Harmondsworth, Penguin Books, 1972. p.203
'Monks; On the pier' *Chicago Review* v.25, no.2, 1973. p.49–51, 63–66
'Landscape; Still life; Still life; The egg; Legend; Spindle form I; Spindle form II; Countryside; Requiem; The lilac garden' Tr. by Hiroaki Sato. *Ten Japanese poets*. Hanover, N. H. Granite Publications, 1973. p.102–113
Lilac garden. Tr. by Hiroaki Sato. Chicago, Chicago Review Press, 1976. 110p.
'Still life no.1; Still life no.2; Paul Klee's dining table; Nude woman' Tr. by Hiroaki Sato. *Contemporary Japanese literature*, ed. by Howard Hibbett. N. Y. Knopf, 1977. p.338–341
'Picking saffrons' Tr. by Fukuda Rikutaro. *Japanese Literature Today*, no.3, March 1978. p.10

YOSHIOKA Zenjidō 吉岡禅寺洞 1889–1961

Haiku 俳句

'1 haiku' *A history of haiku v.2*, by R. H. Blyth. Tokyo, Hokuseido, 1964. p.243

YOSHIUE Shōryō 吉植庄亮 1884–1958

Tanka 短歌

'A pale sun; Little wounds; Spinaches; A peony' Tr. by Asataro Miyamori. *Masterpieces of Japanese poetry, ancient and modern*. Tokyo, Maruzen, 1936; Tokyo, Taiseido, 1956; N. Y. Greenwood Press. 1971. p.708–710
'2 tanka' Tr. by H. H. Honda. *The Reeds*, v.5, 1959. p.144

YOSHIYA Nobuko 吉屋信子 1896–1973

Atakake no hitobito 安宅家の人々

Le cœur des Ataka. Tr. par J. G. Mills et M. L. Battaille. Paris, Stock, 1957. 281p. Genève, Sie und Er, 1958. 1v.
Familien Ataka. Übers. von Ingeborg Stemann. København, Aschehoug, 1961. 201p.

'The Ataka family' Tr. by Takehide Kikuchi. *Info*, Mar. Apr. May, June-July, Aug. Sept. Oct. Nov. Dec. 1964. Jan. Mar. April, May-June, July, 1965 in 13 parts.

Awajishima no kahi 淡路島の歌碑

'아와지섬의 歌碑' 崔貞順訳 「日本代表作家百人集 3」 서울 希望出版社 1966. p.22–47; 「日本短篇文学全集 3」 서울 新太陽社 1969. p.170–195

Essay エッセイ

'Shigeko san no tamatebako' Tr. by Yasutaro Kanzaki. *Eisakubun Zasshi*, July 1922.

YOSHIYUKI Junnosuke 吉行淳之介 1924–

Anshitsu 暗室

The dark room. Tr. by John Bester. Tokyo, Kodansha International, 1975. 170p.

Chōjū chūgyo 鳥獣蟲魚

'鳥獣蟲魚' 呉成鎭訳 「日本代表作家百人集 5」 서울 希望出版社 1966. p.98–114; 「日本短篇小説全集 6」 서울 新太陽社 1969. p.10–26

Genshoku no machi 原色の街

'原色의거리' 崔雲權訳 「日本新鋭文学作家受賞作品集 1」 서울 青雲社 1964. p.101–185; 「戦後日本短篇文学全集 1」 서울 日光出版社 1965. p.101–185

Fui no dekigoto 不意の出来事

'Неожиданное происшествие' Перевод Л. Громковской. *Японская новелла 1960–1970*. Москва, Прогресс, 1972. p.51–63

Kaban no nakami 鞄の中身

'Personal baggage' Tr. by John Bester. *Japanese Literature Today*, no.1, March, 1976. p.4–8

Sabita umi 錆びた海

'Rusted sea' Tr. by Warren Carlisle. *Japan P.E.N. News*, no.20, Sept. 1967. p.106

Sara no ichigo 皿の苺

'Erdbeeren' Übers. von Margarete Donath. *Japan erzählt*. Hamburg, Fischer, 1969. p.94–102

Shōfu no heya 娼婦の部屋

'In Akiko's room' Tr. by Howard Hibbett. *Contemporary Japanese literature*, ed. by Howard Hibbett. N. Y. Knopf, 1977. p.401–411

Shūu 驟雨

'驟雨' 金光稙訳 「芥川賞小説集」 서울 新丘文化社 1960. p.165–185; 「깊은江」 서울 三耕社 1971. p.165–185
'소낙비' 崔雲權訳 「日本新鋭文学作家受賞作品集 1」 서울 青雲社 1964. p.187–207; 「戦後日本短篇文学全集 1」 서울 日光出版社 1965. p.187–207; 「現代日本代表文学全集 1」 서울 平和出版社 1973. p.187–205
'Sudden shower' Tr. by Geoffrey Bownas. *Japan Quarterly*, v.19, no.4, 1972. p.446–457; *New writing in Japan*. Harmondsworth, Penguin Books, 1972. p.99–122

'驟雨' 劉慕沙訳 「芥川賞作品選集 1」 台北 大地出版社 1972. p.109–137

Suna no ue no shokubutsu gun 砂の上の植物群

「노을은알고있다」 姜惠訳 서울 토픽出版社 1966. 281p.

Criticism and Essay 評論・エッセイ

'Day face, night face' *This is Japan*, v.11, 1964. p.224–225
'川端康成傳' 邱素臻訳 「睡美人」 台北 林白出版社 1969. p.101–142

YOSHIYUKI Rie 吉行理恵 1939–

Poems 詩

'Sacrificial victim' *The burning heart*, tr. and ed. by Kenneth Rexroth and Ikuko Atsumi. N. Y. Seabury Press, 1977. p.126

YOSHIZAWA Shōji 吉沢しょうじ 1937–

Poems 詩

'Eye' Tr. by Harry and Lynn Guest and Shozo Kajima. *Post-war Japanese poetry*. Harmondsworth, Penguin Books, 1972. p.157

YOSHIZUKA Kinji 吉塚勘治 1909–1972

Poems 詩

'給焼死了的茜' 適夷訳 「譯文」 1955年8月 p.65–66

YUASA Katsue 湯淺克衛 1910–

Natsume 棗

'붉은대추' 金元基訳 「日本代表作家百人集 3」 서울 希望出版社 1966. p.428–448; 「日本短篇文学全集 4」 서울 新太陽社 1969. p.188–208
'대추' 李吉雄訳 「世界文学속의韓国 6」 서울 正韓出版社 1975. p.265–275

Onna Tāzan 女ターザン

'Woman Tarzan of Korea' *Ukiyo*. Tokyo, Phoenix Books, 1954. p.181–202

YŪKI Aisōka 結城哀草果 1893–1974

Tanka 短歌

'1 tanka' Tr. by Shigeshi Nishimura. *The Current of the World*, v.17, no.2, 1940. p.131

YUKI Shigeko 由起しげ子 1902–1969

Mayonaka no kao 真夜中の顔

'Il volto nella notte' Tr. di Ester Maimeri. *Novelle giapponesi*. Milano, Martello, 1969. p.183–223

INDEX OF TRANSLATORS

INDEX OF TRANSLATORS

INDEX OF TRANSLATORS

INDEX OF TRANSLATORS

Vorgaard-Jepsen, Viggo 143
Voropanov, Gheorghe 205, 240
Vulpitta, R. 51, 112, 148, 169, 170, 184, 207, 222, 226, 261, 278
Vulpitta, Romano 25
Vuorisalo, Katri 233
Vũ Minh Thiều 17, 18, 20, 22, 24, 25, 29

Wada, Den 266
Wadagaki, Kenzo 48, 144, 231
Wahlund, Erik 106, 148
Wakameda, Takeji 127
Wakisaka, Katsunori 29, 211
Waley, Arthur 29
Walsh, Clara A. 144, 229, 231
Warburton, Th. 193
Ward, Henry P. 173
Wargo, Robert 124, 178
Warren, Virgil A. 150
Waseda, Yutaka 171
Wassongowa, Elzbieta 60
Watanabe, K. 20
Watanabe, Kakuji 22, 25
Watanabe, Yoshihiro 167
Watson, Burton 49, 75, 156, 160, 182, 185
Weatherby, Meredith 31, 147, 150
Weidinger, Karl 91, 173
Wells, Warner 53
Wendt, A. 178
Wessely, László 240
Whang, Insu 146
Whitehouse, W. J. 15, 162, 184
Wiersholm, Grete Grieg 110
Wilamowitz-Moellendorff, **Fanny** 198
Will, Frederic 72, 73
Williams, Kenneth 166, 175, 187,

263, 267
Wilson, Graeme 31, 35, 54, 55, 56, 69, 167, 183, 184, 185, 201, 202, 209, 216, 229, 230, 239, 241, 242, 249, 272, 273, 279
Wilson, William R. 161, 162
Windfeld-Hansen, Karina 103, 104
Winkelhöfer, J. 10, 11
Winkelhöferová, Vlasta 9, 10, 11, 38, 39, 59, 190, 223, 244, 252, 260, 265, 276, 277
Winkler, Ursula Eleonore 186, 231
Wolf, Norbert 191
Wolfe, Stephen 56
Wright, Harold P. 51, 54, 55, 118, 231, 239, 240, 249, 250
Wuriu, Yasushi 62, 75

Yada, Kenzoh 173
Yaguchi, Y. 249
Yamada, Kazuo 24, 75, 82, 97, 103, 116, 234, 278
Yamada, Yoshinari 281
Yamagata, Isoh 90, 91
Yamagiwa, Joseph K. 69
Yamaguchi, Hideo 55, 145, 156, 167, 176, 210, 234, 241, 259
Yamaguchi, M. 176
Yamakawa, Sakujiro 89
Yamamoto, Kyohei 129, 227
Yamamoto, Makiko 142
Yamamura, Saburo 86, 167
Yamasaki, Kyoko 36, 242
Yamashiro, José 78, 192
Yamata, Kikou 173, 204, 250, 253
Yamazaki, Fumiko 203
Yamazaki, Isaio 260
Yampolsky, Philip 114
Yanagisawa, Kazouko 152, 274

Yano, Eiko 279
Yashima, Taro 164
Yasuda, Kenneth 32, 40, 65, 71, 75, 83, 87, 89, 108, 139, 143, 158, 165, 173, 174, 178, 185, 187, 190, 205, 206, 208, 212, 213, 225, 235, 238, 242, 259, 265, 266, 270
Yasuda, Yukichi 181
Yasui, Eiitschi 11
Yasukawa, Mariko 268
Yatsushiro, Sachiko 104, 105, 107, 147, 149, 150, 251, 252
Yeğinobali, Nihal 107
Yokoo, Sadamichi 73, 78
Yonekawa, Blanka 41, 71, 124, 225
Yonezawa, Naoto 113
Yoshida, K. 171
Yoshida, M. 171
Yoshida, Masao 164, 172
Yoshida, Yuriko 281
Yoshie, Takamatsu 261
Yoshimura, A. T. 100
Yoshino, Yujiro 207
Yoshioka, Seison N. 194
Yoshioka, Toranosuke 272
Yoshitomi, M. 33, 71, 94, 112, 129, 130, 138, 189, 242, 256
Yoshiye, Takamatou 261
Yu, Beongcheon 15, 17, 24, 26, 183
Yuasa, S. 27, 129, 183, 203, 235
Yuasa, T. 22
Yukawa, Kyoko 79, 242

Zalupsky, Imrich 20, 240
Zamfirescu, Violeta 47
Zolbrod, Leon 73, 106, 128, 146, 161, 275
Zori, Tomira 233

RUSSIAN

Абдукалыков, Ж. 77
Абдуллаев, А. 114
Адарьян, Н. 29
Айвас-Огру, В. 207
Александрова, Е. 251
Алыбаев, Ж. 72, 110, 140, 191, 204, 256, 260, 269
Алыши, Ж. 109
Ариев, К. 240
Арыков, Т. 180
Атыгаев, Е. 190, 241
Андреев, Д. 61, 62

Бабинцев, А. 72, 180, 193, 265
Бабкина, Л. 186, 244
Байзаков, Т. 164, 201, 205, 207
Бейко, Б. 160, 205
Беливанов, А. 72
Бережков, С. 10, 11
Берлин, Я. 61, 72, 107, 188, 265
Брок, Г. 33
Брок, Е. 33
Бугаева, Д. 59, 87, 225, 228

Вардуль, И. 16, 24
Виноградова, Т. 41, 59, 273
Винокуров, Е. 46, 77, 82, 88, 110, 205, 269
Войнюш, О. 14, 73, 180
Воловьев, П. 240

Гладков, А. 163
Глускина, А. 83, 163, 180
Головнин, И. 14, 23
Горбштейн, Г. 116
Горегляд, В. 89

Гребликене, Л. 99
Гребов, Н. 179, 272
Гривнин, В. 10, 11, 12, 15, 22, 23, 28, 29, 106, 117, 193,
Григориев, М. 16, 19, 21, 22, 24, 28, 29, 111, 112, 113, 182
Григорьев, С. 106
Григорьева, Т. 72, 84, 100, 153, 222, 265
Громковская, Л. 180, 283
Гусев, М. 14
Гутерман, С. 12, 43, 71, 101, 105, 123, 142, 172, 182, 189, 253

Делюшная, Т. 38, 39
Джеров, Н. 69, 83, 108, 118, 138, 145, 199, 209, 215, 279
Дзюб, И. 10, 15, 16, 17, 18, 20, 22, 23, 25, 26, 27, 28, 29, 100, 102, 143, 184, 193
Доли, М. 133
Долин, А. 37, 46, 96, 126, 153, 218, 252, 253
Дудин, М. 267

Ералиев, С. 266
Ермакова, Л. 18, 26, 27, 178
Ефимов, М. 257

Жданов, Л. 258
Журавлев, В. 191, 260
Жусуев, С. 47
Жяпаридзе, М. 144

Завяровко, Л. 133

Ибрагимов, А. 144
Иванова, Г. 9, 49, 56, 84, 116
Иммерман, Г. 74, 180, 193, 214, 250, 257
Исабеков, Б. 226

Канев, Х. 257
Карлина, Р. 51, 89, 121, 182
Каспаров, Г. 230
Келгенбаев, Ш. 105, 107
Керекелуватамас, Е. 144
Кетелаури, С. 43
Ким, Минэ 40
Ким, Р. 19, 24, 28, 134
Коваленко, Г. 257
Кожевников, И. 79
Коломиец, А. 79, 175
Конрад, Н. 183
Константинов, В. 84, 155, 177, 228
Коршиков, П. 184
Костерева, В. 162

Левин, Л. 84, 205, 206
Лейферт, А. 62, 63, 179, 254
Лобачев, Л. 16, 21, 26
Логучнов, В. В. 84
Логунова, В. 12, 34, 52, 65, 84, 114, 127, 154, 155, 228, 240, 269
Львова, И. 11, 19, 21, 24, 26, 53, 61, 64, 65, 72, 84, 98, 115, 121, 122, 189, 194, 197, 205, 240, 257, 258

Маймулов. С. 180
Максимова, Г. 76, 178
Мамонов, А. 29, 32, 35, 38, 40, 42, 46, 47, 49, 55, 57, 58, 59, 63, 72, 76,

292

CHINESE

Alphabetical order according to the
Wade system.

INDEX OF TRANSLATORS

294

KOREAN

Alphabetical order according to the
McCune-Reischauer system.

INDEX OF TITLES

INDEX OF TITLES

INDEX OF TITLES

INDEX OF TITLES